The Political Economy of Africa

The Political Economy of Africa addresses the real possibilities for African development in the coming decades when seen in the light of the continent's economic performance over the last half-century. This involves an effort to emancipate our thinking from the grip of western economic models that have often ignored Africa's diversity in their rush to peddle simple nostrums of dubious merit.

The book addresses the seemingly intractable economic problems of the African continent, and traces their origins. It also brings out the instances of successful economic change, and the possibilities for economic revival and renewal. As well as surveying the variety of contemporary situations, the text will provide readers with a firm grasp of the historical background to the topic. It explores issues such as:

- employment and poverty
- social policy and security
- structural adjustment programmes and neo-liberal globalization
- majority rule and democratization
- taxation and resource mobilization

It contains a selection of country-specific case studies from a range of international contributors, many of whom have lived and worked in Africa. The book will be of particular interest to higher level students in political economy, development studies, area studies (Africa) and economics in general.

Vishnu Padayachee is Senior Professor and Head of the School of Development Studies at the University of KwaZulu-Natal, South Africa.

The Political Economy of Africa

Edited by Vishnu Padayachee

LONDON AND NEW YORK

First published 2010
by Routledge
2 Park Square, Milton Park, Abingdon, Oxon, OX14 4RN

Simultaneously published in the USA and Canada
by Routledge
270 Madison Avenue, New York, NY 10016

*Routledge is an imprint of the Taylor & Francis Group,
an informa business*

Typeset in Times by
RefineCatch Limited, Bungay, Suffolk
Printed and bound in Great Britain by
CPI Antony Rowe, Chippenham, Wiltshire

British Library Cataloguing in Publication Data
A catalogue record for this book is available
from the British Library

Library of Congress Cataloging-in-Publication Data
The political economy of Africa / edited by Vishnu Padayachee.
    p. cm.
  Includes bibliographical references and index.
  1. Africa – Economic policy.   2. Africa – Economic conditions.
  I. Padayachee, Vishnu.
  HC800.P638 2010
  330.96—dc22   2009041887

ISBN 10: 415-48038-8 (hbk)
ISBN 10: 0-415-48039-6 (pbk)
ISBN 10: 0-203-85422-5 (ebk)

ISBN 13: 978-0-415-48038-3 (hbk)
ISBN 13: 978-0-415-48039-0 (pbk)
ISBN 13: 978-0-203-85422-8 (ebk)

Contents

Figures

Tables

Acknowledgements

I was very chuffed, but somewhat intimidated, to have received the invitation from Rob Langham at Routledge some two years ago to edit a volume on the political economy of Africa. Although I had done work and writing on aspects of African integration and civil society which led me to visit colleagues in many parts of the continent, and had been deeply involved in research and policy debates on South African economic issues for a few decades, I would not describe myself as an Africanist. I believed that it was important for the School of Development Studies, which I currently head, to be associated with such a volume, given both the School's and the University's academic mission in respect of our continent, and I accepted his invitation on these grounds. So I thank Rob Langham and his team at Routledge, UK, for their confidence in me and their unfailing support and generosity over the last two years.

The editorial advisory team, which I assembled to assist me, was indispensable to the successful realization of my mandate. Chris Cramer, Bill Freund, Keith Hart and Nicolas Pons-Vignon have provided invaluable support: in helping me think through the book proposal, in securing contributors from among their own networks on our vast continent, in reading and commenting on chapter drafts, and in being there whenever I needed advice and encouragement. I would like to say a special thanks to Keith Hart, who makes frequent visits to Durban (where he now has a home) and the School of Development Studies (where he is an Honorary Professor). Keith deserves more credit than that of editorial adviser, and I express my appreciation to him, for his friendship, wisdom and counsel. As the other Durban-based adviser, Bill Freund, my PhD supervisor from few decades ago, has remained a trusted friend and confidant. His own towering contributions to research on Africa are recognized world-wide and I thank Bill for steadying me over anxious times.

I have been incredibly lucky to have secured contributions from so many exceptional scholars of the African economy – all of whom have either lived or worked on our continent for extended periods, and remain committed through their work and their activism to the goal of a prosperous and proud Africa. I cannot thank them enough for the work they have put into their chapters and into this book project.

My colleagues at the School of Development Studies understood the pressures that I faced in finalizing this volume over the second half of 2009. The support staff put up with my moody moments with good humour, even on occasions when the administration of the department took second place. I acknowledge William Munro (University of Illinois-Wesleyan), who was a Visiting Professor in the School for much of 2009, for being so willing to read and comment on chapters in which he had particular expertise.

Finally, I thank my wife Nishi for providing the stability and love on the home front that allowed me to get on with my work with peace of mind. She has never failed me, even when on occasions, I have failed her. My beautiful and spirited 5-year old daughter, Sonali, is the joy of my life, and I am delighted and thrilled to dedicate this edited collection to her.

Vishnu Padayachee

Contributors

Ward Anseeuw is a research fellow at the Agricultural Research Centre for International Development (CIRAD) attached to the Post-Graduate School of Agriculture and Rural Development of the University of Pretoria. He has conducted research for the last 10 years in Southern Africa and the African continent, more particularly on the issues of agricultural restructuring, land conflicts, agrarian and land reforms. He has published extensively on these issues in scientific journals and with renowned publishers, including *The Renewal of Agricultural Policy in Africa-NEPAD's Efforts Scrutinised* (University of Pretoria, working paper series, 2008); *Land, Liberation and Compromise in Southern Africa*, with Chris Alden (Palgrave Macmillan, 2009).

Claire Bénit-Gbaffou is a former fellow of École Normale Superieure (Ulm). She is currently a Senior Lecturer in the School of Architecture and Planning, University of Witwatersrand, Johannesburg (South Africa). Her main research area is the study of urban governance, community participation and party politics. She is currently editing a book on 'The Privatization of Security in Sub Saharan African cities' (Karthala-IFAS), and is coordinating a research programme on 'The voice of the poor in urban governance: participation, mobilization and politics in South African cities'.

James K. Boyce is Professor of Economics at the University of Massachusetts, Amherst, and director of the programme on development, peacebuilding, and the environment at the Political Economy Research Institute (http://www.peri.umass.edu/). He is the co-editor of *Peace and the Public Purse: Economic Policies for Postwar Statebuilding* (Lynne Rienner, 2007).

Christopher Cramer is Professor of the Political Economy of Development, School of Oriental and African Studies, University of London, where he also convenes the MSC programme in Violence, Conflict and Development. He has a PhD in Economics from Cambridge University, and his research interests are in the political economy of conflict and the transition to peace, rural poverty alleviation in southern Africa; labour markets;

privatization in LDCs; and the political economy of inequality. His books include *Civil War is not a stupid thing: accounting for violence in developing countries* (London, Hurst, 2006); and (as co-author) *Supporting Ownership: Swedish Development Cooperation with Kenya, Tanzania, and Uganda* (2 Vols) (Stockholm, SIDA).

Stephen Devereux is a Fellow at the Institute of Development Studies, University of Sussex, an Honorary Research Fellow at the School of Development Studies, University of KwaZulu-Natal, and a Director of the Centre for Social Protection. He works mainly on issues related to poverty and rural development in Africa. His books include *Food Security in Sub-Saharan Africa* co-edited with Simon Maxwell (ITDG, 2001), *The New Famines* (Routledge, 2007) and *Social Protection in Africa* co-authored with Frank Ellis and Phillip White (Edward Elgar, 2009).

Jonathan Di John is a Lecturer in Political Economy of Development at the School of Oriental and African Studies (SOAS), University of London. He is also a Research Fellow on the Crisis States Research Centre at the London School of Economics. His research has focused on historical political economy in the following areas: taxation and tax reform in less developed countries, especially sub-Saharan Africa and Latin America; industrial policy and economic growth in Latin America, especially Venezuela; governance and growth in oil economies. His latest book is *From Windfall to Curse? Oil and industrialization in Venezuela*, 1920 to the present (Penn State University Press, 2009).

Ben Fine is Professor of Economics at the School of Oriental and African Studies, University of London. He was a co-editor of the 'MERG Report', and served as an international expert advisor on the South African Presidential Labour Market Commission. He is co-author with Zavareh Rustomjee of *South Africa's Political Economy: From Minerals-Energy Complex to Industrialization*. Recent books include *The New Development Economics: A Critical Introduction*, edited with K. S. Jomo, Delhi: Tulika, and London: Zed Press, 2006; *Privatization and Alternative Public Sector Reform in Sub-Saharan Africa: Delivering on Electricity and Water*, Basingstoke: Palgrave Macmillan, co-edited with K. Bayliss, 2008; *From Political Economy to Economics: Method, the Social and the Historical in the Evolution of Economic Theory*, awarded the 2009 Gunnar Myrdal Prize. *From Economics Imperialism to Freakonomics: The Shifting Boundaries Between Economics and Other Social Sciences*, awarded the 2009 Deutscher Prize, both with Dimitris Milonakis, London: Routledge; and, with London: Pluto Press, are the fifth edition of *Marx's Capital*, 2010, co-authored with Alfredo Saad-Filho, and *Theories of Social Capital: Researchers Behaving Badly*, 2010.

Bill Freund has taught at universities in Nigeria and Tanzania as well as in South Africa. He is Emeritus Professor of Economic History at the

University of KwaZulu-Natal where he was Head of the Department of Economic History and Development Studies at the University of Natal until 2004. His books include *The Making of Contemporary Africa, The African Worker* and, most recently, *The African City: A History*. He has written many articles and book chapters on political economy and development issues in South Africa.

Hazel Gray is a doctoral student in the Department of Economics at the School of Oriental and African Studies. Her thesis is on comparative political economy of growth and the state in Tanzania and Vietnam. She teaches in the Economics Department and the Centre for International Studies and Diplomacy. Previously she worked as an economist at the Ministry of Finance in Tanzania.

Keith Hart is an economic anthropologist who lives in Paris. He is Honorary Research Professor in the School of Development Studies, University of KwaZulu-Natal, Durban and Professor of Anthropology Emeritus, Goldsmiths University of London. He has held teaching positions in a dozen universities around the world. He was Director of the African Studies Centre, Cambridge University (1992–1998). He has carried out research in Ghana, South Africa and the Caribbean. He contributed the concept of the informal economy to development studies. His books include *The Political Economy of West African Agriculture* (1982); (edited with J. Lewis) *Why Angola Matters* (1995); *The Memory Bank: Money in an Unequal World* (2000); and (edited with C. Hann) *Market and Society: The Great Transformation Today* (2009). Many of his recent writings may be found at www.thememorybank.co.uk.

James Heintz is Associate Research Professor at the Political Economy Research Institute of the University of Massachusetts, Amherst. He has conducted research on employment policies for Ghana, Kenya, South Africa, the Gambia, and Madagascar and on alternative macroeconomic policies for sub-Saharan Africa. This research programme was sponsored by various UN agencies, including the ILO, UNDP, and UNECA. Recent books include *An Employment Targeted Economic Program for Kenya* (with Robert Pollin and Mwangi wa Githinji) and *An Employment Target Program for South Africa* (with Robert Pollin, Gerald Epstein, and Léonce Ndikumana), both published by Edward Elgar.

Raphael Kaplinsky is Professor of International Development at the Open University in the UK. He pioneered the establishment of the Asian Driver research network which focuses on the impact of China and India on low income economies, and cooperates closely with the African Economic Research Consortium on their Asian Driver programme. Currently he is engaged in a collaborative research programme with the University of Cape Town on Making the Most of Commodities in Africa, and is establishing a global network of researchers focusing on innovations in China and India which are targeted at low income bottom-of-the-pyramid consumers.

Mushtaq Khan is Professor of Economics at the School of Oriental and African Studies, University of London. He previously studied and taught at the universities of Oxford and Cambridge, gaining his PhD in Economics from Cambridge. His research interests are in institutional economics, the economics of governance and the role of the state in catching up and in industrial policies. He is a member of the Task Force on Africa set up by Joseph Stiglitz and the Initiative for Policy Dialogue, and a regular lecturer in APORDE (the African Programme on Rethinking Development Economics) based in South Africa.

Peter Lawrence is Professor of Development Economics at Keele University in the UK. He has researched and written widely on development issues in Tanzania, Uganda, India and the transition economies of east and central Europe. His current research interests are in economic and financial liberalization and water poverty. He is a founding editor of the *Review of African Political Economy*.

Francie Lund is a Senior Research Associate in the School of Development Studies, University of KwaZulu-Natal, Durban. She was an Associate Professor at the school for many years and has contributed widely to academic and policy debates on social policy in South Africa and elsewhere over an extended period. She is also Director of the Social Protection Programme of WIEGO (Women in Informal Employment: Globalizing and Organizing). A longstanding research interest has been the impact of South Africa's pensions and grants in mitigating poverty and redressing inequality. She is engaged locally and globally in research and policy advocacy around informal workers, especially regarding local government intervention, and around the provision of social security. She is a Research Associate at the Brooks World Poverty Institute, University of Manchester.

Zoë Marriage is Senior Lecturer in the Development Studies Department of the School of Oriental and African Studies (SOAS), University of London where she teaches an MSc course in Security. She has researched extensively in countries affected by conflict in Africa, and her current work investigates the relationship between security and development in the Democratic Republic of Congo. She is the author of *Not Breaking the Rules, Not Playing the Game. International Assistance to Countries At War* (2006, Hurst & Co).

Showers Mawowa is a Zimbabwean scholar currently studying for a PhD in the School of Development Studies at the University of KwaZulu-Natal, Durban.

Dorothy McCormick is a Research Professor at the Institute for Development Studies, University of Nairobi. She holds MA and PhD degrees in International Studies from the Johns Hopkins University, an MBA from the Wharton School of the University of Pennsylvania, and a BA from Trinity University, Washington, DC. She has a long history of research and teaching in the area of industrialization and enterprise development in Africa. Her work has dealt with the institutions and enterprise development, enterprise clusters, value chains, and most recently, the impact of the rise of China and India on African enterprises and workers.

David Moore is Professor of Development Studies and Head of the Department of Anthropology and Development Studies at the University of Johannesburg. He has a doctorate in Political Science from Toronto's York University. His research focuses on Zimbabwean political history and political economy, the political economy of war and reconstruction in Africa, and development discourse more broadly. He edited *The World Bank: Poverty, Development, Hegemony*, published by the University of KwaZulu-Natal Press in 2007.

Mike Morris is Director of the Centre for Social Science Research, a Professor in the School of Economics, University of Cape Town, and formerly Senior Professor in the School of Development Studies, University of KwaZulu-Natal. He has a PhD from Sussex University. Professor Morris is a project leader of the 'Making the Most of Commodities Programme' (commodities industrialization paths for Africa), and is a steering committee member of the African Economic Research Consortium project on the Impact of the Asian Drivers on sub-Saharan Africa. He has published widely in the areas of globalization, global value chains and international competitiveness, industrial development and policy, clusters and learning networks, clothing and textiles, automotive and furniture sectors. He has also worked with the International Trade Centre (Geneva) and the United Nations Industrial Development Organization (Vienna). He has undertaken research and policy work for a number of international agencies including the EU, DANIDA, DANSET, and IDRC.

Léonce Ndikumana is Director of Research at the African Development Bank. Formerly Associate Professor of Economics at the University of Massachusetts, Amherst, and Chief of Macroeconomic Analysis at the United Nations Economic Commission for Africa (UNECA), Léonce Ndikumana has contributed to various areas of research and policy analysis with a focus on African countries. His research investigates the role of financial systems for domestic investment and growth; external debt and capital flight from African countries; private capital flows; macroeconomic policies for growth and employment; the politics and economics of conflict and civil wars in Africa; and fiscal policies in the context of post-conflict reconstruction. He is an active member of major research networks around the world including the African Finance and Economics Association (AFEA) of which he is a former President, the African Economic Research Consortium (AERC) where he serves as resource person, and others.

Kako Nubukpo is Head of the Department of post-graduate studies and research in the Faculty of Economics and Management at the University of Lome in Togo. He has a PhD from the University of Lyon 2 (France). He has worked at the Head Office of the West African States Central Bank (BCEAO) in Dakar, and has held senior positions at the Institute of Sahel in Bamako, Mali and at the School of Management in Lyon, France. He is also a research fellow at the Agricultural Research Centre for International Development (CIRAD) and Cotton Technical Advisor at The Commission of West African Economic and Monetary Union (WAEMU), Ouagadougou, Burkina Faso. His publications cover a range of issues related to central banking and finance in West Africa, and the economics of the cotton industry in that region, among others.

Carlos Oya is Senior Lecturer in Political Economy of Development, Development Studies Department, School of Oriental and African Studies, University of London. He has done primary research mostly in Mozambique, Senegal and Mauritania, focusing on agrarian issues, rural labour and poverty, about which he has published widely. He has also done substantial work on rural accumulation and agrarian capitalism in Africa, particularly in Senegal. He worked for several years for the Government of Mozambique, at the Ministry of Planning and Finance, where he developed an interest in the political economy of foreign aid relations and policy space in aid-dependent countries.

Vishnu Padayachee is Senior Professor and Head of the School of Development Studies at the University of KwaZulu-Natal. He has a PhD from the University of Natal. His research interests cover a variety of disciplinary fields, including macroeconomic policy; finance, banking and monetary policy; and the politics of race and sport. His latest books (2002) include *(D)urban Vortex* (with Bill Freund); *Blacks in Whites: A Century of Cricket Struggles in KwaZulu-Natal* (with Ashwin Desai, Krish Reddy and Goolam Vahed); and *The Development Decade? Economic and Social Change in South Africa, 1994–2004*. He is an African Associate at Cambridge University's African Studies Centre and a former non-executive director of the South African Reserve Bank (1996–2007).

Nicolas Pejout is Associate Researcher at the Centre d'Étude d'Afrique Noire (CEAN, Bordeaux, France) and Senior Consultant at Eurogroup, the first independent French consulting firm in strategy and organization. His current research focuses on the development of the information society in developing countries, particularly in Africa. He is investigating two main dynamics: the emergence of e-government/e-politics and the development of an ICT-based 'new economy'. He received his PhD in Development Socio-Economics from the École des Hautes Études en Sciences Sociales (EHESS, Paris, France) in 2007.

Nicolas Pons-Vignon is a Senior Researcher at the Corporate Strategy and Industrial Development (CSID) centre in the School of Economic and Business Sciences, University of the Witwatersrand, South Africa. He holds a BA and an MA from Sciences-Po (Paris), and an MSc from SOAS (London). After graduating from SOAS, Nicolas worked in Morocco with an international NGO, before joining the OECD Development Centre in Paris where he researched land-related violent conflicts. Nicolas is doing his PhD in Political Economy at EHESS (Paris), and has spent three years as a Research Fellow at the French Institute of South Africa (IFAS) in Johannesburg. He is the founder and Course director of the African Programme on Rethinking Development Economics (Aporde).

Caroline Skinner is a senior researcher at the African Centre for Cities at the University of Cape Town in South Africa. She is also the Urban Policies Programme Coordinator for the global research policy network Women in Informal Employment: Globalizing and Organizing (WIEGO) and a Research Associate in the School of Development Studies at the University of KwaZulu-Natal. She has worked on the informal economy, urban planning and labour markets in South Africa and Africa over an extended period, and is completing her PhD at the School of Development Studies in this research area. She has published most recently (with Richard Dobson) 'Working in Warwick: including street traders in urban plans'.

Alex Warren-Rodríguez is economic policy advisor with the United Nations Development Programme (UNDP) in Vietnam. Prior to his current position with UNDP, he worked for several years in Mozambique as a consultant and technical advisor for the ministries of finance and planning and development on trade, public finance, development planning, and private sector development issues. He holds a BA in economics from the Autonomous University of Barcelona and an MSc and PhD in development economics from the School of Oriental and African Studies of the University of London. His research focuses on the analysis of technology acquisition and industrial development dynamics in developing countries, with a particular focus on sub-Saharan Africa.

1 Introducing the African economy

Vishnu Padayachee and Keith Hart

The strategy of this book

Since the millennium, some observers have seen evidence of economic recovery in parts of Africa. This was fuelled partly by a rise in world prices for the continent's minerals exports (see Freund below), partly by hot international money in the last years of the credit boom, partly by various endogenous developments. Thus in 2008 Angola had the highest annual growth rate in the world at 23 per cent, as a result of high oil prices, infrastructure reconstruction after three decades of civil war and the renewal of local enterprise. Some countries like Ghana seem to have embarked on a path of political democracy and economic growth, a factor in President Obama's choice of that country to launch a new model of international partnership with Africa. East Africa is a world leader in low-cost computing and the use of mobile telephony for banking, commercial and administrative purposes. As we write, the global economic crisis is said to have snuffed out this precarious revival, with foreign investments drying up and commodity prices collapsed. But this judgment is premature.

This book stands back from such ephemeral journalistic perspectives to address the real possibilities for African development in the coming decades when seen in the light of the continent's economic performance over the last half-century. This involves an effort to emancipate our thinking from the grip of western economic models that have often ignored Africa's diversity in their rush to peddle simple nostrums of dubious merit. We look forward to a time when much of Africa recovers strongly from the setbacks of the immediate post-colonial period and when analysis of its economies will be more securely grounded in local conditions. Neither of these developments has yet occurred. So we introduce here a collection produced by scholars who mostly live and work in Africa, one which keeps an eye open for constructive developments, while surveying the variety of contemporary situations and giving readers a firm grasp of the historical background to our topic.

For two decades, the 1980s and 1990s, Africa seemed to many to have resumed its traditional place as a backward, poor and violent region with only weak connections to the rest of world society, 'the dark continent'.

Whereas, at the start of the twentieth century, Africa's raw material exports and its demand for manufactures were crucial to western industrialization, by its end the region accounted for a tiny part of world trade and only 2 per cent of total purchasing power. This was the heyday of neo-liberal globalization ('the Washington consensus') which deliberately opened up the continent to capital flows and, in the name of 'structural adjustment', dismantled its governments' ability to protect their citizens. The prevailing mood, both at home and abroad, was one of 'Afro-pessimism', a hopeless perspective that saw only the four horsemen of the apocalypse (famine, war, pestilence and death) rampaging through Africa and a regressive 'politics of the belly' there that left many Africans worse off than in colonial times.

It was not always so. The immediate post-independence mood in Africa was optimistic and not without justification. Much progress was made in many newly independent African countries (see Lawrence below). In 1960, Ghana, the world's leading cocoa producer and proud possessor of Africa's most developed middle class, had an economy larger than Indonesia's and a per capita income on a par with South Korea's. The youth of western countries, alienated from their own imperialist traditions, looked to the region and others like it for new directions in world political economy. Things began to change in the early 1970s, when the post-war exchange rate system collapsed and the energy crisis threw the world economy into depression (especially markets for non-oil commodities).

The half-century or more since the Second World War offers a striking contrast between its two main periods. In the 1950s and 1960s, global economic growth was strong and this was reinforced by a universal commitment to the developmental state, the idea that governments could raise their national economies through an emphasis on public spending. There was a genuine desire to reduce global inequality by harnessing the resources of the rich to the development needs of the poor. After the watershed of the 1970s, a renewed emphasis on the free market saw the privatization of public commitments and a retreat from the substance of international development. Rather, financial flows from the poor to the rich countries were higher than at any time in the heyday of colonial empire. Africa was one of the principal victims of this trend.

It is easy to forget how quickly national economic fortunes can turn around. In the period between the two world wars, China was the poorest region in the world and torn apart by warlord violence; 80 years later it is seen as a contender with the United States for world leadership. Africa's economic prospects in the coming decades could well be brighter than most people currently consider. As the most striking symbol of an unequal world society structured along racial lines – with whites at the top, browns and yellows in the middle and blacks at the bottom – Africa has much to gain from the current shift in economic power from the West to Asia. At the very least, dominance by the societies of the North Atlantic is being undermined, making for a more fluid world economy than at any time in the modern era.

The present volume thus aims to overcome three obstacles to effective thinking about Africa's economic development. The first is a tendency to lump the continent's many regions together in a vague abstraction, 'Africa', which can then be made the subject of oversimplified general theories, themselves often swinging between polarized extremes. We do not discount the importance of a continental approach to Africa's economic problems (see Hart and Hart and Padayachee below), but this is an historical project with a long way yet to go and it should not divert us from engaging with Africa's diversity now. The second problem concerns how 'development' might be imagined. In the past this has often been represented as a leap from one idea to its negation, from 'colonialism' to 'independence', from 'capitalism' to 'socialism', whereas historical reality is always a more gradual shift in emphasis between plural institutions that coexist across time and space. The third concerns political agency. African politicians and intellectuals often talk as if development were a free choice from a smorgasbord of historical or comparative examples, to follow the American, Russian, Korean or Chinese route regardless of the constraints imposed by world political economy at a given moment.

The intellectual problem here concerns a widespread inability to keep more than a single idea in one's head at a time, to think dialectically about the global and the national, about the state, the market and popular institutions, about the here and now versus other times and places conceived of in the long run. The strategy of this volume is to take systematic steps towards redressing this problem. Its form to some extent mirrors its content. We start with African political economy seen in overview, proceed to analyses that have general application in Africa, move then to particular case studies which reflect more accurately conditions on the ground and finally engage with new directions in the continent's political economy. We do not claim that we have resolved all the issues that stand in the way of an adequate conceptualization of Africa's development dilemmas. But we hope that the design of the book and its range of chapters point towards a more positive construction of its economic problems and their potential solution.

In what follows we will consider the meaning that might be attached to our title and the tension between external and internal voices when it comes to analysing and prescribing paths of African development. Then we will summarize the contents and organization of the chapters. We will finally offer some brief conclusions.

An African political economy?

Every person of African descent, whatever their actual history and experience – they could be Barack Obama, for example – suffers the practical consequences of being stigmatized by colour in a world society that has been built on racial difference. The United States and South Africa stand out for their racist oppression of black people, whether under slavery, colonialism or apartheid. But many Africans do not share this extreme history. Nigeria in West Africa, for example is a populous region that suffered the predations of the slave trade for centuries, but never had to accommodate white settlers and endured colonialism for a relatively short period. One in six Africans is a Nigerian and it makes no sense at all to approach their history through the lens of colonial empire – before, during and after.

There is already some precedent for viewing Africa as a unity. The African Union, NEPAD and other continental institutions do exist after all. Africa's relative poverty has increased in the last half-century, but, from being the most sparsely populated and least urbanized major region around 1900, Africa's seventh of the world's population now equals its share of the total land mass; and urbanization there is fast approaching the global average of around a half. Africa is divided into three disparate regions – North, South and Middle (West, Central and East Africa); but a measure of convergence between them is now taking place, raising the prospect of economic and political union, as once envisaged in Pan-Africanist ideology. This prospect has been boosted by commitments and time lines agreed by the AU for monetary union, as well as by the recent election as AU President of Libya's Colonel Muammar Gaddafi, a champion of a 'United States of Africa', as once promoted by Ghana's Kwame Nkrumah. Such a process draws on the collective aspirations of black people for their long-delayed emancipation, but it is a matter of universal concern since the blight of racism affects us all.

So, the idea of 'Africa' may be most suitably conceived of as a continental territory – Africans, Arabs and Europeans alike – possibly embarked on a march towards economic and political union. But the legacy of imperialism means that race and development are still linked in symbolic and practical terms; and dreams of African emancipation have global, not just regional implications. It would not be surprising if an economics conceived of in universal terms found it difficult to embrace such an historical and dialectical notion of Africa. And this has indeed been the case. Most writing about African economy borrows wholesale from western mainstream economics as practised at hegemonic institutions such as the World Bank (see Fine below). We have adopted the term 'political economy' because it draws attention to the variable political institutions that structure African economy over time. It follows from this that we are sensitive to the question of how far economic ideas and policies concerning Africa originate from outside or inside the continent.

There is no African 'personality' in economics. There is no 'African' economic theory as such that has been developed for and is applicable only to Africa. Most of the writing on economics and economic development problems and theory is usually presented in general terms applicable to all the world or to all of the underdeveloped world. Much of this is relevant to Africa and often has been the result of research on Africa, but the conclusions are generalized into theory which is not limited to Africa alone. However, there are aspects of economic problems which are especially applicable to Africa, as well as specifically African manifestations of general economic phenomena (Kamarck, 1965: 221).

Is there something that can be described as an African economics, distinguishable from economics in general or western economics? Or, put another way, do 'we have to avoid the accusation (and reality) of eurocentrism' (see Fine below)? This poses quite a challenge (see Freund below and elsewhere), since a coherent African tradition of economic theory and policy is indeed hard to find. Maloka dissents from this view: 'While African leaders can be faulted in many ways, they have made a series of heroic efforts since the early 1970s to craft their own indigenous development paradigms in the light of their own perceptions' (2002:1); and his book reproduces some key documents produced within Africa since then.

A number of factors do appear to have restricted African intellectual production in recent decades. Amina Mana lists the poor state of Africa's universities, autocratic national regimes and the influence of international financial institutions as major contributory factors. 'African underdevelopment' is thus intellectual as well as economic. Yet she insists that 'Africa's more critical intellectuals have contributed significantly to the emergence of the alternative theories, analyses, and methodologies' (2006: 214–15). Mahmood Mandani argues that African intellectuals must also share the blame. Following independence,

> We celebrated. We had arrived. We read off the social history of the national movement as a national history of the social movement. We reduced social history to political history and political history sometimes to political biography of national leaders. We articulated a state nationalism . . . We did not touch the question of popular struggle.
>
> (1992: 193–4)

The disciplines associated with development and political economy are just as uneven. Continental networks such as the African Economics Research Consortium and the African Capacity Building Foundation have done sound work, but could be said to have stayed too close to the orthodoxy of the Bretton Woods institutions. The ACBF has been partly funded by the World Bank and UNDP; it is a co-sponsor of the AERC and supports Nepad's development goals. A more heterodox and some would say progressive source of research and collaborative networks are the somewhat older institutions, Council for the Development of Social Science Research in Africa (CODESRIA) and the Association for African Women for Research and Development (AAWORD). The Egyptian-born, French-trained Marxist economist, Samir Amin, heads the Dakar-based Third World Forum, which links African, Asian and Latin American scholars concerned to articulate alternatives to the standard options associated with globalization. Amin has made major contributions to the theory and practice of development (especially *Unequal Development*, 1976), including exchanges with André Gunder

Frank and others in the influential debates over dependency in the 1970s. He has long insisted on 'delinking' as a precondition for more self-sustaining national development models in developing countries. The Kampala-based Centre for Basic Research was established by a group of scholars and trade unionists with the aim of reversing a situation where 'academics were increasingly being drawn into short-term consultancies to cater for immediate financial needs, thus making long term research and critical intellectual discourse a prerogative of non-national academics and agencies' (www.cbr-ug.org).

Vishnu Padayachee has had direct experience of the situation in South Africa in the run up to democracy and immediately after. Progressive South African economists joined forces then with their western-based, mostly Marxist counterparts, as well as with local progressive social movements and trade unions, and later the African National Congress itself to debate and formulate appropriate development strategies and economic policies for the post-apartheid dispensation. A strong local cadre was based mainly in the liberal universities of Cape Town, Witwatersrand and Natal, and the historically-black Universities of Durban-Westville and Western Cape. They set up research networks such as the Economic Trends Research Group (ET) and the Industrial Strategy Group (ISP). The ANC alliance itself established, with financial support from Canada and other western donors, the Macroeconomics Research Group (MERG) to articulate a macroeconomic policy framework for post-apartheid reconstruction and development. Its recommendations were then dumped by the ANC leadership in favour of an approach more consistent with the Washington Consensus (Padayachee, 1998).

When the ANC seemed determined to toe the line of the World Bank and IMF, many progressive economists quickly shed their 'radical' tag for the resources and prestige of association with these powerful global actors. There may have been other reasons why they caved in. Fine and Rustomjee note that the social sciences in South Africa have been 'insulated or cushioned from intellectual developments elsewhere' (1996: 248). Although some key ideas were imported there, 'economics has been underdeveloped even from orthodox perspectives and political economy has tended to be practiced more by those originating in other disciplines' (1996: 248). Relative isolation, a lack of innovative thinking, the absence of a rigorous tradition of economic debate and the fact that most economists working with social movements were not trained as such, left them vulnerable to the neo-liberal juggernaut, when right-wing ideas, backed by powerful global institutions entered South Africa in a big way after 1990 (Padayachee and Sherbutt, 2007).

Desai and Bohmke (1997) trace this 'retreat' in the thinking and practice of progressive South African social scientists from the mid-1980s in a blistering polemic. The mainly white, male economists in the ET were at first closely allied to the non-racial trade union movement and were unafraid to criticize the tactics and strategies of the ANC, when necessary. An anti-apartheid, 'Bohemian-style' sub-culture knit this exclusive group together. But with the demise of apartheid the 'bottom fell out of their market'. As the 'new government moved to the right', the research work and theoretical disposition of progressive economists, 'moved in tandem' (1997: 30–1). Most of the ET group tossed their main weapon – critique – into the sea and sought their own political rehabilitation as power shifted by becoming consultants to the ANC and then providing academic rationalizations for neo-liberal economic philosophy. 'Because this same set had so dominated left-thinking in South Africa, their betrayal has all but crushed a critique of the transition' (1997: 32).

This implosion of a South African cohort of progressive economists after 1994 probably made less of an impact on policy formulation for post-apartheid reconstruction and development than seemed the case at the time. Nor have they left a model for future generations of how progressive scholars might relate to their governments (Padayachee, 1998, Padayachee and Sherbutt, 2007). So perhaps the emergence of a distinctive South African school of political economy was not so exceptional after all.

The chapters

The sequence of chapters moves from the most inclusive approaches to Africa as a whole to the quite specific local case studies. There are grouped as follows:

Part I   African political economy in overview
Part II   Analytical perspectives on Africa
Part III   African case studies
Part IV   New directions

Overviews

The first three chapters address Africa's recent economic history in very general terms. They deal with the empirical record, social history and economic ideas, respectively.

Peter Lawrence reviews Africa's economic performance since the 1960s. Until then African economies had experienced healthy growth rates, increasing investment, and fast-rising exports, mostly agricultural. Substantial foreign aid and investment made up for low national savings rates. At the same time, many social indicators – life expectancy, infant mortality, access to clean water, school enrolment and literacy rates – were unacceptably low. In the last two decades this situation has been reversed, with remarkable progress in some social indicators, while economic performance has deteriorated badly and debt burdens have built up, severely straining external accounts in many countries. This record is highly variable across Africa, but the continent has stagnated relative to much of Asia. Indonesia's per capita income is now 3.5 times higher than Ghana's and South Korea's 47 times higher! Lawrence lists several explanations for this 'African tragedy', both exogenous and endogenous. He concludes that mineral resources might support infrastructure development and related industries, but it could merely enrich foreign companies and local political elites, as so often before.

Bill Freund suggests that economic growth figures in Africa largely reflect the rise and fall of export commodity prices. He prefers to look at underlying trends in the continent's social history since 1960, including urbanization, the decline of agriculture and emigration. This sets a framework for analysing the sociology of Africa's political economy: the scope of the 'informal economy', the labour market, accumulation and the state. In each case, it is important to emphasize differences between regions. Freund also argues that it now makes little sense to exclude South Africa from general discussions of African development.

Ben Fine shows how development thinking emerged after the Second World War and how this classical model differs from the development economics of recent times, before launching a blistering attack on that (neo-liberal) economics. Africa is regarded as being both exceptional *and* homogeneous, leading to a search for the source of the elusive African 'dummy', the statistical artefact that explains the continent's poor performance. Fine does point to a possible 'renaissance of political economy approaches to Africa that are sensitive to both systemic and contextual influences' that would emphasize the traditional factors: class, power, conflict of interests and the state. We need to understand the nature of contemporary capitalism in the light of a financial crisis that ought to open developing thinking to new approaches (G. Hart forthcoming). Like Lawrence and echoing Freund's argument, Fine points to how endogenous social forces need to capitalize on any temporary gains from commodity exports to make durable investments.

General perspectives

Carlos Oya questions the prevailing pessimism over Africa's agricultural economic performance, finding rather substantial but uneven evidence of success. He discusses the diversity of agrarian structures and processes of change in relation to shifts in policy regime, particularly the recent withdrawal of the state. A Green Revolution in Africa would raise rural incomes and reduce poverty through a renewed commitment to production of export crops. Market liberalization has impaired the ability of small farmers to remain on the land, leading to masses of footloose labour living precariously between rural and urban areas. 'African performance in agriculture has not been bad', he concludes, 'but it could have been very much better given the favourable international demand conditions', especially when compared with Asia.

According to Ward Anseeuw, some African countries have been sensitive to the potential for a reinvigorated agriculture, among them Senegal and Kenya. Kenya has a more 'capitalist' system than Senegal's 'African socialism', yet both states once intervened directly in the agricultural sector. But in times of severe economic crisis both countries abandoned such approaches and, under IMF and World Bank structural adjustment programmes, they began to liberalize, with disastrous results. In 2004, both countries changed tack again, now emphasizing the promotion of new forms of governance (particularly in the framework of Nepad). Anseeuw finds that so far neither country has followed through on plans for greater consultation in agriculture. This leads inevitably to food crises in a general context of agricultural failure.

Jonathan Di John explores the fiscal crisis of the state in Africa through the theme of taxation. Tax policy and systems are vital to viability of states. Taxes on trade taxes account for a third of revenues in Africa and economic liberalization has made it harder to raise such taxes. Di John examines the strengths and weaknesses of the Ugandan tax reform process, while exploring how Mozambique and Zambia have fared in transforming commodity bonds into increased tax revenue. As well, he discusses how South Africa has established autonomous revenue authorities to great effect. He shows how these countries set about their tax reforms and draws some implications for other countries. Above all, his study demonstrates the value of an understanding of history and politics in enabling policy-makers to design effective and sustainable tax systems.

Ndikumana and Boyce address the perplexing problem of the 'revolving door': the use of borrowed funds to finance capital flight. Large-scale capital flight from Africa predates the debt crisis that began in the early 1980s. Africa is a net creditor to the rest of the world in that private assets held abroad exceed the continent's liabilities. So why are Africans so poor? 'Private external assets belong to a narrow, relatively wealthy stratum of the population, while public external debts are borne by the people though their governments.' Newly democratic governments may argue that responsibility for debts incurred by dictatorial regimes does not lie with the current government, but with the individuals 'whose personal fortunes are the real counterpart of the debt'. Such an approach might induce more responsible lending by western financial institutions and more accountable debt management by African governments.

Devereux and Lund review the evolution of welfare policy in Africa from pre-colonial to post-colonial times, and then explore welfare interventions with a primary focus on social security, using a life course approach: children, working age adults and older persons (where there is evidence of the increasing burden of care imposed on older persons by the impacts of HIV and AIDS). A romanticized image of pre-colonial Africa as a 'more caring and sharing' and less materialistic society, permits, underpins, in part, the argument mounted by the World Bank and the like, against the extension of state welfare interventions.

Significant differences exist across the continent in social security provisions, with evidence of a rapid and innovative expansion of social protection in recent decades in North Africa (especially Algeria, Egypt and Tunisia).

Within SSA, South Africa and to a lesser extent Namibia and Botswana, have extensive formal social security and somewhat higher rates of formal employment, though high rates of HIV/AIDS infection and falling formal employment more recently, suggest that the picture even here is not an entirely comfortable one. Apart from these regions there is very little left in the field of social security on the continent. The authors call for a shift in welfare provision from an ad hoc, unaccountable donor-driven social protection model (built in part around emergency food aid) to an indigenized, democratized 'social assurance' model. Yet there appears to be a perplexing dormancy of civil society in much of Africa, with regard to mass mobilization and participation around welfare rights (cross reference).

Carlos Oya and Nicolas Pons-Vignon make a compelling case for increased aid to economic potential in the long term. A period of increased aid beginning in the 1970s was succeeded by the 'aid fatigue' of the 1990s. Since then China has emerged as a new source. The demands placed on African civil services by this aid has drained administrative capacity, while the narrow good governance discourse of the New Aid Agenda in Africa reduced the role of states to being just an instrument of pro-poor service delivery. They offer severe criticism of arguments such as Paul Collier's (2006) that, because aid can attract rents which generate corruption, it should be made even more conditional. The example of American aid to South Korea combines much corruption with significant economic results. They argue that donors should get back to basics (infrastructure, for example) and avoid social engineering exercises, with a view to reducing reliance on aid in the long term through focusing more on domestic resource mobilization.

James Heintz reviews employment in Africa, examining the link with poverty and the bias in policy towards the informal employment. Not much has changed since the work of Hart (Ghana) and the ILO (Kenya) in the early 1970s. His overview of five countries (Ghana, Mali, Kenya, Madagascar and South Africa) shows that, while agriculture remains a critical source of employment, informal employment and the public sector have larger shares of the total. South Africa remains an exception. Women's employment, is lower in North Africa. Heintz finds that limited employment opportunities cannot be attributed to over-regulated or rigid labour markets. Rather, the main challenge is to improve employment opportunities in agriculture. Working conditions in the informal sector should be improved, but a focus on agrarian livelihoods and on expanding formal employment opportunities are equally indispensable.

Caroline Skinner's discussion of street trading in Africa starts from a review of trends in urbanization, migration and economic development. The evidence points to a recent surge in street trading, partly as a result of economic liberalization policies. She assesses developments in policy, planning and governance affecting street trade. State responses range from violent evictions to (rarely) more inclusive approaches. Street traders' organizations reflect this political struggle. Many traders are not part of such organizations.

Skinner concludes that they should be included in urban planning and identifies gaps in research that might inform policy and advocacy. Her chapter draws on a substantial number of case studies in the literature, but she found none from Africa's largest economy, Nigeria.

Nicolas Pejout's essay points to what Africa, with its large informal sector, can achieve by becoming integrated into what he calls the 'ICT-based New Economy'. Africans have sometimes combined the best of both worlds, through investment in three pillars: ICT manufacturing (where South Africa and Nigeria are already big players); call centres (already mushrooming in South Africa and Senegal) and business process outsourcing. Success in this area would include a conducive legal and institutional framework, an appropriate telecoms infrastructure, and a well-balanced skills development strategy. Despite its relative advantage in business processing, South Africa, perceptively described by Pejout as a 'gated new economy', has some way to go in all these areas.

Case studies

Alex Warren-Rodriguez's chapter on state intervention and industrial development in Mozambique shows how successive attempts to industrialize, from the late colonial period through early post-independence (where a flawed strategy of rapid and heavy industrialization was tried) to the current era of reliance on private sector development have all failed. State intervention of varying kinds gave way to a phase of liberalization from the mid-1980s. The latter strategy has set back the state's strategic capacity to intervene effectively to promote industry, and has weakened the institutional framework for industrial policy formulation and implementation. The prospects for achieving broad-based manufacturing development in the country have been dealt a massive blow. Mozambique has been seen as one of Africa's success stories, so this rather gloomy account of industrial developments is sobering.

It is worth pointing here to the contrast offered by another Portuguese ex-colony on the Atlantic seaboard, Angola. From being one of the poorest countries in the world, wracked by civil war and foreign intervention, the country's recent economic performance is remarkable. The government's own figures state economic growth of 15.5 per cent in 2006, though other sources range from 14.2 (Economist Intelligence Unit) to 26 per cent (OECD). Predictions of GDP growth are even higher: 31 per cent (IMF) and 30 per cent (World Bank) in 2009. The Angolan boom has been based on an increase in oil production in 2009. At the same time, inflation has been brought under control and foreign investment has increased.

Claire Benit deconstructs the idealized opposition between good democracy and bad clientelism, showing how much talk about decentralization, participation and democracy rests on unrealistic notions of political life. While seeking to unravel the complex mechanism of party politics in urban government, she reflects on how close decentralization, corruption and poverty alleviation are in practice. She holds that more localized development can actually lead to *more* corruption. Four stories of what she calls 'mild' clientelism in Johannesburg point to social variations in her analysis. Benit's concluding appeal for closer empirical analysis has wide relevance for contemporary Africa.

Zoe Marriage looks at how security concerns, especially those emerging from world society, have shaped the Congolese economy. Her analysis operates at three levels: external competition for control of Congo's economic and political resources; struggles between sub-national groups for land, identity and resources; and the conflict between political leaders and the population at large. In the period 2002–6, substantial inputs from foreign donors supported programmes offering higher returns for the less violent alternatives of demobilization and participating in peacetime politics. Marriage maintains that western support should be seen as a 'loss-leader', allowing donors to regain some influence after their exit in the early 1990s, in the face of China's new challenge. Congo's recent economic growth has been 'disconnected from domestic politics and development and has been achieved through violence'.

Mawowa and Moore address 'primitive accumulation' in Zimbabwe's violent mineral economy. State actors with access to foreign currency, global networks and the means of coercion play crucial roles beyond mere 'rent-seeking'. The state's responses to smuggling and violence in the informal minerals sector have been highly contradictory. They point to how structural adjustment accelerated the growth of a capitalist class in finance and services, while unemployment, inequality and poverty intensified. Violence-based accumulation projects, mainly in unregulated mining, could be seen as a 'war of position' (Gramsci via Cramer). Primitive accumulation in Africa offers neither self-sustaining capitalist development nor much of a future for kleptocrats like Mobuto and Mugabe.

Hazel Gray and Mushtaq Khan approach the question of 'good governance' through a critique of the new institutional economics. They show how the doubtful evidence of econometric models has been used to support this agenda. Asia offers numerous examples of how rent creation has led to sustained economic growth, but in Africa state-created rents do no more than line the pockets of functionaries and politicians. But, by trying to wipe out state-created rents, the narrow good governance agenda 'has reduced the institutional and political capacity of many African countries to deal with significant market failures'. In Tanzania, while problems in public finance management and certain areas of poor governance have been addressed, many critical areas fall outside this agenda (land management, industrial policy, natural resource management). The Tanzanian state's historical attitude to business has compromised its ability to manage rent in relation to land and industrial policy. The idea that *good governance* tends to favour foreign investors is a consistent theme here.

Kako Nubukpo provides a detailed account of how the imposition of the CFA Franc in its former West and Central African colonies was a way of maintaining French control by stealth. The currency, which is still minted in France, is clearly overvalued, with negative consequences for local producers and exporters. Tight monetarist management of the CFA franc has damaged growth prospects. The sharp devaluation of 1994 did resolve the problems created by its being pegged to the euro. Nubukpo proposes a floating exchange rate system within a band negotiated between the authorities of the regional zone and those of the euro zone. The less rigid exchange rate would send more regular signals to the African populations concerning the overall state of their economies. The import-hungry urban class that currently benefits from a strong convertible currency would lose some of their privilege, while millions of small producers who battle daily for self-sufficiency would be favoured.

New directions

Keith Hart asks how Africa's 'urban revolution' of the twentieth century might prepare the way for significant economic development in the decades ahead. To answer that question he returns to the traditional contrast between kinship-based societies south of the Sahara and the agrarian civilizations of Europe, Asia and North Africa. The model of development offered to African countries after independence was based on 'national capitalism'; but only one country achieved anything like that, South Africa. The rest essentially built a form of agrarian civilization in which new state-made urban elites lived off the surpluses of an intensified agriculture. Any hope of economic growth in the near future must harness the social forces unleashed as part of this process.

The unregulated markets that characterize Africa's burgeoning cities are known principally through the idea of an 'informal economy'. Hart reviews the history of this concept's uses and its limitations, concluding that more attention should be paid to the actual social organization of small-scale urban commerce. He identifies five factors that could be harnessed in a new economic synthesis: the energies of youth and women; religious revival; the explosion in the modern arts; the digital revolution; and links between the new African diaspora and people at home. But what might Africans produce for the world market from their urban heartlands? Hart focuses on the potential of cultural commodities in sectors such as entertainment (including sport), education, the media and information services generally. The United States's leading exports today are films, music and software. There is no reason why Africans should not follow suit. After all, Nigeria's film industry ('Nollywood') has already overtaken Bollywood as the second largest in the world.

The last two chapters examine the recent rise of two new players, China and South Africa, to challenge traditional North Atlantic hegemony in Africa. This allows our volume to conclude on a more forward-looking and speculative note.

Kaplinsky *et al.* address the potential impact of China's economic re-engagement with Africa. During the Cold War, China offered decolonizing Africa moral, political and even military support, as well as economic aid. This chapter covers trade, production, direct investment and aid since 1990. The authors are cautiously optimistic about the potential for Africa of rapid trade expansion with China, but warn about possible costs to some national industries. Thus in Ghana and South Africa, clothing and furniture manufactures have been displaced by Chinese imports. Similar evidence can be found elsewhere. The employment impact falls disproportionately on women with severe impacts for families and poverty. Investment has been in both directions, on the African side, mainly from South Africa.

Chinese aid includes financial support for strategic projects, debt relief, technical training, tariff exemptions and peace-keeping. But Chinese aid has been criticized for its lack of attention to good governance, human rights, environmental protection and social justice. China's economic relations with Africa have been carefully watched by Europe and the United States, not least out of concerns for their own influence in the region. African countries themselves need to weigh up how much they wish to rely on China (and other BRIC countries like India) in their current and future development paths, as opposed to developing closer relations within Africa itself. This point is taken up in the volume's final chapter which focuses on South Africa as a potential catalyst for greater continental cooperation.

There we explore how South Africa might assume a role of political and economic leadership in Africa, starting with its own hinterland. This requires us to dispense with the myths surrounding that relationship, by identifying what South Africa's relations with Africa and the world really have been, both when it was thought to stand apart from the continent and now when it is included. Any sustainable future for Africa as a whole must be consistent with effective solutions to South Africa's long-running attempt to evolve from an export-oriented mining enclave to a modern industrial economy. To this end, we draw on a critique of the concept of 'national capitalism', the dominant model of 'development' in the twentieth century. South Africa is the only country in Africa to have come close to implementing this model, and then only within the benefits of whites in mind.

We identify the persistent problem of South Africa's economic history: its contradictory attempt to make the transition from a mining enclave to a modern economy. The British imperialism that gave birth to modern South Africa was succeeded by two variants of national capitalism: the racially exclusive version devised by the Afrikaner National Party and that pursued by the ANC since the early 1990s. At this time of global economic crisis, the underlying problem of South Africa's development remains unsolved. Regional integration is one path towards a solution; but South Africa has a complicated history of relations within its own region. We propose a more active African strategy for South Africa as a precondition for its own transition to economic democracy. Such a regional perspective must also embrace

African unity in a meaningful way. Rather than return to a mid-century model of industrial development, we base South Africa's (and Africa's) economic future on cultural services, along with finance, transport, construction, energy and minerals.

Concluding remarks

There have been considerable shifts in economic and political power across the world over the past decade. Now, when Africa's lost decade of the 1990s was becoming just a memory, the global economic crisis of 2008–9 has thrown the continent's economic development back into jeopardy. Like other parts of the world, Africa has experienced deep dislocations from the effects of the current global recession. A generation after the Berg report, it is now possible to assess the actual impact of structural adjustment from a better perspective and with more robust data. The aid scene is dominated by new paradigms, but the capacity of the richer African countries to pay back debt has also given them more bargaining power. Because Africa produces so little original research, external accounts of its economic challenges prevail, however ill-founded and self-fulfilling. Thus, the poor condition of the state in much of Africa was worsened by structural adjustment programmes and is now being reproduced through a vicious aid cycle where most projects are run by an *ad hoc* administration rather than by developing the capacity of governments to run them. This African-led volume, while facing up to the continent's long-term problems, aims to dissipate some of the most enduring myths about African political economy. It sets the stage for renewed reflection on how to accelerate development there, helping Africa to catch up with Latin America and Asia, building on its own potential economic powerhouses, such as Egypt, Nigeria and South Africa.

African countries grew steadily by 5 per cent on average from 2002–7, but the economic crisis now threatens to reverse much of these gains: we are seeing massive capital flight as foreign banks retreat to their home markets; credit is increasingly unavailable for exports and long-term infrastructure projects; overall levels of aid to Africa declined even before financial crisis and can be expected to fall even more. African countries called at the G20 summit for a three-fold response to their common plight: a stimulus package to support African recovery; a new and more inclusive architecture of global economic governance; and a halt to protectionist practices by rich countries in finance and trade. The G20 leaders promised a US $1.1 trillion package, but much of this merely repackaged existing commitments. No doubt, in the decades ahead, this short-term perspective too will be overturned by events.

References

Amin, S. (1976): *Unequal Development. (Le développement inégal)*. Monthly Review Press, New York.

Desai, A. and H. Bohmke (1997): The Death of the Intellectual, The Birth of the Salesman. *Debate 3*.

Fine, B. and Z. Rustomjee (1996): *The Political Economy of South Africa, from Mineral Energy Complex to Industrialization*. Witwatersrand University Press, and Hurst, Johannesburg and London.

Kamarck, A. (1965): Economic Development, in Robert Lystad (ed.) *The African World: a survey of social research*. London: Pall Mall Press.

Maloka, E. (2002): Introduction: Africa's development thinking since independence, in Eddy Molaka (ed.) *Africa's Development Thinking Since Independence, A Reader*. Africa Institute of South Africa, Pretoria.

Mama, A. (2006): Critical capacities: Facing the challenge of intellectual development, in Africa, in Amanda Alexander, (ed.). *Articulations: A Harold Wolpe Memorial Lecture in Africa*, Centre for Civil Society, Durban.

Mandani, M. (1992): Comment on 'Research and social transformation', special issue *Transformation*, 18/19.

Padayachee, V. (1998): Progressive academic economists and the challenge of development in South Africa's decade of liberation. *Review of African Political Economy*, Vol. 25, No. 77.

Padayachee, V. and G. Sherbutt (2007): Ideas and power; academic economists and the making of economic policy, SDS Working paper, 43.

Part I

African political economy in overview

2 The African tragedy

International and national roots

Peter Lawrence

Introduction

The course of sub-Saharan Africa's development over the last 50 years has been frequently referred to as the 'African tragedy' (Leys, 1994, Easterly and Levine, 1997, Artadi and Sala-i-Martin, 2003). The tragedy of the last 50 years has been played out through war (among many examples, Biafra, Rwanda, Darfur, Angola, Congo/Zaire), disintegration of economies and states (most notably in Somalia and now Zimbabwe), and perhaps most depressingly given the advances in medical science elsewhere in the world, disease. In sub-Saharan Africa in 2007,[1] 1.6 million people died from AIDS, 76 per cent of the world total, and 61 per cent of them women. Malaria kills almost 1 million people a year, while TB, often a side effect of AIDS, kills hundreds of thousands. And if that were not bad enough, road deaths kill 200,000 people in Africa each year. When some parts of the continent suffer drought, as in Somalia in 2008, others suffer floods, as in Southern Africa in the same year. The consequence of all these factors taken together is food shortage causing malnutrition, hunger and death and seriously negative effects on output and on the quality of the labour force, with consequent effects on productivity, costs and competitiveness.

Fifty years ago there was considerable optimism about Africa's development prospects.[2] African economies exported a range of agricultural crops and minerals. Most countries produced most if not all of their domestic basic food needs. Some countries had emerging industrial sectors, mainly food processing, usually owned by foreign investors, or after independence set up as joint ventures by foreign firms and the government. Economic and social infrastructure in the form of schools, hospitals, roads, railways and power generation was growing.

However, the 1960s also saw the Nigerian war with breakaway Biafra, the Congo war with breakaway Katanga, and the coup, nine years into independence in Ghana which overthrew one of the founding fathers of African liberation, Kwame Nkrumah. Alongside these upheavals came the growing liberation struggles to free the Portuguese colonies, and the white minority regimes in Rhodesia and South Africa. This was a pattern of things to come in which the pessimism of post-independence instability was more than balanced by the optimism of further liberation. Finally, great power rivalry was never far away, with different regimes and liberation movements lining up with the US, USSR and China. In Tanzania, while the Chinese were building the railway to Zambia, the Americans were building a road in the same direction. Great power rivalry for a while improved African countries' bargaining power in the pursuit of aid and investment.

This chapter reviews SSA's economic performance since the 1960s, looks at explanations that have been given for this performance and assesses the policies derived from them. The next section details economic performance and social developments. The following section considers explanatory factors both internal and external to African economies, while the final section draws conclusions for framing future development policy.

Sub-Saharan Africa's economic performance since the 1960s

The 1960s was a period of healthy growth rates and increasing investment. Eleven of the 29 countries for which there is data available had export growth rates of between 10 and 26 per cent a year, and all but seven had growth rates over 5 per cent a year. Exports were dominated by agricultural primary commodities. Of the 24 countries for which there is data, agricultural output grew by over 3 per cent a year in half of them. Eleven of the 35 countries for which data is available had positive external balances, while of those that averaged negative balances over the 1960s, nearly half of them amounted to less than 5 per cent of GDP. Of the 32 countries for which there is data available, nine had growth rates of over 5 per cent a year and a further 13 over 3 per cent a year.

Almost a quarter of the 34 countries for which there is data available were investing on average over 20 per cent of their GDP, while almost half were investing more than 15 per cent. Seventeen of 29 countries had investment growth rates ranging from 5 to 31 per cent.

Most countries' savings rates were well below investment rates, implying substantial foreign aid and investment. More than half of the countries for which data is available showed industrial growth rates of more than 6 per cent a year.

The social indicators were much less healthy, some literally so. Life expectancy at birth ranged from 32 years in Sierra Leone to 61 in Mauritius. Infant mortality rates across the decade ranged from 91 deaths per 100 live births in what was then Rhodesia to 255 in Mali. In most countries access to clean water was restricted to between 10 and 30 per cent of the population and fewer than 20 per cent of the adult population could be classed as literate. Primary school enrolment rates in the majority of countries fell below 40 per cent, while secondary enrolment rates were between 2 per cent and 6 per cent of the age cohort and tertiary rates were normally below 1 per cent.

Comparing the data for the 1960s with recent data for the same set of

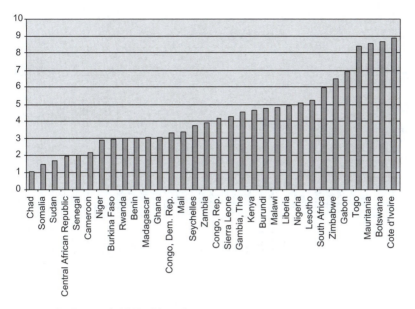

Figure 2.1 GDP growth 1960s (% p.a.).

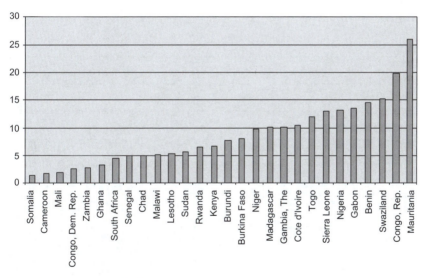

Figure 2.2 Export growth 1960s (% p.a.).

countries, there are signs of substantial progress in socio-economic development. Looking at changes in the indicators considered above, there are several countries in which life expectancy has increased by 20–30 years (although the impact of AIDS in some countries has led to a fall) and infant mortality

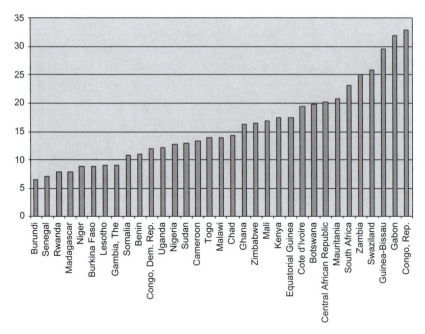

Figure 2.3 Investment as % of GDP 1960s.

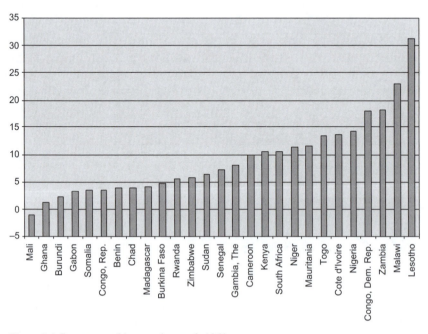

Figure 2.4 Investment % annual growth 1960s.

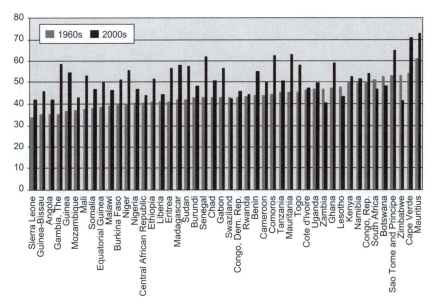

Figure 2.5 Life expectancy 1960s and 2002–6 (average).

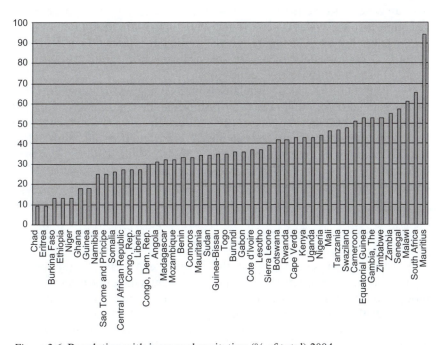

Figure 2.6 Population with improved sanitation (% of total) 2004.

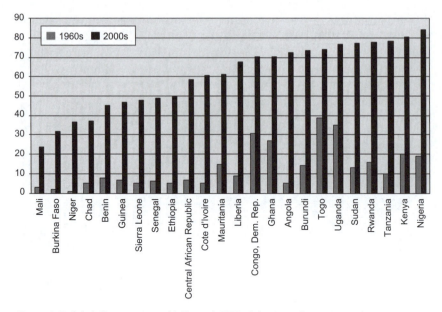

Figure 2.7 Adult literacy rates 1960s and 2002–6 (averages).

rates have fallen dramatically. The proportion of the population with access to clean water has doubled and in some cases trebled, although of the bottom 40 countries in the Water Poverty Index, 33 of them are in SSA. Literacy rates have risen impressively. Primary school enrolment is over 60 per cent in a majority of countries. Secondary school enrolment rates have increased massively, as have those for tertiary education.

However, countries which saw relatively high GDP growth rates in the 1960s have experienced declining rates of growth, while the opposite has happened in some countries especially those where oil or other key raw materials have been discovered and/or have seen an increase in world demand. Both industrial and agricultural growth rates have dropped. Manufacturing growth is down on the rates of the 1960s and in some cases is severely negative. Most countries have deficits in external balances, savings ratios have fallen, though there appears to have been some increase in investment ratios in several countries. Infrastructural development remains poor as evidenced by the data on electricity consumption, the proportion of paved roads, and the number of telephone lines, although there has been an enormous increase in the use of mobile telephony since the end of the last decade. A further factor impacting on African development has been the continent's high rate of population growth. In the last four decades Africa's total population has increased more than threefold, in spite of the impact of HIV/AIDS and other killer diseases. More interestingly, the urban population has increased eightfold putting greater pressure on urban service provision and infrastructure but

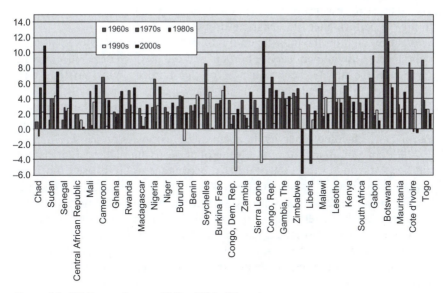

Figure 2.8 GDP growth rates 1960s–2000s (% p.a.).

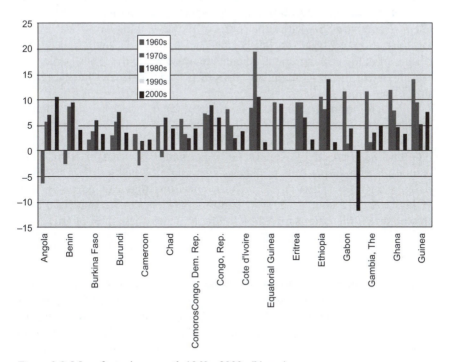

Figure 2.9 Manufacturing growth 1960s–2000s (% p.a.).

also increasing the proportion of the total population dependent on the improved performance of the agricultural sector.

Figuring high on the international public policy agenda has been Africa's debt, its consequent debt service burden, and the need for debt relief and aid to reverse the negative consequences of this burden. While Africa's debt service burden may be falling in recent years, partly as a result of the HIPC (Highly Indebted Poor Countries) initiative which wrote off a large amount of some countries' debt, it still eats up a considerable proportion of export earnings which could otherwise be spent on development projects.

The 'debt mountains' arose as a result of previous multilateral and bilateral aid flows starting in the 1960s. Aid as a percentage of GNI rose from 2 per cent in 1960 to over 7 per cent in 1995, falling to 4 per cent in 2000. This ratio has increased in the last few years. Aid per capita has followed much the same trajectory but has risen sharply in the last few years. However, the overall picture for SSA disguises the extent to which aid has been channelled to post-conflict countries and it is not clear how much of this is peacekeeping and some of those countries are beginning to find their debt service burden increasing as a result.

What this brief overview of SSA's economic performance shows is that there is substantial variation in performance across countries and sectors. Some countries have done better than others and many have undergone substantial changes in structure. Significant progress has been made in some areas of health and education and economic infrastructure. However, it is when we compare SSA with other parts of the developing world that we see why the notion of Africa's variously labelled 'tragedy' or 'growth tragedy' has taken root in the popular and academic literature. Since the 1960s, while SSA has stagnated, the developing countries of the East Asia and Pacific region have grown rapidly.

In 1960, for example, the GDP per capita of Ghana was three times that of Indonesia and one and a half times that of South Korea. By 2006, Indonesia's was nearly 3.5 times and Korea's 47 times that of Ghana. Nigeria, which in 1960 had 85 per cent of Korea's GDP pc, had 3 per cent in 2006, while Indonesia, with 59 per cent of Nigeria's pc GDP in 1960 had 2.25 times its GDP pc in 2006. There are similar comparisons that can be made with Malaysia and Thailand. The next section considers factors that have been presented as explanations for SSA's failure to match these rates of growth.

Explanations

So why have even the better performing countries of SSA failed to fulfil the growth potential envisaged after political independence? What explains the differences in performance between different countries? What explains the differences in performance between the sub-Saharan African and East Asian countries?

Taking the last question first, are there any differences in 'initial' conditions

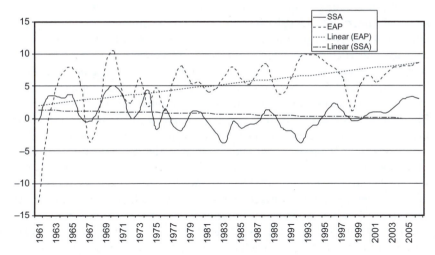

Figure 2.10 Growth in EAP and SSA 1961–2006 (% p.a.).

back in 1960, broadly within the same range in terms of economic structure, which might help understand why these two sets of countries took such different tracks? One answer lies in education. The Asian countries had much higher primary, secondary and tertiary enrolment rates than the African ones, and consequently higher literacy rates. Primary enrolment and adult literacy were roughly double those of the African countries, while secondary and tertiary enrolments were up to five times higher (WDI Online). This suggests that the differences in educational achievement were so big back in 1960 to make this appear to be a key component in successful development in the second half of the twentieth century.

The reason for the differences in the levels of educational attainment can largely be traced to the nature of the colonial regimes. Sub-Saharan Africa was eventually colonised by five countries: Britain, France, Portugal, Belgium and Spain. While each of the colonisers operated different legal systems and different degrees of integration with the imperial centres, they all saw the colonies as sources of mineral and agricultural wealth. The colonial state's function was to assist in the extraction of this wealth and therefore whatever 'development' took place was directed to this end. The developmental phase of colonial state activity came quite late in the day in a somewhat hasty preparation for political independence, as universities were established and more schools were built, and other economic and social infrastructure was expanded.

Countries with a relatively large European settler population – most notably, South Africa and (Southern) Rhodesia – developed in a different way that privileged the white population. Their later transition to black majority rule created a different set of development problems than for the countries that became independent in the late 1950s and 1960s. In these two countries, as in the Portuguese colonies of Mozambique, Angola and Guinea-Bissau, successful liberation struggles involving military campaigns created very different outcomes after liberation. The Zimbabwean government under Robert Mugabe inherited a relatively successful independent economy resulting from the previous white government's fight against economic boycott. Both Zimbabwe and South Africa were restricted in their development policy by external pressures, especially from the World Bank and IMF. In the case of Zimbabwe, this resulted in the demise of a successful import substitution industrialisation, an economic decline in which those with power sought to ensure their share of the economic spoils, and the descent into its current economic and political chaos. In South Africa, in an as yet different outcome, the black-led governments have so far avoided those excesses by protecting the property rights of foreign capital and persuading the white minority capitalist class to share some of its economic power with the new rising black bourgeoisie. In Mozambique and Angola, liberation was followed by civil war, with the rebel groups in each country supported by the white minority regime in South Africa.

Elsewhere, the French colonial regimes pursued a policy of educating an elite of the colonised and even giving them representation in the French parliament. The British colonisers preferred to pursue a different policy, first indirect rule through the local chiefs, and then switching towards the objective of local self-government. The consequence of both approaches was to integrate the local 'elites' into the structures set up by the colonial state so that at independence the institutional inheritance was not one created organically out of the development of the institutions of 'traditional' rule but one superimposed by colonial rule. It then took on the developmentalist mantle it inherited from the colonial state. However, as Cooper (2002) has observed, this 'developmentalist' state had also to fulfil the role of a 'populist-clientalist' state. Governments were expected to reward their supporters in ways which contradicted the developmentalist project of effective allocation of resources to maximise growth. Thus the initial conditions at independence embodied much continuity from the colonial regimes with some changes of policy emphasis to accompany the change in regime, most notably in those countries that adopted nationalisation of productive enterprises as their preferred method of state intervention.

There are several other plausible explanations for the differences in African and East Asian performance which can be broadly categorised as nationally and internationally based. Nationally based explanations usually begin with the failings of early development policy, although a prior factor in explaining SSA economic development needs to lay some emphasis on class and class structure. For our purposes the important issue was the absence of an accumulating and investing local capitalist class. While there were relatively small scale entrepreneurs and traders and some exceptional, usually Asian, large scale traders and plantation owners, who formed an incipient local capitalist class, it was the state that would have to perform the function of such a class. Those countries that chose a broadly 'socialist' path regarded the state as representative of peasants and workers, but in most cases these states formed alliances with foreign capital to generate investment in productive activity.

Early development emphasis was on infrastructural development led by the 'development state' to assist this process of capital accumulation and investment. The argument ran that if the government built roads and power stations, then this would attract investors who would repay the costs of infrastructure through the tax system and user charges. Investment was unlikely to be attracted without a strong infrastructure, not just economic, but also social – health and education in particular. To generate high rates of growth required high rates of investment growth, especially in manufacturing which, because of rapid technical change, would generate the highest increases in productivity. There was even a number attached to this 'incremental capital output ratio'.

But the argument for state direction of economic development went further. To attract investors, some state involvement was necessary not least to reduce the investment risk. Joint ventures in which the state took a share of ownership was one model. Governments with a more 'socialist' ideology believed that nationalisation or part nationalisation of existing enterprises was an effective way of ensuring that the enterprises concerned were managed in the national interest (or that of peasants and workers in the more explicitly class based versions) and that surpluses were invested domestically rather than repatriated as dividends to shareholders in the developed countries. Overall industrialisation strategy was based on import substitution (ISI), the domestic manufacture of goods previously imported.

This argument for state control was carried into other markets. Price-setting for essential agricultural food products, and for agricultural export crops was accompanied by strict controls over interest rates and foreign exchange rates. For a while this set of policies, carried out to varying extents, was relatively successful with the generally respectable rates of growth described earlier.

However, there were many problems with these policies and with their implementation – not always the ones flagged by the World Bank and other critics of state-led development. Government plans for industrial and agricultural expansion depended on having the means to implement them effectively. Capacity to effect plans was limited by the absence of a sufficiently large well-trained managerial and public service cadre, part of the 'initial conditions' discussed above. Industrial planning was limited to the degree to which foreign capital could be persuaded to invest in new activity. Governments entered into joint ventures with foreign, and some domestic, private capital, in which it took majority or even 100 per cent ownership with the private sector partner providing the managerial and technical expertise in addition to whatever share capital the contracts required them to contribute. For the private investors, there was the possibility of providing fixed and working capital inputs as well as managerial services at inflated prices as a means of generating the high returns to their shareholders that justified investing in what was, and still is, seen as a risky environment (Collier and Pattillo, 2000).

As noted above, there have been substantial variations in manufacturing industrial performance across SSA. The conventional explanation for many countries' poor manufacturing performance has been the import substitution strategy. This has been unsuccessful because of small domestic markets for the goods produced, and consequential inability to take advantage of economies of scale to reduce unit costs and so be competitive with imports, except through protection. Furthermore the production of previously imported goods required the importing of the machine tools and other capital goods needed to produce these new outputs. Often the costs of importing and manufacture were greater than the price of the previously imported good. The prohibition of competitive imports produced domestic monopolies who raised the price to cover their higher costs. This protection without any kind of regulation reduced competitiveness. This and a number of other obstacles to exporting the new products, most notably the prohibition on exports to countries where the foreign partners had established markets, generated increased inefficiencies.

The agricultural sector was no less seen as an arena for state intervention. The estates and plantations of the colonial period were targets for nationalisation. Small scale agriculture could only become more productive with assistance from government agencies. But this assistance could only be delivered if farmers were brought together. Whether these agricultural organisations were titled group farms, *ujamaa* villages, settlement schemes, or irrigation schemes, their principal objectives were to take advantage of perceived economies of scale in farming and in the provision of farm services. Such initiatives largely failed for several reasons. The first was that the architects of the schemes that involved re-settlement of farmers or mechanised agriculture, failed to relate to the characteristics of the farming systems which they sought to replace or improve. Mechanisation of agriculture, for example, assumed that there was a cadre of technical specialists who could maintain agricultural equipment and that such equipment was suitable for the soils and terrain of the areas into which they were introduced. Resettlement of farmers ignored the rationality of shifting cultivation. Tanzania's well-known attempt to bring farmers together into *ujamaa* villages ran up against all these problems, but also a more fundamental one: who controlled the villages – the farmers themselves, or the state agricultural bureaucracy?[3] In many ways, policies as they were implemented had much more to do with political control than economic development.

Most importantly, political independence gave political actors control over the state and the machinery of government. The assumption was made that a constitution that comprised a formal executive, normally the President of the nation, a legislature elected by guaranteed democratic elections and a judiciary formally independent of the other two arms of government, would create a framework of government, and a set of governance principles that would prevent abuse of power. However, this took little if any account of prior government, and governance, principles on the basis of which pre-independence societies functioned. Consequently, it is not too surprising that those with political power saw it as quite legitimate to reward their friends and relatives and fellow ethnic group members with whatever patronage their possession of state power and privilege gave them. Although this still happens in societies with a much longer history of democratic constitutions, the checks and balances are not as strong in African countries as they are in longer established democracies and so the frequency of such 'corrupt' activities is lower.

It is therefore frequently argued that the absence of 'good governance' is an important factor explaining Africa's slow rate of development and distinguishes African countries from other faster-growing developing economies (Collier, 2007, Ndulu and O'Connell, 1999). There are several indices of governance and corruption which reflect the perception of a range of individuals about the relative levels of governance around the world. These indices are based on perceptions by leading actors in the development process (for example, foreign government and non-government organisations, businesses, bankers and traders). As we note below with other measures of African 'difference', they are subject to the problem of endogeneity, that is, the differences that explain lower growth may also be explained by the low growth. The other problem with the catalogue of 'differences' is that they constitute differences with some East Asian countries but not with others. Where African countries are different are in their specific cultural, economic and political history, in their colonial backgrounds and in their post colonial starting points which in turn can be explained by their specific histories.[4]

However, other, largely ahistorical, notions of African 'difference', have become a key feature of 'explanations' for Africa's growth record. According to Collier (2007) not only do the SSA countries differ in their levels of governance, but they also display other characteristics that have a negative effect on growth. Coupled to poor governance is the proliferation of ethnic groups, or 'ethno-linguistic diversity'. Leaders who come from one ethnic group promote the interests of that group against the others thus generating disaffection and ethnic rivalries resulting in coups or civil war. The consequent higher risk of civil war, especially if a country had already had one constitutes another 'difference'.

The within-country fragmentation of African societies is duplicated on the continental scale. Africa, Collier argues, has too many small countries which lack sufficient urban agglomeration to make investment attractive. African countries show few inter-country spillover effects compared with other parts of the world. Resource rich, but landlocked countries, are limited by lack of access to the coast, while coastal countries which are resource poor are unable to do what other resource poor coastal countries, such as those in East Asia, have done in the past and provide trading posts and manufacturing investment bases. The reason offered for this latter problem is that relatively to East Asia, at a crucial point in its development, African labour was relatively expensive and so international companies chose East Asia to expand their activities and lower their costs.

There is certainly a communications infrastructure problem which could also be linked to SSA's primary product resource base. As Rodney (1972: 228) put it so well:

> All roads and railways led to the sea. They were built to extract gold, or manganese, or coffee, or cotton. They were built to make business possible for the timber companies, trading companies and agricultural concession firms and for white settlers.

Telecommunications linked the colonies to the colonial powers, so telephone calls between African countries were routed through European capitals. The same was true for airlines. In the last five decades, while there has been expansion of paved roads and intra-African airline services, and internal communications have been revolutionised by mobile telephony, the pattern of communications remains much the same.

The richness of SSA's mineral resources coupled with the fragmentation of African societies generates different aspects of a resource curse. There is the competition for the spoils which leads to changes in governments by coups d'état, or to civil war. There is the rent-seeking by dominant political groups which reduces the degree to which the surpluses generated by the export of the resources can be invested in manufacturing. There are the exchange rate effects of commodity price booms which distort import and export prices and reduce the possibilities for capital accumulation.

Now some of these findings are not surprising, but the variables that are said to explain why Africa is different need some explanation themselves. It is not always the case for example, that countries are too small to grow, as Taiwan and Singapore have demonstrated. In the case of ethno-linguistic diversity, there is the question of how to balance Tanzania's ethnic and first language diversity with its Swahili *lingua franca* to produce a measure of its ethno-linguistic diversity. Other questions relate to whether the distribution of ethnic groups matters and whether the identified ethnic groups in these indices are reflective of how people identify their loyalties and how much information both contemporary and historical, and of what kind, has gone into the ethno-linguistic indices.

Many of the relationships which prove statistically significant are endogenous. For example, if the propensity to civil war is explained by ethnic diversity, maybe we can also explain the levels of ethnic diversity by the propensity for civil war. It is not implausible to theorise that civil wars cement diversity through promoting ethnic identity and thus generating more civil wars. Similarly poor levels of governance could be a function of growth rates rather than vice versa. Correlation is demonstrated to be sure, but not causation.

The same problem applies to empirical work which seeks to explain manufacturing performance in SSA. A typical finding of recent literature is that successful manufacturing performance in SSA is associated with growth of manufactured exports (Lawrence, 2005). However what this literature fails to explain is why the conditions for export-led growth exist in some countries but not in others. Poor infrastructure, low education levels and political instability, all play a role in deterring the necessary foreign investment, but what needs to be explained is why these factors persist. Such explanations are likely to be different for different countries and will involve differences in institutional development and culture. One problem has been the reluctance of neo-classical economic orthodoxy to see a role for the state in direction of investment, such as underpinned the Korean state in its manufacturing strategy, and therefore the importance of state institutions and their level of competence (Wade, 2004).

Low levels of financial development are also regarded as explaining SSA's relatively low rates of growth. The World Bank believes that financial development (financial sector institutions and markets) "contributes significantly to growth;" "is central to poverty reduction;" "directly benefits the poorer segments of society;" and "is associated with improvements in income distribution" (World Bank, 1989). However, empirical work on the first assertion suggests that the causative relationship between financial liberalisation and growth may run both ways or not at all, depending on country and time period, findings that accord well with common sense (Lawrence, 2006). There are good reasons for this. Informal sector institutions play a much more important role in supplying credit in developing countries than they do in developed countries. The liberalisation of financial markets and institutions meant that banks could no longer be protected by the state and the central bank from lax lending. More care about the selection of borrowers meant that less risky lending was undertaken. The overall effects of this were not to deepen the financial sector to any measurable degree, at least not in the first few years. Less economic activity was generated and therefore opportunities for the poorer section of society were reduced. In any case they would be excluded from formal lending and have to rely on informal lending. Paradoxically, studies have shown that in SSA, informal lending increased after financial liberalisation rather than the expected reverse, another example of what appears to be a robust policy having perverse effects (Nissanke and Aryeety, 1998).

The increased emphasis on the development powers of the financial sector was probably derived from the experience of the financial sector boom following the liberalisation of markets in developed countries in the 1980s. This no doubt contributed to increased growth in those countries. But here the financial sector was well-developed and operating in high income countries was able to take advantage of the changes to develop new markets and products, not to mention having a level of economic activity which generated substantial demand for credit services. However, the financial crises of 2008–9 suggest that there are limits to financial development and the financial sector can accelerate negative growth even more than it might contribute positively to growth.

The international factors explaining SSA's performance can be broadly grouped into two main areas: first, the dependence of SSA economies on world markets for primary products and on foreign investment and aid; second, the policies that the international financial institutions have required SSA governments to follow as a condition for aid. At political independence, the cash economies of SSA were dominated by the production and export of agricultural and mineral primary commodities and the foreign exchange earnings were almost entirely derived from the export of primary products. World markets for these commodities have seen considerable price fluctuations, but the general tendency has been for prices to decline over time. Yet the foreign exchange earnings from primary commodities were intended to be the basis for investment in imported capital goods to develop the nascent manufacturing sector and to supply the spare parts necessary to maintain the sector's growth. In the early stages of post-colonial development this model worked reasonably well with the relatively high growth rates described earlier. However, SSA suffered from a technology gap with the developed countries: the absence of a well-qualified technocracy required not only that new manufacturing activity was carried out by foreign enterprises, but that these enterprises supplied the managerial and technical expertise required to set up and maintain them.

Governments highly dependent on earnings from primary commodities and with a low tax base required foreign aid especially to build the necessary infrastructure to encourage foreign investment and also required budgetary support for maintaining the infrastructure to offset the strain on budgets heavily constrained by the low tax base. However, aid flows to SSA ran well below what was required to fund the necessary expenditure. The consequence was that although there were the advances noted earlier in such areas as paved roads and electricity generation, there were problems in maintaining the infrastructure in subsequent years. As we have noted, infrastructure remains a major issue to this day.

The 1970s saw an increasing level of indebtedness of SSA economies. The oil price hikes of the 1970s and the increasing need to import food as a consequence of the droughts that affected various parts of the continent at different times, left SSA economies even more dependent on aid. In 1981 the World Bank published a report on the state of African economies (World Bank, 1981), which called *inter alia* for liberalisation of internal markets, trade and exchange rates, cuts in government expenditure and in the size of government, elimination of subsidies and other forms of price control, and the privatisation of state enterprises.

Following this report the World Bank and the IMF offered aid and import support to SSA on condition that governments committed to 'structural adjustment programmes' (SAPs) which implemented these liberalisation policies. While there was considerable resistance by governments to implementing such policies, the need for aid effectively forced them to commit to doing so. SAPs have been the subject of intense debate over the last 25 years. The devaluations and subsequent liberalisation of exchange rates coupled with trade liberalisation left many countries with worsening trade balances. Pent-up demand for imports prior to liberalisation sent import bills soaring once controls were lifted. Exports did not increase for a considerable time after exchange rate adjustments, if at all. While the liberalisation of domestic trade did result in an increase of prices to producers of primary products, thus giving them an incentive to increase output, producer response was weak. The long period of low prices had encouraged them to switch into the production of food or to engage in non-agricultural rural activity. In any case, some primary products such as coffee required several years before new production could come on stream. Competition from imports made it difficult for domestic manufacturing to compete, resulting in a form of de-industrialisation across the continent (Jalilian and Weiss, 2000). Privatisation of state-owned enterprises has proved a difficult and lengthy process as the private sector whether foreign or domestic has been unwilling to take over loss-making enterprises, or unable to raise bank credit, in economic contexts in which investment is highly risky, although where it has happened it has largely improved firm performance (Nellis, 2003).

Much attention has been given to finding policy approaches that are likely to have greater success than those so far attempted. It is true that the IFIs believe that SAPs have been a success when they have been properly implemented. For the last two and a half decades, the World Bank has argued that countries which have strongly adopted these policies have done better than countries that have weakly adopted them or not adopted them at all: in other words, 'good' policies work. There are major problems with the methodologies employed by the Bank to arrive at such conclusions. And the Bank itself has begun to realise that in focusing its attention on markets, it has neglected the importance of institutions in explaining differences in performance and in implementation of Bank policies. Nonetheless, the belief persists that liberal market policies are the solution, even though these may not match countries' existing institutional development. Solutions are therefore still seen in an expansion of conditional aid, and in liberal policies. We shall consider these in turn.

There has been considerable debate about the usefulness of aid (Easterly, 2006, Riddell, 2007). Easterly notes that while 'the West' has spent $2.3trillion on aid, it has not delivered 12 cent medicines to prevent half of all malaria deaths, nor 4 dollar mosquito nets to poor families, nor 3 dollars to each new mother to prevent 5 million child deaths. Aid projects are often poorly designed, badly implemented and do not deliver the income stream that enables debt to be repaid. Little consideration is given to the maintenance costs of infrastructural projects and the burden they present to government budgets.

In spite of these failures, aid continues to be a major part of the panacea for economic development in sub-Saharan Africa. Pressures for increased aid from developed countries stemmed from periodic international commissions (CID, 1968, WCED, 1987, Africa Commission, 2005). A common thread running through these initiatives is that aid from the developed world is an essential part of the solution to the problems of development in regions such as SSA. In 2000, the UN Millennium Declaration set eight goals to be reached by 2015. The Africa Commission Report establishes these goals as targets for SSA, which can only be achieved with very large injections of aid to African governments who adopt 'good' policies. Of the eight targets, one, achieving gender equality in primary and secondary school enrolment, may be met, but the other seven are not on track to be achieved. The headline target, to halve, between 1990 and 2015, the proportion of people whose income is less than $1 a day has seen that proportion drop to 41 per cent from its 1990 figure of 47 per cent. In spite of the increase in aid noted above, an increase below the target set by the Africa Commission, progress is slow either in spite of aid or because it is not enough, or possibly a combination of the two.

The thread running through the three reports is that helping the developing countries to develop will increase our own welfare through increasing demand for what we produce, that we all have to tackle environmental issues because they have global effects, and of course more recently, that poverty in a large part of the world affects security here. The implicit assumption is that as poor country governments have clearly failed to develop their economies, they need to be shown how.

Conclusions

These are issues of practicality within a framework that sees the international financial institutions spearheading the so-called global community into a combined effort to solve Africa's problems. Debates about what is to be done usually take place without reference to the dominant capitalist economic system, what drives that system and what place the different economic and geographical regions of the world hold within it.

In the case of Africa, the continent's place in this system has been marginalised. However, the continuation of this marginalised state is not necessarily inevitable. Two developments suggest that Africa is heading in a new direction. The first development is the expansion of South Africa into Africa. South Africa's foreign direct investment into the rest of Africa rose sixfold between 1994 and 2004, but this could be overshadowed by the rise of Chinese and Indian involvement (Corkin, 2008). There are clearly contradictory forces at work, but the renewed drive to exploit Africa's mineral resources could repeat earlier colonial and post-colonial experiences but could conversely, through infrastructural development consequent on this raw material exploitation, generate local industrial activities linked to the raw materials industries. Both China and India could also move some manufacturing to Africa. The rapid growth of urbanisation means there is a substantial and relatively low-wage labour force waiting to be exploited. It is widely argued that it was the presence of such an urbanised and cheap labour force in East Asia which led to investors going there rather than to Africa, where urbanisation was less advanced. Whether the state or a local capitalist class is able to take advantage of these trends is the question.

Whether these developments are sufficient grounds for a new optimism remain to be seen. There are no easy answers, but what the last 40 years suggests is that the economic development of SSA will not be achieved by major policy interventions on the part of outsiders. How it will be achieved is another matter, but it will more likely be achieved following the emergence of a governing class or elite (whether leading a state directed development strategy, or a private capitalist one) committed to an agenda which seeks to develop the productive forces and accumulate capital for re-investment in partnership with foreign investors who are willing to work under a regulatory framework established by the local state. Aid may have a part to play, as it did in the development of the East Asian economies, but the paraphernalia of international financial institution policies and conditions will not.

Notes

1 The data in this and the following section is sourced from the *World Development Indicators Online* supplemented by the CIA World Fact Book.
2 There are several recent histories of sub-Saharan Africa since independence, which cover the period in much more detail, including Ayittey, 1992, Cooper, 2002, Nugent, 2004, Meredith, 2005 and Dowden, 2008.
3 Much has been written about the ujamaa villages in Tanzania. Among the best accounts and discussions are: von Freyhold (1979), Coulson (1975), Raikes (1975).
4 Rodney, 1972, Cooper, 2002 and Davidson, 1989, among others are especially useful in emphasising the importance of the historical shaping of the post-independence African societies and economies.

References

Africa Commission, 2005, *Our Common Interest*, London: Penguin Books.
Artadi, E.V. and X. Sala-i-Martin, 2003, The Economic Tragedy of the 20th Century: Growth in Africa, *NBER Working Paper* No. 9865. July
Ayittey, G.B.N., 1992, *Africa Betrayed*, New York: St Martins Press.
Collier, P., 2007, *The Bottom Billion*, Oxford: University Press.
Collier, P. and C. Pattillo, 2000, *Investment and Risk in Africa*, New York: St Martins Press.
CID (Commission on International Development), 1968, *Partners in Development*, New York: Praeger.
Cooper, F., 2002, *Africa since 1940: The past of the present*, Cambridge: Cambridge University Press.
Corkin, L., 2008, Competition or collaboration? Chinese and South African transnational companies in Africa, *Review of African Political Economy*, 115: 128–33.
Coulson, A., 1975, Peasants and bureaucrats, *Review of African Political Economy*, 2, 3: 53–8.

38 *Peter Lawrence*

Davidson, B., 1989, *Modern Africa*, London and New York: Longman.

Dowden, R., 2008, *Africa: Altered States, Ordinary Miracles*, London: Portobello Books.

Easterly, W., 2006, *The White Man's Burden: Why the West's Efforts to Aid the Rest Have Done So Much Ill and So Little Good*, New York: Penguin.

Easterly, W. and R. Levine, 1997, Africa's growth tragedy: policies and ethnic divisions, *Quarterly Journal of Economics* 112 (November): 1203–50.

Freyhold, M. von, 1979, *Ujamaa Villages in Tanzania: Analysis of a Social Experiment*, London: Heinemann.

Jalilian, H. and J. Weiss, 2000, De-industrialization: myth or crisis?' in Jalilian, H.M. Tribe and J. Weiss (eds), *Industrial Development and Policy in Africa* pp. 147–58. Cheltenham and Northampton, MA: Edward Elgar.

Lawrence, P., 2005a, Explaining sub-Saharan Africa's manufacturing performance. *Development and Change*, 36(6): 1121–41.

—— 2005b, Finance and development: why should causation matter? *Journal of International Development*, 18 (7): 997–1016.

Leys, C., 1994, Confronting the African tragedy, *New Left Review* I/204, March–April.

Meredith, M., 2005, *The State of Africa: A History of Fifty Years of Independence*, London: The Free Press.

Ndulu, B.J. and S.A. O'Connell, 1999, Governance and growth in Sub-Saharan Africa, *The Journal of Economic Perspectives*, 13 (3) (Summer): 41–66.

Nellis, J., 2003, 'Privatization in Africa: what has happened? What is to be done?' *Working Paper Number 25*, Center for Global Development (February) 34pp.

Nissanke, M. and E. Aryeetey, 1998, *Financial Integration and Development: Liberalization and Reform in sub-Saharan Africa*, London: Routledge.

Nugent, P., 1984, *Africa Since Independence: A Comparative History*, Basingstoke and New York: Palgrave Macmillan.

Raikes, P.L., 1975, Ujamaa and rural socialism, *Review of African Political Economy*, 2, 3: 33–52.

Riddell, R., 2007, *Does Foreign Aid Really Work?* Oxford: Oxford University Press.

Rodney, W., 1972, *How Europe Underdeveloped Africa*, London: Bogle-L'Ouverture Publications and Dar es Salaam: Tanzania Publishing House.

Wade, R., 2004, *Governing the Market: Economic Theory and the Role of Government in East Asian Industrialization*, Princeton: Princeton University Press.

World Bank, 1981, *Accelerated Development in Sub-Saharan Africa, An Agenda for Action*, Washington: The World Bank.

World Bank, 1989, *World Development Report: Financial Systems and Development*, Washington: World Bank.

WCED (World Commission on Environment and Development), 1987, *Our Common Future*, Oxford: Oxford University Press.

3 The social context of African economic growth 1960–2008

Bill Freund

A brief history of modern African development

From this volume readers should be able to obtain a clear sense of the growth (or otherwise) of African economies over the past half century as measured in quantitative indices (see Lawrence above). African societies have changed rapidly over this time period but these indices have captured relatively little of this; instead, it is the central argument of this essay that they have largely demonstrated the ups and downs on global markets of the resource commodities mined and export crops grown in Africa. As a result, they tell us relatively little about development understood in a more holistic and structural sense.

The emergence of an integrated concept of development in intellectual history, as opposed to a moral idea or imperative, can be said to belong to the period of World War II and its immediate aftermath, including measurable indices such as economic growth figures. In the case of the African continent, almost entirely colonised at that time, development plans were set against what was recognised very widely as deep poverty, a population with few resources, in poor health and little ability to access the modern world effectively, together with only a low level of economic activity which had clearly set limits on African participation in the war, beyond being a scene of battle in the north and east and a source of some manpower recruitment.

Buttressed by favourable commodity prices which increased meagre colonial revenues, the post-war years brought about substantial efforts at development promoted by the state, notably the Fonds pour l'Investissement en Développement Economique et Sociale (FIDES) in the French colonial sphere and the Colonial Development Corporation and its activities in the British (Havinden and Meredith, 1993). It is also arguable that the United Party government of General Jan Smuts in South Africa promoted more actively than any predecessor by far an overarching interest in industrialisation, South African activity in the continent and the beginnings of an urban and social welfare policy, constrained as it was by the racism of the white electorate. A comparable initiative can be said to have been the Plan of Constantine, initiated in the twilight of French rule in Algeria (Ruedy, 2005),

Colonial regimes moved to promote health and education programmes although the largest expenditures were laid aside for roads, bridges and other forms of physical infrastructure. They acknowledged the rapid growth of towns and established urban plans and policies with the beginnings of urban self-government in some locations. They tolerated the legalisation of trade unions and, as Fred Cooper has shown for both British and French empires, experimented with modernist labour legislation (Cooper, 1996). In many colonies, there was a rapid growth in white settler populations (British Kenya and the Rhodesias, Portuguese Angola and Mozambique, the Belgian Congo) which colonial regimes continued to assume were an excellent stimulus to overall development. David Low and John Lonsdale have notably referred to the post-war years as a second colonial occupation, thinking particularly of the depth of social and economic interference in the lives of East Africans (Low and Lonsdale, 1976).

The tasks that the late colonialists set themselves were however enormous. The militarist logic utterly oblivious to any sort of indigenous, or indeed even expert colonial, knowledge, doomed the immensely expensive Groundnut Scheme in Tanganyika (Havinden and Meredith, 1993). The ambitious irrigation plans of the Office du Niger had to be dramatically toned down and adapted to local conditions in the French Soudan (van Beusekom, 2002). Outside expert agricultural advice that frequently flew in the face of local political conditions and labour requirements led to conflict and resistance in numerous districts (Feierman, 1990; Dixon-Fyle, 1977, amongst many others). Much of the settled conditions of the colonial springtide had depended on the imposition of forced labour and massive and expensive recruitment systems. Now the growing number of paid workers brought about strikes with a dramatic potential for political organisation while reminding colonialists that it would not be possible to introduce European style labour conditions to Africa except at very considerable cost (Cooper, 1987, 1996). Increases in settler numbers helped fuel violent conflict in Kenya, Cameroon, Madagascar and Algeria and antagonised African political organisers who were quickly learning how to operate at territory-wide level and link up with labour demands.

Metropolitan awareness of the real costs that would have been entailed by investing in and sustaining imperial rule over a long period of time was matched by the faltering of the mid-century commodities boom in the late 1950s. In the most important economic circles in Western countries, the desirability of coming to terms with African nationalism and of a partial withdrawal from colonial economic designs of the past became common sense (Marseille, 1984; Gouverneur, 1971). In British West Africa, political decolonisation was matched by the effective withdrawal from many economic activities by the United Africa Company, which had dominated pre-war trade (Fieldhouse, 1994). In the Belgian Congo, the first signal for a decolonisation plan was issued by the Institut Solvay, which played a key role as a think-tank for Belgian capital. Bond sees the rapid industrialisation from very low levels in post-war Southern Rhodesia as reaching a point of exhaustion through what he terms overaccumulation, partly sustained under hothouse wartime conditions in the 1970s but unable afterwards to find further traction (Bond, 1998).

The picture was complicated by the growing discovery and exploitation of industrial raw materials in Africa such as uranium and iron ore but especially petroleum in, for instance, Algeria and Nigeria. These activities were not curtailed but there was an abandonment of any plans to use them as a basis for socio-economic transformation such as had taken place on the Witwatersrand or, to a lesser extent, the Northern Rhodesian Copperbelt or the Congolese province of Katanga. Thus corporate activities, coupled in places with strategic Western military sites, would function as enclaves having minimal trickle-down effect on the broader economy apart from the rents that they engendered, by and large. These rents, when it came to oil primarily, could of course be substantial.

The argument here is that independence for Africa largely meant corporate withdrawal from Africa. Colonisation could have involved the wholesale introduction of capitalism in terms of infrastructure, institutions and values but it did so only to a limited extent, even where white settlers or significant foreign trading diasporas were an important part of colonial society. Ideally the conquest and colonisation in Africa had been intended to create a harmonious world of centre and periphery. Africa would buy European manufactured commodities and it would provide a range of raw materials, especially tropical products and scarce minerals. Even in the case of South Africa, the overwhelming dominance of Britain as trading partner and investor indicates that it was hardly an exception. In the post-war world, however, this kind of centre-periphery structure, while it certainly continued along lines frequently denounced as neo-colonial, became less and less significant to international business. The great multinational firms concentrated instead on commerce between industrialised countries and eventually on sourcing goods from efficient and cheap producers; as protectionism declined under the post-World War II international trade regime, the need for trade barriers around politically controlled colonies diminished.

Moreover, the centre-periphery model itself is too structured and harmonious to give a clear sense of colonial realities. Numerous problems, environmental and human, blocked the working out of plans conceived in salubrious headquarters. Anne Phillips' brilliant study of coastal British West Africa convinces the reader that what she calls an essentially makeshift solution that allowed modest forms of local, and slightly more impressive forms of metropolitan, accumulation was essentially what was put into place; it did not really lay the foundations for further development very effectively (Phillips, 1989). Samir Amin has long ago explained why the best cases of cash crop agriculture as a form of new wealth in West Africa were apparent 'miracles' that in the end went no further than the rise of a small class of professional, administrative and commercial elites (see also Hecht, 1984).

In consequence, the African countries which found their way to independence in the 1950s (North Africa), 1960s (British and French colonies elsewhere) and 1970s (Portuguese colonies) experienced at first a continuation of colonial policies assisted by aid deals in the context of the Cold War and punctuated by radical attempts to break away in a nationalist spirit in various locations. (Nkrumah's Ghana, Touré's Guinea, Nyerere's Tanzania, Nasser's Egypt, revolutionary Algeria). These radical ventures, which aimed at self-reliance on a rapid timetable, lacked the material basis for lasting success although they have in some cases left a salient political legacy. As other contributions to this volume make clear, broad patterns of African economic activity measured as growth reveal a mixed trend during the 1960s and 1970s in which a key feature was favourable pricing of some commodities typical of the African economic relationship with the wider world for some of the time (for example, coffee, tea, base metals and after 1973 oil) while others stagnated (sisal, groundnuts, cotton) faced with the competition from artificial substitutes or a glut of competitors. Africa's share in international commerce diminished as did her ability to attract outside investment overall.

This was followed by two disastrous decades, the 1980s and 1990s, when African terms of trade with industrialised countries were very unfavourable and African economic indicators showed negative growth in many cases.[1] It was this period when the influence of the more generous Cold War competitive environment for aid disappeared, the prices of almost all raw materials fell dramatically compared to industrial products and when concerted policies aimed at encouraging Africa in the 'right direction', so-called structural adjustment, were devised and enforced. The most industrialised part of Africa, South Africa, lurched into a crisis that seemed to entangle the economic with the political as its future became more uncertain and the *apartheid* experiment to perpetuate a state based on whites-only citizenship lost its way and incurred mounting internal resistance and external scepticism. Pressures on some areas with weak administrative carapaces and fading centrifugal political forces bred the collapse of 'fragile' states and violent conflict. Neo-colonial structures and arrangements buckled under the weight of conflict and decay.

The picture is now somewhat rosier in the early twenty-first century. Once again, however, the main cause has been the shift towards far better prices for many raw commodities and especially minerals. This has even led to boom conditions in a few African countries, notably oil-rich Angola and the tiny former Spanish colony of Equatorial Guinea. At the same time, countries such as Burkina Faso, Rwanda and Mozambique remain critically aid-dependent in terms of their maintenance of current levels of state activity and inevitably, the flow of aid powerfully determines the direction of development plans.

It is difficult to deny the aptness of the take on the world of a recent book by an often lauded author on economic development in Africa, Paul Collier – Africa is the principal, albeit not the only, site of the 'bottom billion' of the world's population (Collier, 2007). While the rapid growth of India and China and the impressive structural shifts in some other parts of Asia and

Latin America are turning around the picture of a world divided between the Western minority powered by the industrialisation of the eighteenth and nineteenth centuries and everyone else, Africa in this distanced, globalised view by and large seems relatively stagnant, resistant to pressures for further transformation. Moreover, Collier, full of nostrums as one would imagine a specialist to be, is also surprisingly downbeat about the prospect of many African countries, especially those landlocked countries with low populations, poor infrastructures and 'bad' governance; he does not imagine change of any sort there for a very long time to come. It was after all a study of Liberia in the period where timber and iron ore exports were creating relatively prosperous conditions, in the 1960s and even after, that a team coined the phrase 'growth without development' – the idea that economic growth figures could when more closely examined mask a lack of genuine development, in fact one of the insights that undoubtedly fed into the harsh policies prescribed for Africa from 1980 onwards (Clower *et al.*, 1966).

Capturing economic change

How then do we consider key facets that lie behind Africa's growth figures? It is a task bedevilled by two powerful binaries, one more ideological and one more methodological, that dominate a very extensive literature. The first focuses on Africa's relationship with the wider world, especially the West. One powerful perspective, still very widely held by educated Africans, is that African backwardness is effectively held into place as a residue of the colonial economic relationships which still prevail in important ways. For structural reasons, peripheral countries struggle to free themselves from constraints deeply embedded in treaties, mentalities, and institutions for which the answer must ultimately be political. The metropolitan riposte is that the failings of the economy occur despite successes of ex-colonies elsewhere in the world, that they lie embedded in 'uncaptured' Africa's forms of political authority and social nexus (Hyden, 1980), its incapacity to follow the Western model. This liberal perspective would identify the genuine needs of capital as being linked to a sophisticated, complex capitalism emerging everywhere, exchanging primarily innovative products embodying human ingenuity rather than being stuck in exchanges of raw commodities. Both these perspectives contain far more than a grain of truth. Industrial products are indeed the main source of wealth and commerce in our time; however, control over key raw materials with probably oil as the most dramatic case, is far from finished as an important motive for powerful global actors. African governments have themselves oscillated between attempting to break the neo-colonial chains and struggling to get the best deal they can within those surviving neo-colonial institutions and structural arrangements that do exist, in both cases understandably.

The other binary which we shall try to see behind lies in the gulf between approaching African society in terms of positivist, verifiably quantitative, universal categories, with which those trained in economics are most comfortable on the one hand and those from the so-called soft social sciences who have dominated the study of Africa with a strong emphasis on particularity, on the cultural and on 'voice', in Albert Hirschman's terms, rather than 'loyalty'. This is the province of historians and anthropologists who specialise in micro-studies, are suspicious of quantitative indicators and are apt to stand the idea of development on its head (Ferguson, 1990). Here we could point to the work of James Ferguson, with his powerful and harsh assessment of development projects in the mountain kingdom of Lesotho or his bittersweet evocation of how Copperbelt Zambia, in decline, understands modernity as culture and consumption but struggles ever more to access it (Ferguson, 1999). Another important contemporary voice would be that of Jane Guyer, who sees a large swathe of forested western Africa as an economic world which has long been monetarised and involved in commodity exchange but which internalises ideas about money and exchange into an understanding of the world in which capitalist accumulation and development fit only super-ficially or tangentially (Guyer, 2004). A third anthropological voice stresses 'fiscal disobedience' and accumulation while focusing on borders and appar-ent voids of control in the wake of state incapacity (Newbury, 1986; Roitman, 2004). As state capacity weakens, enterprise is drawn away from the capital to the uncontrolled national frontiers which structure chunks of economic life (Flynn, 1997). To take one famous economic anthropologist of the present citing another of the past generation:

> Lacking evidence to the contrary, it should be assumed that all statistics covering whole countries or large states, which relate to such matters as agricultural yields, crop values and production, are bound to include a large element of estimation – to the point that they may not indicate the right trends.
>
> (MacGaffey, 1987: 138, citing a then recent review by Polly Hill)

Development, after all, is a contestable, and arguably an ethical, construction although it continues to have a sticky relationship to dull phenomena like tarred roads, manufacturing in fixed plants and inoculation campaigns. It is very difficult for an economic historian to find common ground between these poles even though both sides might reluctantly admit that areas of uncertainty would suggest a need to turn elsewhere than their own discipline for answers some of the time. This essay cannot hope to reconcile these approaches but it can flag them. What follows is a brief attempt to point to some incontrovertible and some major discussable areas of concern however in an attempt to bridge both gaps to which we have referred.

Economic and social change considered: the basics

We need to begin with the elemental, the biological. The first two genera-tions of post-colonial life in Africa have coincided with quite spectacular population increases in most parts of the continent. The continental population has increased from approximately 200 million in 1950 to perhaps 470 million in 1980 and 850 million by 2003. It is important to note that this is not some kind of unique African process outside history. In the early colonial period, a violent era characterised by forced labour and drastic shifts in economic patterns, many parts of Africa so far as historians could tell, went through phases of catastrophic decline and depopulation and this in turn followed a very dramatic and conflict-ridden nineteenth century including the last and most intense phases of the slave trade. Parts of Africa (i.e. Zambia, Angola, Gabon, the French Congo, etc.) were sufficiently thinly populated as to worry colonial ideologues with the possibility of a potential extinction of human populations, in fact. Stabilisation and modest growth rates characterised the inter-war years and the big demographic leaps were just beginning as late as 1940 or 1950. At the same time, recent evidence in the early twenty-first century is showing a levelling in birth rates where Africans, as with people elsewhere in the world, respond to far better survival rates amongst children than in the past. This is conventionally dubbed 'fertility transition'. It is true that fertility transition is moving rather slowly in North and West Africa and that, again as is the universal pattern, there is a distinctive intermediate phase where the consequences of very high birth rates and declining death rates include a 'demographic bulge' – ballooning absolute growth. Having said this, the developmental consequences of rapid population growth are very variable. In pre-modern times, Malthusian patterns can well take effect: people will be forced to cultivate less and less favourable natural environments and will become more vulnerable to natural catastrophes. Yet particularly since the disastrous famine that led directly to the final overthrow of the Ethiopian monarchy in 1974, it is more and more the case, that major droughts, floods, earthquakes, etc., now receive an international response in terms of charitable aid which makes the survival of distressed populations far more possible although in ways that may even worsen the survivors' chances to resume their previous way of life.

Population increase is going to create the biggest problems where a largely rural population is forced to share poverty, to partition out rural livelihoods without the possible intervention of any significant increase in productivity. In practice, Africans have tended to respond through adjusting their farming techniques to cope or, very commonly, seeking forms of off-farm cash income, widely attested in such varied countries as Tanzania, Kenya, Zimbabwe and Nigeria. In South Africa, where Africans have been excluded except as labourers from most productive land for a considerable time period, the end of apartheid actually signalled a further decline in African peasant food production from the very low level that existed in 1994.

The availability of plentiful labour can lead to intensified productivity and be made use of by entrepreneurs. Increasingly one can argue Africa's biggest single problem is that the current mix of global trends and local social and economic forces is doing this very little. This sticks increasing numbers of

Africans in a no man's (or woman's) land of low productivity and economic activity focused on survival. Most of the economic indicators on African growth therefore tend to measure the remaining neo-colonial structures that contribute to international trade. By contrast, the time and effort of most Africans is spent in the residue, is disappointingly limited in its outcome and difficult to measure.

In the southern half of the African continent, from the 1990s, the HIV immune deficiency led to deaths from AIDS on such a scale as to affect population growth with spectacular declines in the average age of Africans at time of death. These figures have to a certain extent improved with Uganda the somewhat deceptively shining example of an evident turnaround by the middle of the first decade of the twenty-first century. However, in some countries figures remain extreme, especially in South Africa, Botswana and Swaziland, where over 10 per cent of the entire population are infected (much higher figures for women of childbearing age) and the systematic application of anti-retroviral medicine to control the condition is just beginning to show significant results to scale. Accompanied as it is by debilitating sickness, creating large-scale problems of orphanage and of taking away individuals at the most productive time of life, this has hardly been a salutary intervention in a demographic challenge. It is, however, impossible to quantify the economic impact of this pandemic (Iliffe, 2006).

Demographic pressures feed into the broader pattern that Bryceson and Jamal have referred to as deagrarianisation and/or depeasantisation (Bryceson, 2004; Bryceson and Jamal, 1997). Structural adjustment propaganda at its peak often contained the absurd message of 'urban bias', the assumption that African elites, comfort-loving and mimetic, focused on life in cities which were provided with services while the countryside was milked of what wealth it had, starving possibilities of accumulation. The idea that financial convertibility, the destruction of state institutions that 'meddled' in rural life and the apparent provision of fair prices for the farmer would lead to a blossoming of African agriculture has proven to be foolish at best. The most convincing scholars such as Peter Gibbon, Stefano Ponte and Carlos Oya have found that it is literally impossible to correlate better agricultural prices to increases in agrarian production and economic activity (Gibbon and Ponte, 2005, Oya, 2007). Capital-poor farmers in Africa (or pastoralists) are instead dependent on state inputs in the forms of feed and seed and insecticide to manage more than very marginally. They badly need state storage schemes and often benefit from state intervention in marketing, although this in itself has at times been corrupt and abusive. However where competitive local buyers and even moneylenders do sometimes offer growers the best of prices in a working exchange system, this does nothing about the uneven trade arrangements with powerful and efficient Western buyer companies and financial sources. Farmers certainly need a state that can provide the best possible infrastructure in the form of rail and road transport and quality storage facilities; structural adjustment does not generally allow for these little details. Finally, free trade arrangements promoted by the WTO not only contain loopholes in order to block food imports into wealthy consumer countries but, more importantly, permit the massive introduction of cheap foodstuffs from the West, often tied in with famine and food aid, which do not allow local competition to find much space.

Three broad patterns ensue, all of them with very significant if uneven developmental implications. First of all, there has been a spectacular emigration of rural Africans into cities. Here demographic change has been especially marked during the first two decades after independence. Where there were somewhat over 30 million living in cities on the African continent in 1950, the number was estimated at 203 million in 1990 and is likely to double again to surpass 400 million by 2010 (Pieterse, 2008, 19). The growth of some big cities such as Kinshasa and Luanda accelerated due to warfare in the interior at certain stages. South Africa and the countries of the Mediterranean littoral are now predominantly urban and others, such as Senegal, Nigeria, the Ivory Coast, Angola and Zambia are not far behind. Health conditions in cities, notably the chances of survival of children, are better than in scattered and difficult to reach rural areas, in contrast to the situation in Europe during the early Industrial Revolution (Freund, 2007).

African studies in the colonial era were strongly biased towards rural observation. Cities were viewed as exceptional and problematic. Today it is clear that the real developmental problems are urban. Several dozen African cities have million-plus populations and they are the cradle of most economic activity. The cities are far more convenient centres for the distribution of benefits such as schooling and the diffusion of mass entertainment and new cultural forms; it is here that a new cultural and political Africa is in fact emerging. However, they represent a huge challenge insofar as they have historically been centres of administration and commerce primarily rather than internationally significant forms of production. Contra Hernando de Soto, the great majority of inhabitants do not have little pots of money stowed away under the mattress or distinctive skills that can, if institutionally nurtured, quickly turn into sources of businesses and reasonably rewarded livelihood strategies. Africa has come to face as well the challenge of creating minimally acceptable service standards for urban life in the form of sewage, garbage disposal, housing and the like.

Second, there has also been unprecedented transnational migration of citizens of most African countries, both within Africa to the most economically viable centres but also notably to Europe, the Middle East and North America. Millions of Africans now live outside Africa but, through the means of Western Union despatches, electronic mail and mobile phones, remain in quite regular contact with and still often under the systematic cultural influence of, the world into which they were born. The loss of the skilled and talented is grievous and a severe problem. However, it is also true that many overseas Africans thrive and that the provision of remittances is a massive source of income in countries as diverse as Egypt, Nigeria, Ghana,

Algeria, Eritrea and Mali. A recent World Bank estimate suggested that remittances per annum to Africa amount to perhaps $20billion.[2] Cities such as Bamako, Accra and Dakar contain thousands of substantial homes constructed by those who are absent. This income is not usually captured by national economic figures. Whether this kind of migration can become a source of investment internally and, more generally, whether it can help to breed and spread new ideas with economic ramifications, is still an open question. So far it is largely devoted to prestige spending or to serving the basic reproduction needs of the poor.

Third, the countryside itself is changing. As writers such as Chaléard for the Ivory Coast, Berry and Swindell for different parts of Nigeria or Heyer for the coffee fields of Kenya all note and from different angles, there has been a dramatic shift in many of the more commercially propitious parts of Africa away from the colonial cash crops to the sale of food crops for the burgeoning cities (Chaléard, 1996; Berry, 1996, Swindell *et al.*, 1999, Heyer, 2006). This creates a very diffuse range of new possibilities, creating changes in the formerly male-dominated household economies and new kinds of accumulation possibilities, for those with and without state connections, for a class of well-off and usually urban-dwelling elites. Statistics designed to measure the cocoa or coffee crop capture this kind of phenomenon poorly and much new accumulation is done under conditions of notional or apparent state land ownership legislation (or perhaps nominal ownership by clans or other so-called traditional authorities, arrangements intended to minimise the potential of rural conflict by a state with limited resources). (Bassett and Crummey, 1993). More and more rural dwellers become straddlers who require money and earn an income where and when they can; of course, this is apt to lead some towards wholesale abandonment of the countryside but this creates its own problems where urban poverty is acute (Potts, 2000). There is nothing bad or unhealthy about the shift in agriculture to production for the internal market but it does, of course, make it harder to find the foreign exchange that is still absolutely essential for satisfying consumer needs or mounting any further process of industrialisation. Moreover, it is undoubtedly building up patterns of inequality, breaking down households and chipping away at subsistence activities incommensurate with cash exchange as that becomes more and more universally fundamental.

These basic patterns give rise to what somewhat problematically has been called 'informality' in African social science literature. Very large numbers of people, in some countries clearly the majority, survive through economic activities that are not effectively measured by the state (MacGaffey, 1987). This includes the prevalence of markets with innumerable small-scale buyers and sellers, the provision of very diverse services, including housing and health care and the manufacture of items of food and clothing as well as engagement in activities of which the state does not approve (for instance, the illegal crossing of borders, a subject of increasing fascination to social scientists). The informal sector has many close links to the formal sector and the state and can often be seen as subordinate to it. However, in West Africa, basic provisions (food, clothing, shelter) continue to be constructed in this way and North African countries such as Morocco continue to sustain a craft culture with ancient roots linked back to apprenticeships and guilds but this is now probably less typical than the layered network of distribution of products manufactured elsewhere and often outside Africa. Until the 1970s, informal activities were often seen as an uncontrolled and uncontrollable menace to writers on African development such as Peter Gutkind but a related aspect of the changing development environment was the recognition by others such as Keith Hart and Andrew Hake of the economic prominence and even the positive aspects of 'self-help' activities by the poor – a populism that could jibe with neo-liberalism potentially (Gutkind, 1975; Hart, 1975, Hake, 1977). The informal sector, sometimes joined to a vigorous investigation of women's' initiatives on the part of enthusiasts such as Janet MacGaffey or Aili Tripp, still has its proponents and still repays scholarly investigation richly, given its many cultural and social ramifications (MacGaffey, 1991, Tripp, 1989). Awareness that gender is a key factor in understand changing economic activities in Africa, is growing. The illicit and marginal have also become a field of consideration and study (van Schendel and Abraham, 2005).

There is no question that informal activities make a mockery of the exactitude of statistics in most African cases and often provide a considerable part of the dynamics of economic life. However, it is much less clear whether, deSoto-like, any new accumulation trajectory in Africa rooted in the informal sector has significant implications for economic growth. W. Arthur Lewis and other pioneers of development theory believed that development began with the surmounting and marginalisation of the informal ('unlimited supplies of labour'), although they did not use that term; perhaps they will be proven correct ultimately even while missing observations of much that is going on today. It is also very likely to be the case that if the 'formal' economy and the state achieve successful means of building African economies, they will learn from networks and activities that are now labelled as 'informal' and imitate or absorb them, a process still only very haltingly observable. This point has been particularly effectively made by many observers of urban governance (Ahonsi, 2002; Tati, 2001).

Workers, capitalists and the state

This brings us to what I would describe as the three classic elements needed for economic growth that indeed has developmental implications more broadly as derived from the classic writings of the likes of Marx, Polanyi, Barrington Moore or W. A. Lewis – an available labour force, a dynamic bourgeoisie bent on accumulation and a state that can at worst accommodate and at best define and promote economic development. If we wish to get behind the raw growth statistics, we need to interrogate these areas. The first two seem, in terms of new coinage, the province of civil society but I will remain here in the camp of those who think asking questions about class may be more pertinent than the vaguer term, civil society, with its assumption of a Chinese curtain separating the people from the state. The question of a working class will detain us the least. As has been suggested, there are now very large numbers of men and women in many parts of Africa who are detached or easily detachable from the land and available for productive economic activities. It is also true that low educational levels, limited and uneven exposure to what are now useful craft skills and poor infrastructure limit the value of this. The relationship of land tenure conditions, family structures and skill levels is considerably less favourable than the balance that has prevailed in many Asian countries in the late twentieth century. The sustenance of this population is clearly problematic and the whole thrust of so-called poverty alleviation approaches to development focuses on this; it is perhaps also important to mention therefore the human resource potential that is the other side of the coin.

Through the entire independence era, there has been a continous literature devoted to the prospects, and particularly the limitations, of African businesspeople and the African bourgeoisie. When we look at economic figures for African countries, even beyond the waxing and waning of investment in mining, fishing or related activities, there is the question of the extent to which African initiatives play a crucial part in growth or not. The answers are not particularly encouraging but they are also not particularly consistent or conclusive. An excellent collection of some years back (Berman, 1998 but see also Kennedy, 1980, Lubeck, 1987) contains selections that suggest there are forms of business that thrive in conditions where the state has virtually vanished from sight as in the Congo and where state bureaucrats have become steadily replaced by independent figures in the business world in the Ivory Coast.[3] Beckman and Andrae have uncovered a complex world of clothing manufacture in Nigeria in which local industrialists are prominent and aimed at producing for the local market albeit with growing stresses in the 1990s (1998).

But productive activity rarely goes hand in hand with effective state support. Neo-classicist Robert Bates showed how the Kenyatta regime in Kenya supported and protected the economic complex around coffee growing where the president's supporters made much of their money whilst the successor regime of Daniel arap Moi abandoned this support due to reliance on a different set of economic actors. Catherine Boone has depicted the Senegalese state as losing its interest in protecting local industry in favour of the growing influence of import-orientated merchant capital (Boone, 1992). The importers are members of Senegalese religious brotherhoods while most of the industrialists have been Frenchmen. While Tim Mitchell has signalled the struggles faced by industry in Egypt under the dominance of neo-liberal financial markets, (Mitchell, 1999) privatisation in Algeria has enabled some entrepreneurs to strike out for themselves with the abandonment of socialist planning. By contrast, yet others stress the extent to which capitalists depend on state favours and find it difficult to compete or function without them. These cruder bonds clearly are problematic as engines of growth: indigenisation strategies have made individuals wealthy but have not acted as a nursery for economic activities that could have wider implications; they have merely somewhat shifted the balance of forces between foreign actors and their indigenous agents. This balance has however shifted again with the pressure on African states to privatise over the past twenty years.

There has also been a question raised by African nationalists and their sympathisers of the extent to which Bulawayo textile manufacturers, Mauritian clothing exporters, Lusaka greenhouse flower growers and Nairobi industrialists, largely white, Indian or Chinese in origin, are to be described as African. These often now very small minorities have nonetheless been the beneficiaries of the new post-2000 prosperity in much of Africa (Gibbon, 2002). State collapse in the desperate circumstances of Liberia and Sierra Leone, for example, seems to have enriched key Lebanese businessmen first and foremost (Reno, 1998). Behind these successful individuals lies the broader question of a middle class, which studies of economic development used to assume was an essential element, because it was from this class that entrepreneurs can emerge, because their class character can promote a modernising mass society and because their consumer habits can become a seedbed for accumulation models. In this sense, the settler populations of colonial times were in fact a model civil society for the planting of capitalist values and structures. Where such populations have effectively disintegrated or disappeared, their absence has pushed economic development back if perhaps solving political problems. Nonetheless it is important to signal the gradual emergence in Kenya, to take one example, of a more significant middle class of African origin in post-colonial times.

Recent years have perhaps brought up some straws in the wind. One positive factor is the AGOA legislation, promoted through pressure by black American members of Congress, which through giving free entry to the US market has aided a few African countries, notably Lesotho, South Africa and Kenya, to introduce industrial exports there (Gibbon, 2002). This is however a fragile opportunity which could easily be eliminated by legislation. Tunisian industry is heavily geared through investment by Mediterranean European countries towards the EU market; it is now being threatened by competition from the Far East (White, 2001). In the new millennium, Africa witnessed the first major entrance of a successful local businessman as president aiming to make economic development strategies predominate in Marc Ravalomanana's Madagascar and the arrival (at least in the media) of Mo Ibrahim, the Sudanese mobile phone king who promotes good governance in Africa through his support of prize money for best practice. However indigenous they may be, it is clear that African capitalists will be inevitably individuals who find their niche in globalised supply and demand chains to a large extent; they are unlikely to rise up from depths of isolation to compete in global markets without international linkages. It is equally important not to underestimate their capacity to make their mark within those constraints rather than idealising a utopian autonomy, just as the real significance of locally based capitalists, despite their personal origins, fragmented and often limited as they currently are, will inevitably weigh heavily in any substantial capitalist development on the continent.

Even richer and more various is the literature on the African state. With rare exceptions, it is clear that so far the post-colonial state has been weak in forming institutions that can promote accumulation nationally, not to speak of transnational structures. Basil Davidson, arguably the doyen of writing on modern Africa in the English language, penned his doubts about the artificiality of the African state hobbled by its colonial legacy (Davidson, 1992), and yet the European model of the nation-state should at least have served as a successful template for accumulation – as one could argue it does today in South Africa. Writers such as Chabal and Daloz (1999) and Jean-François Bayart (1993) have tried to theorise the deeper nature of the state which arises from clientelist linkages deeply moored in civil society. This kind of patrimonial state is incapable of breaking with the past in order to promote interests that might work against those who currently profit from the sort of state that is up to its neck in clientage. Bayart emphasises African hostility to transparency of the 'rhizoid' state, for instance. Indeed, while Chabal and Daloz emphasise the contradiction between the model of an effective modern state and the real life African state that strews disorder precisely in order to sustain its potency, Bayart moved on to dissect actual criminal patterns in the state at the heyday of structural adjustment (Bayart *et al.*, 1997).

In the final quarter of the last century, things reached a more extreme pattern in some cases. Reno has considered instances whereby, in patrimonial but weak states shaken by declining revenues and also the site of mineral resources such as diamonds, men with arms and determination could use income from such resources as a power base. This can lead to political power effectively hollowed out of normal state-like functions – 'failed states' dominated by warlords who have effectively sloughed off all the accoutrements of the post-colonial state Davidson condemned (Reno, 1999). Here the crudified state extracts in tandem with a capitalism equally hollowed out beyond mineral extraction enclaves. This kind of extreme pattern could be observed in Sierra Leone and Liberia on the West African coast or in Somalia which has now lacked unified government for almost twenty years; Mobutu's Zaïre by the 1980s was certainly a prime model. Yet Reno exaggerated when he proposed Nigeria was evolving the same way; even in the contemporary Democratic Republic of the Congo, the state has retained significance. In truth, the failed state shadows real state functions just as the informal sector relies on the formal. Most of Africa's conflicts display political complexity and have beginnings and ends; they cannot be reduced to resource conflicts or warlord states in ascendancy (Cramer, 2006). The more extreme warlord manifestations have also been in recession since 2000.

Nonetheless the state is a complex force in society. No state is or can be purely a development agency, frustrating as this may be for Western observers, even in Western countries themselves; in reality, the state always is at the play of indigenous local social forces which may project profound barriers to needed changes. In most cases, the post-independence states had a sincere commitment to a version at least of developmentalism; they were not simply a class project of the few hoping to get rich. Corruption and big man authoritarianism went together with the provision of very generous funding for education in particular (this is again noticeable now in countries such as Zambia, Kenya and Tanzania) as well as commitment to projects that were seen as developmental as well as prestigious. Thus the construction of the Akosombo dam and the planned industrial town of Tema were part of Nkrumah's early strategy in Ghana just as were some outrageously corrupt and manipulative politics. It is possible to look at a state like Algeria, where large-scale oil revenues encouraged massive interventions in social policy as well as industrial construction that proved very inefficient and unsustainable and imagine that the number one requirement is for the state to be removed from economic life in Africa as much as is possible. This ideological current has slackened in recent years. The World Bank and equivalent agencies have become extremely sensitive to the need for manifest open governance, balanced budgets and transparency. However this is certainly insufficient without strategy. Indeed bringing WB and other trained Africans to high state office has created a bias towards financial fundamentals at the expense of other important functions and away from coherent development strategies from within key ministries in countries such as Tanzania (Holton, 2005). The structural adjustment strategies forced on Africa were more likely to devastate parts of the state that performed important functions than to eliminate so-called rent-seeking activities.

One of the most elegant observers of this conundrum is the political scientist Colin Leys. In commenting on the so-called Kenya debate where battle was waged over whether the Kenyan state was actually able to promote capitalism and a rounded development beyond just human development indicator interventions and indigenisation decrees, Leys finally concluded that the Kenyan state had largely failed to do just this. The goals of the state were too directed towards ethnically coloured clientage and overly dominated by the concerns of overseas investors. However, he did not think that it was structurally impossible for the state over time to acquire more capability to intervene in decisive ways. He rejected the absolute determinism that marks much of the dependency theory of the 1960s and 1970s, including that found in his own writing of the time (Leys, 1996). A romantic view perhaps would imagine totally new economic forms swirling out of the informal sector to create an indigenous and original growth path. Perhaps there is a bit of truth in this but more likely, significant qualitative change in Africa will be marked by increasing state capacity in areas such as infrastructure, financial impact, ability to collect revenue through taxations and promotion of education, particularly technical education.

Uneven development

Finally, just as it seems important for this chapter to consider the whole of Africa as an entity, to be comprehensive, it is equally noteworthy that, as with Latin America and Asia, there are important differences between African countries. The unconscious inclination to exclude South Africa from general surveys during *apartheid* times makes no sense anymore. South Africa is a relative powerhouse which experienced an important history of diversified industrialisation albeit one distorted by the dominance of mining and related activities. (Fine and Rustomjee, 1996, Feinstein, 2001, Gelb, forthcoming.) Forms of state intervention critically assisted in this process. Parts of the state are efficiently run, well able to collect revenue and run parastatals while a large and now racially mixed middle class forms an important consumerist base and a modest welfare redistribution function is vital to the survival of the poorest third of the population. On this platform, South Africa has itself generated so-called world class firms in a variety of spheres, and is an increasingly important exporter of automobiles. It is an important investor in and very advantageous trader with, southern African countries particularly. Yet it has some features that fit the general pattern – a stock market extremely vulnerable to flows in and out from overseas, the dominance of primary products as an exporter, phases of economic stagnation or slow growth caused by political uncertainty or poor international prices for commodities. It suffers particularly from the large scale of structural long-term unemployment, partly the consequence of deagrarianisation. Amongst the smaller southern African countries, stable Namibia mirrors South Africa on a modest scale but its eastern neighbour, Botswana, seems to buck some of the generalisations with its small population, stable formal democracy and consistently relatively high GNP growth figures over time (but see Taylor, 2003, for a critical assessment of Botswana). By contrast, Zimbabwe, the second largest economy of the region, has been governed by a ruling party that brought government by a racialised minority to an end and is determined to stay in power come what may against the weight of international sanctions and the logic of structural adjustment that was introduced but not sustained. Here one of the most developed sub-Saharan economies has gone into free fall from the late 1990s.

At the other end of the continent, the countries of the Mediterranean littoral exhibit patterns that are also somewhat distinctive as read from statistics. Industrialisation plays a significant role in development but perhaps most striking is the gradual if uneven long-term improvement in human development indicators focused on health and education. Apart from turbulent Algeria, they have experienced no overthrow of the executive for decades although they also have failed to experience the democratisation wave promoted with uneven intensity by the West since 1980. The general pattern here is of moderate growth over the long term with limited structural change but high levels of under- and un-employment and rapid population increase creating social tensions, all of this on the watch of some very authoritarian but stable regimes (Noland and Pack, 2007). It seems both legitimate and useful to read far more off the statistical data available for this region as for the other sub-regions noted in this section than elsewhere.

We might finally point to insular Africa where essentially Creolised populations have seemed to anchor stabler government and a more positive trajectory than elsewhere. One such island, Mauritius, has perhaps had the most successful record of any African country over a range of political, social and economic indices. Here we have the example of a small country, fertile but lacking in special natural resources, which was judged to be overpopulated and with a dim future at the time of independence, that has diversified and found jobs for the large majority of its working-age population. A dynamic bourgeoisie with access to capital independent of the state, white or Chinese, have been critical to accumulation while a conservative but well-structured politics organising the mass of descendants of Indian indentured workers has diffused wealth.

Finally it is perhaps clearer today than half a century ago that amongst the countries 'in between', there are far better prospects in certain key territories whether based on a more developmental colonial trajectory or long-standing mineral resources. The overall advance of African economies depends particularly on Nigeria (home to two-thirds of all West Africans), Ghana, Senegal, the Ivory Coast, Kenya, Tanzania, Zimbabwe to which we can perhaps add Zambia, Angola and Uganda. The populous Cinderella countries are Ethiopia and the Democratic Republic of Congo. This is where, apart from the far south and north, the pattern of development in the future is likely to be written. How well they can build on the more propitious terms of trade and the growing historic distance from the crudely neo-colonial patterns of the early years of independence in the early twenty-first century will be a measure of whether longer-term and structurally deeper advances can be expected any time soon. However, the mere chance of valuable mineral deposits and the measure of 'foreign direct investment' is unlikely itself to bring such advances about.

Notes

1 Between 1980 and 2003, according to the Atlas method of calculating Gross National Income (which includes estimates of remittances from overseas), 29 of 49 African countries with available figures experienced per capita income *decline* and three (Democratic Republic of Congo, Liberia and Sierra Leone) absolute decline. Only Egypt, Tunisia, Botswana, the island nations of the Seychelles and Mauritius plus the expanding oil producers, Angola and Equatorial Guinea, are estimated to have grown their economies by more than 50 per cent per capita over almost a quarter century. If one takes the figures on to 2007, after the commodities boom started to take effect, the figures look considerably better: the countries still in per capita decline from 1980 are reduced to 11 or 12 while 25 or more reached over 50 per cent increases. But from the more turbulent waters of 2008, how secure are even these rather modest gains likely to be? These estimates are taken from World

Bank calculations supplemented with a consideration of the GNP figures of the
Africa Contemporary Record, XIV, 1981–2 (Africana, New York, 1982).
2 Anne-Cecile Robert and Jean-Christophe Servant, 'Africa's Imported Wealth',
Le Monde diplomatique, 16 January 2009 citing Dilip Ratha and Zhimei Xu,
Migration and Remittances Factbook, World Bank, Washington, 2008.
3 For an excellent survey of the literature up to the time of publication, MacGaffey,
1987 is invaluable.

References

Ahonsi, Babatunde, 'Popular Shaping of Metropolitan Forms and Processes in
Nigeria: Glimpses and Interpretations from an Informed Lagosian', in *Under Siege;
Four African Cities: Freetown, Johannesburg, Kinshasa, Lagos*, Hatje Cantz, Kassel
Art Fair Documenta 11, Platform 4, Kassel, 2002, 182–97.
Bassett, Thomas and Donald Crummey, eds., *Land in African Agrarian Systems*,
University of Wisconsin Press, Madison, 1993.
Bayart, Jean-François, *The State in Africa; The Politics of the Belly*, Longman,
Harlow, 1993.
Bayart, Jean-François, Stephen Ellis and Béatrice Hibou, *La criminilisation de l'État
en Afrique*, Editions Complexe, Paris, 1997.
Beckman, Bjørn and Gunilla Andrae, *Union Power in the Nigerian Textile Industry;
Labour Regime and Adjustment*, Nordiska Afrikainstitutet, Uppsala, 1998.
Berman, Bruce, ed., *African Capitalists in African Development*, Lynne Rienner,
Boulder and London, 1998.
Berman, Bruce and John Lonsdale, eds., *African Capitalists in African Development*,
Lynne Rienner, Boulder and London, 1998.
Berry, Sara, *No Condition is Permanent; The Social Dynamics of Agrarian Change in
Sub-Saharan Africa*, University of Wisconsin Press, Madison, 1996.
Bond, Patrick, *Uneven Zimbabwe; A Study of Finance, Development and Under-
development*, Africa World Press, Trenton, NJ, 1998.
Boone, Catherine, *Merchant Capital and the Roots of State Power in Senegal, 1930–85*,
Cambridge University Press, Cambridge, 1992.
Bryceson, Deborah, 'Agrarian Vista or Vortex: African Rural Livelihood Policies',
Review of African Political Economy, 102, 2004, 617–29.
Bryceson, Deborah and V. Jamal, *A Farewell to Farms; De-agrarianization and
Employment in Africa*, African Studies Centre, Leiden, 1997.
Chabal, Patrick and Jean-Pascal Daloz, *Africa Works; Disorder and Political Instru-
ment*, James Currey and Indiana University Press, Oxford and Bloomington,
1998.
Chaléard, Jean-Louis, *Temps des Villes, temps des vivres; l'essor du vivrier marchand en
Côte d'Ivoire*, Karthala, Paris, 1996.
Clower, Robert, W.G. Dalton, M. Harwitz and A. Walters, *Growth Without Develop-
ment; An Economic Survey of Liberia*, Northwestern University Press, Evanston,
1966.
Collier, Paul, *The Bottom Billion; Why the Poorest Countries are Failing and What Can
Be Done About It*, Oxford University Press, Oxford, New York *et al.*, 2007.
Cooper, Frederick, *On the African Waterfront; Urban Disorder and the Transformation
of Work in Colonial Mombasa*, Yale University Press, New Haven and London,
1987.

——— , *Decolonization and African Society; The Labour Question in French and British Africa*, Cambridge University Press, Cambridge, 1996.

Cramer, Christopher, *Civil War is Not a Stupid Thing; Accounting for Violence in Developing Countries*, Hurst, London, 2006.

Davidson, Basil, *The Black Man's Burden; Africa and the Curse of the Nation-State*, James Currey, London, 1992.

Dixon-Fyle, Mac, 'Agricultural Improvement and Political Protest on the Tonga Plateau, Northern Rhodesia', *Journal of African History*, XVIII, 1975.

Feierman, Steven, *Peasant Intellectuals; Anthropology and History*, University of Wisconsin Press, Madison, 1990.

Feinstein, Charles, *An Economic History of South Africa; Conquest, Discrimination and Development*, Cambridge: Cambridge University Press, 2005.

Ferguson, James, *The Anti-Politics Machine; Development, 'Depoliticization' and Bureaucratic State Power in Lesotho*, Cambridge University Press and James Philip, Cambridge and Cape Town, 1990.

——— , *Expectations of Modernity and Meanings of Urban Life*, University of California Press, Berkeley, 1999.

Fieldhouse, David, *Merchant Capital and Economic Decolonization; The United Africa Company 1929–89*, Clarendon Press, Oxford, 1994.

Fine, Ben and Zavareh Rustomjee, *The Political Economy of South Africa; From Minerals-Energy Complex to Complex Industrialisation*, Westview Press, Boulder, 1996.

Flynn, Donna, ' "We Are the Border"; Identity, Exchange and the State along the Nigeria-Bénin Frontier', *American Ethnologist*, XXIV, 2, 1997, 311–30.

Freund, Bill, *The African City; A History*, Cambridge University Press, Cambridge, 2007.

Gelb, Stephen, 'Macroeconomic Policy in South Africa: From RDP through GEAR to ASGISA', in Bill Freund and Harald Witt, eds., *Development Dilemmas in South Africa*, ms.

Gibbon, Peter, 'Present-Day Capitalism, the New International Trade Regime and Africa', *Review of African Political Economy*, 91, 2002, 95–112.

Gibbon, Peter and S. Ponte, *Trading Down; Africa, Value Chains and the Global Economy*, Temple University Press, Philadelphia, 2005.

Gouverneur, Jacques, *Productivity and Factor Proportions in Less-Developed Countries; The Case of the Congo*, Oxford, 1971.

Gutkind, Peter, 'The View from Below; The Political Consciousness of the Urban Poor in Ibadan', *Cahiers d'études africaines* 15, 1975, 5–35.

Guyer, Jane, *Marginal Gains; Monetary Transactions in Atlantic Africa*, University of Chicago Press, Chicago, 2004.

Hake, Andrew, *African Metropolis; Nairobi's Self-Help City*, Sussex University Press, London, 1977.

Hart, Keith, 'Informal Income Opportunities and Urban Employment in Ghana' *Journal of Modern African Studies*, 11, 1973, 141–69.

Havinden, Michael and David Meredith, *Colonialism and Development; Britain and its Colonies 1850–1960*, Routledge, London, 1993.

Hecht, Robert, 'The Ivory Coast Economic "Miracle": What Benefits for Peasant Farmers?', *Journal of Modern African Studies*, XXI, 1983.

Heyer, Amrik, 'The Gender of Wealth: Markets and Power in Central Kenya', *Review of African Political Economy*, 107, 2006, 67–80.

Holton, Duncan, 'Reconsidering the Power of the IFIs: Tanzania and the World Bank 1978–85', *Review of African Political Economy*, 106, 2005, 549–67.

Hyden, Gøran, *Beyond Ujamaa; Underdevelopment and an Uncaptured Peasantry*, Heinemann, 1980.

Iliffe, John, *The African AIDS Epidemic: A History*, Ohio University Press, James Currey and Double Storey, Athens, O, Oxford and Cape Town, 2006.

Kennedy, Paul, *Ghanaian Businessmen: From Artisan to Capitalist Entrepreneur in a Dependent Economy*, Weltforum Verlag, Munich and London, 1980.

Leys, Colin, *The Rise and Fall of Development Theory*, EAPH, Indiana University Press and James Currey, Nairobi, Bloomington and Oxford, 1996.

Low, D. A. and John Lonsdale, 'Towards the New Order 1945–63', in D. A. Low and Alison Smith, *History of East Africa*, III, Clarendon Press, Oxford, 1976.

Lubeck, Paul, ed., *The African Bourgeoisie; Capitalist Development in Nigeria, Kenya and the Ivory Coast*, Lynne Rienner, Boulder, 1987.

MacGaffey, Janet, *Entrepreneurs and Parasites: The Struggle for Indigenous Capitalism in Zaire*, Cambridge University Press, Cambridge, 1987.

MacGaffey, Janet, ed., *The Real Economy of Zaïre*, University of Pennsylvania Press and James Currey, Philadelphia and Oxford, 1991.

Marseille, Jacques, *Empire colonial et capitalisme français: histoire d'un divorce*, Albin Michel, Paris, 1984.

Mitchell, Timothy, 'No Factories, No Problems: The Logic of Neo-Liberalism in Egypt', *Review of African Political Economy*, 82, 1999, 455–68.

Newbury, David, 'From "Frontier" to "Boundary": Some Historical Roots of Peasant Strategies of Survival in Zaire' in Nzongola-Ntalaja, *The Crisis in Zaïre; Myths and Realities*, Africa World Press, Trenton, 1986, 87–97.

Noland, Marcus and Howard Pack, *The Arab Economies in a Changing World*, Peter Peterson Institute for International Economics, Washington, 2007.

Oya, Carlos, 'Agricultural Maladjustment in Africa: What Have We Learned After Two Decades of Liberalisation?', *Journal of Contemporary African Studies*, XXV, 275–97, 2007.

Phillips, Anne, *The Enigma of Colonialism, British Policy in West Africa*, Indiana University Press and James Currey, Bloomington and London, 1989.

Pieterse, Edgar, *CityFutures; Confronting the Crisis of Urban Development*, Zed Press and University of Cape Town, London and Cape Town, 2008.

Potts, Deborah, 'Worker-Peasants and Farmer-Housewives in Africa; The Debate about "Committed" Farmers, Access to Land and Agricultural Production', *Journal of Southern African Studies*, XXVI, 2000, 807–32.

Reno, William, *Warlord Politics and African States*, Lynne Rienner, Boulder and London, 1998.

Roitman, Janet, *Fiscal Disobedience: An Anthropology of Economic Regionalism in Central Africa*, Princeton University Press, Princeton, 2004.

Ruedy, John, *Modern Algeria; The Origins and Development of a Nation*, Indiana University Press, Bloomington, 2nd edition, 2005.

Swindell, Kenneth, M.A. Iliya and A.B. Mamman, 'Making a Profit, Making a Living; Commercial Food Farming and Urban Hinterlands in North-West Nigeria', *Africa*, LXIX, 1999, 386–403.

Tati, Gabriel, 'Responses to the Urban Crisis in Cameroon and Congo: Patterns of Local Participation in Urban Management', in Arne Tostensen, Inge Toerten and

Mariken Vaa, ed., *Associational Life in African Cities*, Nordiska Afrikainstitutet, Uppsala, 2001, 182–97.

Taylor, Ian, 'As Good As It Gets; Botswana's "Democratic Development" ', *Journal of Contemporary African Studies*, XXI, 2003, 215–31.

Tripp, Aili, 'Women and the Changing Urban Household Economy in Tanzania', *Journal of Modern African Studies*, XXVII, 1989.

van Beusekom, Monica, *Negotiating Development; African Farmers and Colonial Experts at the Office du Niger, 1920–1960*, Heinemann, James Currey and David Philip, Portsmouth NH, Oxford and Cape Town, 2002.

van Schendel, Willem and Itty Abraham, eds., *Illicit Flows and Criminal Things; States, Borders and the Other Side of Globalization*, Indiana University Press, Bloomington, 2005.

White, Gregory, *A Comparative Political Economy of Tunisia and Morocco; On the Outside of Europe Looking In*, State University of New York Press, Albany, 2001.

4 From the political economy of development to development economics

Implications for Africa[1]

Ben Fine

Introduction

The purpose of this chapter is less to elaborate an elusive economics or even political economy of Africa than to outline the more general evolution of development economics within which Africa has been located as an object of study. This is primarily an exercise in the history of economic thought but, as such, should not be confined to economics alone but is also attached to interdisciplinarity (especially relations with development studies) and to the broader material and intellectual circumstances (including policy stances and practices) that have interacted with development economics as a field of study (including teaching) and research and advocacy (including the externally funded).

These broader considerations are particularly salient in view of the current global financial crisis. It is widely acknowledged that it has created a crisis of neo-liberalism, not least with the extensive US state intervention to support its financial system and quite apart from the loss of legitimacy claimed by those purest of free markets, the financial. This raises questions over whether we are witnessing a crisis of neo-liberalism or its dissolution – in which case with what will it be replaced? But, even before the current crisis, questions were being raised over whether the notion of neo-liberalism had any coherence, given both diversity of experience and ideology associated with it,[2] as neatly expressed in appeal to a strong but minimal (and hence weak?) state, one that *intervenes*, often extensively, to make *free* markets work in and of themselves and in institutional and social support to the market, neutrally conceived but inevitably reflecting particular interests.

These conundrums surrounding neo-liberalism can be resolved by appeal to three factors. The first is to disentangle its separate elements as ideology, advocacy or rhetoric, its scholarship, its policy in practice and its putative representation of reality. These are not necessarily mutually consistent with one another; they shift over time and place in relation to one another and topic, but they are not, thereby, totally independent of one another. Second is to highlight the extent to which neo-liberalism has been about state intervention to underpin the promotion of markets by which is meant private capital in general but of finance in particular. For the latter, it has not simply been a matter of the proliferation and expansion of financial markets but their increasing penetration into ever more areas of economic and social reproduction. In the political economy literature, this has become known as financialization, and it has underpinned the longevity of a contemporary period of capitalism that might be designated as neo-liberal since the character of contemporary ideology, policies, scholarship and representations of the economy have been dominated by, although not reduced to, the imperatives associated with financialization. And third, then, is to distinguish between two broad phases of neo-liberalism, the first running from roughly the recognizable crisis of Keynesianism through to the early 1990s when state intervention took the form of promoting private capital through a generalized shock therapy, most notably in the push for privatization, deregulation and constraints on government expenditure. The second phase followed, if unevenly across different aspects, and has had two aspects, both to temper the dysfunctional impact of the first phase upon economic and social reproduction and, thereby, to promote continuing financialization (Fine, 2008a).

We are now entering, if not the demise, at least a major crisis of this second phase of neo-liberalism, which had already witnessed some retreats from the extremes of the first phase especially with what is known as Third Wayism or the social market. And corresponding shifts in development economics, from Washington Consensus to post Washington Consensus, are indicative of a heightened sensitivity to the supposedly dysfunctional market and institutional imperfections associated with the first phase. But, as argued elsewhere, such an approach has no handle on the systemic character of contemporary capitalism in general or in its historically evolved attachment to financialization, and might be justifiably caricatured as 'zombieconomics', living but dead, for it has nothing new to contribute to the understanding of development and the economy other than to interpret any aspect as yet another instance of market or institutional imperfection. As such, zombieconomics feeds upon and degrades other contributions from across social theory (Fine, 2008b and 2009b).

In this light, I begin in Section 2 by explaining how the old or classic development economics emerged after the Second World War with an entirely different character than the new development economics that prevails today. Successive sections chart how the old gave way to the new, and highlighted the corresponding implications for how development is now understood within mainstream economics as something that should not be distinctive from how any economy is addressed. Consequently, the 'economics of Africa' has been unduly homogenized, especially in method, and subject both to degraded and idiosyncratic scholarship. The concluding remarks, however, point to the possibility, if not the certainty, of a renaissance of political economy approaches to Africa that are sensitive to both systemic and contextual influences.

From old development economics . . .

As an academic field of study, development economics is very new, usually perceived to have emerged after the Second World War, especially in response to the challenges of decolonization. This is not to suggest that the study of what we would now term development did not exist before. But it was primarily the domain of economic historians or of classical political economy with a focus upon those now developed countries which, in Chang's (2002) telling phrase borrowed from the nineteenth-century German protectionist List, have subsequently 'kicked away the ladder' to development. The embryonic development economics was, then, born in the unique material circumstances defined by the post-war period *and*, as will be seen, a particularly telling intellectual environment.

For a defining moment for modern economics is the marginalist revolution of the 1870s. This established what might be termed the technical apparatus and architecture that prevails to the present day. It put aside the classical political economy that preceded it, associated with Smith, Ricardo, Mill and Marx, together with issues of distribution, class and accumulation. In its place was offered an apparatus based on utility and production functions, now familiar to every student and practitioner from the lowest to the highest levels within the discipline. The corresponding architecture involves a set of methods and concerns around individual optimizing behaviour, efficiency and equilibrium, with an accelerating pre-occupation over the current period with econometric methods.

Crucial, though, to the initial content and status of what is now termed the old or classic development economics is that the technical apparatus and architecture were themselves only fully established as the core of the discipline by the 1950s, too late to claim development economics as residing within their orbit. Thus, whilst Lionel Robbins had already (in)famously defined economics as the allocation of scarce resources between competing ends in the early 1930s, this was to anticipate what was only on the horizon for the time-being. Both within the economics discipline itself, and especially amongst those drawn to address development, the methods and content of the technical apparatus were judged to be totally inappropriate for the subject matter involved. Indeed, the 1930s witnessed the emergence of (Keynesian) macroeconomics as distinct from the microeconomics of the technical apparatus, as the latter was perceived to be inadequate to explain the systemic dysfunction of the macroeconomy. In addition, in the United States itself, what is known as the old institutional economics was at least as strong within the profession as the new technical principles. And, whilst the old institutional economics went into rapid decline after the Second World War, the gap between the methods and substance of macroeconomics and microeconomics remained significant over the period of the post-war boom. It was complemented by a strong if subordinate commitment to applied and policy economics, with a strong descriptive content.

In short, the nature of economics as development economics first emerged meant that the microeconomic principles associated with its technical apparatus only filled out a part of the discipline, one that would not intersect with the study of development itself. The principles were perceived only to explain a small part of individual behaviour (pursuit of self-interest through the market) and to be incapable of addressing systemic issues such as the massive recession of the 1930s, business cycles more generally, and the emergence and role of economic and social institutions and structural change widely conceived. In practice, the passage from the 1870s to the 1950s witnessed a remarkable 'implosion' around the microeconomic principles.[3] The goal was set of extracting technical results from the principles – what the formal, i.e. mathematical, deductive consequences are of assuming an optimizing producer or consumer – with everything else sacrificed along the way to get those results whether it be realism or method. This explains the adoption of what are surely still bizarre assumptions to the new student of economics until inured to their use – preferences, endowments and technologies are taken as given, as are human automatons as consumers and producers, prices are given, and technical conditions are assumed to allow for equilibrium and efficiency. On this basis, the technical apparatus/architecture was completed with the general equilibrium theory of the 1950s as most clearly associated with Arrow and Debreu.

Thus, as development economics was born, significant limitations prevailed over the scope of application of microeconomic principles. This is so even though the 1950s also witnessed what has been described as a formalist revolution within economics, as mathematical and statistical techniques came rapidly to the fore. This certainly eased the way for microeconomic principles to gain greater purchase on the substance as opposed to the form of the discipline and for the corresponding professionalization of economics in this respect also to be an Americanization as the US increasingly took the lead in research and teaching.

But this was by no means immediate. And, for development, two further factors were of significance. First, within the United States, economic history had traditionally been located within economics departments and a core part of the curriculum, in part a reflection of the influence of the old institutionalism. As a result, development economics tended to be taken up by (economic) historians. Second, the Cold War rendered imperative the offering of a non-Soviet alternative in the era of decolonization. It came most overtly and prominently in the form of the book by the economic historian Rostow's (1960) with his *Stages of Economic Growth: A Non-Communist Manifesto*. Brushing over the details, this understood development as the passage though five stages of transition to the modern (US) economy, with developing countries reaching a state of modernization (and drive to mass consumption) through emulating the stylized and homogenized history of their predecessors. In short, for varieties of reasons, and especially the memory of the 1930s and the Soviet experiment as potential alternative, neo-liberalism was off the agenda for developed and developing economies in the Keynesian era.

In addition, whatever the merits of, and rationale for, Rostow's stages, it is indicative of a number of much more general characteristics of the newly emerging field. First is its use of an inductive method, i.e. the examination of the historical record in broad outline in order to derive empirical regularities as the basis for understanding the process of development. Second, although often falsely perceived as such in retrospect by mainstream economics for lack of use of its own microeconomic principles and methods, the classic development economics was not without theory. Rather, it was pitched at the systemic level, concerning the role agriculture played in industrialization, for example, or the state in promoting industry and modern institutions. Third was a concern with the processes of development as involving economic and social change as opposed to pre-occupation with individual optimization, efficiency and equilibrium. Fourth, then, attention was explicitly drawn to systemic economic and social factors rather than reducing the analysis to the role of optimizing individuals. Fifth, this all also entailed a strong inter-disciplinary component, in light of the economic and social change associated with development. Sixth, not surprisingly then, the rise of development economics was soon accompanied by that of development studies to address the non-economic aspects of development and their interaction with the economic. Significantly, though, this did not occur in the United States where development as such, outside economics departments, was studied within other disciplines rather than in dedicated and newly-formed departments of development studies. Seventh, quite apart from its special position within economics, the classic development economics was also highly contested with alternatives on offer through the intersecting strands from radical political economy, from development studies and opposition to the notion of homogeneous modernization, and from the alternatives on offer in scholarship and practice from the Third World itself whether inspired by a Soviet model or otherwise (with Africa offering a number of models).[4]

The old development economics, then, emphasized economic and social transformation, thereby incorporating structural change and systemic understanding, one that drew favourably upon parallel contributions from other disciplines, with the role of the state as an agent of nation-building and modernization of considerable significance.[5] Accordingly, development economics in its classic phase enjoyed something of a buffer against the incursions of microeconomic principles. But such protection proved short-lived. With the microeconomic principles established by the 1950s through the implosion that allowed for them, their application then exploded out of the limits imposed by attention to supply and demand alone. Underlying this has been one crucial aspect of the logic of the principles themselves – that pursuit of self-interest and the technical apparatus of utility and production functions have no historical or social bounds. The result has been to seek to apply these principles universally and not just to supply and demand. An early example of such 'economics imperialism' has been public choice theory, with politics perceived as the pursuit of self-interest through other (non-market) means.[6]

... Through newer to newest development economics

But equally striking has been the extent to which microeconomic principles have been deployed to claim the terrain of economic analysis itself. This was given a huge boost by the critique and demise of Keynesianism, following the collapse of the post-war boom, and the corresponding rise of both neo-liberalism and monetarism as its intellectual counterpart. Ultimately, monetarism took the form of the new classical economics in which, remarkably, the response to economic disaster was to dig deeper into the methods associated with the technical apparatus. Markets were presumed to work perfectly unless interfered with; individual agents were presumed to optimize over use of information as well as goods; the economy was constructed on the basis of representative individuals (such as a household and a firm), and the state was deemed to be ineffective at the macro level other than in inefficiently distorting the economy on the microeconomic supply-side. As the leading new classical economist, Lucas (1987: 108) was to put it, 'the term "macro-economic" will simply disappear from use and the modifier 'micro' will be superfluous'.

This is, of course, intended to signal the end of systemic analysis (with this itself understood to be confined to Keynesian macroeconomics). Not surprisingly, similar major incursions were soon to be felt by development economics, and the new development economics was born in which the idea was to apply microeconomic principles to development. Initially, in the 1970s, such initiatives were associated with anti-statism and were not too influential within the discipline itself, primarily because of the lack of standing of the new practitioners as far as formal models were concerned, and a lingering attachment to traditional divisions of labour between micro, macro and other fields.[7]

Matters changed very rapidly with the shifting stance adopted by the World Bank. Symbolically, the arrival of Anne Krueger as Chief Economist in 1982 marked the clearing out of the old-style development economists. Such intellectual shifts underpinned the emergence of the Washington Consensus, heralded for Africa by the Berg Report of 1981, even if weakly relative to what was to materialize over the next decade, with its emphasis on a mean and lean state and reliance upon market forces.[8] Krueger's (1986: 62) own view on, or manifesto for, development economics from an article, published in the first issue of the *World Bank Research Observer*, could not have been expressed more clearly, emphasis added:

> Once it is recognized that individuals respond to incentives, and that 'market failure' is the result of inappropriate incentives rather than

non-responsiveness, the *separateness* of development economics as a field largely disappears.

In a sense then, just as the formalist revolution of the 1950s marked a watershed in the evolution of economic theory in general (with shift from implosion to explosion around microeconomic principles), so the 1980s offered a similar watershed as those principles were turned upon development economics, promoting the new at the expense of the old or classic. Further, the policy and ideological thrust of the new development economics was to displace all aspects of modernization other than promotion of, and reliance upon, the market.

Nonetheless, the Washington Consensus and the new development economics did not prevail without considerable opposition. It should be observed that, though possibly relatively limited in its effects until the mid-1990s, such contestation was strong compared to its presence within economics more generally for other fields where economic imperialism in its internal colonization of the discipline proved especially powerful. For, over the post-war period, mainstream economics has evolved to exhibit a lack of interest in its own history, in methodology, in other disciplines (except as fields of application) and in heterodox alternatives – all tending to be dismissed without debate as irrelevant and/or lacking scientific rigour.

Drawing upon its traditions, the strength and nature of the opposition to the rapidly emerging new orthodoxy pinpointed two issues. First, almost exclusively around the experience of the East Asian NICs, was the notion of the developmental state, and the sheer lack of empirical rationale for the postulates of the Washington Consensus in light of both their miraculous economic performance and the heavy state intervention that had accompanied it. Such a focus more or less completely excluded attention to Africa.[9] Second, though, considerable emphasis was placed upon adjustment with a human face, and the extent to which Washington Consensus policies placed an unduly heavy burden on the impoverished irrespective of their merits otherwise. Ultimately, with the poor continuing results of the policies emanating from the World Bank and the IMF, these organizations experienced a crisis of legitimacy and, by the late 1990s, the Washington Consensus had given way to the post Washington Consensus, PWC.

Here again, though, it is imperative to locate the shifts in development economics within the context of the broader shifts within economic theory itself. For, within the discipline, there had been a reaction against the extremes of the new classical economics which was based on the presumption that markets, unless interfered with, work both perfectly and instantaneously. Instead, with economists such as Joe Stiglitz to the fore, emphasis was placed upon the imperfect working of markets, especially because of informational imperfections. As a result, so it was argued, whether for second hand cars, insurance for the aged, or anything else, markets might not be efficient, might not clear, and might not exist at all. Further, the presence of non-market institutions – the state, culture, custom, habit, trust, apparently irrational behaviour and so on – could be explained as a response to the presence of those market imperfections. This offered a perspective on the world in which it was viewed through the prism of the microeconomic incidence, or not, of market (and corresponding institutional) imperfections that could potentially be corrected (or not depending upon the motivations and imperfections attached to those who might do the correcting).

Significantly, the shift to market imperfection economics expanded both the scope of application of microeconomic principles *and* their palatability to the other social sciences. Whilst the old-style economics imperialism was based upon the idea that the non-market factors should be treated as if they were equivalent to the presence of a market,[10] the new style emphasized that history and institutions mattered in their own and distinct if derived right. The result was to reinvigorate economics imperialism, with the emergence or renewal of a new range of applications in and around the discipline – the new growth theory, the new economic sociology, the new institutional economics, the new economic geography, and so on.

And, of course, the same applied to the reinvention of the new development economics and, putatively, detached it from its neo-liberal origins to become what might be termed the newer development economics, especially associated with the post-Washington Consensus. Not surprisingly, there has been understandable debate over the extent to which the PWC does or does not depart from the Washington Consensus (and the new development economics). In addressing this, it is, as with neo-liberalism, essential to distinguish between the rhetoric, the scholarship, the policy in practice and the (empirical) representation of reality that each incorporates. The rhetoric and scholarship are clearly different with one emphasizing market perfection as opposed to market imperfections. Yet, these differences should not be exaggerated. For the newer development economics, as Stiglitz (2000: 23), for example, puts it, 'Economics is the study of scarcity, how resources are allocated among competing uses'. The issue is how to make the market work better rather than to rely upon it to the maximal exclusion of state intervention.

Moreover, the breach with the methods and technical apparatus of the orthodoxy are minimal if not non-existent. This is brought out explicitly in Dani Rodrik's (2007: 3) retrospective manifesto that has such striking resonances with, even development of, that previously furnished by Krueger:[11]

> First, this book is strictly grounded in neoclassical economic analysis. At the core of neoclassical economics lies the following methodological predisposition: social phenomena can best be understood by considering them to be an aggregation of purposeful behaviour by individuals – in their roles as consumer, producer, investor, politician, and so on – interacting with each other and acting under the constraints that their environment imposes. This I find to be not just a powerful discipline for

organizing our thoughts on economic affairs, but the only sensible way of thinking about them. If I often depart from the consensus that 'mainstream' economists have reached in matters of development policy, this has less to do with different modes of analysis than with different readings of the evidence and with different evaluations of the 'political economy' of developing nations. The economics that the graduate student picks up in the seminar room – abstract as it is and riddled with a variety of market failures – admits an almost unlimited range of policy recommendations, depending on the specific assumptions the analyst is prepared to make. As I will argue in the chapters to come, the tendency of many economists to offer advice based on simple rules of thumb regardless of context (privatize this, liberalize that), is a derogation rather than a proper application of neoclassical economic principles.

Rodrik is motivated by the wish, like the newer development economics, to shift away from the one model fits all of the new development economics and its neo-liberal Washington Consensus. But he is equally attached to what might be termed a 'one economics of one model does not fit all'. The results are significant both for policy and realism. For, whilst the Washington Consensus deployed neo-liberal rhetoric not to withdraw state intervention but to use it on behalf of select interests, usually those of private capital in general and of finance in particular, so the PWC has provided a rationale for such discretionary, piecemeal intervention, and on a broader economic and social terrain.[12] And, the Washington Consensus has, unlike its modernization predecessor, offered no notion of development itself. Rather there is a way to achieve it – reliance upon the market – but without much by way of what will be achieved. And exactly the same is true of the PWC, with development as the correction of market and institutional imperfections but with no account of to what end. This is symptomatic of the loss of the concerns and methods of the old development economics, and of its understanding of development as marking economic and social transition across a number of dimensions.

The last decade or so has, then, witnessed the passage from the new to the newer development economics. And the process has been completed by one further step. Once again, broader shifts within economics as a whole are of relevance. At one level, the market imperfection model is as far as the micro-economic principles can be stretched, being applied intensively in context of market imperfections and extensively by subject matter across the traditional domains of other social sciences through economics imperialism. The only remaining avenue for originality and continuing scope of application and appeal has been to complement the optimizing individual with other motivations or with other arbitrarily chosen factors, even if not individualistically grounded. This necessarily leads to 'dirty' or mixed models with a presumption in favour of rationality at the individual level but an acceptance of other factors for convenience and in light of subject matter.

Such is the 'newest' economics imperialism, and it has attained cult popularity under the aptly named 'freakonomics' (Levitt and Dubner, 2006). The corresponding economic theory of almost everything (Frank, 2008), has addressed topics as diverse as the fixing of sumo wrestling contests and why drug dealers live with their mothers. As already indicated, the predisposition to draw upon the technical apparatus of economics is complemented by appeal to any other speculatively or empirically derived factor and, to be strongly highlighted, heavy reliance upon statistical methods. As will be seen, there is no reason why the putative economics of Africa should not be treated as akin to the fixed sumo wrestling or the domiciled drug dealer!

Africa as freak or zombie?

Initially, though, it is necessary to place the passage from new to newest in development economics in the broader context both to locate its own position and the potential for dissent. For seven trends across both development economics and studies have been of extreme importance. First, with the emergence of the Washington Consensus, the World Bank has increasingly set the agenda for development economics, primarily as one of market versus the state, and has also shifted the balance of debate in favour of the market. Second, despite the shift from Washington Consensus to PWC, the developmental state paradigm has primarily remained outside orthodox discourse which has eschewed systemic approaches and failed to engage with them in deference to at most commitment to piecemeal analyses and interventions to improve the workings of the market. Third, development economics has increasingly distanced itself from development studies and the incorporation of interdisciplinarity other than on its own terms. Fourth, it has been able to do so to some extent because of the absence of the counterweight of development studies as a discipline within the United States, as well as the capture of economic history by the mainstream within economics departments in the United States. Fifth, there has been an increasing emphasis on policy, external funding and contract research as opposed to critical understanding of the nature of development. Sixth this has been complemented by the turn against political economy and the turn to postmodernism within development studies.[13] Last, and by no means least, the Americanization of economics has been especially pronounced in the training of academics and practitioners, with the disproportionate production of economic doctorates in the United States for export to the rest of the (developing) world whose own universities have increasingly emulated the US model of economics to the exclusion of alternatives.

The preceding account, then, is intended to explain how development economics currently got its spots and exactly what those spots are. Both the process and the outcome could be illustrated by reference to the application of development economics to Africa but space constraints do not allow for this in detail but see other Chapters in this volume. And some further preliminary comments are still necessary before offering some minimal if revealing illustrations from the most recent literature alone.

First, the 'economics of Africa' as such is a nonsense given the diversity of countries and conditions involved.[14] Nonetheless, the idea that there is such a thing gathered strength with the rise of the Washington Consensus and the new development economics in the wake of the Berg Report. With, initially, a singular set of policy prescriptions and, subsequently, a continuity of economic method across the transition from Washington Consensus to PWC, there has been an inevitable tendency to homogenize across diversity and to admit the latter only in the limited sense of selectively chosen differences across market and institutional imperfections broadly conceived.

Second, development economics in general and in its application to Africa has been subject to waves of fashion, often dictated by the World Bank, and its consistent thrust in finding shifting ways of supporting the market in posing an agenda of market versus the state. The result has often been to incorporate a heavy dose of idiosyncrasy in terms of what is considered and how. At times, Africa has been marginalized as an object of study, as with debate around the developmental state; at other times, it has assumed prominence especially in terms of poverty, democracy and (violent) conflict.[15] As widely recognized with the 2008 World Development Report on agriculture, despite its significance for African livelihoods, this has been sorely neglected (and possibly the most incoherent in its mish-mash of scholarship, rhetoric, policy and representation of reality (Oya, 2011)).

Third, the dominance of the World Bank, its lack of engagement with critics, and the imperative of policy (and rhetoric) over understanding have together constituted a set of ingredients, the recipe from which has been a source not only of idiosyncrasy but also of impoverished scholarly standards even by those of the mainstream itself. Within the new, newer, and newest development economics, there is very little theory, limited relation of the theory to the statistically investigated hypotheses, and poorly undertaken statistical investigation itself (in terms of standard problems such as correlation versus causation, omitted variables, problems with cross-section over time-series and so on). I have, for example, demonstrated the appalling level of theory underpinning financial programming from its origins with the Polak model of 1957 through to the PRSPs of the present day (Fine, 2006) and see below.

Such conclusions have been sharply confirmed by the Deaton Report (2006) on World Bank research over the period 1998–2005, commissioned by the Bank itself and conducted exclusively by mainstream economists. One of the main messages from the Report, and especially by reference to the Bank's research on aid and growth, is that its conclusions are not warranted but that they were nonetheless widely propagated in order to promote the Bank's own position. Thus,

> the panel has substantial criticisms of the way that this research was
> used to proselytize on behalf of Bank policy, often without expressing

appropriate scepticism. Internal research that was favorable to Bank positions was given greater prominence, and unfavourable research ignored
. . . balance was lost in favour of advocacy . . . there was a serious failure
of the checks and balances that should separate advocacy and research.

(p. 6)

These themes around advocacy, proselytizing and balance recur. For,

putting too much weight on preliminary or flawed work could [why not
'does'?] expose the Bank to charges that its research is tailored or selected
to support its predetermined positions, and the panel believes that, in
some cases, the Bank proselytized selected new work in major policy
speeches and publications, without appropriate caveats on its reliability
. . . this happened with some of the Bank's work on aid effectiveness.

(p. 38)[16]

Of course, the Bank's research does not fill out the world of development
economics but it has a profound influence by setting the terms of debate and
by situating itself within the discipline (and as a source of resources and prestige, all of this to an increasing and unprecedented extent). Consider, then,
one of the most cited contributions on 'African Economic Performance'
(Collier and Gunning, 1999). It seizes upon the notion of social capital to
explain poor outcomes. This is undoubtedly because social capital was a
buzzword in vogue at the time, especially at the World Bank in promoting the
transition from Washington Consensus to PWC, and as a means to finesse a
detachment both from neo-liberalism and state intervention in deference to
civil society.[17] So important is social capital to Collier and Gunning that they
reference the term over thirty times (usually preceded by 'lack of' in the
African context). But this is to offer an entirely arbitrary and unsupported
explanation. As one of the commissioned background papers for Deaton
suggests in response to the question, 'Are the conclusions consistent with the
research findings?', the answer is 'No. The paper jumps to conclusions about
social capital, while there is nothing in previous research or even in this paper
that suggests that social capital is a major factor'. And for the question
'If applicable, are policy recommendations commensurate with the findings?
No. The evidence does not support social capital and the related policy
recommendations' (Fine, 2011) for further details.

A little less then a decade later, African economic growth is being addressed
by Collier (2007a) in a background paper for the Spence Commission. His
substantive analysis begins, 'Africa is too large and diverse a region to be
treated as a single aggregate . . . it is an enormous region and cannot sensibly
be analysed as a single entity'. But this diversity is addressed through the
simple expedient of emphasizing physical geography across two single-valued
dimensions, allowing for four ideal-types. For, his second paragraph answers the diversity conundrum, 'Potentially, these two distinctions create four

possible categories: resource-rich and landlocked; resource-rich and coastal; resource-scarce and landlocked; and resource-scarce and coastal', (p. 4).[18] Of course, other variables can also be added, such as those attached to human geography in the limited sense of ethnic diversity and levels of population, but this is all indicative of the arbitrary selection and promotion of particular variables to positions of prominence, their incorporation into heavy statistical exercises, and an underlying presumption of markets and democracy as the way forward to an unspecified developmental outcome (other than of higher growth and, by World Bank proselytizing, through neo-liberal policies with poverty reduction as outcome). Stunningly, though, the variable in vogue just a short time previously is simply not mentioned. Social capital does not appear once.

This is all indicative of how the economics of Africa has evolved around a shifting content and interaction across scholarship, advocacy, policy and representation (of the putative African economy). First and foremost, Africa is both exceptional *and* homogenized. This is most readily recognized in the search for the source of the elusive African 'dummy', the statistical artefact that explains the continent's poor performance once selection from a wide range of other standard variables are taken into account (Englebert, 2000) for example. If only that dummy could be found, it could be addressed by policy (or not if 'physical').

Second, in the 1980s following Berg, if not put in these terms, the African dummy within orthodoxy was perceived to be the failure to rely upon the market. As a result of its poverty and poor economic performance, and its heavy level of indebtedness,[19] the continent has been disproportionately dependent upon aid and the associated conditionalities attached to them. These have failed to deliver, however much dispute might persist over the impact of adjustment programmes across different methods of assessment – by comparisons of with and without such programmes, of before and after, and of targets with outcomes. Whether adjustment has had some positive impact or not is not really the issue, for what stands out is the extent of absolute failure irrespective of the outcome of this debate on what can only at best have been marginal improvement on the most favourable judgement.[20] Such considerations do not arise in case of the successes of east Asian NICs, whereas SAPRI (2004, pp. 173/4) concludes for Africa:

> [We] have identified four basic ways in which adjustment policies have contributed to the further impoverishment and marginalization of local populations, while increasing economic inequality. The first is through the demise of domestic manufacturing sectors and the loss of gainful employment by laid-off workers and small producers due to the nature of trade and financial-sector reforms. The second relates to the contribution that agricultural, trade and mining reforms have made to the declining viability and incomes of small farms and poor rural communities, as well as to declining food security, particularly in rural areas.

Third, the retrenchment of workers through privatizations and budget cuts, in conjunction with labour-market flexibilization measures, has resulted in less secure employment, lower wages, fewer benefits and an erosion of workers' rights and bargaining power. Finally, poverty has been increased through privatization programs, the application of user fees, budget cuts and other adjustment measures that have reduced the role of the state in providing or guaranteeing affordable access to essential quality services.

And, Mkandawire (2005) identifies 27 African countries that have been designated as good adjusters at one time or another by the Washington institutions, on 60 separate occasions between 1981 and 1998. So, it would appear that even when the policies are adopted, they do not work over the longer term or cannot be sustained. Further, he also shows that the successful adjusters do not always show successful performance even by the limited standards of growth alone.

With most African economies subject to renewal of adjustment programmes every few years, the extent of *interventions* to promote the putative free market has been remarkable over the past 30 years. For, following the emergence of Washington Consensus policies in the wake of the Berg Report, pressure has been exerted on levels and composition of government expenditure, fiscal balance and tax reform, deregulation of both domestic and international financial markets, encouraging devaluation, privatization, deregulation of business, and trade liberalization, increasing flexibility in labour markets, and guaranteeing secure property rights especially for inward foreign investment. But these measures, both in principle and as exercised in practice, should not be seen as the simple move towards some ideal pure market system. Rather, they represent continuing intervention with considerable discretion to place the highest priority on freedom of manoeuvre for private capital.

As a result we have witnessed the rhetoric of free markets alongside the ever more pervasive imposition of conditionalities. Paradoxically, this has even accelerated with the discrediting of the Washington Concession and its displacement by the post-Washington Consensus, PRSPs and mission creep. For the response of the Washington institutions to the failure of its policies to sustain improved performance within Africa, and elsewhere, has been to bemoan their lack of implementation in the first instance and, to extend their scope, and the rationale for them, with the shift to the market/institutional imperfections paradigm. And, as conditionalities expand, so they are not met, leading to a further cycle of measures designed to deal with these deficiencies. As UNCTAD (2002, p. 17) report, 'IFI conditionality, loosely defined, in 13 sub-Saharan countries over 1999–2000 amounted on average to 114 for each country, of which 82 were governance related'. Not surprisingly, then, 'with the rise in the number of structural conditions in the 1980s and 1990s, the degree of compliance with programmes declined'. Indeed, 'if disbursement of 75 per cent or more of the loans was taken as a measure of compliance with Fund policy conditionality, less than half of Fund-supported programmes met the test during 1973–97. The decline was particularly dramatic in the 1990s: during 1993–7 only 27.6 per cent of the 141 arrangements could be considered in compliance'.

Consider, for example, the growing intervention of the World Bank in social policy (Fine, 2009) for detail. Despite its now extensive intervention, from within, Moser (2008, p. 47), for example, possibly complains:

> The World Bank does not have a specifically defined social policy as such. Within the institution, three predominant social policy 'domains' can be identified: social sectors, social protection, and social development. The fact that each has a distinct location within the organization has served to create artificial conceptual and operational barriers to a holistic social policy.

Yet, the Bank's own review of social protection is extraordinarily revealing (Holzman (ed.) 2009). Between 2000 and 2007, it implemented 25 risk and vulnerability assessments across SSA. In doing so, it provided a mere $2billion in aid over the last five of these years to cover social funds, safety nets, pensions, and labour markets. In short, netting out the costs of the assessments themselves, we are talking something less than $1 per year per person for a major say in the formation of social policy, teasing out the figures from Holzman *et al.* (2009, pp. 6–7). And, both analytically and policy-wise, the World Bank's position has become one in which (temporary?) individual household vulnerability depends upon and interacts with everything in principle, so that discretionary piecemeal intervention is pervasively justified but without any notion of a developmental or welfare state agenda as strategic guide. So the absence of the systemic and of the corresponding permanence of poverty (and welfare provision more generally) is implicitly overlooked rather than addressed.

In short, if the African dummy has been reluctant to yield to adjustment programmes, it might be that the dummy is to be found, at least in major part, in the programmes themselves. But, instead, the result has been, third, a focus on the virtues and vices of aid as a support for adjustment. Orthodoxy sought initially to explain the persistence of the dummy by too much state intervention, and a corresponding culture and practice of rent-seeking. This had, in turn, by the 1990s given way to an emphasis upon corruption and the failure of African governments to implement policies rather than the failure of the policies themselves. On the one hand, this has now induced a discourse of country ownership of adjustment programmes (possibly to be interpreted as doing what the World Bank and IMF want without being told to do so). On the other hand, failure to adopt the right policies ought itself to have been taken into account in proposing them. Consequently, Africa in particular has been subject to a new political economy of aid in which donor support moves from being conditional upon levels of need and future adoption of policy to an appropriate policy environment already being in place (van Waeyenberge, 2007).

Fourth, as indicated, the last decade has begun to witness a shift in scholarship, towards accepting a greater, if piecemeal, role for the state both in promoting development (if ultimately this is predominantly the market) and in alleviating poverty in the interim. Not surprisingly, the economics of Africa has increasingly been reduced to the economics of poverty, itself incorporating or gathering together more or less disparate topics around factors such as migration, geography, violence, institutions, corruption, ethnicity, race, urbanization, micro-finance, gender, education, fertility, and so on.[21] As discussed next, these have been incorporated into economic analyses, an ideal illustration of economics imperialism, with development studies especially in the firing line, not least with the economics of Africa.

Fifth, then, the big stories are still told around Africa's growth or economic performance. They have come to reflect an extraordinary tension around the confidence with which the same economic *principles* are deployed (despite their inability to explain the economy) and the extension of those principles to the non-economic to supplement explanation albeit through their introduction in a piecemeal and arbitrary fashion. These have ranged over the physical (geographical), the biological (susceptibility to disease), and the social (violence, corruption, institutions and so on). Ironically, such work is often heavily grounded in statistical methods whose results, when not proselytized, are indicative of what has to be explained as opposed to offering an explanation. And the results are generally inconsistent with the theoretical principles that they are deemed to investigate. Thus, for example, empirical estimation of models of growth show that it is not steady, being subject to both rapid periods of expansion and of collapse. If only the pro-market bias and underlying theory could be shed, there is almost a resonance with the inductive method of the old development economics!

Sixth, these features taken together have had the effect of creating eclectic and frequently shifting initiatives in the amalgam of scholarship, rhetoric and policy, not least with the PRSPs and the Millennium Development Goals. The Spence Report of late 2008 is an outstanding example of the newest development economics, if marginally more progressive and modest than most. Like NEPAD that preceded it in 2001, and with only a few pages on Africa itself, it characteristically takes the virtues of the market or globalization at most as point of departure in an age of reaction against the extremes of neo-liberalism.[22] Significantly, the only macroeconomic model underpinning PRSPs for a number of years made the astonishing assumption that the labour market was characterized by both full employment and a single, uniform wage. As unemployment and low wages are the two single most important sources of poverty, the model had the effect of precluding its consideration at the outset![23] More than 30 PRSPs are now in place in SSA, most dating from 2000, and all without proper analytical underpinnings (although critical attention has been more focused on the lack of genuine government ownership and participation).

As I have shown more generally, in the treatment of financial programming, the theory underpinning the policy stances of the Washington institutions, as it goes about its macroeconomics, fits somewhere between the ridiculous and the elementary, often both at the same time (Fine, 2006) for this and what follows. The Polak model, now in its sixth decade, that continues to provide the framework for financial programming in the era of poverty reduction, has always been about the dynamics around a given *equilibrium* and, as a consequence, can say nothing about growth let alone the broader process of development as economic and social transformation. When in the late 1980s, an attempt was made at a theoretical marriage between the IMF's goal of short-run adjustment and the World Bank's mission of long-run growth, the result was a model in which growth declined to zero in the long run (although this remained unnoticed as attention focused only on what happened in the short run, after which the advisors would return for a new assessment). As has been pointed out by the Deaton Report, World Bank research is often of low quality and high profile as long as it conforms to the message of the day. It should be added that even where it is of high quality by the standards of techniques that are sacrosanct to the discipline, this is no guarantee either of the relevance or validity of the research.

There is, then, at most a loose connection between the ideology and scholarship of the World Bank and its policies in practice. The ideological scholarship of those such as Collier have an enormous impact but their attachment to aid policy in practice is limited and/or uncertain.[24] As van Waeyenberge (2007) has shown in her close assessment of the aid practices of the World Bank, and its use of the CPIA (Country Policies and Institutions) tool in particular, to determine aid allocation in the first instance (before political considerations enter), the last ten years has witnessed a tightening on the conditionalities associated with the Washington Consensus. The one, at first sight, perverse exception is the absence of insistence upon elimination of capital controls – until it is realized that by now this is more or less taken for granted! This is so much so that in order to guard against short-run capital flight, developing countries are now accumulating large dollar reserves to the benefit of the United States and at significant expense to themselves (Rodrik, 2006).

But whilst the ideology and the scholarship of the new, newer and newest development economics may not be a decisive influence on the incidence and impact of aid and conditionalities, this is far from suggesting that it has had no influence. Sen (2006) is surely too generous in closing his commentary on Easterly (2006), yet another grand World Bank diatribe against aid, with the suggestion that,

> there is a strong case for judging a book by its best contributions, not its weakest points. My hope is that the 'searchers' among the readers of *The*

White Man's Burden will look for the convincing arguments Easterly does provide rather than for those he does not.

The same generosity is certainly not appropriate, however, to the world of development economics, especially in its application to Africa, where a particular version of Gresham's Law of currency prevails, and the bad and unconvincing go further than driving out the good and convincing and do not even allow them to emerge. Such is the stranglehold of the World Bank on who does what research, how and for what purpose, not least with its huge influence as knowledge bank over the resources for research and training whether at academic, government or training levels (van Waeyenberge, 2007). No wonder that African economies are so poorly served by African economists.

Concluding remarks

This chapter has painted an extremely pessimistic picture of the way in which development economics has evolved over the post-war period, coming under the influence (in scholarship, rhetoric, policy and agenda setting) of the World Bank, detaching itself from heterodoxy (including the previous orthodoxy of the old or classic development economics) and from interdisciplinarity and development studies (other than as an opportunity for economics imperialism), degenerating both in scholarly quality and relevance, and generally supporting market-conforming policy at the expense of understanding the processes of development and more progressive stances on how to achieve it.

But the picture is not entirely bleak. As argued elsewhere, the social sciences are currently going through a dual retreat from the extremes of both postmodernism and neo-liberalism, with a corresponding renewal of interest in understanding the nature of contemporary capitalism (Fine, 2004a). Together with the issues posed by the current financial crisis, this has meant that the social sciences are as open in direction and content as they have been for some time. Both within and across individual disciplines, and in their integration within development studies, there is an increasing interest and need in offering a political economy of capitalism, one that both addresses the general trends associated with what has been termed globalization, as well as their intersection with particular conditions and processes that were previously associated with, and identified by the old development economics. This will also involve the reintroduction or strengthening of the presence of the traditional variables of political economy and social theory, those of class, power, conflict and the state. Attention will necessarily be given to the meaning of such variables in specific contexts rather than their homogenized reduction to statistical variation. But, ultimately, the renewal of African political economies will depend less upon departure from the new development economics or the economics of Africa and more upon the extent to which progressive movements upon the continent themselves gain some purchase.

Notes

1 This Chapter draws in part upon earlier work, especially (Milonakis and Fine, 2009) and (Fine and Milonakis, 2009). Thanks to editors and others for comments on earlier drafts
2 See, for example (Castree, 2006) and (Ferguson, 2007).
3 Interestingly, as outlined in (Fine, 2007a), this implosive reductionism involved a recognition of qualifications by those pushing it forward, only for them to be forgotten step by step. In contrast, in the evolution of economic theory following the formalist revolution (see next paragraph), the extension of scope of application of the orthodox principles is both more rapid and lacking in sensitivity to potential reservations.
4 See Helleiner (1968), Loxley (1971), Arrighi and Saul (1973), Wuyts (1989) and Sender and Smith (1990) for some reflection of and on these. The presence, prominence and conditions for emergence of African voices in dissent have worsened to the point almost of extinction from the period of the Washington Consensus onwards.
5 For coverage of the old development economics, see Jomo (ed.) (2005 and 2006).
6 Thus (Bates, 1981) is at least as interesting for its timing as for its content.
7 Thus, the earliest neo-liberal developmentalists such as Basil Yamey, Peter Bauer and Deepak Lal, were treated as eccentrics and, even later, gained more ideological than scholarly prestige. For the latter, 'the demise of development economics is likely to be conducive to the health of both the economics and the economies of developing countries' (Lal, 2000, p.109).
8 For an early critique of the Berg Report, and some of it left critics, see Sender and Smith (1985).
9 See (Mkandawire, 2001) and, for overview of developmental state literature (Fine, 2007b and 2010d).
10 As Buchanan (1984, p. 14) puts it the '[utility] function defines or describes a set of possible trade-offs among alternatives for potential choice, whether the latter be those between apples and oranges at the fruit stand or between peace and war for the nation'. This has, of course, become extremely important in orthodox economic analysis of civil war, especially in Africa.
11 Rodrik's other requirements, apart from the first, are to sift the empirical evidence, to have some faith in government, to be context specific, to prioritize, and to be modest. For my own critique of where this leads in practice (more in the breach than the observance), with reference to South Africa, see (Fine, 2010a and b) in debate with (Hausmann and Andrews, 2009).
12 A further point is of significance in passing – that John Williamson, originator of the latter term, has persistently argued that the differences between it and the PWC can only be exaggerated (especially by Stiglitz and Rodrik), not least to promote claims to distinctiveness (Williamson, 2008) for example.
13 The work of Sen is significant if an exception in these respects. Although extremely influential within development studies, it has had little impact upon, or against, the trends in development economics as such, and has not offered alternatives in terms of causal political economy (Fine, 2004b) for some account.
14 For this argument in the specific context of labour markets, see Sender *et al.* (2005).
15 Here Paul Collier has been to the fore (Collier, 2009) most recently but see also below. He has, literally, blundered on through social capital, aid effectiveness, policy conditionalities, ethnic diversity, poverty, geography, violence and dem-

ocracy without regard to criticism not least from within orthodoxy itself, most devastating in this respect from the Deaton Report (2006) and its assessors. See also Cramer (2002) on violence and ethnicity that has been particularly prominent in the World Bank's African mythology.

16 For a wide-ranging critical assessment of Deaton, see Bayliss *et al.* (eds) (2011).
17 For a full account of the remarkable rise and fall of social capital at the World Bank, see (Fine, 2010c).
18 Collier takes his cue from Jeffrey Sachs (2005) who has himself gone through a remarkable reinvention from shock therapist to aid advocate, in moving from Eastern Europe to Africa and elsewhere, whilst relying upon a heavy dose of geographical determinism in analytical terms, (Unwin, 2007) for critique.
19 So much so that net aid flows to Africa are frequently found to be negative when setting interest payments against receipts.
20 For discussion of the results of adjustment on Africa, see (SAPRI, 2002) and Mkandawire and Soludo (eds) (2003) for example.
21 See other chapters for some detail on how these topics have been addressed.
22 *The Growth Report: Strategies For Sustained Growth And Inclusive Development*, http://www.growthcommission.org/index.php?option = com_content&task = view&id = 96&Itemid = 169 for details; and *The New Partnership for Africa's Development*, http://www.nepad.org/2005/files/documents/inbrief.pdf
23 See the rehashing of the piece in various guises by Devarajan *et al.* (2000) and Fine (2006) for a critique.
24 For a trenchant and wide-ranging critique of Collier (2007b), see Grove (2008) who concludes:

> *The Bottom Billion* is not an economics book. It is a confused and disordered array of conflations, fallacies, and falsehoods. Collier's one achievement is to have written so many distortions, contradictions, untruths, and fatuous arguments that he still manages to hang himself without even supplementing footnotes.

References

Arrighi, G. and Saul, J. (1973) *Essays on the Political Economy of Africa*, New York: Monthly Review Press.
Bates, R. (1981) *Markets and States in Tropical Africa: The Political Basis of Agricultural Policies*, Berkeley: University of California Press.
Bayliss, K., Fine, B., and van Waeyenberge, E. (eds) (2011) *The World Bank and the Future for Development Research*, forthcoming Buchanan, J. (1984) 'Politics without Romance: A Sketch of Positive Public Choice Theory and Its Normative Implications', in Buchanan and Tollison (eds) (1984).
Birch, K. and V. Mykhnenko (eds) (2010) The Rise and Fall of Neoliberalism: The Collapse of an Economic Order?, London: Zed Press.
Buchanan, J. and Tollison, R. (eds) (1984) *The Theory of Public Choice – II*, Ann Arbor: University of Michigan Press.
Castree, N. (2006) 'Commentary', *Environment and Planning A*, 38 : 1–6.
Chang, H-J. (2002) *Kicking Away the Ladder – Development Strategy in Historical Perspective*, London: Anthem Press.
Collier, P. (2007a) 'Growth Strategies for Africa', a paper prepared for the Spence Commission on Economic Growth, http://www.growthcommission.org/storage/cgdev/documents/ThemesPapers/Paper%20Collier.pdf

—— (2007b) *The Bottom Billion: Why the Poorest Countries Are Failing and What Can Be Done about It*, Oxford: Oxford University Press.

—— (2009) *Wars, Guns, and Votes: Democracy in Dangerous Places*, New York: Harper Collins.

Collier, P. and J. Gunning (1999) 'Explaining African Economic Performance', *Journal of Economic Literature*, 37: 64–111.

Cramer, C. (2002) 'Homo Economicus Goes to War: Methodological Individualism, Rational Choice and the Political Economy of War', *World Development*, 30: 1845–64.

Deaton, A., Banerjee, A., Lustig, N., Rogoff, K. (2006) 'An Evaluation of World Bank Research, 1998–2005', available at http://siteresources.worldbank.org/DEC/Resources/84797-1109362238001/726454-1164121166494/RESEARCH-EVALUATION-2006-Main-Report.pdf

Devarajan, S., Go, F., Charlier, A., Dabalen, W., Easterly, H., Fofack, H. Izquierdo, J. and Koryukin, L. (2000) *A Macroeconomic Framework for Poverty Reduction Strategy Papers*, Washington, DC: World Bank, http://www.worldbank.org/research/growth/pdfiles/devarajan%20etal.pdf, subsequently with an application to Zambia, 2002, http://www.worldbank.org/files/12937_TK_Paper_Chap_13_Devarajan_Go.pdf.

Easterley, W. (2006) *The White Man's Burden: Why the West's Efforts to Aid the Rest Have Done so Much Ill and so Little Good*, New York: Penguin.

Edigheji, O. (ed) (2010) Constructing a Democratic Developmental State in South Africa: Potentials and Challenges, Cape Town: Human Sciences Research Council Press, forthcoming.

Englebert, P. (2000) 'Solving the Mystery of the AFRICA Dummy', *World Development*, 28: 1821–35.

Ferguson, J. (2007) 'Formalities of Poverty: Thinking about Social Assistance in Neoliberal South Africa', *African Studies Review*, 50: 71–86.

Fine, B. (2004a) 'Examining the Idea of Globalisation and Development Critically: What Role for Political Economy?', *New Political Economy*, 9: 213–31.

Fine, B. (2004b) 'Economics and Ethics: Amartya Sen as Point of Departure', ABCDE Conference, Oslo, June, 2002, published in *The New School Economic Review*, 1: 151–62, http://www.newschool.edu/gf/nser/articles/0101_fineb_econan dethicssen_ fall04_final.pdf

—— (2006) 'Financial Programming and the IMF', Jomo and Fine (eds) (2006).

—— (2007a) 'The Historical Logic of Economics Imperialism and Meeting the Challenges of Contemporary Orthodoxy: Or Twelve Hypotheses on Economics, and What is to Be Done', paper presented at EAEPE Conference, 1–3 November 2007, Porto, Portugal, https://eprints.soas.ac.uk/5620/

—— (2007b) 'State, Development and Inequality: The Curious Incidence of the Developmental State in the Night-Time', paper presented to Sanpad Conference, Durban, June 26–30, http://www.iippe.org/wiki/images/1/1a/Ben_Fine_State_Development_Inequality.pdf.

—— (2008a) 'Looking at the Crisis through Marx: Or Is It the Other Way about?', mimeo, https://eprints.soas.ac.uk/5921/1/isrfin.doc

—— (2008b) 'Zombieconomics: The Living Death of the Dismal Science in the Age of Neo-Liberalism', Paper for ESRC Neoliberalism Seminar, April 2008, http://www.cppr.ac.uk/centres/cppr/esrcneoliberalism seminar/, to appear in abbreviated form in Birch and Mykhnenko (eds) (2010).

—— (2008b) 'Development as Zombieconomics in the Age of Neo-Liberalism', Third World Quarterly, vol. 30, no 5, pp. 885–904.

—— (2008d) 'Can South Africa be a Developmental State?', in Edighedi (ed) (2010), forthcoming.

—— (2009) '*Social Policy and the Crisis of Neo-Liberalism*', conference paper for "The Crisis of Neo-Liberalism in India: Challenges and Alternatives", Tata Institute of Social Sciences (TISS) Mumbai and International Development Economics Associates (IDEAs), 13–15 March, http://www.networkideas.org/ideasact/jan09/PDF/Fine.pdf.

—— (2010) 'Submission to the COSATU Panel of Economists On "The Final Recommendations of the International Panel on Growth (The Harvard Panel)" ', *Transformation*, 69: 5–30.

—— (2010b) 'Rejoinder to "A Response to Fine's 'Harvard Group Shores up Shoddy Governance' ", *Transformation*, 69: 66–79.

—— (2010c) *Theories of Social Capital: Researchers Behaving Badly*, London: Pluto Press.

—— (2011) 'Social Capital and Health: The World Bank through the Looking Glass after Deaton', in Bayliss *et al.* (eds) (2011).

Fine, B. and Milonakis, D. (2009) *From Economics Imperialism to Freakonomics: The Shifting Boundaries Between Economics and Other Social Sciences*, London: Routledge.

Frank, R. (2008) *The Economic Naturalist: Why Economics Explains almost Everything*, London: Virgin.

Grove, S. (2008) 'A Review of Paul Collier's *The Bottom Billion*', http://www.monthlyreview.org/mrzine/grove150808.html

Hausmann, R. and Andrews, M. (2009) 'Why We Still Believe Exports for Jobs Will Lead to Shared Growth: A Response to Fine's "Harvard Group Shores up Shoddy Governance" ', *Transformation*, 69: 31–65.

Helleiner, G. (1968) *Socialism, Self Reliance and the Second Plan : A Public Lecture*, Dar es Salaam: Economic Research Bureau, University College, ERB Paper, no 68.9.

Holzman, R. (ed.) (2009) *Social Protection and Labor at the World Bank, 2000–2008*, Washington: World Bank.

Holzman, R., Sipos, S. and the Social Protection Team (2009) 'Social Protection and Labor at the World Bank: An Overview', in Holzman (ed.) (2009).

Jomo, K. (ed.) (2005) *Pioneers of Development Economics: Great Economists on Development*, Delhi: Tulika, and London: Zed Press.

—— (2006) *Origins of Development Economics: How Schools of Economic Thought Addressed Development*, Delhi: Tulika, and London: Zed Press.

Jomo, K. and Fine, B. (eds) (2006) *The New Development Economics: After the Washington Consensus*, Delhi: Tulika, and London: Zed Press.

Krueger, A. (1986) 'Aid in the Development Process', *World Bank Research Observer*, 1: 57–78.

Lal, D. (2000 [1983]) *The Poverty of "Development Economics"*, second revised and expanded U.S. edition, Cambridge: The MIT Press.

Levitt, S. and Dubner, S. (2006) *Freakonomics: A Rogue Economist Explores the Hidden Side of Everything*, London: Penguin.

Loxley, J. (1971) *The Domestic Finance of Development Projects in Tanzania*, Dar es Salaam: Economic Research Bureau, University of Dar es Salaam.

Lucas, R. (1987) *Models of Business Cycles*, Oxford: Blackwell.

Milonakis, D. and Fine, B. (2009) *From Political Economy to Economics: Method, the Social and the Historical in the Evolution of Economic Theory*, London: Routledge.

Mkandawire, T. (2001) 'Thinking about Developmental States in Africa', *Cambridge Journal of Economics*, 25: 289–313.

—— (2005) 'Maladjusted African Economies and Globalisation', *Africa Development*, XXX: 1–33.

Mkandawire, T. and Soludo, C. (eds) (2003) *African Voices on Structural Adjustment. A Companion to: Our Continent, Our Future*, Dakar: CODESRIA.

Moser, C. (2008) 'A Framework for Asset-Based Social Policy', in Moser and Dani (eds) (2008).

Moser, C. and Dani, A. (eds) (2008) *Assets, Livelihoods, and Social Policy*, Washington: World Bank.

Oya, C. (2009) 'Agriculture in the World Bank: Blighted Harvest Persists', in Bayliss *et al.* (2011).

Rodrik, D. (2006) 'The Social Cost of Foreign Exchange Reserves' *International Economic Journal*, 20: 253–66.

—— (2007) *One Economics, Many Recipes*, Princeton: Princeton University Press.

Rostow, W. (1960) *The Stages of Economic Growth: A Non-Communist Manifesto*, Cambridge: Cambridge University Press, third revised edition, 1990.

Sachs, J. (2005) *The End of Poverty: How We Can Make It Happen in Our Lifetime*, London: Penguin.

SAPRIN (2002) 'The Policy Roots of Economic Crisis and Poverty. A Multi-Country Participatory Assessment of Structural Adjustment', based on the results of the joint Sen, A. (2006) 'The Man without a Plan', *Foreign Affairs*, March/April, http://www.foreignaffairs.org/20060301fareviewessay85214/amartya-sen/the-man-without-a-plan.html

SAPRIN (2003) *Structural Adjustment: The SAPRIN Report: The Policy Roots of Economic Crisis, Poverty and Inequality*, London: Zed Press.

Sender, J. and Smith, S. (1985) 'What's Right with the Berg Report and What's Left of Its Critics?', *Capital and Class*, 24 (Winter): 125–44.

Sender, J. and Smith, S. (1990) *Poverty, Class and Gender in Rural Africa : A Tanzanian Case Study*, London: Routledge

Sender, J. *et al.* (2005) *Unequal Prospects: Disparities in the Quantity and Quality of Labour Supply in Sub-Saharan Africa*, Working Paper, No. 0525, World Bank Social Protection Discussion Paper Series, https://eprints.soas.ac.uk/5791/1/WB_SenderCramerOya_2005.pdf

Stiglitz, J. (2000 [1986]) *Economics of the Public Sector*, 3rd edn, New York: Norton & Company.

Stiglitz, J. (2002) *Globalization and Its Discontents*, New York: W.W. Norton and Co.

UNCTAD (2002) *Economic Development in Africa, From Adjustment to Poverty Reduction: What is New?*, Geneva: UNCTAD.

Unwin, T. (2007) 'No End to Poverty', *Journal of Development Studies*, 43: 929–53.

Van Waeyenberge, E. (2007) 'Exploring the emergence of a new aid regime: selectivity, knowledge and the World Bank', unpublished thesis, University of London.

Williamson, J. (2008) 'Letter: The Spence Commission and the Washington Consensus', *The Economists' Voice*, 5, Article 4, www.bepress.com/ev/vol5/iss4/art4/ World Bank/Civil Society/Government Structural Adjustment Participatory Review Initiative Network, available at: www.saprin.org/SAPRIN_Findings.pdf

Wuyts, M. (1989) *Money and Planning for Socialist Transition: The Mozambican Experience*, Aldershot: Gower.

Part II

Analytical perspectives on Africa

5 Agro-pessimism, capitalism and agrarian change

Trajectories and contradictions in Sub-Saharan Africa

Carlos Oya

Introduction

The importance of agriculture in Sub-Saharan Africa (SSA) appears to be obvious and is widely noted in the literature on African[1] development. For example, the Commission for Africa (2005) states that 'agriculture contributes at least 40 per cent of exports, 30 per cent of GDP, up to 30 per cent of foreign exchange earnings, and 70 to 80 per cent of employment'. There is however wide variation across countries in the relative importance of agriculture measured in terms of its contribution to GDP and exports, as well as aggregate evidence that agriculture's share of GDP has declined significantly in many countries. Still, the significance of agriculture as an occupation (either as 'main' or 'secondary' occupation in both rural and peri-urban areas) is well established.

Conventional wisdom tends to present us with two images. First, one hears that there is significant potential for agricultural development, often understood in static terms of comparative advantage.[2] This informs agriculture-centred development strategies where 'agricultural productivity gains must be the basis for national economic growth and the instrument for mass poverty reduction and food security' (World Bank, 2007: 19).[3] Second, this potential is regarded as severely constrained for several reasons and aggregate agricultural performance is judged to have been disappointing if not dismal. The literature on Africa, especially in the aftermath of the global recession of the 1970s, has been largely pessimistic, and despite some more nuanced assessments in recent times, 'Agro-Afro-pessimism' continues to permeate policy discourse.

The pessimism around agricultural performance, coupled with the optimism about its potential and the necessity of agriculture as an engine of development, combine to inform many of the most popular agriculture-centred policy recommendations for Africa, notably the quest for an 'African Green Revolution' to boost farm productivity and the promotion of smallholder export production to raise farmers' incomes, drive growth and reduce poverty all at the same time.[4] These policy fads and conventional platitudes, albeit containing some sensible ideas about which it is hard to disagree, tend to obscure tensions between intended and unintended outcomes, and power relations and inequality, as they are often presented in terms of simplistic win-win scenarios. Thus, it is expected that a Green Revolution is not only possible, but that it can help masses of smallholders out of poverty. It is assumed that export crop expansion will raise incomes thereby not only lifting masses of smallholders out of poverty but turning them into successful and viable entrepreneurs. The contradictions involved in agricultural development processes are therefore neglected: the fact that accumulation and generally 'development' can be both a progressive and awful process that 'varies only, and importantly in its awfulness' (Kitching, 1989: 195); that there are no easy answers or panaceas; that also large-scale commercial farmers, despite their superior means, need strong support from the state to thrive; that markets open opportunities but are discriminatory; that, despite pro-liberalization rhetoric, 'economic agents' do not like competition and will do all they can to stifle it; that smallholders can expand their production and incomes by deepening the exploitation of their household members, notably women and youth; that the expansion of relatively decently remunerated wage employment in agribusiness farming comes with tough working conditions and uncertainty. All these dialectic tendencies, rather than ignored, should be an analytical and empirical starting and fundamental point.

This chapter has two overarching aims. First, it attempts to question generalized 'agro-pessimistic' assessments of agricultural development in SSA, by emphasizing the substantial evidence of success, the marked unevenness in agrarian/rural development trajectories between and within countries and the diversity in initial conditions at the time of independence. Second, the chapter will discuss the diversity of agrarian structures and processes of change by referring to analyses of the uneven development of capitalism in the continent, particularly in relation to shifting agricultural policy regimes towards liberalization and state withdrawal. In conclusion, the chapter will briefly explore the challenges and implications of globalization and in particular the emergence of global value chains for African agriculture and prospects of capitalist development, with a final reflection on the challenges faced by African states.

Getting the record straight: The foundations of 'Agro-pessimism' in Africa

Devereux and Maxwell emphatically assert that 'SSA is the only region in the world currently facing widespread food insecurity as well as persistent threats of famine' (Devereux and Maxwell, 2001: 1). Many studies and reports on rural Africa stress the significant levels of undernourishment and malnourishment and its association with increasing poverty in the last 30 years, to highlight the disaster facing most African populations.[5] There is no question that undernutrition is a serious problem in SSA and indeed that, in comparison with other developing regions, some indicators of nutritional status are particularly alarming.[6] It is also true that some countries still face

episodes of famine, increasingly related to conflict and much less to production problems or food availability (Devereux, 2001). However, it is misleading
to overemphasize the bleak picture and ignore the progress made despite the
enormous challenges and constraints. These pessimistic accounts risk falling
into the trap of advocating costly and unrealistic programmes of food self-
sufficiency, which numerous African governments have drafted since the
1960s without much success. An often-cited statistic by agro-pessimists is
the rate of decline in per capita food production on aggregate terms (see
Figure 5.1). Unfortunately, both the food production data and the population
data used to illustrate this decline are extremely unreliable. Besides, 'average
calorie intake has serious limitations as a nutrition indicator' (Deaton and
Drèze, 2008: 70). Ignoring these problems for the moment, the apparent
decline in per capita food production in SSA was especially marked in the
period 1970–84, but it should be noted that food production over the last
decade has grown in line with population and has been significantly faster
than the rate of growth of the rural population.

Much of the 'gloom and doom' literature, indeed, presents evidence that
compares the situation in the 1970s with the situation in 2000. In other words,
the assessments tend to be confined to the period of global recession followed
by neoliberal globalization. In order to make a more reasonable assessment
one needs to go further back in time and get a sense of what has happened in
the long term.[7] 'Agro-pessimism' was a view shared by advocates of liberalization at the time when the World Bank published the Berg Report in 1981
and by 'neo-populists'. The former were particularly critical of the performance in the 1960s and 1970s blaming 'agrarian crisis' on excessive government
intervention and policy 'mistakes' (Sender and Smith, 1984). The latter

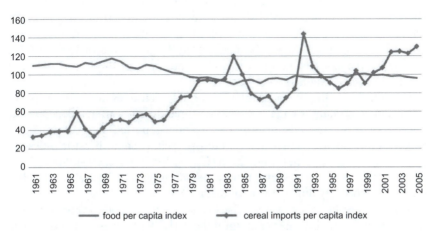

Figure 5.1 Food production and cereal imports per capita.

Source: FAOSTAT

criticized both 'modernist' state interventions and subsequent liberalization efforts, suggesting that smallholders and especially food producers had been systematically discriminated against by successive policy regimes in SSA and that an excessive focus on export crops had undermined household food security (Amara and Founou-Tchuigoua, 1990; World Bank 2007; Hyden, 2006). There are, however, strong empirical reasons to cast doubts on these pessimistic accounts.

First, it is imperative to consider data quality for food production more seriously. The quality of agricultural statistics may have improved recently but in many countries annual staple production statistics remain guesstimates. This means that if we have an aggregate figure of a decline of 15 per cent in aggregate farm production per capita recorded between 1965 and 1995, the thesis of 'crisis' 'depends on being sure of the numbers to within 15 per cent accuracy, a figure well within the range of errors in data' (Wiggins, 2002: 102).[8]

Another problem is that data quality varies a great deal from country to country and from period to period. One source of unreliability is precisely how raw data are generated. In many countries and for many years food production statistics have been routinely produced by government officials in provincial or district departments where production levels are 'guessed' after various factors are taken into account, such as rainfall in the region, input distribution and so on (cf. Svedberg, 1999). The problem is that rainfall and input distribution are likely to be very variable even within small administrative units and this variability cannot be captured by even the most well-intentioned officials. Less well-intentioned officials may have incentives to inflate or deflate food production statistics depending on the implications of the figures, whether it is to pretend to have met government-set targets and score points within the administration or to attract more funds and projects from donors, which may generate much needed rents at the local level.[9] In general, however, the main constraint on the generation of good annual agricultural data is material. Statistical offices are under-resourced, especially at local level, and getting accurate production information from sparsely populated areas where many farmers hardly keep records of their output, especially where some production is consumed within the household, is a massively demanding task.

Second, the quality of agricultural data has been uneven across crops. In particular, especially for the first two or three decades after independence, many SSA countries did not produce or under-reported data on roots and tubers (yam, cassava, sweet potato, etc.) as well as small livestock, despite their massive importance for nutrition (Guyer, 1987; Berry, 1984; Sender and Smith, 1986: 100). As a result, food production may well have been under-estimated especially during the period 1960–85.

Third, reported discrepancies between recorded food production and increases in calorie intake at least until the early 1980s suggest that domestic production estimates were biased downwards by the evidence of fast rising food imports (see Figures 5.1 and 5.3 for official series).[10] This matches

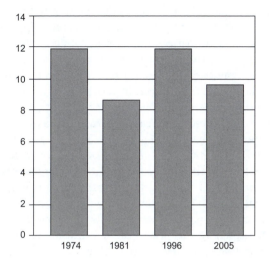

Figure 5.2 Food imports as a proportion of total imports: 1974–2005.

Source: World Development Indicators 2008 (World Bank)

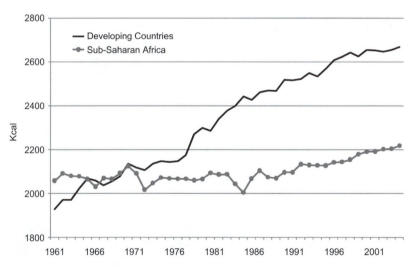

Figure 5.3 Food consumption trends in comparative perspective.

Source: FAOSTAT

micro-level evidence on nutrition and domestic food supplies in urban centres, which is inconsistent with the idea of a production crisis (see Guyer, 1987; Berry, 1984; Wiggins, 2002). In other words, rapid urbanization, industrialization and changes in diet patterns could have been accompanied by increases in imports that did not necessarily imply a reduction in domestic food production. In fact, recent FAO analysis of cereal supply sources shows that over the last 40-year period and especially since the mid 1990s *both* domestic production and imports increased on aggregate (Kidane *et al.*, 2006: 9). In many countries, food imports (40 per cent of which is usually accounted for wheat, rarely produced in SSA) did not compete or displace domestic production (with exceptions like rice in Senegal and meat in Côte d'Ivoire),[11] and often import increases were more associated with trade and industrial policies than with alleged domestic production shortfalls (Mortimore, 2003). Nor have food imports become an increasing drain on foreign exchange since their relative share of total merchandise imports has stagnated at around 10–11 per cent in the last decade (Figure 5.2). Finally, problems with African food trade data also vitiate the reliability of production estimates at country level. The notorious problem of smuggling is well documented and, arguably, the process of liberalization and currency devaluations during the 1980s and 1990s may have made 'visible' output flows previously concealed by conspicuous inter-country smuggling, especially for cocoa between Ghana and Côte d'Ivoire, coffee between Ethiopia and Kenya (Dercon y Ayalew, 1995) and groundnuts around Senegal.

A critical review of food production statistics and trends also offers insights into another debate that has preoccupied pessimists, namely the effects of 'cash-crop' or export-crop expansion in African farming systems. Aggregate trends show significant increases in export crop production from the colonial period onwards (Sender and Smith, 1986; see also Figures 5.4–5.6 and Table 5.1). In aggregate, it is hard to discern a negative relationship between

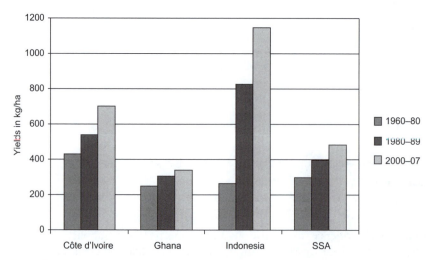

Figure 5.4 Export crop productivity increases: comparisons for cocoa.

Source: FAOSTAT

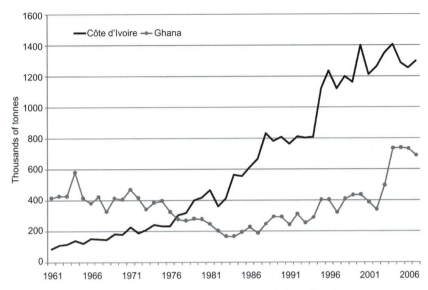

Figure 5.5 A contrast of agricultural tales: Ghana and Côte d'Ivoire.

Source: FAOSTAT

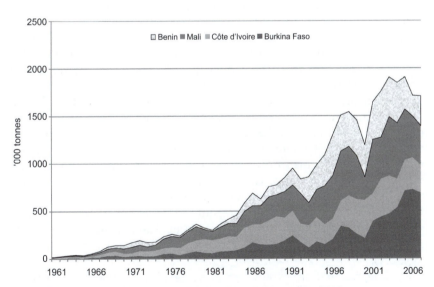

Figure 5.6 Cotton production expansion in West Africa, 1960–2007.

Source: FAOSTAT

Table 5.1 Growth of vegetable production (index 1980 = 1000)

		Côte d'Ivoire	Kenya	South Africa	Zambia
1	1960–9	48	60	66	62
2	1970–9	69	79	85	83
3	1980–9	118	114	113	114
4	1990–2002	188	299	128	127
	ratio 4/1	3.9	5.0	1.9	2.0

Source: FAOSTAT

food production and export crop production in absolute or per capita terms. The variability of export crop performance across countries and periods does not seem to mirror any opposite trends in food production. In fact, as Mortimore (2003) shows for a sample of West African countries, significant increases in export crop production were accompanied by equally impressive food production trends. Micro-level evidence has consistently shown a positive relationship between engagement with cash/export crops and household food security as well as child nutrition, and no convincing evidence of competition between cash- and food-crops (see studies referred to in Maxwell, 2001 and Sender and Smith, 1986; see also von Braun and Kennedy, 1986, Peters, 2006 and Benfica *et al.*, 2005).

The foundations of 'agro-pessimism' also shake if one offers a more balanced interpretation of actually published statistics and when the significant number of agricultural success stories are considered. Sender (1999) argues that annual agricultural growth rates of 2.34 per cent between 1965 and 1995 (and 3.1 per cent after 1984) cannot be regarded as unimpressive especially if compared with 1.5 per cent growth rates in the now advanced capitalist countries during the early stages of their industrialization. For a more extended period, between 1961 and 2005 the compound annual agricultural growth rate in real terms is still 2.4 per cent. Part of this growth was due to a rather good, albeit uneven, performance in export crop production, especially for tea, cotton, cocoa and tropical fruits – mangoes, pineapples – (with SSA annual growth rates of 4.7 per cent, 3.3 per cent, 2.6 per cent and around 2.8 per cent between 1960 and 2007), tobacco (until 1999) and less impressive for coffee and groundnuts (less than 1 per cent p.a.). This growth has been possible not only through land expansion, as the land frontier became more closed in some areas, but also and more significantly through notable yield increases, even though not as fast as other Asian competitors (in the case of cocoa, for example, see Figure 5.4). The growth of non-traditional agricultural exports (fruits and vegetables and cut flowers) has also been impressive since the 1990s (see Table 5.1).

These aggregate statistics, however, mask significant variation across countries, another reason to question generalizations about 'African agriculture'. A number of countries have attained real agricultural growth rates superior to 3 per cent (especially the protagonists of the 'cotton revolution' – see below and Figure 5.6.-i.e. Côte d'Ivoire, Benin, Burkina Faso; and also Kenya, Nigeria and Malawi, all for different reasons). Some countries have performed much worse, with growth rates below 1 per cent, as is the case of small states and islands (e.g. Equatorial Guinea, Seychelles) and some countries severely affected by conflict (e.g. Sierra Leone and the Democratic Republic of Congo). Some particular contrasts are illustrative of the importance of diversity, history and context to assess agricultural performance in SSA. For example, cocoa production and exports followed quite different trends in Ghana, where performance was very disappointing until the 1990s, and Côte d'Ivoire, where cocoa production expanded continuously on the basis of both expansion in cultivation land and significant increases in yields (see Figures 5.4–5.5). Differences in agrarian structures, agro-industrial linkages and policy regimes account for much of this divergence between the two neighbouring countries. The disparity also serves to question the hypothesis that underperformance of agriculture in Africa is mostly due to unfavourable external conditions, especially to declines in world market prices. For other crops, the 'cotton revolution' in West Africa (Burkina Faso, Mali, Côte d'Ivoire, and Benin) contrasts with less impressive cotton performance in Eastern and Southern Africa.[12] Similarly cereal production and yield growth is significantly better in Southern and Eastern Africa than in Middle and West Africa. In contrast, performance in roots and tubers in West Africa has been much better than in Southern Africa. Contrasts can also be drawn within countries. In Zambia the Northern and Western provinces are, in terms of both export and food production, very disadvantaged compared with the Central Province, the corridor linking Lusaka with the Copperbelt and parts of the Eastern Province where cotton contract growing has flourished. In Mozambique, the relative agricultural dynamism of the provinces of Manica, Tete and Zambezia clearly contrast with the poor agricultural record of Inhambane and Gaza provinces. Over time, Zimbabwe has in a fairly short time span moved from being one of the most successful agricultural exporters and grain producers in the continent until the 1990s to a situation of humanitarian emergency amidst agricultural and economic collapse.

The diversity stressed above and some of the good performance that a more balanced account of long-term trends would show are illustrated in Figure 5.5 and Table 5.1 and also reflected in a significant number of 'success stories' (see Wiggins, 2005; Gabre-Madhin and Haggblade 2004; Maredia *et al.*, 2000). These can be classified into supply-side and demand-side success trajectories. The first (supply-side) group includes impressive performance in a range of situations typically associated with agricultural research and technological diffusion (Gabre-Madhin and Haggblade, 2004)[13] such as: (a) regional-research-led improvements in cassava yields as well as product quality, which made cassava also a profitable cash crop in West Africa; (b) fast increase in rice production in Mali, through irrigation and better seed variety and especially the creation and diffusion of NERICA 'New Rice for Africa', an African rice variety very successfully introduced in several countries (in terms of yields and pest resistance); (c) research on and diffusion of HYV (high-yield seed varieties) of maize in Eastern and Southern Africa (especially Zambia, Zimbabwe, South Africa and Malawi), resulting in significant yield increases and better commercialization of maize; or institutional arrangements like in the case of (d) the excellent performance of cotton production and marketing through state-led vertically integrated chains in West Africa (Mali, Burkina Faso, Senegal). These supply-side stories generally confirm the decisive role that state intervention can play in agriculture, where establishing the basics is essential for agricultural development (Dorward *et al.*, 2004, see also Lele and Christiansen 1990). The second category of success stories (demand) includes cases such as: (i) the horticultural, fruit and cut flower export drive, spurred by a combination transnational agribusiness demand and state support, particularly in Kenya, Zambia, Côte d'Ivoire, and more recently Ethiopia, partly led by global agribusiness in search of new sourcing locations and partly in connection of state-led programmes; (ii) the dairy sub-sector in Kenya; (iii) the thriving belts of agriculture around cities and small towns, which have responded to urban demand for vegetables, fruit, livestock produce and grain and local dynamism even in contexts of apparent macroeconomic stagnation (see Guyer, 1987 and Wiggins, 2002); (iv) the effective (and guaranteed) demand created by parastatal marketing boards until the early 1980s, which helped even small farmers in isolated regions to engage in cash crop and more input-intensive farming through implicit and explicit subsidies (especially on transport and inputs), thereby addressing the market failures that have eventually become so obvious with market liberalization.

In this section I have so far questioned the foundations of pessimism on African agricultural performance. However, the same empirical evidence can also be used to show the below-par performance of *many* African countries in comparison with the massive success of several Asian, particularly East and South-east Asian competitors. In other words, African performance in agriculture has not been bad but could have been very much better given the favourable international demand conditions. A good indicator of this differential performance is the loss (and low levels) of *market shares* in global markets for several agricultural commodities, especially 'traditional exports', in which many SSA countries had positions of dominance until the 1970s.[14] This is especially the case for coffee, palm oil, oilseeds, tea, cotton, cashew nuts and oilseeds, and, in particular, for all measures of agricultural productivity. This evidence shows that on average SSA has performed inadequately in comparison with better performers, particularly in Asia.[15] There are structural and historical reasons for this relative underperformance as Karshenas (2001) shows. First, initial conditions were very different in SSA and Asia, if one takes the early 1960s as a point of departure. By that time, most African countries were already severely disadvantaged in terms of the infrastructure and production conditions required for agricultural modernization. In most SSA territories high land/labour ratios were the norm in contrast with massive labour abundance and much greater land pressure in Asia (Barrett *et al.*, 2001, Austin, 2005).[16] Low demographic densities (Table 5.1) and the related lack of sufficient infrastructural investments during both the colonial and post-colonial periods marked the conditions for a more extensive and precarious agricultural development path in most African regions. Labour constraints and relative land abundance (although with lower soil quality) have indeed been a hindrance to more rapid intensification and to the emergence of capitalist forms of production, whereas in Asia pressures to intensify and accumulate appear earlier and more forcefully. However, the experience in 'settler' economies in Southern Africa has also shown how natural conditions can be changed with accumulation through forced dispossession, resulting in contradictory outcomes of dynamism with social injustice, labour repression and gross inequality (notably South Africa). At the same time, the emergence of coalitions of interests to support agrarian accumulation and modernization through state intervention (e.g. Côte d'Ivoire, Mauritius, Kenya and Zimbabwe) also attenuated some of the structural obstacles highlighted by Karshenas. These structural features and the differences in historical trajectories reflect the uneven development of capitalism in African agriculture and the historically-contingent agrarian dynamics that have characterized SSA from the colonial into the post-colonial times. The next section will discuss these matters.

Table 5.2 Agricultural population per hectare of arable land (persons/ha)

	1990–2	*1995–7*	*2003–5*
Developing regions	2.6	2.7	2.7
Northern Africa	1.7	1.6	1.6
Sub-Saharan Africa	1.9	1.9	2.0
Latin America and the Caribbean	0.8	0.7	0.6
Eastern Asia	6.2	6.1	5.3
Southern Asia	3.0	3.2	3.4
South-Eastern Asia	2.7	2.8	2.6
Western Asia	0.9	0.9	0.9

Source: FAOSTAT

The uneven development of capitalism in African agriculture

Rural capitalism and capitalists

An initial appreciation of the uneven development of capitalism in African agriculture and the contingency of agrarian dynamics as a result of interactions between 'internal' and 'external' factors can be made by highlighting the variety of agrarian structures in terms of land distribution and forms of production. Despite the common image of African agriculture as characterized by 'smallholders' or an 'amorphous peasantry' (cf. Hill, 1968), one can note very important variations in the distribution of land by farm size, particularly within the small-to middle-scale range (0–20 ha). A basic comparison between selected countries on the basis of agricultural census data illustrates this variety by showing that the proportion of total cultivated land in farms below 1–2 ha and farms above 5 ha varies markedly from country to country, even among those countries lacking forms of large-scale industrialized agriculture (see Figure 5.7).[17] This wide range of land concentration and farm-sizes reflects the legacy and current variety of labour regimes, with more or less reliance on family labour, casual hired labour, seasonal migrant labour and, in the past, slave labour. The variety in forms and scale of rural accumulation is also marked, especially if one compares extremes such as the settler economies of South Africa, Kenya and Zimbabwe with the predominantly pastoral societies of parts of the Sahel and the Horn of Africa (Oya, 2007b).[18]

This diversity is associated with the way 'agrarian questions' have been addressed and resolved or not in SSA. According to Bernstein (2004), Africa has faced great difficulty in resolving the 'classical' agrarian question, i.e. in achieving a transformation towards capitalist forms of production; the disappearance of 'peasantries'; and creating political alliances between urban, rural labour and an organized proletariat. Thus, in SSA, agriculture has made only a limited contribution to primary accumulation for industrialization. Bernstein's pessimism also extends to the prospects for the formation of a national bourgeoisie and the emergence of developmental states in Africa. However, on this matter there is no consensus. While some argue that (rural) capitalist classes, albeit still weak and unevenly developed, have emerged

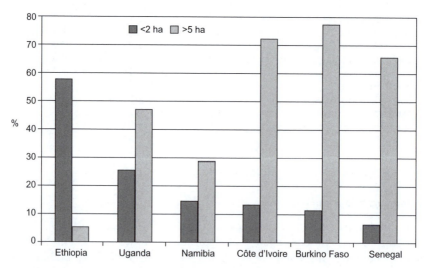

Figure 5.7 Land concentration and smallholdings: selected cases.

Source: Author's elaboration from FAOSTAT (Agricultural Censuses) http://www.fao.org/ES/ess/census/wcares/default.asp

and continue to do so in most of SSA (cf. Oya 2007b; Hill 1970; Sender and Smith 1986; Austin 2005; Rapley 1993; Ghai and Radwan 1983), other authors are more sceptical about the idea of an emerging African capitalist bourgeoisie, especially in the countryside, where an 'uncaptured peasantry' persists (cf. Hyden 2006, Chapter 4; Berry, 1993). The uneven emergence of rural accumulators, in some views, is consistent with the relatively low incidence of landlessness in African social formations, which has partly led Berry (1993) to defend a thesis of 'accumulation without dispossession',[19] despite survey evidence of growing polarization and land pressures in the era of neoliberal globalization (Raikes, 2000; Peters, 2004). Berry (1993), in this respect, has always advanced the idea that class, kinship (social networks) and various sectional interests are not mutually exclusive in Africa and that class differentiation can occur within kinship networks, which shape the incidence of redistribution and kin-related patronage that is frequently observed in the continent.[20] In Oya (2007b) I have argued that the stories of African rural capitalists provide some evidence of the sort of 'grass roots' capitalist development mentioned by Warren (1980), and other researchers of African capitalism (Rapley, 1993; Hill, 1970; Austin, 2005). Whereas available evidence points to a dominance of 'capitalism from below' (through smallholder differentiation),[21] there is no shortage of evidence concerning accumulators originating from a variety of 'ruling' classes, whether pre-capitalist landed rural elites or members of a rising urban petty bourgeoisie of merchants, bureaucrats and politicians (Oya 2007b, Kitching 1980).

Rural social differentiation

Some of the disagreements and unanswered questions above are a result of problems with the evidence, both in terms of availability and quality. In fact, studies of rural capitalists and rural accumulation are extremely scarce; research has tended to concentrate on 'peasants' and 'small farmers' as if these were the only or even most appropriate empirical and analytical categories. In fact, agricultural expenditure and income data disaggregated by class of farmers have not been collected on any systematic and consistent basis. Nevertheless, scattered quantitative and qualitative evidence, mostly through micro-surveys and in-depth studies, tends to strongly support the hypothesis of marked rural social differentiation, partly reflecting a process of polarization within rural areas, partly as a process of formation of various classes of farmers different from one another in terms of farm size, productivity, input intensity, labour hiring practices and forms of income diversification (Barrett *et al.*, 2001; Raikes 2000; Oya 2007a; Ghai and Radwan 1983).

For example, it is well documented that colonial penetration had already provided an impetus to processes of rural differentiation, particularly with the spread of 'legitimate commerce', cash cropping and tax-related cash needs. For this period Sender and Smith (1986: 21) provided a long list of rural surveys on different parts of Africa, which 'unambiguously demonstrate that some rural entrepreneurs operate extensive tracts of land', often land previously occupied by smaller farmers. More recently, several studies based on national rural household surveys have identified distinct classes within the smallholder population and in particular a top 'third' or 'quintile' who are larger in farm size, more market oriented and much more reliant on hired labour than the poorer small farmers in the same villages and regions, i.e. an incipient class of small-middle-scale rural capitalists (for relevant survey data see Jayne *et al.*, 2003, Barret *et al.*, 2001; Mortimore 2003; Peters 2006).[22] These are the farmers that hold the key for the expected successful integration of smallholders in high-value agribusiness chains (World Bank 2007). Conversely, the significant and increasing proportion of smallholder farmers who are net buyers of food attests to the growing 'proletarianization' of small farmers and their families, and their increasing inability to survive on their miniscule farms (Staatz and Dembele, 2007; Devereux, 2001; Raikes, 2000).[23] However, given the inadequate growth of demand for wage labour in rural areas and the bleak prospects for good jobs in towns, particularly in the post-liberalization context of de-industrialization, their access and attachment to land remains conspicuous as a last ditch form of insurance.

The state and shifting policy regimes towards liberalization

The role of the state has obviously been critical in determining agrarian dynamics and the uneven development of capitalist production relations. State intervention, both before and after the era of the Washington Consensus, had contradictory and uneven effects on agrarian transitions and the formation of incipient agrarian capitalism. On the one hand, the efforts to modernize agriculture and to accelerate the growth of productive forces in the country-side through a combination of marketing boards and rural development agencies for research, extension and input distribution, did indeed create conditions for the emergence of middle- and large-scale farmers whose dynamism underscores some of the success stories, especially in export crops, outlined above. Some of these farmers emerged from the ranks of smallholder producers and rural merchants, and gradually accumulated to become potential capitalists (Oya 2007b). On the other hand, indiscriminate, pan-territorial and pan-seasonal state support (mostly through official guaranteed prices and subsidized inputs), together with legislation to constrain private property rights (in favour of a combination of state control and customary rights), encouraged the survival of poor peasants in remote areas, i.e. acted as a form of rural 'welfare state' that helped poor farmers achieve simple reproduction on the basis of access to land and casual work for richer farmers or in towns, without being compelled to disappear as peasants (Wiggins, 2002).[24] In fact, the (still predominant) ideological commitment to small farmers, together with public expenditure cuts, donor pressures on policies and reduced aid flows to agriculture in SSA have been obstacles to the spread of capitalist relations of production in a large number of African countries.

During the same period there were also sharp contrasts between regimes inclined to support the emergence of a national (rural) capitalist class (e.g. Kenya, Côte d'Ivoire, Malawi) and regimes that embraced an anti-capitalist and pro-peasant rhetoric, soon reflected in deliberate or unintended measures, often driven by dreams of food self-sufficiency and peasant communes, which eventually constrained accumulation in rural areas thereby affecting the possibility of surplus creation for more sustainable industrialization (see Sender and Smith, 1990 on Nyerere's Tanzania; also cases of Ethiopia, Nkrumah's Ghana, Sekou-Toure's Guinea and post-Independence Mozambique). As some newly independent states managed the space to develop their own agricultural 'modernization' plans (often in the image of old 'colonial' plans and doctrines) they also legislated to demonstrate national resistance to plantation systems and a commitment to the Africanization of capital, land and labour. Nationalist movements and governments, unable to provide sufficient social infrastructure and livelihoods to a growing but scattered rural population, often opted to play the card of showing 'that "foreigners" and colonialists would no longer dominate agricultural production' (Sender and Johnston, 2004: 143). Outcomes in both sets of regimes were not homogenous and, as in the case of Côte d'Ivoire, Ivoirien capitalists advanced neither at the expense of foreign capital (with which they allied) nor at the expense of the peasantry (Rapley, 1993).

Nevertheless, structural adjustment and liberalization altered the rules of the game and weakened states[25] to an extent that agriculture has increasingly become a space of 'social Darwinism' where farmers' differentiation has become more visible and ruthless. The anti-state bias and wave of structural reforms brought by the Washington Consensus in agriculture actually reflected that 'the first impulse towards agricultural adjustment really came from the imperatives of macroeconomic reforms and the concomitant fiscal and financial squeeze of deflationary policies in the 1980s' (Oya, 2007a: 278). In other words, agricultural policies were effectively subordinated to macroeconomic stability and the idea of a minimal role for the state, marking the end of broad-based 'modernist' nationalist strategies for agriculture at the service of industrialization. The 'one-size-fits-all' structural adjustment agenda was promoted regardless of marked documented diversity across countries, crops, classes of farmers and without consideration of external opportunities and constraints. Not surprisingly then, during the past thirty years, the effects of market liberalization have been contradictory although generally negative for agricultural performance, especially with regards to some traditional export crops, land and labour productivity and marginal small farmers. With liberalization, farmers could no longer rely on a stable and guaranteed source of cash income, as prices began to fluctuate markedly, and states gradually stopped providing a guaranteed market outlet, altogether increasing the high risks faced by most African farmers. Furthermore, the collapse of public input distribution systems and the general increasing costs of previously subsidized inputs, especially imported fertilizers, seed, and fuel made real incomes not only erratic but also declining in many countries and for a majority of producers. In addition, some of the progress made in agricultural research and in the availability and dissemination of improved varieties was partly undone by the same deterioration of public input distribution and subsidy systems in many African countries, with Zambia and Malawi providing particularly stark examples in the 1990s (Pardey *et al.*, 1997; Havnevik *et al.*, 2007).[26]

The 'Social Darwinism' induced by agricultural reforms is noteworthy but not surprising. First, market forces have exposed the inability of large segments of the smallholder population to reproduce themselves in a 'Chayanovian' fashion under more competitive conditions and facing much greater risks (in both production and marketing). This has resulted in accelerated processes of differentiation (growing rural inequalities) leading to growing incidences of wage labour in the countryside, migration and distress-driven non-farm activities (Bryceson, 2000; Reardon, 1997; Raikes, 2000; Ponte, 2002).[27] Barriers to entry into the most lucrative segments of the non-farm economy (very heterogeneous in itself) have also increased rural inequality (Reardon, 1997; Raikes, 2000). These trends have exacerbated pressures on many households' simple reproduction and unevenly spurred the gradual formation of rural labour markets, where poorly paid casual labour is a widespread phenomenon (Ponte, 2002). They have also exacerbated land conflicts (Peters, 2004). The demise of labour institutions in urban Africa in the era of structural adjustment has also contributed greatly to the informalization of labour and to complex patterns of labour circulation, migration, 'footloose' working households straddling economic activities, employment status and residence. It is in this precarious context that the still limited opportunities offered by globalization for access to markets and employment creation often appear as 'saviours' in the eyes of the promoters of liberalization, given the failure to sustain the industrialization efforts of the 1960s and 1970s (cf. World Bank 2007). Second, the process of liberalization and adjustment in the countryside has not only left 'losers', as winners emerge by reaping the opportunities open by a liberalized environment with declining state regulation. Arguably, large-scale capitalist farmers in many countries were able to withstand the effects of state withdrawal thanks to their higher level of capitalization and their greater capacity to gain access to global commodity chains (see below). However, large farmers had also benefited from pre-reform interventions and were likely to suffer from the relative scarcity of yield-enhancing inputs and technology as well as from the credit squeeze in agriculture (Oya, 2007b). Similarly, a small segment of better-off smallholder farmers who managed to integrate in agribusiness chains also benefited from higher incomes and the opening of more lucrative markets in non-traditional exports, even though still exposed to the risks and uncertainties associated with entry to these highly demanding and mobile global chains (Peters, 2006; Jayne *et al.*, 2003: Gibbon and Ponte 2005). Amongst the main beneficiaries, richer traders (as opposed to street vendors) and moneylenders stand out. Despite the expectation that markets would become more competitive with the abolition of parastatal marketing boards,[28] the pervasiveness of market failures in output and input marketing[29] as well as the squeeze in publicly provided credit meant that a class of richer rural and urban-based traders (and moneylenders, often one and the same thing) have made the most of seasonal and territorial price volatility, by using the huge transport costs to their own advantage through oligopsonistic power at village level (see Mosley, 2002; Oya, 2007a: 286–87).

Concluding remarks in light of the globalization challenges

The reforms towards liberalization have coincided with (and partly facilitated) global capital restructuring and a marked increase in the power of global agribusiness and buyer-driven agricultural commodity chains (Gibbon and Ponte, 2005; Watts, 1994). The challenges and opportunities presented by globalization in African agriculture will be very briefly reviewed here in light of the historical overview presented above. There are three main issues and related policy questions to address.

First, is the extent to which globalization and the new global food regime make the agrarian question of capital obsolete in developing countries (Bernstein, 2004). In other words, a context in which global food giants, controlling large shares of value chains between production and retail as well as input markets, may no longer need a transformation of production relations in agriculture towards fully-fledged agrarian capitalism as long as a selected class of peasant (smallholder) farmers can be successfully incorporated into the chains. This is indeed the hope that the World Bank exhumes in its analysis of the relations between (small) farmers in developing countries and high-value global markets (cf. World Bank 2007). However, a closer examination of previous experiences of 'small farmers' with global agribusiness (usually via contract farming) tends to show that: (a) some become disguised wage labourers bearing the risk of fluctuating world prices decided elsewhere (Bassett, 2008, and Watts, 1994) or the risk of crop failure – which effectively may be a preferred option for flexible agribusiness not too concerned about product quality and reliability (cf. Watts, 1994); (b) more often than recognized, the main beneficiaries of direct and stable connections with agribusiness chains, particularly in high-value dynamic markets (horticulture, cut flowers, fresh fruits), are either fully established large-scale capitalist farmers or dynamic mid-scale producers (frequently equated with the 'top third' of the smallholding population mentioned before). This is largely because existing global value chains, increasingly dominated by retail giants, pose very stringent demands on quality, traceability, timeliness and even 'social responsibility' that only a minority of dynamic farmers can meet (Gibbon and Ponte, 2005; Amanor, 2005; Dolan and Sutherland, 2002). Therefore, the success of connections with the 'global food regime' in actually nurturing domestic agrarian capitalists cannot be assumed away. The question is also whether such a trend would be capable of generating an adequate rate of growth of employment for the growing labour surplus population (Bernstein, 2004; Dolan and Sutherland, 2002). These are indeed important empirical questions that require more substantial research.

Second, accelerated processes of commodification typical of neoliberalism *cum* globalization are affecting social dynamics in rural Africa, as elsewhere in the developing world. Some have already been discussed in the previous section. One trend shared with other developing regions seems to be the process of de-agrarianization, widely attributed to the inability of large segments of the small farming population to survive on their own farms in a context of market liberalization, withdrawal of direct and indirect state support and competitive pressures from global markets.[30] This process entails a growing mass of footloose labour floating between urban and rural areas in coping migration patterns in search of casual jobs or a variety of forms of low-productivity self-employment. They also reflect a growing significance of the so-called 'rural non-farm economy' as a site of distress-driven labour surplus absorption (Reardon, 1997). The available accounts tend to tell stories of distress, where whole households or individuals within households, men and women, leave farming and search any alternative available in rural or urban areas (Raikes, 2000; Breman, 2000). In this context, the strategies of investing in 'social relations' noted by Berry (1993) may indeed be breaking down as evidence on changes in labour mobilization patterns from social negotiation to individual contracts as well as increasing conflicts over land seem to suggest (Ponte, 2002; Peters, 2004). Sometimes, the rural non-farm economy opens sites of accumulation but this may result, according to some authors, in a constraint on *agrarian* accumulation if returns are disproportionately invested in diversified activities especially in the sphere of circulation (trade, transport).[31] There is also some (less cited) evidence of distress-induced re-agrarianization, particularly in countries that urbanized earlier and later experienced a gradual but continuous deterioration of living conditions in towns. The most obvious example is Zambia, where, according to Census data, the fastest increase in agricultural households has taken place in the predominantly urban areas of Lusaka and the Copperbelt. The main reasons for this counter-tendency are found in declining employment opportunities in towns, notably the crisis of the Copperbelt corridor and its industries as well as the impact of HIV/AIDS, which compels affected people to return to rural areas.

The processes noted above can be interpreted in a pessimistic fashion that contrasts with the more optimistic account I have given above. In fact, the gradual demise of smallholder farming is often seen as the culmination of African 'agrarian disasters', particularly by those (read neo-populists) who strongly believe in the desirability and viability of small farmers in Africa. However, arguably these processes mainly reflect the ongoing Social Darwinism that may well be consistent with fairly positive trends in terms of aggregate production, export growth, export diversification towards higher-value crops and so on. Is neoliberalism *cum* globalization exposing the structural weaknesses and vulnerabilities of small-scale farming in SSA? Probably yes. Are (small-scale) farming populations shrinking elsewhere in Asia and Latin America? Indeed they are, and 'agro-pessimism' does not abound there, particularly in Asia (Rigg, 2006). The key difference does not lie in agriculture so much as in the failure of most African countries to have sustained adequate rates of industrialization from very low levels at Independence, largely as a result of the 1970s crisis and ensuing market reforms that killed infant industry policy options.

Third, after years of adjustment-led withdrawal from interventions in agricultural markets and years of erosion of capacities to generate home-grown long-term strategies, most African states find themselves facing the daunting task of having to cope with multiple, and often contradictory agendas brought by the donor aid agencies on which they partly depend, and trying to achieve the need to generate sufficient employment and foreign exchange to maintain growth and political stability. The policy space and range of tools to achieve these competing demands is now very narrow, after decades of donor-induced economic and institutional neoliberal reforms, particularly as most agricultural policy initiatives normally require some form of subsidy, which has been out of the policy menu since the 1980s (Raikes, 2000).[32] The loss of policy space in agricultural policies is unquestionable but perhaps equally worrying is the decline in resources devoted to agriculture by governments and donor agencies. The World Bank, which remains one of the leading donors in Africa for agricultural development, reduced its lending portfolio for this sector from a peak of 32 per cent of World Bank lending in 1976–78 to only 6.5 per cent during the period 2000–2005 (Pincus, 2001: 196; World Bank data).

Nowadays, token measures of selective protection within WTO rules (such as Senegal's attempts to ban imports of palm oil affecting its domestic and recently privatized vegetable oil industry) and 'disobedience' with regards to fertilizer subsidies (e.g. Malawi since 2007) are unlikely to be sufficient to meet the employment and globalization challenges lying ahead. Instead, bolder and longer-term approaches will be necessary, especially: substantial increases in public investments in infrastructure (particularly in irrigation and land improvement), making use of labour-intensive public works also designed to tighten rural labour markets; a revamp of agricultural research and innovation to fulfil the obvious potential to improve crop yields on a large scale; careful attraction of agribusiness investments to transform productivity in segments of the agricultural sector and open access to high-value markets on conditions of monitorable employment and net foreign exchange generation; development of national food markets and systems of provision in a way that benefit both a class of dynamic market-oriented farmers and the mass of poorer net buyers of food for whom low and stable food prices are key for survival; all complemented by sustainable forms of universal protection through, perhaps, unconditional cash transfers such as basic income grants. Of course, only specific combinations of *some* of these measures may be politically and economically feasible in the short-term, especially in aid-dependent countries, but these may work as long as they are framed within a longer-term development strategy where agriculture may play an important, even if perhaps not central, role. As Scoones *et al.* (2005 : 9) conclude: 'No single scenario is inevitable, no single policy solution is appropriate'.

Notes

1 From here any reference to Africa will mean Sub-Saharan Africa.
2 The World Bank (2007) places most African countries in the group of 'agriculture-based countries' where agriculture is a major source of growth and most of the poor live in rural areas.
3 Several countries in SSA put agriculture at the centre of development strategies, particularly in the Poverty Reduction Strategy Papers, more or less following the same static logic cited above. Ethiopia is one particularly interesting example of a move towards agriculture-centred development strategies.
4 The World Bank calls for a 'smallholder-based productivity revolution in agriculture' (World Bank 2007: 232). The Commission for Africa report (CFA 2005: 237) calls for developed countries to support 'measures to improve production and the efficiency of African agriculture' while addressing unfair subsidization of agriculture in OECD countries that affects African smallholder farmers' incomes (see also Bassett, 2008). The NEPAD Comprehensive Africa Agriculture Development Programme states that 'African governments have agreed to increase public investment in agriculture by a minimum of 10 per cent of their national budgets and to raise agricultural productivity by at least 6 per cent' http://www.nepad-caadp.net/about-caadp.php#Vision
5 According to FAO data, the percentage of undernourished in the total population is close to 30 per cent in aggregate in SSA followed by slightly over 20 per cent in South Asia.
6 But see Svedberg (1999) for a more nuanced and empirically careful approach to nutrition data in Africa. Svedberg also shows that despite high levels of undernourishment in the 1990s, there had been a decline since the 1970s. He also suggests that there are biases in undernutrition figures for SSA, as discrepancies with anthropometric data show.
7 For example, food production per capita did increase by almost 20 per cent between 1960 and 1970, before the 'crisis'.
8 Svedberg (1999) reports studies showing margins of error in the 15–46 per cent range.
9 See Ponte (2002) and Berry (1984) on data politics and Devereux (2001) with reference to famines.
10 Schatz (1983) triangulates sources to finally contend that in aggregate food production per capita may have actually increased in the period 1960–82. During this period food imports to Africa almost quadrupled. Between 1980 and 1994 food import growth slowed down partly as a result of foreign exchange constraints, but import volumes still increased from 8 million tonnes in 1980 to 12 million in 1994.
11 In practice Asian rice imported to Senegal (particularly Thai broken rice) has long been preferred for its taste and culinary properties by Senegalese households thereby reducing the actual substitution effects between domestically produced and imported rice.

12 See Bassett (2001) for an in-depth historical account of the 'cotton revolution' in Côte d'Ivoire and the role of small and mid-scale farmers in this success story.

13 A success story that combines supply and demand drivers but that is essentially about farmers' adaptability to situations of land and demographic pressure is the story of agricultural intensification, growing commercialization and income improvements in the Machakos district in Kenya (Tiffen et al., 1994).

14 According to FAO data, SSA's shares in global agricultural exports fell from about 8 per cent in the 1960s to nearly 2 per cent nowadays (Kidane *et al.*, 2006: 35).

15 Comparisons with Asia are frequently made to highlight the relative under-performance of African agriculture.

16 However, as noted by Austin (2005), shifting factor ratios mean that labour abundance and land pressure (with conflicts) become increasingly widespread across Africa (see also Peters, 2004).

17 The contrast is particularly stark between the more egalitarian and land scarcer Ethiopia, and some West African countries where small-to-mid-scale dominates and agricultural growth has taken mostly an extensive pattern.

18 Despite its frequent association with 'traditional' forms of survival, areas dominated by pastoralism have increasingly become subsumed by capitalism and displayed capitalist tendencies, especially through the development of cattle markets within countries and across borders in Mauritania (Ould Cheikh, 1990) and parts of the Horn of Africa, where livestock exports are a basic source of accumulation and not just survival. Water-related conflicts also become the site of new enclosures and accumulation by dispossession and differentiation.

19 Berry (1993) thus claims to question an historical materialist approach, which she limits to the 'Lenin model' of polarization and dispossession (Bernstein, 2004: 122).

20 See Bernstein (2004) for a critical view on Berry's thesis and her functionalist superficial interpretation of Lenin's model of agrarian transition from below.

21 Especially if one includes settler capitalists of Southern Africa as emerging from the ranks of migrant (white) peasant farmers.

22 Smallholder differentiation is intimately associated with the rise of middle-scale farmers. Bernstein (2004: 131) notes that the consolidation of a 'middle' peasantry and marginalization of poor peasants unable to reproduce themselves as capital is a widespread outcome of the competition between small farmers (petty commodity producers in Bernstein's terms).

23 In a review of several country studies the proportion of net buyers among smallholder farmers ranged from 30 per cent to 67 per cent (Staatz and Dembele, 2007).

24 To a certain extent many African states in the 1960s and 1970s were victims of their own optimism about their capacity to please many constituencies at the same time and build up legitimacy in a late process of state formation (Oya, 2007a: 284). See also Raikes (2000).

25 Weakened in terms of the available policy space, political will and capacities to deal with short- and long-term imperatives for agricultural transformation.

26 For extensive reviews and a variety of conclusions on different aspects of agricultural liberalization see Kherallah *et al.* (2002), Oya (2007a), Havnevik *et al.* (2007), Mkandawire and Soludo (1999), Raikes (2000), Peters (2006) and Amanor (2005).

27 Peters (2006) shows substantial micro-level evidence of rapid increasing inequality in Malawi (the income ratio of top and bottom income quartiles increased from 3 to 11 between 1986 and 1997) and a significant degree of household 'churning' between income classes, related to their insertion in tobacco growing schemes.

28 Obviously, from a previous situation of near state-monopsony, competition in

marketing networks somewhat increased but not to the extent expected by reformers (Oya, 2007a, Kherallah *et al.*, 2002). Moreover some of this additional competition in reality reflected the new 'visibility' of hitherto illegal trade practices.

29 In fact there is no substantial evidence that marketing margins and costs were reduced by market liberalization, thus questioning one of the most basic rationales for reforms (Oya, 2007a: 281).

30 See collection of essays in Bryceson *et al.* (2000) as well as Reardon (1997) and Rigg (2006).

31 See Bernstein (2004: 131) and Berry (1993).

32 Some exceptions of resistance start to emerge. Since 2007, Malawi defied the World Bank and the IMF by reintroducing fertilizer subsidies, which, according to government claims, have boosted maize production. In response, traditionally 'anti-subsidy' agencies like the World Bank have begun to accept the idea of temporary 'market smart' subsidies (whatever this means) to stimulate input markets (World Bank 2007: 232), 'but the conditions for using them efficiently are demanding' (World Bank 2007: 152).

References

Amanor, K.S. (2005) 'Agricultural Markets in West Africa: Frontiers, Agribusiness and Social Differentiation', *IDS Bulletin* 36 (2): 58–62.

Amara, H.A. and Founou-Tchuigoua, B. (eds.) (1990) *African Agriculture: the critical choices*, London: Zed Books.

Austin, G. (2005) *Land, Labor and Capital in Ghana: from slave to free labor in Asante, 1807–1956*, Rochester NY: University of Rochester Press.

Barrett, C. B., Bezuneh, M., Clay, D. C. and Reardon, T.A. (2001) 'Heterogeneous Constraints, Incentives and Income Diversification Strategies in Rural Africa', Department of Applied Economics and Management Working Paper, WP 2001–25, Ithaca: Cornell University.

Bassett, T.J. (2001) *The Peasant Cotton Revolution in West Africa: Côte d'Ivoire, 1880–1995*, Cambridge: Cambridge University Press.

—— (2008) 'Producing Poverty: Power Relations and Price Formation in the Cotton Commodity Chains of West Africa' in *Hanging by a Thread: Cotton, Globalization, and Poverty in Africa*, William G. Moseley, Leslie C. Gray (eds.) Center for International Studies, Ohio University: Ohio University Press.

Benfica, R., Miguel, A., Zandamela, J. and Sousa, N. (2005) 'The Economics of Smallholder Households in Tobacco and Cotton Growing Areas of the Zambezi Valley of Mozambique', DAP/MSU, Research Report No. 59E, Maputo: Ministry of Agriculture of Mozambique. Available from http://www.aec.msu.edu/fs2/mozambique/wps59E.pdf

Bernstein, H. (2004) 'Considering Africa's Agrarian Questions', *Historical Materialism* 12 (4): 115–44.

Berry, S. (1984) 'The food crisis and agrarian change in Africa: a review essay', *African Studies Review*, 27 (2): 59–112.

Berry, S. (1993) *No Condition is Permanent: The Social Dynamics of Agrarian Change in Sub-Saharan Africa*, Wisconsin: University of Wisconsin Press.

Breman, J. (2000) 'Labour and Landlessness in South and South-east Asia', in *Disappearing Peasantries? Rural Labour in Africa, Asia and Latin America*, Bryceson, D., Kay, C. and Mooij, J. (eds.) London: ITDG Publishing.

Bryceson, D. (2000) 'African Peasants' Centrality and Marginality: Rural Labour

Transformations', in *Disappearing Peasantries? Rural Labour in Africa, Asia and Latin America*, Bryceson, D., Kay, C. and Mooij, J. (eds.) London: ITDG Publishing, 37–63.

Bryceson, D., Kay, C. and Mooij, J. (eds.) (2000). *Disappearing Peasantries? Rural Labour in Africa, Asia and Latin America*, London: ITDG Publishing.

Commission for Africa (2005) *Our Common Interest. Report of the Commission for Africa*, London.

Deaton, A. and Drèze, J. (2008) 'Nutrition in India: Facts and Interpretations', available at SSRN: http://ssrn.com/abstract = 1135253

Dercon, S. and Ayalew, L. (1995) 'Smuggling and Supply Response: Coffee in Ethiopia', *World Development*, 23 (10): 1795–813.

Devereux, S. (2001) 'Famine in Africa', in *Food Security in Sub-Saharan Africa*, Devereux, S. and Maxwell, S. (eds.) London: ITDG, 117–48.

Devereux, S. and S. Maxwell (2001) 'Introduction', in *Food Security in Sub-Saharan Africa*, Devereux, S. and Maxwell, S. (eds.) London: ITDG.

Dolan, C. and Sutherland, K. (2002) 'Gender and employment in the Kenya horticulture value chain', Globalisation and Poverty Discussion Paper No. 8. Globalisation and Poverty Research Programme. Institute of Development Studies, Brighton.

Dorward, A., Kydd, J., Morrison, J. and Urey, I. (2004) 'A Policy Agenda for Pro-Poor Agricultural Growth' *World Development* 32 (1): 73–89.

Gabre-Madhin, E.Z. and Haggblade, S. (2004) 'Successes in African Agriculture: Results of an Expert Survey', *World Development* 32 (5): 745–66.

Ghai, D. and Radwan, S. (1983) 'Agrarian change, differentiation and rural poverty in Africa: a general survey', in *Agrarian policies and rural poverty in Africa*, Ghai, D. and Radwan, S. (eds.) Geneva: ILO, 1–30.

Gibbon, P., and Ponte, S. (2005) *Trading Down: Africa, Value Chains, and the Global Economy*, Philadelphia: Temple University Press.

Goetz, S. (1993) 'Interlinked Markets and the Cash Crop: Food Crop Debate in Land-Abundant Tropical Agriculture', *Economic Development and Cultural Change* 41 (2): 343–61.

Guyer, J. (ed.) (1987) *Feeding African Cities*, London: I.A.I.

Havnevik, K., Bryceson, D., Birgegard, L.E., Matondi, P. and Beyene, A. (2007) 'African Agriculture and The World Bank: Development of Impoverishment?' Policy Dialogue n. 1, The Nordic Africa Institute, Uppsala.

Hill, P. (1968) 'The Myth of the Amorphous Peasantry: A Northern Nigerian Case Study'. *Nigerian Journal of Economic and Social Studies*, 10: 239–60.

Hill, P. (1970) *Studies in Rural Capitalism in West Africa*, Cambridge: Cambridge University Press.

Hyden, G. (2006) *African Politics in Comparative Perspective*, Cambridge: Cambridge University Press.

Jayne, T. S., Yamano, T., Weber, M., Tschirley, D., Benfica, R., Chapoto, A. and Zulu, B. (2003) 'Smallholder income and land distribution in Africa: implications for poverty reduction strategies', *Food Policy* 28: 253–75.

Karshenas, M. (2001) 'Agriculture and economic development in sub-Saharan Africa and Asia', *Cambridge Journal of Economics*, 25: 315–42.

Kherallah, M., Delgado, C., Gabre-Madhin E., Minot, N. and Johnson, M. (2002) *Reforming Agricultural Markets in Africa*, London: Johns Hopkins.

Kidane, W., Maetz, M. and Dardel, P. (2006) *Food security and agricultural development in sub-Saharan Africa: Building a Case for More Public Support*, Rome: FAO.

Kitching, G. (1980) *Class and Economic Change in Kenya: the Making of an African Petite-Bourgeoisie*, New Haven: Yale University Press.

—— (1989) *Development and Underdevelopment in Historical Perspective*, London: Routledge.

Lele, U. and Christiansen, R.E. (1989) 'Markets, Marketing Boards, and Cooperatives in Africa: Issues in Adjustment Policy', MADIA Discussion Paper n. 11. Washington DC, World Bank.

Maredia M., Byerlee, D. and Pee, P. (2000) 'Impacts of food crop improvement research: evidence from sub-Saharan Africa', *Food Policy* 25: 531–59.

Maxwell, S. (2001) 'Agricultural issues in food security' in *Food security in Sub-Saharan Africa*, Devereux, S. and Maxwell, S. (eds.) London: IDS/ITDG, 32–66.

Mkandawire, T. and Soludo, C. (1999) *Our Continent, Our Future*, Trenton NJ: Africa World Press.

Mortimore, M. (2003) 'The future of family farms in West Africa: What can we learn from long-term data?', Issue paper no. 119, International Institute for Environment and Development, Drylands Programme, Kent.

Mosley, P. (2002) 'Agricultural marketing in Africa since Berg and Bates: results of liberalisation', in *Renewing Development in sub-Saharan Africa: Policy, Performance and Prospects*, Belshaw, D. and Livingstone, I. (eds.) London: Routledge, 176–90.

Ould Cheikh, A.W. (1990) 'Mauritania: nomadism and peripheral capital' in *African agriculture: the critical choices*, Amara, H.A. and Founou-Tchuigoua, B. (eds.) London: Zed Books, 68–99.

Oya, C. (2007a) 'Agricultural Mal-Adjustment in Africa: What Have We Learned After Two Decades of Liberalisation?', *Journal of Contemporary African Studies* 25 (2): 275–97.

—— (2007b) 'Stories of Rural Accumulation in Africa: Trajectories and Transitions Among Rural Capitalists in Senegal', *Journal of Agrarian Change* 7 (4): 453–93.

Pardey, P.G., Roseboom, J. and Beintema, N.M. (1997) 'Investments in African Agricultural Research', *World Development* 25 (3): 409–23.

Peters, P. (2004) 'Inequality and Social Conflict Over Land in Africa', *Journal of Agrarian Change* 4, 3: 269–314.

—— (2006) 'Rural income and poverty in a time of radical change in Malawi', *Journal of Development Studies* 42 (3): 322–45.

Pincus, J. (2001) 'The Post-Washington Consensus and Lending Operations in Agriculture: New Rhetoric and Old Operational Realities', in *Development Policy in the Twenty First Century: Beyond the Post-Washington Consensus*, Fine, B., Lapavitsas. C. and Pincus, J. (eds.) London: Routledge, 182–218.

Ponte, S. (2002) *Farmers and Traders in Tanzania*, London: James Currey.

Raikes, P. (2000), 'Modernization and Adjustment in African Peasant Agriculture' *Disappearing Peasantries? Rural Labour in Africa, Asia and Latin America*, Bryceson, D., Kay, C. and Mooij, J. (eds.) London: ITDG Publishing, 64–80.

Rapley, J. (1993) *Ivoirien Capitalism. African Entrepreneurs in Cote d'Ivoire*, London: Lynne Rienner.

Reardon, T. (1997) 'Using Evidence of Household Income Diversification to Inform Study of the Rural Nonfarm Labor Market in Africa', *World Development* 25 (5): 735–47.

Rigg, J. (2006) 'Land, Farming, Livelihoods, and Poverty: Rethinking the Links in the Rural South', *World Development* 34 (1): 180–202.

Scoones, I., Devereux, S. and Haddad, L. (2005) 'Introduction: New Directions for African Agriculture', *IDS Bulletin* 36 (2): 1–12.

Sender, J. (1999) 'Africa's Economic Performance: Limitations of the Current Consensus', *Journal of Economic Perspectives* 13 (3).

Sender, J. and Smith, S. (1984) 'What is Right with the Berg Report and What's Left of its Critics?', *IDS Discussion Paper 192*, Sussex.

Sender, J. and Smith, S. (1986) *The Development of Capitalism in Africa*, London: Methuen.

Sender, J. and Smith, S. (1990) *Poverty, Class and Gender in Rural Africa: a Tanzanian case study*, London: Routledge.

Sender, J. and Johnston, D. (2004) 'Searching for a Weapon of Mass Production in Rural Africa: Unconvincing Arguments for Land Reform', *Journal of Agrarian Change* 4 (1 and 2): 142–64.

Shatz, S.P. (1986) 'African Food Imports and Food Production: an Erroneous Interpretation', *Journal of Modern African Studies* 24 (1): 177–8.

Staatz, J.M. and Dembele, N.N. (2007) 'Agriculture for Development in Sub-Saharan Africa', Background paper for the WDR 2008.

Svedberg, P. (1999) '841 Million Undernourished?', *World Development* 27 (12): 2081–98.

Tiffen, M., Mortimore, M., and Gichuki, F. (1994) *More People Less Erosion: Environmental Recovery in Kenya*, Chichester, UK: John Wiley & Sons.

Von Braun, J. and Kennedy, E. (1986) 'Commercialization of Subsistence Agriculture: Income and Nutritional Effects in Developing Countries', International Food Policy Research Institute (IFPRI), Working Papers on Commercialization of Agriculture and Nutrition, No. 1.

Warren, B., (1980) *Imperialism: Pioneer of Capitalism*, London: Verso.

Watts, M.J., (1994) 'Life under Contract: Contract Farming, Agrarian Restructuring and Flexible Accumulation', in *Living Under Contract: Contract Farming and Agrarian Transformation in Sub-Saharan Africa*, Little, P. and Watts, M.J. (eds.) Madison: University of Wisconsin Press, 21–77.

Wiggins, S. (2002) 'Smallholder Farming in Africa: Stasis and Dynamics', in *Renewing Development in sub-Saharan Africa: Policy, Performance and Prospects*, Belshaw, D. and Livingstone, I. (eds.) London: Routledge, 101–20.

—— (2005) 'Success stories from African Agriculture: What are the Key Elements of Success?', *IDS Bulletin*, 36 (2): 17–22.

World Bank (2007) *World Development Report 2008. Agriculture for Development*, Washington DC: The World Bank.

6 The political economy of taxation and resource mobilization in sub-Saharan Africa

Jonathan Di John

Introduction

The process of tax collection is one of the most powerful lenses in political economy to assess the distribution of power and the legitimacy of the state and of powerful interest groups in civil society. The collection of tax not only requires substantial coercive power, but more importantly requires a state to be legitimate since the vast majority of tax is collected when there is a high level of voluntary compliance (Levi, 1988). Douglass North, for instance, *defines* the state in terms of taxation powers: ". . . an organization with a comparative advantage in violence, extending over a geographic area whose boundaries are determined by its power to tax constituents" (North, 1981: 21). Long before that Edmund Burke remarked: "Revenue is the chief preoccupation of the state. Nay more it is the state" (quoted in O'Brien (2001: 25).

Taxation is inherently political. In the early twentieth century, Joseph Schumpeter once wrote: "Taxes not only helped create the state; they helped form it." Schumpeter also famously observed: "The fiscal history of a people is above all an essential part of its general history" (Schumpeter, [1918] 1954). Indeed, there is a long history of thinking in political economy and history that links the process of state-building with the capacity of rulers to collect taxation (Tilly, 1990; Brewer, 1990).

Tax collection also reflects basic core capacities of states to collect vast amounts of information which is essential for the formulation of informed policy decisions. The administrative apparatus required to collect and monitor the information required to develop a tax base is one of the most challenging technical and political functions a state can undertake. Thus taxation has always acted as a key incentive for states to create competent bureaucracies.

In sum, taxation and tax reform is central to state-building for several reasons: first, governments must be able to ensure sustainable funding for social programs, and for public investments to promote economic growth and development. Because aid generally diminishes over time and is often volatile, domestic resources are necessary to sustain these institutions and programs.

Second, taxation is the main nexus that binds state officials with interest groups and citizens. Not only can taxation enhance government accountability, it also provides a focal point around which interest groups (such as producers groups, labor unions, and consumer groups) can mobilize to support, resist, and even propose tax policies. In other words, taxation is as constitutive of state formation as it is of interest group formation. Third, taxation, particularly in the form of land and property taxes, customs and border collection can help increase the territorial reach of the state. The diversity of the tax base is a telling indicator of the ability of the state to engage with different sectors and regions and is indicative of the degree to which state authority permeates society. There is a long history of evidence that supports the notion that economic and political development can not easily happen without a consolidated central state. Fourth, fiscal capacities are needed to build a legitimate state. Democratic elections do not themselves ensure state legitimacy. Neither do "quick impact projects" in which aid agencies seek to fill urgent needs. Legitimacy comes in large part from government delivery of services that people want and need. Elections provide an avenue for the citizenry to voice demands; responding to those demands requires capacity to mobilize, allocate, and spend public resources effectively.

In the wake of fiscal crises of the state in sub-Saharan Africa and indeed other regions, designing tax systems that can provide incentives for growth, can meet distributional demands and can increase revenue collection is central to state viability and effectiveness (Toye, 2000). In post-war economies on the continent, reconstruction of the revenue base is essential for the reconstruction of a viable state and sustained peace (Addison *et al.*, 2002). In sub-Saharan Africa, improving taxation to meet developmental needs is one of the main challenges facing the region (Gupta and Tareq, 2008). The average tax-to-GDP ratio in sub-Saharan Africa has increased from less than 15 percent of GDP in 1980 to more than 18 percent in 2005 compared to an average tax-to-GDP ratio of 30 percent in advanced industrial countries. The overall tax base in high-income countries is, of course, much higher than the tax-to-GDP ratios suggest because the level of GDP is significantly higher compared with sub-Saharan African countries.

But virtually the entire increase in tax revenue in sub-Saharan Africa came from natural resource taxes, such as income from production sharing, royalties, and corporate income tax on oil and mining companies. Non resource-related revenue increased by less than 1 percent of GDP over 25 years. Even in resource-rich countries, non resource-related revenue has essentially been stagnant (Keen and Mansour, 2008).

Also, in many of Africa's low-income oil importers, domestic revenue mobilization has not kept pace with rising public spending. As a result, a growing share of current spending is financed by aid. For example, from 1997–99 to 2004–6, the share of current spending financed by aid (including debt relief) increased fivefold, from 16 percent to 36 percent in Ghana, from 22 percent to 40 percent in Tanzania, and from 60 percent to 70 percent in

Uganda (Gupta and Tareq, 2008). Thus, improved taxation is the only route out of aid dependence.

While there has been considerable work on the technical aspects of tax administration, the focus of the chapter will be on the historical, political and political economy factors that influence tax reform in the context of low levels of income and given the challenges of globalization. Where possible, case study examples of what works and what does not in terms of tax reform and the political and economic factors behind these trajectories will be illustrated.

The reasons for an historical and political economy focus are not only to do with the abundant work on tax administration but also due to the limitations of a purely administrative approach to taxation. Administrative constraints are often identified as the main constraint to the ability of states to collect revenues in general and direct taxes such as income tax in particular (Bird, 2007). As Bird and Casanegra (1992) argue: "In developing countries, tax administration *is* tax policy."

While identifying administrative constraints needs to be central when designing short-term tax policies, the longer-run goal of improving tax capacity (and therefore state-building) also needs to be part of policy interventions. There are many shortcomings to the administrative approach. First, the conception of capacity is static. There is no attempt to explain why and how administrative capacities change. Second, there is no explanation as to why tax capacities differ across countries in countries at similar levels of per capita income. Third, there is often little analysis as to why sound tax policies are not enforced. Although not often emphasised, low levels of legitimacy are often behind a state's inability to ensure compliance (Levi, 1988) and the genesis and variation in this legitimacy is not analyzed in the administrative approach. Finally, the emphasis on discouraging the collection of taxes with high information requirements (such as income tax) does not provide the impetus for countries to improve administrative tax collection capacity for such taxes.

The main goal of the chapter is to move beyond the technical features of tax reform and develop a more historical and political economy view of the difficult yet central process of taxation and tax reform and their relationship to state formation and consolidation. The case examples cited and the issues covered are not meant to be exhaustive but to highlight the importance of how an understanding of history and politics can help policy-makers think strategically, and propose tax reforms in a way that is more likely to be feasible and sustainable given the relevant political and economic context.

Economic structure and the tax base in Africa: theory and evidence

The traditional economic approach to tax focused on the *structural reasons* why the tax base is low and why direct taxes are relatively low in the context of underdevelopment (e.g. Burgess and Stern, 1993). An important component of the applied literature on tax indeed concentrates on why the level and composition of taxes in less developed countries differs from more advanced countries. One important set of factors concerns the economic structure of developing countries. These include: first, a large share of (subsistence) agriculture in total output and employment; second, large informal sector and occupations; third, many small establishments; fourth, small share of wages in total national income; and fifth, small share of total consumer spending made in large, modern establishments. Combined, these factors mean that the take as a percentage of GDP tends to be much lower than in countries with greater levels of per capita income.

In comparison with OECD, the most striking differences of LDCs include:

- low usage of social security taxes (largest values are in ex-socialist transition economies);
- high revenues from trade taxes;
- high levels of non-tax revenue (especially from mineral rents);
- higher share of tax revenue from companies rather than individuals (thus much lower personal income tax);
- much more narrow base of tax payers (hence the importance of large taxpayers office (LTOs));
- higher rates of tax evasion.

It is, however, important to note that there are substantial variations among countries with similar per capita incomes. An example of the variation of taxation can be seen within sub-Saharan Africa, as indicated in Table 6.1.

There are several points worth considering with respect to the data in the table. First, as standard theory predicts, low tax countries tend to have much lower income per capita and tend to be much more reliant on trade taxes which means that the fiscal consequences of trade liberalization can be devastating if alternate forms of tax are not quickly increased. However, income per capita is not necessarily associated with higher tax takes. For instance, there are many countries with a lower income per capital than the Central African Republic and Uganda that collect a much higher share of taxes as a percentage of GDP. Second, the level of tax collection does not necessarily indicate that the state has the capacity to promote rapid economic growth. Uganda, Mozambique and Tanzania have been among the fastest growing African economies in the period 1900–2005 yet have relatively low tax capacity. South Africa and Zimbabwe have higher tax capacity but have not had nearly as impressive growth rates over the same period. Finally, tax levels do not necessarily indicate that a state or government is legitimate. Recent episodes of political violence in Kenya and Zimbabwe, two relatively high tax states, are examples that relatively high tax collection does not preclude violent challenges to state authority. In these two cases, further research is needed to

Table 6.1 Tax collection and composition in selected sub-Saharan African countries

Lower tax countries	Years	Tax revenue (as % of GDP)	Trade taxes (as % of total taxes)	GDP/cap (market prices*)
Congo (DR)	1998–2002	4.5%	32.0%	$600
Central African Rep.	1992–6	6.1	39.0	1,055
Chad	1994–2000	6.5	34.0	801
Niger	1994–2000	7.9	57.0	678
Rwanda	1993–9	9.3	18.0	931
Tanzania	1992–9	9.6	35.0	524
Uganda	1998–2003	11.4	16.0	1,167
Mozambique	1993–9	11.4	18.0	799
Ethiopia	1993–7	12.9	40.0	814
Mali	1991–2000	12.9	30.0	784
Malawi	1993–2000	14.2	15.0	583
average		9.7	30.3	814
Higher tax countries				
Botswana	1993–8	32.5%	18.0%	$8,347
South Africa	1998–2002	25.5	13.0	8,764
Zimbabwe	1992–7	22.5	19.0	2,498
Kenya	1992–2001	23.1	17.0	1,033
Zambia	1990–9	18.1	12.0	785
Côte d'Ivoire	1991–9	18.0	40.0	1,582
Senegal	1992–8	16.0	28.0	1,427
Nigeria	1992–2000	15.2	18.0	854
Average		21.4	20.6	2,420
Average (excl. Botswana, S.Africa)				1,363

Source: IMF, Government Finance Statistics

Note: * at $US 2000, market prices

explain if high tax rates were the result of compliance/consent, administrative effectiveness, or unsustainable levels of coercion.

The fiscal challenges of economic liberalization in Africa

Perhaps the greatest challenge facing low income African economies is how to replace declining trade taxes in the face of economic liberalization. Trade taxes represent over one-third of all tax revenues in sub-Saharan African (SSA) economies. This degree of dependence on trade taxes is substantially higher in SSA compared with other regions (Bird and Zolt, 2005). Trade taxes are often the main source of revenue in weak and low income states. Problems of domestic revenue-raising have been exacerbated by a global shift away from trade taxes as a principal source of revenue. This has been one of the consequences of trade liberalization policies over the last 20 years. It has posed particular problems for low income countries. IMF research shows that, whereas rich countries have managed to offset the decline with other sources of revenue, notably VAT, the poorest countries have at best replaced about 30 percent of lost trade taxes (Baunsgaard and Keen, 2005).

However, research suggests that while many low-income countries have experienced real difficulty in dealing with the revenue consequences of trade liberalization, there are others that have managed to cope (IMF, 2005). This study examines the experience of a sample of eight low-income countries (six of which are in Africa). These countries have in common a decline in the collected tariff rates over the past 20 years, but differ in the extent of revenue recovery. In Kenya, Sri Lanka, Egypt and Cote d'Ivoire lost trade tax revenues were not replaced. In Malawi, Uganda, Senegal and Jordan, they were. The conclusions of this study were as follows:

1   Those countries which did recover total tax revenue also increased domestic consumption tax revenue, often by an amount broadly corresponding to the loss of trade tax revenue.
2   The presence of a VAT does not in itself appear to enhance the ability to recover revenue, a result similar to the econometric evidence provided by Baunsgaard and Keen (2005).
3   In those countries with high recovery, there has also been a strengthening of income tax revenues, suggesting that the burden of adjustment has not been borne solely by shifting to taxes on consumption. This result is important since it contradicts the conventional wisdom that consumption taxes are the main source offsetting trade tax revenue. Such a broad-based tax effort is also likely reduce the possibilities that the tax system becomes regressive since improved income tax collection is generally progressive.
4   Reductions in tax/GDP ratios in low- and middle-income countries are not confined to those undertaking trade reform. Of the 14 low-income countries in which collected tariff rates did not decline over the past two decades, nine experienced a decline in the tax ratio. This suggests that while trade liberalization poses particular challenges to maintaining revenue collection, there are other political economy factors that need to be researched.

In sum, trade liberalization needs to be purposively sequenced with domestic tax reform and donors need to focus on this issue. This is especially the case since high levels of informality in post-conflict economies may make the collection of taxes from value-added taxes particularly difficult in the short-run (Emran and Stiglitz, 2005; though see Keen, 2008 for an opposing view). While tariff protection may not necessarily create much productive capacity given the weak state of domestic business capacity, the role of moderate tariffs in preventing a collapse in fiscal revenues may be a reasonable "second best" solution to the problem of tax collection in low-income contexts, at least in the short-to-medium run. As discussed above, further research is needed to explain why low-income countries find it difficult to replace lost trade taxes with domestic revenues, and the condition under which VAT is potentially more conducive to tax capacity-building in LDCs.

Case study: Uganda

The experience of Uganda provides one exception to the trend of low income countries experiencing a reduction in tax revenues. Under the Museveni regime, trade liberalization (that is the decline in import and export tariffs) was imposed *gradually* over the period 1986–98. Rodrik (2004) classifies Uganda as a case, not of shock therapy liberalization, but one of moderate and gradual reform. Non-tariff barriers were removed for the first time in 1991; six years after Museveni took power. In 1995, there were still import quotas on beer, beverages, and auto parts. In 1999, all non-tariff barriers were eliminated.

It was only in the early 1990s that the structure of trade taxes was switched from export taxation to import taxation, but import tariffs were introduced at a high level. There were few options available for alternative types of taxation, a characteristic of very poor economies with weak fiscal institutions. As a result, import taxes necessarily led fiscal resource mobilization in the 1990s. In 1996, ten years after the National Revolutionary Movement (NRM) regime took power, trade taxes still accounted for more than 50 percent of total tax revenues.

This gradualism of trade liberalization proved crucial to maintaining fiscal revenues until the political and administrative problems of introducing VAT could be overcome. The tax revenues in Uganda increased from 7 percent of GDP in 1986 to nearly 11 percent by the mid-1990s. While this is still below the sub-Saharan African average, the fiscal consequences of more rapid trade liberalization could have been devastating. The case against rapid tariff reduction as a means for maintaining and increasing fiscal resources, a key element in state consolidation and state-building, is one of the main lessons in the political economy of the Ugandan post-war reconstruction.

It is important to consider however that trade taxes can create disincentives for production and distortions in the economy and thus the impact of trade taxes on economic performance need to be carefully monitored. Collier and Reinikka (2001), for instance, argue that the substitution of export with import taxes created greater inefficiencies in Uganda because import taxes were subject to greater dispersion of tax rates since the latter were subject to more tax rates than the former.

In theory, this could have proved to be a problem, but there were several factors that allowed the Ugandan economy to overcome this problem. First, the replacement of export taxes was important in improving incentives for exports. Second, the substitution of export taxes with import taxes (however much dispersion) was essential for maintaining resource mobilization, which was central to state-building. Third, a dispersion of import taxes allows the state to provide selective rents (and therefore incentives) for the development of particular sectors. A uniform import rate provides much less scope for industrial and agricultural strategies. Fourth, tariffs provide a fiscally more sustainable mechanism to promote domestic industry in low income countries. While export subsidies may be less distortionary than tariffs, fiscal constraints in low income countries prevent the extensive use of subsidies as a tool of industrial policy. Finally, the argument that trade policy created static inefficiencies does not explain why Uganda achieved one of the fastest growth rates in the developing world over the period 1986–99. Tariffs on commodity exports, for example, while potentially providing some disincentives to production, were the only mechanism to tax the incomes of wealthy farmers.

Export tariffs thus can provide a functional substitute to weak income tax capacity in low income/post-war economies. In the Ugandan case, such tariffs did not coincide with a decline in export growth, but rather were compatible with relatively rapid export and production growth in commodities (Di John and Putzel, 2005). The Ugandan strategy ultimately favored a greater reliance in import tariffs rather than on high export tariffs although this emerged as a result of trial-and-error. To understand the political economy dynamics of this, it is important to consider initial conditions of the economy in 1986.

Mineral booms and tax policy

Notwithstanding the potential danger of mineral booms for growth and governance, recent commodity booms do offer an important opportunity for mineral abundant countries to generate significant tax revenues, and increase their policy space. Thus, the fiscal and productive impact of attracting mineral investment and natural-resource-based industrialization is of central concern for many low-income countries, particularly in sub-Saharan Africa The potential revenue capture from such booms often far outweighs aid flows. However, recent experience suggests that, in sub-Saharan Africa, at least, this potential is not always being realized. Two recent examples that illustrate the challenges of mineral-based development are Zambia and Mozambique. Consider first the case of Zambia.

Case study: Zambia

Zambia is one of the poorest countries in sub-Saharan Africa. It is a land-abundant but sparsely-populated country of 11 million inhabitants. Copper is the dominant export industry and the development of export diversification has been further hampered by the fact that the country is landlocked and is surrounded by five countries which have experienced civil wars and political disorder. By any conceivable measure, the growth performance of Zambia has been dismal, a chronicle of decades of relentless economic decline as indicated in Table 6.2:

Table 6.2 Zambia's per capita growth rates in comparative perspective 1961–190

Country	1961–4	1965–9	1970–4	1975–9	1980–4	1985–9	1990–4	1995–2000
Zambia	.7	.8	.5	–4.0	–2.2	–.8	–2.7	–.2
Sub-Sahara African Average	2.2	1.5	3.3	.9	–.5	.5	–1.4	2.0
Zambia's rank:	16/26	20/31	22/32	30/32	29/36	26/40	32/41	34/41

Source: World Development Indicators.

The reasons for the decline in Zambian economic performance are complex, but include a combination of the disruption of regional trading routes, the nationalization of the copper industry before the development of skilled workers and managers emerged on the domestic scene, and mismanagement of the state-owned copper industry (see Weeks *et al.*, 2004). Copper production declined from 600,000 tons in the 1960s to just over 300,000 tons by the end of the 1990s.

The response of the government in the late 1990s was to privatize the copper industry and lower mineral royalties in order to attract foreign investment. This was undertaken in the context of desperation, namely historically low world copper prices, declining copper production, and an unsustainable debt burden. Its privatization strategy for copper included a reduction in the corporate tax rate from 35 to 25 percent; exemption from customs duty on imports up to US$15million; reduction of the mineral royalty from 2.0 percent to 0.6 percent; exoneration from excise duty on electricity; an increase in the period for which losses could be carried, from ten to 20 years; and, exemption from the withholding tax on interest, dividends, royalties and management fees (Fraser and Lungu, 2007).

Indeed, the mining sector contributes less to government revenues than either the finance or telecoms sectors. In sum, the mining companies effectively paid almost no income taxes in the period 2000–2006. The effect of these so-called incentives was that it would be decades before the government received substantial revenue from the new mining companies.

While the government in 2008 has considered raising the royalty rate to 2.5 percent with the support of the IMF, this rate is still low by the standards of Zambia's neighbours – an IMF survey of tax and royalty rates in developing countries found no other African country charging royalties with rates below 2 percent, and some with rates as high as 20 percent (Baunsgaard, 2001). As a result, taxes as a percentage of GDP declined from 18.4 percent in 1996 to 17.0 percent in 2005. In 2006, the government received just $25million in copper royalties out of a $US2billion turnover in copper sales. This substantially hampers the extent to which the government can finance improvements in physical infrastructure which are essential for reviving productive capacity and growth in non-copper sectors in agriculture and light manufacturing.

Case study: Mozambique

Mozambique is considered one of the success stories of post-war reconstruction. A turbulent post-independence period and long civil war coincided with declines in economic activity. In the period 1974–86, real GDP per capita declined by one-third. Economic reforms, begun in 1987, and the end of the civil war in 1992, helped revive the economy. In the decade from 1987, annual growth averaged 5.3 percent, and accelerated further to over 8 percent per year in the period 1996–2006. Growth has been fuelled by substantial levels of foreign aid, which has financed approximately one-half of government expenditures over the period 1985–2005 (Virtanen and Ehrenpreis, 2007: 17), which has coincided with an increase in the tax take, which has risen from 11.7 percent of GDP in 1995 to 14.6 percent of GDP in 2004 (USAID 2004: Table I-1, p. I-13).

The main pole of growth and exports has been generated through foreign-owned mega-projects in mining and natural-resource-based industrialization. The leading project in this is Mozal, a large aluminium smelter (completed in 2000) on the outskirts of the capital city, Maputo. Mozal cost $2.4billion to build and produces 512,000 tons of aluminum ingots. South African mining interests control two-thirds of the project, as is the case in most mega-projects in Mozambique. As of 2004, Mozal contributes 75 percent of manufacturing exports, and 42 percent of total export revenues of Mozambique (Castel-Branco, 2004). Aluminium represents nearly half of total manufacturing output.

Tax policy has been central in attracting foreign investment in mega-projects. Mozal was given Free Industrial Zone (FIZ) status. This means that it is exempted from paying duties on imports of material inputs, and equipment. It is also exempted from valued-added taxes, and corporate income taxes are limited to 1 percent of sales! The failure of the government to develop a more revenue-enhancing tax package was the result of it not seriously considering the offers of rival aluminum producers (Kaiser, a US multinational, made initial offers in the late 1990s but was rejected by the Mozambican government on the grounds that it did not have enough of an influence on world markets to succeed). Irrespective of the reasons for rejecting the Kaiser bid, an important policy lesson is that governments can use competition among multinationals to produce more lucrative tax packages out of mineral-based investments. The increased interest of Chinese corporations in mineral development in Africa may provide an opportunity for governments to reap the fiscal rewards of competitive bidding among multinationals.

While Mozal has undoubtedly contributed to the export and production capacity of the Mozambican economy, there are several issues that are of concern for the prospects of long-run economic development and productive capacity-building. First, the negligible tax payments Mozal makes to the government limits the fiscal linkage such projects can generate (Castel-Branco, 2004). This limits the extent the government can invest in developing productive capabilities and infrastructure elsewhere in the economy. Second, the mega-projects have focused FDI and manufacturing production around the capital city and this has induced a substantial regional concentration in manufacturing production (in 2003, 81 percent of industrial activity was generated in Maputo Province [USAID 2004, Table 12–13, p. 3]). Manufacturing production outside the capital is negligible. Third, most of the economic linkages of Mozal are with firms in South Africa, not in Mozambique. This is mostly because Mozambican firms do not have the technical capacity to provide inputs that Mozal needs, but also because there is no wider industrial strategy to provide either carrots or sticks for Mozal to develop important supplier contracts with Mozambican firms.

There are several policy implications that it is possible to draw from the Zambian and Mozambican cases. First, there is an urgent need for mineral abundant states to enter into a renegotiation of mining contracts when they are unfavourable. Second, there is a need for governments to develop productive strategies that exchange mineral rights for local content conditions, whereby foreign investors are obligated to use domestic suppliers on an increasingly greater scale. Local content management has been one of the main ways in which FDI can be utilized for the benefit of national productive capacity. Finally, capacity-building in the geological survey capacity in sub-Saharan Africa needs to be developed in order to improve the bargaining power of states vis-à-vis multinationals. This is an area where the international financial institutions can play a leading role.

Thinking strategically about the politics of administrative reforms: the case of autonomous revenue authorities

In terms of institutional design, international financial institutions and aid donors have developed the proposition that, in weak states, revenue collection authorities are more effective when they operate *autonomously* from the state (and particularly the finance ministry), as a commercial entity at arms length from the government rather than as a department within the government administration (Taliciero, 2004). This is the reasoning behind the promotion of the so-called autonomous revenue agencies (ARAs).

This line of thinking follows much the line of New Public Management, which stresses that agencies be run on business principles, where directors can circumvent the institutional obstacles of weak public sectors, which include multiple layers of principles and agents, cumbersome rules and regulations, low pay, antagonistic unions and so on (Therkilsden, [2003: 2]; see also Fjeldstad and Moore, [2008] for a discussion of the extent to which the introduction of semi-autonomous revenue authorities have enhanced state capacity in sub-Saharan Africa). According to this argument, autonomy protects revenue authorities from political interference. In short, the creation of parallel agencies is favoured over the restructuring of existing tax institutions.

While there is some evidence in Africa and Latin America that autonomous revenue authorities may have been instrumental in initiating reforms, it is less clear that such arrangements are sustainable. Such a technical approach to tax policy abstracts from politics in at least three ways. First, the reasons why such reforms were politically feasible in the first place are not addressed. Second, there is little analysis of why such autonomy is acceptable to relevant political coalitions over time. Third, there is no accepted definition of autonomy. Since tax policy, which is the domain of finance ministries, cannot practically be divorced from tax collection, which is the domain of newly created ARAs, it is not ultimately possible for the latter to function in purely autonomous ways. In effect, autonomy can never be complete where there are inter-dependencies among agencies and thus is always a contested notion.

Case study: Uganda

As with many cases of tax reform, fiscal and economic crisis provided the catalyst for reform in Uganda. The previous tax administrations were riddled with inefficiency linked to the high levels of clientelist pressures and the power of interest groups to gain exemptions in all areas of tax.

Museveni took power in 1986 on an anti-corruption, anti political party platform in the midst of a collapsing state and following the economic decline during the Amin and second Obote regimes. In 1991, the state, with the financial support of Britain, set up the Uganda Revenue Authority (URA). While internal staff relations and hiring followed New Public Management principles, salaries were increased by eight times the public sector average; poorly performing staff were either dismissed or moved to other ministries. The URA's autonomy vis-à-vis donors and the Ministry of Finance initially increased as it was put in charge of determining tax revenue targets. The initial results were encouraging as tax collection as a percentage of GDP increased from 7.0 percent in 1991 to 12 percent in 1999. Thereafter, cases of corruption and a worsening of tax collection occurred. By 2001, tax collection declined to 10.7 percent of GDP. In comparative perspective, Uganda's tax performance was indeed poor. By the late 1990s, Uganda's tax take of 11 percent of GDP remained well below the African average of 20 percent of GDP. Neighbouring Kenya's tax collection was over 20 percent of GDP, while Tanzania tax collection was 15 percent of GDP during this period (Kayizzi-Mugerwa, 2002: 2).

To the extent that tax capacity reflects legitimacy, it may not be unreasonable to think that both the Ugandan revenue authority and the Museveni regime may have experienced a decline in legitimacy in the post-2000 period. The extent to which this decline in legitimacy matters for the government's political survival, of course, depends on the emergence of a sufficiently powerful opposition.

Several political problems emerged that compromised the functioning of the URA. First, while there have been substantial pay increases to senior managers in the URA, there has been growing wage differentials with respect to staff at lower levels, which has created discontent (Robinson, 2006: 22–5). Such wage differentials were also a factor in the growth of corruption in the URA (ibid.) Second, while the internal autonomy of the board of the URA vis-à-vis its employees may have increased, external autonomy was limited. Relations with the finance ministry soured after the first three years as the URA failed to meet target objectives. The latter claimed the targets set were unrealistic. Finally, the encroachment of clientelism in affecting recruitment and promotion within the URA and growing interference of well-connected members of the executive, the finance ministry and the parliament contributed to the widespread perception that corruption grew substantially within the URA after 1995 (ibid.).

Likewise, relations with the President, initially very strong, soured. There were at least two sources of this tension. First, the introduction of semi-military operations to prevent smuggling and tax evasion became unpopular among not only large taxpayers but also the ordinary public, who viewed these measures as unduly harsh. In 1996, Museveni pledged to drop these units and used the URA as a scapegoat. Second, the introduction of VAT, which had the support of Museveni initially, proved very unpopular in a country where tax payments were notoriously low. Tax revolts over the introduction of VAT induced Museveni to make the URA a scapegoat in 1996.

The Ugandan experience along with other instances of personalist rule provides several important lessons for tax reform.

First, the role of macroeconomic and particularly fiscal and inflationary crises has provided opportunities for leaders to gain leverage over the reform process. This is part of the wider story on the role of threat, war and crisis as a constitutive element in the construction of tax states (see Schumpeter, [1918] 1954; and Tilly, [1990]).

Second, centralized public authority and executive support is essential for tax reform to be undertaken.

Third, public relations and communications are as important as coercive capacity in improving tax collection. The perceived legitimacy of a tax by the majority of the tax payers is important to revenue collection. Levi (1988), for instance, argues that increases in tax capacity are intimately related to the voluntary compliance of large sections of the population.

Fourth, the creation of a (semi-) autonomous revenue authority paradoxically can increase the political attention it receives. If presidential support sours, then the ARA can become a political scapegoat. The political strategy of anti-party politics makes the revenue authority vulnerable to shifting policies and coalitional and/or electoral calculations of the President. It is no accident that tax reforms have not been consolidated in Uganda since the consolidation of effective tax authorities elsewhere has relied on the support of strong, centralized political party structures such as in South Africa and Malaysia (Di John, 2006: 7–8).

Fifth, the pressure on governments (whether they are experimenting with ARAs or not) to meet revenue targets can create tensions between the state and interest groups which can undermine the tax authority's legitimacy. Pressure to meet revenue targets can result in tax administrations responding with some combination of (a) an even tighter squeeze on registered tax-payers; and (b) quasi-military "raids" on other businesses on which they do not have detailed information.

In Uganda, operations against smuggling and tax evasion have been staffed by military personnel creating a militarization of the revenue collection. Therkildsen (2003) argues that, by pushing for unrealistically high revenue targets, the Ministry of Finance contributed to undermining the reputation and credibility of the Uganda Revenue Authority in the eyes of the public. Attempts to meet externally set tax-to-GDP targets may undermine demo-cratic accountability if legal processes and taxpayers' rights are set aside in response. Thus, the drive toward rapid revenue collection can come at considerable political and economic cost.

While pressure to increase tax reforms from international donors is unlikely to be the only source of such tensions, the larger point is that how taxes are collected is as important as whether they are collected by ARAs. The Ugandan case provides some indication that a more gradual approach to increasing tax revenues may avoid rapidly increasing coercion in the tax col-lection effort. In this perspective, foreign aid can lessen the need to increase tax collection so rapidly and so may contribute to episodes of coercive methods which can undermine state legitimacy. For this to be realized, donors and international financial institutions need to take a much *longer* time horizon perspective (see section on post-conflict countries for policy advice on the role aid can play in improving tax collection in a longer-term perspective).

Lessons from a successful ARA: the case of South Africa

In the mid-1990s, South Africa reformed its tax administration and granted the revenue authority greater autonomy. Tax collection has been very success-ful as well as being very progressive. In the period 1997–2002, the tax taken as a percentage of GDP in South Africa averaged over 25 percent compared with the middle-income country average of 15 percent of GDP and income tax collection averaged 14.6 percent of GDP compared with the Latin American average of 3.9 percent and the East Asian average of 6.9 percent.

While there has been a coincidence of impressive revenue collection with increased autonomy, there are several historical and political factors under-lying this success. First, the highly successful income and overall tax collec-tion capacity of the South African state is not a new feature of the state's tax capacity. In the period 1960–2000, South African tax collection as a percent-age of GDP has consistently been the highest among middle-income coun-tries. In the period 1997–2002, the tax take as a percentage of GDP in South Africa averaged over 25 percent compared with the middle-income country average of 15 percent of GDP. The South African state was already particularly successful in collecting direct taxes in the form of corporate and personal income taxes, which are generally the most progressive types of tax. In the period 1975–8, income tax collection averaged 12.9 percent of GDP compared with the Latin American average of 5.0 percent and the East Asian average of 5.7 percent.

The factors that permitted this high level of income tax collection capacity have been the subject of considerable analysis (Lieberman, 2001; Friedman and Smith, 2004). First, there has been a high degree of cooperation between the state and upper-income white groups which supported state-led reforms. This challenges the idea that simply instituting an autonomous revenue agency is central to effective tax collection. Second, the introduction of computerization in the 1960s greatly enhanced the ability of the Department of Inland Revenue to calculate and issue assessments, to record payments, and to register and monitor large tax payers, and maintain controls on tax payments more generally. Third, the introduction of a withholding pay-as-you-earn (PAYE) system also greatly enhanced tax collection. This system made employees responsible for withholding taxes on a monthly basis. The willingness of business owners to cooperate greatly reduced the transaction costs of implementing the PAYE system.

In the post-apartheid state there are several key political and institutional features that marked the continued success of SARS in tax collection capacity.

First, there has been a high degree of administrative cooperation within the state, particularly between SARS, the Finance Ministry and the Central Bank. Such cooperation allowed for exchange in information that improved budget planning and tracking tax evasion. It should be mentioned, however, that while SARS has had success in widening the number of tax payers for personal income and corporate tax over the period 1998–2002 (Smith, 2003: 8), it has been much less successful in taxing the informal sector (ibid, 2003: 11). More research is required to explain why this has been the case. To the extent that this is true is reflective of the difficulty of taxing the informal sector even in the context of a middle-income country with one of the best tax administrative capacities among developing countries.

Second, the state has historically maintained a cooperative relationship with upper-income groups, including large firms, which helped reduce the transaction costs of collecting income taxes.

Third, the reforms were introduced with substantial consultation with representatives from the state, political parties, business chambers, labour unions, and national and international tax and legal experts. This allowed for the design of policies that were technically and politically feasible. This contrasts with the more top-down, executive-led approaches of Uganda where much less consultation took place before introducing tax reforms, including the introduction of ARAs.

Fourth, SARS was formed in the context of a strong national political party, the African National Congress (ANC). The ANC as the governing party provided an important platform of wider legitimacy for the reforms.

Moreover, The ANC also possessed substantial amounts of political capital as it was the leading political organization in the struggle to end apartheid. Its leading role in the liberation struggle is where it largely derives its legitimacy (Hlope and Friedman, 2002).

Fifth, tax compliance is aided by the fact that most business leaders agree that there must be some redistribution from the top down given the legacy of apartheid and the very unequal distribution of income; there is little political room to contest progressive taxation as fundamentally unfair; or to complain that a particular sector or region is being overtaxed at the expense of another. Several CEOs in South Africa comment: "We can't make progress without black empowerment."

The tax system thus has become one of the central institutions targeted for righting past wrongs. By equating corporate taxation with the taxation of whites, and VAT payment disproportionately burdening the poorer blacks, unions and community leaders have managed to generate a national discourse which has in turn produced a nationally distinctive interpretation of democratization that emphasizes equitable development.

In conclusion, it is worth noting that the South African example illustrates that state capacity to tax at high levels does *not* necessarily translate into equally effective state capacities to collect specific types of taxes or govern the economy in *other* policy areas. In other words, state capacity is not necessarily uniform across administrative functions. For example, while SARS has had success in widening the number of tax payers for personal income and corporate tax over the period 1998–2002 (Smith, 2003: 8); it has been much less successful in taxing the informal sector.

The fact that state capacity is not monolithic suggests that aggregate indicators of state capacity or failure may be an inappropriate way to address state reform more generally. The policy implication is that designing reforms requires an historical and political understanding of the coalitions opposing and supporting reforms for specific policy areas within a country. There is no reason why the political economy dynamics and obstacles will be the same for each reform issue.

Export taxes, production strategies and the territorial reach of the state

Export taxes on agriculture are generally inadvisable for developing countries because of the well known disincentives they provide for producers. However, there are some examples of the developmental role these taxes can play when they are explicitly part of a production strategy to improve agricultural productivity. For such taxes to work, they need to the earmarked directly to finance infrastructure investment in agriculture. Apart from this, such taxes have played an important role in expanding the territorial reach of the state and the territorial dimension of state-society relations. Let us examine some country examples.

In the case of Mauritius, export taxes on sugar, the main export commodity in the nineteenth and most of the twentieth centuries had several positive effects on state-society relations and in increasing the productive capacity of the sugar sector (Bräutigam, 2008). First, the tax was an effective substitute for income taxes, and was generally progressive as it shifted the burden of taxation and redistributive spending on the wealthy and middle classes. This contributed to the public sense of fairness and solidarity and thus enhanced state legitimacy. Second, the tax was used by the state to finance research and development, infrastructure, and marketing which enhanced production and productivity growth in the sugar sector. An often neglected aspect in tax analysis is to explain how tax reform can be linked to productive strategies (which Grabowski [2008], for instance, argues was central to successful agricultural development in Japan, South Korea, and Taiwan). Third, the export tax helped the private sector organize, and it built their capacity to interact with the government over time. Fourth, it helped both the state and society to solve collective action problems they faced in building skills and in supporting research on sugar. Finally, the export tax helped develop the territorial reach of the state since the tax affected the main employer in the countryside and promoted mutually beneficial rights and obligations between the state and farmers, both large and small.

A second important example concerns the important role agricultural marketing boards have played in some countries in expanding the territorial reach of the state and in linking rural interest groups to the state. Marketing boards were also an important source of state resource mobilization through the mechanism of monopolizing the purchase of cash crops at below world market prices and selling such crops abroad at world market prices. The surplus generated was often of similar magnitude to formal total tax collection levels, particularly in sub-Saharan African economies in the 1960s and 1970s. Marketing boards were effective in some countries such as Taiwan, South Korea, Indonesia, and India because the state gave something in return to producer groups such as services, infrastructure, research, and price stability.

By the 1980s, however, an extensive critique of marketing boards developed in the wake of worsening agricultural performance, particularly in sub-Saharan Africa (Bates, 1981). It was generally viewed that the system worsened the terms of trade by paying farmers less than what the state received for the products at the world market. This often created disincentives for farmers to produce, and/or led to smuggling – both of which reduced the resource mobilization capacity of African states. Economic liberalization of agriculture was promoted as the cure for the growth-retarding effects marketing boards had in many contexts.

Despite these concerns, there are other important factors to consider in terms of the role marketing boards played in state-building. A principal task of policy-makers is to understand why some marketing boards performed better than others. The historical evidence suggests that the political power of the state and the nature of the political coalitions underpinning the central state are significant factors determining the effectiveness of marketing boards. For instance in Taiwan during the 1960s, the ability of the state to undertake land reform removed the power of large landowners who historically resisted state penetration of the countryside (Amsden, 1985). This state penetration allowed the state to tax rice farming in return for financing inputs that improved the productivity of rice production.

To take a sub-Saharan African comparison, Bates (1995) argues that the Kenyan coffee board was, in the 1970s and 1980s more effective than the Tanzanian coffee board because the nature of the political coalition in power differed in the two countries. In Kenya, large and medium-sized coffee farmers were a powerful interest group; whereas in Tanzania, coffee farmers were not a powerful group in the national government's support base. As a result, policies were in Kenya were developed in ways that extracted much fewer *net* resources from coffee producers than in Tanzania.

Even where marketing board policies were relatively ineffective such as in Tanzania and Zambia, they have played an important role in increasing the territorial reach of the state, developing state-rural interest group links, and in providing social infrastructure and services. In these two countries, the reach of the state was a by-product of the development of nationally-based political parties which developed an inclusive system of patronage across all agricultural regions (see Hesselbein, Golooba-Mutebi and Putzel, 2006 on Tanzania; and Di John, forthcoming on Zambia). There is also evidence that the inclusive reach of marketing boards contributed to the maintenance of political stability and nation-building in both these cases. Further comparative historical work is required to assess the differential impacts marketing boards have had in state-building and in enhancing the territorial reach, and legitimacy, of the state.

Conclusion

The stakes of deepening the tax mobilization capacity in African economies are great. Tax contributes to making the social contract operational, and in particular, to creating the mutual obligations between state decision-makers and relevant political actors. Of critical importance is the development of bargaining mechanisms between the state and elite groups, who generally control much of the production and export sectors of the economy. It should also be remembered that success of tax reforms should not only be measured by meeting feasible targets but should also be judged by the extent to which they enhance the institutionalization of state-interest group bargaining and policy dialogues. In any case, a major challenge of research for the development community is to develop a more strategic, historical, and politically informed basis to promote the more difficult tax reforms.

There are some other important issues worth remembering when examining the process of tax reform. First, the sequencing of tax reform is essential in the context of the decline in trade taxes. Very rapid trade liberalization in the absence of constructing alternative revenue sources can make the tax base even weaker, especially in low-income contexts. Second, the pace of tax collection should not take precedence over political stability and legitimacy. Over ambitious tax collection goals can be self-defeating if they lead to excessive coercion and government predation. Third, while tax collection efforts are central to state-building, it should not be assumed that effective tax collection is the only, or even the main source of state legitimacy. In low-income countries, economic growth may be a more important source of legitimacy if it is providing increases in employment, which is the main source of increasing incomes and reducing poverty. Finally, tax reform should not be undertaken in isolation but needs to be part of effective production strategy initiatives, especially if the tax base is to be widened to include informal sector firms, and create incentives for investment among larger formal enterprises.

While the technical aspects of tax reform are crucial, an understanding of the sustainability of reforms is not possible without understanding how reforms become legitimate. Because taxation affects incentives and distribution simultaneously, tax reform requires either a degree of social consensus that such policies are in the collective interest and/or it requires a state with the ability to coerce those who challenge its allocations. The focus on institutional designs (such as the degree of autonomy) and other technical issues of tax is incomplete since it ignores the political nature of taxation.

Further reading

Boyce, J. and O'Donnell, M. eds. (2007) *Peace and the Public Purse: Building State Capacity after Violent Conflict*. Boulder, CO, Lynne Rienner.

Brautigam, D., Fjeldstad, O-H. and Moore, M. (2008) *Capacity and Consent: Taxation and State-building in Developing Countries*. Cambridge, Cambridge University Press.

Di John, J. (2006) *The Political Economy of Taxation and Tax Reform in Developing Countries, World Institute of Development Economics Research (WIDER)*. Research Paper No. 2006/74, Helsinki: United Nations University-WIDER.

Herbst, J. (2000) *States and Power in Africa: Comparative Lessons in Authority and Control*. Princeton, Princeton University Press.

Hobson, J. (1997) *The Wealth of States: A Comparative Sociology of International Economic and Political Change*. Cambridge, Cambridge University Press.

Levi, M. (1988) *Of Revenue and Rule*. Berkeley, University of California Press.

Lieberman, E. (2003) *Race and Regionalism in the Politics of Taxation in Brazil and South Africa*. Cambridge, Cambridge University Press.

Tilly, C. (1990) *Coercion, Capital and European States: 990–1992*. Oxford, Blackwell.

References

Addison, T., Chowdhury, A., and Murshed, S.M. (2002) Taxation and Reform in Conflict-Affected Countries, paper presented at the conference on 'Taxing

Perspectives: A Democratic Approach to Public Finance in Developing Countries, Institute of Development Studies, Sussex, 28–29 October.

Amsden, A. (1985) The State and Taiwan's Economic Development. In: Evans, P., Rueschemeyer, D. and Skocpol, T. eds. *Bringing the State Back In*. New York, Cambridge University Press, pp. 78–106.

Bates, R. (1981) *Markets and States in Tropical Africa*. Berkeley and Los Angeles, University of California Press.

—— (1995) Social Dilemmas and Rational Individuals: An Assessment of the New Institutionalism. In: Harriss J., Hunter, J. and Lewis, C. eds. *New Institutional Economics and Third World Development*. London, Routledge, pp. 27–48.

Baunsgaard, T. (2001) A Primer on Mineral Taxation, IMF Working Paper WP/01/139.

Baunsgaard, T. and Keen, M. (2005) Tax Revenue and (or?) Trade Liberalization, *IMF Working Paper* 05/112.

Bird, R. (2007) Tax Challenges Facing Developing Countries, background paper for DFID project: "Taxation for Effective Governance and Shared Growth". London: Department for International Development.

Bird, R. and Casanegra, M. eds. (1992) *Improving Tax Administration in Developing Countries*. Washington DC, International Monetary Fund.

Bird, R. and Zolt, E. (2005) Redistribution via Taxation: The Limited Role of Personal Income Tax in Developing Countries. *UCLA Law Review*, vol. 52, no. 6, pp. 266–92.

Bräutigam, D. (2008) Contingent Capacity: export taxation and state-building in Mauritius. In: Bräutigam, D., Fjeldstad, O-H., and Moore, M. eds. *Taxation and State-Building in Developing Countries: Capacity and Consent*. Cambridge, Cambridge University Press, pp. 135–59.

Brewer, J. (1990) *The Sinews of Power: War, Money, and the English State, 1688–1783*. Cambridge, MA., Harvard University Press.

Burgess, R. and Stern, N. (1993) Taxation and Development. *Journal of Economic Literature*, 31, no.2, pp. 762–830.

Castel-Branco, C.N. (2004) What is the Experience and Impact of South African Trade and Investment on the Growth and Development of Host Economies? A View from Mozambique. Paper presented to Conference on: "Stability, Poverty Reduction and South African Trade and Investment in Southern Africa", sponsored by the Southern African Regional Poverty Network and the European Union, Pretoria, South Africa, 29–30 March.

Collier, P and Reinikka, R. (2001) Reconstruction and Liberalization: An overview. In: Reinikka, R. and Collier, P. eds. *Uganda's Recovery: The Role of Firms, Markets and Government*. Washington, DC, The World Bank.

Di John, J. (2006) The Political Economy of Taxation and Tax Reform in Developing Countries. *World Institute of Development Economics Research (WIDER) Research Paper*, No. 2006/74, Helsinki, United Nations University-WIDER.

—— (forthcoming) Zambia: State Resilience against the Odds: An Analytical Narrative on the Construction and Maintenance of Political Order. Crisis States Research Centre Working Paper, London School of Economics, London.

Di John, J. and Putzel, J. (2005) Institutional Change for Growth and Poverty Reduction in Low Income Countries: The Case of Uganda, paper presented for Conference on "When Institutions are Weak: Strategies for Change, 6–7 July, Washington, D.C., International Monetary Fund,

Emran, M. S. and Stiglitz, J. (2005) On Selective Indirect Tax Reform in Developing

Countries (http://ideas.repec.org/a/eee/pubeco/v89y2005i4p599-623.html) *Journal of Public Economics*, 89(4): 599–623.

Fjeldstad, O-H. and Moore, M. (2008) Revenue Authorities and State Capacity in Anglophone Africa. Bergen, Christian Michelsen Institute, Working Paper 2008: 1.

Fraser, A. and Lungu, J. (2007) For Whom the Windfalls? Winners and Losers in the Privatisation of Zambia's Copper Mines, Mine Watch Zambia (www.mine watchzambia.com), manuscript funded by Christian Aid, UK.

Friedman, S. and Smith, L. (2004) Tax and Society in South Africa, in Moore, M., and Schneider, A. Taxation, Governance, and Poverty: Where do the Middle Income Countries fit? *IDS Working Paper* 230.

Grabowski, R. (2008) Modes of Long-run Development: Latin America and East Asia. *Journal of Institutional Economics*, 4 (1), pp. 1–24.

Gupta, S. and Tareq, S. (2008) Mobilizing Revenue. *Finance and Development*, vol. 45, no. 3, pp. 44–7.

Hesselbein, G., Golooba-Mutebi, F. and Putzel, F. (2006) Economic and Political Foundations of State-making in Africa: Understanding State Reconstruction, Crisis States Research Centre Working Paper 3 (series 2), London School of Economics, London.

Hlope, D. and Friedman, S. (2002) And Their Hearts and Minds Will Follow? Tax Collection, Authority and Legitimacy in Democratic South Africa. *IDS Bulletin*, vol.33, no.3, pp. 67–76.

IMF (2005) Dealing with the Revenue Consequences of Trade Reform. Background Paper for Review of Fund Work on Trade. Washington, D.C., International Monetary Fund, February.

Kayizzi-Mugerwa, S. (2002) Fiscal Policy, Growth and Poverty Reduction in Uganda. *WIDER Discussion Paper* No. 33. Helsinki, UNU/WIDER.

Keen, M. and Mansour, M. (2008) "Revenue Mobilization in Sub-Saharan Africa: Key Challenges from Globalization," paper presented at the conference, "Globalization and Revenue Mobilization," Abuja, Nigeria, February.

Levi, M. (1988) *Of Revenue and Rule*. Berkeley, University of California Press.

Lieberman, E. (2001) National Political Community and the Politics of Taxation in Brazil and South Africa in the Twentieth Century. *Politics and Society*, Vol. 29, No. 4, pp. 515–55.

North, D. (1981) *Structure and Change in Economic History*. New York, Norton.

O'Brien, P. (2001) Fiscal Exceptionalism: Great Britain and Its European Rivals. Working Paper No. 65/01, Department of Economic History, London School of Economics.

Robinson, M. (2006) The Political Economy of Governance Reforms in Uganda, Institute of Development Studies (IDS) Discussion Paper No. 386, May.

Rodrik, D. (2004) Rethinking Growth Strategies. *WIDER Annual Lecture* 8, Helsinki, WIDER.

Schumpeter, J. (1918) 1954. The Crisis of the Tax State. *International Economic Papers*, No. 4. Reprinted in 1954.

Smith, L. (2003) The Power of Politics: The Performance of the South African Revenue Service and Some of its Implications. *Policy: Issues and Actors*, vol. 16, no. 2, pp. 1–17.

Taliceiro, R. (2004) Designing Performance: The Semi-Autonomous Revenue Authority Model in Africa and Latin America. *Policy Research Working Paper* 3423. Washington, D.C., The World Bank.

Therkilsden, O. (2003) Revenue Authority autonomy in sub-Saharan Africa: The case of Uganda, Draft Paper for NFU conference on "Poverty and Politics", Oslo, 23–24 October.

Tilly, C. (1990) *Coercion, Capital and European States: 990–1992*. Oxford, Blackwell.

Toye, J. (2000) Fiscal crisis and reform in developing countries. *Cambridge Journal of Economics*, vol. 24, no. 1, pp. 21–44.

USAID (2004) *Removing Obstacles to Economic Growth in Mozambique*. Washington, D.C., US AID, vol. 2.

Virtanen, P. and Ehrenpreis, D. (2007) Growth, Poverty, and Inequality in Mozambique. *International Poverty Centre Country Study* no. 10. Brasilia: UNDP.

Weeks, J., Chisala, V., Geda, A., Dagdeviren, H., McKinley, T., Oya, C., and Saad-Filho, A. (2004) Economic Policies for Growth, Employment and Poverty Reduction: Case Study of Zambia. London, Centre for Development Policy and Research, School of Oriental and African Studies (SOAS), University of London; New York, United Nations Development Programme Bureau for Development Policy.

7 Africa's revolving door
External borrowing and capital flight in sub-Saharan Africa

*Léonce Ndikumana and
James K. Boyce*

Introduction

External borrowing can be a good thing, or a bad thing, from the standpoint of the well-being of a country's people. If the money is invested productively, in activities that yield a rate of return high enough to repay the debt with interest and still come out ahead – in theory, the underlying premise of development finance – then it is a good thing. Even if the money is used to purchase items for consumption, rather than invested, this can be a good thing if it helps the populace through lean times and lets them repay when the economy improves, a consumption-smoothing logic akin to the life-cycle behavior of individuals who borrow in their younger years and repay later when the have higher incomes. Indeed, in such circumstances external borrowing can be a blessing. But if neither of these conditions holds – if the borrowed funds are neither invested productively nor used for consumption needs – then external borrowing can be a bad thing, burdening future governments and citizens with debt service costs without commensurate benefits.

If, for example, the money is used for unproductive purposes, such as buying arms and paying security forces to enable an unpopular leader or faction to retain political power, then external borrowing can be regarded as a bad thing from the standpoint of the society as a whole (however good it may be for those currently in power). Similarly, if the money is illicitly diverted into private accounts abroad, while the debt accrues to the public of the borrowing country, external borrowing is a curse rather than a blessing. Unfortunately, there are many examples of both of these adverse impacts of external borrowing in developing countries in general, and in sub-Saharan Africa (SSA) in particular.

This chapter is focused on the second of these problems: the use of borrowed funds to finance capital flight, a "revolving door" that creates both public debts and private assets. Our aim is to quantify the dimensions of this phenomenon in sub-Saharan Africa. To do so, we engage in some statistical detective work. First, we estimate the magnitude of capital flight from the subcontinent in the period 1970 to 2004. Next, after briefly reviewing various explanations for capital flight, we summarize econometric results that provide an estimate of the proportion of borrowed funds that were used to fuel capital flight. Finally, we offer some thoughts on the policy implications of our findings, suggesting that the moral and legal legitimacy of external debts can be called into question where there has been widespread debt-fueled capital flight.

Africa's hidden balance of payments: estimating the magnitude of capital flight

Studies have revealed large amounts of capital outflows from SSA countries over the past decades. The estimated magnitudes of capital flight vary, primarily due to differences in data and time-period coverage.[1] The standard methodology is to calculate capital flight as the residual difference between capital inflows and recorded foreign-exchange outflows. For country i in year t, capital flight is computed as follows (Boyce and Ndikumana, 2001):

$$KF_{it} = \Delta DEBTADJ_{it} + DFI_{it} - (CA_{it} + \Delta RES_{it}) + MISINV_{it} \qquad (1)$$

where $\Delta DEBTADJ$ is the change in the country's stock of external debt (adjusted for cross-currency exchange rate fluctuations, so as to take into account the fact that debt is denominated in various currencies and then aggregated in US dollars); DFI is net direct foreign investment; CA is the current account deficit; ΔRES is the change in the stock of international reserves; and $MISINV$ is net trade misinvoicing.

This method is a variant of the one used by the World Bank (1985) among others, based on the difference between the inflows of foreign exchange from external borrowing (as reported in the World Bank's *World Debt Tables*) and the uses of foreign exchange reported in the IMF's *Balance-of-Payments Tables*. In effect, this "residual" method estimates capital flight as the recalculated "net errors and omissions" after the often incomplete data on external borrowing that are reported in the capital account of the official Balance-of-Payments (BoP) tables are replaced with more accurate and comprehensive data compiled by the World Bank.

The trade misinvoicing adjustment corrects for another source of errors in the official BoP data: the export and import data in the current account. On the export side, the official BoP data of African countries often under-report the true value, as exporters use underinvoicing to conceal earnings from the domestic authorities in order to evade taxes or foreign exchange controls. On the import side, there can be overinvoicing for similar motives: inflated invoices reduce nominal profits and serve as a mechanism to move foreign exchange out of the country. At the same time, however, "pure" smuggling (where imports are unrecorded) and "technical" smuggling (where imports are recorded but their value is understated), both motivated by the desire to evade import duties, have an opposite effect, reducing officially reported payments for imports below their true level.

The misinvoicing adjustment corrects for the resulting errors by using the IMF's *Direction of Trade* statistics to compare the import and export data from African countries with those of their industrialized-country trading partners, whose official data are taken to be more accurate. The discrepancies are calculated after adjustment for the costs of freight and insurance. Depending on the relative magnitudes of export underinvoicing and import overinvoicing on the one hand, and smuggling (i.e. import underinvoicing) on the other, the net effect of the misinvoicing adjustment on the residual estimate of capital flight can be either positive or negative. If the former dominate, the misinvoicing adjustment increases the estimate of capital flight, since these types of misinvoicing represent unrecorded outflows of foreign exchange. If smuggling dominates, the misinvoicing adjustment decreases the estimate of capital flight, since some of the "missing money" otherwise captured by the residual method was actually used to finance unrecorded or underinvoiced imports.[2]

Here we have refined this measure by incorporating further adjustments for (i) the impact of exchange rate fluctuations on the dollar value of external debt; (ii) the effect of debt write-offs on changes in the debt stock; and (iii) the underreporting of remittance inflows in the BoP current account.[3]

Table 7.1 summarizes results for the sample of 40 sub-Saharan African countries between 1970 and 2004. Including imputed interest earnings, the accumulated stock of capital flight was about $607 billion at the end of 2004. Together, this group of SSA countries is a "net creditor" to the rest of the world in the sense that their private assets held abroad, as measured by capital flight including interest earnings, exceed their total liabilities as measured by the stock of external debt. The region's external assets are 2.9 times the stock of debts owed to the world. The region's net external assets (accumulated flight capital minus accumulated external debt) amounted to approximately $398billion over the 35-year period. For some individual countries, the results are even more dramatic: for Côte d'Ivoire, Zimbabwe, Angola, and Nigeria the external assets are 4.6, 5.1, 5.3, and 6.7 times higher than their debt stocks, respectively.

The data indicate that capital flight is not solely a phenomenon dating from the onset of the debt crisis of the 1980s (see also Ndikumana and Boyce, 2003). The outflows of the 1970s were often comparable to, and in some cases greater than, those of more recent decades. Over the period, a number of countries appear to have experienced episodes of capital flight reversal (that is, net outflows followed by net inflows), but in the period as a whole, estimated outflows more than outweigh estimated inflows for all but seven countries in the sample (Benin, Comoros, Mali, Mauritius, Niger, Senegal, and Togo).

Causes of capital flight

Previous studies have found that the volume of external borrowing is an important determinant of capital flight. In an earlier study of 30 SSA

Table 7.1 Total capital flight (million 2004 dollars and % of GDP), stock of accumulated capital flight (million dollars and % of debt stock) over 1970–2004 period

Name	Real KF	Stock of KF in 2004	Net foreign assets in 2004	Total KF/GDP (%)	Stock of KF/debt (%)
Angola	42178.8	50950.6	41430.0	215.6	535.2
Benin	−3989.7	−7663.9	−9580.3	−98.6	−399.9
Botswana	1127.9	−1086.9	−1610.9	12.6	−207.4
Burkina Faso	3076.9	4670.6	2934.6	73.6	269.0
Burundi	2073.6	2566.6	1181.2	312.2	185.3
Cameroon	18378.9	27287.7	17791.8	116.5	287.4
Cape Verde	2190.9	2707.1	2190.1	231.1	523.6
Central African Republic	1943.8	2774.1	1696.4	148.7	257.4
Chad	1337.7	2345.6	644.3	31.1	137.9
Comoros	−176.3	−168.7	−474.5	−47.8	−55.2
Congo, Dem. Rep.	19572.5	36737.6	24896.7	295.1	310.3
Congo, Rep.	14950.4	17474.8	11645.4	344.3	299.8
Côte d'Ivoire	34349.4	54000.6	42261.2	222.0	460.0
Ethiopia	17031.5	22526.0	15951.9	175.0	342.6
Gabon	8580.8	11997.6	7847.9	118.7	289.1
Ghana	8503.7	11208.4	4173.3	98.7	159.3
Guinea	551.2	1048.9	−2489.6	14.6	29.6
Kenya	2665.4	6369.3	−456.9	16.6	93.3
Lesotho	407.4	893.4	129.8	29.8	117.0
Madagascar	7430.9	9570.8	6108.5	170.3	276.4
Malawi	2527.8	3825.4	407.5	132.9	111.9
Mali	−372.0	−425.4	−3741.8	−7.6	−12.8
Mauritania	2319.1	4006.0	1709.2	151.2	174.4
Mauritius	−962.8	650.1	−1643.8	−16.0	28.3
Mozambique	10677.7	14273.4	9622.9	180.6	306.9
Niger	−5975.7	−8732.6	−10682.6	−195.7	−447.8
Nigeria	165696.7	240781.0	204891.3	230.0	670.9
Rwanda	3366.8	5889.5	4233.8	183.5	355.7
São Tomé and Príncipe	723.3	1059.1	696.9	1265.9	292.4
Senegal	−8885.0	−13077.3	−17015.7	−114.3	−332.0
Seychelles	2700.9	2986.3	2371.5	384.1	485.7
Sierra Leone	4607.7	7005.4	5282.6	424.7	406.6
South Africa	18266.0	17492.3	7552.7	8.5	176.0
Sudan	9218.7	16325.0	−3006.7	43.0	84.4
Swaziland	1263.9	1342.6	872.5	50.2	285.6
Tanzania	5185.2	9963.4	2163.9	45.8	127.7
Togo	−3481.6	−4064.6	−5876.9	−168.9	−224.3
Uganda	4982.0	6853.7	2031.4	73.0	142.1
Zambia	9769.5	19814.3	12535.5	180.2	272.2
Zimbabwe	16162.0	24556.0	19758.5	344.2	511.9
Sample total	419975.7	606733.7	398433.6	81.8	291.3

Sources: Ndikumana and Boyce 2003; series updated (1997 to 2004) and sample expanded using information from: IMF, *International Financial Statistics*; IMF, *Balance of Payments Statistics*; IMF, *Direction of Trade Statistics*; IMF, various country online information in "Selected issues and statistical appendix"; World Bank, *Global Development Finance*; World Bank, *World Development Indicators*.

Note: For Burkina Faso, last year where KF is available is 2003; so totals, stocks, and ratios refer to 2003.

countries over the period 1970–96 (Ndikumana and Boyce, 2003), we found that for every dollar of external borrowing in a given year, on average, roughly 80 cents leave the country as capital flight. Our results also supported the hypothesis that debt overhang has an independent effect on capital flight: a one-dollar increase in the stock of debt adds an estimated 3.5 cents to annual capital flight in subsequent years. Collier *et al.* (2004) report an almost identical result, with a one dollar increase in the stock of debt leading to 3.2 cents of capital flight.

The causal relationships between capital flight and external debt can run both ways; that is, foreign borrowing can cause capital flight, while at the same time capital flight can lead to more external borrowing. Boyce (1992) distinguishes four possible causal links. First, foreign borrowing causes capital flight by contributing to an increased likelihood of a debt crisis, worsening macroeconomic conditions, and the deterioration of the investment climate. In such cases of *debt-driven capital flight*, "capital flees a country in response to economic circumstances attributable to the external debt itself" (Boyce, 1992: 337). High levels of debt also may be interpreted as a signal of higher tax rates in the future as the government seeks to service the debt. These effects will deter domestic investment while inducing capital flight.

Second, foreign borrowing provides the resources as well as a motive for channeling private capital abroad, a phenomenon Boyce (1992: 338) terms *debt-fueled capital flight*. In such cases, funds borrowed abroad (by the government or by private borrowers with government guarantees) are re-exported as private assets. In some cases, the funds may never even leave the creditor bank, simply being transferred into an international private bank account at the same institution (Henry, 1986).

In the other two linkages, capital flight causes foreign borrowing. In the case of *flight-driven external borrowing*, capital flight drains national foreign exchange resources, forcing the government to borrow abroad.[4] In the case of *flight-fueled external borrowing*, flight capital directly provides the resources to finance foreign loans to the same residents who export their capital, a phenomenon known as "round-tripping" or "back-to-back loans," motivated by the desire to obtain government guarantees on foreign borrowing, or by the need to devise a pretext for unexplained wealth.

Prior studies also reveal that capital flight tends to persist over time: all else being equal, past capital flight "causes" more capital flight, which suggests *hysteresis* in the dynamics of capital flight. Ndikumana and Boyce (2003) interpret this result as a *habit formation effect*, as private actors gain experience in smuggling capital abroad. The result may also reflect a *contagion effect*, as capital flight corrodes the legitimacy of capital controls, particularly if the flight capitalists include government authorities. At the same time, capital flight may contribute to the deterioration of the macroeconomic environment, in turn sparking further capital flight. Collier *et al.* (2004) find that the effects of past capital flight last up to a decade, suggesting that portfolio adjustment is a slow process. This suggests that it may take a long time before countries are able to reap the dividends from policy reforms aimed at curbing capital flight.

Good economic performance, measured simply in terms of higher economic growth, has been found to be associated with lower capital flight (Ndikumana and Boyce, 2003). Higher economic growth is a signal of higher expected returns on domestic investment, which induces further domestic investment and thus reduces capital flight. High and sustained economic growth also gives confidence to domestic investors about the institutional and governance environment of the country. It constitutes the most palpable evidence that the country's institutions and governance system are favorable for private economic activity, whereas stagnation and economic decline are an indication that the government has lost control over the economy.

High political risk has played a significant role in the capital hemorrhage experienced by SSA countries over the past decades. In a case study of South Africa, Fedderke and Liu (2002) find that both the change in political rights dispensation and an index of political instability are positively related to capital flight. In a cross-country study, Collier *et al.* (2004) find that more durable regimes experience significantly less capital flight, while countries prone to civil wars experience higher capital flight. However, the result on the effects of regime durability should be taken with some caution given the history of political change in Africa. Frequent regime changes are typically associated with higher political instability, which discourages domestic investment and induces capital flight. It does not necessarily follow, however, that durable regimes are associated with a better political environment. Some regimes in Africa have persisted because they were able to establish an oppressive apparatus that suppressed demand for political opening. Examples include the regimes of Mobutu in the Congo and Mugabe in Zimbabwe. Such regimes are associated with high risk of expropriation and uncertainty, which deters domestic investment and induces capital flight. Moreover, under such regimes, capital flight is high as government leaders engage in smuggling the country's assets, including natural resources, borrowed funds, and official aid (for evidence on the case of the Congo, see Ndikumana and Boyce, 1998).

Corruption has figured prominently in discussions of the problem of capital flight from sub-Saharan Africa. There are various ways to understand the effects of corruption on capital flight. First, capital flight consists of assets which often are acquired illegally domestically and channeled abroad illegally as well. Corruption facilitates both the illegal acquisition as well as the illegal transfer of private assets. Second, countries experience high capital flight partly as a result of its "contagious" nature. As government officials engage in capital smuggling and embezzlement of national resources, private agents are induced to engage also in illicit transfers of assets abroad as a result of the collapse of the mechanisms of control and accountability. In general, high levels of corruption are a symptom of failure of the governance system, which results in high economic risk. In such an environment, private agents cannot fully internalize the costs of corruption and choose to hold assets abroad as a means of hedging against uncertainty.

Finally, price distortions are often thought to be a cause of capital flight. Agents choose to hold assets abroad to shield their portfolios from the effects of changes in relative returns arising from external shocks and policy uncertainty. Empirical studies have found a significant effect of the black market premium on capital flight (see Collier *et al.*, 2004). The black market premium constitutes an effective subsidy on assets held abroad and symmetrically a levy on assets held domestically. Market distortions therefore can have important regressive effects, disproportionately hurting the general public relative to the political and economic élites who are able to hold assets abroad.

The revolving door: estimating the magnitude of debt-fueled capital flight

The econometric analysis that follows builds on the prior research on the determinants of capital flight from SSA countries. In particular, we explore further our earlier findings that show a positive and significant relationship between capital flight and both annual flows of external borrowing and the cumulative stock of external debt, suggesting that capital flight is both *debt-fueled* and *debt-driven* (Ndikumana and Boyce, 2003). In other words, external borrowing appears to provide resources for capital flight while growing indebtedness provides a motive for private agents to export capital. Prior studies also show that capital flight exhibits a high degree of *hysteresis*, or persistence. Furthermore, it is negatively related to the growth rate of per capita GDP, possibly implying that growth is a signal for returns to domestic capital so that high growth is a disincentive for exporting capital and an incentive for investing domestically.

Based on this evidence, we formulate the econometric model as follows:

$$KF_{it} = \sum_{j=1}^{q} \theta_j KF_{i,t-j} + a_1 DEBT_{it} + a_2 growth + \boldsymbol{\beta}'\mathbf{X}_{it} + \eta_i + \varepsilon_{it} \qquad (2)$$

where for a country i at time t, KF is the ratio of real capital flight to GDP (and $j = 1 \ldots q$ is the number of lags), $DEBT$ is alternatively the ratio of the annual inflows of debt (change in debt stock) to GDP or the ratio of the debt stock to GDP (we also run regressions with change in debt and the stock of debt simultaneously), $\mathbf{X}$ is a vector of control variables, η_i is a country-specific intercept representing unobservable individual country characteristics, and ε is a white-noise error term.

Among control variables we explore are the effects of the macroeconomic environment, interest rate differentials, financial development, natural resources, and governance. An unstable macroeconomic environment increases uncertainty over expected returns to domestic capital, which reduces incentives for investing domestically, thus inducing capital flight. We proxy macroeconomic uncertainty by inflation variability, measured as the absolute value of the difference between actual inflation and predicted inflation.[5] Including the real interest rate differential – proxied by the real US Treasury bill rate minus the African country's real deposit rate – permits us to test whether the conventional portfolio theory prediction that capital flight is driven by higher world interest rates relative to domestic rates holds for this sample of African countries. As a measure of financial development, we use bank credit to the private sector as a ratio of GDP. The natural resource endowment is included as a potential source for both exportable funds and embezzlement of exports. As a proxy for this, we use the share of fuel exports in the country's total exports.[6] We explore the role of governance by interacting natural resources with a polity measure.[7] The rationale for this interaction is that a natural resource-rich country with a corrupt regime will experience more capital flight as the leaders embezzle the proceeds of exports and channel them into private assets held abroad. Descriptive statistics for the regression variables are provided in the Appendix (Table 7.A1).[8]

Table 7.2 reports our findings on the relationship between capital flight and external debt. The first column of the table contains results with robust OLS estimation, the second regression results add country fixed effects, and the last results are from the instrumental variable approach where change in debt is considered endogenous. The results clearly indicate a positive and significant relationship between capital flight and the annual inflows of external debt (change in the stock of debt). The estimated coefficient on change in debt implies that up to 62 cents out of each dollar borrowed abroad between 1970 and 2004 has left sub-Saharan Africa in the form of capital flight. The results provide strong support for the revolving door phenomenon, or debt-fueled capital flight, whereby borrowed funds are captured and converted into private assets in foreign banks.

The results also show a strong positive effect of the stock of external debt on capital flight. The results again are robust to country-specific effects and any potential two-way causation between capital flight and debt as can be seen in the regressions with the instrumental variable approach where external debt is considered endogenous (column 6). These results suggest that an increase in the stock of debt by 1 dollar leads to 3 to 4 cents of capital flight in subsequent years. There are two related possible explanations for this effect. First, in a highly indebted country, investors may expect that future economic performance will be lower, implying lower overall returns to investment. This reduces incentives for investing domestically, encouraging capital flight. Second, private agents may expect that high future debt service obligations associated with high debt stock will force the government to raise more taxes to meet debt service commitments. Higher future taxes reduce expected after-tax returns to capital, which further reduce incentives for investing domestically, leading to higher capital flight.

In the last column of Table 7.2, both the debt flow and debt stock are

Table 7.2 External borrowing and capital flight

Variables	Regressions with debt flows (change in debt)			Regressions with debt stock			Combined regression
	OLS^a (1)	FE (2)	iv_(FE)^b (3)	OLS^a (4)	FE (5)	iv_(FE)^b (6)	FE^c (7)
Change in debt	0.606 (0.00)	0.603 (0.00)	0.451 (0.00)				0.625 (0.00)
Debt stock (2nd lag)				0.045 (0.00)	0.044 (0.00)	0.049 (0.00)	0.033 (0.00)
1st lag of capital flight	0.280 (0.00)	0.172 (0.00)	0.180 (0.00)	0.269 (0.00)	0.157 (0.00)	0.158 (0.00)	0.174 (0.00)
2nd lag of capital flight	0.129 (0.00)	0.031 (0.19)	0.032 (0.20)	0.132 (0.00)	0.031 (0.26)	0.032 (0.25)	0.022 (0.36)
Lagged real GDP growth	-0.084 (0.00)	-0.066 (0.01)	-0.069 (0.01)	-0.056 (0.06)	-0.044 (0.17)	-0.039 (0.22)	-0.073 (0.00)
F (with p-value)	41.6 (0.00)	108.9 (0.00)	4.1 (0.00)	17.6 (0.00)	15.8 (0.00)	3.4 (0.00)	90.9 (0.00)
overall R-sq	0.39	0.37	0.39	0.22	0.20	0.20	0.37
between R-sq (FE)		0.71	0.77		0.69	0.67	0.60
within R-sq (FE)		0.28	0.27		0.05	0.05	0.29
Observations	1137	1137	1117	1138	1138	1137	1136

Notes:
The numbers in parentheses are p-values.
a OLS = with robust standard errors, taking account of outliers.
b iv_FE = instrumental-variable fixed-effects estimation where change in debt and stock of debt are considered as endogenous.
c The combined regression includes the second lag of the stock of debt, given that by construction, the change in debt is dependent on the contemporaneous and first lag of the stock of debt.

included simultaneously in the regression. The coefficients on both the flow and the stock measures are statistically significant. This specification incorporates both the *debt-fueled* capital flight (with change in debt) and *debt-driven* capital flight (with debt stock) channels. As the results indicate, the linkages between capital flight and external borrowing in this sample of African countries operate through both channels. In the following exploration of the effects of other factors, we use this specification that includes both the flow and stock of debt and apply the fixed-effects estimation methodology.

Table 7.3 reports estimates of the effects of measures of macroeconomic instability (inflation variability), the real interest rate differential, financial development (credit/GDP), natural resource endowments (fuel exports), and governance. The results indicate that the inflation effect is positive and statistically significant at the 10 percent level. This suggests that to some extent, macroeconomic instability plays an important role in portfolio decisions by investors. High uncertainty over inflation discourages domestic investment by raising the discount rate applied to expected profitability of investment. As a result, more savings flow into foreign assets. Investors may also interpret inflation variability as a sign of lack of control by the government over the macroeconomic policy, which reduces confidence in the performance of the local economy.

Somewhat surprisingly, the results show that the real interest rate differential does not have a statistically significant impact on capital flight. This suggests that other motivations – such as the desire to safeguard illicit wealth – have been more important than conventional portfolio investment criteria in explaining capital flight from sub-Saharan Africa.

The results indicate that financial development has no impact on capital flight. Financial development is proxied by the ratio of bank credit to the private sector over GDP. The evidence does not support the presumption that the development of the financial system, and the ease of conducting transactions that accompany it, may facilitate the export of capital. Indeed, the SSA countries with the most developed financial systems have relatively low levels of capital flight (e.g. Kenya, Mauritius, Seychelles, South Africa).

We also investigated the effects of natural resource endowment on capital flight, under the premise that natural resource exports are subject to embezzlement by leaders as well as smuggling and misinvoicing by private operators, which would lead to a high correlation between natural resource endowment and capital flight. This exercise is severely hindered by the poor quality of data on natural resource exports. We experimented with various measures of natural resource endowment, including the share of various natural resources in total exports as well as a dummy taking the value of one if the share of natural resources in total exports is greater than 75 percent and zero otherwise. We report the results with the share of fuel in total exports as a proxy for natural resource endowment. The coefficient on the share of fuel exports in total exports is positive and statistically significant in robust OLS estimations (not reported here), but it becomes statistically insignificant (and negative) when country-specific fixed effects are included (Table 7.3). This is not surprising given that natural resource endowment is likely to be one of the key country fixed effects that is unaccounted for in the OLS.

One possible linkage between capital flight and natural resource endowments is that the exports proceeds are embezzled by leaders. This would imply that the link would be stronger under non-democratic regimes, suggesting that the quality of governance affects the resource-capital flight link. We explore this possibility by adding to the regression the polity index of the quality of governance and its interaction with the share of fuel exports. We expect the coefficient on the polity indicator to be negative, implying that more democratic regimes (with a higher value of the index) experience less capital flight than more autocratic ones. Contrary to this expectation, the estimated coefficient on the polity indicator is positive and statistically significant.[9] The coefficient on fuel exports and the interaction term both are statistically insignificant.

Table 7.3 Determinants of capital flight: effects of other factors

Explanatory variable	Inflation differential (1)	Interest rate differential (2)	Credit/ GDP (3)	Fuel exports/ total exports (4)	Fuel export share*Polity2 (5)
Change in debt	0.644	0.550	0.531	0.591	0.494
	(0.00)	(0.00)	(0.00)	(0.00)	(0.00)
Debt stock (2nd lag)	0.043	0.044	0.049	0.045	0.029
	(0.00)	(0.00)	(0.00)	(0.01)	(0.15)
1st lag capital flight	0.121	0.139	0.110	0.091	0.241
	(0.00)	(0.00)	(0.00)	(0.01)	(0.00)
2nd lag capital flight	0.047	0.036	0.051	0.023	0.019
	(0.08)	(0.22)	(0.03)	(0.51)	(0.69)
Lagged growth	−0.052	−0.059	−0.068	−0.072	−0.063
	(0.05)	(0.02)	(0.00)	(0.07)	(0.09)
Inflation variability	0.015				
	(0.09)				
Interest rate differential		−0.0005			
		(0.86)			
Credit/GDP			−0.037		
			(0.27)		
Fuel exports				−0.019	−0.018
				(0.75)	(0.79)
Polity2 index					0.39
					(0.02)
Fuel exports*Polity2					−0.005
					(0.28)
overall R-sq	0.39	0.26	0.22	0.21	0.30
between R-sq	0.49	0.17	0.18	0.08	0.40
within R-sq	0.40	0.28	0.25	0.29	0.29
observations	719	784	976	496	364

Notes:
The numbers in parentheses are p-values.
All equations are estimated with country fixed effects.

One possible concern with our econometric estimates of the relationship between capital flight and external borrowing is that the results may be driven by the way in which our measure of capital flight was constructed. Given that the change in the stock of debt is one component of the capital flight measure, errors in this variable could lead to a spurious relation. To address this concern, we re-estimate the model using a proxy for capital flight that is unrelated to debt. This proxy is the deposits held by non-bank African agents in Western banks, that is, the liabilities of foreign banks vis-à-vis the African non-bank private sector.[10] Reported holdings in Western banks represent only a small fraction of total capital flight; this measure omits non-bank financial holdings, real estate and other property holdings, and bank holdings for which the African identity of the depositor is concealed, as well as capital flight that was used to finance overseas consumption. For the 40 African countries in our sample, recorded bank deposits in 2004 amounted to $35.3 billion, less than 10 percent of our measure of cumulative capital flight for the 1970–2004 period ($420billion in 2004 dollars).[11]

Table 7.4 reports the results of the regressions with the foreign bank liabilities vis-à-vis the African private sector. The results confirm the positive effects of external debt, both for annual flows and stock of debt, on capital flight, although as expected the estimated magnitude is much smaller. In the regression including both the flow and stock of debt, the estimated coefficients imply that one dollar of new borrowing results in 15 cents of deposits by Africans in foreign banks and one extra cent annually in subsequent years. As expected, given that the BIS data on bank deposits capture only a fraction of total capital flight, the magnitude of the coefficient on external borrowing is smaller than the results reported in Tables 7.2 and 7.3. But using this alternative proxy as a measure of capital flight clearly supports the conclusion that there is a positive and significant relationship between capital flight and external borrowing.

Policy implications: Africa's odious debts

The evidence presented in this chapter indicates that sub-Saharan Africa is a net creditor to the rest of the world, in the sense that private assets held abroad exceed the continent's liabilities to the rest of the world. If so, why are so many of its people so poor? The answer is that the subcontinent's private external assets belong to a narrow, relatively wealthy stratum of its population, while public external debts are borne by the people through their governments. To the extent that these private assets were accumulated using the external borrowings that were intended to develop the countries, this raises the question of the legitimacy of much of the debts owed by African countries. In other words, there is a moral and legal basis for claiming that a substantial fraction of Africa's debts are "odious."

A country's debts are considered "odious" if three conditions hold (see Sack, 1927; Khalfan, 2003; King, 2007; and Howse, 2007): (1) *absence of*

Table 7.4 Regression results with an alternative proxy for capital flight (foreign bank liabilities)

Variables	Regressions with debt flows (change in debt)			Regressions with debt stock			Combined regression
	OLS^a (1)	FE (2)	$IV\_(FE)^b$ (3)	OLS^a (4)	FE (5)	$IV\_(FE)^b$ (6)	$IV\_(FE)^b$ (7)
Change in debt	0.013	0.009	0.145				0.151
	(0.00)	(0.30)	(0.00)				(0.00)
Stock of debt				0.0003	0.018	0.002	0.010
				(0.00)	(0.00)	(0.62)	(0.01)
1st lag of foreign bank liabilities	0.822	0.676	0.663	0.796	0.661	0.675	0.659
	(0.00)	(0.00)	(0.00)	(0.00)	(0.00)	(0.00)	(0.00)
2nd lag of foreign bank liabilities	0.056	0.072	0.129	0.061	0.040	0.065	0.102
	(0.00)	(0.04)	(0.06)	(0.00)	(0.26)	(0.07)	(0.01)
Lagged real GDP growth	−0.016	−0.001	0.004	−0.014	0.011	0.0002	0.0006
	(0.00)	(0.87)	(0.62)	(0.00)	(0.17)	(0.98)	(0.95)
F (with p-value)	3260	203.3	1.52	3150	219	1.98	1.50
	(0.00)	(0.00)	(0.02)	(0.00)	(0.00)	(0.00)	(0.03)
overall R-sq		0.754	0.681		0.710	0.752	0.65
between R-sq (FE)		0.996	0.968		0.852	0.991	0.88
within R-sq (FE)		0.469	0.342		0.488	0.474	0.34
Observations	962	962	959	963	963	962	962

Notes:
The numbers in parentheses are p-values.
a OLS = with robust standard errors, taking account of outliers.
b iv_FE = instrumental-variable fixed-effects estimation where change in debt is considered as endogenous.

consent: the debts were incurred without the consent of the people, which is typically the case when the debts were borrowed by an undemocratic regime; (2) *absence of benefit:* the borrowed funds were used not for the benefit of the people, but instead for the interests of the rulers, possibly for acts of repression against the same people that these funds were nominally intended to help;[12] (3) *creditor awareness*: creditors were aware or should have been aware of conditions (1) and (2).

The doctrine of odious debt draws from both international law and domestic law, including that of the United States and United Kingdom, to whose jurisdiction dispute resolution often is assigned in loan agreements. One particularly strong backing of the doctrine is the principle of *domestic agency*, which states that "every power of making a binding commitment for another person carries with it the special responsibility of acting in the interest of that person" (Khalfan, 2003: 3). Thus, while the agent (the government) has the power to make binding debt commitments in the name of the principal (the people), it also has the fiduciary obligation of doing so in the latter's interest. When it fails to do so, there is a well-established legal basis for challenging the legitimacy of the resulting liability. Moreover, under domestic law in most countries, a third party can be held liable for assisting an agent in the breach of his obligation toward his principal. This implies that if a bank knowingly assists a government official or private citizen in robbing a country, the bank is liable for the losses incurred by the nation and its people.[13]

The practice of servicing external debts regardless of the uses to which the borrowed money was put gives rise to a moral hazard problem: insured against the risk of malfeasance, creditors lack adequate incentives to act to minimize this risk. One way to improve international financial governance would be to improve the institutional arrangements for repudiation of odious debts. This would encourage due diligence by creditors and curtail the phenomenon of debt-fueled capital flight in future years.

The literature on odious debts has outlined two main strategies with regard to the question of repayment of debts that are presumed odious. In the first strategy, odious debts are defined as loans issued to a government that has been designated as "odious" *ex ante* by an international institution (Kremer and Jayachandran, 2002, 2003). Under this scenario, governments can repudiate only those debts incurred after the "odious government" status has been established and made public by the appropriate international institution. The second strategy is for debtor countries to repudiate past debts unilaterally. Here we focus on the latter, which we refer to as the *ex post* strategy.

It is difficult to distinguish between legitimate debts and odious debts. Putting the burden of proof on the shoulders of debtor countries to establish the "odious" nature of debts in many cases would impose insuperable transaction costs. An alternative approach is to put the burden of proof on the creditors to demonstrate the legitimacy of the debts contracted by previous dictatorial regimes.[14] Sub-Saharan African governments would inform their creditors that outstanding debts will be treated as legitimate if, and only if, the real counterparts of the debts can be identified and shown to have benefited the people of the country. If the creditors can document where the money went, and show when and how it benefited citizens of the borrowing country via investment or consumption, then the debt would be regarded as a *bona fide* external obligation of the government (and hence an external asset of the creditor bank or government). But if the fate of the borrowed money cannot be traced, then the present African governments must infer that it was diverted into private pockets associated with the former regimes, and possibly into capital flight. In such cases, it can be argued that the liability for the debt lies not with the current government, but with the private individuals whose personal fortunes are the real counterpart of the debt.

In adopting such a strategy, Africans can invoke as a precedent the US government's stance a century ago toward the creditors of the erstwhile Spanish colonial regime in Cuba after the Spanish-American war: the creditors knew, or should have known, the risks they faced when they made the loans to the predecessor regime, and they "took the chances of the investment."[15] Regarding the burden of proof, they can invoke the further precedent of the Tinoco Arbitration, in which US Supreme Court Justice William Howard Taft ruled in favor of the Costa Rican government in a dispute over external credits that had been diverted for the personal use of the dictator Federico Tinoco and his brother: Taft required the creditor "to discharge the burden of proving that the Costa Rican governments had used the money for legitimate purposes, something which it could not do."[16]

In effect, this strategy would accord symmetric treatment to Africa's external assets and liabilities. On both sides of the balance sheet, the burden of proof in establishing the legitimacy of claims and realizing their face value would lie with the creditors: African governments seeking to reclaim flight capital, and banks and creditor governments seeking to collect debt-service payments. The case for symmetry is reinforced by the past complicity of sub-Saharan Africa's external creditors in sustaining the power of corrupt rulers and in helping them to spirit their ill-gotten gains abroad. As *The Financial Times* (2000) remarks, in an editorial comment on the freezing of General Abacha's Swiss bank accounts, "Financial institutions that knowingly channeled the funds have much to answer for, acting not so much as bankers but as bagmen, complicit in the corruption that has crippled Nigeria." Capital flight from Nigeria under the Abacha regime was simply a particularly egregious example of a more widespread phenomenon in the subcontinent.

One concern with debt repudiation is the potential retaliation by lenders who may refuse to lend to countries whose governments opt to exercise the odious debt doctrine. However, this concern may be exaggerated. First, many African countries currently in fact receive little in terms of net flows of debt; indeed many are experiencing negative net transfers, paying more in debt service than they receive in new money. Thus such debtor countries can easily endure the "punishment" of credit rationing. Second, the invocation of the odious debt doctrine is not equivalent to unilateral across-the-board debt repudiation. Legitimate creditors have no reason to fear, given that all legitimate loans will be duly repaid. Applying the odious debt doctrine will enforce and reward responsible lending practices by western financial centers as well as transparent and responsible debt management by leaders in the South. Thus with respect to future lending the strategy will yield a win-win outcome for lenders and borrowers.

On the other hand, there is a risk that debtor countries would adopt an overly expansive definition of what constitutes an "odious debt" if they could repudiate such debt unilaterally, without recourse to legal proceedings to assess the merits of the case. Governments that abused the odious debt doctrine presumably would be denied further credit even for legitimate purposes, but this may not be a strong deterrent for the reason stated above. To address this concern, it would be useful to establish an international institution to adjudicate questions of debt legitimacy.[17]

In sum, the strategy of challenging the legitimacy of parts of African debts is based on three crucial arguments. First, the evidence of strong year-to-year correlations between external borrowing and capital flight implies that a substantial proportion of the borrowed funds ended up in private assets through debt-fueled capital flight. Thus, past borrowing practices failed the test of benefiting the people. Second, historical evidence gives strong indications for complicity of the lenders, who in many instances were aware (or should have been aware) of the embezzlement and mismanagement of borrowed funds and the corrupt nature of the borrowing regimes. Thus, historical evidence establishes the test of creditor awareness. Third, the debts were borrowed in the name of the people without their consent, which is obvious in the case of undemocratic regimes. These regimes only exercised their prerogatives of agents of the people in committing the nations to binding debt obligations, while reneging on their attendant obligation of acting in the interest of the people. Thus, borrowing practices did not meet the condition of consent by the people. Consequently, much of Africa's accumulated debts may be deemed as odious and their legitimacy challenged by the people of debtor nations.

We argue that the burden of proof of legitimacy of debts must rest on the lenders. Indeed, given the practices of secrecy in western financial centers, it will be impossible for African governments to locate more than a very small fraction of the stolen funds that are stashed in foreign banks or other investments. Enforcing the doctrine of odious debt will result in a win-win situation for borrowers and lenders in future years. By inducing responsible lending by Western financial institutions and accountable debt management by African governments, the strategy will both maximize the gains from external resources for African economies and minimize the risk of default, maximizing profits for western bankers. As the African continent searches for ways to reach financial stability and increase resources for development financing, we believe that the strategies outlined in this paper for addressing the problem of capital flight must feature prominently in debates at the national level as well as in the international development assistance community.

Appendix

Table 7.A1 Descriptive statistics and sources for variables used in the econometric analysis

Variable	Observations	Mean	Std. Dev	Min	Max	Source
Capital flight/GDP (%)	1218	7.16	22.53	−158.67	188.66	Authors' calculations (see text)
Total debt/GDP (%)	1287	106.61	88.75	0.79	806.16	Global Development Finance (CDROM); IFS for South Africa
Change in debt/GDP (%)	1253	8.04	16.28	−143.60	162.13	Authors' calculations from total debt adjusted for exchange rate fluctuations
Real GDP growth (%)	1268	7.58	17.53	−74.35	139.56	World Development Indicators (WDI), CDROM
Inflation variability	820	28.08	111.53	0.12	1392.39	Authors' computation using data from WDI as the absolute value of the difference between actual inflation and predicted inflation (obtained from a linear regression of inflation on time)
Private credit/GDP (%)	1096	25.34	21.91	−77.38	144.25	WDI
Interest rate differential	862	14.91	162.97	−19.07	4000.07	Computed using data from WDI as: (real US Tbill rate) − (real deposit rate for the African country)
Fuel exports (% of total exports)	584	16.46	28.11	0.00007	99.66	World Bank Africa Database ("mineral fuels", SITC Section 3)
Polity2 index	847	−2.26	5.97	−10.00	10.00	Polity IV Project database
Non-bank private deposits in foreign banks (% of GDP)	1047	8.91	8.11	0.00	82.35	Bank for International Settlements: http://www.bis.org/statistics/bankstats.htm.

Notes

1 For discussions of the methodology for the computation of capital flight, see Lessard and Williamson (1987); Ajayi (1997); and Boyce and Ndikumana (2001).

2 This misinvoicing adjustment methodology, first applied by Gulati (1987), has been widely used in capital flight estimation.

3 For details on the first adjustment, see Boyce and Ndikumana (2001); for details on the second two, see Ndikumana and Boyce (2008).

4 Kahn (1991, p. iv) suggests that in the South African case, in some periods "the need to finance capital flight might account for all the accumulation of external debt."

5 Predicted inflation is obtained from a linear regression of inflation on time.

6 "Fuel exports" consist of "mineral fuels" (SITC Section 3) as reported in the World Bank Africa Database (and World Development Indicators).

7 As a proxy of governance we used the Polity2 index from Polity IV Project's database which ranges from −10 (strongly autocratic) to +10 (strongly democratic).

8 In our estimation procedure, we account for outliers by using the robust ordinary least squares estimation technique.

9 Again the use of country fixed effects, which mask inter-country differences in the polity index, may be part of the explanation. Summary statistics for our sample show that capital flight is lowest in countries with either the most democratic or the most autocratic regimes, and highest in countries in the intermediate range implying a nonlinear relationship.

10 These data are published by the Bank for International Settlements, available online at http://www.bis.org/statistics/bankstats.htm.

11 This proxy of capital flight is positively correlated with our measure of capital flight. The correlation coefficient (using time series, i.e. including time and cross-sectional dimensions) between capital flight and foreign bank liabilities is 0.33 (significant at 1 percent level).

12 A good example is the case of debt issued to the apartheid regime in South Africa which by and large was used to consolidate the oppressive regime. Since all the lenders knew very well that the regime was illegitimate and violated all human rights, the post-apartheid regime could have claimed that past debts are odious. See Walker and Nattrass (2002) for a discussion of the South African case.

13 For discussion, see Jochnick (2006) and Buchheit *et al.* (2007).

14 Referring to domestic law, Buchheit *et al.* (2007, p. 1252) write: "We believe that governmental corruption in some countries is so suffocatingly ubiquitous that a U.S. court could legitimately shift onto the plaintiff [i.e. a creditor seeking redress for non-repayment] the burden of showing that a particular transaction was *not* tainted by corruption. . . . Against a showing of pervasive corruption, is it unreasonable to ask the plaintiff/lender to explain how it alone had managed to preserve its virtue in dealing with the corrupt regime?"

15 For discussion, see Hoeflich (1982) and Ndikumana and Boyce (1998).

16 Howse (2007, p. 15); for discussion, see also Buchheit *et al.* (2007).

17 The Norwegian government has called for the creation of an "international debt settlement court" for this purpose. See the Soria Moria Declaration on International Policy, October 2005; available at http://www.dna.no/index.gan?id = 47619&subid = 0.

References

Ajayi, I. S., 1997. "Analysis of external debt and capital flight in the severely indebted low income countries in Sub-Saharan Africa," IMF, Working Paper WP/97/68.

Boyce, J.K., 1992. "The revolving door? External debt and capital flight: a Philippine case study." *World Development*, 20 (3): 335–49.

Boyce, J.K. and L. Ndikumana, 2001. "Is Africa a net creditor? New estimates of capital flight from severely indebted sub-Saharan African countries, 1970–96." *Journal of Development Studies*, 38(2): 27–56.

Buchheit, L.C., G.M. Gulati and R.B. Thompson, 2007. "The dilemma of odious debts." *Duke Law Journal*, 56: 1201–62.

Collier, P., A. Hoeffler and C. Pattillo, 2001. "Flight capital as a portfolio choice," *World Bank Economic Review*, 15 (1): 55–80.

——, 2004. "Africa's exodus: Capital flight and the brain drain as portfolio decisions." *Journal of African Economies*, 13(2): 15–54.

Fedderke, J.W. and W. Liu, 2002. "Modeling the determinants of capital flows and capital flight: with an application to South African data from 1960 to 1995." *Economic Modeling* 19: 419–44.

Gulati, S., 1987. "A Note on Trade Misinvoicing." in D.R.Lessard and J. Williamson (Eds.), *Capital Flight and Third World Debt*. Washington, D.C.: Institute for International Economics. pp. 68–79.

Henry, J., 1986. "Where the money went: Third World debt hoax," *The New Republic*, (April 14), 20–3.

Higgins, M.L., A. Hysenbegasi, and S. Pozo, 2004. "Exchange-rate uncertainty and workers' remittances." *Applied Financial Economics*, 14: 403–11.

Hoeflich, M.E., 1982. "Through a glass darkly: reflections upon the history of the international law of public debt in connection with state succession." *University of Illinois Law Review* 1: 39–70.

——, 2007a. "The concept of odious debt in public international law." Geneva: United Nations Conference on Trade and Development (UNCTAD), Discussion Paper No. 185.

International Monetary Fund 2007b, *Balance of Payment Statistics*, CD ROM edition.

——, 2007. *Direction of Trade Statistics*, CD ROM edition.

Jayachandran, S. and M. Kremer, 2006. "Odious debt." *American Economic Review*, 96(1): 82–92.

Jochnick, C., 2006. "The legal case for debt repudiation." In C. Jochnick and F.A. Preston, eds., *Sovereign Debt at the Crossroads*. Oxford: Oxford University Press, 132–57.

Kahn, B., 1991. "Capital flight and exchange controls in South Africa." London: London School of Economics, Centre for the Study of the South African Economy and International Finance, Research Paper No. 4.

Khalfan, A., 2003. "Advancing the odious debt doctrine." CISDL Working Paper (March).

King, J.A., 2007. "Odious debt: The terms of the debate." *North Carolina Journal of International Law and Commercial Regulation*, 32: 605–68.

Kremer, M. and S. Jayachandran, 2002. "Odious debt." NBER working paper 8953.

——, 2003. "Odious debt: when dictators borrow, who repays the loan?" *Brookings Review*, 21 (2).

Lessard, D.R. and J. Williamson (Eds.), 1987. *Capital Flight and Third World Debt*. Washington, D.C.: Institute for International Economics.

Ndikumana, L. and J.K. Boyce, 1998. "Congo's odious debt: external borrowing and capital flight in Zaïre." *Development and Change*, 29: 1995–217.

——, 2003. "Public debts and private assets: explaining capital flight from sub-Saharan African Countries." *World Development*, 31 (1): 107–30.

——, 2008. 'New estimates of capital flight from Sub-Saharan African countries: linkages with external borrowing and policy options,' Amherst, MA: Political Economy Research Institute, Working Paper No. 166.

Sack, A.N., 1927. *Les effets de transformations des états sur leur dettes publiques et autres obligations financières*. Paris: Recueil Sirey.

The Financial Times, 1999. "Nigeria seeks help in tracing billions 'taken' by former military leaders." 23 July, p. 5.

Walker, R. and N. Nattrass, 2002. "Don't owe, won't pay! a critical analysis of the Jubilee SA position on South African government debt." *Development South Africa*, 19 (4): 467–81.

World Bank, 1985. *World Development Report 1985*. Washington, D.C.: World Bank.

8   Democratising social welfare in Africa

Stephen Devereux and Francie Lund

Introduction

This chapter explores the main historical and contemporary trajectories of social welfare policy in Africa, a continent where vulnerabilities and needs for social assistance have consistently exceeded provision, often by orders of magnitude. Across the world, social policy is seen as a residual component of public policy, an add-on after macroeconomic policy and investment in 'productive' sectors, ameliorating the unequalising effects of capitalism. In sub-Saharan Africa, social welfare has been equated for decades in the popular imagination with humanitarian relief, delivered by western donors in the form of emergency food aid. This is, however, overly simplistic and ahistorical.

Africa's complex history of welfare has its genesis in pre-colonial systems of mutual support and indigenous risk-pooling mechanisms, which have their contemporary counterparts in informal institutions such as savings clubs and burial societies. During the colonial period these mechanisms were overlaid by imported models of social security, which took different forms in anglophone and francophone territories. Further layers of complexity were added in the post-colonial period, when government policies and programmes were complemented or subverted by donor agendas and NGO projects.

Characteristic of all these mechanisms and institutions are eligibility criteria that define the rules of inclusion and exclusion. Wealthier, formally employed urban individuals generally enjoy preferential coverage and security; informal workers, smallholder farmers and minority groups generally remain uncovered and unprotected against life-cycle and livelihood shocks. Even today, these groups rely on the benevolence of governments, donors and NGOs. Whether they receive social assistance or not, who benefits, by how much and for how long, is largely a matter of chance.

The anchoring argument of this chapter is that 'welfare' in Africa must be upgraded from discretionary, supply-driven, *ad hoc* interventions that are largely externally financed and benefit relatively few vulnerable individuals, to institutionalised systems that respond adequately to needs and are grounded in citizen rights, legislation and accountability – a 'social contract' between the state and citizens. A fundamental distinction must be drawn between imported (donor-driven) social protection projects and indigenous (government-owned) social welfare systems. The former model is a necessary but highly imperfect and risky step on the road towards the latter. In short, what is needed is the 'democratisation of welfare' in Africa.

The chapter proceeds with a brief review of the evolution of welfare policy in Africa, from pre-colonial to post-colonial times. Next, welfare interventions are explored, focusing mainly on social security and social assistance (not education, health or social services), and following a 'life-course' approach as a framing construct – children, working-age adults, and older persons. The discussion of children draws a sharp contrast between government pro-grammes, using South Africa's Child Support Grant as a case study, and donor-supported initiatives such as 'child-sensitive social protection'. The discussion of working-age adults draws a distinction between first, people who are contractually covered by social security provisions and second, people in the informal sector and self-employment, who are potentially covered by initiatives to extend workers' rights and protections to these sectors. A third group – mostly rural farming families – are entirely uncovered, and depend for social protection on indigenous mechanisms and erratic, inadequate provision of public works employment or (most recently) 'social cash transfers'. Finally, the main welfare provision for older persons is social pension schemes, which are spreading throughout southern Africa, partly as a response to the increasing burden of care imposed on older per-sons by the impacts of HIV and AIDS.

Historical trajectories

Before the 1990s, little systematic scholarship about social welfare dealt with the African continent as an entity. Addressing the political economy of wel-fare requires a framework for dealing with the continent as a whole, for characterising historical and contemporary trends. The contemporary work on 'welfare regimes' relies heavily on a few seminal sources – Mouton's sys-tematic description of social security systems in Africa (1975); Midgley's analysis of social security and inequality in 'the Third World', including Africa (1984); and Iliffe's volume on the poor in Africa (1987) which has extensive data on non-formal as well as formal systems. All of these follow a similar periodisation – pre-colonial, early missionary influences, early and late colonial developments, the independence period and beyond.

Iliffe (1987) noted that in the pre-colonial period there was a reliance on family networks and patronage, in largely rural, subsistence-oriented soci-eties. Countries in which there was a strong Islamic presence practised *zakat*, in which a proportion of personal income was (and still is) given to provide support for the poor and needy. In the period of early European influence, Christian orders had the primary purpose of religious conversion, and also introduced welfare systems to support the poor and indigent.

For the pre-colonial period, one strand of historical work has constructed a romanticised image of African communities and kingdoms, which are presented as having had complex consumption smoothing and risk-pooling mechanisms, such as village grain banks and 'chief's fields', which supported vulnerable community members and provided some protection against bad years. These societies were not in fact egalitarian, but extremely hierarchical. The 'dark side' of the moral economy was reflected in subordinate community members becoming indebted to powerful families, or pawning their daughters as servants or child brides. Also, while these traditional mechanisms were effective against minor to moderate shocks, they could not protect against severe or protracted shocks, which often resulted in community-wide destitution (Watts, 1983). This debate has relevance to contemporary social protection debates, because the 'myth' persists that African society is more 'caring and sharing' and less acquisitive and materialistic than are other societies. This view has been invoked in the World Bank argument that public transfers might merely 'crowd out' private transfers and savings, providing a justification for limited public welfare interventions (Cox and Jimenez, 1995).

Mouton (1975) and Iliffe (1987) drew attention to the differences in social provision between countries in Africa settled by France and by Britain, showing how they reflected different forms of colonial domination. French colonies were ruled as extensions of France, staffed by the French, with power centralised in Paris. More generous social security benefits were provided than those first introduced by British colonial administrations, and legislation was introduced sooner to extend benefits to local workers. Cooper (1996) showed how different approaches to the relationship between a modernising and industrialising (mostly male) workforce and family life reflected different traditions in the respective metropoles. The French were more open to a broader conception of the family wage and family allowances – their minds doubtless focused by the 1946 general strike in Senegal, which pursued a demand that workers in the colonies should have identical work conditions, including social benefits, as workers in France. The British had a more restrictive and ambiguous approach, as emerged in the early 1950s, when ILO member countries were actually required to implement the ILO conventions on family wages and allowances (Cooper, 1996: 330). In parallel, after 1948, post-colonial South Africa proceeded apace with the implementation of 'separate development' policies which had at their core the separation of male labourers from their families, thrusting responsibility for the reproduction of African family life on to rural non-wage-earning household members.

Social security schemes were introduced first to support the colonial administrations, then civil administrations and the military, but excluded most poor people, specifically those in rural areas. Their rapid expansion in Africa in the thirty years from the 1950s to 1970s coincided with the independence of many African countries. Reviewing this expansion, Midgley (1984) concludes that social security schemes had on the whole served to reinforce and amplify existing inequality, and entrenched the division between 'modern' and 'subsistence' sectors. Midgley (1984: 111) suggested that this differential colonial influence extended also to the broader welfare sector: the informal 'mutual benefit societies' in Belgian and French territories (Congo, Algeria) were based on the European 'friendly society' model. By contrast, Britain's 'indirect rule' in Africa led to more local control, but often with racial rules of inclusion and exclusion, and with more categories of worker being excluded.

In 1990, Esping-Anderson's pioneering work on welfare state regimes in industrialised countries transformed the political analysis of social policy (Esping-Andersen, 1990). His central concern was the role of the state in contemporary advanced welfare states, and how welfare provision moulds class formation in terms of both the receivers (the effects of getting free health care, housing, state pensions, for example), and of the providers. His work generated a new wave of interest in global social policy, and the extent to which welfare state (now welfare regime) analysis could be applied to regions outside 'the north' (see for example Barrientos (2004) for Latin America, and Gough (2004) for East Asia).

Turning to Africa, Bevan (2004) suggests that sub-Saharan Africa can be characterised as an 'in/security regime'. The factors that accompanied colonial domination – urbanisation, migrant labour, separation of men from families, insertion of women into labour markets – weakened and eroded 'traditional' forms of support. Bevan suggests that Africa is so diverse that it defies regional regime analysis, and she goes so far as to look inside individual countries for different elements of 'in/security regimes': some (usually small) segments of the population have access to relatively advanced and secure welfare provision, either sourced domestically or purchased outside, while others rely on informal traditional security mechanisms, and many depend directly on dangerous and illegal work and networks to survive. This 'inside one country' approach appears to be at odds with the purpose of regime analysis, however. Cooper's (1996) deeply historical exploration of one aspect of welfare provision – in his case, a comparison of work-related social security in French and British colonies – could be a more fruitful approach to understanding the forces that shaped the exceptionally uneven welfare provision that exists in Africa today.

Destremau with Yaghi (2007) attempt to apply a welfare regime analysis to a selection of countries in the Middle East and North Africa (MENA) region. They capture the commonalities between Arabic-speaking states, especially the fundamental influence of religious and cultural norms in determining women's and men's differential access to social security. They note a recent 'renaissance' of religious forms of involvement with charitable work, from declared Islamic political parties, members of royal families, well-known politicians and others (Destremau with Yaghi, 2007: 6). At the same time, there are clear differences within the region: Algeria, Egypt and Tunis, in particular, have a version of 'restricted Bismarckian professionalism' with a relatively good public health service, the extension of social protection, and inclusion within social security systems of new groups of workers such as agricultural workers and the self-employed (Destremau with Yaghi, 2007: 37). They hold that this is an identifiably different type of welfare regime to the much more restricted state provision that pertains to Morocco, and to the statist patrimonial systems in the Gulf States.

Globally, some argue that sovereign states have come to have less autonomy over their social policies, with social aspects of citizenship developing regional and international dimensions (Deacon *et al.*, 1997: 17), related to the fact that international forces are shaping the policy agendas of national governments (Alcock and Craig, 2009: 5). In Europe for example, old and new European Union members try to harmonise their actions, in the interests of greater economic competitiveness and regional citizens' solidarity. In highly aid-dependent countries, international financial institutions (IFIs) and donors have imposed increasingly homogenised poverty reduction strategies and social protection policies. Some of these externally designed approaches to social welfare in Africa are discussed below.

Welfare over the life-course

Children

Fulfilled, healthy and productive adulthood depends on certain building blocks being put in place in the first few years of a child's life. Later programmes – in primary and secondary education, in post-school bridging and remedial education, in industrial training – cannot remedy early deficits in nutrition and cognitive development. Children face multiple and inter-related vulnerabilities – malnutrition, orphanhood, lack of shelter, displacement as refugees, poor access to health and education, abuse and violence, participating as child combatants in war. Children are excluded from consideration in most of development economics, and indeed in development studies. In this section we consider different routes through which children in Africa have been included in, or excluded from, social welfare provision.

A striking difference between social security in Francophone and Anglophone countries in Africa was the introduction in the former of child allowances (as distinct from family allowances discussed above) as part of the benefits attached to formal waged work in the public and/or private sector. A child benefit was introduced in Arab-speaking French colonies in the 1940s, and in much of Francophone and Belgian Africa through the mid-1950s (Midgley, 1984: 120). These benefits were financed through a payroll tax on employers, set at a percentage of the minimum wage, and were often subsidised by government. They varied as to how many children were eligible – three in Tunisia, six in Senegal, for example. These schemes largely covered only the urban formal labour force, with agricultural and informal workers being specifically excluded. Attempts to withdraw such schemes after independence were resisted by those organised workers who benefited from them. In North Africa, the family allowances that remain accrue automatically to the man's salary, for his wife and children. Senegal retains child and family allowances in legislation, but very few children are now covered, because of the small numbers of workers in regular formal employment. South Africa, on the other hand, went a different route, implementing a family allowance that was not linked to formal employment.

State social assistance: South Africa's child support grant

South Africa's post-apartheid government inherited a means tested cash transfer that was initially designed to protect white women and children, and by the 1970s went predominantly to coloured and Indian women in urban areas, and to very few Africans (Lund, 2008: 14–17). It was based on a model of nuclear family life that was inappropriate to South Africa. The post-apartheid government sought to introduce a system of support for children and families that would reach the poorest children, especially in rural areas, and that could be administered despite the diverse and complex family structures, high rates of orphanhood and high rates of 'granny care'. An unconditional cash transfer for children in poor households was introduced in 1998, replacing the old state maintenance grant for women and children (see Lund, 2008, for an account of this reform). Within ten years it was being paid to the primary caregivers of over 10 million children. It was introduced at a very low level (R100* per month) for children up to the age of seven. Over the next decade, strong advocacy from children's rights organisations articulated with progress made by the post-apartheid revenue services in collecting taxes, and a significant part of the annual fiscal surplus went to extending the grant. Age eligibility has been gradually extended to 15 years, and since 2002 small increases have been made annually, to the level of R200 per month at the end of 2008. Early studies of its performance show positive effects on school enrolment (Case *et al.*, 2005).

The grant is means tested, which makes it expensive to administer, and the amount is not enough to cover the actual costs of caring for children. Despite these shortcomings, it is based on the child's constitutional right to social security, and it is written into legislation. It is funded from general government revenue, and there are (usually) annual increments. It reaches significant numbers of children in need. There is ongoing contestation between government and advocacy groups about improvements in the level and administration of the grant. There are relatively transparent monitoring arrangements, with government regularly releasing data about take-up. It therefore contains some of the essential elements of a democratised system.

---

* Rand–dollar rate at time of writing (March 2010): US$1 = R7.42.

Donor-supported assistance: orphans and other vulnerable
children (OVC) projects

Recognising the particular vulnerabilities of children, especially in contexts of high AIDS-prevalence as in much of Africa, several governments and donors have recently initiated social protection programmes targeted at children or their carers. Drawing from the Convention on the Rights of the Child (CRC) and the African Charter on the Rights and Welfare of the Child, UNICEF (2008) argues for a range of interventions to provide both 'child protection' (against violence and social deprivation) and 'child-sensitive social protection' (against poverty and economic deprivation). Under the child protection objective, governments are encouraged to reform their legal and judicial systems to provide equal protection to women and children, and to draft comprehensive Children's Acts.

Under the social protection objective, several donors are implementing cash transfer programmes targeted at poor families, usually calibrated by household size and often using high dependency ratios as an eligibility criterion, in order to reach orphans and female-headed households. An evaluation of one pilot programme in Malawi found statistically significant positive impacts on children in intervention *versus* control households, including: lower reported sickness in children, lower incidence of malnutrition (wasting, stunting and underweight), higher expenditure on children's health-care and education, and a reduction in child labour (Miller *et al.*, 2008).

Two concerns have been raised about child-focused cash transfer projects. The first is that they depend on a model of intra-household relations that might not hold in reality – for instance, cash transfers collected by men might not reach children as directly as would food transfers under the control of women (Slater and Mphale, 2008). The second is that the fashion for cash transfers (discussed below) might deflect resources away from other interventions that target vulnerable children directly, such as community-based growth promotion and community-based management of acute malnutrition (Vaitla *et al.*, 2009).

Supporting advocacy for children

Children cannot advocate for themselves, and for the majority, their female carers are likely to be vulnerable as well. They are spoken for by international organisations such as UNICEF, Oxfam, CARE and Save the Children. Within Africa, there are some highly effective organisations and networks focusing on getting a better deal for children. All are grounded in a child rights framework, and some bring, in addition, sophisticated technical skills to their advocacy work. The Children's Budget, initiated in South Africa and also active in Ghana and Uganda, is an offshoot of the 'gender budgeting' stream of work. It aims both to make governments more aware of how their budgetary allocations help and hinder child development, and to give civil society organisations the tools to advocate for better provision for children. The African Child Policy Forum, based in Addis Ababa, scores and ranks African governments in terms of their 'child-friendliness' according to a set of specific indicators. The Forum aims to encourage governments to move beyond the promises made in innumerable treaties, conventions, declarations and accords, into concrete progress towards meeting these commitments.

People of working age

Welfare provision in industrialised societies is based on assumptions about what working people will be able to contribute, throughout their working lives, to the management of their own risk, and to the security of the next generation of workers. Demographic changes, in conjunction with changes in the structure of the labour market – including gendered changes in labour force participation – have meant that worldwide there is a mismatch between welfare needs and welfare provision for people of working age.

Heintz and Valodia (2008), working with data from sub-Saharan African countries, make the following broad generalisations about the structure of employment informal. Employment accounts for a larger share of total employment than does formal employment (for example, formal workers constitute only 13.6 per cent of all employment in Kenya, 8.7 per cent in Ghana, and 10.9 per cent in Mali); women work disproportionately in informal employment; agricultural and non-agricultural self-employment are significant sources of employment for both men and women; agricultural employment remains important; the public sector remains an important source of formal employment; men have greater access to both formal and informal wage employment (Heintz and Valodia, 2008: 10). The situation in North Africa is different from the rest of Africa, and indeed from the rest of the world: formal employment constitutes a larger share of women's employment than men's; women have a higher share of agricultural work than men; within the informal sector, informal wage employment is more important than own account work; and women have a very high rate of working as unpaid workers in family enterprises (Heintz, 2008).

There are direct implications for work security and social security. First, the majority of workers in Africa are excluded from core labour legislation, by the nature of their category of work – agricultural workers, domestic workers, family workers, the self-employed. Then there is a second round of exclusion, from social security provision. In this section, we outline the provisions first for contractually covered workers, then for informal and casualised workers, and then describe public works programmes for unemployed people of working age.

Contractually covered work

Employment-related social security was initially introduced through colonial governments to cover their own staff, then expatriate and local civil servants, then extended to local populations in formal employment (Midgley, 1984: 116). This social insurance was funded by employer and employee contributions, sometimes with government subsidising and/or under-writing as well. Typically it covered invalidity, compensation for work-related disability, benefits for survivors in the case of death of the worker, and retirement schemes. It rarely reached rural areas, and therefore excluded agricultural workers and smallholder farmers. Midgley (1984) speculated that because of the structure of labour markets leading to limited coverage, such work-related schemes would serve to 'amplify inequalities'. They would transfer resources from those not covered (the poor) to better-off (urban) formal workers in more secure, albeit low-paid, jobs. Such schemes typically also have a strong bias against women. More men than women are in formal employment, and spouses and children get benefits through working males.

The civil service has been important as a source of secure employment, for women as well as for men. In North Africa, Destremau with Yaghi (2007) describe fairly good social security coverage of those in the formal public and private sectors. However, the long arm of structural adjustment has reached into North Africa, with accompanying reduction in the size of civil services which will affect the long-term security of both women and men, including especially women with higher education such as teachers and nurses.

Falling between properly informal and properly formal workers are those who hold temporary contracts. There is a paradox here: in both North Africa and South Africa, workers' rights and benefits have been enhanced through progressive legislation, but employers who want to evade the associated costs and responsibilities have responded by 'casualising' their workforces: permanent workers have become seasonal workers, day workers or contractualised (though full-time) workers. Instead of enjoying greater protections and rights, affected workers have lost the limited benefits they previously enjoyed, and have become more vulnerable than before.

There is a growing increase worldwide in the service sector, and in the numbers of women who migrate in search of domestic employment. For many poorer workers, migration is a step into increasing vulnerability. Women from West Africa who travel to the Middle East for domestic work are typically contracted through labour brokers and undergo complex formal procedures, including health examinations. Once in the homes of employers, many 'disappear' from view, hand over their passports, and are neither protected by labour legislation nor covered by social security (Esim and Smith, 2004). In South Africa on the other hand, domestic workers are now covered by basic labour legislation, and by some social security measures such as unemployment insurance. South Africa also receives large numbers of Zimbabwean and other African migrants who do domestic work or farm labour; as visitors, they have no rights to South African social security. More generally, Africa's high numbers of migrant workers face problems of accessing social protection and social security in destination countries, and limited 'portability' of benefits from their country of origin (Sabates-Wheeler and Macauslan, 2007).

Informal work

Informal employment (including the unregistered self-employed, and wage workers) comprises the majority of all non-agricultural employment in sub-Saharan Africa, averaging 72 per cent (ILO, 2002). There is a strong gender dimension: 84 per cent of all African women who work, work informally, compared to 63 per cent of men. Informal work is by definition work with no employer-related social protection. How do informal workers save, and manage risk?

Across the world, poorer informal workers say that their greatest work-related needs are for reliable incomes and better incomes. Thereafter, a high priority is freedom from harassment by local authorities, pointing to the vital role that local, not national, government plays in determining everyday working conditions of the majority of workers – those who work in public places (streets, pavements, parks), and in their own homes.

Rotating savings and credit associations (ROSCAs) are found throughout Africa (see Skinner, 2008: 24, 25 for a review of ROSCA practices among African street traders), and are a useful financial management tool for millions of (mostly) women. They seldom reach the poorest of the poor, because of the need to make regular contributions; further, high HIV and AIDS prevalence rates (as are found in many African countries) are associated with stress on such indigenous mechanisms, as members draw down savings more often to pay for health and funeral costs. Informal burial societies are a widespread mechanism for ensuring dignified death ceremonies. With growing numbers of AIDS-related deaths, formal insurance institutions in southern Africa have been quick to extend their coverage, in some places making linkages with the informal societies.

East Africa is particularly noted for its micro-savings and micro-insurance schemes, whereas Francophone West Africa has a stronger tradition of mutual health insurance ('mutuelles'). Both types of schemes face problems of financial sustainability and expanding membership (Atim, 1999; Ekman, 2004; Coheur *et al.*, 2007: 5). It is hard for poor people to co-insure against risk, and expensive for organisations to increase coverage to go to scale in contexts where financial institutions, transport and technology are scarce and expensive for the poor (Dercon, 2004). Micro-schemes rely heavily on women's voluntary work, and under-estimate the amount of time and money already spent by poorer people, again mostly women, in caring for the increasing numbers of AIDS-infected people who have inadequate access to formal health services.

The ILO has committed to extending social protection to all, as part of its 'Decent Work for All' agenda (ILO, 2006). However, actually extending formal social security to informal workers is very hard to achieve. South Africa introduced a minimum wage 'sectoral determination' for domestic workers (about 1 million, largely poor women) in 2002, and these workers were included in the unemployment insurance fund (UIF). In Mauritius, workers who left formal employment were encouraged to remain in the insurance scheme and to continue making voluntary contributions, but the numbers who did so were very small.

Additional and new institutional relationships and linkages are necessary. The Ghanaian Trade Union Congress (GTUC) is one of the few formal worker organisations worldwide to have attempted to create linkages between formal and informal workers. Prompted by its rapid decline in membership because of structural changes in employment, the GTUC has enabled partial membership status of informal workers. They are allowed to contribute to union savings schemes even though there is no matching employer contribution, and they can use union savings as collateral for securing small loans from banks. Skinner (2008: 25) reports similar emerging links between formal unions and members of informal trader organisations in Malawi, Mozambique and Zimbabwe.

A new type of north-south partnership is being planned by the Global Social Trust, and facilitated by the ILO. Luxembourg workers who belong to a trade union would contribute a small part of their monthly income to enable Ghanaian women workers to receive a small conditional cash transfer, during and after pregnancy. The ILO is facilitating this intervention. Whether or not this initiative is implemented, it has raised the possibility of a model that could be adapted by other, larger international worker federations, and could also draw in employer organisations. Other possible innovative routes to pursue for improved social benefits for informal workers are through trade agreements, fair trade and ethical trade initiatives.

The changed nature of the labour market and employment relations needs to be factored in to economic and social theory. Dominant economic theories assume a surplus labour market, rather than recognising the barriers to entry to formal employment, and the difficulties of moving between informal and formal employment. They assume a predominantly waged labour market, whereas in most African countries, self-employment in the informal economy constitutes a significant proportion of all employment (more so for men than for women). More realistic models are important, both for macroeconomic theory and for understanding the scope and limitations of social protection (Heintz, 2008).

Public works

Public works programmes are an active labour market intervention that responds to problems of seasonal underemployment, deagrarianisation and rural landlessness, as well as high levels of structural unemployment caused by limited job creation potential in low-income economies. Food-for-work programmes have been one of the most popular anti-poverty interventions with governments and donors in Africa for decades, partly because they aim to address two problems faced by the chronically poor – food insecurity and unemployment or underemployment – and partly because the work requirement supposedly ensures self-targeting, avoids perceived 'welfare dependency' (behavioural changes allegedly induced by social grants, such as disincentives to seek work) and resonates with ideological constructs of the 'deserving poor'. Self-targeting in public works is achieved both by lowering the benefits, through setting the wage below local market rates and paying participants with food (food-for-work) rather than with cash, and by raising the costs of accessing these benefits, through requiring participants to perform heavy manual labour.

Public works programmes are controversial. Critics argue that they create few useful assets; that the quality of assets created is sub-standard; that inadequate attention to maintenance results in their rapid deterioration; that the work requirement excludes the most vulnerable people; that paying low wages is unethical and counterproductive to poverty reduction objectives; and that paying people with food rations is demeaning (Devereux and Solomon, 2006; McCord, 2008). In response, efforts have been made to ensure that public works assets such as rural feeder roads and micro-dams are directly beneficial to the workers who construct or maintain them, and 'decent work' principles have been introduced on some projects, such as paying fair wages. Ethiopia's Productive Safety Net Programme addresses the vulnerability of people who cannot perform manual labour by complementing public works (for approximately 85 per cent of 'able-bodied' participants) with 'direct support' (free cash or food transfers to approximately 15 per cent of 'labour-constrained' participants).

Recognition of gender inequities in public works programmes has also led to some progressive modifications being adopted. First, gender quotas have been applied, though this can be counter-productive if it forces women to take on heavy additional workloads simply to acquire food that was previously provided by men. Second, work intensity and time expenditure can both be reduced for women. On some food-for-work projects in Ethiopia, activities are classified as 'light', 'medium' or 'heavy', with women being allocated only 'light' and 'medium' tasks (e.g. providing child-care at worksites); women also work fewer hours than men, in recognition of their heavier domestic responsibilities. Sometimes projects are selected because they have labour-saving implications for women, such as digging boreholes and planting trees, to reduce women's 'drudge time' on water and firewood collection. South Africa has introduced public works programmes in the areas of home-based care work (caring for ill and frail elderly people), and pre-school care.

Finally, public works rarely operate on a scale adequate to meet employment needs. Reviewing the evidence from South Africa and Malawi, McCord

(2008: 169) concludes that 'the effectiveness of small-scale, temporary public works programmes in the context of chronic poverty and mass under- or unemployment is trivial'. Government as employer of last resort works best in employment guarantee schemes, as in India where the National Rural Employment Guarantee Act entitles every poor rural Indian household up to 100 days of work a year at the local minimum wage.

Democratising public works includes ensuring that assets created are directly useful to participants, that wages are not set unethically low as a self-targeting mechanism, that women are neither neglected nor over-burdened, and that public works are complemented with interventions that reach all needy people who are unable to work. Ultimately, though, public works programmes have largely failed as an anti-poverty intervention in Africa. Effective labour market intervention requires more innovative models, such as wage subsidies or demand-driven employment guarantee schemes.

Cash transfers

The main form taken by donor-provided social assistance to Africa until the early 2000s was emergency food aid, which was heavily criticised for its ineffectiveness in addressing either chronic poverty or the underlying causes of hunger and food insecurity. In response, several donors started promoting 'predictable social cash transfers' as a form of minimal social welfare for poor families, in countries too poor to afford comprehensive social welfare or social security systems.

Evaluations of many cash transfer programmes have found powerful positive impacts on a range of outcome indicators, from poverty and food security to education and health. Predictable cash transfers allow vulnerable families to protect their assets instead of selling them to meet basic needs, and to invest in farming and micro-enterprises. A panel survey of participants in Ethiopia's Productive Safety Net Programme found that their real incomes had increased by more than 40 per cent in two years, while the real incomes of a non-beneficiary control group had fallen by 20 per cent (Devereux *et al.*, 2008).

Concerns about the 'dependency' effects of social grants are empirically unsubstantiated. There is no evidence, for instance, to support the popular belief that South Africa's Child Support Grant (CSG) has caused an increase in teenage pregnancies because it provides financial incentives to poor women and girls to have children (Steele, 2006; Makiwane and Udjo, 2006). Steele (2006: vii) finds that: (1) 'South Africa already had a relatively high teenage fertility rate before the introduction of the CSG'; (2) 'teenagers claiming the CSG were considerably lower (13 per cent lower) than the proportion of teenage mothers in the South African population'; and (3) 'no link could be established between the availability of the CSG and the fertility behaviour of teenagers in the South African population'. Concerns that cash transfers might be misused by men have also proved to be unfounded beyond the anecdotal level, and this possibility has been circumvented in many programmes by disbursing cash transfers directly to women.

Four critiques of cash transfer pilot projects are commonly made, relating to fiscal affordability, purchasing power, administrative capacity and political commitment. First, they often operate outside government structures and are heavily dependent on external financing and technical expertise, raising questions about democratic accountability and sustainability. Second, cash transfers are vulnerable to erosion of purchasing power due to seasonal price rises or price spikes during food crises, which undermine their effectiveness in ensuring access to adequate food. This effect was highlighted by the global food price rises of 2008, which drastically eroded the value of (non-indexed) cash transfers throughout Africa. Third, pilot projects implemented at district level are rarely scaled up to national coverage, because of administrative constraints. Finally, cash transfers are generally less popular with governments than are other food security interventions such as fertiliser subsidies, raising questions about government commitment to these donor-driven programmes (Devereux and White, 2008).

Nonetheless, the momentum behind cash transfers is strong, and in cases where governments have taken the lead in introducing and financing such programmes, as with social pensions in several southern African countries (discussed below), they have rapidly become politically irreversible pillars of social policy.

Older people

The main social protection instruments targeted specifically at older people are pensions, either contributory or non-contributory ('social pensions'). Occupational and private pension schemes are activated by retirement from formal employment, and are partly funded by personal and employer contributions. Social pension schemes, which are not related to employment status and are non-contributory, are best classified as unconditional cash transfers targeted at older persons.

Although 'social protection' is a recent addition to the policy agenda in Africa, social pensions have been implemented in southern Africa for 80 years. Two waves of adoption can be discerned. South Africa introduced a social pension in 1928 and extended this to Namibia (then South-West Africa) in 1949. More recently, social pensions have been adopted by Botswana (1996), Lesotho (2004) and Swaziland (2005). Zambia has been piloting a social pension in one district since August 2007. During 2008, Malawi debated the feasibility of introducing a social pension.

There are important differences between the two waves of adoption (pre-1950 and post-1990). The 'early adopters' imported social pensions from European (Bismarckian) models of social security. In South Africa, heavily influenced by British and Dutch social policy thinking, the Old Age Pensions Act of 1928 established the right to a state-funded pension for all 'white' and 'coloured' citizens aged 65 years or older. This was a welfarist response to the structural poverty that followed the discovery of gold and diamonds, the expansion of capitalist agriculture and the subsequent displacement of small farmers into urban areas. Africans were initially excluded from the Old Age Pension on the grounds that 'Native custom makes provision for maintaining dependent persons' (Human Awareness Programme, 1983: 3). Only in 1944 was eligibility extended to Africans, but at a lower rate, the spurious justification being that Africans faced lower living costs. In Namibia – under South African administration until 1990 – Africans only became eligible for the Old Age Pension in 1973, and a complex hierarchy of seven racially defined payment levels was implemented, with white Namibians receiving seven times more than African residents of Caprivi, Okavango and Owamboland. Racially discriminatory pension payments persisted until the democratically elected SWAPO government came to power in Namibia in 1990 and just before the ANC government came to power in South Africa, in September 1993 (Devereux, 2007).

The 'late adopters' introduced social pensions for entirely different reasons. As noted above, the HIV and AIDS pandemic in Africa has its epicentre in southern Africa, the region with the highest HIV prevalence rates in the world. Much of the burden of care is falling on older persons (especially on older women), as the King of Swaziland noted when motivating the introduction of the Old Age Grant in 2005.

> HIV and AIDS continues to kill a lot of our young people who leave behind orphans and uncared for elderly parents. Some of these elderly people sometimes go without basic support and yet they are expected to also care for the orphans ... Government has decided to increase the annual allocation to the social security fund to E30 million for the benefit of our elderly poor citizens.
>
> (quoted in Ellis *et al.*, 2009: 18)

In both Lesotho and Swaziland, social pensions have become 'positively politicised'. In November 2006, a cash-flow disruption within the Department of Social Welfare meant that thousands of social pensioners in Swaziland did not receive their Old Age Grants. In a rare display in Africa of civil society activism around a social protection issue, affected pensioners lobbied their local Members of Parliament, who took up the issue in the House of Assembly. The government immediately appointed a task team comprising several Cabinet ministers and the Governor of the Central Bank, and after seven days a comprehensive plan was devised and the problem was solved.

During the February 2007 general election in Lesotho, the main opposition party campaigned on a manifesto promise to treble the Old Age Pension, forcing the government to pledge to reconsider the payment level. A post-election survey revealed that many voters decided which party to support on the basis of their respective commitments on the pension. In his first budget statement after the election, the Minister of Finance announced a 33 per cent increase in the pension level.

Surveys of social pension impacts have found significant reductions in household poverty and food insecurity in South Africa (Ardington and Lund, 1995; Barrientos, 2003; Samson *et al.*, 2004), Lesotho (Croome and Nyanguru, 2007) and Namibia (Devereux, 2007). In all three countries, social pensions are used mainly for buying food and groceries, but also to pay for health and education fees, clothing and other expenses of household members. Grandchildren of pensioners are the main secondary beneficiaries, and especially granddaughers of female pensioners (Duflo, 2003). Social pensioners also enjoy preferential access to informal credit from local stores, because of their guaranteed regular transfer income.

Although social pensions appear to be spreading, at least in southern Africa, there are constraints to further expansion across Africa. It is often argued that only middle-income countries (like Botswana, Namibia and South Africa) or small and highly unequal economies (like Lesotho and Swaziland) can afford to implement universal social pensions. Lesotho has a high poverty headcount (58 per cent) but a comparable level of inequality (a Gini coefficient of 0.66), which provides the necessary fiscal basis for redistribution. In countries with much larger populations, widespread poverty, infrastructure deficits and a small tax base (say, Ethiopia or Sudan), it is doubtful whether a social pension would be fiscally and administratively feasible. On the other hand, Lesotho's successful introduction of the pension for older citizens, with no donor support and against the advice of the IMF, suggests that the crucial ingredient for any social protection programme is political commitment.

Conclusion: 'democratising welfare' in Africa

This chapter has pointed to a number of innovations in the provision of social welfare in African countries, and to progress that has been made with programmes that deliver real resources to large numbers of people. It is a complex picture, however. We have shown that it is problematic to generalise about the continent as a whole, or even about regions within the continent. North Africa is different from sub-Saharan Africa, and within North Africa, Algeria, Egypt and Tunisia perform better than their neighbours in the provision of vital social services. Within sub-Saharan Africa, South Africa is distinctive with its large economy and relative wealth – but persistent inequality and high prevalence of AIDS mean that prospects for the poor remain bleak, and the extension of social welfare in a context of over 30 per cent unemployment has been critiqued as government's way of avoiding the underlying structural problems. Botswana, Namibia and Mauritius are similarly better placed than other countries in sub-Saharan Africa, since they have the most extensive social security systems as well as higher rates of formal employment. Bevan (who did not include South Africa in her analysis) points out that removing these three countries from the sub-region leaves very little in the field of social security, (Bevan 2004). Moreover, this is in a context of rapid urbanisation, but with very limited jobs of the sort that offer a living wage or any kind of security. A range of welfare and religious organisations offer social assistance and other services, as do donor organisations, but these are typically patchy and uneven, do not reach deep rural areas, and are not reliable for many people.

We have shown how progress has been made recently in a number of countries in introducing and sustaining cash transfers for groups of vulnerable people, in particular non-contributory pensions for elderly people. Some initiatives, such as those in Lesotho and Swaziland, have been driven by governments themselves. Others, such as those in Zambia, were introduced as pilots by external donors and are vulnerable to changing donor commitments. The 'Livingstone Call for Action', under the auspices of the African Union but robustly supported and driven by externally supported NGOs, seeks to galvanise continent-wide commitment to greater social spending, especially on cash transfers. Initiated in 2006, it is too early to say what progress will be made. It is concerned especially with those vulnerable groups outside the labour market. In another social policy terrain closely associated with the World Bank, however, there are social policy proposals that seek to dismantle the employment-related social security benefits attached to formal work altogether (see Bourguignon, 2005; Levy's (2008) proposals for Mexico; Perry *et al.*, 2007), and to substitute these with a minimum core of universal provision by the state. The implications of this for weak states, and for poor states, are alarming, with high prospects for elite co-optation, and for inadequate services. This is not the 'universalism' that the advocates for cash transfers are seeking – parallel campaigns for universal benefits could in fact erode rather than add to resources and services for poorer people, and especially for people in informal work.

Social and economic policies are related to each other. Resources allocated to education, health and social services provide for only a small part of the totality of caring and reproductive work that has to be done in all societies to ensure survival, productivity and well-being. More recognition needs to be given to unpaid care work done by family and kin. Formal and informal structures of provision are underpinned by voluntarism and (mostly women's) unpaid work in the care economy. Ironically, it may be that the AIDS pandemic will make this work more visible, with a new body of scholarship around the time and costs of unpaid care work by household members in caring for the prematurely ill. These analyses include Tanzania and South Africa (Budlender, 2008) and reveal the gendered differences in time allocated by men and by women to care work. Where formal health services are scarce or inaccessible, this care work is an additional burden on all generations of women, with lasting ill-effects on their productivity.

Finally, fundamental shifts are needed, away from unaccountable donor-driven 'social protection project' models to indigenised social welfare models. Yet there is a perplexing dormancy of civil society in much of Africa, with regard to mass mobilisation and participation around welfare rights. What forces and pressures would create *domestic* demand for accountable, contractual social protection? These would include regular elections; freedom of association and civil society mobilisation; transparent budgetary procedures; robust research evidence on the effectiveness and performance of pilot projects and longer term programmes; and ongoing parliamentary advocacy, with members of parliament able to pose questions, and receive clear answers, about efficacy and equity outcomes of public spending.

References

Alcock, P. and Craig, G. (2009) 'The international context', Chapter 1 in Alcock, P. and Craig, G. (eds): *International Social Policy: Welfare Regimes in the Developed World*, Second Edition, Houndmills, Basingstoke: Palgrave Macmillan.

Ardington, E. and Lund, F. (1995) 'Pensions and development: social security as complementary to programmes of reconstruction and development', *Development Southern Africa*, 12(4): 557–77.

Atim, C. (1999) 'Social movements and health insurance: a critical evaluation of voluntary, non-profit insurance schemes with case studies from Ghana and Cameroon', *Social Science and Medicine*, 48: 881–96.

Barrientos, A. (2003) 'What is the impact of non-contributory pensions on poverty? Estimates from Brazil and South Africa', *CPRC Working Paper*, No. 33, Manchester: Chronic Poverty Research Centre, University of Manchester.

Bevan, P. (2004) 'The dynamics of Africa's in/security regimes', in Gough, I. and Wood, G. with Barrientos, A., Bevan, P., Davis, P. and Room, G. (eds) *Insecurity and Welfare Regimes in Asia, Africa and Latin America*, Cambridge: Cambridge University Press.

Bourguignon, F. (2005) 'Development strategies for more and better jobs', paper presented at the conference 'Help Wanted: More and Better Jobs in a Globalised Economy', organised by the Carnegie Endowment for International Peace, Washington D.C., 14 April.

Budlender, D. (2008) 'The statistical evidence on care and non-care work across six countries', *Gender and Development Paper*, No. 4. Geneva: United Nations Research Institute for Social Development.

Case, A., Hosegood, V. and Lund, F. (2005) 'The reach and impact of the Child Support Grant in South Africa: evidence from KwaZulu-Natal', *Development Southern Africa*, 22(4): 467–82.

Cichon, M. and Hagemejer, K. (2007) 'Changing the development paradigm: investing in a social security floor for all', *International Social Security Review*, 60(2–3): 169–96.

Coheur, A., Jacquier, C., Schmitt-Diabaté, V. and Schremmer, J. (2007) 'Linkages between statutory social security schemes and community-based social protection mechanisms: a promising new approach', *Technical Report*, 09, Geneva: International Social Security Association.

Cooper, F. (1996) *Decolonisation and African society: the labour question in French and British Africa*. Cambridge: Cambridge University Press.

Cox, D. and Jimenez, E. (1995) 'Private transfers and the effectiveness of public income redistribution in the Philippines', in van de Walle, D. and Nead, K. (eds), *Public Spending and the Poor*. Baltimore: Johns Hopkins University Press.

Croome, D. and Nyanguru, A. (2007) 'The impact of the old age pension on hunger and vulnerability in a mountain area of Lesotho', report written for the Regional Hunger and Vulnerability Programme. Maseru: National University of Lesotho.

Deacon. B. with Hulse, M. and Stubbs, P. (1997) *Global Social Policy: International Organisations and the Future of Welfare*, London: Sage Publications Ltd.

Dercon, S. (ed.) (2004) *Insurance against Poverty*. Oxford: Oxford University Press.

Destremau, B. with AbiYaghi, M.N. (2007) 'The social protection challenge: how can informal workers enjoy social rights in Arab countries? A regional gendered perspective', paper presented at the ILO/ CAWTAR regional research workshop on *Gender and Rights in the Informal Economies of Arab States*, Tunis, November.

Devereux, S. (2007) 'Social pensions in Southern Africa in the twentieth century', *Journal of Southern African Studies*, 33(3): 539–60.

Devereux, S. and Solomon, C. (2006) 'Employment creation programmes: the international experience', *Issues in Employment and Poverty: Discussion Paper 24*. Geneva: International Labour Office.

Devereux, S. and White, P. (2008) 'Social protection in Africa: can evidence, rights and politics converge?' paper presented at the international conference on *Social Protection for the Poorest in Africa: Learning from Experience*. Entebbe, Uganda, September.

Devereux, S., Sabates-Wheeler, R., Slater, R., Tefera, M., Brown, T. and Teshome, A. (2008) 'Ethiopia's Productive Safety Net Programme (PSNP): 2008 Assessment Report', report commissioned by the PSNP Donor Group. Brighton: Institute of Development Studies.

Duflo, E. (2003) 'Grandmothers and granddaughters: old-age pensions and intra-household allocation in South Africa', *World Bank Economic Review*, 17(1): 1–25.

Ekman, B. (2004) 'Community-based health insurance in low income countries: a systematic review of the evidence', *Health Policy and Planning*, 19(5): 249–70.

Ellis, F., Devereux, S. and White, P. (2009) *Social Protection in Africa*. London: Edward Elgar.

Esim, S., and Smith, M. (eds) (2004) *Gender and Migration in Arab States: The Case of Domestic Workers*. Beirut: International Labour Office.

Esping-Anderson, G. (1990) *The Three Worlds of Welfare Capitalism*. Cambridge: Polity Press with Blackwell Publishers.

Gough, I. (2004) 'Welfare regimes in development contexts: a global and regional analysis', in Gough, I. and Wood, G. with Barrientos, A., Bevan, P., Davis, P. and Room, G. *Insecurity and Welfare Regimes in Asia, Africa and Latin America*. Cambridge: Cambridge University Press.

Heintz, J. (2008) 'Revisiting labour markets: implications for macro-economics and social protection', *IDS Bulletin*, 39(2): 11–17.

Heintz, J., and Valodia, I. (forthcoming) The informal self-employed in Africa', in Aryeetey, E., Devarajan, S., Kanbur, R. and Kasekende, L., (eds) *The Oxford Companion to the Economies of Africa*. Oxford: Oxford University Press.

Human Awareness Programme (1983) *Pensions: An Assessment – How They Affect Black People in South Africa*. Johannesburg: Human Awareness Programme.

Iliffe, J. (1987) *The African Poor: A History*. Cambridge: Cambridge University Press.

International Labour Office (ILO) (2002) *Women and Men in the Informal Economy: A Statitical picture*. Geneva: ILO.

International Labour Organisation (ILO) (2006) 'Social security for all: Investing in global social and economic development', *Issues in Social Protection: Discussion Paper*, 16. Geneva: ILO.

Levy, S. (2008) *Good Intentions, Bad Outcomes: Social Policy, Informality and Economic Growth in Mexico*. Washington D.C.: The Brookings Institution.

Lund, F. (2008) *Changing Social Policy: The Child Support Grant in South Africa*. Cape Town: HSRC Press.

McCord, A. (2004) 'Public works: policy expectations and programme reality', *CSSR Working Paper*, 79. Cape Town: Centre for Social Science Research, University of Cape Town.

—— (2008) 'The social protection function of short-term public works programmes in the context of chronic poverty', in Barrientos, A. and Hulme, S. (eds), *Social Protection for the Poor and the Poorest: Concepts, Policies and Politics*. Houndmills: Palgrave Macmillan.

Makiwane, M. and Udjo, E. (2006) 'Is the child support grant associated with an increase in teenage fertility in South Africa? Evidence from national surveys and administrative data', Final Report for the Department of Social Development. Cape Town: Human Sciences Research Council.

Meth, C. (2008) 'Basic Income Grant: There is no alternative!' Unpublished paper. Durban: School of Development Studies, University of KwaZulu-Natal.

Midgley, J. (1984) *Social Security, Inequality, and the Third World*. London: John Wiley and Sons.

Miller, C., Tsoka, M. and Reichert, K. (2008) 'Impact evaluation report: external evaluation of the Mchinji Social Cash Transfer Pilot'. Boston University: Center for International Health and Development (CIHD).

Mouton, P. (1975) *Social Security in Africa: Trends, Problems and Prospects*. Geneva: International Labour Office.

Perry, G., Maloney, W., Arias, O., Fajnzilber, P., Mason, A. and Saavedra-Chanduvi, J. (2007) *Informality: Exit and Exclusion*. Washington D.C.: The World Bank.

Sabates-Wheeler, R. and Macauslan, I. (2007) 'Migration and social protection: exposing problems of access'. *Development*, 50(4): 26–32.

Samson, M., Lee, U., Ndlebe, A., MacQuene, K., van Niekerk, I., Gandhi, V., Harigaya, T. and Abrahams, C. (2004) 'The social and economic impact of South Africa's social security system', report commissioned by the Economics and Finance Directorate, Department of Social Development. Cape Town: Economic Policy Research Institute.

Slater, R. and Mphale, M. (2008) 'Cash transfers, gender and generational relations: evidence from a pilot project in Lesotho', report commissioned by World Vision International. London: Humanitarian Policy Group, Overseas Development Institute.

Skinner, C. (2008) 'Street traders in African cities: a review', *School of Development Studies Working Paper*, No. 51. Durban: University of KwaZulu-Natal.

Steele, M. (2006) 'Report on incentive structures of social assistance grants in South Africa'. Pretoria: Department of Social Development.

UNICEF (2008) *Social Protection in Eastern and Southern Africa: A Framework and Strategy for United Nations Children's Fund*. Nairobi: UNICEF-ESARO.

Vaitla, B., Devereux, S. and Hauenstein Swan, S. (2009) 'Seasonal Hunger: A neglected problem with proven solutions', *Public Library of Science (PLoS) Medicine*. 6(6): 1–4.

van Ginneken, W. and McKinnon, R. (2007) 'Introduction. Extending social security to all', *International Social Security Review*, 60(2–3): 5–16.

Watts, M. (1983) *Silent Violence: Food, Famine and Peasantry in Northern Nigeria*. Berkeley: University of California Press.

9 Aid, development and the state in Africa

Carlos Oya and Nicolas Pons-Vignon

Introduction

Sub-Saharan Africa (SSA)[1] as a region currently receives the highest share of Official Development Assistance (ODA) in the world with around one third of overall net ODA flows during the period 2000–7 (Figure 9.1). It is also the leading region in aid receipts in per capita terms (Figure 9.2). A significant number of countries can be classified as 'aid-dependent' in the sense that aid represents 15 per cent or more of their GNI (Table 9.1). To an extent, the contemporary history of many SSA countries is closely tied in with what we can call the 'aid complex', which includes the various international and national institutions funding and implementing aid projects, the financial and in-kind flows, associated technical assistance, and the various African government and non-government institutions dealing with or created by donor agencies over the past four decades. Foreign aid in Africa has had multiple and contradictory effects. It has, for example, shaped state formation (and 'deformation') and state-society relations, affected regional geopolitics, moulded and driven policy regimes, assisted in emergencies, prevented *and* fuelled conflict, and provided much needed services, infrastructure and capital injections. For some critics, ODA in Africa is mainly an expression of Western imperialist projects (Petras and Veltmeyer, 2005), perhaps even including Chinese aid, which is also interpreted as a new form of imperialism taking advantage of SSA's vulnerabilities and weak bargaining power (see quotes of this view on Chinese aid in Alden *et al.*, 2008). For others, who are less pessimistic and 'functionalist', ODA remains the only realistic and reliable source of foreign finance at least for the medium term, and particularly in a context of global financial crisis.

The MDG (Millennium Development Goals) agenda has provided further impetus to calls for more aid, by establishing a series of universal targets. The adoption of the MDGs in some ways signals a victory of what Reinert (2007) calls 'palliative economics', where 'instead of attacking the sources of poverty from the inside through the production system – which is what development economics used to be about – the symptoms are addressed by throwing money at them from the outside' (p. 240). Underlying the MDGs is Jeffrey

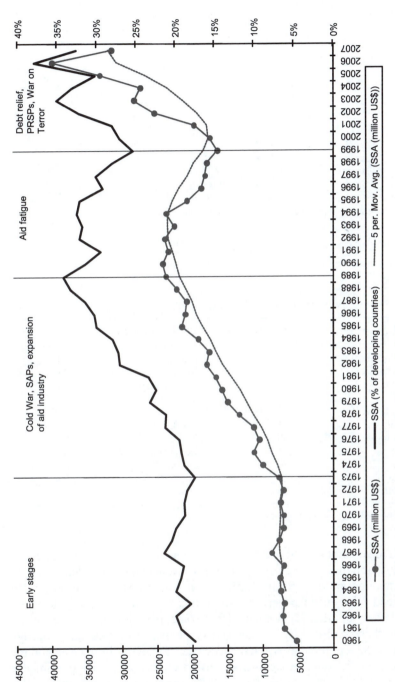

Figure 9.1 Foreign aid to Africa: broad trends and periodization 1960–2007.

Source: Own elaboration from OECD/DAC 2008 database.

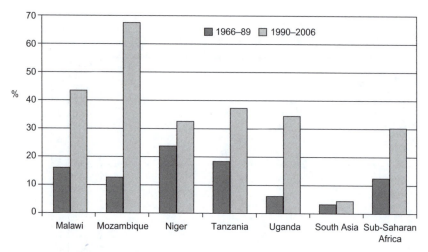

Figure 9.2 Aid per capita: a comparison of selected recipients.

Source: Own elaboration from WDI 2008 database

Table 9.1 Aid dependence in % of GNI 2004

Highest dependence	% of GNI	Lowest dependence	% of GNI
São Tomé and Príncipe	70	Kenya	3.6
Guinea-Bissau	39	Sudan	2.9
Sierra Leone	36	Congo, Rep.	2.8
Eritrea	36	Swaziland	2.3
Congo, Dem. Rep.	32	Zimbabwe	2.2
Burundi	31	Seychelles	1.9
Mozambique	30	Nigeria	0.7
Malawi	25	Botswana	0.6
Liberia	24	Gabon	0.5
Rwanda	20	South Africa	0.4
Mauritania	20	Mauritius	0.4

Source: World Development Indicators 2006

Sachs's idea, embraced by a remarkable number of donors, NGOs, and pop singers, that poor countries need a 'Big Push', that can be provided by aid, to lift them out of poverty (Sachs, 2005). This is possibly where the problem lies: to lift countries out of poverty is not seen as premised on lifting them out of underdevelopment. This renewed but sometimes superficial case for aid is somewhat weakened by an excessive emphasis on the African 'tragedy'. However, the economic situation of Africa has not always been bleak and the data to support 'tragic' diagnostics is to an important extent questionable (Sender, 1999; Jerven, 2008). Before 1980, policies pursued by nationalist post-independence governments nurtured serious hopes of economic take-off,

as the frequency of growth episodes was significant and evidence of indigenous capitalist development was noteworthy (Sender, 1999). The evidence is
less ambiguous on the fact that things started going wrong in the wake of the
debt and global crisis of the late 1970s, with the 1980s characterized as a 'lost
decade' (not uniquely though, as the Latin American experience also shows).
Despite the potential importance of aid for growth and improvements in
living standards in Africa since the 1950s, what went wrong during the neo-
liberal phase of the 1980s and 1990s, we argue, has much to do with aid. The
more recent forms it has taken, following the 'good governance' agenda, and
the gradual reforms of the aid complex are far from an improvement. If the
importance of aid in economic development cannot be denied, in Africa it
has proven problematic ever since it became extremely intrusive into policy
decisions and processes and, more crucially, weakened already fragile states.
Evidence of the beneficial impact of aid, largely found in East Asia (Wade,
1990; Amsden, 1989), suggests that it should support not a universal
unhistorical set of 'good policies', but context-specific long-term development strategies which are nationally owned, negotiated and implemented.
Unfortunately, the weakening of state capacity in Africa driven by
aid-induced conditionality, reforms and interference represents a major
obstacle to an effective use of aid for development.

This chapter will first provide a somewhat traditional but still compelling
macroeconomic case for aid to Africa. It is followed by a brief overview of
trends in aid to SSA, in terms of volume, approaches, historical drivers and
different time and regional patterns. Here we will emphasize the unequal
distribution of aid flows especially in the wake of the rise of foreign aid
'starlets' and moves towards country selectivity, typical of the 'New Aid
Agenda'.[2] Second, the chapter engages with some of the issues emerging from
the vast literature on aid effectiveness. We focus on two sets of issues. First,
the possible negative macroeconomic effects of aid, such as disincentives to
save, Dutch disease and aid volatility. We stress the significance of the latter
and raise doubts about the former two. Then, we briefly review the move
towards a good governance agenda that has become central to the Western
aid complex in Africa since the 1990s.

In this regard, we focus on the further *loss of policy space*[3] that the New
Aid Agenda entails in comparison with the old Washington Consensus (WC),
and the lack of evidence supporting the link 'good governance'-development.
The paper pays particular attention to the erosive effects of aid relations
on African states, especially in the context of aid dependence. Thus we ask
the question whether dependence on aid is becoming a 'resource curse' for
some African countries, and thereby assess whether dependence on aid
should be reduced as a priority in favour of domestic resource mobilization
(see McKinley, 2005 and Di John, 2006).

An important but often under-researched issue that the chapter addresses
are the perverse effects that the complex and demanding delivery of ODA
has had on the functioning of state administrations. The burden of aid

management, coordination and execution, as well as the biases introduced in public administration through technical assistance and conditionality-led loss of policy space, have contributed to the formation of states (a) that now seem unable to deal with long-term strategic issues; (b) are ill-suited to creative and innovative policy thinking; (c) are far too constrained by the fragmentation and ideological biases of the aid complex; and (d) remain more preoccupied with managing and maximizing aid than with long-term development goals.

Why Africa needs aid

The macroeconomic and developmental case for aid and even for *more* aid to Africa is perhaps not particularly fashionable nowadays, but arguably its macroeconomic and historical rationales remain powerful. A historically- and analytically-informed case for more aid ought to link aid to the process of establishing the basics for countries to step up their development efforts and get into a more sustained growth-with-redistribution development path, in other words, towards increasing long-term growth *potential*. Here we summarize some of the main arguments for maintaining or increasing aid flows to low income African countries.

First, history teaches us that most successful accumulation processes and late industrialization strategies have been associated with significant foreign capital inflows, which have taken a variety of forms, and been mobilized through economic or extra-economic (including violent) means. For example, the 'imperialist' industrialization of Britain and France was of course not simply based on domestic forces of accumulation, if one considers the role of unequal treaties and extra-economic force exerted on African and Asian colonies (Chang, 2006). Meanwhile, the economic recovery in post-war Europe, Japan, and Korea could not have been possible, at least not as rapid and sustained, without 'Marshall Plans'. Generally the East Asian episodes of economic and industrial catching-up (especially South Korea, Taiwan, Thailand, Malaysia from the 1960s onwards), also underscore the importance of foreign capital flows and especially of large volumes of aid in the early stages. In other cases, ranging from Russia to several Latin American economies, debt through foreign state banks was actively sought to finance late industrialization in the late nineteenth and early twentieth centuries (Schwartz, 2000). In most of these experiences one of the key challenges was the long gestation period between the inflows of foreign finance, particularly in the form of debt (concessional or not), technological catch-up and the subsequent build up of export competitiveness in manufactures with increasing technological sophistication (Schwartz, 2000: 248). Arguably, some of the most successful late industrialization stories, such as South Korea, Taiwan and other East Asian 'tigers' partly hinged on a combination of time, luck and capacity to manage substantial capital inflows in the form of commercial debt, development assistance and foreign direct investment, which eventually served to fund accumulation strategies that paid off in the long term by dynamically shifting competitive advantages (Amsden, 1989: 38–9; Schwartz, 2000).

Second, most capitalist accumulation strategies require systematic real increases in imports and technology transfer that cannot be simply financed by current domestic resources, especially in low surplus-low savings economies, because of the known savings, foreign exchange and fiscal gaps (McKinley, 2005; Taylor, 1993; Schwartz, 2000). Equally aid, as a non-market and concessional form of foreign finance, if absorbed and well spent, can provide the necessary foreign exchange to distribute benefits across several developmental outcomes, such as promoting rapid improvements in welfare (health, education), developing basic infrastructure necessary for accumulation and industrialization, enhancing dynamic linkages for poverty reduction, facilitating technological adoption and catching up, and strengthening productivity-enhancing institutions (which could be a more effective and stronger state). Of course, aid 'pessimists' question the aid-investment-growth link with specific basket cases like Zambia (Easterly, 2001). One could indeed be tempted to argue that there has been no shortage of aid in SSA, otherwise characterized by below-par performance, especially since the 1980s. This is, however, not a strong enough argument against aid *per se* but rather, an argument about *how* aid is managed, absorbed and spent. The same can be argued for other forms of foreign capital (Eatwell and Taylor, 2000; Chang and Grabel, 2004). Moreover, the aid 'pessimism' of the 1990s, mostly based on cross-country growth regression analysis, has been questioned on technical grounds (Roodman, 2008) and by alternative specifications and samples (Karras, 2006; Minoiu and Reddy, 2006).[4]

Finally, if one accepts the less demanding proposition that flows of foreign capital (in general) may have an important contribution to growth and long-term development, the question for Africa is: what are the possible realistic sources of external finance in the short to medium term? Overall long-term net capital flows into developing countries declined in the 1990s by almost 25 per cent in nominal terms, which means that the decline is more acute in real terms.[5] Moreover, foreign direct investment (FDI) flows tend to consistently concentrate in very few countries (among developing countries and *within* developing regions, e.g. China, India, Indonesia, and within Africa, Nigeria, Angola, South Africa, etc.). Despite some important increases in FDI to SSA after the late 1990s, the region still receives a marginal proportion of FDI directed to developing countries (5 per cent), while two thirds of this volume go to Latin America and East Asia. Even the most recent recorded increases in FDI to SSA are very concentrated in few countries, for some years (2001–2) largely accounted for by some individual massive investments (such as Mozal, the aluminium smelter in Mozambique), and privatization processes, mergers and acquisitions, thus not much 'Greenfield' investment (UNCTAD, 2005: 32). Moreover, until 1996 the largest recipients of FDI in SSA, such as Angola, Nigeria, Côte d'Ivoire and Cameroon have also been some of the most affected by capital flight, leading to extremely large *net outflows* of capital (UNCTAD, 2005: 32 and Table 9.5).

Aid thus still represents the bulk of external finance to Africa and, according to UNCTAD, the only reliable source in the medium term. African and generally Least Developed Countries (LDCs) find it very hard to raise funds through bank consortia, public debt or portfolio equity flows. FDI is likely to go to countries where a minimum of basic infrastructure and funds to maintain it are in place, and is thus likely to follow ODA rather than precede it (Chang and Grabel, 2004). Therefore, agencies like UNCTAD have supported the idea that, given the paucity of private capital flows, the vicious circle of low growth and aid dependence can only be broken with combinations of a big push in official aid and a revision of WC policies, in other words, a 'Marshall Plan' with policy space. We will come back to some of these questions below.

Why and how aid is *not* helping Africa so much

Aid distribution: trends and composition of flows

A simple inspection of data on aid flows, trends and composition suggest some stylized facts that can be summarized as follows (see Figures 9.1–9.3 and Table 9.1).

- First, African countries have received overall *increasing* volumes of aid, particularly after the take off in the 1970s, then sustained over the 1980s.
- Second, fluctuations have been important both in the region as a whole and within countries, as evidence of marked aid volatility clearly attests (see below and Figure 9.3). In aggregate terms, the aid flows declined in constant terms and also in relative terms as a proportion of total aid to developing countries during the 1990s. Thus the data clearly shows that the combined 'aid fatigue'-effects of the end of the Cold War and failed structural adjustment were felt particularly in Africa.
- Third, there are significant differences in average annual net aid flows across countries between the 1960s and the 2000s (Figures 9.2 and 9.3). Some countries have received much more than others, notably Tanzania, Ethiopia, Kenya, Mozambique and Sudan, in comparison with a range of small countries, and some success stories like Mauritius, Gabon and Botswana (themselves with relatively small populations).
- Fourth, aid per capita has also followed trends similar to those of total volumes of aid (Figure 9.2), but small countries receive substantial and higher than average volumes of aid per capita, suggesting there is some minimum threshold for aid flows into a country. In fact, many small countries tend to be particularly dependent on aid in terms of proportions of several macroeconomic aggregates like GNI (gross national income), investment and government expenditures (see Table 9.1). Moreover, some

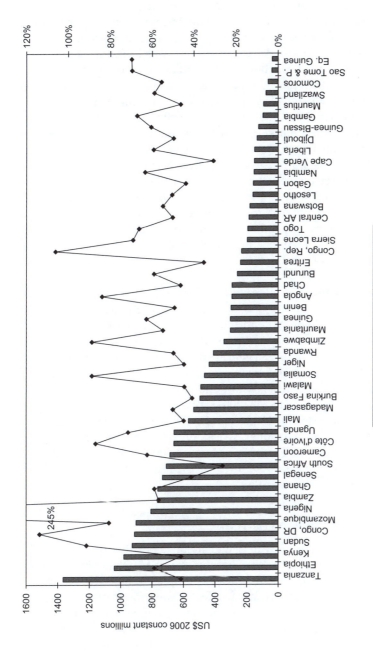

Figure 9.3 Aid distribution by country and volatility: 1965–2007.

Source: Own elaboration from OECD/DAC 2008 database. CV – coefficient of variation

countries with similar levels of income per capita have also received markedly different volumes of aid per capita also as a result of donor preferences for particular destinations (Figure 9.2).

- Fifth, as advanced above, despite recent increases in FDI and other forms of private capital flows, aid remains by far the most important source of foreign savings for most African countries, which, in turn receive the largest share of total ODA flows (at around one third) (Figure 9.1).

- Finally, aid to Africa has become increasingly multilateral as the rise of the World Bank, IMF, UN agencies, and regional banks (like the African Development Bank) has offset the negative effect of the end of the Cold War on bilateral aid flows. However, bilateral aid flows today are to a significant extent pegged to the endorsement of recipient government policies by multilateral institutions thereby significantly increasing the bargaining power of the latter beyond their financial muscle. With the rise of multilateral aid and policy conditionality, aid delivery has grad-ually moved from project towards programme support with a more recent drive towards general budget support (GBS) although this is still quantitatively quite marginal (around 20 per cent in Mozambique, one of the top receivers of GBS).

Increasing aid to Africa has indeed followed and driven at the same time the exponential growth of the world's 'aid complex'. As Riddell (2007) shows, the number of official donors, implementing agencies, projects and NGOs has expanded exponentially over the last three decades. There are over 100 major (large) official aid donors. There are many more smaller agencies oper-ating in most African countries. Each individual recipient country deals with an average of 26 different official donors and several African countries exceed this figure. According to Riddell (2007), over 35,000 separate official aid transactions were reported in 2004 to the OECD/DAC. He also quotes aston-ishing figures about how individual African ministries are overloaded by aid proliferation. For example, Tanzania had over 2,000 donor projects ongoing in the early 1990s, while the Ministry of Health in Mozambique alone managed over 400 projects recently.

Aid to Africa from an historical perspective

Aid was born out of World War II and its first, possibly most successful incarnation – the European Recovery Programme, or Marshall Plan – allowed massive transfers from the United States to Europe. The objective was clearly stated: to help restore prosperity in war-affected countries in order to prevent them from becoming communist. This philosophy was applied to other parts of the world, from Latin America to Africa and in particular Asia – 'We have learned in Europe what to do in Asia', said Paul Hoffman, the first adminis-trator of USAID.[6] However, aid to non-European countries was granted substantially lesser means. As far as African countries were concerned, the aid flows they received still reflected their colonial ties, especially with Britain and France, except when they decided to break away from the latter's grip and to pursue socialist policies. Tanzania, Guinea and Mali (until the devaluation of the Malian franc in 1967) were among those and received aid from the Soviet Union. In the 1960s and 1970s, aid flows to Africa increased thanks also to the emergence of multilateral and Scandinavian donors (or the 'Nordic group', which includes The Netherlands), the latter asserting a more disinterested approach than the US or Western European countries.

It is striking to note that the share of aid in Western governments' spending grew smaller over time (except in a few Scandinavian countries), only to increase temporarily when the Cold War became more intense. Aid, moreover, soon became tied, a trend that spread from the US to other donors because it limited the impact of aid on their balance of payments and promoted national 'interests'. Tied aid is aid which has to be used entirely on (usually intermediate and capital) goods bought from the country which supplies the loan (one should also include consultancy services, of course). This further limited the positive impact aid may have had since, as Amsden puts it, '(t)ying prevents an aid recipient from shopping worldwide for the best bargain, and from building an experienced local cadre of executives, managers, and engineers, with the result that the real value of aid is lower than the nominal value' (Amsden, 2007: 60).

With the emergence of the WC and the debt crisis which hit numerous developing countries from the late 1970s, stabilization and structural adjustment programmes (i.e. BWI aid with its attached conditions) were forced on many African countries, with consequences which continue to be felt today (see below). The collapse of the Soviet Union gave way to a brief belief in the end of history, which would imply the advent of liberal democracy all over the world. From François Mitterrand's speech in La Baule in 1991 – where he warned African leaders that they should democratize to continue receiving French support – to the numerous 'democracy enhancing' programmes organized in order to promote 'good governance' (see section below), a Post-Washington Consensus (PWC) emerged which in Africa entailed, for example, a focus on (technical) aspects of democratic life, such as elections and various 'institutional fixes' designed to make economic reforms (i.e. liberalization, privatization, public sector restructuring, etc.) 'work'. It is in this period that the rise of multilateral aid in Africa accelerated, with the World Bank becoming the largest single donor in several countries.

Yet, Africa has not ceased attracting aid for geopolitical reasons after the end of the Cold War; first, as a battlefield of the War on Terror driven by the US; second, as a focus of immigration-limiting measures, particularly in Europe; and, third, as an arena of scramble for mineral and oil resources, spearheaded by the fast increasing presence of China in the continent (Alden *et al.*, 2008). The War on Terror – based on a very flexible definition of terror and terrorism – is directing US aid flows to Eastern Africa, to the Sahel and to Muslim areas in general. As security (of the Western world) becomes a key concern informing foreign and aid policy, it also becomes a criterion for the selection of recipient countries and accounts for the increased amounts invested in post-conflict reconstruction programmes, in order to prevent fragile states emerging from conflicts from becoming havens for terrorist activities. Post conflict reconstruction in poor countries is, as shown by Cramer (2006), very reminiscent of the Morgenthau plan, which aimed to make Germany harmless by turning it into a pastoral country. Programmes aimed at fragile, failed or ghost states are, as we will discuss in the subsequent sections, not geared towards putting these countries on a developmental path (as the Marshall plan did with Europe); they rather aim to minimize the risks associated with them.

Growing flows of African immigrants associated with persistent under-development and an acceleration of population growth on the continent are another major preoccupation of European donors. The European Union and several of its key member states, especially those situated on the Mediterranean (France, Italy and Spain), are outsourcing immigration control to African countries (Blanchard and Wender, 2007). This has taken the form of the creation of buffer zones (from Morocco to Turkey to Guinea-Bissau), with formal 'aid for increased migration control' deals, as well as of a growth in a new form of tied aid, namely aid tied to keeping would-be immigrants in their own countries. In France, Nicolas Sarkozy created upon his election in 2007 a Ministry of National Identity, Immigration and '*Co-développement*' (joint development) with this very purpose in mind.

Geopolitical issues have thus played a central role in the allocation of Western aid to Africa, although the issues informing it have varied over time. They have also probably reduced effectiveness, by introducing biases in aid allocation across countries, its sector composition and the extent to which it has been used to further particular political projects.

Geopolitics also seems to characterize the recent emergence of 'new' donors in Africa, notably China, which primarily aims at securing access to natural resources for its expanding manufacturing sector and at establishing diplomatic alliances to support its rise as a key power in multilateral institutions (Alden *et al.*, 2008). As growing evidence suggests, China, devoid of the superiority complex of formal colonizers, and of any preoccupation with governance or other noble aims, takes a very pragmatic approach to aid and investment and brings new, less cumbersome, and more effective modalities of aid delivery[7] (Davies *et al.*, 2008). For example, in a war-torn country like the Democratic Republic of the Congo, Sinohydro Corp and China Railway Engineering Corp, supported by EXIM bank and the Chinese government, have acquired a 68 per cent stake in a joint venture with Congolese state copper miner Gecamines, with rights to two large copper and cobalt concessions, in exchange for a $9 billion investment plan for the refurbishment of mines and massive infrastructure projects, expected to expand and upgrade the DRC's road (4,000 kilometres) and rail (3,200 km) systems.[8]

Debates on aid effectiveness and shifting aid agendas: towards a new aid agenda?

The 'aid fatigue' of the late 1990s was partly informed by pessimism emerging from debates on aid effectiveness in general and in Africa in particular, mostly based on cross-country growth regression analysis. Despite an illusion of false econometric precision, the fact is that the empirics of aid-growth relations is marred by biases, spuriousness and data controversy (particularly reverse causality). In fact, the vast literature based on cross-country regressions over large heterogeneous samples of countries has provided a wide range of contradictory results:

- that aid does not cause or barely affects growth (see Roodman, 2008 for a good review of this literature);
- that aid is good for growth (Sachs, 2005);
- that aid only works in 'good-policy' environments (Burnside and Dollar, 2000);
- that 'developmental' aid (as opposed to 'geopolitical' aid) does positively affect growth in the long term (Karras, 2006; Minoiu and Reddy, 2006).

Perhaps more interesting than the *average* correlation (rather than causality) between aid and growth across several countries, are specific aspects of aid relations and the dynamics of aid flows which may significantly reduce its positive impact on national economies and states and even result in perverse effects. In this chapter we focus on some of the most significant problems.

The perverse macroeconomic effects of aid

Despite the compelling macroeconomic rationale for aid based on the need to close savings, fiscal or foreign exchange gaps, there is also a risk of perverse macroeconomic effects that has often been mentioned by critics of aid-giving to Africa. 'Dutch disease' is often mentioned as one of these problems, particularly in the case of aid surges, and now quite popular among the sceptics with regards to aid 'scaling up' in Africa (cf. Collier, 2006; Easterly, 2002). The danger is that large inflows of foreign grants and credits could keep foreign exchange rates above levels that would prevail in the absence of foreign aid, resulting in an appreciation of the exchange rate, with pernicious effects on the international competitiveness of the economy.[9] However, a substantial body of evidence fails to corroborate this hypothesis as instances of aid-related 'Dutch disease' symptoms in SSA are very rare (IMF, 2005). A critical issue is that to understand the implications of scaling up aid 'the composition of government expenditures and the composition of net imports do matter' (McKinley, 2005: 11).

Much more serious for aid effectiveness is the volatility of aid flows (see Figure 9.3). UNCTAD (2000) shows that foreign aid receipts are more volatile than export revenues and more volatile than government revenues (excluding grants) in most of the least developed countries, especially in Africa.[10] Even more alarming is the frequently perverse pro-cyclical character of aid flows, particularly in a context of country selectivity in which better performers receive more aid *ex-post*. This pro-cyclical pattern also implies that aid cannot stabilize fluctuations in domestic consumption (Fielding and Mavrotas, 2005: 1).

Empirical research also shows that aid volatility affects economic performance and the impact of aid *negatively*, so much that after controlling for uncertainty, aid volumes have a significant positive effect on growth, through their effects on domestic investment – private and public – via *crowding-in* (Fielding and Mavrotas, 2005, Lensink and Morrisey, 2000).[11] In practice, especially in aid-dependent countries, fiscal planners in SSA governments prepare their medium-term expenditure projections on the basis of assumptions on future aid flows and expected revenues to calculate the 'resource envelope'. The latter is invariably conservative due to aid volatility, in countries with binding fiscal constraints, and has prevented more effective public investment with long maturity and the design of long-term strategies. The reality is that, despite continuous rhetorical calls from Western donors to make aid flows more predictable and long-term (as in the 2005 Paris Declaration), the logic and incentives of the aid delivery system seem inimical to these proposals (Riddell, 2007, see more below). In fact, Poverty Reduction Strategy Papers (PRSPs) and associated aid flows have generally *not* resulted in less volatility but, as an IMF report shows, have actually exacerbated volatility on average, especially in countries like Benin, Lesotho, and Uganda (Bulir and Hamann, 2006).

Even advocates of aid to SSA suggest that there is also a potential risk of negative impact on long-term domestic savings rates, which are already too low in most of SSA (McKinley, 2005). In other words, aid may simply not be absorbed and spent in long-term investment while in some circumstances it may instead create a disincentive to mobilize domestic resources through various forms of taxation (including more taxation on transnational business in extractive industries, for instance). This may indeed significantly reduce the long-term impact of foreign aid on growth. The problem is compounded by debt-creating aid, i.e. flowing in the form of concessional loans, like most multilateral aid. A vicious circle between low savings, aid dependence and indebtedness may set out and some African countries have found themselves in such traps during the 1980s and 1990s. In fact, a significant proportion of 'new' aid being disbursed to African governments from the mid-1980s onwards was earmarked or directed to meeting international debt obligations, which were particularly stringent in the case of debt with the IMF and the WB.[12] Even mainstream economists (and former WB employees) like Easterly (2002 and 2005) have shown that engagement with policy-conditioned loans over protracted periods is associated with a lower or negative impact of aid on growth.

Aid, the 'good governance' agenda and loss of policy space

Conditionality is indeed a contentious issue. With the more recent New Aid Agenda, reflecting the post-Washington Consensus, African countries have been subject to the 'good governance' conditionality framework. To understand the emergence (and importance for aid) of the focus on promoting good governance, it is useful to briefly look at the emergence of this idea. Following Khan (2006), one can identify three phases in the evolution of the link between governance and development in the discourse and practice of aid donors. Essentially, in the 1950s–1960s and into the 1970s, governance was seen (cynically) as instrumental in promoting growth; the idea that an enlightened autocrat could play a decisive role in development take-off was more or less explicitly accepted in different versions of modernization theory, since growth would derive from a strategic selection of sectors to support. Under what Amsden (2007) calls the 'First American Empire', the nature of the regime and its economic policies, as long as it stayed away from Communist temptations, was not a central concern of donors. With the emergence of a Second American Empire, much more preoccupied with the content of development policies, and with ideology, and epitomized by IFI-sponsored programmes of macroeconomic stabilization and structural adjustment, the idea of state intervention or even regulation became synonymous with ineffective resource allocation and rent-seeking. Following the radical 'rent seeking' argument of the Public choice school, all the economic woes associated with (and following) the debt crisis were seen as a result of 'government failure' (as opposed to market failure) – and the main governance objective became to 'roll back' the state.[13]

While the results of aid-induced WC policies in the 1980s and early 1990s were clearly disappointing, particularly in Africa, a new (post-Washington) consensus emerged in the mid-1990s around the idea that, in order to make markets work (for growth, for poverty reduction and so on), the 'right' institutions should be put in place. This way the substance and rationale of WC policies was never seriously questioned and the focus was placed on the conditions for their applicability in Africa and elsewhere.[14] The central feature of the good governance agenda, intellectually underpinned by the emergence of New Institutional Economics, is, first, its belief that institutions *currently* in place in developed countries, particularly the 'Anglo-American model', are the most appropriate for economic development and that they should be created in poor countries to allow economic take-off. Second, the new agenda has established the principle that states should be instruments of 'pro-poor' service delivery. In this picture of 'institutional and technical fixes', history, structural relations of inequality and political (class) conditions are largely left out.

The resulting New Aid Agenda is clearly reflected in the PRSPs, which have become the new benchmark for most African countries to access external finance through bilateral and multilateral sources.[15] PRSPs exemplify the double preoccupation with institutional change and 'pro-poor' focus in public service delivery, and show that, while geopolitical considerations play an important part in aid allocation (see above), the importance of adhering to the good governance agenda is now essential. The World Bank, by far the largest donor in sub-Saharan Africa, thus relies on Country Policy and Institutional Assessments (CPIAs) to allocate funds according to the principles of this new agenda. These assessments are a way of giving countries scores which reflect their adherence to a large set of predefined 'good' policies (Van Waeyenberge, 2008). It is important to note here that, like the WC of the 1980s, the good governance agenda is not preoccupied with drawing lessons from successful episodes of economic development, whether past or contemporary, for instance in China or Vietnam.[16] Rather it represents a refined version of the neoliberal agenda which is incredibly more pervasive than the WC, since it directly engages with 'civil society' to advance a broad project of social, political and institutional transformations (Harrison, 2004).

Therefore, aid conditionality in Africa has evolved from a clear set of economic policies primarily concerned with macroeconomic stability and the obsession with 'getting prices right' through deregulation (i.e. the 'old' WC) to a far-reaching agenda of institutional, political and economic reforms, whose outreach and implications are more wide-ranging. In fact, the ample gamut of 'new' reforms, 'benchmarks' and performance criteria amounts to a transformation of states (via 'governance states') and societies (through social engineering as 'embedding neoliberalism') into an 'ideal' and stable type conforming to the fantasies and values of neoliberal ideology in general and the World Bank's current development model in particular (Harrison, 2004: 128; see also essays in Pincus and Winters, 2002, especially Sender, 2002). The practical result of this process of expanding conditionality and increasing selectivity is obviously a deepened shrinkage of policy space. As Chang (2006) notes 'these days, there is virtually no area on which the Bank and the Fund do not have (often very strong) influence – democracy, judicial reform, corporate governance, health, education, and what not'.[17] The other outcome is confusion and lack of strategic prioritization (Rodrik, 2006). In fact, 'good governance' is so encompassing and vague at the same time that there is no real consensus among donors on (a) definitions and (b) what constitutes a concrete set of 'good enough governance' reforms to promote.[18]

Furthermore, by imposing a never-ending list of technical recommendations and programmes aimed at correcting some of the disasters caused by the curtailing of African civil services, the good governance agenda makes it effectively impossible for African states to (re)build any real capacity to resume a much-needed path of economic development. Darbon (2003) highlights that all of these quick-fixes stay clear of any engagement with the political nature of the state, as well as from an attempt to understand what is really happening in African states. The accommodation of imported norms has produced a political and administrative reality which, if it is not understood, cannot be oriented towards developmental policies (Mkandawire, 2001).

This apparently clear trajectory towards a new (good governance) aid agenda is not devoid of contradictions on the ground. In fact, the 'good governance' agenda appears to clash with the effective reality of donor-government relations in showcases such as Uganda, Tanzania and Mozambique. These countries, whose embrace of neoliberalism and substantive economic reforms have placed them at the top of the ranking of World Bank 'starlets', have shown signs of governance deterioration, particularly with regards to corruption, pluralism and political accountability (Harrison, 2004; Hanlon and Smart, 2008). Taking the 'good governance' agenda seriously in these successful countries may in fact 'disrupt the post-conditionality regime, with its image of partnership, progress and powerful claim to showcase status' (Harrison, 2004: 94). Instead, donors prefer to cherry-pick aspects of the agenda that are politically feasible and turn a blind eye to the more serious slippages so that the showcase is preserved.[19]

Aid dependency and state erosion

Aid dependency: a case of 'resource curse'?

It is clear from the previous sections that little attention has been given by aid agencies to understanding the political economy of development and underdevelopment in recipient countries. This may account for the emergence, since the early 2000s, of a series of mainstream analyses of African economic development claiming to draw on 'political economy'. In lieu of political economy, one finds rather an amalgamation of political science and mainstream economic theory, or rational choice applied to political 'agents'.

An important argument warning of the possible ill effects of aid has thus been developed, in particular by Collier (2006) and Auty (2007). This argument likens aid to a 'rent' and sees recipient countries as likely to fall prey to 'Dutch disease' (i.e. the inability to diversify beyond 'easy' sources of income).[20] Auty (2007) thus writes that '(a)id shares with natural resource rent and contrived (i.e. government monopoly) rent the property of being a large revenue stream that is detached from the economic activity that generates it, and elicits political contests for its capture'. Both papers draw on econometric studies highlighting the alleged 'retarding' effects of aid on development (with some level of distinction between different forms of aid) but fail to capture the causal relationship and mechanisms between aid and underdevelopment. Results are analysed through a conservative 'political economy' of poor countries which dubs aid recipients 'immature political economies'.[21] In line with the Post-WC, the problem is seen as being a result of underdevelopment of recipients, and related inadequacy of their institutions, rather than of aid or aid relations themselves. Unsurprisingly, it is suggested to condition aid to 'good' policies to avoid rent seeking; moreover, in line with the claim to a political economy approach, Auty makes the following statement: '(t)he political economy (*sic*) should inform reform policies and reformers should ensure they build political constituencies to back such policies' (p.15).[22]

This qualification of African countries as 'immature' reveals a problematic lack of understanding of their actual functioning. The fact that aid attracts interest and can generate corruption is hardly debatable; what is on the contrary very important is that this does not imply a deterministic impossibility of development: there was plenty of corruption associated with American aid in South Korea, which nonetheless performed remarkably well. Rather than understanding rents within a rigid neoclassical framework, it seems more useful to follow Khan and Jomo (2000) in their attempt to identify under which political conditions (i.e. political settlements and class structures/ alliances) rents can be reinvested in the domestic economy and mobilized to support a process of long-term economic development, rather than accumulated without any productive linkage, for instance in foreign accounts.[23] Instead, Auty and Collier's approaches do not help to understand how aid can work, because they do not consider political economies from a structural perspective; they only draw on a schematic (and remarkably loose) typology of regimes.[24] Uganda and Mozambique, both purportedly immature countries, thus received a lot of aid, yet did not suffer any resource curse, and are normally used as showcases by Western donors. In the following section, we will argue that the problem with aid is not so much that it is a 'free flow', but has to do with the modalities of and conditions attached to its disbursement and the perverse incentive systems that it trends to create on both donor and government sides.

Aid delivery systems and state capacity 'de-building'

The abundant literature on aid in Africa has not taken issues of perverse incentives and failures in aid delivery systems seriously enough, although there are important exceptions (see review of relevant studies in Riddell, 2007: 361–6, Wuyts, 1996 and Hanlon and Smart, 2008: 120–34). Despite growing emphasis on 'capacity building' by donor agencies, there is some irony in this discourse for several reasons that suggest that aid flows have been associated with what we could call instead state capacity 'de-building'.

First, many years of structural adjustment and macroeconomic stabilization policies drove the fiscal squeeze that led to public sector downsizing, reductions in real salaries in the public sector and increasing dependence on project-funding for normal operations, including recurrent expenditure. This process resulted in diminished material incentives for public employment at a time when public sector reform and the management of aid posed fresh and *greater* demands on civil servants, especially those at the middle-high level of public management.

Second, IMF-related fiscal targets have often created blocks for the necessary expansion of government services, especially in education and health (Action Aid International, 2005). The IMF argument has often been that donor-funded service expansion cannot always be trusted and that the fiscal implications in terms of hiring of more civil servants (teachers, nurses and so on) may be serious in the long-term. Thus, the IMF has somewhat cynically used the argument of bilateral aid volatility in its favour. As a result, either the expansion of education and health provision has not proceeded with the required speed, or workers have been contracted on a temporary basis without becoming civil servants and therefore unprotected by employment law.

Third, the proliferation of projects, and project units within state bureaucracies, has created different layers of bureaucrats either excluded or included in the management of such projects, which often offer additional compensation in the form of top-up salaries, daily allowances and other perks of great appeal to poorly paid civil servants.

Fourth, the fragmentation of aid as well as complex (and multiple) delivery and reporting mechanisms have created a massive burden on increasingly demoralized public sector workers and shifted attention away from work routines necessary for a good day-to-day management of public finances, not least to improve domestic tax mobilization.[25] In this context it is not surprising that an increasing number of highly paid international consultants are hired to fill gaps and 'assist' governments to carry out their normal duties (what often counts as 'capacity building').

More significantly, these mechanisms of state capacity 'de-building' alter the system of incentives in African bureaucracies and align them with those of donor agencies in many ways. As Castel-Branco (2008) argues on Mozambique, one of the government's primary goals has become to maximize aid. Thus policy processes and institutions are shaped to meet this goal. By mistaking the outcomes of development with its means, the Post-WC in fact pushes African countries – the weakest states, hence the least challenging guinea pigs of aid fads in the world – to adapt continuously to changing recommendations. As Bergamaschi (2008) notes in the case of Mali, the focus of government policy, stripped of most its capacity by previous (WC) reforms, is now entirely on attracting aid and pleasing donors: 'Aid is not a mere financial and technical tool to support national initiatives, but rather it has replaced national political reflections on development' (p. 224).[26]

Moreover, the persistent erosion of 'old' sources of state power and rents such as public employment, salaries, parastatals, credit, among others, provoked by years of fiscal austerity and public sector reforms, has also had two further effects in terms of the consolidation of neoliberal agendas, affecting policy space and the legitimacy of state intervention in Africa. First, a larger pool of qualified and semi-skilled workers have had to find work in the expanding informal business, NGOs or donor agencies, thereby facing different constraints and articulating new interests (Rapley, 2007).[27] Whereas public sector employees would tend to be more unionized and advocates of state interventions in the economy, informal sector operators are mostly interested in the removal of obstacles to their activities, which often amounts to a defence of a market deregulation agenda. Public sector retrenchments and freezing of state salaries have therefore pushed a significant workforce towards alternative non-state mediated livelihoods. The second effect is related to the increasing retreat of the state from a number of public services hitherto provided to the population. Thus the elimination of rural development agencies and the progressive NGOization of some social services, including education and health, have in many cases diminished the expectations of the population from the government.[28] The lack of trust in what states have to offer inevitably strengthens anti-state discourses and the articulation of demands from those who provide services, either NGOs or the private sector.

In such context of declining material and 'moral' incentives within African bureaucracies, donor efforts to introduce 'state-of-the-art public management practice' may compound the problem. Darbon (2003) highlights that the attempted implementation of the prescriptions of New Public Management in Africa is an essentially technical approach to state functions which has on purpose ignored the *political* dimensions and choices. The failure of technical quick fixes is hardly surprising given the essentially political nature of economic development, which implies the emergence of new classes of interests and the demise of others. Perhaps most representative of the neoliberal onslaught against the state is the suggestion that tax collection should be carried out by 'autonomous revenue authorities', insulated from the possible predatory intentions of the state apparatus. It is the most obvious contradiction of the external attempts to reform African states because tax collection is at the very core of building state capacity and legitimacy, as shown by Di John (2006). The failure of the state in Africa, a subject of much discussion in political science and economics, may have less to do with Africa's 'cultural differences' (or natural tendencies towards 'neo-patrimonialism')[29] than with the way in which development aid has attempted to impose some of the features of what it saw as efficient states while weakening the structural conditions which actually allow states to emerge and consolidate themselves.

The process of state capacity erosion, both in material and non-material terms, has indeed contributed to the erosion of policy space discussed above. This has been in the form of accommodating 'subservience' to donor demands and ideological principles (Hanlon and Smart, 2008). One important source of 'consent construction' is the production of knowledge and the creation and reproduction of a new kind of intelligentsia that is 'neoliberal-friendly'. The role of the World Bank (through funding, the World Bank Institute and consultancy contracts), private foundations providing scholarships and Western academic institutions has been crucial in this respect.[30] There are of course instances of 'forced consensus' (i.e. the new technocrats cynically articulating a convenient way of policy making that matches donor's preferences), but our hypothesis is that much of the 'new intelligentsia', especially younger African economists with no experience of liberation struggles or nationalist development programmes of the 1960s and 1970s, is indeed neoliberal in ideology and practice and has in many countries managed to occupy spaces of significant responsibility.[31]

Donor agencies have devoted significant funding to the production of knowledge in the form of consultancies and grey reports to which the members of the 'new intelligentsia' (including frustrated academics) have significantly contributed (thereby also making good additional money). Indeed, this additional source of funding attracts not only qualified civil servants, but also the 'intellectuals' hitherto busier in providing alternative discourses (often 'anti-structural adjustment'). This way the sources of 'alternative views' and intellectual resistance from within have probably shrunk in a large majority of African countries.[32] Interestingly, connivance with broadly 'market-friendly' policies and principles may be perfectly compatible with instances of increasing corruption in open 'liberal democratic' regimes. Indeed there seems to be a trade-off that donors are prepared to accept so that the neoliberal *cum* 'good governance' project remains intact.[33]

Under the conditions described above, recent calls to move towards direct general budget support (GBS) are generally welcome, especially by officials in Ministries of Finance who have to bear the burden of managing fragmented aid. The problem is that this commitment may come at a price. Despite the dearth of empirical research on the factors behind budget support implementation and its implications, an evaluation of recent experiences reports concerns about attempts by donors to micromanage policy processes in recipient countries through newly established GBS-related institutional mechanisms (IDD and Associates, 2006: 97). Hanlon and Smart (2008) elucidate this trend with reference to GBS in Mozambique and how this new 'technical fix' has provided further space to enhance donor power in domestic policy processes, thereby expanding donors' influence from policy *content* to policy *process*.

Conclusions

Africa has had a long relationship with foreign aid, and as this chapter shows, partly contradictory and tortuous, but not unique. As Amsden puts it, '(f)oreign aid was like the hallucinogen called angel dust – it felt good, but it had a lot of bad side effects. Most developing countries never got hooked on it and, thanks to the First American Empire [which allowed them to conduct their policies freely], could go their own way' (2007: 71). However, most African countries *did* get hooked on aid, as shown in Table 9.1 and Figure 9.1. Aid intensity varies from country to country but aid dependence is a phenomenon more common in SSA than anywhere else. Critics of aid to Africa abound and reasons for pessimism are plentiful, but this chapter has begun to argue that the economic and developmental case for aid remains compelling. Many SSA countries do need aid, as alternative sources of finance are hard to come by and may be at least as problematic as aid. And history shows that aid *can* work and pay off in the long-term.

Nevertheless, we have also highlighted a series of common problems with foreign aid in Africa, which are widely documented. Specifically, we have placed particular emphasis on two types of negative effects. First, the steady weakening of states, which years of aid-induced conditionality and perverse incentive systems in aid relations have brought about, has rendered the possibility of genuinely home-grown long-term development strategies unlikely for now. Second, the loss of policy space associated with the neoliberal project, which remains embedded in the 'good governance' discourse of the New Aid Agenda in Africa, has probably been the highest price paid by SSA countries to access Western development assistance. Associated with these two effects is a state-adverse agenda (in theory and practice and, of late, mostly in practice) which maintains faith in institutional and technical fixes. The Post-WC (good governance) and New Aid Agenda, despite an apparent greater openness to the role of the state in development, place strong emphasis on inadequate or weak state capacity in Africa, which has become a justification for a limited range of state interventions and the denial of any possibility of replicating lessons from East Asia, especially on trade and industrial policies. However, as Sender (2002: 194) points out: 'Inadequate state capacity in Sub-Saharan Africa has been a self-fulfilling prophecy; the outcome of a bet rigged by those in a strong position to influence results. The Washington institutions have consistently demanded initiatives that impair governments' capacity for policy formulation and implementation'.

From a long-term perspective, aid in SSA should be seen as a temporary push. Therefore, the political economy of domestic resource mobilization requires urgent attention. Meanwhile, Western donors should seriously consider 'going back to basics' (e.g. basic infrastructure) and avoid social and institutional engineering excesses. Development banks, such as the World Bank, should concentrate and focus precisely on what they have been designed for and where their comparative advantage lies: providing long-term finance for large-scale developmental projects like any development bank (Pincus and Winters, 2002). At least China, an emerging donor in Africa with obvious geopolitical and national interests, seems to be partly following this principle of 'back to basics'.

Notes

1 We will use the terms 'Africa' or 'SSA' interchangeably throughout the text.
2 On various important aspects, contradictions and problems with the New Aid Agenda, see Killick (2004).
3 The 'policy space' can be seen as the space or room for manoeuvre that African states should have to design and implement 'an appropriate "policy mix" or "diversity of policies" tailored to the specific situation of each country, rather than a one-size-fits-all approach' (UNCTAD, 2007: 4). It also refers to the space 'to use the very instruments and tools that many industrialized nations took advantage of to reach their current levels of development' (Gallagher, 2005: 1).
4 The econometric evidence on aid-growth linkages is increasingly contradictory, partly as a result of endogeneity problems (reverse causality) (Roodman, 2008). See also section below on aid effectiveness debates.

5 Since the late 1990s, FDI flows to developing countries have increased substantially, partly as a result of the pull from China and India and partly in response to sweeping privatizations in other countries, but these trends are easily reversible in a recession context.

6 Quoted in Amsden (2007: 56).

7 More effective in terms of cost effectiveness, speed of delivery, absence of excessive strings, and generally as in-kind support, i.e. without involving actual money transfers (see Davies *et al.*, 2008).

8 See Jiang (2009) for more details.

9 See McKinley (2005) who argues that the 'Dutch disease' symptoms may simply be a reflection that real foreign exchange resources are being transferred into the country. If both increasing government expenditures and boosting net imports are allowed so that ODA is spent and absorbed (rather than sterilized by restrictive macroeconomic policies), Dutch disease symptoms may be manageable and not worrying.

10 Figure 9.3 shows very high variability of aid commitments (hovering around a 70 per cent coefficient of variation) in most SSA countries, despite significant differences in *average* aid inflows per year across countries.

11 Even an IMF study concedes that 'public investment can crowd-in private investment in [sub-Saharan Africa]. Crowding-in likely reflects the complementarity of private investment with some components of public investment, especially infrastructure' (Gupta *et al.*, 2005: 25) quoted by McKinley (2005: 14).

12 Likewise a significant proportion of 'new' aid flows in the post-1999 period merely reflected the accounting of the savings from debt relief and cancellations, even though some countries were not actually repaying much of this debt. See also Killick (2004).

13 Despite donor proliferation, the increasing dominance of the World Bank, the IMF and like-minded bilateral donors as the main sources of external finance in Africa from the 1980s quickly helped introduce the WC agenda in most African aid recipients (Sender, 2002).

14 See Pincus and Winters (2002) and Fine *et al.*, (2001) for comprehensive and substantive critiques of the intellectual and empirical basis of the Post-Washington consensus.

15 PRSPs were initially required to reach the completion point for the HIPC initiative and consolidated afterwards as the main policy framework to inform government-donor relations. By September 2008, 30 African countries had completed PRSPs and 20 had also approved a second PRSP (the strategies normally have a five-year span). SSA is therefore the main 'laboratory' of PRSPs.

16 For a discussion of how aid donors, in particular the World Bank, attempted to convince the Vietnamese government to adopt more orthodox economic policies in the wake of the East Asian crisis, denying the positive impact of the policies it was following, see Masina (2002).

17 See also Rodrik (2006).

18 See Riddell (2007: 370–4) for an illustration of this lack of consensus and clarity.

19 Showcases are particularly important since donors, notably the World Bank, prefer to base recommendations on crafted notions of 'best practice' and require relevant showcases (therefore countries from the same region or similar characteristics) to make their case more credible.

20 See section on macroeconomic effects above.

21 Auty thus writes of Africa's fastest growth period (the immediate post-independence period) that it created the conditions for idle rent accumulation because '*fashionable* policies to override markets [were followed] that inadvertently increased the risk that rent-seeking groups would capture natural resource rent

and contrived rent to the detriment of sustained long-term wealth creation' (p.14) (emphasis added).

22 This also resonates the PWC call for 'ownership' largely defined in terms of buying into donors' agendas (Killick et al., 2005, Hanlon and Smart, 2008).

23 For a convincing discussion of Bangladesh's development impasse using this perspective, see Khan (2004), as well as the chapter by Gray and Khan on Tanzania in this volume for an application to an African country.

24 See also Allen (1995) for a more useful account of the variety of political trajectories in Africa and more historically-informed typologies.

25 See Riddell (2007) on the existence of perverse incentive systems and substantial loss of institutional memory in donor agencies, which affect the logic and practice of aid giving.

26 Bergamaschi thus shows that much of the scarce state capacity in Mali has been mobilized in recent years to design and implement a decentralization programme, for the sole reason that it is an important item on the donors' wish list. Of the aid-induced institutional reforms which have been pushed since the 1990s, decentralization has been one of the most destructive, forcing states to surrender power and resources while leaving poor populations at the mercy of local political power holders.

27 This has also been reflected in the severe deterioration of public universities, which has probably had two significant effects. First, a generation of young graduates has either migrated to further training in mainstream academic institutions or found jobs in the very agencies advancing the neoliberal agenda across Africa. Second, a large pool of academic staff, partly frustrated by developments in the 1980s and 1990s, has gradually 'abandoned' core duties in universities to tap the more lucrative niches of donor-driven consultancy business.

28 See Ferguson (2006) for a lucid discussion and examples. See also Sinha (2005) for a more general overview of this process.

29 See Mkandawire (2001) for a discussion and critique of the 'neo-patrimonial' thesis in African politics.

30 An example of this process may be the African Capacity Building Foundation.

31 There is no systematic empirical research on this aspect, but an account of the life stories of Ministers of Finance, governors of Central Banks and other high-level bureaucrats in Ministries of Finance from the 1990s onwards would surely confirm this process.

32 See Harrison (2004) and Hanlon and Smart (2008) for illustrations of these processes.

33 See Harrison (2004: 93–4) on various cases and Hanlon and Smart (2008: 101–37) for a very provocative yet well documented account of Mozambique's case, one of the 'darlings' of donors in Africa.

References

Action Aid International (2005) *Real Aid: An Agenda for Making Aid Work*, Johannesburg. Available at: http://www.actionaid.org.uk/doc_lib/69_1_real_ aid.pdf.

Alden, C., Large D. and Soares de Oliveira, R. (2008) *China Returns to Africa. A Superpower and a Continent Embrace*, London: C. Hurst & Co Publishers Ltd.

Allen, C. (1995) 'Understanding African Politics', *Review of African Political Economy*, 22 (65): 301–20.

Amsden, A. (1989) *Asia's Next Giant: South Korea and Late Industrialization*, Oxford: Oxford University Press.

—— (2007) *Escape from Empire. The Developing World's Journey Through Heaven and Hell*, Cambridge (MA): MIT Press.

Auty, R.M. (2007) 'Aid and Rent-Driven Growth. Mauritania, Kenya and Mozambique Compared', UNU-WIDER Research paper no. 2007/35.

Bergamaschi, I. (2008) 'Mali: Patterns and Limits of Donor-Driven Ownership', in *The Politics of Aid. African Strategies for Dealing with Donors*, Whitfield, L. (ed.), Oxford: Oxford University Press, 217–45.

Blanchard, M. and A.-S. Wender (eds.) (2007) *Guerre aux migrants. Le livre noir de Ceuta et Melilla*, Paris: Syllepse.

Booth, D. (2008), 'Aid Effectiveness after Accra: How to Reform the "Paris Agenda" ', ODI Briefing Paper n. 39, London.

Bulir, A. and Hamann, A.J. (2006) 'Volatility of Development Aid: From the Frying Pan into the Fire?', IMF Working Paper no. 06/65.

Burnside, C. and Dollar, D. (2000) 'Aid, Policies, and Growth', *American Economic Review* 90 (4): 847–68.

Castel-Branco, C.N. (2008) 'Aid and Development: A Question of Ownership? A Critical View', Instituto de Estudos Sociais e Económicos, Working Paper n. 1, Maputo. Available from http://www.iese.ac.mz/lib/publication/AidDevelopment Ownership.pdf

Chang, H-J. (2006) 'Policy Space in Historical Perspective–with Special Reference to Trade and Industrial Policies', *Economic and Political Weekly*, February 18–24, XLI (7): 627–33.

Chang, H-J. and Grabel, I. (2004) *Reclaiming Development: An Alternative Economic Policy Manual*, London: Zed Books.

Collier, P. (2006) 'Is Aid Oil? An Analysis of Whether Africa Can Absorb More Aid', *World Development* 4, (9): 1482–97.

Cramer, C. (2006) *Civil War Is Not a Stupid Thing. Accounting for Violence in Developing Countries*, London: Hurst.

Darbon, D. (2003) 'Réformer ou reformer les administrations projetées des Afriques? Entre routine anti-politique et ingénierie politique contextuelle', *Revue française d'administration publique*, 105–6: 135–52.

Davies, M. with Edinger, H., Tay, N. and Naidu, S. (2008) *How China Delivers Development Assistance to Africa*, Report of the Centre for Chinese Studies prepared for the Department for International Development (DFID), Beijing. www.ccs.org.za/downloads/china-dev-africa-sum.pdf.

Di John, J. (2006) 'The Political Economy of Taxation and Tax Reform in Developing Countries', UNU-WIDER Research Paper no. 2006/74

Easterly, W. (2001) *The Elusive Quest for Growth: Economists' Adventures and Misadventures in the Tropics*, New York: Macmillan.

—— (2002) 'The Cartel of Good Intentions: The Problem of Bureaucracy in Foreign Aid', *Journal of Policy Reform* 5 (4): 223–50.

—— (2005) 'What did Structural Adjustment Adjust?: The Association of Policies and Growth with repeated IMF and World Bank Adjustment Loans', *Journal of Development Economics* 76 (1): 1–22. Volume 76, Issue 1, February 2005, Pages 1–22.

Eatwell, J. and Taylor, L. (2000) *Global Finance at Risk: The Case for International Regulation*, New York: The New Press.

Ferguson, J. (2006) *Global Shadows: Africa in the neoliberal World Order*, Durham and London: Duke University Press.

Fielding, D. and Mavrotas, G. (2005) 'The Volatility of Aid', WIDER Discussion Paper no. 2005/06.

Fine, B., Lapavistas, C. and Pincus, J. (eds) (2001) *Development Policy in the Twenty-first Century. Beyond the Washington Consensus*, London and New York: Routledge.

Gallagher, K.P. (2005) 'Globalization and the Nation-State: Reasserting Policy Autonomy for Development', in Gallagher, K.P. (ed.) *Putting Development First: The Importance of Policy Space in the WTO and International Financial Institutions*, London: Zed Books.

Gupta, S., Powell, R. and Yan, Y. (2005). 'The Macroeconomic Challenges of Scaling Up Aid to Africa'. September draft. IMF Working Paper WP/05/179, Washington DC: IMF.

Hanlon, J. and Smart, T. (2008) *Do Bicycles Equal Development in Mozambique?*, London: James Currey.

Harrison, G. (2004) *The World Bank and Africa. The Construction of Governance States*, London: Routledge.

IDD and Associates (2006) *Evaluation of General Budget Support: Synthesis Report*, International Development Department, University of Birmingham, May. Available at: http://www.oecd.org/dataoecd/42/38/36685401.pdf.

IMF (2005) 'The Macroeconomics of Managing Increased Aid Flows: Experiences of Low-Income Countries and Policy Implications', August, Washington D.C.: IMF.

Jerven, M. (2008), 'African Economic Growth Reconsidered: Measurement and Performance in East-Central Africa, 1965–95', PhD Dissertation, London: London School of Economics.

Jiang, W. (2009) 'A Chinese "Marshall Plan" or business?', Asia Times online, 14 January, http://www.atimes.com/atimes/China_Business/KA14Cb01.html

Karras, G. (2006) 'Foreign Aid and Long-Run Economic Growth: Empirical Evidence for a Panel of Developing Countries', *Journal of International Development*, 18 (1): 15–28.

Khan, M. (2004) 'Power, Property Rights and the Issue of Land Reform: A General Case Illustrated with Reference to Bangladesh', *Journal of Agrarian Change*, 4 (1 and 2): 73–106.

—— (2006) 'Governance and Development', Paper presented at the 'Workshop on Governance and Development' organized by the World Bank and DFID in Dhaka, 11–12 November.

Khan, M. and Jomo, K.S. (eds) (2000) *Rents, Rent-Seeking and Economic Development: Theory and Evidence in Asia*, Cambridge: Cambridge University Press.

Killick, T. (2004) 'Politics, Evidence and the New Aid Agenda', *Development Policy Review*, 22 (1): 5–29.

Killick, T., Castel-Branco, C.N. and Gerster, R. (2005) 'Perfect Partners? The Performance of Programme Aid Partners in Mozambique, 2004'. Report to the Programme Aid Partners and Government of Mozambique, Maputo.

Lensink, R. and Morrissey, O. (2000) 'Aid Instability as a Measure of Uncertainty and the Positive Impact of Aid on Growth', *Journal of Development Studies* 36 (3): 31–49.

McKinley, T. (2005) 'Why is the "Dutch Disease" always a disease? The macroeconomic consequences of scaling up aid', International Poverty Centre Working Paper no. 10, UNDP.

Masina, P. (2002) 'Vietnam and the Regional Crisis: The Case of a 'Late Late-Comer' ', *European Journal of East Asian Studies* 1 (2).

Milonakis, D. and Fine, B. (2007) 'Douglass North's Remaking of Economic History: A Critical Appraisal', *Review of Radical Political Economics* 39 (1): 1–31.

Minoiu, C. and Reddy, S.G. (2006) 'Development Aid and Economic Growth: A Positive Long-Run Relation', Working Papers 29, United Nations, Department of Economics and Social Affairs.

Mkandawire, T. (2001) 'Thinking About Developmental States in Africa', *Cambridge Journal of Economics* 25 (3): 289–313.

Moss, T., Pettersson, G. and Walle, N. (2005) 'An Aid-Institutions Paradox? A Review on Aid Dependency and State Building in Sub-Saharan Africa', Mario Einaudi Centre for International Studies, Working Paper no. 11–05.

Petras, J. and Veltmeyer, H. (2005) 'Foreign Aid, Neoliberalism and US Imperialism', in *Neoliberalism: A Critical Reader*, Saad-Filho, A. and Johnston, D. (eds) London: Pluto Press, 120–26.

Pincus, J. and Winters, J. (eds) (2002) *Reinventing the World Bank*, London: Cornell University Press.

Rapley, J. (2007) *Understanding Development: Theory and Practice in the Third World*, Third edition, Boulder, CO: Lynne Rienner.

Reinert, E. (2007) *How Rich Countries Got Rich . . . And Why Poor Countries Stay Poor*, London: Constable and Robinson.

Riddell, R.C. (2007) *Does Foreign Aid Really Work?*, New York: Oxford University Press.

Rodrik, D. (2006) 'Goodbye Washington Consensus, Hello Washington Confusion', Harvard University paper prepared for the *Journal of Economic Literature*, accessed online on 8th August 2009 at http://ksghome.harvard.edu/~drodrik/Lessons%20of%20the%201990s%20review%20_JEL.pdf

Roodman, D. (2008) 'Through the Looking Glass, and What OLS Found There: On Growth, Foreign Aid, and Reverse Causality' Working Paper n. 137, Washington D.C.: Center for Global Development, January.

Sachs, J. (2005) *The End of Poverty: Economic Possibilities for Our Time*, London: Penguin Press.

Schwartz, H.M. (2000) *States versus Markets: The Emergence of a Global Economy*, 2nd edition, London: Palgrave.

Sender, J. (1999) 'Africa's Economic Performance: Limitations of the Current Consensus', *Journal of Economic Perspectives* 13, (3): 89–114.

—— (2002) 'Re-Assessing the Role of the World Bank in Sub-Saharan Africa', in *Reinventing the World Bank*, Pincus, J. and Winters, J. (eds) London: Cornell University Press, 185–202.

Sinha, S. (2005) 'Neoliberalism and Civil Society: Project and Possibilities', in *Neoliberalism: A Critical Reader*, Saad-Filho, A. and Johnston, D. (eds) London: Pluto Press, 163–9.

Taylor, L. (ed.) (1993) *The Rocky Road to Reform*, New York: Macmillan.

UNCTAD (2000) *The Least Developed Countries Report 2000. Aid, Private Capital Flows and External Debt: The Challenge of Financing Development in LDCs*, Geneva: UNCTAD.

—— (2005) *Economic Development in Africa: Rethinking the Role of Foreign Direct Investment*, New York: United Nations.

—— (2007) *Reclaiming Policy Space: Domestic Resource Mobilization and Developmental States*, Geneva: UNCTAD.

Van Waeyenberge, E. (2008) 'The World Bank as a Knowledge Bank: beyond

Deaton', Article presented at the School of Oriental and African Studies / London International Development Centre as part of the seminar series on 'Scholarship, Advocacy and Policy (after Deaton): The World Bank through the Looking Glass'.

Wade, R. (1990) *Governing the Market: Economic Theory and the Role of Government in Taiwan's Industrialization*, Princeton: Princeton University Press.

Wuyts, M. (1996) 'Foreign Aid, Structural Adjustment and Public Expenditure Management: The Mozambican Experience', *Development and Change* 27 (4): 717–49.

10 Employment, poverty and inclusive development in Africa

Policy choices in the context of widespread informality

James Heintz

The structure of employment in most African countries is characterized by a relatively small share of private industrial employment, a dominance of agricultural employment, and widespread self-employment in informal, non-agricultural enterprises. Of course, exceptions exist (e.g. South Africa) and there is noticeable heterogeneity in employment arrangements among countries with similar economic structures. However, coherent employment policies that explicitly recognize the structure of employment often remain elusive and underdeveloped. This chapter examines the nature of employment in Africa, the importance of the employment-poverty linkage, and the biases implicit in standard employment policies through the lens of informal employment and the informal sector.

The concept of employment in the informal sector was first developed and applied in the African context. Two widely cited early studies are Keith Hart's (1973) research on the informal sector in Accra, Ghana and the report of the well-known ILO mission to Kenya (ILO, 1972). These studies identified the variety of livelihood activities in which individuals were engaged, but which did not correspond directly to standard categories of wage employment and traditional farming activities. These activities collectively constituted the informal sector in which formal regulations did not apply and in which access to formal institutions, such as commercial banks, was non-existent or sharply curtailed. Since that time, the idea of the informal sector and informal employment has been used to describe labour markets around the world and informality remains a defining feature of employment in African countries.[1]

The new concept of the informal sector supplanted, at least in part, surplus labour models of labour markets in developing countries (e.g. Lewis, 1954). In surplus labour approaches, the jobs provided by the formal economy at the prevailing wage falls short of total labour supply. Individuals who cannot find formal employment work in subsistence activities. Informal employment therefore becomes an undifferentiated residual – a kind of employment of last resort. As an economy develops, productivity improvements in the formal economy would increase labour demand and reduce the amount of surplus labour. Eventually, the informal residual would disappear. Informality becomes a marker of underdevelopment and economic 'backwardness'.

For economists adopting this residual concept, informal employment may be associated with inefficiency, as labour is allocated to activities with very low levels of productivity.[2]

In contrast, Hart (1973) and the ILO's mission to Kenya introduced a different conceptualization of the informal sector. They saw the informal sector as consisting of a diverse set of activities that represented a critical source of employment income, particularly for the urban poor. Hart stressed the heterogeneity of informal employment, in which barriers to entry might exist, depending on the specific type of activity. Informal employment often supplemented income from formal employment, particularly in the context of high inflation and falling wages. The ILO report on Kenya argued that the development of informal activities could constitute an important element of an overall employment strategy.[3] Economic policies could be developed to explicitly improve working conditions in the informal sector.

This alternative view suggested that the solution to problems of low productivity, poverty, and precarious earnings associated with the informal sector was not to eliminate informal employment over time, but rather to improve conditions among individuals working in these activities. Instead of viewing the informal sector as an indicator of underdevelopment and 'backwardness,' this new approach viewed the informal sector as a potential basis for improving employment opportunities, if appropriate strategies were adopted.[4] These conflicting viewpoints – informality as underdevelopment versus informal employment as an important livelihood strategy – continue to influence employment policies and development strategies today.

As the empirical review presented later in this chapter suggests, the structure of employment in many African countries has not changed significantly from that described in these early studies of employment in the informal sector. Moreover, productivity and earnings remain low and poverty is widespread. This raises the important question of what framework is appropriate for formulating employment policies in Africa, given the context of widespread informality. We return to this question at the end of the chapter.

Employment and poverty

Policies to promote economic growth will only reduce poverty and mitigate inequalities if the benefits of such growth are widely shared. In African countries, the improvement of employment opportunities represents a critical channel through which the additional income associated with faster growth can be distributed throughout the population. Labour is the one factor of production which poor and low-income households typically command in abundance (Islam, 2006; Khan, 2006; Squire, 1993). Therefore, policies which more fully employ labour resources and which raise the returns individuals can expect to earn from their paid work create a foundation for more egalitarian growth and development.

Development strategies that aim to distribute the benefits of growth through improved employment opportunities must do so along a number of dimensions. First, the policies must address problems of insufficient labour demand. In African countries, problems of open unemployment may not be as significant as wide-spread underemployment. This is particularly true outside urban areas and in informal activities. However, both unemployment and underemployment have a common root cause: lack of sufficient labour demand, recognizing that labour demand is derived, in part, from the demand for other goods and services.

Second, economic policies to address poverty should support improvements in the quality of employment. Possibilities for raising the quality of employment opportunities are often constrained by low productivity and the inability of workers to capture the benefits of productivity improvements. We can think of raising the returns to labour in terms of improving labour's terms of trade – that is, the income received from work relative to the costs of sustaining workers and their families. In African countries, workers often face unfavourable terms of trade – i.e. remuneration is low relative to the costs of living (Fox and Gaal, 2008). Finally, workers must enjoy sufficient economic mobility to take advantage of new and better opportunities when they become available. Barriers to mobility – including labour market segmentation in which individuals are excluded from certain employment relationships or activities – limit the redistributive impact of an employment-centred development strategy.

Poverty is typically defined and measured at the household level while the attributes of employment are assessed at the level of the individual or job. Therefore, two sets of institutions shape the employment-poverty connection: the labour market and the household. These institutions are closely intertwined and exhibit highly gendered dynamics. For example, women's participation in remunerative employment is partly determined by conditions in the household. However, women's access to paid employment also impacts total household income and the risk of poverty. Similarly, extended family networks in African countries frequently mean that the benefits from a single source of employment are distributed widely. The impact on poverty rates are therefore more broad-based than they would first appear to be if we only focused on individual earnings and welfare. Differences in household composition, the structure of employment, returns to labour, and the segmentation of the labour force shape the dynamics of employment and poverty.

Structure of employment in Africa: examples from five countries

Knowledge of the structure of employment – specifically in terms of the economic arrangements and institutional settings in which labour is exchanged – is important for prioritizing and focusing policy effort. Labour can be exchanged through various channels and this is broadly reflected in the status in employment categories. For paid employees, labour is directly exchanged for a wage. For the self-employed, individuals realize the returns to their labour through other forms of market exchange. There are hybrid forms – e.g. piece-rate workers – who may effectively be working as paid employees, but are treated as self-employed, albeit in highly dependent forms of self-employment.

In addition, employment relationships are differently regulated. Employment arrangements for paid employees are typically regulated through labour legislation and by non-government forms of regulation (e.g. collective bargaining). However, paid employees are not always covered, *de facto* if not *de jure*, by regulatory protections and collective agreements. These workers, lacking basic legal and social protections, represent informal paid employees. In contrast, the self-employed are excluded from the regulatory system which governs wage employment. Instead, the enterprises in which the self-employed work are the subject of regulation, not the employment relationship itself. Self-employment is deemed to be informal if the enterprise falls outside the regulatory sphere (i.e. it belongs to the informal sector).[5]

Table 10.1 presents estimates of the distribution of employment by employment status and informality status which give a useful overview of the structure of employment for five countries: Ghana, Mali, Kenya, Madagascar, and South Africa.

We can draw a number of broad inferences from Table 10.1 which are generally indicative of the structure of employment in many sub-Saharan African countries, recognizing that South Africa remains an exception. First, the agricultural sector is a critical source of employment opportunities. Second, informal employment accounts for a significantly larger share of total employment than does formal employment. Third, informal self-employment – both agricultural and non-agricultural – provides a large number of economic opportunities. Fourth, the public sector remains an important source of formal jobs in African countries.

As mentioned, South Africa is an exception among the countries featured in Table 10.1. Formal wage employment in the private sector is the dominant form of employment in South Africa. Informal self-employment and agricultural employment are significantly less important when compared to other African countries. Wage employment accounts for a larger share of agricultural employment than does self-employment – in the other four African countries, agricultural self-employment is dominant. The public sector is an important source of formal jobs, but the private sector dominates formal employment arrangements. Finally, South Africa currently has very high measured rates of open unemployment – i.e. the unemployed do not enter into informal self-employment at a rapid rate (Heintz and Posel, 2008). The distinct structure of employment in South Africa has important implications for the political economy of employment policy – a theme to which we return later.

Although South Africa is clearly unique among the countries examined here, the other four countries also exhibit diversity in the structure of employment. Employment in Africa cannot be taken as homogeneous or

Table 10.1 Structure of employment in five African countries. Distribution of formal and informal employment by employment status.

	Kenya (2005)	Ghana (1998/9)	Mali (2004)	Madagascar (2005)	South Africa (2004)
Total formal employment					
Formal, private wage employment	6.9%	1.0%	n/a	2.5%	40.8%
Formal, public wage employment	5.4%	4.1%	n/a	2.7%	16.5%
Total formal wage employment	12.3%	5.1%	5.8%	5.2%	57.3%
Formal, self-employment	1.3%	3.6%	5.1%	1.6%	4.2%
Informal employment (agricultural and non-agricultural)					
Informal wage employment	18.0%	9.3%	11.0%	9.3%	22.8%
Informal self-employment	64.8%	81.6%	78.1%	83.8%	14.4%
Other/undeclared	3.6%	0.4%	0.0%	0.0%	1.3%
Total	100%	100%	100%	100%	100%
. . . of which . . .					
Agricultural wage employment	n/a	1.2%	0.9%	3.3%	10.6%
Agricultural self-employment	50.0%	52.3%	41.2%	77.2%	4.7%
Additional ratios					
Informal non-agricultural self-employment (% of total)	14.8%	29.3%	36.9%	6.6%	9.7%
Informal as a % of non-agricultural employment	66%	80%	81%	65%	27%

Source: Kenya, authors' calculations based on the 2005 Household Integrated Budget Survey; Ghana, authors' calculations based on the 1998/9 Ghana Living Standards Survey; Mali, ILO Bureau of Statistics; and South Africa, Heintz and Posel (2007). See appendix for detail on definitions.

invariant across countries. For example, in Ghana and Mali, non-agricultural informal self-employment is particularly important, accounting for one-quarter to one-third of all employment. However, in Kenya and Madagascar, informal non-agricultural wage employment is as important as informal self-employment outside agriculture. In Ghana, Mali, and Madagascar, formal wage employment represents a small fraction of total employment. In Kenya, the share of formal wage employment is twice as large as in the other three cases.

Table 10.1 does not contain an example of a Northern African country. Northern African countries exhibit a distinct structure of employment when compared to sub-Saharan countries, particularly in terms of women's employment. Official measurements of women's labour force participation rates, and hence rates of employment, are significantly lower in North African economies compared to the rest of the continent. In the Arab States, a particularly large share of women work as unpaid contributing family workers in informal enterprises, both agricultural and non-agricultural (Heintz, 2007).

In African countries, earnings are typically lowest and poverty rates are highest in agricultural employment (see, for example, Chen *et al.*, 2005; Pollin *et al.*, 2008; Epstein *et al.*, 2008). In non-agricultural informal employment – both wage employment and self-employment – earnings are higher than in agricultural employment, but lower than in formal employment. Exceptions exist – for example, informal employers who hire other workers can earn more on average than formal wage workers. Apart from these employers, individuals in formal employment enjoy the highest earnings, and lowest risks of poverty. Given these patterns of earnings, migration out of agricultural and into non-agricultural informal employment often represents a step upwards in terms of earnings and economic mobility, even though poverty rates are high among households that depend on informal employment as the primary source of income. Therefore, movement into non-agricultural informal activities, in both urban and rural settings, represents an intermediate step in the transition out of agriculture, particularly in the context of widespread informality. It also helps explain rural-to-urban migration, in which individuals leave agriculture to work informally in cities.

Labour market regulation and employment

Economists often identify labour market rigidities – due to excessive regulation or the bargaining activities of trade unions – as the primary constraints to employment growth. It is argued that such rigidities tend to increase labour costs and reduce labour demand relative to supply. If wages cannot fall so as to 'mop up' the excess supply, the result will be an overall reduction in labour demand. This line of argument was central to the Washington Consensus and neoliberal approach to addressing problems of unemployment and underemployment.

Note that this proposition only applies to formal *wage labour* markets – in which regulations are binding and in which the supply of labour can be easily distinguished from the demand for labour. Standard dualist theories of labour markets frequently argue that high labour costs due to labour market rigidities constrain employment growth in the formal economy (e.g. Harris and Todaro, 1970; Fields, 1975).[6] Formal job opportunities are rationed and those without formal jobs work in 'traditional' activities (i.e. agricultural or informal activities) or are openly unemployed. Under these assumptions, labour market rigidities cause either informal employment or open unemployment. To the extent this holds true, informalization could be reduced by removing all rigidities. In effect, this would 'informalize' formal jobs by removing the regulatory structure.

Arguments that high wages and excessive regulation are responsible for a lack of formal employment, high unemployment, or widespread under-employment have only limited relevance for most African countries. As we have shown, formal (i.e. regulated) private wage employment typically accounts for a small fraction of total employment – often well below 10 percent of all employment. Although labour market regulations may slow the growth of formal employment, they cannot be fully responsible for the exist-ence of unemployment or informal employment in African countries, given the small size of the regulated workforce (Heintz and Pollin, 2008). Only in a country like South Africa, with a large share of regulated wage employment, would those labour market institutions have the potential to have large-scale impacts on employment dynamics. It is not surprising, therefore, that con-flicts about employment policy in South Africa often focus on the degree of regulation of wage employment. This is not to say that labour market rigid-ities are the primary cause of unemployment in South Africa, but rather to point out that the structure of employment shapes the political economy of employment policy.

It is also important to recognize that not all imperfections in labour mar-kets can be attributed to formal regulations. Non-regulatory market failures are commonplace in all labour markets (Heintz, 2008). These include real costs associated with labour market participation, job search, and monitoring (i.e. positive transactions costs); imperfect information; costly enforcement of contracts (both explicit and implicit); and unequal degrees of market power among economic actors, including the various intermediaries operating in the informal economy. Researchers have found evidence of barriers to mobility between formal and informal employment, and between different forms of informal employment in African countries (Heintz and Posel, 2008; Günther and Launov, 2006). Similarly, Hart (1973) emphasizes the importance of a variety of barriers to entry, including the role of kinship networks for determining access to employment in Ghana. Such non-regulatory barriers can be more important in determining access to employment opportunities than the system of formal labour market regulations.

The significant point of this discussion is that limited employment opportunities in Africa are not primarily the result of over-regulation of formalized labour markets and rigidities in the governance of wage labour. The solution to most employment problems must therefore be found outside the formal wage labour market institutions and involve additional factors such as market access, financial services, agricultural dynamics, and urban policy. In other words, the challenge of creating decent jobs in African coun-tries is a development challenge, one that requires a comprehensive set of employment-focused policies.

Beyond the labour market: improving informal employment opportunities

Many constraints operate to limit the quality and quantity of employment in African countries and, as stressed above, these are not restricted to distortions caused by the regulation of wage labour. If labour market rigidities are not to blame for the persistence of low-quality employment, what are the real constraints to improving employment opportunities? As suggested above, the solution to employment problems in Africa requires addressing constraints found outside the labour market. We demonstrate the relevance of this argument by exploring constraints in three areas that are particularly important for informal employment: the financial sector, market access, and urban policy. We focus on non-agricultural employment, specifically informal non-agricultural employment, because other chapters in this volume address issues concerning agricultural livelihoods in detail (the chapters by Oya and Anseeuw).

The financial sector

Banks remain the dominant financial institutions in much of Africa. In most African countries, the developmental role of the banking sector is circumscribed by limited access to the appropriate type of financial services that would encourage an expansion of productive activities. Barriers to credit and financial markets are a particularly severe problem for smaller enterprises, those operating in the informal economy, and agricultural activities. Not only is access to credit limited, the cost of credit is typically high throughout Africa. Financial market rigidities frequently have a more profound negative impact on the quality of employment in African countries than labour market inflexibility.

A number of factors are particularly important in contributing to the relatively high costs of credit in African banking systems. First, the risk premium that borrowers must pay in formal credit markets is extremely high. This is due to perceptions, often incorrect, that most creditors are high risk borrowers and not bankable (Atieno, 2001). The reliance on perceptions is important, since many commercial banking sectors never developed the capacity to collect information on the creditworthiness of potential borrowers outside their traditional clientele (Kimuyu and Omiti, 2000; Nissanke and Aryeetey, 1998; Steele, *et al.*, 1997). For small-scale and rural borrowers, transactions costs may also raise the cost of credit from commercial banks. Because many banks in Africa have traditionally extended credit to the public sector or to finance international trade, they may be inefficient in managing loans to small producers (Steele *et al.*, 1997). A second contributing factor to the sizeable interest rate spreads observed in Africa is the market structure of the banking system itself. Banking tends to be highly concentrated, with a few large banks dominating the sector. Finally, central bank policies which target low rates of inflation often yield excessively high real interest rates (Heintz and Pollin, 2008).

One reason behind the low quantity of credit extended to the private sector is that banks in sub-Saharan Africa currently tend to hold excess liquidity (Sacerdoti, 2005; Mkandawire, 1999; Steele *et al.*, 1997). That is, commercial banks prefer to hold short-term government securities rather than extending loans to borrowers whom they perceive to be high-risk. Under these conditions, credit to the private sector is rationed. Credit rationing is likely to be particularly severe for rural and small-scale borrowers for the same reasons that interest rates are extremely high: lack of credit information systems and perceptions of risk.

In short, institutional barriers in the banking sector limit the availability of credit to small-scale producers and the informal self-employed. Since these individuals tend to have limited access to capital assets, credit represents one channel through which this constraint could be relaxed. However, the informal self-employed are effectively excluded from participating in the formal financial sector and, when they do have access to credit, the terms under which they must borrow are unfavourable. Such economic exclusion, and unfavourable inclusion, limits the scope to improve the quality of employment opportunities by, for example, investing in capital equipment which could raise productivity and living standards.

Market access

For the informal self-employed and those working in small enterprises, the domestic market is the primary source of demand for goods and services. For example, research has found that, in Ghana, informal employment depends on domestic demand in local markets (Barwa, 1995). In Kenya, informal enterprises rely almost exclusively on domestic markets (Pollin *et al.*, 2008). Therefore, barriers to market access and insufficient local demand will limit the ability of these individuals to realize income from their productive efforts. A number of factors contribute to enhancing market access. For example, public investments in roads, storage facilities, and communications infrastructure improve access. Macroeconomic policies have a direct impact on the level of domestic demand and the development of markets. Often, substandard infrastructure and restrictive macroeconomic policies constrain access to domestic demand.

In many cases, the majority of the informally self-employed in African countries, outside agriculture, are engaged in the provision of services (see, for example, Pollin *et al.*, 2008). This has important implications for how we think about policies to improve earnings and productivity. Productivity in services is distinct from productivity in manufacturing and other industrial activities. Productivity in services, and by extension earnings in service activities, is strongly influenced by the level of demand and development of markets. For example, a street trader's productivity will be largely determined by the quantity of goods she sells within a given time period. In manufacturing, productivity is often thought of as a 'supply-side' factor, linked to the nature of production technology. In services, the boundary between the supply-side and demand-side is blurred in the determination of overall productivity – issues of domestic demand and market access become crucially important.

Institutional barriers to direct market access can affect earnings in other ways. In some cases, informal workers must go through various intermediaries in order to access markets. This worsens their terms of trade, since the intermediaries capture a significant share of the value produced along the supply chain. Often specific interventions can increase direct market access and improve the terms of trade. For example, in South Africa, the municipal government of Durban/eThekwini established buy-back centres in the city to allow companies to purchase recyclable materials directly from self-employed waste collectors. Prior to the establishment of the buy-back centres, waste-collectors often had to rely on intermediaries for market access. In this way, a targeted, municipal-level intervention was able to increase market access and to create a type of market exchange which was not prevalent before (Chen *et al.*, 2005).

Urban policies

The governance of urban space in general – and public space in particular – is central to the livelihood strategies of many of the informal self-employed. Moreover, the issue will only become more important in the future, given the rates of rural-to-urban migration and the projected growth rates of the urban population in Africa. The informal self-employed need space in order to operate their enterprises. However, because the majority of these workers are asset-poor, they lack private property rights over such space. In some cases, it is possible to operate the informal business from a residential structure. Even then, the tenure rights of these households may be uncertain. In other cases, the activities cannot be restricted to private homes. For example, street traders need to go to their markets – their markets may not come to them.

Urban public space may be considered a type of public asset – although with specific properties. For example, access may not be entirely unrestricted or non-monitored, some level of exclusion is possible. Moreover, the use of urban public spaces by one individual does not necessarily preclude its use by others (e.g. mobile roadside retailers), but issues of congestion and diminishing returns can become serious problems. One approach to addressing problems of congestion, insecure tenancy, and 'tragedy of the commons' effects is to increase the excludability of such space by defining enforceable private property rights (de Soto, 1989). The benefits of privatization is a common theme of the neoliberal policies which have dominated the development strategies of most African countries over the past several decades.

However, privatizing public space may not produce welfare improvements when informal use of public space generates synergies among informal activities (e.g. clustering of informal activities facilitates the development of markets and higher levels of demand), economies of scale exist (e.g. when multiple uses of public space are possible without significantly raising the costs or lowering the productivity of other users), or there are concerns over equity (e.g. if the poor are unable to secure access to privatized property rights). Therefore, a viable regulatory framework for the urban environment is needed, one that improves the security of access to public assets among the informal self-employed. Some of the approaches to the management of competing uses of urban spaces, adopted by municipal governments in many African countries, which aim to 'clean up the streets' can be disastrous for the livelihoods of the informal self-employed. The so-called 'backwardness' of informal employment is deemed to be inconsistent with a modern urban setting and so-called 'world class cities'. However, this style of urban management will undermine attempts to improve the employment opportunities of the poor and thereby reduce poverty.

African employment in the context of widespread informality

We now return to the question raised at the beginning of the chapter: what is the appropriate employment strategy for African economies in which informal employment tends to be the rule, rather than the exception?

It is hard to escape the fact that informal employment, in all its diversity, represents an important source of livelihoods. Given the low level of private industrial employment in most African countries, even if formal employment opportunities were to grow rapidly, informal employment will remain critically important for decades. However, because informal employment is seen as a marker of underdevelopment, it has been marginalized in policy discussions and development strategies.

Instead, the blame for poor quality employment is often levied on labour markets, despite the paucity of evidence in support of this proposition. Financial and industrial policies typically cater to larger firms, with more political and economic influence. Moreover, the banking sector will resist reform when the current way of doing business is quite profitable. Exporters also disproportionately influence the direction of economic policy. An emphasis on exports *de facto* excludes informal enterprises, which are linked to domestic markets. Those individuals and households relying on informal employment have little voice, and therefore employment policies remain disconnected from the reality of people's livelihoods in Africa. Since policies are often not crafted with informal employment in mind, it is not surprising that the constraints outlined in the previous section – in terms of finance, market access, and urban space – continue to limit earnings and productivity among informal workers.

What is needed is a shift in thinking and politics to re-orient employment policy towards removing the constraints that limit productivity and mobility in informal employment. At the same time, we must acknowledge that this is only a partial answer. Informal employment in most African countries is concentrated in service activities where the scope for productivity improvements is limited. Own-account workers in informal manufacturing cannot capture the benefits of economies of scale due to the nature of informal enterprises. In short, there are real limits to productivity improvements in informal activities that go beyond the institutional and policy constraints highlighted earlier. Nevertheless, informal employment will not disappear any time soon – the informal sector remains as relevant today as when it was first discussed by the ILO with regard to Kenya and Hart with regard to Ghana.

Therefore, efforts to improve the working conditions of informal workers must be seen as complementary to, and not a substitute for, a broader economic development agenda that includes an emphasis on agrarian livelihoods and expansion of formal employment opportunities. The policy playing field is not level – systematic biases against informal employment exist, and these must be eliminated. Employment strategies must be inclusive of informal activities and aim to integrate them more closely into development policy. This involves a particular process of 'formalization' of informal employment, one that goes well beyond the notion of registering the unregistered enterprises – i.e. extending to the informal economy economic services (e.g. finance), appropriate regulation (e.g. urban policy), and stronger linkages with the domestic economy (e.g. market access). Moreover, the kinds of barriers to mobility discussed earlier represent impediments to the fuller integration of formal and informal spheres of the economy. Identifying and removing these barriers would also encourage greater economic inclusion.

In conclusion, it is useful to reiterate the observation that improving employment opportunities in Africa is a development challenge, one that requires a variety of specific interventions, the precise nature of which depends on the structure of employment and the particulars of the institutional setting. Informal employment must be included in broad-based strategies for economic development and poverty reduction, but with an ultimate aim of transforming these employment arrangements so that they are no longer marginalized in terms of economic institutions and policy formulation. The creation of such an inclusive, employment-centred approach to economic development is necessary to lay the foundation for egalitarian growth in Africa.

Appendix

Notes on country-specific definitions of informal employment

Ghana

For the self-employed: individuals who work in unregistered enterprises. For paid employees: formal employees had access to paid leave and/or some kind of pension.

Kenya

For self-employed: individuals who work in an unregistered household enterprise. For paid employees: based on the sector of the employer, given the design of the Kenya Integrate Household Budget Survey. Employees are considered to be formal if they work in private corporations, government departments, public enterprises, or national/international NGOs. Employees of individuals or other categories of employers are considered to be informal.

Madagascar

For the self-employed: individuals who work in unregistered household enterprises (without a número statistique). For paid employees: informal employees have no access to a pension, or any social protection in the form of medical coverage.

Mali

For the self-employed: individuals who work in an unregistered enterprise. For paid employees: employees are informal if there are no employer contributions to the social fund, no paid leave, and no sick leave.

South Africa

For self-employed: individuals who work in an unregistered enterprise. For paid employees: employees are formal if they have an employment contract or if the employee receives both paid leave and pension contributions.

Notes

1 In 2003, the seventeenth International Conference of Labour Statisticians made a distinction between informal employment and employment in the informal sector. We use this distinction in this chapter. The informal sector is defined in terms of the nature of the enterprise. Informal enterprises are not registered with a government body or subject to the full set of formal regulations. In contrast, informal employment uses a jobs-based definition. Informal employment refers to jobs that are not covered by a basic set of social and legal protections.
2 Santiago Levy makes a similar argument about the inefficient employment of labour in informal activities in Mexico, but in this case, he assumes that informality is freely chosen. He argues that distortions introduced by Mexico's social security system create incentives for individuals to enter informal employment. The allocation of labour to low-productivity activities hinders economic growth (Levy, 2008).
3 For example, the ILO report argues that 'the informal sector is not a problem but a source of future growth' (ILO, 1972, p. 505).
4 Hart raises the question, 'Does the 'reserve army of urban unemployed and underemployed' really constitute a passive, exploited majority in cities like Accra, or do their informal activities possess some autonomous capacity for generating growth in the incomes of the urban (and rural) poor?' (Hart, 1973, p. 61).

5 Hussmanns (2004) presents a more detailed discussion of the international definitions of informal employment, based on the recommendations of the International Conference of Labour Statisticians.

6 For a review of various theories of informality, including dualist approaches, see Kucera and Roncolato (2008).

References

Atieno, Rosemary (2001) 'Formal and informal institutions' lending policies and access to credit by small-scale enterprises in Kenya: an empirical assessment', AERC Research Paper 111, Nairobi: African Economic Research Consortium.

Barwa, S.D. (1995) 'Structural adjustment programmes and the urban informal sector in Ghana,' Issues in Development Discussion Paper 3, International Labour Office, Geneva.

Chen, M., Vanek, J., Lund, F., Heintz, J., Jhabvala, R., and Bonner, C. (2005) *Progress of the World's Women 2005: Women, Work, and Poverty*, New York: UNIFEM.

de Soto, Hernando. (1989) *The Other Path: The Invisible Revolution in the Third World*, New York: Harper and Row.

Epstein, Gerald, Heintz, James, Ndikumana, Léonce, and Chang, Grace. (2008) 'Employment, Poverty and Economic Development in Madagascar: A Macroeconomic Framework', Policy report prepared for the International Labour Organization.

Fields, Gary (1975) 'Rural-urban migration, urban unemployment and under-employment, and job-search activity in LDCs' *Journal of Development Economics*, 2(2): 165–87.

Fox, Louise and Sekkel Gaal, Melissa. (2008) *Working Out of Poverty: Job Creation and the Quality of Growth in Africa*. Washington, DC: World Bank.

Günther, Isabel and Launov, A. (2006) 'Competitive and segmented informal labor markets', IZA (Forschungsinstitut zur Zukunft der Arbeit) Discussion Paper No. 2349.

Harris, John R. and Todaro, Michael P. (1970) 'Migration, unemployment, and development: a two-sector analysis', *American Economic Review*, 60(1), 126–42.

Hart, Keith. (1973) 'Informal income opportunities and urban employment in Ghana', *Journal of Modern African Studies*, 11(1), 61–89.

Heintz, James. (2007) 'The structure of employment in the Arab States: a comparative statistical analysis of informality, gender equity, and social protection,' Chapter prepared for the project of the ILO and Center for Arab Women Training and Research on Gender Equality and Workers' Rights in the Informal Economies of the Arab States, Beirut Office: ILO.

——— . (2008) 'Revisiting labour markets: implications for macroeconomics and social protection' *IDS Bulletin* 39(2): 11–17.

Heintz, James and Pollin, Robert. (2008) 'Targeting employment expansion, economic growth, and development in sub-Saharan Africa: outlines of an alternative economic program for the region', United Nations Economic Commission for Africa (UNECA) Working Paper.

Heintz, J. and Posel, D. (2008) 'Revisiting segmentation and informal employment in the South Africa labour market,' *South African Journal of Economics*, 76(1): 26–44.

Hussmanns, Ralf. (2004) 'Statistical definition of informal employment: guidelines endorsed by the 17th International Conference of Labour Statisticians', Paper prepared for the 7th Meeting of the Expert Group on Informal Sector Statistics (Delhi Group), New Delhi, Feb. 2–4.

ILO. (1972) *Employment, Incomes, and Equity: A Strategy for Increasing Productive Employment in Kenya*, Geneva: International Labour Office.

Islam, Rizwanul (2006) 'The nexus of economic growth, employment, and poverty reduction: an empirical analysis,' in R. Islam, ed. *Fighting Poverty: The Development-Employment Link*, London: Lynne Rienner.

Khan, Azizur Rahman (2006) 'Employment policies for poverty reduction', In R. Islam, ed. *Fighting Poverty: the Employment-Development* Link. London: Lynne Rienner, pp. 63–103.

Kimuyu, Peter, and Omiti, John. (2000) 'Institutional impediments to access to credit by micro and small scale enterprises in Kenya', Institute of Policy Analysis and Research Discussion Paper 26, Nairobi: IPAR.

Kucera, David and Leanne Roncolato (2008) 'Informal employment: two contested policy issues', *International Labour Review*, 147(4): 321–48.

Levy, Santiago (2008) *Good Intentions, Bad Outcomes: Social Policy, Informality, and Economic Growth in Mexico*. Washington, DC: Brookings Institution.

Lewis, W. Arthur. (1954) 'Economic development with unlimited supplies of labour', *Manchester School of Economic and Social Studies*, 22(2): 139–91.

Mkandawire, Thandika. (1999) 'The political economy of financial reform in Africa', *Journal of International Development* 11: 321–42.

Nissanke, Machiko and Aryeetey, Ernest. (1998) *Financial Integration and Development: Liberalization and Reform in sub-Saharan Africa*. London and New York: Routledge.

Pollin, Robert, Githinji, Mwangi wa, and Heintz, James. (2008) *An Employment-Targeted Economic Program for Kenya*. Aldershot and Northampton: Elgar.

Pollin, Robert, Epstein, Gerald, Heintz, James, and Ndikumana, Léonce Ndikumana. (2006) *An Employment-Targeted Economic Program for South Africa*. Aldershot and Northampton: Elgar.

Sacerdoti, Emilio (2005) 'Access to bank credit in Sub-Saharan Africa: key issues and reform strategies', IMF Working Paper 166, New York: International Monetary Fund.

Squire, Lyn (1993) 'Fighting poverty', *American Economic Review*, 83(2): 377–82.

Steele, William, Aryeetey, Ernest, Hettige, Hemamala, Nissanke, Machiko (1997) 'Informal financial markets under liberalization in four African countries,' *World Development* 25(5): 817–30.

11 Street trading in Africa

Demographic trends, planning and trader organisation

Caroline Skinner [1]

Street trading is a core component of the informal economy across the African continent. This chapter critically analyses what is known about this phenomenon. First urbanisation, migration and economic development trends are reviewed and the available data on street traders reflected. The evidence suggests that there has been a surge in the numbers of street traders, partly caused by structural adjustment processes and this is and will continue to be exacerbated by the 2008/2009 global financial crisis. Section 2 critically analyses trends in policy, planning and governance. Research on the issue suggests that state responses to street trading form a continuum from violent sustained evictions to an inclusive approach, but that an inclusive approach is rare. What is clear from this, is that the processes of incorporation or exclusion of street traders is part of everyday political struggle. The ways in which street traders are organised, articulate their concerns and wield power, is therefore critical. Section 3 thus focuses on trends in street traders' organisations. Although there are promising examples of street trader organisation, existing evidence suggests that many traders are not part of organisations. The conclusion makes the case for including street traders into urban planning.

In his discussion in this volume on the use value of the notion of the 'informal sector / economy' forty years on, Keith Hart notes that the term allows academics and bureaucrats to incorporate the teeming street life into abstract models 'without having to know what people are really doing'. He states 'we need to know how formal bureaucracy works in practice and, even more important, what social forms have emerged to organise the informal economy'. This chapter hopes to go someway in responding to his call.

This chapter draws largely on existing literature. As will be detailed below, there have been studies on street trading in West Africa (Senegal, Guinea-Bissau, Ivory Coast and Ghana); Central Africa (the Democratic Republic of Congo); Southern Africa (Zambia, Zimbabwe, South Africa, Lesotho) and East Africa (Tanzania, Kenya). The most striking gap is the absence of research on North Africa. Also no research was found on street trading in Africa's second biggest economy, Nigeria. The literature search was confined to research written in English and there is thus a bias towards Anglophone experiences. The broad trends identified need to be qualified by these biases.

Street trader trends over time

In Africa the informal sector as a whole is estimated to account for 60 per cent of all urban jobs and over 90 per cent of all new urban jobs. After home-working, street trading is estimated to account for the largest share of these jobs. (Charmes, 2000). Trends in street trading over time are integrally linked to urbanisation, migration and economic development processes. Therefore before reflecting on what data there is, each of these will be considered in turn.

As Mitullah (1991:16) notes urbanisation in African countries is a relatively recent phenomenon except for West Africa and some coastal East African towns. Table 11.1 below presents urbanisation figures in 1995 and 2008 as well as projected urban growth rates for 2005–10.

Despite the fact that, for the first time in history, in 2008 one in every two people lived in urban areas, overall urbanisation in Africa is lower than in Asia and in Latin America and the Caribbean. However what is clear from the table is that there are significant regional differences within Africa. North and Southern Africa are highly urbanised in contrast, for example, to East Africa. In the space of thirteen years – a relatively short period in demographic time – the percentage of the total population that is urban has increased by 5 per cent. Again there are regional differences with increases in urbanisation rates being particularly pronounced in Middle, East and West Africa. The final column of the table uses current figures to project the urban growth rate. These predictions suggest that urbanisation processes in Africa will proceed faster than in other continents. Due to low barriers to entry, newcomers to the city often opt for street trading as a way of surviving. These figures seem to suggest that the current congestion on the streets is likely to intensify.

A further dimension of urbanisation processes that swells the number of street traders is international migration. As Landau (2007:61) points out

Table 11.1 Percentage of total urban population

	1995	2008	Urban growth rate 2005–10
Latin America and the Caribbean	74	79	1.7
Asia	35	41	2.5
Africa	34	39	3.3
Eastern Africa	22	23	3.9
Middle Africa	33	42	4.3
Northern Africa	46	51	2.4
Southern Africa	48	58	1.5
Western Africa	37	43	3.8

Source: United Nations, 1997, United Nations, 2007, United Nations, 2008

'international migration is an inexorable response to regional economic inequalities'. Not only are there significant inequalities between African countries, but Africa has long been the site of a number of political crises and civil wars. Somalia, Liberia, Sierra Leone, the Democratic Republic of Congo, Rwanda, Burundi, Ethiopia and Eritrea have generated high levels of forced migration. More recently issues in the Darfur Region as well as Zimbabwe are generating flows of migration both within Africa and elsewhere. In a continent where there is large scale unemployment and underemployment, the trend is for migration legislation to be designed to protect locals from competition for jobs. Foreign migrants, like their rural counterparts, often have no choice but to work in segments of the economy where barriers to entry and set up costs are low. Street trading is thus what many foreign migrants opt to do. Another group of foreigners involved in street trading are cross border traders. Again this is an activity that has been going on for some time. Lourenço-Lindell (2004:87) points out that Dyulas – West African, cross border traders – have been active for centuries and that for many villages they are the primary source of supplies. Cross border traders either supply domestic street traders or sell their goods directly (see Peberdy, 2000 for one of the few surveys of this group).

A critical factor driving up the numbers of street traders in Africa has been the Structural Adjustment Programmes (SAPs) of the 1980s and 1990s. As has been discussed in detail elsewhere (see among others, Iyenda, 2001, Freund, 2007, Lourenço-Lindell, 2004, Tsitsi and Agatha, 2000) the cocktail of privatisation, restructuring of the public sector and the opening up of African economies to foreign goods, led to a dramatic shrinking of the formal economy in Africa. This resulted in a substantial increase in the numbers of those informally employed. SAPs, however, did often encourage a more tolerant attitude to the informal economy, particularly for example in the former (African) socialist states. Lourenço-Lindell (2004) details this for Guinea-Bissau and Nnkya (2006) for Tanzania.

Ongoing privatisation and liberalisation efforts on the continent continue to impact on the size, nature and dynamics within the informal economy, in general, and street trading in particular. Consider, for example, the implications of the increase in numbers of those working informally, on gender dynamics. Although often more dominant in terms of numbers, in many countries, women tend to predominate in areas of trade which are less lucrative. With greater competition, there is evidence that either women get displaced or forced into even more marginal areas of trade (see for example Transberg Hansen (2004:72) on street traders in Zambia). The combination of greater competition among informal traders and a shrinking demand for goods due to shrinking economies, has led to individual incomes decreasing.

The implications for informal traders of trade liberalisation are also complex. Liberalisation of African economies has lead to an increase of imports with the final point of sale for many of these goods being informal traders. This has become particularly pronounced with the dramatic increase in imports from China to Africa over the last ten years. The greater availability of a diverse range of goods can be positive for informal traders. But trade liberalisation has often had devastating impacts on local industry. Baden and Barber (2005), for example, reflect on the impact of second hand clothes trade on local clothing manufacturing in West Africa. This has not only led to job losses, especially for women, but also a shrinking customer base for informal trade. The overall welfare implications, for this segment of the informal economy, of recent economic policies require further examination.

As the International Labour Organisation's (2002:51) compilation of informal economy statistics outlines, despite the numbers and visibility of street traders there are few good estimates of the number of traders. Many population censuses and labour force surveys do not contain a question on 'place of work' with relevant alternative responses. Over and above this, however, street trade is inherently difficult to measure. As the report notes there is a great variance in the number of street vendors counted depending on the time of day, day of the week, time of month or the season of the year.

Despite these issues the ILO managed to pull together estimates for selected countries. They found that informal traders in the African countries for which data is available contribute between 85 and 99 per cent of total employment in trade and between 46 and 70 per cent of total value added in trade (2002:53). In most African countries, other than North African Muslim countries, women represent at least 50 per cent, if not more, of the total number of traders. In matrilineal societies of West Africa there is a long standing tradition of informal markets largely controlled by women (Charmes, 2000, see Lyons and Snoxell, 2005b: 1308 among others). Adiko and Anoh Kouassi (2003) in their survey of over 1,700 market and street vendors in Ivory Coast for example, found that over 70 per cent of traders were women. Although there are regional differences there appears to be a trend of women selling food products and men selling non-food products, which are often more lucrative.

Although there is no time series data available on this particular worker group the combination of urbanisation, migration and economic development trends suggests that there has been a rapid increase in the numbers of street traders operating on the streets of African cities. Preliminary evidence suggests that this is being and will continue to be exacerbated by global financial crisis. Interviews were conducted with street traders in Nakuru (Kenya), Blantyre (Malawi) and Durban (South Africa) in June and July of 2009 for a broader project assessing the impact of the global financial crisis on the informal economy.[2] Preliminary findings suggest that the global recession is leading to greater numbers of street traders and pushing existing traders and their families further into impoverishment. The respondents, who were predominantly women, reported that in the first six months of 2009 there was a significant decline in the demand for their goods while the price of inputs on the whole was increasing. In most cases traders did not increase the prices of their products for fear of losing customers. Traders also reported an increase in the number of traders on the streets as those retrenched from the formal economy started trading. Many of these new comers are men. This suggests that the economic crisis will result in a reconstitution of the nature of trading and the dynamics within it.

Policy and planning trends

The co-ordinator of the international alliance of street vending organisations, who has substantial direct experience of city policies and street trading across Africa warns:

> There are no policy 'best practises' with street trading. Where there have been windows where better practices emerge, there tends to be a continuity problem. There is a change in the bureaucracy, a big event or an election, and the approach changes . . . With street vending things are particularly fluid.

> (Interview, 16/04/07)

Mindful of the dynamism of state responses to street trading, this section reviews policy planning and governance trends.

There is substantial evidence of large scale sustained evictions of street traders. Possibly the largest and most violent eviction of street traders on the continent in the last decade was in Zimbabwe in May 2005 – Operation Murambatsvina.[3] Street traders and those living in informal housing were targeted. The UN Habitat mission to Zimbabwe estimated that some 700,000 people in cities across the country lost either their homes, their source of livelihood or both (Tibaijuka, 2005:7). Sites where informal sector workers gathered to market their wares, as well as formal markets, some of which had been in operation for decades, were targeted. Potts (2007: 265) estimates that in Harare alone 75,000 vendors were unable to work from late May, 2005. A local civil society support group described the impact of Operation Murambatsvina on street traders as follows:

> The Government, under the auspices of the Ministry of Small and Medium Enterprises Development, began by arresting 20,000 vendors countrywide, destroying their vending sites, and confiscating their wares. Thousands more escaped arrest, but have lost their livelihoods. This process took one week in the first instance. Harare was among the worst affected cities: police action was brutal and unannounced. . . . Vendors, who have been operating in the same places without complaint or interference for their entire working lives, were confronted with riot squads without any warning, were rounded up, arrested, and watched helplessly while their source of livelihood was destroyed. Within days, bulldozers have moved in to take away remains.[4]

In explaining these events many analysts have pointed to the fact that since 2000 the urban electorate had voted overwhelmingly for the opposition – the Movement for Democratic Change (MDC). Since Tibaijuka (2005) estimates that one in every five Zimbabweans was affected by Operation Marumbatsvina, not only MDC supporters were affected. Political affiliations, although critical, are only one part of the rationale behind these actions.

Although not on the scale of Zimbabwe there are other cases of widespread evictions. Transberg Hansen (2004:66–7) in her study of street traders in Zambia notes how in April 1999,

> council workers, police and paramilitary in riot gear razed the temporary market structures of Lusaka's city centre, extending the demolition the following night and weeks all across the city, into townships and residential areas . . . In June, similar operations took place on the Copperbelt and in the towns along the line-of-rail.

Transberg Hansen identifies a leadership change in the local authority as a key reason for the evictions. She notes (2004:68) a new mayor and council members had come into office in Lusaka and they were 'bent on cleaning up the capital'. In a Ghanaian context, King (2006) reflects a similar finding. She argues that the new system of decentralisation where there are more frequent changes in local authorities leads to evictions of street traders which is seen as 'a common way to impress the public' (2006:117).

There are a number of historical cases where national governments have established systems of trader repression. In South Africa, the apartheid state's complex web of national and local laws effectively banned street trading. Rogerson and Hart (1989:32) argued that South African urban authorities 'fashioned and refined some of the most sophisticated sets of anti-street trader measures anywhere in the developing world'. This, however, was in a context of high levels of unemployment and poverty so traders continued to attempt to operate. They were consistently harassed and periodically violently removed. Rogerson and Hart (1989:32) point out that until the early 1980s hawkers in South Africa were subject to 'a well-entrenched tradition of repression, persecution and prosecution'. Treatment in socialist states was equally harsh. In Tanzania, Nnkya (2006) relays how in the mid-1970s the Tanzanian government rounded up street traders operating in Dar es Salaam and forcibly removed them to villages on the coast. In 1983 a penal code was enacted that branded all self-employed people as 'unproductive, idle and disorderly' (Nnkya, 2006:82). These actions were justified on the basis that street trading was a subversive activity that challenged socialist principles. Lourenço-Lindell (2004) describes a similar situation in newly independent Guinea-Bissau.

Sporadic evictions of street traders often precede major public events. In Maseru (Lesotho) Setsabi's (2006) lists the many times street traders were removed – in 1988 when Pope John Paul II visited the city, in 1991 when

President Nujoma from Namibia came on a state visit and street traders were threatened with eviction when President Mandela came in 1995. In this last case the street traders diverted the action by agreeing to clean the streets. In Zimbabwe, Potts (2007:270) notes that street traders were removed just before Harare hosted the Non-Aligned Movement conference in 1984. There are already cases of street traders being removed in South Africa ahead of the 2010 Football World Cup (www.streetnet.org). Bromley (2000) in his review of street trading, drawing on over two and a half decades of related research and international policy, confirms this as an international trend. He (2000:12) notes 'Aggressive policing (of street traders) is particularly notable just before major public and tourist events, on the assumption that orderly streets improve the image of the city to visitors'.

Ongoing and low level harassment of informal traders is pervasive across African cities. Lourenço-Lindell (2004) outlines that in Bissau, although a more permissive approach has been adopted since the SAP of 1986, municipal agents have essentially remained hostile to them. In surveys street traders cite that they are frequently bribed, complaining of the 'oppressiveness and arbitrariness of public agents' (2004:94–5). Of the 355 street traders interviewed in Abidjan in Adiko and Anoh Kouassi's study, 69 per cent feared being chased off their current site (2003:55). A group that is particularly vulnerable to this are foreign street traders. Hunter and Skinner's (2003) survey of foreign street traders operating in Durban (South Africa), for example, found that they frequently reported that police elicited bribes. Few of these foreigners have proper documentation, nor do they have access to bank accounts and are thus easy targets. Kamunyori (2007:33) reports that in Nairobi the council inspectors make several times their monthly salaries on bribing street traders. She records the monthly salary of these so called 'askaris' as approximately US$50. This points to a more systemic problem – until local officials in African cities are better paid, this kind of corruption will be difficult to root out.

City development and urban planning paradigms are critical to understanding these trends. Kamunyori (2007:11) points out there is a tension between modernisation of African cites and what are often perceived as 'non modern' activities like street trading. This issue of how street traders are perceived reoccurs. In the case of violent removal of street traders in Zambia, Transberg Hansen (2004:70) points out that these actions were condoned by national government who argued that the presence of street traders was discouraging international investors. Further, as previously noted, street traders are often removed prior to international events as part of city 'beautification' processes. As Bromley (2000:12) argues there is a widely held view that street trading is 'a manifestation of both poverty and underdevelopment' thus 'its disappearance is viewed as progress'.

This is connected to the focus in urban studies, policy and practice on 'world class' cities. Beaverstock *et al.*, (2002) is a classic text in this literature. They establish a roster of world cities. In their analysis mention is made of only one African city – Johannesburg. Robinson (2002:563) contends that the notion of 'world' or 'global' cities has the effect of 'dropping most cities in the world from vision'. The position and functioning of cities in the world economy thus becomes the dominant factor in urban economic development planning. The implicit economic development policy prescriptions are that international investment should be pursued above all else. Informal activities, like street vending, in this paradigm, are seen as undesirable and their contribution to local economies is not recognised. Robinson (2002:531) argues that the notion of world class cities imposes 'substantial limitations on imagining or planning the futures of cities'. This is particularly the case in the developing world.

Urban planning traditions play an important role in shaping local authority responses to these issues. Freund (2007:156) argues, in his reflections on post colonial African cities, that planning ordinances and decrees often show little real variation from colonial patterns. This lies at the heart of more nuanced analyses of the rationale behind Operation Murambatsvina. Potts (2007) details how colonial approaches extended on into the post colonial period. She demonstrates that there was a long history of anti-informality sentiments in both national and local government. She (2007:267–8) notes that although street traders were present, they were 'very contained and on a minor scale *in comparison with* the bustle and competitive selling of goods and services so typical of cities from Luanda to Kinshasa to Lagos to Dakar'. She argues (2007:283) that the 'adherence to the ideology of planned and orderly cities remained a core belief for many'. This combined with anger against the urban electorate was a fertile field for those who always desired urban 'order' to gain ground. In many other countries colonial laws remain in place. Transberg Hansen (2004:63) in the case of Zambia for example states 'post colonial regulations on markets, trading licensing, town and country planning and public health restricted trading ... to established markets'. Kamunyori (2007:10) points out that in Nairobi, although street trading is legal according to the city by-laws, colonial era legislation (The General Nuisance by-law) is used to supersede this provision. The General Nuisance by-law allows city officials to arrest any individual that they deem to be 'creating a "general nuisance" in public spaces'.

There are however (albeit very few) examples where street traders have been accommodated. In Dar es Salaam, Tanzania by the early 1990s street traders had been issued licenses and were allowed to operate. Nnkya (2006:88) states that 'street trading in the central business district (CBD) is well managed and trader associations have good relations with the city authorities'. Nnkya (2006) identifies the 1992 Sustainable Dar es Salaam Project (SDP) as a turning point from the state's previous approach to trader repression. This project, a collaboration between United Nations agencies and the state, identified petty trading as a key issue. By the mid-1990s, as a direct consequence of the SDP, a Working Group on Managing Informal Micro-Trade was established. This group identified constraints street traders faced and made numerous recommendations. A consequence of the SDP was the Guidelines for Petty Trade adopted by the City Commission in 1997 which set out the framework for managing street trade. Nnkya does however point out that there are implementation inconsistencies – with management being haphazard in parts – and that while some are included, others (most notably women traders) are not, particularly in the more lucrative trading sites in the CBD. In comparison to many other cities in African overall, he argues, Dar es Salaam has created an enabling environment for street traders.

Adopting new approaches to urban planning are common to the more inclusionary practices cited above. In Tanzania the 1992 Sustainable Dar es Salaam project stemmed from an invitation by the state to the United Nations Development Programme to review the Dar es Salaam Master Plan. As Nnkya (2006:83) notes, instead the UN staff persuaded the city council to pursue a new approach to planning, based on participatory or collaborative principles.

The other case that has been cited as better practice in the management of street trading is Durban, South Africa. Although there has been recent harassment of traders in Durban, there was a period were Durban's approach was identified as particularly progressive, especially in respect of the policy adopted in the inner-city district that contains the main transport node – the Warwick Junction (for a detailed analysis see Dobson and Skinner, 2009). On a busy day the area is estimated to accommodate 460,000 commuters, and at least 8,000 street traders. In 1996 the city council launched an area based urban renewal initiative. In careful consultation with traders, trader infrastructure was established. For example nearly 1,000 traditional medicine traders were accommodated in a new market and corn-on-the-cob sellers and those cooking and selling the Zulu delicacy, bovine heads, were provided tailor-made facilities. Through this, the Project piloted an economically informed, sector by sector approach to supporting street traders. In parallel with infrastructure development there was a focus on improving management of the area. The area-based team established a number of operations teams to deal with issues as diverse as curbside cleaning, ablution facilities, child care facilities and pavement sleeping. In 2001 the local authority in the city – the eThekwini Municipality – adopted an Informal Economy Policy. This policy acknowledges the informal economy as an important component of the city's economy and, drawing on some of the lessons learnt from the Warwick Junction Project, suggests a number of management and support interventions. This was an attempt to standardise a progressive approach across the city. Since 2007, Durban adopted a much more conservative stance to street trading issues and in 2009 announced plans to build a shopping mall in the centre of Warwick Junction confirming Horn's contention.

Dobson and Skinner's analysis of the Warwick Junction Project suggest that participation was central to the project's approach. A street trader leader described the council's staff approach as affording 'informal traders the opportunity to participate on a sustained and continuous basis in negotiations about their needs and priorities ... in a low-key way, often on an issue-by-issue basis' (Horn, 2004:211). Dobson and Skinner (2009) argue that consultation dissipated conflict, facilitated interventions genuinely informed by user needs and led to users having a sense of ownership of the area. This, in turn, led to high levels of volunteerism that resolved a number of urban management issues like crime and cleaning. These are good examples of what Healey (1998) would describe as planning by multi-stakeholder collaboration and planning by negotiation and contract. The dynamism of street vending lends itself to this style of management. Sandercock's (1998:30) arguments although reflecting largely on contexts in the north are applicable to the challenges of planning in developing country contexts. She argues for the need to develop a new kind of multicultural literacy which she explains as follows:

> An essential part of that literacy is familiarity with the multiple histories of urban communities, especially as those histories intersect with struggles over space and place claiming, with planning policies and resistances to them, with traditions of indigenous planning and with questions of belonging and identity and acceptance of difference.

Trends in organising among street traders

Traders who have been incorporated into urban plans, tend to be well organised. Nnkya (2006) identifies this as a factor in Dar es Salaam. He (2006:84) points out that by 1997, about 240 self-help groups representing 16,000 members had been formed, 'enabling traders collectively to address problems and access services'. There is an umbrella organisation – the Association of Small Scale Businesses – which 'acts as a lobbyist and pressure group and is involved in the selection of public space for business activities'.[5] In Durban, street traders were well organised during the redevelopment of the Warwick Junction area. Traders were organised into product groups and block committees (Dobson and Skinner, 2009). The Self Employed Women's Union (a sister to the much larger Self Employed Women's Association in India), was also very active in the area (Devenish and Skinner, 2006). In both cases this meant that there were negotiating partners for local authorities.

Unfortunately, existing information on street trader organisation is patchy. The research that is available suggests that many traders are not affiliated to any organisation at all. Where trader organisations do exist, they focus on one or more of three concerns – financial services, lobbying and advocacy particularly at a local level and product specific issues. The role of trade unions appears to be increasingly important. Concerns about the internal organisational dynamics have also been raised. Each of these issues is considered in turn with a focus where possible on regional trends.

There is some evidence that organisation densities among street traders are low. Lund's (1998:33–4) re-analysis of data in South Africa, for example, found that in the two large surveys of street traders that had been conducted, in Johannesburg 15 per cent of traders reported to belong to an association, while in Durban 12 per cent of the men and 16 per cent of the women traders were members of associations. Alilo and Mitullah's (2000) interviews with over 300 street traders operating in four different Kenyan cities found that 67 per cent had no knowledge of associations that addressed street vending issues (2000:18). More recently in Nairobi there has been the formation of the Nairobi Informal Sector Confederation (NISCOF). According to Kamunyori (2007:14–15) NISCOF was registered in 2005 and as of 2007 had 23 member associations representing approximately 15,000 individual traders. Although this is a positive development, Lyons and Snoxell (2005b:1078) suggest there may be as many as 500,000 street traders operating in the city. NISCOF thus represents 3 per cent of the total number of traders.

There is evidence of a high prevalence of rotating savings and credit associations (ROSCA's). As is the case in other parts of the world, these members deposit a mutually agreed sum with the group at regular intervals. Each member has a turn to receive the total money collected. Some ROSCA's also provide loans to their members. As Lyons and Snoxell (2005a:1089) note this guarantees the periodic availability of a capital sum, through peer pressure to save. Of the 124 traders interviewed in Nairobi in Lyons and Snoxell's (2005b:1089) study, 58 per cent were part of a ROSCA. They conducted a similar study in two markets in Ghana and found that 49 per cent of 144 traders interviewed were members of a savings group (2005a:1312).[6] Although not quoting exact figures, Alila and Mitullah (2000: 11) and Tsitsi and Agatha (2000: 10) find a similar situation in Kenya and Zimbabwe respectively. All of these studies note that there is a particularly high prevalence of membership of savings groups among women. In the face of poor access to banking services, these systems of financial services and support play an important role.

In 2005 War on Want (2006) in collaboration with the Workers' Education Association of Zambia conducted research explicitly focused on the organising and advocacy strategies of informal economy associations in Ghana, Malawi, Mozambique and Zambia. Interviews were conducted with 62 organisations, the majority of which were street or market trader organisations. This research concluded that the majority of organisations were established in specific markets or trading areas and have been dealing with urgent issues arising in these locations, such as harassment from the police and solving disputes and conflicts among vendors. The relationship between organisations and the state was examined and the researchers conclude that street trader organisations largely had confrontational relations with local government (WoW, 2006:31–2). Lund and Skinner's (1999) study of 22 organisations of street traders in five cities in South Africa found that many of them focused on negotiating with local authorities. They were however not formally structured and tended to be vocal when issues arose but often difficult to find in between. These trends were confirmed in more recent studies (Thulare, 2004, Motala, 2002).

Evidence suggests that traders are comparatively well organised in West Africa. King (2006) for example, reflecting on the situation in Kumasi Ghana, found that trader organisations were well established and widely respected. She notes that the Market Traders Association – an umbrella group of various product associations, has a representative on the Kumasi Municipal Authority's General Assembly. This association launched a successful challenge in court when the local authority threatened to increase market fees by 300 per cent (King, 2006:108–9). The Ghana Trade Union Congress (GTUC) has had an informal sector desk for many years. In February 2003 the GTUC initiated a national alliance of market and street traders – the StreetNet Ghana Alliance. As of 2006 they had 19 trader associations with a total of 5,810 individuals (War on Want, 2006:36). Adiko and Anoh Kouassi's (2003) study in the Ivory Coast found that organisational membership was high among traders – varying between 36 per cent and 42 per cent of interviewees depending on their location.[7] Traders were members of a range of organisations including unions, co-operatives and ROSCAs.

The research pays less attention to collective action that directly supports the business of trading. Lund and Skinner's (1999) found that a number of street trader organisations in South Africa are primarily focused around the bulk purchase of goods. War on Want found a number of product-specific trader organisations in Ghana, Malawi and Zambia. They give the example of an organisation of wholesalers that supplies street traders – a banana sellers' association. Their primary aim is to ensure regular and adequate supply of products and to negotiate the terms of trade with the primary suppliers. Although this is not explored in any detail, Adiko and Anoh Kouassi's (2003) study in the Ivory Coast suggests co-operatives have been formed among traders.

Given the decreasing numbers of those formally employed in Africa, there is evidence of trade unions, particularly the national federations, paying increasing attention to organising among the informally employed. These initiatives either entail direct organising efforts, encouraging appropriate affiliates to organise or supporting or expanding on existing organising efforts. In May 2002 the Zimbabwe Congress of Trade Unions (ZCTU) launched an informal sector desk which is tasked with directly organising, among other groups, street traders (Tsitsi and Agatha, 2000:12).[8] The Malawi Congress of Trade Unions assisted in the formation of the Malawi Union for the Informal Sector. This union has street traders among its members. As previously noted the Ghana Trade Union Congress has been very actively involved in encouraging its affiliates to organise in the informal economy. The Mozambique trade union federation (OTM) played an important role in forming the Association of Informal Sector Operators and Workers (ASSOTSI). ASSOTSI has 26 branch committees within 59 markets in Maputo and in 2005 claimed membership of over 40,000 (War on Want, 2005:43). The War on Want research does, however, find that there are often tensions between the national federations and informal worker organisations.

Concerns are raised in this literature about two aspects of internal organisational dynamics – how organisations are constituted and women's roles. The War on Want study (2005:30) found that trader associations 'often show low levels of participation and leadership accountability'. For example of the 20 trader organisations interviewed in the Ghana study, nine reported that their method of choosing leadership was by appointment rather than elections (War on Want, 2006:95–6). Lund and Skinner (1999) raised a concern about organisations not being formally constituted. At the time of their study there was only one organisation – the Self Employed Women's Union[9] – that had functioning democratic structures and regular elections.

Although members are often predominantly women, the leaders of street trader organisations are often men. This was found in studies of street trader organisations in Malawi, Zambia and Mozambique (War on Want, 2006) and in South Africa (Lund and Skinner, 1999). For example, in Malawi of the 16 organisations interviewed, only one had a majority of women in leadership positions (War on Want, 2006:97–8). Lyons and Snoxell's (2005:1082) study of markets in Nairobi found that both market committees were compromised entirely of men and that no women had ever been an official. The opposite however held true in Ghana where of the 33 organisations interviewed 22 had a majority of women in leadership positions. Women seem to play a much more dominant role in leadership positions in markets in the matrilineal societies of West Africa. However, again there are exceptions particularly in predominantly Muslim states. In Senegal the Mouride Brotherhood largely controls trading activities and is politically very powerful.

StreetNet International, an alliance of street trader organisations, since its launch in 2002 is an increasingly important player in street trader organising on the continent. Membership-based organisations directly organising street and market traders, are entitled to affiliate to StreetNet. They currently have members not only in Africa but also in Latin America and Asia. One of StreetNet's primary aims is to build the capacity of street trader organisations so as to strengthen their organising and advocacy efforts. This is done through providing direct leadership training, exchange visits which allow sharing of experiences among traders and documenting and disseminating better practices. Another area of activity is assisting with the expansion of organising efforts to the national level. StreetNet was instrumental in the establishment of both the Alliance for Zambia Informal Economy Associations and the formation of the national alliance of trader organisations in Ghana. These kinds of organisations will help traders to play a more influential role in policy particularly at national level. At an international level StreetNet advocates for the rights of street traders within international bodies like the International Labour Organisation but also the international trade union federations. Currently their primary campaign is at the moment is the World Class Cities Campaign. This aims to challenge the notion of 'world class' cities and the trend to remove traders when cities host international events. The campaign has started in South Africa in response to the 2010 Football World Cup (www.streetnet.org.za).

The research on street trader organisations thus suggests that many traders are not members of organisations. Given the importance of collective action to inclusive planning, this constitutes a challenge both to existing organisations and trade unions but also to local authorities. Concerns have been raised about the internal dynamics within organisations and who is represented in organisations. Bromley (2000:14) claims street trader associations 'typically represent older, established and licensed traders'. The research reviewed here suggests that women should be added to this list.

Conclusion

There are a number of reasons why an inclusive approach to street trading is desirable. Pragmatically, demographic and economic trends indicate that these activities are on the increase, thus street trading is a reality that is unlikely to go away. From a developmental perspective street traders are often responsible for large numbers of dependants. There are also a disproportionate number of women working as street traders. Research demonstrates that women are more likely than men to spend their income on the household needs (Levin *et al.*, 1999 demonstrate this for vendors particularly). From a planning perspective, street traders provide urban residents and particularly the urban poor, with goods and services in appropriate quantities and forms, and at times of day and in parts of the city that contribute to the functioning of cities. Although the individual incomes are often low, these activities' cumulative contribution to local economies and to local revenue collection are not insignificant. Inclusive planning however does not imply unbridled street trading. Local authorities need to balance the interests of many different stakeholders using public space. Traders themselves report not wanting to work in badly managed environments. Further, as previously noted, given limited consumer demand there is a direct trade off between the number of traders and individual incomes earned. Innovative approaches to policy, planning, urban design and management can maximise the gains from these activities.

Notes

1 This paper is a reworked and shorter version of a paper published in an edited volume entitled 'Street Vendors in the Global Urban Economy' published by Routledge, New Delhi.
2 This research is being done by the global research policy network Women in Informal Employment: Globalising and Organising or WIEGO.
3 While Government translated this to mean 'Operation clean-up', the more literal Shona translation of 'murambatsvina' is 'getting rid of the filth' (Potts, 2007).
4 Source: http://sokwanele.com/articles/sokwanele/opmuramb_overview_18june 2005.html.

5 Unfortunately he does not detail how the organisation is constituted nor how representative these organisations are, particularly of poorer and women traders.
6 Lyons and Snoxell (2005a) also surveyed a similar number of traders in two markets in Senegal and found only 17 per cent were members of a savings group. The majority of these traders were men. This reinforces again the importance of avoiding any blanket generalisations.
7 It should be noted that a number of traders were reluctant to report on their organisational membership.
8 The ZCTU is aligned to the opposition in Zimbabwe. Given the current repression of the opposition it is difficult to get any recent information about, for example, how many informal worker members the ZCTU has organised.
9 This organisation has since closed.

References

Adiko, A. and Anoh Kouassi, P. (2003) Activities and Organisations of Traders on the Markets and Streets of Ivory Coast: A Case Study of Cocody, Treichville, Yopougon Communities and Some Streets in Abidjan. Paper Commissioned by Women in Informal Employment: Globalising and Organising. Abidjan, University of Cocody.

Alila, P. and Mitullah, W. (2000) Women Street Vendors in Kenya: Policies, Regulations and Organisational Capacities. Paper Commissioned by Women in Informal Employment: Globalising and Organising. Nairobi, Institute for Development Studies, University of Nairobi.

Baden, S. and Barber, C. (2005) The Impact of the Second-Hand Clothing Trade on Developing Countries. Oxfam International. (www.maketradefair.com/en/assets/english/shc_0905.pdf)

Beaverstock, J., Taylor, P. and Smith, R. (2002) A Roster of World Cities. *Cities*, Vol. 16, No. 6.

Bromley, R. (2000) Street Vending and Public Policy: A Global Review. *International Journal of Sociology and Social Policy*, Vol. 20, No. 1–2, 29.

Charmes, J. (2000) Informal Sector, Poverty and Gender: A Review of Empirical Evidence. Paper commissioned for World Development Report 2000/1. Washington D.C., World Bank.

Devenish, A. and Skinner, C. (2006) Collective Action for those in the Informal Economy: The Case of the Self Employed Women's Union. In Ballard, R., Habib, A. and Valodia, I. (Eds.) *Voices of Protest: Social Movements in Post-Apartheid South Africa*. Durban, University of KwaZulu-Natal Press.

Dobson, R. and Skinner, C. (2009) *Working in Warwick: Including Street Traders in Urban Plans*, Durban, School of Development Studies, University of KwaZulu-Natal.

Freund, B. (2007) *The African City, A History*, Cambridge, Cambridge University Press.

Healey, P. (1998) Collaborative Planning in a Stakeholder Society. *Town Planning Review*, Vol. 69, No.1.

Horn, P. (2004) Durban's Warwick Junction: A Response. *Development Update*, Vol. 5, No. 1, pp. 209–14.

Hunter, N. and Skinner, C. (2003) Foreigners Working on the Streets of Durban: Local Government Policy Challenges. *Urban Forum*, Vol. 14, No. 4, 301–19.

International Labour Organisation (2002) Women and Men in the Informal Economy: A Statistical Picture. Geneva, International Labour Office.

Iyenda, G. (2001) Street Food and Income Generation for Poor Households in Kinshasa. *Environment and Urbanisation*, Vol. 13, No. 2.

Kamunyori, W. (2007) A Growing Space for Dialogue: The Case of Street Vending in Nairobi's Central Business District. *Department of Urban Studies and Planning*. Boston, Massachusetts Institute of Technology.

King, R. (2006) Fulcrum of the Urban Economy: Governance and Street Livelihoods in Kumasi, Ghana. In Brown, A. (ed.) *Contested Space: Street Trading, Public Space, and Livelihoods in Developing Cities*. Warwickshire: Warwickshire, Intermediate Technology Publications.

Landau, L. (2007) Discrimination and Development? Immigration, Urbanisation and Sustainable Livelihoods in Johannesburg. *Development Southern Africa*, Vol. 24, No. 1.

Levin, C., Ruel, M., Morris, S., Maxwell, D., Armar-Klemesu, M. and Ahiadeka, C. (1999) Working Women in an Urban Setting: Traders, Vendors and Food Security in Accra. *World Development*, Vol. 27, No. 11.

Lourenço-Lindell, I. (2004) Trade and the Politics of Informalisation in Bissau, Guinea-Bissau. In Transberg Hansen, K. and Vaa, M. (Eds.) *Reconsidering Informality, Perspectives from Urban Africa*. Uppsala, Nordic Africa Institute.

Lund, F. (1998) Women Street Traders in Urban South Africa: A Synthesis of Selected Research Findings. *CSDS Research Report No. 15*. Durban, University of Natal (www.sds.ukzn.ac.za).

Lund, F. and Skinner, C. (1999) Promoting the Interests of Women Street Traders: An Analysis of Organisations in South Africa. CSDS Research Report No 19. Durban: University of Natal.

Lyons, M. and Snoxell, S. (2005) Sustainable Urban Livelihoods and Marketplace Social Capital: Crisis and Strategy in Petty Trade. *Urban Studies*, Vol. 42, No. 8.

Mitullah, W. (1991) Hawking as a Survival Strategy for the Urban Poor in Nairobi: The Case of Women. *Environment and Urbanization*, Vol. 3, No. 2.

Motala, S. (2002) Organising in the Informal Economy: A Case Study of Street Trading in South Africa. *Seed Working Paper No. 36*. Geneva, International Labour Organisation.

Nnkya, T. (2006) An Enabling Framework? Governance and Street Trading in Dar es Salaam, Tanzania. In Brown, A. (Ed.) *Contested Space: Street Trading, Public Space and Livelihoods in Developing Cities*. Warwickshire, Intermediate Technology Publications.

Peberdy, S. (2000) Mobile Entrepreneurship: Informal Sector Cross-border Trade and Street Trade in South Africa. *Development Southern Africa*, Vol. 17, No. 2.

Potts, D. (2007) City Life in Zimbabwe at a Time of Fear and Loathing: Urban Planning, Urban Poverty and Operation Murambatsvina. In Myers, G. and Murray, M. (Eds.) *Cities in Contemporary Africa*. New York, Palgrave Macmillan.

Robinson, J. (2002) Global and World Cities: A View from off the Map. *International Journal of Urban and Regional Research*, Vol. 26, No. 3.

Rogerson, C. and Hart, D. (1989) The struggle for the streets: Deregulation and Hawking in South Africa's Major Urban Areas *Social Dynamics*, Vol. 15. No. 1.

Sandercock, L. (1998) *Making the Invisible Visible: A Multicultural Planning History*, Los Angeles, University of California Press.

Setsabi, S. (2006) Contest and Conflict: Governance and Street Livelihoods in Maseru, Lesotho. In Brown, A. (Ed.) *Contested Space: Street Trading, Public Space, and Livelihoods in Developing Cities*. Warwickshire, Intermediate Technology Publications.

Thulare, P. (2004) Trading Democracy? Johannesburg Informal Traders and Citizenship. *Centre for Policy Studies, Policy: Issues and Actors*, Vol. 17, No.1.

Tibaijuka, A. (2005) Report of the Fact-finding Mission to Zimbabwe to Assess the Scope and Impact of Operation Murambatsvina by the UN special envoy on Human Settlements Issues in Zimbabwe. (www.un.org/News/dh/infocus/zimbabwe/zimbabwe_rpt.pdf).

Transberg Hansen, K. (2004) Who Rules the Streets? The Politics of Vending Space in Lusaka. In Transberg Hansen, K. and Vaa, M. (Eds.) *Reconsidering Informality, Perspectives from Urban Africa*. Uppsala, Nordic Africa Institute.

Tsitsi, N. and Agatha, T. (2000) Women Street Vendors in Zimbabwe. Women and Law in Southern Africa Research and Education Trust, Paper commissioned by Women in Informal Employment: Globalising and Organising.

United Nations (1997) State of the World Population 1997 Reproductive Rights and Reproductive Health. (www.unfpa.org/swp/1997/swpmain.htm).

—— (2007) State of the World Population 2007 Unleashing the Potential of Urban Growth. (www.unfpa.org/swp/2007/presskit/pdf/sowp2007_eng.pdf).

—— (2008) State of World Population Reaching Common Ground: Culture, Gender and Human Rights http://www.unfpa.org/swp/2008/presskit/docs/en-swop08-report.pdf.

War on Want (2006) Forces for Change: Informal Economy Organisations in Africa. London (www.waronwant.org).

12 Africa and the 'second new economy'

How can Africa benefit from ICTs for a sustainable socio-economic development?

Nicolas Pejout

Introduction

After J.H. Boeke (1953) and A. Lewis (1954), in 2003, former President Thabo Mbeki submits the idea of *two economies* co-existing in South Africa: a *first-world economy* (first economy) and a *third-world economy* (second economy). The first one is 'an advanced, sophisticated economy, based on skilled labour, which is becoming more globally competitive'. The second one is 'a mainly informal, marginalised, unskilled economy, populated by the unemployed and those unemployable in the formal sector' (Mbeki, 2003a; Mbeki, 2003b). The relationship between these two economies varies between deconnection and a trickle-down effect.

Simultaneously, since the 1990s and 2000s, the ICT-based *new economy* (NE) has been growing exponentially, but not for everyone. Although there is diversity of *new economies* (Boyer, 2004; Amable, 2005), one major trend is that the NE is fostering a socio-economic dualisation, particularly the polarisation of the labour market (Brender and Pisani, 2004; Milkman and Dwyer, 2002; Artus, 2000; Wright and Dwyer, 2003). One explanation is the skill-biased technological progress that is at the heart of the NE.

How can the *second economy* and the *new economy* be reconciled? How can Africa, that is mainly characterised by the *second economy*, get into the *new economy* given its assets and weaknesses? Answering this question is key for designing a socio-economic scenario that positions the NE as a tool to foster a sustainable growth and, above all, a self-sustainable social contract. The NE is a *total social fact* (Mauss, 1927). As such, it is *embedded* (Polanyi, 1944) in a both specific and diverse socio-economic and institutional context that represents both a set of constraints and opportunities.

In our view, Africa (at least some African countries) can (and some are already doing so) develop a *second new economy* that combines the *best of both worlds* to set ICT-intensive industries that are the heart of the NE as key engines of socio-economic development to achieve GDP growth, job creation and skills enhancement. For that, one strategy (or one tactic, cf. De Certeau, 1990) would be to invest in one of the following three:

- ICT (re-)manufacturing industry: Nigeria and South Africa are already important players in this sector and the availability of a huge secondhand stock from Europe (EU directives compel firms to recycle or reuse such equipment) can be an opportunity for local industry players to emerge;
- Call centres: they have already mushroomed in some English-(South Africa) and French-speaking (Senegal) African countries and could get more numerous, with the creation of many jobs;
- Business Process Outsourcing (BPO): the externalisation of all activities that are not a core business for a firm (for instance, customer relationship management or data management) can be outsourced and offshored to some African countries; that would set Africa in competition with India.

These three sectors are of major strategic interest for Africa to develop a sustainable *second new economy* that creates jobs and therefore injects additional revenues. For this scenario to be realistic, some conditions are required: appropriate telecom infrastructures; a conducive legal and institutional framework; a well balanced skills development strategy. As for political will, the coordination of a second *NE Plan* at the NEPAD level could be an option to look at. In the end, that all looks to a certain *Africanisation of the NE* meaning that this economy can fit into the socio-economic priorities of the continent, in parallel to the US NE, the Indian NE, the Scandinavian NE . . .

* * *

Information and communication technologies (ICTs), telecoms and Africa[1]

Before wondering whether and how Africa can grasp some benefits out of the NE, one should consider the overall situation of ICTs on the continent. Africa hosts 30.6 million main fixed telephone lines, with a teledensity of 3.2 per 100 inhabitants, ranging from 0.01 per cent in Democratic Republic of the Congo to 15 per cent in Egypt. The continent also hosts 275 million mobile cellular phone subscribers, i.e. a teledensity of 28.5 per 100 inhabitants, ranging from 1.45 per cent in Ethiopia to 87 per cent in Gabon and South Africa.

As for the Internet, Africa hosts 11 million subscribers, with an Internet penetration rate of 1.25 per 100 inhabitants from 0.03 per cent in Chad to 9 per cent in South Africa. If we look at Internet users, figures look better: there are 52 million Internet users, with an Internet penetration rate of 5.5 per 100 inhabitants. The continent also counts 2 million broadband Internet subscribers, reaching an Internet penetration rate of 0.2 per 100 inhabitants. Though Africa counts for 14 per cent of the world population, its presence on the ICT map is not up to that: it gathers 6.2 per cent of mobile phone users, 3.4 per cent of Internet users, 2.2 per cent of landline phones and 0.4 per cent of broadband subscribers. Using the Digital Opportunity

Index (DOI[2]), the average rank for an African country is 140, from the lowest 181 (Niger) to the highest 58 (Morocco).

These few figures show that Africa is still struggling to be fully connected to the world telecom and IT infrastructures. In this context, it is a challenge for the continent to grasp all the benefits of the new economy. It is all the more difficult since this new economy is not necessarily adapted to the current socio-economic challenges of Africa.

The new economy and socio-economic dualism

Understanding the new economy as an elitist socio-economic scenario only for highly qualified people would be misleading. This economy rather fuels a socio-economic dualism that might cause sustainability problems to most African countries.

Robert Boyer (2004) and Bruno Amable (2005) recall the diversity of new economies: the long-dominating American NE model is not exclusive. The rising inequalities occurring with the rising NE is not a *necessary entry condition into modernity* (Boyer, 2004). Nevertheless, with a Gini coefficient of 51 per cent Africa has the worst income distribution in the world. The ratio of income of the richest 10 per cent of countries to the poorest 10 per cent of countries rose from 10.5 in 1975 to 18.5 in 2005. This inequality is a determining factor in the social and political stability of countries (McCord, 2003).

The socio-economic dualism that characterises the NE refers to the polarisation of the labour market: on one side, the creation of numerous *high value added* jobs; on the other, the multiplication of *low value added* jobs. The number of *middle value added* jobs is stagnating since the 1980s, as shown in the US (Brender and Pisani, 2004). Between 1992 and 2000, high revenues have rocketed, low revenues have diminished and middle revenues have stagnated (Milkman and Dwyer, 2002). For Brender and Pisani (2004), during the 1990s, the gap between the top and bottom of the revenue scale has grown. Many other authors diagnose these dynamics: Paulré (2000), Baudchon and Fouet (2000), Artus (2002).

Milkman and Dwyer (2002) explain this dualism by various factors such as deindustrialisation, deregulation and the low union rate. But they also identify the NE as a key cause, as a *geographically bounded entity, highly concentrated in particular industries and sectors*. Because the NE is requiring complex human capital, it is valorising higher socio-professional categories that are highly qualified. For Artus (2000), two dynamics are at work: first, by moving towards the key sectors of the NE, the capital drives with it highly qualified jobs, which increases wages; second, non- or low-qualified jobs are being replaced by capital. Another strong move is depicted by Artus (2002): people who want to make the most of the NE have to adapt themselves – no matter their qualifications – constantly to the rapidly changing working conditions.

This dualism fuelled by the NE is contemporary with that of African economies. The representation of economic duality has been used by J.H. Boeke (1953) and Arthur Lewis (1954) to characterise the coexistence of an informal economy and a formal economy. This duality echoes the representation of the South African economy as a two-economy country. Although this is particularly true for South Africa, this can be extended to other African countries. Thabo Mbeki (2003a, 2003b) has indeed depicted South Africa as the coagulation of two economies:

> the *first world economy* that becomes ever more integrated in the global economy and the third world economy or second economy that is structurally disconnected [. . .] and incapable of self-generated growth and development. The latter constitutes the structural manifestation of poverty, underdevelopment and marginalisation in the country.
>
> (Mbeki, 2004)

The NE clearly belongs to the first economy.

These two economies are interlinked by an ambivalent relationship. On the one side, they seem to be disconnected leaving the first economy growing without a necessary positive impact on the second: the managers of start-up incubators are well aware of this *economic gated community* syndrome. On the other, the successes of the first economy can generate the resources that are necessary to tackle the problems that are endured by the second one, thanks to a trickle-down effect. The problem with this later interaction is time: how much time can people living in the second economy wait for the first one to succeed adequately for them?

This tension refers to the possibility of economic development to provide enough resources to share so that a virtuous circle of sustainable socio-economic development can settle. Putting a country on the map of the *first economy* on most dynamic sectors is highly desirable in the middle to long run from a macro-economic point of view. However, it cannot necessarily answer people's everyday aspirations that are to be – at least partially – addressed in order to ensure stability and sustainability. This is all the more true when we consider the unemployment and poverty rates in Africa. Though the unemployment rate is officially around 8 per cent in sub-Saharan Africa, 75 per cent of workers are considered as extreme working poor (1.25 US$ daily) and close to 80 per cent are enduring vulnerable employment (unpaid contributing family workers and own-account workers).

But do African countries really have to choose between these two economies? Though some of them are already on the map of the NE with specific advantages, they can also invest in the parts of NE that correspond to the second economy. These parts can foster the creation of jobs and thus make the NE scenario both economically relevant and socially sustainable.

Africa and the mainstreaming of the new economy

The mainstreaming of the new economy for African countries can be implemented through three moves. The first one is the specialisation on ICT (re-) assembly industry: Nigeria and South Africa are already important players in this sector and the availability of a huge secondhand stock from Europe (EU directives compel firms to recycle or reuse such equipment) can be an opportunity for local industry players to emerge. The second one is the specialisation in call centres: they have already mushroomed in some English- (SA) and French-speaking (Senegal) African countries and could become more numerous, creating many jobs. The third and last specialisation targets the Business Process Outsourcing (BPO) sector: the externalisation of all activities that are not a core business for a firm (for instance, CRM or data management) can be outsourced and offshored to some African countries; that would set Africa in competition with India. The main common point of these three specialisations is their potential for job creations. The NE can be sustainable if it benefits most of the people, the first benefit being earning one's living with one's work.

Opportunity 1: IT (re-)manufacturing industry

Although the NE is often depicted as the playground for virtual and immaterial activities, it cannot exist without hardware. Two sectors are particularly interesting to reconcile the NE, ICTs and sustainable development through job creation: the IT hardware assembly industry and the IT hardware recycling industry.

As for the first one, some African firms are already in place: for instance Mustek and Sahara from South Africa and Zinox from Nigeria. Mustek was founded in 1989 by David Kan, the son of the then Taiwanese trade consul in South Africa. He set up his first PC assembly line in 1987 near Pretoria and established his own PC brand in 1989 with plants in Cape Town, Durban and Port Elizabeth. In 1992, Mustek was the no. 1 PC seller. Between 1998 and 2003, its turnover grew from 1.1 to 2.9 billion rand. Headquartered in Midrand, South Africa, it now employs about 1,500 people with a network of sub-contractors. On its side, Sahara was established in 1997 and is currently running with a turnover of 1.4 billion rand. Although it is mainly based in South Africa, it is expanding across Africa: for instance, the firm was expected to open a 3,000-unit per month PC manufacturing plant in Mozambique by September 2008. As for Zinox, it is a joint venture between Mustek, the Nigerian firm Stan Tech and the French firm Alhena. In 2005, it had an assembly plant located in Lagos with an operational capacity of 200 to 350 computers per day. It also employs 200 people in Ghana. Zinox computers are the only Microsoft Authorised Original Equipment Manufacturer partner in West Africa, Intel's largest premier partner in sub-Saharan Africa, and the first and only certified system built in sub-Saharan Africa. Some other IT manufacturing players are in place such as Geniac, Omatek and Beta Computers in Nigeria, or Matomo Technologies, SourceCom Technology Solutions and Tellumat in South Africa. Beyond job creation, the other advantage for having local IT assemblers is their commitment to corporate social responsibility programmes that benefit the population regarding public IT access and literacy through the promotion of cybercafés and PC equipment for schools for instance.

Beyond these local firms that have managed to grow internationally, some international players are committing themselves to assemble PCs in Africa, not just for job creation but this is a positive direct consequence thereof. For instance, in South Africa, because PC firms want to make the most of the local workforce, they are to foster the development of local sub-contractors given the positive discrimination dynamics embedded in the Black Economic Empowerment (BEE) programme. Beyond firms, some IT manufacturing clusters have developed such as the Otigba Computer Village with about 10,000 employees at the end of 2004, or the Alaba market, both in Nigeria (Oyelaran-Oyeyinka, 2006).

Another strong dynamic can boost the African market for local PC or, more generally, IT manufacturing: the blooming market of e-waste. If this market is not regulated it can be catastrophic and transform Africa into a huge dustbin carrying environmental disasters, given the electronic and chemical content of IT equipment. The green IT movement and particularly the European Union directives are compelling IT firms and customers to recycle their equipment. One way for African economies to make the most of this dynamic is to capture the unwanted secondhand equipment coming from Northern countries, disassemble, select spare parts and re-assemble equipment when possible. That can only be performed by people.

In collaboration with HP and the EMPA Institute, the Digital Solidarity Fund (DSF), an international mechanism focusing on innovative financing for ICT projects in developing countries, is implementing an e-Waste programme in Africa, aiming at developing a sustainable e-waste management system, with recycling and re-manufacturing local capacities especially in the informal sector. One specific concern is to foster a local economic activity around this new business, without creating an unfair competition with already established local manufacturers.

Opportunity 2: call centres

The second sector on which Africa could focus more and more in order to make the most of the NE for a sustainable socio-economic development if that of call centres. This contact industry can be an innovative way to reconcile a strategic positioning on the worldwide NE and a sustainable micro-economic policy aimed at creating not just value but also jobs. Africa enjoys many advantages: common languages with call centres' foreign customers (English, French and Portuguese); no more than a three hour time difference with European countries; more and more countries authorising Voice over Internet Protocol (VoIP) and cheaper labour costs. A call centre agent in Africa earns from $8,900 to $22,100 whereas the range is from $24,500 to $33,100 for a call centre worker in the UK and Europe and from $22,000 to $36,200 in the Asia-Pacific region (Dimension Data, 2006). The biggest African player in the call centre industry is South Africa. In 2001, it had 410 call centres of 20 seats or more, i.e. as many as in Belgium, Ireland, Scotland, the Philippines, Italy or Spain (Mitial, 2002). There were also 135 micro-call centres. The biggest one (900 seats) is operated by Old Mutual. The average number of seats per call centre is 116, which is higher than in Europe. On average, a South African call centre is twice as big as a German call centre and two thirds bigger than a French and an English call centre. The higher than 20 seat call centre industry employs about 80,000 people. The industry has grown by 8 per cent a year since 2003 and contributes about 1 per cent to South Africa's GDP.

The strong French-speaking presence in South Africa has enabled local industry to set up call centres dealing with both English- and French-speaking customers. In that regard, South Africa can compete with other French-speaking African countries. South Africa can enjoy low salaries in the sector: the basic salary of a South African call centre director is about a third of its British, Dutch or Irish counterpart. The average annual salary of a South African call centre operator is about 90,000 rand, twice as cheap as in England. And the leading fixed line operator, Telkom is proposing special tariffs for call centres that are using more than 1 or 3 million minutes per month. Another advantage for South Africa is that the accent of the English-speaking population is regarded as being easily understood: research carried out by Mitial in 2001 shows that UK and Irish consumers are much happier dealing with South Africans than Indians. Indian operators are requested to change their diction and their accent by watching British TV programmes such as *Eastenders* and *Blackadder* during their training sessions. But they can also use software that neutralises their accent (Genesis, 2003). Dutch companies are also interested in South African contact centres because of the similarity between Dutch and Afrikaans.

In the French-speaking part of Africa, Senegal, Tunisia and Morocco are leading the market. At the end of 2008 in Tunisia, 17,500 people were working in 200 call centres. In Morocco, 20,000 people are working in call centres. In Senegal, the call centre operator PCCI is the first employer of the country in the formal economy, with 1,400 people. Of course, working conditions in call centres are not necessarily comfortable (Lewis, 2000) and they might be the electronic assembly lines of the new economy as depicted by Phil Jennings, Secretary-General of the Union Network International. But a position as a call centre operator can be a good start for young people who are not necessarily qualified enough for high added-value positions. It can be a step-up to the middle class.

African governments are implementing specific policies to attract call centres. For instance, in South Africa, the Western Cape province which hosts about 12,000 call centre operators has launched the public-private partnerships CallingTheCape in 2001 to support the local call centre industry. The Gauteng province also has its regional initiative, ContactInGauteng, as well as the KwaZulu-Natal province with its KZNonSource. These three regional initiatives and the Department of Trade and Industry have created the South African Contact Centre Community in 2004 to coordinate their efforts better. In Senegal, the public investment agency APIX is also promoting the call centre industry.

Opportunity 3: offshore BPO

The last sector to be considered for positioning the NE at the heart of a sustainable socio-economic development in Africa is Business Process Outsourcing (BPO). A firm is implementing BPO when it outsources its non-core activities to a service provider. It is offshore BPO when this provider is abroad. BPO is a highly IT-intensive industry especially when it refers to the outsourcing of accounting, customer relationship management or data management. Despite the risks of BPO (losing control, service discontinuity, data integrity, and the risk of locating in a politically unstable country), it does answer some business requirements: focusing on core activities and value; cutting costs; contracting quality of service; accessing specific technologies (Genesis, 2003). The global BPO industry is estimated to be worth 120 to 150 billion US$. Within this category, offshore BPO is estimated to range from 10 to 40 billion US$. In 2004, South Africa was rated seventeenth by A.T. Kearney in its BPO global ranking, showing positive figures for the availability of semi-qualified human resources, low attrition rate, sound business environment, solid financial infrastructures and a satisfactory Intellectual Property Rights regime (A.T. Kearney, 2004).

India is the historical BPO leader with 35 per cent market share. The Philippines represent 15 per cent of the offshore BPO market. General Electric and Amex inaugurated the BPO movement in the 1980s. In 2008, the BPO was employing 245,000 people in India which lists 50 BPO-centric industrial parks (TBDS, 2002). India offers many advantages; amongst them is the conducive tax policy aiming at facilitating the delocalisation of BPO to India and an average salary of a BPO worker that is four times lower than in South Africa. But some factors are putting Africa on the map, competing with India. India has indeed an erratic power grid, a high attrition rate (up to 50 per cent) and some issues with the CRM-style of Indian BPO centres' operators.

South Africa is leading the African BPO market and intends to position itself on financial BPO, i.e. the outsourcing of financial activities such as the administration of life insurance and loan contracts and asset management (Wesgro, 2003). In that regard, the South African Department of Trade and Industry's SAVANT initiative is focusing on BPO; it notably aims at making the most of the similarity of the South African financial regulatory system with the British one, in order to attract BPO activities from the UK. The Investment and Trade Promotion Agency for the Western Cape (Wesgro) was expecting to host 1,000 BPO jobs by the end of 2008, generating 1 billion rand (Wesgro, 2003).

Because South Africa has robust IT infrastructures and a good average qualification rate of its workforce, it intends to position itself as a BPO hub that is managing BPO service providers offshore. This is particularly relevant given the expertise of South African groups in the financial services industry, such as Old Mutual, Sanlam and Metropolitan (TBDS, 2002). The South African firm Computer Sciences Corporation is the biggest BPO out-sourcer in the insurance sector in the US with the management of about 4.5 million insurance policies and pension files (CITI, 2003). By creating a BPO precinct in central Johannesburg, the city expects to create 50,000 jobs, rising from the current 360 BPO centres. At the national level, the macro-economic policy Accelerated and Shared Growth Initiative of South Africa (Asgi-SA) identifies the BPO as one of the top three priority sectors to stimu-late growth and job creation. In 2009, the government expects the BPO sector to create 25,000 direct and 75,000 indirect jobs and contribute up to 8 billion rand to the national economy.

Towards the Africanisation of the new economy

As we mentioned it earlier, there is not one single model of the new economy; Boyer (2004) and Amable (2005) have documented the plurality of new econ-omies. If one could identify an African model of the new economy, one could say that it is built around one priority: positioning the new economy (and IT) at the heart of a sustainable socio-economic development strategy that builds on three main pillars: the IT (re-)manufacturing industry, the call centre industry and the offshore BPO industry. Such a strategy could both position Africa on the map of the New Economy and bring shared development through job creation. This Africanisation of the NE refers to an appropriation or an endogenisation tactic as understood by De Certeau (1990). It refers to the use of imported exogenous technologies that are not just adopted but rather adapted or absorbed in order to address local needs (Emmanuel, 1981). Bayart (1996) depicts this movement as *extraversion*.

To fulfil this Africanisation of the NE, four main conditions need to be met: appropriate telecom/IT infrastructures; a conducive legal and insti-tutional framework; a relevant skills development strategy; a strong political will such as a 'second NE Plan' at the NEPAD level.

Condition 1: appropriate telecom/IT infrastructures

One basic condition for Africa to develop its NE is to have the right infra-structures in place. Twenty-eight African countries are not connected to any international fibre connection, with a severe negative impact on their competitiveness. In 2005, Africa's 900 million inhabitants only had access to 20,000 international circuits, i.e., just 0.16 per cent of the global total of 12.2 million international circuits. Many network initiatives are currently on track to strengthen the connection of the continent to the international backbone: four Afritel subregional projects, East African Submarine Cable System (EASSy), the East African Digital Transmission Project, COM-7, Boucle de Nord, Boucle de Sud, NIGAL, Infinity West African Cable, GLO-1, West African Festoon System, East African Backhaul System, TEAMS, FLAG, Infraco, NEPAD SPV. As for the IT (re-)manufacturing sector, the requirements are even more basic such as a stable power supply, a good road network for logistics, a sound business environment for registering firms, etc . . .

Condition 2: appropriate institutions

The appropriate institutions must also be in place for the market to function appropriately with public safeguards. Two main institutions are crucial. The first one is fair competition between players. As the International Telecommunications Union notes, looking at 19 sectors,[3] competition is prevailing in half of African countries whereas 25 per cent still have a monopoly and 25 per cent have partial competition. The competition is very well established in the mobile markets but is still scarce regarding international gateways. And too few African countries have liberalised Voice over Internet Protocol (VoIP) so far. The second one is the set up of Universal Service Funds that are usually alimented by market players in order for public authorities to develop information society programmes such as the set up of Internet public access and training points. In 2005, only eight African countries had such funds: Burkina Faso, South Africa, Uganda, Nigeria, Tanzania, Mozambique, Zambia and Madagascar.

Condition 3: a multi-layered skills development strategy

The third condition is to gather the right human capital so that as many Africans as possible can participate in this economy. Kraak (2003) rightly calls for a multi-layered skills development policy that enables the different categories of people – considering their resources – to find their place in this environment. Three layers have to be developed: high, intermediate, low. These three layers correspond to different economic sectors. The intermediate and low layers could refer to the three sectors we have mentioned earlier. If a part of the economic strategy is to go up the added-value chain notably by focusing on foreign direct investments, one condition is to have an adequate workforce. For many African countries, the right human resources are not available, particularly due to the absence or the lack of relevant skills. Therefore a supply-side policy cannot build the African model of the NE on its own. A balance must be set with an approach that focuses on the need to create jobs with added value, i.e. in the three sectors we have identified. This is not an easy path since the demand for non- or low-qualified workers is oriented downwards. For instance, in South Africa, between 1995 and 2001, the number of semi- and un-skilled workers in the IT sectors has diminished from 23.4 per cent to 21.6 per cent whereas the number of highly skilled workers has gone up from 15.6 per cent to 17.4 per cent (Pillay, 2003).

Condition 4: A NEPAD-led 'second NE plan'

The New Partnership for Africa's Development (NEPAD) considers Telecoms and ICTs as a priority in terms of infrastructure investments. The objective is to capitalise on ICTs as a tool in enhancing livelihoods and creating new business opportunities. The NEPAD has created the Information Society Partnership for Africa's Development (ISPAD), a public-private partnership aiming at bridging the digital divide. It also relies on the e-Commission for Africa that is based on the Council for Scientific and Industrial Research campus in Pretoria. The NEPAD is already focusing on two main projects. The first one is the NEPAD ICT Broadband Infrastructure Network; it aims to connect all African countries to one another and, in turn, to the rest of the world through broadband fibre-optic submarine cables. The Commission is working towards the development of two regional networks, one for Eastern and Southern Africa and the other for Central West and North Africa. The Eastern and Southern integrated ICT Broadband backbone is based on governance principles that have been signed in the Kigali Protocol by 12 countries in 2006. The submarine segment of the NEPAD network is named Uhurunet and the terrestrial segment is named Umojanet.

As for the Central, Western and Northern African countries, the integrated ICT Broadband backbone was agreed in 2005. The second project is the NEPAD e-Schools initiative. It was launched in 2003 and aims to equip all African primary and secondary schools with ICT apparatus and to connect them to the Internet. It involves 600,000 schools across the continent and is based on a public/private partnership organising five consortia led by AMD, Cisco, HP, Microsoft and Oracle. In parallel to these projects, the NEPAD should take a strong lead on one or more of the three sectors that we focused on: IT (re-)manufacturing, call centres, BPO offshore. They truly complement the two NEPAD projects by facilitating professional achievements for learners and by strengthening the case for a superior bandwidth capacity. That would be a second new economy NEPAD plan.

Conclusion

The new economy is full of promises, but not for everyone. Africa can definitely grasp the benefits thereof. Some firms, individuals and countries are already well positioned in this economy. But the vast majority of the continent is less well positioned. For the continent to make the most of the new economy, private and public actors should not only focus on the high value niche markets but also promote the sectors that foster job creations. We have identified three NE segments that could directly impact on the everyday life of some African people: IT (re-)manufacturing, call centres, BPO offshore. Of course, some African countries are already well positioned in the upper part of the value chain, especially South Africa (Péjout, 2006), and this is a sound investment for the future. Nevertheless, it does not bring a rapid and significant transformation in most people's lives. That is why a specific focus on the middle-to low strata of the NE is necessary.

Though these can be considered as the electronic assembly lines of the new economy, they are key to securing a social contract that is using the new economy to promote a sustainable socio-economic development. This multi-layered strategy is already implemented by some countries that are accumulating the necessary conditions for this scenario to happen. But it is also a matter of coordination at the continental level. Reconciling the new economy with the so called *third world* second economy is possible and desirable to ensure social progress.

Further reading

Headrick, D.R., 1991, *The Invisible Weapon: Telecommunications and International Politics, 1851–1945*, Oxford, Oxford University Press.

International Telecommunications Union, 2008, African Telecommunication / ICT Indicators, Geneva, ITU.

James, T., 2003/2004, *Information and Communication Technologies for Development in Africa*, Dakar/Ottawa, Codesria.Idrc, 3 volumes.

Noam, E.M, 1999, *Telecoms in Africa*, New York, Oxford University Press.

Schiller, D., 1999, *Digital Capitalism: Networking the Global Market System*, Cambridge, MA, MIT Press.

Notes

1 All figures are from the International Telecommunications Union (http://www.itu.int/ITU-D/ict/). We do not include the Seychelles and Mauritius when focusing on minima and maxima.
2 The DOI uses 11 separate indicators of ICT performance to monitor three clusters of opportunity, infrastructure and utilisation. This index was endorsed by the World Summit on the Information Society at the Tunis Phase in 2005.
3 Local services, domestic fixed long distance, international fixed long distance, wireless local loop, data, DSL, cable modem, VSAT, leased lines, fixed wireless broadband, mobile, paging, cable TV, fixed sat., mobile sat., GMPCs, IMT 2000, Internet services, international gateways.

References

Amable, B., 2005, *Les Cinq Capitalismes – Diversité des Systèmes Economiques et Sociaux dans la Mondialisation*, Paris, Seuil.

Artus, P., 2000, 'Nouvelle Economie, Nouveaux Problèmes', in Le Cercle des Economistes, *Espérances et Menaces de la Nouvelle Economie*, Paris, Descartes and Cie, pp. 21–42.

——, 2002, *La Nouvelle Economie*, Paris, La Découverte, 2nd Ed.

Baudchon, H. and Fouet, M., 2000, *L'Economie des Etats-Unis*, Paris, La Découverte.

Bayart, J.-F., 1996, *L'Illusion Identitaire*, Paris, Fayard.

Boeke, J.H., 1953, *Economics and Economic Policy of Dual Societies as Exemplified by Indonesia*, New York, Institute of Pacific Relations.

Boyer, R., 2004, *Une Théorie du Capitalisme est-elle Possible?*, Paris, Odile Jacob.

Brender, A. and Pisani, F., 2004, *La Nouvelle Economie Américaine*, Paris, Economica.

Cape Information Technology Initiative (CITI), 2003, *ICT Census Report*, Cap, CITI.

De Certeau, M., 1990, *L'Invention du Quotidien 1. Arts de Faire*, Paris, Gallimard.

Dimension Data, 2006, *Merchants' Global Contact Centre Benchmarking*, Johannesburg, Dimension Data.

Emmanuel, A., 1981, *Technologies Appropriée ou Technologie Sous-Développée?*, Paris, P.U.F.

Genesis Analytics, 2003, *Business Process Outsourcing and the Contact Centre Industry in South Africa*, Johannesburg, Genesis Analytics.

A.T. Kearney, 2004, *Making Offshore Decisions – AT Kearney's 2004 Offshore Location Attractiveness Index*, Chicago, A.T. Kearney.

Kraak, A., 2003, 'HRD and the Skills Crisis', *Human Resources Development Review*, Pretoria, HSRC.

Lewis, A., 1954, 'Economic Development with Unlimited Supply of Labour', *Manchester School of Economic and Social Studies*, no. 22, May, pp. 139–91, in Agarwala, A.N., Singh, S.P. (Dir.), 1988, *The Economics of Underdevelopment*, New York, Oxford University Press.

Lewis, C., 2000, *Call Centres in South Africa: A Labour Perspective*, Johannesburg, COSATU.

McCord, A., 2003, 'Overview of the South African Economy', in HSRC, *Human Resources Development Review : Education, Employment and Skills in South Africa*, Pretoria, HSRC, pp. 33–63.

Mauss, M., 1927, 'Divisions et Proportions des Divisions de la Sociologie', *Année Sociologique*, New series, 2.

Mbeki, T., 2003a, 'Characteristics of South Africa's First and Third World Economies', Johannesburg, *ANC Today*, 28 August.

——, 2003b, *Address to the National Council of Provinces*, Cap, 11 November.

——, 2004, 'State of the Nation Address', Cap, Joint Sitting of Parliament, 6 February.

Milkman, R. and Dwyer, R.E., 2002, 'Growing Apart : The "New Economy" and Job Polarization in California, 1992–2000', University of California Institute for Labor and Employment, eScholarship Repository, University of California, available at: <*http://www.repositories.cdlib.org/ile/scl2002/MilkmanDwyer*>, accessed on 2005, 19th March.

Mitial Research, 2002, *South Africa 2002/2003 – Call Centre Country Report*, October.

Oyelran-Omyeyinka, B., 2006, *Learning Hi-tech and Knowledge in Local Systems: The Otigba Computer Hardware Cluster in Nigeria*, Maastricht, United Nations University, January.

Paulre, B., 2000, 'De la "New Economy" au Capitalisme Cognitif', *Multitudes*, 2, May, pp. 25–43.

Pejout, N., 2006, 'L'hypercapitalisme dans les pays du Sud: Performance économique, temporalités et contrat social', *Terminal*, 95–96, Spring, pp. 47–63.

Pillay, P., 2003, 'The Skills Requirements of Specific Economic Sectors', in HSRC, Resources Development Review: Education, employment and skills in South Africa, Pretoria, HSRC, pp. 87–111.

Polanyi, K., 1983, *La Grande Transformation: Aux Origines Politiques et Economiques de Notre Temps*, Paris, Gallimard.

Trail Business Development Services (TBDS), 2002, *Offshore Business Process Outsourcing and South Africa – An Investigation into the Business Case for Gauteng-based Companies*, Johannesburg, Blue IQ, October.

Wesgro, 2003, *ICT Census*, Cap, Wesgro.

Wright, E.O. and Dwyer, R., 2003, 'The Patterns of Job Expansions in the USA: A Comparison of the 1960s and 1990s', *Socioeconomic Review*, 1, pp. 289–325.

Part III
African case studies

13 Agricultural policy in Africa – renewal or status quo?

A spotlight on Kenya and Senegal

Ward Anseeuw [1]

Since the spring of 2008, not a single week passed without new riots erupting against the expensive life in the countries of the South, most particularly in sub-Saharan Africa. While the crisis has also touched the purchasing power of the Western consumer, the rapid escalation of the prices of goods – foods of first necessity in particular – affected the political stability of certain developing countries. Social unrest has spread quickly: the FAO identified more than 30 countries where the sharp rise in the price of staples resulted in demonstrations and, sometimes, provoked riots and violence. To use the terms advanced by *Time* magazine, these events and subsequent acts could be a cause of massive destabilisation.[2] Riots caused 40 deaths in Cameroon in February and generated violence in Ivory Coast, Burkina Faso, Mauritania, Morocco, Mozambique, Egypt, Senegal, Sierra Leone, Somalia, etc. (CCFD, 2008). Populations that seemed affected by food issues are today exposed to hunger. The importance of these popular movements, their spontaneity, and sometimes their violence, must be considered as messages addressed towards policy and decisions makers at a time when the need for regulatory measures is becoming more coercive (Anseeuw and Wambo, 2008). Questioning indeed the legitimacy of globalised development models and internationally recognised institutions,[3] it also draws attention to the situation of Africa's agriculture and its own capacities to overcome this crisis.

Although the food crisis was addressed and initiated local and international responses, it accentuated and made more visible the present syndrome of Africa's agricultural malaise. The latter is not new for Africa: although it is very diverse, the image of Africa's agriculture is rather dark. With stagnant productivities since the 1970s, Africa has become, in 40 years, a net importer of agricultural commodities and staple foods. The continent imports more than 15 per cent of its basic consumption, at a cost of $88billion in 2006 and $119billion in 2007. The UN reports that the total bill for cereal imports of the least developed countries increased by more than 50 per cent in 2007, accounting for an increase of more than $7billion. This situation is all the more catastrophic since Africa is comprised of a majority of 'Agricultural Based Countries' (as qualified by the World Bank), dependent on agriculture as a major component of their development trajectories (29 per cent of GDP) and of the livelihoods of the bulk of its population (68 per cent population in agriculture) (World Bank, 2007). Yet, many of these countries suffer from hunger and malnutrition and presently depend on food imports, even during their more prosperous periods (Fleshman, 2008; Von Braun, 2008).

In opposition to the rather conjunctural character of the crisis (increase of price of petrol, competition with the biofuels, increased consumption of proteins, decrease of cereal stocks, climatic disturbances, etc.) often insisted on by analysts, these longer tendencies of agricultural stagnation emphasise that the vacuity of agricultural policies and the multiplication of intervention frameworks without any real contents since more than two decades constitute at least as important structural constraints. Two major reasons are often advanced for the lack of tangible agricultural policies: first, national contexts are often marked by a decline and loss of administrative legitimacy to pilot the agricultural policy processes (including a decline of national administrations, multiplication of the number and types of actors intervening in the agricultural sector, the importance of external constraints such as WTO, EPA, etc.); second, hard to decipher national policies and strategies (i.e. comprising a profusion of strategy documents – with, as a consequence, an absence of strategy, weak operational potential of the documents, weak ownership of the policies) (Ribier and LeCoq, 2007). Initiated during the implementation of the Structural Adjustment Programmes (SAP) proposed by the World Bank and The International Monetary Fund in the 1980s in counterpart of aid which many of the countries affected by crises could not decline, this tendency has been accentuated by the opening up of markets negotiated within the framework of the WTO and bilateral, regional or multilateral commercial agreements. In addition, in many African cases, existing policies – or more precisely measures and/or projects – do not consider the long-term needs of the sector, but more the short-term ones regarding the economy in general, and of the urban elites in particular. This situation seems to be the reflection of a laissez-faire policy of African administrations to a sector that remains in any case, according to their administrations, anarchic, with few structural and electoral stakes and with little significance for their national growth or poverty alleviation strategy. The choice of favouring food provision at low prices to increasing urban populations has often been realised to the detriment of the farmers, who – in addition – were often taxed in order to induce industrial development or, in the worst case scenario, to feed State resources (Anseeuw and Giordano, forthcoming).

However, some countries have, since the early 2000s, recognised the need for the agricultural sector to be revitalised.[4] As such, Senegal and Kenya developed new agricultural policies in 2004: the 'Loi d'orientation agro-sylvo-pastorale (LOA-SP)' (Agro-pastoral and Forestry Orientation Act) and the Strategy for Revitalising Agriculture (SRA), respectively (République du Sénégal, 2004; Republic of Kenya, 2004).[5] Both are considered to be innovative and are a call for fundamental policy changes, institutional, legal and regulatory reforms, in order to achieve food and nutritional security and facilitate the shift from subsistence to market oriented production. This chapter's objective is to understand the renewal of agricultural policy in these two countries and to analyse whether it offers a coherent response to the present critical socio-economic situation and to the subsequent call for revitalisation of the agricultural sector. Aiming to contextualise better Senegal's and Kenya's present agricultural situations, policies and future options, the first section details, in the framework of the historical evolution of the countries' agricultural policies, the significance and structural aspects of the agricultural sector and, subsequently, the importance of their present crises. Secondly, the LOA-SP and the SRA and the renewal of agricultural policies in Senegal and Kenya (respectively) are presented from a development process and content perspective. In conclusion, the chapter discusses the lack of transformation, ownership and commitment implied by the renewed policies, therefore questioning the legitimacy of these pieces of legislation in the broader context of the countries' political economy.

The progressive political and economic agricultural crises in Kenya and Senegal

Although Kenya's history as a 'settler state' implied particular interactions between settlers and indigenous populations, differing from the merely extractive practices seen in Senegal, broad similarities do appear between the two countries and their respective agricultural sectors. In order to promote raw material provision for Britain's or France's industrial production and food revolution, production in the colonies, as well as transport towards the metropolises, had to be enhanced. While, initially, this was achieved through the peasantification of the African households, more constraining practices for the local populations were soon implemented. As such, Kenya increased its export revenues by encouraging white settlement and production mainly through heavy support,[6] and through African proletarianisation by limiting African farming activities and accumulation (Maxon, 1992). France established a triangular system between religious marabouts, French local administrative chiefs and intermediary Syrian-Lebanese traders, which enhanced the agricultural provision (mainly of ground nuts) to French companies organising export to France (Cruise O'Brien *et al.*, 2002). Both systems were implemented in a way that avoided the development of a local political elite and independent economic production bases, subsequently leading to uncompetitive local producers and even to the proletarianisation of the indigenous population providing cheap labour for white development – particularly in Kenya (Anseeuw and Rahal, 2007; Anseeuw *et al.*, 2008).

After independence in the 1960s, although Kenya opted for a more capitalistic system than Senegal's African Socialism oriented policies, both governments intervened directly in the economy, including in the agricultural sector, with the aim of achieving political and macroeconomic stabilisation. The new African governments acted quickly to lay, promulgate and to institute policy frameworks designed to ensure a smooth transfer of power and responsibility, to establish African unity and to Africanise the economy and the agricultural sector. As such, the state played a paternalistic role, characterised by heavy government expenditure and donor involvement (Nyagito, 1999; Faye, 2005). To attain the awaited returns from independence within this framework, Kenya complemented large-scale land reforms[7] with activities aimed at professionalising agricultural activities (agricultural support services such as credit, research, extension, and access to inputs) (Ogonda, 1992). Kenya also transformed the pre-independence agricultural commodity boards into government parastatals that continued to control not only production, pricing and marketing, but also input supplies and credit disbursements (Gamba and Kibaara, 2007). To achieve the same returns, Senegal nationalised the entire agricultural sector, mainly by establishing large, centralised companies, which not only engaged in huge infrastructural programmes in the provision of all agricultural services including extension, inputs and transport, but also regulated flows, fixed prices and transformed and commercialised production. At local level, the reorganisation of the agricultural sector took place through the establishment of state-controlled cooperatives (Faye, 2005). Both countries gave the domestic market the chance to thrive successfully and protected it from external forces.[8]

There were major breakthroughs with the emergence of a commercialised smallholder sector, which contributed significantly to total agricultural production and marketed volume (cash crops, such as tea and coffee in Kenya; mainly groundnuts in Senegal). However, where government intervention had to make up for lack of indigenous capital, this led to an increasingly controlled economy, dependent on a new elite and patronage networks. On the one hand, Kenya's Africanisation of the settler areas unduly focused on establishing a rural – primarily Kikuyu – elite in agriculture, thereby creating an African bourgeoisie that left a large majority of the Kenyan peasants poor and without means to develop a viable agricultural activity (Lofchie, 1989; Chege, 1998).[9] In Senegal, the socialist cooperative system has led to an economy of plunder and clientelism that orchestrated a double, complementary, system of patronage: the use of resources for private use by the State and a religious network of marabouts exercising their influence on the farmers and their production. In both cases, inefficiency, mismanagement and corruption led to high costs, which, combined with the world recession and the international debt crisis of the late 1970s, negatively affected their economies.

Due to severe economic and financial crises, Senegal was the first country in Africa in 1979, followed by Kenya in 1980, to abandon the state-controlled phase, subsequently having to engage in market reforms through the IMF and WB fronted structural adjustment programmes (SAP). Focusing more on macro-economic stability, this new era discarded sectoral policies. In agriculture, this shift to a more competitive economy, by privileging markets and providing an enabling environment for enhanced private sector participation, broadly meant the retreat of the state, the liberalisation of prices and marketing systems, international trade reforms, government budget rationalisation, divestiture and privatisation, cooperative or parastatal reforms, and civil service reforms, among other measures (Gamba, and Kibaara, 2007; Diouf, 1992). The transfer of commercial functions from the public to the private sector was mainly emphasised for efficiency reasons; however, this period saw increased political patronage and fulfilment of self-interests by the political elite, leading to abuse instead of popular capitalism (Okello and Owino, 2005; Dahou, 2004). The restructuring process of state ownership to private ownership resulted in a private concentration of state capital in the hands of a few who were close to those in power, and transformed public interests into private ones. In addition, the withdrawal of the state, combined with frequent policy reversals (because of the reluctance to reform confusing the private sector players),[10] led to the collapse of essential services to farmers (TEGEMEO Institute, 2002; Diouf, 1992). In the process of government withdrawal from commercial service provision,[11] the private sector was not in a position, nor was it prepared, to take up roles previously assumed by the state. It resulted in a disruption of service delivery and in an 'abandoning' of the farmers. Moreover, poor institutions, marketing and storage facilities, high transport costs, constraints on investments and underdeveloped services – including inadequate and declining research in agriculture, ineffective extension and delivery systems, and lack of finance to the agricultural sector and related activities – reduced incentives to produce and contributed to the negative situation.[12]

The incomplete and unsuccessful restructurings during the previous period led to disastrous results from the late 1990s to the beginning of the 2000s. The growth of the agricultural sector (whose contribution to GDP the late 1990s decreased to 25 per cent in Kenya and 20 per cent in Senegal) has declined in Kenya from a rate of 4.4 per cent in 1996 to 1.8 per cent in 2004, with an all time low of –2.4 per cent in 2000 (Ministry of Agriculture, 2006), and was on average 0.4 per cent in Senegal, with a low of over –10 per cent in 2002 (Faye *et al.*, 2007). In Kenya, with the liberalisation of pricing and marketing within the agricultural sector in the 1990s, there was a producer price increase in all commodities except rice.[13] However, although the impacts on the production of crops have been mixed with tea production growing, production volumes indicate a poor response to the price increase. This is explained by the strong fluctuation of real producer prices, high input prices, and of various domestic taxes and deductions along the domestic marketing chain, which decreased farmers' benefit from increased prices (Gamba and Kibaara, 2007). During the same period in Senegal, on the contrary, overall producer prices have decreased by 22 per cent (under the pretext that world prices – mainly of peanut oil – had decreased), while input costs had quadrupled.

The liberalisation process has also made Kenya's and Senegalese farmers more vulnerable and sensitive to exogenous shocks. Regarding Kenya, Legovini notes that 'among them are the severe droughts of 1997–2000, the 1998 El Niño floods and the rising HIV/AIDS virus prevalence, which have contributed to loss of livestock, crops and income, and threatened family structure and the viability of social services' (2002, p. 6). This is even more acute because a large segment of Kenya's agricultural production is fed by rain and depends on variations in the weather.[14] Similar characteristics apply to Senegal, which, besides the lower profitability of its agricultural activities, saw an acceleration of soil degradation and a decrease of soil productivity with 25 per cent compared to 1980 (Faye *et al.*, 2007).

These negative evolutions were once more aggravated when confronted by a series of external shocks and decreasing world prices for most export crops. Cheap imports affected producer prices and created competition for domestic supplies. The liberalisation of trade in agricultural commodities has led to an increase in imports of almost all basic goods (rice, wheat, and sugar; a sector that supported about 5 million Kenyans; rice, meat and many horticultural products for Senegal), mainly from other respective COMESA and ECOWAS countries but also from Western countries often disposing of surpluses.

The issues described are all the more dramatic since agriculture remains the most important sector, playing a major role in the Kenyan and Senegalese economies. In the beginning of the new millennium, over 80 per cent of the 32.5 million Kenyans still lived in rural areas, with agriculture-related activities, directly or indirectly, as their main livelihood source (Ministry of Agriculture, 2006). The sector still contributes about 25 per cent of GDP, employing 75 per cent of the labour force and contributing to 60 per cent of export earnings. In Senegal, although the contribution of agriculture to GDP decreased to 19.9 per cent, 51 per cent of the population still remains rural with agriculture employing 73 per cent of the total work force. The declining state of the agricultural sector led to rising unemployment and increasing poverty levels. Poverty increased in Kenya from 49 per cent in 1981–2 to 60 per cent in 2000 within the rural areas, and from 47 per cent to 57 per cent during the same period at the national level, aggravating the already high inequality levels (Argwings-Kodhek, 2006). In Senegal, the weight of rural poverty has increased from 61.7 per cent in the early 1990s up to 64.9 per cent early in 2001–2, mainly concerning small-scale farmers affected by deteriorating conditions. About 56 per cent of the latter, which is an increase of 5 per cent compared to the early 1990s and is 40 per cent higher than in urban circles, even suffers from food insecurity (Faye *et al.*, 2007).

The renewal of Kenya's and Senegal's agricultural policies in a context of renewed processes and governance

Considering the importance of the agricultural sector on the one hand, and of the crisis affecting it on the other, Kenya and Senegal committed themselves in the early 2000s to revitalise their agricultural sector. Senegal developed and adopted the LOA-SP, which constitutes the development framework for Senegal's agriculture for the following 20 years (République du Sénégal, 2004). Likewise, the SRA was prepared in Kenya as the national policy document for the agricultural sector for the period 2004 to 2014 (Republic of Kenya, 2004), constituting a ten year (2004–14) reference framework for the development of the agricultural sector (Republic of Kenya, 2004). In Kenya, more so than in Senegal, there even seemed to be a consensus on the necessity of the development of the agricultural sector as an integral part of its development trajectory.

The renewal of the SRA and LOA-SP not only represented an answer to the inadequacies of previous policies and a need for the renewal of agricultural policies, they also reflected innovative policy processes that took into consideration the emergence of new governance and decision-making structures. With the continued growth and influence of organised civil society, the governments came under increased pressure to consider new interlocutors in the process of policy development. The negative effects of solo government liberalisation policies and reform programs, combined with political and clientele based economic policy patronage, which complemented mismanagement of public resources, strongly pointed towards the need to reflect on agricultural policy formulation processes. Controversies started to arise concerning the implementation of the previous reforms, which were often perceived by many stakeholders as top-down, donor driven or implemented only under donor terms and conditions. Various stakeholders, civil society and NGOs emphasised that the respective governments had implemented the previous reforms with little or no consultation with the private sector or stakeholders.

In conformity with the need to revamp agricultural policy, the SRA and LOA-SP were developed in a renewed context characterised by the democratisation of public life, the promotion of new forms of governance (particularly in the framework of Nepad) and the implementation of more transparent participatory approaches. Indeed, in Senegal, the 'Conseil National de Concertation des Ruraux' (CNCR, National Council for Rural Co-operation), that was established in 1993 and progressively institutionalised to represent at the end of 1990s a large majority of the Senegalese producers' organisation, became an inescapable interlocutor within the agricultural and rural world. The lobbying of more than 30,000 farmers assembled in the capital in January 2003 to present their farmers' manifesto, obliged President Wade and the involved administration to accept a participative development of the policy. In Kenya, the authorities could not avoid the locally based Kenyan National Farmers Union (KNFU), which was inaugurated in 2000 into the Kenyan Federation of Agricultural Producers (KENFAP) to represent all farmers' interests in Kenya, organised from grassroots level upwards, through commodity group and individual membership.

The LOA-SP consultation process lasted for one year and included 55 contributions, issues by different protagonists, including internal services of the Ministry of Agriculture, civil society, political parties, development partners, etc.[15] The CNCR, aiming to include grassroots points of view, organised with support from international donors, parallel consultation processes at farmer's level. The latter, including more than 3,000 members and non-member farmers, resulted in an entire counter project. The final drafting of the policy, taking into account the different inputs, was conducted by a parity committee composed by the concerned administrations as well as the CNCR and the private sector, representing the major stakeholders (Chaboussou and Ruello, 2007). In opposition to the LOA-SP, the SRA, which is the agricultural component of the 'Economic Recovery Strategy for Wealth and Employment Creation' (ERS) developed in 2003 (Republic of Kenya, 2003), does not present direct consultations during its development. It is, however, based on anterior policy documents, which were widely discussed and debated. The SRA and ERS policy documents are the results of the government's subscription to the Poverty Reduction and Growth Facility (PRGF) developed in 2000 towards the end of the Moi regime, the Interim Poverty Reduction Strategy Paper (IPRSP) and later the Poverty Reduction Strategy Paper (PRSP 2001–14) in 2001 (Republic of Kenya, 2001) and, as a more sectoral product of the latter, the Kenya Rural Development Strategy (KRDS 2001–16). Even though the ideas of these PRSP-related policies were foreign, their development processes included many of the local stakeholders. As such, the PRSP 2001–14 was participatory in its formulation process involving wide stakeholder consultation, including the private sector, at the national, provincial and district levels further down to divisions, locations and villages in some of the districts.[16] The KRDS, too, involved wide stakeholder consultations and is therefore considered by many – although it also benefited from ideas of renowned rural development specialists and local experts – to represent genuine views and aspirations for growth and poverty reduction in the rural areas (Smith *et al.*, 2004). In addition, it must be emphasised that the ongoing implementation of the SRA and the development of the sessional papers are undergoing extensive consultations once again.

Both policy processes were thus – at least in their conception phase – indicators of a more transparent and systematic policy process, with a much larger platform for various stakeholders. These processes enabled the different stakeholders to take ownership of the policy. As such, the CNCR claimed that 70 per cent of its requests stipulated in the counter project were retained in the final Act. In Kenya, Philip Kiriro, the President of the Eastern African Farmers Federation (EAFF), notes:

> There has actually been quite a bit of change. Currently the policies are now being negotiated with farmers' organisations, since 2003. Farmers brought issues on the table. Government has facilitated and even has rehabilitated key farmer led market initiatives, like cooperatives. The farmers have also been linked to boards that used to belong to government before. Through reforms, most of the boards are now managed by the producers. There is some high level partnership at the country level.
>
> (Kiriro, 2008, p. 369)

Henceforth, the more participatory approaches have resulted – although few effective policy measures have been developed yet – into renewed policy orientations for Kenya's and Senegal's agriculture. The strategic guidelines on restructuring the countries' agricultural sector are therefore considered to be highly innovative, presenting a real paradigm compared to previous agricultural policies.

The SRA and the LOA-SP endeavour to transform agriculture into a commercially viable and internationally competitive sector that provides food and nutritional security, increased incomes and gainful employment for their respective populations. They aim at revitalising agriculture through the modernisation and the mechanisation of farm structures, the improvement of the infrastructure, the increase in agricultural services and the improvement of access to domestic and foreign (mainly regional – ECOWAS for Senegal, COMESA for Kenya) markets, as well as an overall revision of the legislation and governance structures. These ideas are often conceptualised alongside the aim of an African green revolution. As such, they intend to reverse the declining trend in agricultural productivity, making the agricultural sector commercially viable and attractive for the private sector. For example, the SRA identifies six fast-track interventions requiring immediate action: first, reviewing and harmonising the legal, regulatory and institutional framework; second, improving delivery of research, extension and advisory support services; third, restructuring and privatising non-core functions of parastatals and ministries to bring about efficiency, accountability and effectiveness; fourth, increasing access to quality farm inputs and financial services; fifth, formulating food security policy and programmes; sixth, taking measures to improve access to markets, for example rural roads and internal taxes (Republic of Kenya, 2004).

On paper, both strategies represent a paradigm shift that if implemented should lead to a cultural and attitudinal change by all stakeholders. The involvement of stakeholders in the policy development processes implied a steady but significant process towards the recognition of more sustainable and equitable growth, through the recognition of different production systems and different roles for service delivery and actors. Not only is there a renewed focus on different agricultural development strategies (through the recognition of both large and small scale farming, as a strategy for development), the emphasis is on policies that are beneficiary/demand driven and that recognise local needs. The LOA-SP, for the first time since the definition of Senegalese agricultural policies, focuses particularly on smallholder agriculture. It projects a vision based on agricultural development as one of the drivers for economic development by increasing the productivity and competitiveness of its structures, through the restructuring of family agriculture (République du Sénégal, 2004). The SRA, in addition to productivity increase, acknowledges the multi-sectoral nature of agricultural development, representing a major shift from the purely sectoral, solely production and growth-oriented development approaches. It emphasises the need to develop a coherent strategy based on a multi-sectoral approach to planning, implementation and the monitoring and evaluation of projects and pro- grammes. While aiming for significant improvement in living standards of people in the agricultural and rural sector, both the SRA and LOA-SP emphasise complementarity with other public sectors such as water, roads, rural electrification and security to its activities. Subsequently, in comparison to the mainly foreign or finance-led policies previously implemented, the office of the Presidency, the Ministry of Public Works in Senegal, and various Permanent Secretaries and Members of Parliament, in Kenya, actively par- ticipated in the development and implementation processes. In addition, the policy restructuring process implies all the agriculture and rural sector related ministries (Agriculture, Livestock and Fisheries Development), without exclu- sion of other administrations necessary for a broader rural transformation (Ministry of Lands, Ministry of Cooperatives, etc.).

The role of the stakeholders is also alleged to change. Between the all-state orientations of the more socialist era and the minimal state interventions of the SAPs, there seems to be a compromise promoting a specific role for government, included in the delivery of certain commercial services. As such, two important roles are identified for governments: first, to carry out a num- ber of regulatory functions that cannot otherwise be enforced through pri- vate self-regulation and industry codes of conduct, and; second, to provide support services that are not taken up by other stakeholders, but which are still needed for the purpose of increasing and sustaining agricultural product- ivity, real incomes, and food security and nutrition. The renewed policies thus address the poor performance of the agricultural sector by considering the overall production-related criteria but also by linking aspects of inequality and redistribution through the redefinition of the roles of government and the private sector in the development of agriculture. The strategies recognise new roles for government and promote, without foreseeing an entire with- drawal, divestment of public enterprises in activities that can be performed by the private sector. The strategies emphasise that for the economy to grow in a sustainable manner the public sector must play a major role,[17] without con- straining the roles to be performed by other private sector stakeholders.[18] Public services could include (among others): security, research and extension, and certification of compliance with sanitary and phytosanitary requirements. But the role of public service is also recognised in poverty reduction, with emphasis on the need for service delivery targeting the most-needy small- scale farmers in more marginalised regions (such as the Arid and Semi-Arid Areas (ASAL) in Kenya or the Casamance region in Senegal); therefore, a major innovation is the recognition of the role of the state in the intra and inter regional redistribution of its resources (Republic of Kenya, 2004; République du Sénégal, 2004).

Effective agricultural transformation or status quo?

The transformations in processes of policy-making and policy contents, demanding the modernisation of farming practices that would achieve food and nutritional security and facilitate the shift from subsistence to market oriented production, call for fundamental effective policy changes, institutional, legal and regulatory reforms as well as for concrete measures on the ground. If the policy changes have been achieved through the development of the SRA and LOA-SP documents, the effective reforms are still outstanding in both cases. In Senegal, the government has been avoiding the implementation of the legislation. Not a single decree or effective policy measure has been implemented since, mainly because the final policy result did not reflect the objectives of the administration (Diop, 2008). In Kenya, the development of the sessional papers has been ongoing for four years now and no consensus seems to be in sight. As Alila and Atieno observe 'the inability to build consensus with the stakeholders at the initial stages of policy review resulted in protracted arguments between the various stake-holders and between the stakeholders and the government' (Alila and Atieno, 2006, p.25).

Alila and Atieno continue, in specific reference to Kenya's case, but the same can be said for Senegal:

> Eventually, the changes were perceived to reflect the interests of the development partners rather than those of the stakeholders. In certain cases, aspirations of the stakeholders were sought when sessional papers and bills had been prepared. That meant, nothing changed and the stakeholders were just called in to 'rubber stamp' donor aspirations.
>
> (Alila and Atieno, 2006, p. 25)

Indeed, if civil society succeeded during the policy development phase to make the specific governments accept different views, mainly regarding the importance of developing small-scale agricultural activities and the role of the different stakeholders (including the state), they did not manage to push their ideas through to effective implementation. Consequently, little has changed and the measures implemented (if there are any) do not reflect the initial structural transformation, the discourses and finally the policy documents required. This observation is as valid for the type of measures implemented as well as for the contents and ideologies the policy documents imply. In Senegal, President Wade, instead of engaging specific government departments and/or different stakeholders (civil society, private sector, etc.) in the implementation of the LOA-SP, implemented several Presidential initiatives focusing on large-scale agri-business project. As such, accompanied by major political clamour and media attention, Wade implemented the REVA ('*Retour à l'agriculture*', Back to Agriculture) plan in 2006 and the GOANA (Grand Agricultural Offensive for Food Security). Despite their titles, both programmes presented multimillion agri-business initiatives, mainly funded through foreign donors. The non-structural transformation is also reflected, although differently, in the Kenyan case, where change is mainly based on a green revolution orientation that incorporates access to inputs, technology and capacity development (through the Kenyan Agricultural Productivity Programme, National Agricultural Accelerated Input Programme (among others), which are often donor funded).[19] Although on paper it is oriented towards small-scale agriculture, Kenya's agricultural overall policy orientation remains, in order to sustain its integration into a globalised economy, trade liberalisation and opening up markets mainly to promote economic growth through trade.[20]

Exclusively project and programme-oriented, these initiatives neglect the policy development processes, the policy consultations and, subsequently, the demands, requests and needs that the different stakeholders lobbied for. It also emphasises the disconnection between the process and the countries' present agricultural debates and completely avoids considerations of structural change in the agricultural sector. As such, the different stakeholders seem concerned about the future of family agriculture, the recognition of food sovereignty, and WTO and EPA negotiations, aspects that will affect them in the near future. However, these issues are entirely absent from the project-oriented approaches implemented. In addition, project and programme-oriented approaches avoid a broader reflection regarding the restructuring of agriculture, hence overlooking the broader political-economy of the countries and the place and role of agriculture in their global development trajectory. On the contrary, the effectively implemented measures, based on project implementation, emphasise a view based solely on productivity and modernisation, entirely omitting the implementation of renewed, broader, coherent and effective policies, which – ironically – were the objectives of the SRA and LOA-SP policy processes.

Serving as examples, several issues based on broader reflections are left out: first, the role of agriculture regarding social and economic transformation, in countries facing significant demographic increases; second, a vision for agricultural development, at a time when in Senegal and Kenya respectively between 51 per cent and 80 per cent of the population depends on it; third, the core question of activities and employment facing the increasing active population in countries where alternatives are low (productivity is important but is not enough)? As such, it appears that reflections concerning the sector's capacities to absorb its activities, and regarding the transformation of the structural aspects of the sector (distribution of assets, recognition of pluriactivity, etc.), are lacking. Other options for a large number of rural people, such as diversification into non-agricultural activities, off-farm employment, or migration (rural-urban or international) might have to be considered and developed;[21] however, none of these options are mentioned or proposed through the measures contained in the SRA or LOA-SP. A broader reflection on agriculture, its evolution in a globalised world and its capacities to respond to Kenya's and Senegal's wider demographic, and social and political contexts seems necessary.

The project and programme-based approaches are often endorsed for their rapid results and their habitually intensive use of land and labour force. Because they result in the improvement of agricultural productivity, mainly through projects based on the green revolution and/or the development of high-value chain principles, they are often presented as an ideal development strategy. However, whereas it has been presented as a solution in many developing countries, the green revolution has also often been criticised for emphasising a solely technical solution. More than three decades after the adoption of these 'modern' technologies, the success of the green revolution in eliminating or reducing poverty and inequalities have to be nuanced (Rahman, 2004).[22] In parallel, considering the transformation of current high-value chains,[23] new requirements, norms and standards, supported by the development of contract arrangements, are imposed on producers and might lead, due to the severe competition from larger producers having the financial and technical basis to meet these demands, to segmentation and exclusion of a large share of the smaller producers and to an amplification of poverty and inequality (Nyoro *et al.*, 2007).

The shift in policy orientations and effective implementations is striking and can be explained by the interest-based decision-making processes, the countries' legislative processes and the still important influence of donors. First, small-scale agriculture is still seen by many as anarchic, and unable to respond in a structured way to the demand of transforming African societies. President Wade's projects that were often foreign-funded seem to present easier options for implementation, resulting in quicker and seemingly more noticeable results. The rapid degree of urbanisation and an increase in powerful urban (often elitist) lobbying groups, tend to justify this choice. Second, the Minister of Agriculture does not have the final word on decisions linked to agriculture, rather the latter must defer to the statutory Ministries, particularly those of Finance and Expenditure. Therefore, with revenues from imports often being considered more important for the state than the profits resulting from agricultural production (as it is in the case of UEMOA's CET for Senegal), it has generally led to the neglect of pro-agricultural policies and initiatives. Third, these choices can also be explained by the positions of the international community and development partners, as well as the countries' dependency on foreign aid, despite its decline in the last couple of years. Although the international partners promote good governance and more participatory and transparent decision-making processes, they still seem reluctant to adopt fundamental economic paradigm changes – even if they are negotiated. As such, the large majority of international donors did not support the LOA-SP for the reason that it was not liberal enough; SRA, on the other hand, was supported but only under certain conditions, linked to management and policy options. Another example is the present EPA negotiations, through which, it has to be noted, bilateral and multilateral cooperation and/or international development organisations are still pushing their own agendas forward.

*   *   *

Africa's agricultural sector has been in crisis for the last three decades. The importance and impact of the recent food crisis only served as an accentuating event of this fact. If many analysts emphasise the conjunctural aspect of the crises, the vacuity of agricultural policies and the multiplication of intervention frameworks without any real contents for more than two decades constitute important structural constraints. To counter this situation, Kenya and Senegal have engaged – at least on paper and through their policy discourses – in a renewal of agricultural policies. Developed through consultative processes, the policy documents represent a paradigm shift from previous, often centrally or foreign-led, policies, that could lead to a cultural and attitudinal change by all stakeholders. As such, they present a renewal of public policy in agriculture, from a point of view of its content (it proposes far-reaching legal and regulatory reforms, new public-private partnerships, etc.) and its processes (focusing on a participatory development approach). However, none of the countries has effectively engaged in the implementation of these policies, nor have they advanced the reflection regarding the broader political-economy of the countries, and the role of agriculture in their global development trajectory, leading to a status quo on the ground.

Since Kenya and Senegal are the forerunners engaged in agricultural policy change in Africa, the above observations question the road African countries must follow if they do not want to be condemned to a repetitive history, characterised by agricultural and food crises. It seems that the response to these imbalances calls for effective changes, requiring in-depth reflection regarding the real needs of its populations without sacrificing its potentialities and resources in the short-term. As Kenya and Senegal have shown, Africa's situation requires a drastic change in policies. As such, every crisis has virtues and would provide opportunities to those who have the courage to respond and to question the development trajectories in which they are engaged.

However, while the crisis had initiating effects, in most African countries it did not galvanise energies to resolve the underlying reasons for Africa's fundamental food and agricultural problems. Many of the countries did not engage in revitalising their agricultural sector or restructuring the related policies; on the contrary, most responded through urgency measures often trying to reduce food prices and enhance food access. To this effect, Liberia, Tanzania, Ghana and Ivory Coast suspended their customs duties on the imports of basic foods. Senegal imposed food price controls; Ethiopia suspended VAT on cereals and flours; Burkina Faso introduced price subsidies on milk, and Tanzania has forbidden exports of foods. South Africa has increased subsidies to the most vulnerable inhabitants to support food consumption (Fleshman, 2008). Short-term measures supporting urban demand

and needs still seemed to be a higher priority, with the result that most African countries tend to neglect a broader reflection on their long-term national growth and poverty reduction strategies and also to overlook the importance and role of agriculture as integral part of the latter. Presently, Africa still seems to exclude itself from initiatives to establish independent, responsible, efficient and harmonised answers to its problems, crises and development, but, on the contrary, still engages in quick-fixes, which are, indeed, often easier and less strenuous to implement, but which neglect the underlying causes of Africa's present situation, not shielding them from, but increasing their vulnerability to, the next crisis.

Notes

1 CIRAD ES-ARENA and the Post-Graduate School of Agriculture and Rural Development, University of Pretoria, Pretoria 0002, South Africa (ward. anseeuw@up.ac.za).
2 Time (2008), 'The World's Growing Food-Price Crisis', published 27/02/2008, http://www.time.com/time/world/article/0,8599,1717572–1,00.html, consulted on 30/08/2008.
3 As such, President Wade of Senegal has accused the FAO of absorbing a major part of the organisation, without achieving any results, and requested immediate closure (see interview with Wade by Ba, D (2008). 'Abolish wasteful world food body – Senegal's Wade', Reuters, published 05/05/2008).
4 Also, at international level, the importance of the agricultural sector has been emphasised, as is the case of NEPAD, which with its CAADP programme has tried to sensitise African leaders to agricultural issues. For more information regarding the latter, see Anseeuw and Wambo (2008).
5 These policy initiatives were followed by Mali, Malawi and Rwanda.
6 The Crown Lands Ordinances (1902 and 1915), which allowed settlers to obtain land on 99 or 999-year leasehold bases, were complemented by the White Highlands policy, providing the settlers with heavy support from the colonial state. Government made available maize and wheat subsidies, low interest loans and direct grants to purchase farming equipment, in addition to a favourable fiscal policy. Besides the provision of transport facilities, such as railway and roads, they also benefited from government sponsored agricultural research and agricultural extension services. In addition, sponsored marketing schemes were initiated and settlers were allowed monopolistic control and marketing of some commodities: several production and marketing boards/organisations were established (Kenya Cooperative Creameries, the Coffee Board, the Pyrethrum board, the Sisal Board, the Flax Board, the Passion Fruit Board, the Pig Industry Board and the Maize and Produce Control Board, the Meat Marketing Board).
7 The Million Acre Scheme, the Haraka Scheme, the Agricultural Land Act, etc.
8 These include quantitative restrictions and controls, high tariffs on competing imports, exchange rate controls, controls on importation and licensing, controls on domestic prices and wages, taxation of exports and the requirement of 'no objection certificates' (to be allowed to export).
9 Large landowners emerged through the reform of the settler highlands, with about 80 per cent of the settler land transferred intact to Kenyan, mainly Kikuyu, farmers. They developed quickly through the support of the state and the assistance of a host of parastatal organisations.
10 For example, as detailed by Nyangito and Okello (1988), in Kenya's coffee and tea

sectors there is general dissatisfaction from stakeholders that the government is still holding on to some controls, mainly in the export market for the cash crops. And, even though maize marketing was liberalised in 1994, random import bans and import tariff imposition are still common. The National Cereal Produce Board (NCPB) continued buying maize at prices above market prices thereby distorting the grain market.

11 The proportion of expenditure in the agricultural sector in Kenya and Senegal has declined respectively from an average of above 10 per cent to an average of 6 per cent during the 1980s.

12 For Kenya, Alila and Atieno observe that

> since the liberalisation of domestic marketing of agricultural products, which reduced the role of marketing boards like Kenya Meat Commission (KMC) and Kenya Cooperative Creameries (KCC), the marketing of livestock and livestock products was left to private traders, who lacked the capacity to take over the role of the state corporations.
>
> (Alila and Atieno, 2006)

13 Rice prices were still under the control of the National Irrigation Board. The increase for food crops was due to a removal of price controls, while for export crops, it was partly due to removal of foreign exchange regulations, which led to higher prices (Nyangito and Okello, 1988).

14 Less than 20 per cent of Kenya's land is suitable for cultivation and only 12 per cent is classified as 'high potential'. Less than 7 per cent of Kenya's cultivated land is irrigated and consequently, 80 per cent of the land is either arid or semi-arid receiving little or erratic rainfall.

15 Out of the 55 contributions, 20 came from different internal services of the Ministry of Agriculture and Livestock, ten were issued by other Ministries, eight from key experts and informants, four from professional organisations, four from political parties, four from development partners, three from consular chambers and one from local electives (Chaboussou and Ruello, 2007).

16 The extensive consultation with stakeholders included parliamentarians, trade unions, professionals, financial institutions, industrialists, ASAL representatives, development partners, civil society and government.

17 As such, the SRA notes: 'The private sector will play a critical role in the provision of physical and social infrastructure, production, processing, input and output marketing, import and export, provision of rural financial services, and the provision of goods and services with strong "private good" characteristics'.

18 The private sector is here considered in a broad way, including farmers and professional organisations, agribusiness institutions, financial institutions, civil society, research institutions, universities and other international centers.

19 In launching the SRA in March 2004, HE President Mwai Kibaki explicitly called on the government, development partners, the private sector and the farming community to cooperate and fully participate in the implementation of '*a Green Revolution in Kenya*' (see President Kibaki's foreword to the SRA, page v) (Republic of Kenya, 2004).

20 The latter is confirmed by the accession to several international agreements, including WTO, COMESA, IGAD, AGOA and ACP-EU entailing the further removal of internal trade tariffs and barriers.

21 The latter corresponds to the options put forward in the latest WDR of the World Bank (World Bank, 2007).

22 Indeed, Lipton and Longhurst (1989) argue that,

in most developing countries, even those with major green revolution areas and significant growth in food output per person at national level, the proportion of people who have moved out of poverty in the dynamic areas has been almost balanced by the proportion that has become poor, especially in rural areas which because their crops or soil water regimes appeared less amenable to research have been little affected by modern seed varieties. Thus, contrary to the vision of its founders, the green revolution has turned into an instrument which marginalized millions of poor people in the Third World countries.

23 The transformation of value chains are linked to the rapid restructuring of agri-food markets at the global level, implying the establishment of new stakeholders such as supermarkets, processors, etc. (Nyoro *et al.*, 2007).

References

Alila, P. O. and Atieno, R. (2006), *Agricultural Policy in Kenya: Issues and Processes*, Paper for the Future Agricultures Consortium workshop, London, IDS.

Anseeuw, W. and Rahal, S. (2007), *Les politiques agricoles sénégalaises: Evolutions et facteur explicatifs*, Montpellier, CIRAD, Document de travail non publié, 83pp.

Anseeuw, W. and Wambo, A. (2008), 'Le volet agricole du NEPAD peut-il répondre à la crise alimentaire du NEPAD?', *Herodote*, 131, 4e semestre 2008, pp. 40–58.

Anseeuw W. and Giordano, T. (forthcoming), ' "L'agriculture familial": un débat légitime mais pas suffisant', *Afrique Contemporaine* (en préparation).

Anseeuw, W., Freguin-Gresh, S., and Gamba, P. (2008), Une nouvelle politique agricole au Kenya: Nécessaire mais suffisante?, In: Deveze, J.C., *Défis agricoles africains*, Paris: Karthala-AFD, pp. 209–35.

Argwings-Kodhek, G. (2006), An inequality and welfare analysis of Kenya's agricultural sector, In: SID, *Readings on inequality in Kenya*, Nairobi: SID, 253–89.

CCFD (2008), *Emeutes contre la faim en Afrique Sub-saharienne*, Document d'analyse, CCFD, juin 2008, http://www.ccfd.asso.fr/ewb_pages/d/doc_1429.php.

Chaboussou, A. and Ruello, M. (2007), *Processus de concertation pour l'élaboration d'une politique publique: La Loi d'orientation agro-sylvo-pastorale du Sénégal*, Dakar, ISRA-BAME, Reflexions et perspectives, Vol. 6, no. 2, 59pp.

Chege, M. (1998), 'Introducing race as a variable into the political economy of Kenya debate: an incendiary idea', *African Affairs*, Vol. 97, no. 387, pp. 209–30.

Cruise O'Brien, D., Coumba-Diop, M., Diouf, M. (2002), *La construction de l'état au Sénégal*, Paris: Editions Khartala, p. 231.

Dahou, T. (2004), *Entre parenté et politique. Développement et clientélisme dans le Delta du Sénégal*, Paris: Khartala, p. 60–61.

Diop, P.A. (2008), *Politiques agricoles au Sénégal. Différences entre l'Etat et les organisations paysannes*, Thiès, FONGS, Document de travail, 10pp.

Diouf, M. (1992), 'La crise de l'ajustement', *Politique Africaine*, no. 45, p. 62.

Faye, J. (2005), *Evolution et impact des politiques agricoles 1960–2005*, Dakar, Forum sur l'arachide, 7–8 Décembre 2005, 16pp.

Faye, J., Dansokho, M., Ba, C.O., and Dièye, P.N. (2007), *Les implications structurelles de la libéralisation sur l'agriculture et le développement rural au Sénégal*, Dakar, rapport Ruralstruc, première phase, 183pp.

Fleshman M. (2008), 'Flambée des prix alimentaires en Afrique : Mesures d'urgence et investissements agricoles', *Afrique Renouveau*, Vol. 22, no. 2, p. 15–20.

Gamba, P. and Kibaara, B. (2007), *Structural implications of Economic Liberalization on Agriculture and Rural Development in Kenya: First Phase: National Synthesis*, Nairobi, World Bank, Ministry of Agriculture, TEGEMEO Institute, Ruralstruc report, 146pp.

Kiriro, P. M. (2008), Prises de position d'un leader agricole kenyan, In: Deveze, J.C., *Défis agricoles africains*, Paris: Karthala-AFD, pp. 367–71.

Legovini, A. (2002), *Kenya: Macro Economic Evolution since Independence*, Washington, World Bank.

Lipton, M. and Longhurst, R. (1989), *New Seeds and Poor People*. London: Unwin Hyman.

Lofchie, M. F. (1989), *The Policy Factor: Agricultural Performance in Kenya and Tanzania*, Boulder, CO: Lynne Rienner Publishers.

Maxon, R. M. (1992), The establishment of the Colonial Economy, In: Ocheing, W.R. and Maxon, R.M., *An Economic History of Kenya*, Nairobi: East African Educational Publishers, pp. 63–74.

Ministry of Agriculture (2006), *Strategic Plan 2006–2010*, Nairobi, Kenya, Ministry of Agriculture, 96pp.

Nyangito, H. (1999), *Agricultural Sector Performance in a Changing Policy Environment. Kenya's Strategic Policies for the 21st Century*, Nairobi, IPAR.

Nyangito, H. and Okello, D. (1988), *Kenya's Agricultural Policy and Sector Performance: 1964 to 1996*, Nairobi, Institute of Policy Analysis and Research, 20pp.

Nyoro, J.K., Ariga, J. and Ngugi, I.K. (2007), Kenya, In: Vorley, B., Fearne, A., Ray, D. *Regoverning Markets: A Place for Small-Scale Producers in Modern Agrifood Chains?*, London, IIED, Research report, 170pp.

Ogonda, R.T. (1992), Land, natural and human resources. In: Ocheing, W.R. and Maxon, R.M., *An Economic History of Kenya*, Nairobi: East African Educational Publishers, pp. 1–16.

Okello, D. and Owino, K. (2005), Socio-economic context of Governance in Kenya, In: Bujra, A., *Democratic Transition in Kenya – The Struggle from Liberal to Social Democracy*, Nairobi: African Centre for Economic Growth and Development Policy Management Forum, 90pp.

Rahman, A.Z. (2004), 'Correlation between green revolution and population growth: revisited in the context of Bangladesh and India', *Asian Affairs*, Vol. 26, no. 3, pp. 41–60.

Republic of Kenya (2001), *Poverty Reduction Strategy Paper (PRSP 2001–2014)*, Nairobi, RoK, 214pp.

—— (2003), *Economic Recovery Strategy for Wealth and Employment Creation*, Nairobi, RoK, 112pp.

—— (2004), *Strategy for Revitalizing Agriculture (2004–2014)*, Nairobi, RoK, 115.

République du Sénégal (2004), *La Loi d'orientation agro-sylvo-pastorale du Sénégal*, Dakar, RduS, 98pp.

Ribier, V. and Le Coq, J.-F. (2007), *Renforcer les politiques publiques et agricoles en Afrique de l'OUest et du Centre: Pourquoi et comment?*, Paris, Ministère de l'Agriculture et de la Pêche, Direction Générale des Politiques Economiques, Européennes, et Internationales, Notes et études économiques, pp. 45–73.

Smith, L., Jones, S. and Karuga, S. (2004), *Agriculture in Kenya: What shapes the Policy Environment?*, Oxford, Policy Management, discussion document, 37pp.

TEGEMEO Institute (2002), *Agriculture and Rural Growth in Kenya*, Nairobi, TEGEMEO, discussion document, 60pp.

Von Braun, J. (2008), *Que faire face à la flambée des prix alimentaires?*, Washington D.C., IFRPI, Discussion brief, avril 2008, http://www.ifpri.org/french/pubs/bp/bp001fr.asp, consulté le 30 aout 2008.

World Bank (2007), *World Development Report 2008 – Agriculture for Development*, Washington, World Bank.

14 Industrialisation, state intervention and the demise of manufacturing development in Mozambique

Alex Warren-Rodríguez

Introduction

Having been, in the early 1970s, the sixth most industrialised economy in Sub-Saharan Africa, industrialisation concerns have traditionally occupied a prominent place in policy debates in Mozambique. Manufacturing development in Mozambique has its origin in the late colonial period, during which there was a fast expansion of manufacturing activities encompassing a relatively broad number of industrial sectors. Independence from Portugal in 1975 led to a massive disruption of economic activity and a fundamental shift in Mozambique's political economy. Yet, industrialisation concerns remained at the top of the economic policy agenda of post-independence governments: first, as a set of interventions aimed at salvaging the industrial infrastructure inherited from the colonial period and resuming manufacturing activity; later as a fundamental component of a broader strategy aimed at achieving rapid economic growth and ending underdevelopment by the 1990s through a process of accelerated industrialisation. Since the mid-1980s, the government has pursued an agenda of comprehensive economic reform and liberalisation. Whilst the adoption of this new approach has involved a radical change in the government's approach to economic development, private sector development remains an important part of its developmental strategy. Liberalisation has coincided with a recovery of economic activity and of aggregate levels of industrial development, but also with a process of growing concentration of manufacturing activities, and a thinning of Mozambique's manufacturing base.

Against this background, this chapter argues that developments taking place in Mozambique in the sphere of industrial development during the past five decades cannot be properly understood without examining the nature of state intervention in the economy. In particular, it argues that after several decades of active involvement of the state in shaping patterns of industrial and economic development, starting in the late colonial period and continuing through the first decade after independence, the liberalisation policy stance adopted by the Mozambican authorities since the mid-1980s has led to a fundamental shift in Mozambique's approach to manufacturing development and of the role of the state in the economy, with a gradual, but unequivocal disengagement of the state from actively aiming to shape the path of economic and industrial development, and the adoption *de facto* of a *laissez-faire* approach to economic and manufacturing affairs. This chapter argues that this policy shift has ultimately undermined any realistic aspiration of manufacturing development in Mozambique. It has done this in three fundamental ways. First, it has led to the neutralisation of the state's ability to articulate strategic interventions in policy areas that are critical to promote industrial development. Second, by focusing solely on business environment concerns, it has shifted policy attention away from the more fundamental problems hindering manufacturing development in Mozambique and from those problems that industrial policy typically aims to address. Third, it has led to a weakening policy and institutional framework for industrial development, further undermining any meaningful attempt by the state to shape patterns of economic and manufacturing development and address the many constraints that the Mozambican manufacturing sector currently faces.

Manufacturing development, industrial policy and the state

The rationale for industrial policy rests on two main premises. First, the presumption that industrialisation yields a series of economic benefits not matched by any other sector. In the specific context of development, this translates into a belief that industrial development drives the process of growth and structural transformation. Second, that the process of industrial development is fraught with a number of problems that the market mechanism on its own cannot address, hence requiring some form of state intervention.

The first premise is based on the idea that industrial production results in large dynamic efficiency gains, associated with the existence of economies of scale, which are less evident in primary sectors. Also on the fact that industrial activities generally involve more complex production processes, allowing for greater technological activity, industrial intensification and the creation of comparative advantages in trade. At the same time, manufacturing production is usually more susceptible to product differentiation, increasing the market power that industrial firms have in local and international markets and, consequently, allowing for larger gains of trade. Furthermore, the use in industry of a large variety of inputs results in important linkages with other parts of the economy and increases the value added incorporated in industrial goods. These traits have led to the idea that industrial development plays a critical role in development processes as an engine of economic growth. Stylised facts of development processes confirm this (Thirlwall, 2002). The traits that convey manufacturing production with this role can also be found in non-industrial sectors, including primary activities, for instance in the production of high-value agricultural commodities (e.g. flowers or branded coffee). Yet, these findings do not invalidate the rationale for industrial policy; rather, they broaden its scope of application (Stewart, 1991, Rodrik, 2004).

It is in this context that industrial policy as an instrument for promoting economic development can be framed. In a neoclassical setting, characterised by rational maximising agents, perfect information, diminishing returns on factor accumulation and constant economies of scale, there is little scope for any specific set of policies to promote industrial development. Unsurprisingly, this view has shaped mainstream policy thinking on these issues, which typically reduces the difficulties that developing economies experience in establishing modern industrial sectors to a question of institutional failure. Hence, governments are portrayed as distorting market signals against prevailing patterns of comparative advantage, as determined by relative factor endowments (Krueger, 1998). They are also seen as corrupt, imposing overly burdensome bureaucratic and regulatory constraints on the private sector. The policy recommendations for private sector development that follow from this conceptualisation are straightforward: liberalisation and investment climate policies for private sector development. Yet, this reading of the constraints faced by industrial sectors in developing economies obviates the fact that the assumptions underlying the neoclassical model rarely apply to the real world.

One approach taken within mainstream economics to overcome the limitations of neoclassical analysis of industrial development has been to extend this framework to incorporate the possibility of market failures, in the form of missing markets, spill-over effects or externalities. These failures affect the generation and management of information (Stiglitz, 1994) or the acquisition and use of new technologies, skills and technical capabilities (Lucas, 1988, Romer, 1986, Lall, 1992). Whilst technically useful, this approach is fraught by the same conceptual problems as more standard neoclassical analyses, from which it stems. Moreover, it obviates the fact that in development environments, the types of phenomena that the market failure approach tries to capture are pervasive (Deraniyagala and Fine, 2001).

In this respect, recent contributions in the literature on industrial policy for development (e.g. Chang, 1994, Rodrik, 2004) provide a more appropriate prism through which to understand the nature of industrial policy and its role in development. These contributions view industrial policy as a device to promote the structural transformation of the economy by promoting investment in areas that are deemed to generate the greatest dynamic benefits and maximising the impact of these investments. This approach sees industrial policy as a multifaceted process playing a variety of interrelated roles. Hence, industrial policy is supposed to provide vision and direction, guiding investment towards specific sectors and technologies and addressing potential bottlenecks and investment coordination problems. It also addresses market failures, especially those of an informational nature that undermine collective learning, and those undermining skill and technological development. Beyond these, mostly, supply-side considerations, industrial policy also consists of measures that shape the path and rate of industrial development by affecting the market and demand conditions that firms face. From this angle industrial policy sets the 'rules of the game' that determine the relative payoffs to different entrepreneurial investments. This may take the form of infant industry policies that promote learning and technology upgrading or, simply, ensure minimum returns on entrepreneurial investments. However, other interventions affecting the returns on investment may be equally as effective, such as mechanisms that generate certainty in investment and mitigate risk, investment coordination policies that help reveal demand interdependencies, market regulations introducing entry and exit barriers or business climate initiatives aimed at reducing the costs of investment.

These developments in the industrial policy literature have taken place alongside a growing body of applied research examining successful cases of economic development, with particular attention given to the rapid industrialisation episode experienced by the newly industrialised economies of east and south-east Asia.[1] A recurring theme in this literature is the decisive role played by the state in promoting industrialisation and growth, leading to the idea of a developmental state (Evans, 1989, 1995). Here, the developmental state is not defined 'ex ante', in terms of an ideal set of institutions that can be replicated in other countries, but rather, as an institutional arrangement, arising from country-specific conditions, which successfully engages all relevant agents in the process of growth and structural transformation. This conceptualisation is formulated in terms of *embedded autonomy* of the state; that is, the ability of the state to act as an autonomous external actor, whilst at the same time being embedded and, in effect, resulting from the social, political and economic reality in which it operates. In practice, the developmental state's success lies in a complex interaction of state bureaucracies with all relevant social, economic and political agents, in which the state successfully allocates incentives in a growth enhancing way. Whilst a large part of this literature has focused on cases of successful industrialisation, this framework has also been applied to analyse other forms of state, such as predatory or failed states, as well to study cases of unsuccessful developmental states.[2]

Mozambique: from colonial developmentalism to liberalisation

It is against this theoretical setting that the following sections examine historical processes of manufacturing development in Mozambique and the role played by the state in this process.

Industrial development during the colonial period

The first signs of industrial activity in Mozambique date back to the late nineteenth century when chartered companies began setting up small processing plants around their plantation operations. During this time, small processing mills also started to appear around urban areas to supply local markets with basic processed foodstuffs. Despite these first signs of industrial activity, during the early colonial period the Portuguese authorities generally discouraged manufacturing activities in an effort to eliminate all competition to the

Portuguese manufacturing industry, in line with the philosophy of economic nationalism that infused Salazar's 'New State' regime.[3]

By the mid-1950s, however, there was a gradual shift in colonial policy, with Portugal allowing for a growing number of manufacturing activities to take place in its colonies and with the colonial authorities playing a very active role in shaping patterns of economic development in Mozambique. Several factors explain this shift. These included the high costs of international transport of raw materials between Mozambique and Portugal, which undercut the competitiveness of the Portuguese manufacturing sector; also, a rapidly growing settler population, which between 1940 and 1960 quadrupled to around 100,000 people, and which needed to be provided with employment. This population provided a pool of semi-skilled workers that could be employed in industry, whilst also leading to an expansion of local markets sufficiently large to sustain an emerging local manufacturing sector, without harming the import of goods from Portugal in a significant way. Finally, the restructuring and modernisation of Portuguese industry also generated a surplus of second-hand equipment that could profitably be used in Portugal's colonies.

As a result of these developments, there was a considerable growth of manufacturing activities in Mozambique throughout the 1950s. By the end of this decade, the Mozambican manufacturing sector had expanded considerably and consolidated a sizeable industrial base,[4] with a relative degree of diversification. Industrial production continued its fast expansion during the 1960s and into the early 1970s, with Mozambique becoming the sixth most industrialised economy in Sub-Saharan Africa by 1973. This process of manufacturing development took place alongside the discrimination of the African population and its exclusion from the industrial workforce, with the bulk of posts in manufacturing covered by Portuguese workers, including senior, middle-ranking and skilled positions, and a large proportion of semi-skilled and unskilled jobs. Racial segregation and exclusion was also extended to the provision of education, where black Mozambicans were effectively barred from schooling beyond primary level, reinforcing the exclusion of black Mozambicans from working in manufacturing and, as a result, undermining the skill and entrepreneurial base of the native workforce.

During this late colonial period, the Portuguese authorities take a very active involvement in shaping the structure and nature of industrial activities in Mozambique. Hence, they articulated protectionist trade policies, justified on the basis of encouraging industrialisation. They also regulated and exercised a tight control over international trade and international financial flows, which enabled them to determine the nature, direction and composition of investment. At the same time, they used the state-owned Banco Nacional Ultramarino, a development bank for the Mozambican colony, to finance private and state companies operating in Mozambique. The active intervention of the colonial state in other spheres of economic activity, especially in labour markets (e.g. by controlling migrant labour, instituting compulsory contract labour and controlling trade unions) and agriculture,[5] where there was an extended use of marketing boards supervising production of key crops, provided further support to this view. Finally, the fact that agro-processing and manufacturing activities in Mozambique were dominated by large Portuguese business conglomerates with strong ties to the Salazar regime – such as the Champalimaud, Entroposto or Espirito Santo groups – suggested the existence of a strong interaction between the colonial authorities and Portuguese business elites.

Altogether, these findings suggested a strong involvement of the colonial state in shaping patterns of economic and industrial development in Mozambique, consistent with the developmentalist ideology of the Salazar regime, which saw strong state intervention in the economy as a natural *modus operandi*. Indeed, the Salazarist regime still saw its involvement in Mozambique as serving the purpose of reinforcing the economic interests of the metropolis. Yet, this was not at odds with a certain degree of development of local productive forces, including manufacturing, with the state playing a very active role managing investment, human and natural resources, articulating policies underpinning this process and, as a result, shaping patterns of economic and industrial development. This process was reinforced by the growing size of the Portuguese settler population, which exerted pressure over the colonial authorities to change the nature of colonial policies in the direction of developing the local economy, in line with their class (and race) interests.

Post-independence: central planning, state intervention and industrialisation

Independence from Portugal in 1975 was followed by a very sharp decline in economic activity, with GDP and manufacturing output contracting by 27 per cent in a period of barely two years. This sharp economic downturn was largely driven by the exodus of around 200,000 Portuguese settlers, representing over 90 per cent of the Portuguese population living in Mozambique at the time. The departure of these people resulted in a very significant loss to the country's skill, knowledge and technological base, which not only affected the manufacturing sector, but also the government administration and transport systems. It also led to a dramatic fall in internal demand, directly as a result of the exodus of the Portuguese population, but also through its multiplicative impact on local employment. In the industrial sector many firms were abandoned after the flight of their Portuguese owners, managers and technicians, leading to an abrupt halt in production in many industries. This situation was made worse by the numerous acts of sabotage on Portuguese assets, which greatly affected the industrial sector via the destruction of manufacturing plants, equipment and basic infrastructures.[6] Finally, the massive capital outflow that followed independence in June 1975 further hampered the rehabilitation and modernisation of damaged industrial plants and infrastructure. The armed conflict with the Rhodesian regime starting in 1976 only added more problems, by increasing insecurity and leading to the destruction of vital infrastructures.

The end of colonial rule led to a fundamental shift in Mozambique's political economy and developmental strategic orientation, yet with the state continuing to be seen as playing a central role in the process of industrial development and economic transformation. The growing role that the state took during this period was partly driven by the ideological orientation of the FRELIMO liberation movement, but was also dictated by the unprecedented disruption that followed independence from Portugal. Hence, the departure of most Portuguese settlers, who had previously run the colonial administration and most manufacturing firms, and the precipitated transfer of power to FRELIMO, a guerrilla liberation movement with little experience of government, policy making or macroeconomic management, in the midst of a period of great political uncertainty and economic turmoil, led the post-independence Mozambican authorities to adopt a strategy of direct intervention in the economy, in an to attempt to avoid the collapse of economic activity, preserve the country's industrial infrastructure inherited from the colonial period and, eventually, re-establish production. As a result of these actions, the initial economic collapse experienced in the aftermath of independence was followed by a brief period of economic recovery between 1978 and 1981, with both GDP and manufacturing value added growing by 11.4 per cent (Castel Branco, 2002).

Beyond these initial interventions, aimed at maintaining a minimum level of economic activity, FRELIMO envisaged a central role for the state in economic planning and management, particularly with regard to industrial development. This vision of the state and of industrial growth as catalysts of economic development was made explicit in FRELIMO's third Congress. Held in 1977, it set out the government's development strategy for the 1980s, establishing the principles for central planning and the centrality of the industrial sector as a 'dynamic factor for economic development' and, in particular, heavy industry as 'the decisive factor for economic development' (Pitcher, 2002: 52). Among other aspects, the resolutions adopted during the third FRELIMO Congress directed the government to: first, consolidate the role of the state as an agent of change and economic transformation, by adopting a system of central planning and reinforcing the role of the state in production; second, accelerate industrialisation, with an emphasis on heavy industry, maximising the use of existing production capacity and promoting both export-oriented and import-substituting industries, and third, develop technical and managerial skills (Word Bank, 1985; Wuyts, 1989). These directives were later reflected in the ten-year Prospective Indicative Plan (PPI) of 1981, which aspired to end underdevelopment in Mozambique in a period of ten years.

The new approach adopted in the third FRELIMO congress led to a substantial reorganisation of the industrial sector and the introduction of mechanisms of direct government management of industrial activities, a process facilitated by the large number of enterprises left abandoned after independence. These firms were merged to create large sector-wide industrial conglomerates. This process of industrial reorganisation, rationalisation and concentration of industrial assets was aimed at achieving greater economies of scale, especially important given the small size of the Mozambican market. Additionally, it contributed to reduce the dispersion of investment, industrial equipment, inputs and scarce skills and technological resources. It also facilitated a more focused approach to industrial technological upgrading and modernisation.

Despite these efforts, the implementation of the PPI and the adoption of central planning were followed by a sharp decline in economic performance from 1982 onwards. Between that year and 1986, GDP, manufacturing value added, industrial investment and manufacturing exports fell by 24, 45, 65 and 81 per cent respectively (Castel-Branco, 2002), with capacity utilisation falling below 30 per cent in many industries (World Bank, 1990). Several factors have been identified to explain this poor performance, such as the disruption caused by the civil war with RENAMO, the continuous incursions of South African apartheid forces into urban and industrial areas around Maputo, the recession that hit the world economy in the early 1980s, or the four-year drought that hit Mozambique between 1982 and 1985. Yet, perhaps more important, was the fact that many of the structural constraints inherited from the colonial period continued to hinder industrial development in Mozambique. These included the persistently weak inter-sectoral linkages with agriculture, which reduced the supply of raw materials to industry and the potential of rural areas as markets for manufactured goods, as well as the strong dependence on imports of raw materials, intermediary goods, spare parts and machinery increased balance of payments imbalances and exacerbated foreign exchange shortages. The general lack of technical and management skills and the growing obsolescence of equipment further hampered any prospects of rapid economic recovery and industrial development. In this respect the FRELIMO government of the time had correctly identified many of these constraints and had made a strong commitment to address them, recognising at the same time the importance of state intervention to solve these problems. Yet, paradoxically, with its strong focus on heavy industrialisation, the PPI intensified many of these constraints by expanding the demand for imported investment goods and, as a result, increasing foreign exchange constraints, at the cost of reducing the availability of foreign currency for other purposes, such as the acquisition of spare parts, machinery and inputs. This strategy also seemed oblivious to the fact that the country lacked the skills and expertise to sustain a process of heavy industrialisation, especially after the departure of most of the Portuguese settler population. Moreover, the excessive role of the state in economic management generated poor incentives, undermining firms' ability to adapt to these adverse conditions, as acknowledged by FRELIMO itself during its fourth congress (Egero, 1987).

In summary, what emerges from the analysis of this period is a situation in which the Mozambican government of the time appears to have correctly identified the main constraints hindering economic and manufacturing development. It had also committed itself to address these problems by putting them at the top of its developmental agenda, as captured in the PPI programme. Yet, ideological and practical reasons, as well as a general lack of experience in economic management led to the formulation of an unrealistic and flawed strategy of heavy industrialisation and rapid industrial modernisation, partly articulated though a system of central planning, which not only was ineffective in addressing these constraints but actually intensified them.

Structural reform and liberalisation

The mid-1980s marked the beginning of a gradual, yet unequivocal change in the government's economic strategy. In 1983 FRELIMO held its fourth congress, which centred on finding solutions to the deteriorating economic situation. This congress agreed on two key issues: the restoration of macroeconomic stability and the reorganisation of the manufacturing sector, putting a greater emphasis on the production of consumer goods, as well as on increasing the role of the private sector. These directives, later reflected in the Economic Action Plan of May 1984, the Economic Rehabilitation Plan (PRE) of 1987 and the Economic and Social Rehabilitation Programme of 1989, initiated a process of economic liberalisation and reform that has continued until the present day. The adoption of this new approach has entailed a gradual transition towards a market economy as well as a radical shift in the government's development strategy, aimed at reducing the state's intervention in the economy and placing the market as the central mechanism governing economic relations.

Liberalisation in Mozambique has involved the articulation of a gradual, yet comprehensive programme of economic reform and liberalisation encompassing a wide range of areas, implemented over a period of two decades. This has included the privatisation of over 1,200 state-owned enterprises and the liberalisation of prices, distribution and profit allocation. Trade liberalisation has been another keystone of the Mozambican structural reform programme, involving the elimination of quantitative restrictions to trade, the simplification and rationalisation of the Mozambican tariff structure, with the conversion of all specific tariffs to *ad valorem* rates, plus successive rounds to reduce MFN rates. Similar liberalising efforts have been directed at foreign exchange markets, aimed at liberalising the allocation of foreign currency and the determination of the exchange rate. One final set of reforms at the core of the Mozambican structural adjustment programme has been financial liberalisation, aimed at reintroducing private market forces and reducing the state's direct involvement in financing activities to the productive sector. Yet, perhaps, more importantly, liberalisation has entailed a redefinition of the role of the state in the economy and the nature of state policy interventions.

In the industrial sector, the implementation of this liberalisation programme was initially followed by a strong recovery in industrial activity, with manufacturing value added growing by 84 per cent between 1986 and 1990 and annual manufacturing investment expanding from USD49million in 1986 to over USD229million in 1990. This recovery was followed by a sharp, yet brief, decline in manufacturing activity lasting until the mid-1990s. Since then, however, there has been a strong performance of aggregate indices of industrial activity, with manufacturing investment and exports more than doubling between 1994 and 2001 and manufacturing value added growing by 247 per cent over the same period. As a result, by 2001 manufacturing accounted for over 15 per cent of GDP, a proportion significantly above the average share for other Sub-Saharan and least developing economies.

However, this recovery has been limited to a select number of industries, mainly agro-processing, non-metallic mineral production and, more recently, the basic metal industry. Hence, by 1999 the already dominant food, beverages and tobacco sector was accounting for 71.4 per cent of industrial production, almost double its share in 1986 (36.7 per cent) and two thirds higher than in 1973 (43.7 per cent), at the height of the colonial period. Meanwhile, other traditionally important sectors have fared less well. Some have almost disappeared, as is the case of textiles and garments, barely accounting for 4 per cent of manufacturing production in 1999, down from 23 per cent in 1988. This sector's decline has continued in more recent years, with textile and garment production falling by an annual rate of 32.2 per cent in 2000 and by a further 41.2 per cent in 2001, and with only one textile plant and one garment manufacturer operating in the country by the mid-2000s (Minor, 2005). Other sectors have experienced a similar fate, such as chemicals, metal-machinery, transport equipment and woodworking sectors. Even within the food, beverages and tobacco and the basic metal sectors, there has been a disparity of outcomes. Furthermore, in agro-processing, the traditionally important cashew-nut industry and, to a lesser extent, tea and rice processing sectors have almost disappeared, with growth concentrated on flower milling, beer production, soft drinks and, more recently, the sugar sector. Even within these successful industries there has been a reduction in the industrial structure, leading to a growing concentration of industrial activities in a small number of firms. Thus, by 1999 only nine firms accounted for 56 per cent of industrial production in Mozambique, with the two largest, South African Breweries and Coca-Cola, responsible for 25.7 per cent of total industrial output in Mozambique (WTO, 2001). This growing concentration of industrial activity has continued into the 2000s with the establishment of several industrial mega-projects. Only MOZAL, an aluminium smelter employing around 1,100 workers operating outside Maputo since 2000, accounted for 6.7 per cent of Mozambique's GDP in 2004, 38 per cent of its growth and 55 per cent of its exports.

State withdrawal and the demise of industrial (policy) development

This process of industrial reduction and concentration should be seen in a context in which structural adjustment and liberalisation programmes implemented during the past two decades have involved a profound change in the nature of policies to support industrial development, as well as in the role of the state in the economy. More specifically, it has involved a gradual withdrawal of the state from the economic sphere and an increasing disengagement of the state from actively shaping patterns of economic development. This process has ultimately undermined any prospect of broad-based industrial development in three fundamental ways, first, by neutralising the state's ability to articulate strategic interventions in the economy; second, by advancing a very narrow understanding of the problems afflicting the Mozambican private sector, centred on business environment issues, which overlooks the more fundamental structural problems hampering manufacturing development in Mozambique and third, by contributing to the progressive weakening of Mozambique's policy and institutional framework for industrial development.

The demise of industrial policy as a tool for strategic policy intervention

Thus, over the past two decades the Mozambican government has largely abandoned any attempt to actively promote manufacturing development through the articulation of strategic policy interventions aimed at priority sectors or at addressing specific bottlenecks hindering economic activity. Eventually, this has reduced its ability to directly influence and shape developments in the manufacturing sector, in a context in which stabilisation policies have imposed severe macroeconomic constraints on the economy. Several examples illustrate this.

Privatisation is perhaps where this transformation is more evident. Privatisation has been a core element of the Mozambican structural adjustment programme, as well as the most significant manifestation of the separation between state and the economy. Overall, results of this process of mass privatisation have been mixed, with final outcomes not meeting initial expectations of industrial recovery and the creation of an indigenous entrepreneurial class.[7] As mentioned earlier, this process did coincide in time with a partial recovery of manufacturing activity. However, it is difficult to ascribe these improvements to the effects of privatisation (Cramer, 2001). In any case, if any, these post-privatisation improvements have been unevenly distributed, with numerous firms closing down, whole sectors collapsing and with job losses directly related to privatisation amounting to over 100,000 workers up until 1996, equivalent to a 40 per cent reduction in industrial employment levels (Cramer, 2001; Pitchcer, 2002). Furthermore, privatisation does not appear to have had any significant impact in the creation of an indigenous entrepreneurial class, despite preferential treatment being given to Mozambican nationals, with a large proportion of privatised firms ending up being purchased by foreign investors. There is also abundant evidence indicating that, in many instances, both national and foreign investors purchased these firms for purposes other than maintaining their manufacturing activities, for example to be used as warehouses or for speculative purposes, or that they had been purchased by investors clearly unfit and unqualified to run these firms.[8]

These mixed and somewhat disappointing results of the privatisation process have generated substantial controversy,[9] with concerns raised regarding the appropriateness of the process, its sequencing, speed, ownership and sovereignty considerations, transparency of the process, divestment methods or asset valuation. Yet, as noted by Castel-Branco *et al.*, (2001), the main underlying problem appears to have been the government's failure to accompany this process with a set of complementary policies and strategic interventions that could guide the privatisation process, promote effective post-privatisation industrial recovery and avoid pernicious practices, such as industrial collusion, price fixing or enterprise divesture. However, privatisation in Mozambique has been part of wider set of liberalisation and structural policy reforms that have generally reduced the government's ability to intervene in the economy and, thus, have undermined the state's role in shaping economic events. It is in this wider context that state disengagement from industrial development and economic management should be viewed in the case of privatisation: not solely as a process of state divesture, but also as part of a wider process which has reduced the state's ability to continue to actively support industrial development.

This process of policy transformation and state disengagement from actively promoting industrial development is also evident in relation to trade policy. In this sphere liberalisation has involved a profound change in the nature of state economic intervention and, in particular, in the use of trade policy as an instrument to support specific sectors. This is evident from the fact that by the mid-2000s only five products benefited from surcharges in addition to their MFN rates: sugar, cement, steel tubes and cashew nuts exports. Of these, only in the case of sugar and, to a lesser extent, cashew exports do these surcharges appear to be part of a comprehensive attempt by the government to support production in these sectors. It is also evident from the prevalent perception that, beyond the general principle of trade liberalisation, tariff policy should focus only on revenue concerns rather than on trade regulation and support of specific sectors. In this sense, the government approach to trade issues is essentially defined along the lines of the new international discourse on trade, poverty and private sector development (e.g. World Bank, 2004). Under this approach, the government has essentially assumed the principle that trade liberalisation is the best trade policy for all purposes, so that any other actions in this sphere should be limited to removing bureaucratic, tax or legal impediments that hold back the full and effective integration of Mozambique in the world economy. There have been some isolated instances in which the government has attempted to articulate strategic policy interventions aimed at supporting specific sectors. This was the case, for instance, of the sugar and cashew nut sectors, for which temporary trade protection was seen as of critical importance to allow for the post-war rehabilitation of these two traditionally important Mozambican industries, in a context where international markets already showed important policy distortions. Yet, these isolated initiatives have typically encountered the strong opposition of the international financial and donor community – in the case of the cashew nut sector, with the government finally acceding to reduce tariffs on cashew nut exports in order to continue receiving the financial support of the donor community, yet at the cost of the ensuing collapse of the cashew nut industry. As a result of these policy developments the government is increasingly constrained in using trade policy to support sectors of strategic importance. The recent introduction of new legislation exempting local manufacturing firms from paying duties on their intermediary goods is a good example of this. Hence, concerns over revenue losses have led to the imposition of very stringent requirements to benefit from these tax exemptions so that, one year after this scheme came into effect in 2003, only 16 firms had qualified for duty exemption under this programme (Nathan Associates, 2004).

Another example illustrating this process of policy transformation and the gradual adoption of a *laissez faire* approach to economic affairs is that of reforms affecting the financial sector and investment financing mechanisms. Liberalisation in this sphere has been aimed at reducing the state's involvement in the financial sector and its ability to give preferential finance to priority areas, limiting the role of the state to that of financial regulator. Reforms in this area led to the separation of commercial and central banking operations in 1992, the subsequent break up, reorganisation and privatisation of the state-owned banking sector, the liberalisation and unification of interest rate setting, and the creation of a stock exchange in Mozambique.

As part of this process, the government has gradually renounced articulating policies aimed at easing specific financial constraints faced by the productive sector and directing scarce financial resources to areas of strategic importance. In this context, the only devices left to the government with which to influence financing conditions faced by the private sector are those offered by standard monetary policy interventions. However, these reforms have coincided with the implementation of a tight monetary policy framework, an intrinsic part of the Mozambican macroeconomic stabilisation programme, which has greatly reduced the availability of credit and raised interest rates to prohibitive levels, at a time when significant investments were required to rehabilitate industrial infrastructure and upgrade obsolete technology and equipment. Hence, whilst average nominal interest rates remained at single digit levels throughout the 1980s, with lower preferential rates given to priority sectors (World Bank, 1985), by 1996 lending rates had risen to 44.2 per cent. More recently, during the 2000s nominal lending interest rates have fallen to more moderate levels, yet are still around 20–25 per cent.

The government and various donor agencies have tried to ease these constraints by creating several funds, micro-credit schemes and other similar instruments. Yet, these initiatives involve very small amounts of money and have not addressed the underlying constraints to enterprise financing and manufacturing development. An illustrative example is PoDE, a donor private sector support scheme that was perhaps the largest of these initiatives operating in the early 2000s. This scheme included a small USD10million credit facility for local firms. Yet, by the end of 2004 only 20 per cent of these funds had been used, mainly because the high interest rates applied to these credits and the general lack of business opportunities deterred local firms from taking such credits in the first place (PoDE, 2004). Other more ambitious initiatives, such as the creation of a rural development bank to facilitate access to finance in preferential conditions to rural enterprises, an idea put forward by the Mozambican government and several civil society and private sector organisations, have been received with general scepticism by the donor community, international financial organisations, as well as by some segments of the Mozambican private sector, making it unlikely that it will be created.

In this context, FDI has emerged as a fundamental source of private sector financing. However, the government has done little to maximise the spill-over effects typically associated with FDI. As discussed earlier, this was particularly evident during the process of mass privatisation of state-owned and intervened enterprises undertaken in the 1990s, which saw many state-owned and intervened firms being sold to foreign investors with little impact on enterprise modernisation and performance. But it is also visible in other areas, including in successful cases of post-war rehabilitation such as the sugar sector, where the absence of policies aimed at promoting linkages between sugar operators and domestic businesses has reduced the impact of these FDI projects on the local economy (Warren-Rodriguez, 2007b). In this sense, investment policy has mostly been limited to the creation of an investment promotion agency in 1997 devised as a one-stop information desk for foreign and local investors, the promulgation of a code of investment benefits and, more recently, the creation of the legal figure for industrial free zones. However, beyond these measures, few efforts have been made to make FDI policy a tool for directing foreign investment to priority sectors, easing the financial constraints faced by Mozambican firms, or maximising the impact of FDI projects on the local economy, in terms of creating employment, generating linkages with local businesses and actively promoting the transfer of technology, skills and know-how. As a result, FDI generates very few linkages with the rest of the economy and few spillover effects (Warren-Rodríguez, 2007b).

Investment climate and the new discourse on private sector development

In this context, private sector debates in Mozambique have been largely reduced to a narrow investment climate discourse. From this perspective the argument is that, whilst structural adjustment and stabilisation programmes were necessary to trigger economic recovery, they have not been sufficient to provoke the expected private sector response due to the pervasive investment climate constraints of doing business in Mozambique. Consequently, it is argued that a second wave of reforms is required that focuses on removing bureaucratic and regulatory barriers that impinge on private investment, so as to improve the conditions in which businesses operate.

Certainly, Mozambique's poor business environment poses important difficulties for investors, as has been repeatedly raised by numerous reports and studies. However, there are a number of problems with how business environment debates have been approached in Mozambique and, more generally, with limiting the problems hindering industrial development to an issue of a poor business environment. Thus, this debate has taken a very narrow understanding of investment climate, limited almost exclusively to issues of excessive regulation and bureaucracy. In other words, it presumes that all investments are beneficial and equally desirable, that all markets operate perfectly and, thus, that any constraints on private sector development arise from institutional failures that take the form of business environment constraints. In this sense, it has ignored other important structural problems impinging on the business climate and which also undermine industrial investment. For example, it fails to recognise the strong competition that many manufacturing firms face from the informal sector, which currently employs an estimated 87 per cent of the working population. It also overlooks the impact that uncompetitive and collusive practices have on the business environment, despite these practices being pervasive in many sectors. More strikingly, it ignores the various structural problems that have afflicted the Mozambican manufacturing sector since the colonial period and have accumulated since, through decades of post-independence turmoil, war, central planning direction and state disengagement. These range from problems of access to credit, the prevalence of old industrial infrastructure, the paucity of the Mozambican technical, skill and capabilities base or the collapse of upstream and downstream sectors.

Policy fragmentation and the chimera of private sector development

The gradual withdrawal of the Mozambican authorities from the economic sphere also has its expression in an increasingly weak and fragmented policy and institutional framework for private sector development, which further undermines any attempt to address the structural problems that the Mozambican manufacturing sector currently faces. At a more basic level, it prevents the state from performing the core functions of ensuring the rule of law in business and providing basic services, such as health inspection, quality control or certification services.

Hence, the general lack of resources, technical assistance and aid devoted to these purposes has further undermined the government's ability to develop an effective policy and institutional framework for industrial development. A good example of this is the 1997 'Industrial Strategy' government policy paper, an ambitious attempt to put forward a coherent and comprehensive strategy for private sector development in Mozambique, which, however, was never developed into a concrete strategy, largely as a result of a lack of financial and technical resources and of political backing. The challenges faced by government agencies working in the area of private sector development have intensified in the last decade as the government's policy priorities and, consequently, financial resources and donor support have shifted towards the implementation of programmes in social sectors. This has left those government agencies in charge of formulating and implementing policies in the sphere of industrial and private sector development underfunded and presenting very weak capabilities. (Castel-Branco, 2002; Warren-Rodríguez, 2007b). Paradoxically, this lack of attention that these government agencies have received, has contributed to worsen the Mozambican business environment. Hence, poorly qualified government employees working in these agencies often have a very rudimentary understanding of the tasks they are expected to perform and of the part that the state plays in facilitating economic and entrepreneurial development. Low wages in the public sector, on the other hand, discourage many of these government workers from taking a more proactive approach to their work, in the best of cases, and opens the door to corruption, in the worst.

In addition to its very weak institutional capacity, what is left of the Mozambican industrial policy framework is excessively fragmented and operating with little inter-agency coordination, with different spheres of industrial policy formulation falling under the responsibility of different ministries, and dozens of frequently uncoordinated private, governmental, donor and non-governmental programmes supporting private sector development initiatives (Warren-Rodríguez, 2007a). A similar situation arises with regard to specific initiatives supporting private sector development, with dozens of public, private, or donor-sponsored initiatives to support private sector development, in the form of business development service providers, micro-credit schemes or training programmes. Overall, this fragmentation comes at the cost of uncoordinated, piecemeal efforts to promote private sector development, further preventing the formulation of a comprehensive policy response to the problems undermining manufacturing development in Mozambique.

Concluding comments

What emerges after two decades of economic liberalisation and structural reform in Mozambique is a gradual process in which the state has gradually disengaged from industrial development affairs and has renounced to articulate policy initiatives aimed at shaping patterns of economic and manufacturing development. This has led to the emergence of a policy and institutional framework for manufacturing development that cannot address the underlying structural problems afflicting the Mozambican manufacturing sector at least since Mozambique gained independence from Portugal in 1975. This occurs in a context in which macroeconomic stabilisation and liberalisation has imposed additional constraints to manufacturing activities and industrial investment, in the form of high interest rates, increased competition or the informalisation of the economy.

Hence, in general, policy reform has led the government to refrain from actively seeking to shape developments in the manufacturing sector for instance, by articulating targeted interventions to promote priority sectors or solve specific constraints hampering manufacturing development, such as those imposed by macroeconomic stabilisation and liberalisation. Instead, the government has, *de facto*, adopted a *laissez faire* approach to private sector development, limited to ensuring an enabling business climate and making available a limited number of services to local manufacturing firms. Yet, even this, it has pursued with little success. Hence, not only have the Mozambican authorities renounced articulating strategic policy interventions, but they have also failed to put together an alternative policy and institutional framework for private sector development that, for instance, ensures the existence of a basic institutional and regulatory framework and the provision of basic business services, enables businesses to operate and supports private sector development. With regard to investment climate considerations, the government has taken a very narrow reading of the factors affecting business conditions in Mozambique, largely ignoring the structural constraints hindering manufacturing development in Mozambique since independence. On the other hand, the current institutional framework for private sector development appears fragmented and with insufficient human, technical and financial resources, further undermining any realistic prospects of achieving broad-based manufacturing development in Mozambique.

Notes

1 See, for instance, Pack and Westphal (1986), Amsden (1989), Wade (1990) or Weiss and Hobson (1995).
2 See Khan (1999) and Herring (1999) for analyses of failed developmental states in Pakistan and India; and Donner and Ramsay (2000), and Hutchcroft (2000) for studies of clientelistic states in Thailand and the Philippines.
3 See Newitt (1981) for an analysis of the Salazar regime's political motivations and how these reflected on Portuguese colonial policies from the 1930s until the end of the Salazarist dictatorship in 1974.
4 Hedges (1999) reports the number of industrial firms growing from 150 in 1947 to 1,025 in 1961.
5 See Hedges (1999) and Wuyts (1989) for a detailed examination of these interventions.
6 See, Hanlon (1984) or Egero (1987) for accounts of specific cases of economic disruption.
7 See Cramer (2001) or Pitcher (2002) for a comprehensive analysis of privatisation outcomes and RPED (1999) for some quantitative results.

8 See Pitcher (2002). This also appeared to be the case of several firms surveyed as part of the research on which this chapter is partly based (Warren-Rodriguez, 2007b). In any case, concerns over this type of outcomes were already raised by the World Bank in its 1990 Industrial Sector Study (World Bank, 1990).
9 See Hanlon (1996), Abrahamson and Nilsson (1995), Pitcher (2002), Cramer (2001) or Castel Branco *et al.*, (2001) for different views on the privatisation process in Mozambique.

Bibliography

Abrahamsson, H. and Nilsson, A. (1995) *Mozambique: The Troubled Transition From Socialist Construction to Free Market Capitalism*. London: Zed Books.

Amsden, A. H. (1989). *Asia's Next Giant: South Korea and Late Industrialization*. Oxford: Oxford University Press.

Castel-Branco, C. N. (1994) 'Problemas Estruturais de Industrialização: A Indústria Transformadora' in (ed.) Castel-Branco, C. N. *Moçambique: Perspectivas Económicas*. Maputo : Universidade Eduardo Mondlane and F. E. Stiftung.

—— (2002) 'An Investigation into the Political Economy of Industrial Policy: The Case of Mozambique'. Unpublished PhD thesis dissertation. School of Oriental and African Studies, University of London.

Castel-Branco, C. N., Cramer, C. and Hailu, D. (2001) *Privatization and Economic Strategy in Mozambique* WIDER Discussion Paper No. 2001 / 64. World Institute for Development Economics Research. United Nations University.

Chang, H. J. (1994) *The Political Economy of Industrial Policy*. London: Macmillan Ltd.

Cramer, C. (2001) 'Privatisation and Adjustment in Mozambique: a 'Hospital Pass'?' *Journal of Southern African Studies* Vol. 27, No. 1: 79–103.

Deraniyagala, S. and Fine, B. (2001) 'New Trade Theory Versus Old Trade Policy: A Continuing Enigma' *Cambridge Journal of Economics*, Vol. 25: 809–25.

Donner, R. F. and Ramsay A. (2000) 'Rent-seeking and Economic Development in Thailand' in (ed.) Khan, M. H. and Jomo, K. S. (2000) *Rents, Rent-Seeking and Economic Development: Theory and Evidence in Asia*. Cambridge: Cambridge University Press.

Egerö, B. (1987) 'Mozambique: a Dream Undone. The Political Economy of Democracy, 1975–84' *Nordiska Afrikainstitutet*. Motala: Uppsala Motola Grafiska.

Evans, P. B. (1989) 'Predatory, Developmental and other Apparatuses: A Comparative Political Economy Perspective of the Third World State' *Sociological Forum*. Special Issue: Comparative National Development: Theory and Fact for the 1990s. Vol. 4, No. 4.

—— (1995) *Embedded Autonomy: States and Industrial Transformation*. Chichester: Princeton University Press.

Hanlon, J. (1984) *Mozambique: The Revolution Under Fire*. London: Zed Books.

—— (1996) *Peace Without Profit: How the IMF Blocks Rebuilding in Mozambique (African Issues)* London: Villiers Publications.

Hedges, D. (1999) *História de Moçambique, Volume 2: Moçambique no Auge do Colonialismo, 1930–1961*. Second Edition. Maputo: Livraria Universitária.

Herring, R. J. (1999) 'Embedded Particularism: India's Failed Developmental State' in (ed.) woo-Cummings, M. *The Developmental State* Cornell University Press, Ithaca.

Hutchcroft, P. D. (2000) 'Obstructive Corruption: The Politics of Privilege in the Philippines' in (ed.) Khan, M. H. and Jomo, K.S. (2000) *Rents, Rent-Seeking and Economic Development: Theory and Evidence in Asia*. Cambridge: Cambridge University Press.

Khan, M. H. (1999) 'The Political Economy of Industrial Policy in Pakistan 1947–71' SOAS Department of Economics Working Paper No. 98, School of Oriental and African Studies, University of London.

Krueger, A. O. (1998) 'Why Trade Liberalisation is Good for Growth' *Economic Journal* Vol. 108: 1513–22.

Lall, S. (1992) 'Technological Capabilities and Industrialization' *World Development* Vol. 20, No. 2: 165–86.

Lucas, R. E., Jr. (1988) 'On the Mechanics of Economic Development' *Journal of Monetary Economics* Vol. 22: 3–42.

Minor, P. J. (2005) *A Mozambique Textile and Garment Industry Strategy* Trade Integrated Programme (TIP) Mozambique Research Report. Submitted by Nathan Associates to USAID. February 2004.

Newitt, M. (1981) *Portugal in Africa: The Last Hundred Years*. London: C. Hurst & Co. (Publishers) Ltd.

Pack, H. and Westphal, L. E. (1986) 'Industrial Policy and Technological Change: Theory Versus Reality' *Journal of Development Economics*, Vol. 22: 87–128.

Pitcher, M. A. (2002) *Transforming Mozambique: The Politics of Privatisation, 1975–2000*. Cambridge: Cambridge University Press.

PoDE (2004) 'Aide Memoire from the Supervision Mission – June/July 2004' Enterprise Development Project (PODE) Credit 3317-MOZ. Draft Version. Maputo, Mimeo.

Rodrik, D. (2004) 'Industrial Policy for the Twenty-First Century.' KSG Working Paper No. RWP04–047. Harvard University.

Romer, P. M. (1986) 'Increasing Returns and Long-Run Growth' *Journal of Political Economy*, Vol. 94, No. 5: 1002–37.

RPED (1999) *Structure and Performance of Manufacturing in Mozambique* RPED Paper No. 107. Prepared by T. Bigs, J. Nasir and R. Fisman. Regional Programme on Enterprise Development. The World Bank. Washington, D.C.

Stewart, F. (1991) 'A Note on "Strategic" Trade Theory and the South' *Journal of International Development*, Vol. 3, No. 5: 467–84.

Stiglitz, J. (1994) *Wither Socialism?* Cambridge, MA: MIT Press.

Thirlwall, A. P. (2002) *The Nature of Economic Growth: An Alternative Framework for Understanding the Performance of Nations*. Cheltenham and Northampton: Edward Elgar Publishing.

Wade, R. (1990). *Governing the Market: Economic Theory and the Role of the Government in East Asia Industrialization*. Princeton: Princeton University Press.

Warren-Rodríguez, A. (2007a). 'Science and technology in the PRSP process; A survey of recent country experiences' *Background Paper for the 2007 Least Developing Countries Report*. United Nations Conference for Trade and Development. Geneva
—— (2007b). 'An Exploration of Factors Shaping Technological Developments in the Mozambican Manufacturing Sector and their Impact on firm-level Performance'. Unpublished PhD thesis. School of Oriental and African Studies, University of London.

Weiss, L. and Hobson J.M. (1995). *States and Economic Development: A Comparative Historical Analysis*. Cambridge: Polity Press.

World Bank (1985) *Mozambique: an Introductory Economic Survey*. Report No. 5610-MOZ. World Bank. Washington D.C., June 6.

—— (1990) *Mozambique: Industrial Sector Study. The Development of Industrial Policy and Reform of the Business Environment*. Report No. 7795-MOZ. The World Bank. Washington D.C., May 22.

—— (2004) *2005 World Development Report: A Better Investment Climate for Everyone*. World Bank. Washington, D.C.

World Trade Organization (WTO). (2001). 'Trade Policy Review of Mozambique'. Trade Policies Review Division. Draft Secretariat Report of 30 October.

Wuyts, M. E. (1989) *Money and Planning for Socialist Transition: The Mozambican Experience*. Institute of Social Studies, Aldershot: The Hague & Gower Publishing Ltd.

15 Local democracy, clientelism and the (re)politicisation of urban governance

Reflections from Johannesburg stories

Claire Bénit-Gbaffou

In a rough sense, the essence of all competitive politics is bribery of the electorate by politicians.

(Dahl, 1946: 68).

Anyway, who cares? We are in power. It is not the councillor who decides on local development anyway.

(ANC PR councillor and local branch leader, after ANC lost both the ward election and the ward committee election, Johannesburg, 2006).

Introduction

The local level is often perceived as more democratic than other levels of government, as it offers citizens the possibility of directly liaising with their elected representative, and therefore hold them to account, especially on local issues that affect their daily lives. Purcell (2006) has warned about the danger of worshipping the local scale, arguing it has nothing 'inherently' more democratic than others. However the local scale is certainly specific in the *potential* it offers for interpersonal contacts between residents and their representatives; for a more 'humane', flexible and locally-grounded state. This potentiality of a greater state accountability has been one of the key driving forces for decentralisation as well as local participation in the last decades, all around the world; the other driving force being also, especially in African societies, the globally-driven, neoliberal attempt to weaken or sideline the central state that is considered corrupt and inefficient. In African cities, this plea for both a greater decentralisation and an enhanced participation of civil society in urban governance is reinforced by the understanding that central states do not control many of the urban dynamics currently shaping African cities (Swilling, 1997) – and local democracy is seen as the way to build democracy and achieve efficient urban governance.

However, when reflecting on what makes the local scale potentially more democratic (an increased level of accountability of office holders thanks to personal, direct and ordinary contacts with the voters), one cannot but be affected by the possible clientelist nature of such links, which rely on personal, binding relationships between elected representatives and their voters. Whereas many South American scholars have seen in the development of local democracy (understood here in its two dimensions of decentralisation and participation) a way out of what they conceive as 'traditional clientelism', or patronage (Abers, 1998; see Gay, 1998 for a synthesis), this paper argues the contrary. Clientelism has been defined in many ways (Médard, 1973; Briquet and Sawicki, 1998; Kitschelt and Wilkinson, 2007) and has taken many names according to contexts, scales and focus (patronage, prebendalism, patrimonialism, neo-patrimonialism . . .) but we shall define it here very broadly as the exchange of public goods for political support. Clientelism is almost universally described as an evil, responsible to a large extent for the failure of democracy in Africa.

What is then the line between 'good'/ 'democratic', and 'bad'/ 'clientelistic' relationships, between a citizen and his/her elected representative? Is there something radically different in the nature of this relationship that could give us analytical tools to understand in what circumstances 'local democracy' leads to clientelism, and in which cases it does not? Or, as argued by a number of Latin American scholars (Gay, 1999, Auyero, 1996, 1999), and also theorists from the North (Kitschelt and Wilkinson, 2007), is there essentially a continuity between local democracy and clientelism? After all, both rely on forms of exchanges of votes for public deliverables and providing a form of accountability. The objective here is not only to provide a subtler understanding of clientelism, as a *de facto* form of accountability in certain conditions (some argue, like Gay about Brazilian cities (1998), that it is the *main* existing form of political accountability to the poor) – but with major effects in terms of fragmentation and dormancy of critical or radical social movements. The objective is also and maybe merely to discuss the founding principles of decentralisation and local participation, which can lead, if uncritically praised, to undemocratic practices and ultimately to the disempowerment of the poor. While several studies already attempt to assess the impact of decentralisation on corruption, poverty alleviation or development (Bhardan and Mookherjee, 2006), few reflect on the theoretical and practical proximity of these three notions, and unravel at the local level the complex mechanisms of party politics in urban governance daily practices (Williams, 2004). This is the approach adopted here.

The chapter is structured in two parts (after a preliminary discussion on the definition of clientelism adopted): the first will provide four stories of (mild) local clientelism in Johannesburg, in its relationship to decentralised and participatory urban governance; the second will draw three broader ideas on the theoretical and practical relationships between decentralisation-participation and clientelism, and their consequences for democracy and the voices of the poor in urban governance.[1] The conclusion will question the specificity of African urban governance in this regard.

Preamble – an operational definition of clientelism

We follow Kitschelt and Wilkinson (2007), when defining political clientelism as 'a direct exchange between a politician and a voter, of public goods (given as 'favours') for political support (vote and other)'. This definition is certainly specific:

– It is not necessarily an individual relationship between two agents, even if it relies on personalised linkages (a 'direct' relationship). It can develop between a politician and a group (local or social) – we will then speak of *collective* clientelism.   ·
– Political clientelism is about the distribution of *public goods* (public housing, employment contracts, access to social services or skills training programmes, distribution of food parcels, information on public tenders, etc.): excluded here are other forms of exchanges and social links between agents with unequal power.
– Political clientelism is not only about enfranchisement, and occurs largely outside the vote, even if its occurrence increases at election times. Political support indeed takes many forms (as outlined by Auyero, 1999): participating in party rallies, campaigning for the party, being the party watchdog in public or local meetings, etc.

Four stories of intertwined clientelist/decentralised/ participatory practices in contemporary Johannesburg

Four stories might illustrate the variety of forms taken by clientelism and the ambiguity of their definition in relationship to the practices of local democracy. They all take place in one low-income, inner city neighbourhood of Johannesburg, divided into two electoral wards, both marked by an important electoral competition – a rather exceptional element in post-apartheid Johannesburg context that has led, in both wards, to the local victory of opposition parties in the 2006 municipal elections: one is led by the Inkatha Freedom Party (IFP) and the other by the Democratic Alliance (DA).

Story 1 – accessing few temporary contracts

The first story is the most clear-cut example of clientelism. Major public works are under way in the vicinity of this area, in the context of the 2010 Football World Cup. The private companies that won the tender have their own construction workers, but they are required to provide some job opportunities for local communities: overall it is extremely limited (two dozen temporary contracts on road construction) – maybe partly because local communities, very fragmented and disorganised, have not been able to put pressure on government or private companies (as can be the case in some townships for instance). The DA ward councillor, through whom these temporary jobs ought to be distributed, has been accused by some community leaders of favouring members of the DA in particular through the Community Liaison Officer she has appointed to make the selection (a DA activist), who supposedly is asking candidates that he does not know personally to show their DA card.

This is a rather classic example of favouritism along party political lines in the distribution of very scarce public resources. But this also raises the question of how to proceed to select the beneficiaries of such resources: for so limited a number of casual contracts (involving un-skilled labour, which abound in the area), what could be a 'fair' process? It also shows how the notion of local economic development and 'public works that benefit local communities' (not to talk about the benefits of the Football World Cup for the poor), embedded in the principles of 'good governance', is limited in its local impacts.

Story 2 – buying social peace with public skills training programmes

The second story is less simple. The City of Johannesburg offers NGOs the opportunity of skills training workshops for their members (carpentry, sewing, baking, etc.). The IFP local councillor has apparently selected one specific NGO (working in the hostels, a traditional stronghold for the IFP) to choose the beneficiaries of these workshops. A municipal employee working 'on the ground', shocked by this practice (similar to the one presented above), has reported this fact to the municipality as well as to the local and provincial ANC structures. However, her statement was ignored – most probably because this minimal form of clientelism is seen as a way to buy social peace in a tense context; there had been political violence between IFP hostel-dwellers and other residents of the neighbourhood in the 1990s.

Here apparently is a case of clientelism that is well known but is tolerated by local government and by the party in power, as a way of managing social and political conflict at the local level.

Story 3 – distributing state-sponsored food parcels through a civic organisation, in order to side-line opposition parties councillors

The third story involves the distribution of public food parcels to the poorest households of the neighbourhood. In the name of closer 'proximity' to the ground and a better knowledge of needy households (who are very numerous in the area), the city asked SANCO (a major civic organisation in the area, which is officially allied to the ANC even if it has some form of local autonomy) to choose the beneficiaries and organise the distribution. It is very likely that SANCO has distributed the parcels to its own members, no less needy than non-members – these types of advantages can explain the civic organisation's sustained popularity in the neighbourhood in spite of many rumours about its dishonest practices. One of these, mentioned by several residents and local leaders, is the collection of fees from members in exchange for a promise of access to public housing.[2]

Here, two forms of clientelism coexist: the municipal administration which sidelines the local (opposition party) councillor to favour an ANC-aligned civic organisation, so that the public food parcels are distributed with an ANC stamp.[3] The SANCO clientelism can use its link with the municipality to access resources and build its membership and local power basis – with an even less democratic accent to it, since SANCO is not an elected body and therefore is less accountable to local residents than a local councillor. Second, it is interesting to see how SANCO leaders can use this newly built local political power to make money for their own profit – if SANCO can indeed provide food parcels for its members, why could it not provide housing? In both cases, this shows the opacity of channels and criteria of allocation of public goods; and the dominant logic of 'favour' over 'rights' in a context of scarcity of public resources.

Story 4 – resistance to eviction by the city and a political bargain with the ANC

The fourth story is the most complex, and its analysis in terms of clientelism can be challenged, but is nevertheless enlightening. A group of residents in the area, about 100 people living in a quite distinct cluster of council houses just next to the stadium (called 'the seventeen houses'), has a distinct collective identity as the result of a shared history of resistance; some residents have been long-standing ANC/SANCO/anti-apartheid activists and have therefore kept quite dense political networks within the party and the state. In the preparation for the 2010 Football World Cup, the municipality intended to destroy this cluster of houses in order to build a shopping centre that would encourage international visitors to spend some money during the one-month event. The residents committee started by contacting an NGO, the Centre for Applied Legal Studies (CALS), well-known for its successful lawsuits against the city of Johannesburg (in particular compelling the city to provide suitable alternative accommodation in case of the displacement of residents). As CALS started sending letters to the city requiring information regarding the fate of its 'clients', the residents' committee suddenly withdrew and attacked CALS; accusing the NGO of being 'racist', 'anti-ANC', betraying the nation as trying to undermine the foundation of the post-apartheid democratic state, trying to promote a culture of rent strikes and orderlessness, etc. What happened is that the residents' committee negotiated with the city of Johannesburg (through their linkages to high ranking ANC city officials) – the trade-off being that the city would abandon the eviction (but for four of the 17 houses), and the residents would drop the lawsuit (and break their relationship with CALS).

Clientelism is not what comes to mind immediately when deciphering the power games that took place. It can be seen as the result of participation from organised residents, oscillating between cooperation and conflict with the municipality, and eventually successful in winning their local fight through a local compromise, negotiated behind closed doors within the ANC to which they all belong at different levels. However, one could argue that there is here an exchange (abandonment of eviction against a form of support to the ANC/the municipality, in the violence of the residents' attack against CALS – which was yesterday's ally-as an 'enemy of the party/of the nation'); and that this exchange is taking the register of favours rather than rights, in its lack of publicisation – and the discrediting of rights-based actions and of CALS, which was hoping to use this case to raise awareness of other cases of eviction in the area.

On the theoretical and practical proximity between clientelism, participation-decentralisation principles, and its consequences on the voice of the poor in urban governance

These stories could be multiplied *ad infinitum*, and not only in politically contested wards. These detailed narratives are useful to question, through residents and local leaders' practices, very rigid conceptual divides that appear less clear-cut in reality and in return help questioning concepts framing our understanding of urban governance and local democracy. Two points can be made at this stage:

There is a practical, but also theoretical proximity between decentralisation-participation and local clientelism

It seems important to stress this as the highly positive connotation usually associated with the first two notions is directly opposed to the generally negative understanding of the second. Both decentralisation and participation have attracted massive intellectual and political support, both from progressive academics and activists, and from neo-liberal global institutions (World Bank, 2000) – although the exact nature of each form of governance is obviously not understood in the same way by each set of actors (the former stressing its democratic and transformative potential; the latter insisting on governance improved efficiency as state institutions roll back).

Critical approaches to decentralisation and participation have remained limited. As far as internal contradictions of participation are concerned, they have focused mainly on the (necessarily) limited representation of participatory democracy as opposed to representative democracy (Abers, 1998) – which is almost a tautology. Others have denounced the capture of local democracy by local elites (or at least 'the empowered'), new or old (Bardhan and Mookerjhee, 2004; Veron *et al.*, 2006), at the expense of more marginal groups which remain voiceless in decentralised structures and participatory platforms (Cooke and Kothari, 2001; Harriss, 2002). Some have also argued that the restriction of public debates around local and immediate issues was an efficient way of depoliticising democratic debates, sedating social movements and avoiding more radical questioning of existing power structures and forces acting at broader levels (Cooke and Kothari, 2001; Mohan and Stokke, 2000).

There is much less literature on the nature of local participation and decentralisation in relationship to democracy, and the potential un-democratic processes it can give rise to (Staniland, 2008, Veron *et al.*, 2006), so entrenched is the idea that 'communities' (especially low-income ones) cannot be wrong or exclusionary, and so the idea of 'conservative participation' (as we could call it) has been theorised. Stressing the proximity of participation and decentralisation to clientelism allows for a less one-sided approach, for a deeper analysis of the relationship between participation-decentralisation and democracy, and for the introduction of party politics in the understanding of urban governance (Cornwall and Coelho, 2007, Williams, 2004).

Kitschelt and Wilkinson's recent work on clientelism is useful in this regard, as they convincingly argue that, in the analysis of the relationship between politicians and voters (in particular in its dimension of account-ability), there is a difference in gradient, more than in nature, between what they call 'programmatic policies' and 'clientelist policies'. They define 'pro-grammatic policies' as policies benefiting a certain social group, in principle, *a posteriori*, and therefore indirectly and rather abstractly (one understands that a political programme lifting taxes on business will rather benefit the economic elite; a programme promoting universal medical aid will primarily benefit the poorest, etc.). 'Clientelist policies' also benefit certain social groups, but in a more direct way, through less abstract and more personal engagement between the politicians and the beneficiaries/voters and possibly *a priori* (if a politician provides electricity to a neighbourhood, (s)he'll expect the neighbourhood to organise massive voting support for him/her). Between what are considered two poles of a *continuum*, there is a variety of policies that define a narrower group of beneficiaries in a relationship that is inter-mediate: not entirely abstract and indirect; not entirely personalised and direct (a policy that would give advantages to a specific ethnic group over the others; to a certain age category; to a specific region or space). What is interesting in Kitschelt and Wilkinson's model is the *continuum* they stress between programmatic and clientelist policies, on the basis that they both rely on a relationship between politicians and voters based on an 'exchange of votes for benefits', those benefits being defined more as abstract 'rights' in the first case, more as personal or localised 'favours' in the second; being given on the basis of an abstract and legally defined rule in the first case; on the basis of a direct, locally defined arrangement in the second.

This *continuum* is even more convincing in African countries, where the scarcity of public resources, made even scarcer in the context of structural adjustment programmes often leads governments to pragmatically trans-form a programmatic policy (for instance, employment of local residents in local development projects) into a clientelist policy (Khan, 2005). This is clearly illustrated by Story 1 – can one start a tender process, fair competition between all job seekers, for 20-odd three month construction contracts? If not, who should get the contracts? The question is also, of course, why there is no collective mobilisation to claim more local benefits from an important public investment such as the 2010 public project.

Going further, decentralisation and participation (whose positive aspects we will return to later) share with clientelist logics two main features:

–   They entail an increased personalisation of the relationships between the state and citizens – far from a Weberian ideal – and in particular between local representatives and their voters: elected local representatives are supposed to be 'closer' to their constituency as constituencies are narrower and more 'local', during election times (decentralisation – meaning they supposedly take into account local needs and requirements in their campaign and political programme) but also between election times (participation – elected representatives supposedly being 'accessible' to solve everyday problems and concerns of their voters, on a flexible and *ad hoc* basis).

–   They also imply a form of local negotiability and adaptability of public policies – following the principle of governance itself,[4] stating that policies should be the result of negotiation, either between different levels of government (decentralisation), where the local level is supposedly the better informed about local needs and contexts; or between the state and 'local' civil society (participation) – in a broad understanding of local civil society including for instance local business groups (or business groups having a stake in the area). This spatial (but also temporal) flexibility, according to local contexts and circumstances, departs from a 'universal', abstract, city, region or nation-wide set of laws and rules – opening the way for local arrangements, or 'negotiated local compromises'.[5]

Personalisation of relationships between politicians and voters on the one hand, flexibility of the general law or policy to be adapted and negotiated at the local level on the other, are at the core of clientelist practices – possibly fostering both a form of greater accountability (in the sense of responsiveness), and a form of opacity of public policies and choices that would tend to lower accountability (in the sense of transparency and questionability).

Coming back to Story 3 in this perspective, one could argue that the implication of a civic organisation (SANCO) in the choice of beneficiaries of state-provided food parcels is following some of the principles of decentralisation (finding a way to gather information that is the most locally accurate in order to be able to focus public policies better and distribute scarce public resource to the neediest) and participation (the civic organisation having more than a role of implementer and information bearer, but actually having a say and control over resource allocation). Some would argue clientelism is a mere perversion of this practice – a double perversion, due to the lack of representation of the civic (not encompassing all needy residents) on the one hand; the dishonesty of its leadership on the other. They would argue that this could have worked if the civic organisation had been 'the good one', disentangled from any partisan affiliation and any monetary temptation. However, this interpretation is rather naïve. The devolution of powers of allocation of public resources to an agent that is not democratically account-able is *in itself* conducive to undemocratic practices (maybe questioning the democratic character, at least in practice, of Arnstein's last rung of the par-ticipatory ladder: 'citizens' control'), whatever the local legitimacy of this agent. Personalisation and opacity of the access to public goods are the rule, and is leading to abuse.

Ambiguities of decentralisation-participation-clientelism regarding the questions of accountability and of the possibility of local democratic debates

The impact of decentralised and participatory governance modes on demo-cratic accountability are far from being obvious, although both pretend to enhance accountability and local democracy by rendering local representa-tives and the state more accessible and more responsive to local needs. The theoretical and practical fine line between those two notions and the one of clientelism has questioned their 'dark side', stressing the potential opacity and arbitrariness of public policies leading to weaken state accountability to citizens. It also underlines the possible 'lighter' side of clientelism, which is also, in spite of all its negative perceptions relying on real democratic shortcomings, conducive to forms of accountability.

Here, the distinction between individual and collective clientelism (as expressed for instance in Gay, 1999) is crucial. Story 1 illustrates clearly a case of individual clientelism (with the distribution, by the local councillor, of the few temporary jobs to selected individuals – members of the same political party but also probably with some kind of local leadership position). Story 4 is a case of collective clientelism, where individuals form a group (defining what can be called a 'community') to fight a public policy, and later to sup-port the party that has granted them 'a favour' after a local bargain. Here, it is the possibility for the group to remain in the area and to avoid demolition of their houses that is at stake (even if the goods 'distributed' are individual dwellings). Stories 2 and 3 are intermediary cases, where collective entities act as mediators for the distribution of public goods to individuals. The point here is that collective clientelism provides for a form of public accountability, as is obvious in Story 4 where the state or the party is finally obliged to take into consideration local residents' claims, rather than simply ignore them. For Gay (1998), collective clientelism is even *the dominant form* of state account-ability to the poor, as he argues that the rhetoric of rights, theoretically to benefit, protect and develop the poor, seldom reaches them due to the scarcity of public resources and inefficiencies of the state, in the context of Brazilian cities. Clientelism therefore becomes the (unique?) means through which the voice of the poor gets a chance to be heard and translated into any form of benefits and access to public goods – collective clientelism leading to the public delivery of collective or at least club goods (the electrification of an area, tarring of roads, provision of a community centre, etc.).

Having stated this, clientelism also enlightens the way in which other forms of accountability are undermined by personalised and flexible public practices of allocation of public goods to local beneficiaries; and, in the same ways, how decentralisation and participation also can lead to such a diminished accountability. In a way, this criticism of decentralisation and participation has been developed already, through the notion of the 'local trap' (Purcell, 2006), of 'the dangers of localism' (Mohan and Stokke, 2000), and the key book by Cooke and Kothari (2001) stressing how the confinement of debates on local and immediate issues legitimise the power structures' *status quo*, since some issues are not questionable at that scale. The link with clientelism, we argue, allows to go further in this criticism, focusing on the micro-politics at play in clientelist (but also in decentralised and participatory) practices, and on the actual, everyday workings of the state (Fuller and Benei, 2001, Corbridge *et al.*, 2005).

Coming back to Story 4, there are several sides to be exposed. As mentioned earlier, this can be seen as a victory for residents of the 17 houses – they obtained what they wanted (not being evicted), through an eventually negotiated process with the city (through ANC networks mainly), thanks to the power gained and CALS' intervention. Local residents have been able to mobilise for their best immediate advantage the political resources they had (NGOs as well as ANC linkages), alternatively using threat, conflict, as well as cooperation and compromise. The result is a success, both practical (no eviction) and political (links with the ANC maintained and maybe reinforced), even though the links with CALS have been sacrificed. It can be seen as a successful form of participation, although through 'invented' rather than through 'invited spaces' (which were non-existent in the neighbourhood around the issue of the 2010 World Cup competition).

However, this success can also be seen as a setback for the broader local community affected by urban renewal and eviction threats – at least they are for CALS which hoped to see and support the emergence of a broader residents' movement fighting evictions in the whole area (an anti-eviction front of sorts). Their moral disqualification (to please the ANC) by residents who are quite powerful local leaders, does not make their future action easy, at least not on a collective scale. The city, on the other hand, has managed to limit the political impact of this victory (in a context where more evictions are taking place, publicly and privately led, in a slow but steady move towards urban regeneration – at the expense of often less organised and less politically-resourced groups of residents). Their final acceptance of residents' claims to stay in their area has not been the result of a public debate and the affirmation of a right of residents to have a say on their neighbourhood; rather, it has been negotiated behind closed doors and given as a favour, due to exceptional circumstances and for the benefit of a specific set of former political activists.

More generally, local negotiations and immediate advantages, be they collective ones (like in Story 4) or, more frequently, individual ones (public goods distributed individually generally benefit influential local leaders, so as to 'buy' their silence or tolerance), lead to the fragmentation of more radical contestations and the silencing of more critical social movements. The importance of party politics, and party allegiance, in civil society organisations, is both empowering (giving access to political networks and resources) and disempowering (allowing the party to socially control individual leaders) (Bénit-Gbaffou, 2008).

How can decentralisation, participation and clientelism be said to simultaneously increase and decrease state accountability to urban citizens? This requires a better understanding of the notion of accountability (an often taken for granted, under-theorised notion), by differentiating between two of its dimensions, somehow different from those proposed by Schedler (1999).[6] A first operational dimension of local state accountability consists in its reactivity and responsiveness to specific contexts (to local needs, to a sudden crisis, to personal requests); the second (more in line with Schedler's) is about local policies and practices' transparency/questionability by any citizens (in particular non-beneficiaries of a specific policy). This would explain why decentralisation, participation and actually, clientelism, can be simultaneously said to enhance a form of accountability (responsiveness or reactivity), at least for those residents who are politically resourced and connected (possibly local leaders also); and to undermine another (transparency or questionability). Although the dichotomy is quite simplistic, the first would put pressure on governance efficiency (in line with the World Bank's attempts to enhance the efficiency of urban governance through structural reforms – decentralisation and participation being some of them); the second one would be more of a democratic and political concern.

Conclusion – are African cities specific in terms of urban governance and clientelist practices?

Existing literature on local democracy in African cities stresses the importance of personal networks as major means of survival (Swilling, 1997; Tostensen *et al.*, 2001; Simone, 2004); the fluidity and ephemeral character of urban governance and power patterns (Simone, 2004; Lindell, 2008); the multiplicity of levels of leadership and group affiliations of various nature and with different, often competing, types of legitimacies (traditional chief, religious leader, traditional healer, local party representative, etc.) (Rakodi, 2002; Simone, 2004; Akinyele, 2006). While one may contest the idea of fluidity and instability of power patterns in African urban governance (which problematically discards the notion of reproduction of unequal power struc-tures, and can be contradicted by the overall stability of political notables or patrons, even if their power platform and alliances might change according to political and economic opportunity), it is interesting to match the other quite specific characters of African urban governance with our reflection on decentralisation, participation and clientelism.

Decentralisation is adding another layer of political legitimacy and of leadership (with the figure of the local councillor) to those already existing; participation is providing another space or arena for interaction, negotiation and access to urban goods – in particular around urban projects, more or less empowering and more or less influenced by international institutions' demands. In this sense decentralisation and participation can empower local residents by broadening[7] the range of existing (few) opportunities to voice their needs and access public goods – not necessarily on a radically different model, as these political opportunities still rely on direct and personalised linkages between client and patron. In another sense however, decentralisa-tion and participation can easily increase the fragmentation of broader social movements as well as promote the sedation of more radical claims for political or structural changes of resource allocation, particularly as their independence from party politics is further compromised (Benit-Gbaffou, 2008; Staniland, 2008).

Indeed, a second hypothesis is that decentralisation and participation dynamics may reinforce the importance of political parties' role in civil soci-ety, as they both attempt to strengthen the power of civil society organisa-tions in urban governance, which therefore become more important a stake for political parties' competition. Existing literature on African cities had already stressed the lack of independence of civil society organisations towards political parties and their embeddedness in clientelistic relationships with the state at all levels, which is said to compromise their ability to challenge the state and work towards the consolidation of democracy or the empowerment of the poor (Tostensen *et al.*, 2001; Rakodi, 2002; Watson, 2002). If this statement seems to match general perceptions of civil society in African cities, it is however seldom comforted by evidence nor is any substantial analysis advanced to explain this African perceived specificity.

As many authors have requested (Low, 2007; Cornwall and Coelo, 2007; Williams, 2004), it is necessary to develop a deeper understanding of the dynamics of party politics at the local level, to shift from normative accounts towards stronger analyses of the workings of urban governance and local democracy. This can contribute to their 're-politicisation', in the literal as well as in the broader sense – challenging a general neglect of party politics that has also been constructed by the (overrated?) hopes in the ability of civil societies, social movements and participatory democracy to challenge urban structural inequalities (Sinwell, 2008), in opposition rather than in alliance with 'older' forms of social transformative action like the one led by trade unions and political parties (Harriss, 2002). Even if the link between civil society and political parties is far from being unambiguous, researchers start to stress the importance of party politics and policies in the successes or failures of a progressive local democracy (Wampler, 2004; Véron *et al.*, 2006). Bringing together literature and research on local democracy and on clientelism is hopefully a step in this direction.

Notes

1 This research is part of an ongoing programme called 'The voice of the poor in urban governance: civil society, the state and party politics in South African cities' (2008–11), funded by the French Ministry of Foreign Affairs.
2 The leader, named Florence, is said to have gone as far as to take all contributors by bus to a place called 'Florence Park', where the houses were supposed to be built, convincing them that she had power to deliver.
3 It also happens that the leader was also the (unsuccessful) local candidate for the ANC in the ward in 2006.
4 Governance meaning a mode of government where power is shared between the state, business and civil society multiple stakeholders (without stating, unlike World Bank enhanced 'good governance', which balance of power should occur between all stakeholders – in particular, not necessarily advocating for a diminished role for the state).
5 See Bénit-Gbaffou and Morange (2008), for a study of local security arrangements in South African cities (or 'flexible governance'), and how they can undermine both broader security policies and the notion of law itself.
6 Who usefully distinguishes between 'answerability' of the power-holders (itself divided into the obligation to provide information and to provide justification for their action) and their 'sanctionability'. However, the notion of 'answerability' does not explicitly encompass the idea of fulfilment of a mandate, or response to constituencies' requests – which is central to the debate on decentralisation and participation (supposed to promote a better responsiveness to citizens' needs); and, more broadly, to the debate on substantive democracy (Harriss *et al.*, 2004).
7 Seldom replacing, as was hoped by several scholars in Latin America – see Abers 1998. See Khan (2005) on a similar argument at the national level.

References

Abers, R. (1998), 'From clientelism to cooperation: local government, participatory policy, and civic organizing in Porto Alegre, Brazil', *Politics and Society*, 26 (4): 511–38.
Akinyele, R. (2006), 'Urban experience in Lagos – white caps chiefs, land grabbers and victims', presentation to the conference 'Inclusive African Cities', DBSA-HSCR-Wits, Johannesburg, 13–15 March.
Arnstein, S. (1969), 'A Ladder of Citizen's participation', *Journal of the American Institute for Planners*, 35: 216–24.
Auyero, J. (1996), 'Performing Evita: Brokerage and problem-solving among urban poor in Argentina', working paper, New York: Center for Studies of Social Change, 26 pp.
—— (1999), ' "From the client's point of view": how poor people perceive and evaluate political clientelism', *Theory and Society*, 28: 297–334.

Bardhan, P. and Mookherjee, D. (2006), 'Decentralization, Corruption and Government Accountability: An Overview', in Rose-Ackerman, S. (eds), *International Handbook of the Economics of Corruption*, Edward Elgar Publishing: 161–88.

Barnett, C. and Low, M. (eds) (2004), *Spaces of Democracy – Geographical Perspectives on Citizenship, Participation and Representation*, London: Sage.

Bénit-Gbaffou, C. (2008), 'Are practices of local participation sidelining the institutional participatory channels? Reflections from Johannesburg', *Transformation: Critical Perspectives on Southern Africa*, 66–7: 1–33.

Bénit-Gbaffou, C. and Morange, M. (2008), 'Sécurité et gouvernance flexible à Johannesburg et au Cap : légiférer pour gouverner?', *Espaces et Sociétés*, 134(3): 19–35.

Briquet, J.L. and Sawicki, F. (eds) (1998), *Le clientélisme politique dans les sociétés contemporaines*, Paris: PUF.

Cook, B. and Kothari, U. (eds) (2001), *Participation: The New Tyranny?*, London: Zed Books.

Corbridge, S., Williams, G., Srivastava, M. and Veron, R. (eds) (2005), *Seeing the State: Governance and Governmentality in India*, Cambridge: Cambridge University Press.

Cornwall, A. and Coelho, V.S. (eds) (2007), *Spaces for Change? The Politics of Citizen Participation in New Democratic Arenas*, London and New York: Zed Books.

Dahl, R. (1956) *A Preface to Democratic Theory*. Chicago: University of Chicago Press.

Gay, R. (1998), 'Rethinking clientelism: demands, discourses and practices in contemporary Brazil', *European Review of Latin American and Caribbean Studies*, 65: 7–24.

—— (1999), 'The broker and the thief: a parable. Reflections on popular politics in Brazil', *Luso-Brazilian Review*, 36(1): 49–70.

Fuller, C.J. and Brunei, V. (eds) (2001), *The Everyday State and Society in Modern India*, London: Hurst and Co.

Harriss, J. (2002), 'Political participation, representation and the urban poor. Findings from research in Delhi', *Economic and Political Weekly*, March 12: 1041–54.

Harriss, J., Stokke, K. and Törnquist, O. (eds) (2004), *Politicising Democracy: the new local politics of democratisation*, New York: Palgrave Macmillan.

Hickey, S. and Mohan, G. (eds) (2004), *Participation: from Tyranny to Transformation: Exploring New Approaches to Participation in Development*, London and New York: Zed Books.

Khan, M. (2005), 'Markets, states and democracy: patron-client networks and the case for democracy in developing countries', *Democratization*, 12(5): 704–24.

Kitschelt, S. and Wilkinson, S. (eds) (2007), *Patrons, Clients and Policies: Patterns of Democratic Accountability and Political Competition*, Cambridge: Cambridge University Press.

Lindell, I. (2008), 'The multiple sites of urban governance: insights from an African city', *Urban Studies*, 45(9), pp. 1879–1901.

Low, M. (2007), 'Political parties and the city: some thoughts on the low profile of partisan organisations in urban political theory', *Environment and Planning A*, 39(11): 2652–67.

Médard, J.F. (1973), 'Corruption in the neo-patrimonial states of Sub-Saharan Africa', in Eisenstadt, S.N. (ed), *Traditional Patrimonialism and Modern Neo-Patrimonialism*, London: Sage.

Mohan, G. and Stokke, K. (2000), 'Participatory development and empowerment: the danger of localism', *Third World Quarterly*, 21(2): 247–68.

Rakodi, C. (2002), 'Order and disorder in African cities: governance, politics and urban land development processes', in Enwezor, O. *et al.*, (eds), *Under siege: Four African cities – Freetown, Johannesburg, Kinshasa, Lagos*, Document 11, Platform 4, Ostiledern-Ruit, Germany: Hatje Cranz, pp. 45–80.

Schedler, A. (1999), 'Conceptualising accountability', in Schedler, A., Diamond, L. and Platner, M. (eds), *The Self-Restraining State: Power and Accountability in New Democracies*, Boulder and London: Lynne Rienner: 13–28.

Simone, A. (2004), *For the City Yet to Come. Changing African Life in Four Cities*, Durham: Duke University Press.

Sinwell, L. (2008), 'Participation as popular agency: the limitation and possibilities for transforming development in the Alexandra Renewal Project', unpublished PhD thesis (Development Studies), University of the Witwatersrand.

Staniland, L. (2008), ' "They know me, I won't get any job": public participation, patronage, and the sedation of civil society in a Capetonian township', *Transformation: Critical perspectives on Southern Africa*, 65–6: 34–60.

Swilling, M. (ed) (1997), *Governing Africa's Cities*, Johannesburg: Witwatersrand University Press.

Tostensen, A., Tvedten, I. and Vaa, M. (eds) (2001), *Associational life in African Cities. Popular Responses to the Urban Crisis*, Stockholm: Elanders Gotab.

Véron, R., Williams, G., Cordbridge, S. and Srivastava, M. (2006), 'Decentralised corruption or corrupt decentralisation? Community monitoring of poverty-alleviation schemes in Eastern India', *World Development*, 34(11): 1922–41.

Wampler, B. (2004), 'Expanding accountability through participatory institutions: mayors, citizens and budgeting in three Brazilian municipalities', *Latin American Politics and Society*, 46(2): 73–99.

Watson, V. (2002), 'The usefulness of planning normative theories in the context of Sub-Saharan Africa', *Planning Theory*, 1(1): 27–52.

Williams, G. (2004), 'Evaluating participatory development: tyranny, power and (re)politicisation', *Third World Quarterly*, 25(3): 557–79.

World Bank (2000), *Reforming Public Institutions and Strengthening Governance: A World Bank Strategy*, Washington DC: the World Bank.

16 Many conflicts, one peace

Congo's economy and global security [1]

Zoë Marriage

The Democratic Republic of Congo[2] has a long history of violence, much of it sustained from outside the country for the economic benefit of various actors. Since the turn of the twenty-first century, northern donors have used interventionist policies to address this violence, and some of it has been brought to a close. This chapter traces how global security concerns have shaped the Congolese economy in the past. It then places the demobilisation and democratisation of 2002–6 in their economic and security context and explores the outcomes for the Congolese economy alongside what kind of peace has been agreed and what violence it accommodates.

Many conflicts

Three major conflicts can be identified in Congo. One is the external violent competition for control of Congo's political and economic resources, which has been pursued at a regional level as well as by countries on other continents. The second conflict is that between subnational groups, and it is centred on land, identity or resource issues. It is manifested in wars, secession movements, dispossession and forced eviction. The third is a conflict between the leadership and the population; it is conducted through attacks and extortion, often by security personnel, and structural violence, involving denial of citizenship, access to basic services, markets and information. These three conflicts take place within changing contexts of global and domestic security, where security 'assumes a field of relationships, including a threatener, the threatened, the protector or means of protection, and the protected' (Fierke, 2007, 46).

The conflicts are intertwined and have historical precedents. The extraction of Congo's resources was the defining characteristic of Belgian rule, and involved mass displacement, forced labour and the deaths of millions of Congolese people charged, amongst other things, with harvesting rubber for the European market (Hochschild, 1999). During the colonial era, the Belgians imposed abusive employment conditions on thousands of Congolese workers (Dibwe dia Mwembu, 2001), steering the economy to maximise the exploitation of resources, particularly copper. At Independence, the international predation became national predation with the establishment of neo-colonial rule and with it a domestic conflict between the leadership and the population. Independence was marked by five years of fighting, secession and interference by Belgium and the USA that ingrained faultlines between the east and the west of the country and between the province of Katanga and the capital.

Joseph Mobutu took power as President in 1965 and his international role was to provide the West with an ally and stability in central Africa. This gave him licence to manipulate the country's resources in answer to his patrons, and thereby effectively granted licence to prey on the population. Global security was defined during the Cold War by the dynamics of East–West relations, and in Africa this placed the onus on national security and maintaining borders.[3] Mobutu was threatened in 1977 and 1978 by incursions by Shaba (Katanga) separatists from Angola but reasserted territorial integrity through the intervention of the CIA and Belgium.

Zaïre's resources were valuable but political alliance was more crucial and Mobutu presided over several phases of economic disorder. First there was a period of ten years of state building (Hesselbein, 2007; Putzel, *et al.*, 2008), which promoted education and established a professional cadre (Ekwa, 2004) but was accompanied by moderate economic decline (Dunning, 2005, 467). This was followed by two phases of economic ruin as Mobutu dismantled the economy through political favour and self-aggrandisement: the 1970s were characterised by radical nationalisation and the 1980s by privatisation. Mobutu used each as mechanisms for rewarding his cronies and punishing his opponents (Nzongola-Ntalaja, 2002) and in favouring some regions he hardened subnational divides and stoked enmity between himself and the population. These conflicts intensified as funds dried up and a diminishing group could be feted on the returns from predation on the rest. Mobutu's antics of personal enrichment were condemned by the West but his allegiance remained a Cold War necessity. There was little in the way of censure, and nine rounds of debt forgiveness sustained Mobutu's position (Wrong, 2001, 194) and with it his abuse of the population (Boyce and Ndikumana, 2001).

In the early 1990s, changes in the global security environment, as defined by the West's Cold War victory, led to the re-configuration of Zaïre's economy. With the easing of Cold War tensions, Western donors withdrew their funding from client states resulting in Mobutu's sudden and dramatic loss of power. The economic situation in Zaïre became more acute and the conflict between the leadership and the population grew increasingly violent as Mobutu guarded the political and economic differential between himself and the people by use of an elaborate apparatus of security forces. The diminished need for buffer zones also saw a dwindling respect for sovereignty in Africa and therefore of the state as the guarantor of security.

The first impact of these changes was seen in the pillage that started in 1991 and caused an estimated $1billion worth of damage for 72 hours (U.S. News and World Report, 1992). All major towns were ransacked with the exception of Bukavu in South Kivu, and further pillaging broke out in 1993. The pillages were carried out by the army, which was embroiled in rounds of unsuccessful pay negotiations and needed little encouragement. Mobutu authorised the troops to 'fend for themselves'[4] and in the lawlessness of the army's activities the population joined in the pillaging (Hoover, 2005). The looting of shops and factories and the attacks on personal property hastened the departure of the relatively few expatriates who remained in Zaïre (Palermo, 1997: 1876, 1883, etc.). The pillages led to food shortages, unemployment and loss of capital particularly in urban areas as the result of the violent reallocation and destruction of economic resources.

The reformulation of global security at the end of the Cold War had a second impact: the tightening economic situation following the withdrawal of bilateral aid and the damage from the pillages fuelled populist support for a divisive political discourse, known as *géopolitique*. This was a rhetorical style directed by Mobutu, and it manifested itself in different ways across the country, exposing and exacerbating regional conflict. The political function of the discourse of *géopolitique* was to institutionalise conflicts between sections of the population, thereby limiting threats to the weakening central power. In foreclosing coalitions, though, *géopolitique* also inspired informal socio-economic semi-autonomy in fragments of the population. In Ituri district, the Kivus and other eastern provinces, tensions were raised between groups on the basis of land claims, nationality, identity and control of economic resources (Malengana, 2001; ODI, Huggins *et al.*, 2005). In the south-eastern copper-belt, a discourse of 'Katanga for the Katangans' was led by the provincial governor in the early 1990s. It resulted in the persecution, death or relocation of thousands living in Katanga whose families originated in the neighbouring province of Kasai, and the further economic decline as much of the educated cadre was uprooted.

The pillages and the physical reordering of populations had internal causes within Zaïre, but took place at the moment when African states were dropped from their strategic positions in maintaining the East-West balance of global security. The violence of the early 1990s also combined the conflicts between subnational groups with those between the leadership and the population. The looting generalised the use of violence in economic activity as the security forces – themselves divided across the country and between the elite core and the rank and file – fed themselves at the expense of the civilians, and parts of the population took advantage of the situation. Previously violence had been used to control or crush the opposition and as such, it was functional to sustaining the leadership. Through the 1990s, though, it became more widespread giving way to the fact that Mobutu was no longer able to dictate and ultimately destroying its perpetrators. The bankruptcy and decline of Mobutu's rule, and the rout of his army by Laurent Kabila's forces, backed by foreign troops, resulted from the ubiquitous violence of pillage, harassment and fighting that tipped the economy and state machinery towards defeat.

Hence, the changes in the global security environment had a third impact on the Congolese economy, and Congolese security, in heightening its vulnerability to regional violent predation by Rwanda and Uganda (Clark, 2002; Jackson, 2002). The multiplicity of pre-existing conflicts shaped the two Congo wars of 1996–7 and 1998–2002 in at least four ways. First, the notion of a national interest had been scrambled as the priorities of the leadership, the administration (including the army) and sections of the population were at odds with each other. Second, the fragmentation that had been pursued by Mobutu to protect himself from political opposition facilitated the formation, during the wars, of disparate self-defence and militia groups. Groups that had been abandoned by the state fended for themselves with violence and were not responsive to governmental chains of command. Third, the differing levels of protection and control across the country led to divergent war trajectories and in some cases to violent secondary conflicts. Fourth, the impoverishment of the population, the disruption of agriculture and industry and the non-payment of salaries had all taken their toll by the time the wars broke out, increasing people's vulnerability to violence and diminishing their ability to cope or survive.

One peace

The emergence of the USA as the unrivalled superpower at the end of the Cold War established neoliberalism as the dominant political paradigm. In promoting liberalisation for economic growth, this became central to interventionist development policies and to the reformulation of global security that was required to protect the market model. The move away from state-centric development analysis inspired a debate, led by the World Bank's researchers, on individuals' economic incentives for civil war (Collier, 2000) and the possibility of addressing conflicts by reworking economic incentives for violent players (Collier *et al.*, 2003).

In a related policy development, a belief in economic growth as an engine for development and effective states (and therefore peace) was reawakened in the early twenty-first century, epitomised by DFID's Business Action for Africa[5] and its Congo Plan, which included reform and regulation of the mining sector as part of its Strategic Objective 1 (DFID, 2008). The notion that underdevelopment was dangerous had been gaining credibility through the 1990s (Duffield, 2001); following the attacks on Washington and New York in 2001 the definition of global security had shifted to incorporate a threat from wars in poor countries[6] and peace agreements were signed in a number of African countries. In Congo, the second war was formally ended following talks in South Africa in 2002.

Congo's transition – which ran from 2002–6 – was sponsored by Northern donors with regional players taking key roles in the negotiations,[7] and demobilisation and democratisation featured prominently in the intervention. The following discussion is not an evaluation of the demobilisation and democratisation in Congo; its purpose is to put the programmes in their security and economic context. Both programmes rest on an economic logic of reorienting incentives for violent behaviour by offering nominally higher returns for less violent alternatives by demobilising or participating in peacetime politics. In examining them it is possible to observe what forms of violence have been neutralised and which have been accommodated and transferred to the emergent political economy.

Demobilisation

The demobilisation carried out during the period of transition involved four major programmes: the national programme, the demobilisation of foreign troops, the demobilisation of minors and a dedicated programme in Ituri, the area of most military activity at the time. All four programmes faced problems arising from short time-lines, the lack of organisational or operational capacity, and the lack of opportunities for demobilised fighters to integrate into society (Nest *et al.*, 2006, 114; Marriage, 2007). Demobilisation was not completed within the four year transition period, and as of August 2008, 102,148 combatants had been demobilised and a further 60–70,000 cases were pending.[8] Some of the ex-combatants who had been through demobilisation remobilised and new militia groups emerged. According to Amnesty International, 50 per cent of the children demobilised in the Kivus were re-recruited between January and May 2008.[9] The same year, Congo entered another phase of demobilisation, headed by the National Programme Execution Unit (UEPN), a new implementing body of the national programme, with a budget of $210.74million.[10]

The logic behind the demobilisation process was that combatants could choose to demobilise and, using the money they received on demobilisation, they could start up some other economic activity. This logic did not take into account the processes identified above that had shaped the Congolese economy and security situation, and it proved weak in the face of extreme vulnerability, forced conscription, fragmented and politicised groups and the associated number of chains of command. Some groups were linked to government forces or became irrelevant and demobilised (IRIN, 2008). Others had support from elsewhere. The remnants of the previous Rwandan regime went through a series of shifts in identity (ICG, 2003; ICG, 2005b; ICG, 2005c) and maintained a force of around 6,000 fighters, known as the FDLR. The Maimai militias mobilised to protect local interests rather than to conform to government policy, and more groups were formed after the peace was signed, destabilising northern Katanga in particular. Other militia forces established themselves round conflicts that were tangentially related to national politics: the conflicts in Ituri and Kivu, whilst concurrent with the main wars, took on dynamics of their own.

The demobilisation relied on mixing these diverse military elements through a process known as *brassage* to form a unified national army. At this stage, the economic and essentially managerial orientation of the programme again overlooked the history of the militarisation, the motivation of the combatants and the lines of power that sustained armed groups. Faultlines between subnational groups, varying experiences of security and differential treatment by the state laid the basis for further mobilisation after the transition was apparently completed. This weakness in the programme had some spectacular fallout, including Laurent Nkunda, who joined the army of the transitional government, but went on to dominate the politics of the Kivus with his National Congress for the Defence of the People (CNDP) anti-governmental forces until his arrest in January 2009.

Given the array of conflicts, including that between the leadership and the population, and the continued violent competition for resources, one of the most significant economic features of the demobilisation is that for individual fighters (as for the majority of the population) life in the east of Congo remains precarious. Despite the economic rationale behind the programme that proposed that ex-combatants could establish themselves in other trades, thousands of ex-combatants returned to an economy that was severely limited and dysfunctional. The demobilisation was not accompanied by the installation of a resolute system of law or bureaucracy, meaning that the economic situation was unfavourable or unviable to newly demobilised ex-combatants.

This is not a politically neutral situation and the economic calamity is not confined to the east: a study by MSF-Belgium found exceptionally high mortality in the western province of Equateur (MSF-Belgium, 2005). The failure of the government to pay adequate salaries on time to public employees, including the army, can be read as a sign of state weakness but it can also be seen as a sign of relative strength in that the population is unable to respond to the negligence. Protests and strikes are routine in Congo and are routinely ignored, which preserves the power differential between the population and the leadership, or agreements are made and subsequently reneged on[11] in a manner of non-negotiation established during the era of Mobutu (Palermo, 1997: 1887). The lack of money entering the economy at the level of salaries or public investment means that there is little currency in circulation and few opportunities for trading or establishing small businesses.

In the absence of industrial or organised agricultural production, the economy depends on non-formal taxation and mineral extraction, areas that have proved violently contentious in the past. The demobilisation policy did not account for the fact that the economy was dominated in regressive ways by those with access to state power and those who had recourse to other forms of violence. Taxation, including the discretionary taxation by security forces, is not procedurally linked to the provision of services and strangles civilian attempts to enter or operate within the economy. The comparative ease of taxing small-traders means that they pay disproportionately high taxes and face obstacles to establishing themselves financially.[12] Thousands of fighters have been demobilised in accordance with the programme that was based on reorienting economic incentives of individual combatants. The fact that these ex-combatants have returned to civilian conditions in which their economic survival is practically impossible carries the implication that these people are not perceived to pose a further security threat.

The outcome of the demobilisation is that many militias have been neutralised allowing for swathes of calm across much of Congo. Nonetheless, there has been an accommodation of the violence of two theatres of war in the east of the country and structural violence that continues to impose economic catastrophe with high loss of life (IRC, 2008).

Democratisation

Alongside the faltering demobilisation, the process of democratisation moved forward from the installation of a transitional government and attendant institutions in 2003, and kept marginally within schedule. The transitional government comprised a president and four vice presidents, thus allocating political positions to former belligerents. A new constitution was passed by referendum in 2006, presidential and legislative elections were held, and the National Assembly and the Senate was established. The elections were supported to the tune of half a billion dollars (Weiss, 2007, 140), and Monuc, which was charged with the security of the elections, was the United Nations' most expensive single-country mission with yearly costs in the region of $1,136,875,200.[13]

Whilst the democratisation has recorded certain successes, particularly in organising and holding elections, claiming these successes has involved overlooking weaknesses, which has incurred costs in terms of the confidence of many Congolese people. The distrust, which entered the democratisation process early on (Weiss, 2007, 141 and 146) is connected to the regional interest bases and the conflict between the leadership and the population. During the transition, the formula of one vice president and four vice presidents precipitated an absorbing and divisive competition between the contenders that manifested itself in a multiplication of taxes as each vice-president gathered funds.[14] There were also links to the international conflict, in that the elections, funded and observed from outside the country, provided an influential role for donor countries in the process of establishing political institutions.

The democratisation was accompanied throughout by violence (Mantuba-Ngoma, Hanf *et al.*, 2006, 5–8) and non-violent players were crowded out of the political scene. No census was taken before electoral registration, and this angered and subsequently isolated the opposition led by veteran politician Etienne Tshisekedi, undercutting confidence in his home region of Kasai and elsewhere. The burning of ballot boxes in the east and of the Supreme Court in Kinshasa is downplayed by international organisations and observers; the Carter Center, for example, described the elections as 'generally peaceful', which obscures the significance of the violence that did take place. Episodes of fighting in Kinshasa occurred at the announcement of the first round results and in March 2007. The violence was perpetrated not by civilians but by rival troops loyal to the two candidates, Joseph Kabila and Jean Pierre Bemba, and confirmed that the presidential playing field was for violent players.

Throughout the democratisation process, there was armed conflict in the east of the country, including re-invasion by Rwanda in November 2004. The politics of the conflicts in Ituri and Kivu were practically overlooked in run-up to the elections, but the violence defined the process: the two front-runners in the presidential elections were the two men with the largest armies at the moment when the peace was signed. Azarias Ruberwa, the vice-president representing the Rally for Congolese Democracy (RCD, formerly the Rwandan-backed insurgent group), was widely despised because of his links with Rwanda and the atrocities committed by the RCD, but still came sixth in the Presidential elections. Of the two non-military vice-presidents one came twenty-third out of 33 presidential candidates (with 0.34 per cent of the vote) and the other did not stand. The manner in which violent players consistently won rounds at the expense of non-violent players allowed previously established forms of power to be reproduced in a democratic setting.

The unpopularity of the way in which democratisation was carried out was demonstrated through the elections. The voting patterns, particularly of the first round, register discontent: in the west, Kabila received little support as he was associated with Rwandan interests and groups.[15] In the east, where the power of the state was weakest, he won enormous majorities. The bloc voting revealed that most people voted for the leader they had not experienced: Kabila had ruled for five years in the west, but was beaten by Bemba there. Bemba was derided in the east by the populations who had suffered under him (and the RCD), yet won support in the west, including in the capital, where he had never held power. Weiss, commenting on the situation, suggests that the question is not 'Who did the Congolese citizenry vote *for?*' but 'Who did the Congolese citizenry vote *against?*' (Weiss, 2007, 142)[16] arguing that there was a near-unified protest vote against the leadership. The population voted strongly against the configuration that had emerged from the internationally orchestrated wars and peace process.

The results of the presidential elections had the trappings not of the conclusion of a political debate but of a military victory, suggesting that the dynamics of the violent conflict remained in place. Bemba, defeated, left the country on medical grounds. He was later arrested and brought before the International Criminal Court charged with war crimes in the Central African Republic, and so was effectively removed from the political scene. Kabila has political and economic support provided through aid by northern donors and there is essentially no organised domestic political opposition.

Congo's economy and global security

The demobilisation and democratisation involved millions of dollars of funding, provided chiefly by northern donors, and apparent shared success. Despite serious setbacks and delays within the programmes and high levels of violence in the country, the interventions continued to be operationalised and the broader peace process was not thrown off-track. By the end of the transition period of 2002 to 2006, the first round of demobilisation was complete in that the government committee charged with its implementation, had spent the money and was disbanded, and the democratisation had led to presidential elections being held across the country.

The success, though, was thin, and critical contortions can be detected in the demobilisation and democratisation programmes. The economic problematisation did not realistically frame the options available for combatants or the political climate for leaders and their relationship with the population as the multiplicity of conflicts meant that decisions were not free or fully informed and were not purely economic. Continuing insecurity and political alliances were key in determining demobilisation (Boshoff, 2004) and in shaping the behaviour of the leadership (including the vice-presidents) through the transition (ICG, 2005a). Consequently, demobilised combatants were returned to a situation of economic collapse, and the democratisation did not install accountability: the analysis notwithstanding, little was done during the transition to address the economic aspects of the war (HRW, 2005).

Why was so much money channelled towards a country that had slipped to the edge of the security map to fund programmes that were unfeasible?[17] The mix of apparent success alongside major shortfalls at policy and implementation is less puzzling when viewed beside the modest economic recovery that Congo was experiencing, as depicted in Figure 16.1.

The graph shows that growth in GDP per capita is linked not to the transition but to patterns established by the invasion of the Rwandan and Ugandan

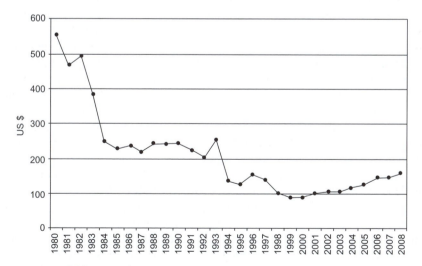

Figure 16.1 GDP per capita DRC, 1980–2008 (Hesselbein 2007, 66).

Source: International Monetary Fund, World Economic Outlook Database, April 2007

armies in 1998. The economic recovery, to the extent that it can be captured by the measurement used, started in 2000, during the second war. This was a time when resources were being plundered from the east of the country (UN, 2001, and subsequent years) and concessions were being agreed with large foreign companies (Lutundula Commission, 2005). There were material returns for companies based in the northern countries that were sponsoring the transition but more significantly the upturn marks a concerted effort to re-orientate the Congolese economy, which had been in decline and largely neglected, to the international market and its logic.

This re-orientation began with mining licences granted during the war that were formalised through the transition, and Joseph Kabila's willingness to approve concessions has been a defining feature of his presidency. He was assisted by the World Bank, which drafted the 2003 Mining Code. The Lutundula Commission, formed as part of the peace accords in 2003 in line with contemporary governance policy, submitted a report, the purpose of which was to examine concessions signed between 1996 and 2003. It found numerous illegalities and little benefit for the Congolese state (Lutundula Commission, 2005). It was followed in 2006 by the UN Group of Experts' report that also raised doubts about a number of the 2,144 concessions listed on the DRC Mining Cadastre (UN, 2006). The World Bank also questioned the transparency of mining contracts and likelihood that they could be of benefit to the development of Congo (le Carre and Stearns, 2006). In April 2007, prompted by the Lutundula Commission's report, the Minister for Mines, Martin Kabwelulu, filed a memorandum indicating that no concessions would be annulled, and a review was published shortly after.[18]

The rounds of laissez-faire surveillance alongside economic growth are connected: according to DFID – 'DRC is ranked bottom in the World Bank's Doing Business survey of 175 countries' and is the 'fifth most corrupt country in the world according to Transparency International' (DFID, 2008, 30). The country is doing well, according to conventional economic indicators, and at the same time, the economy is known not to conform to conventional economic behaviour. The corruption identified by DFID and Transparency International has returns for the companies that are not held to account, and for Congolese individuals who wave through irregularities, but the costs are passed down to the population in predictable ways. Rather than the resources being channelled towards the development outlined by DFID in its economic growth model, the capital is foreign-owned, the state does not manage a profitable deal, and in the persistent economic disaster domestic politics continues to depend on favour, vertical hierarchies and predation on the population.

This chapter has argued that changing formulations of global security placed different demands on the Congolese economy. The economic upturn in 2000 provides further evidence, whilst also explaining why donors were willing to engage in a costly demobilisation and democratisation programmes that were flawed in implementation. These programmes were loss-leaders, allowing northern donors to reassert their influence after their departure in the early 1990s, an about-turn provoked by the appearance of a new and significant challenge: China. Laurent Kabila, who ousted Mobutu and swept to power in 1997, shunned northern interference; but he signed an 'agreement on mutual protection and encouragement of investment' with China and made a state visit in December of the same year.[19] Joseph Kabila, whose son who succeeded him in January 2001, was training at the Military Academy in Beijing when he was called to office and he asserted that he wanted to make Congo 'the China of Africa' (La Revue, 2006). The recent concerted northern interest in Congo has a global security context shaped by the threats posed by the booming Chinese economy.

Mearsheimer (2002) defines first order threats as those that threaten existence of a great power, for example the USA. With China's investment in Africa towards the end of the 1990s, Congo's resources became not simply a matter for violent economic competition, but also a contested area for global security. The rush of companies in recent years has taken Congo from a security backwater; the process was driven by the emergence of a power large enough to challenge the USA economically, and thereby to challenge the entire neoliberal agenda.

The urgency of responding to the challenge posed by China and the lack of due regulation explains the upward curve on Congo's economic trajectory, but if anything it was arguably underestimated during the transition. Parts of Gécamines and Miba, the national mining giants were sold off, and other licences were granted, but the continuing fighting, particularly in mineral-rich areas, and the lack of transparency identified by DFID made investment risky and laborious for individual companies, despite the strategic importance of committing. In September 2007, the year after the end of the transition, China declared its intention to invest $5billion on infrastructure in Congo in return for minerals. The announcement was reported by the *Financial Times* as causing 'alarm,' in donor circles, and it came as the IMF and World Bank were inching towards resumption of budgetary support to Congo.[20] In April 2008, the figure was upped to $9billion.

The global security concerns have catalysed some macroeconomic improvement but the majority of the population have no contact with the exploitation of resources or indeed the formal sector more broadly. As foreign firms vie for concessions, once again the leadership answers to investors and donors, rather than to its constituency. Given that the conflict between the leadership and the population has survived the transitional processes of demobilisation and democratisation, the returns from ostensible compliance with licensing, aid demands, resource management, security sector reform and other interventions, are likely to aggravate the situation as they strengthen the state's arm relative to the population.

The interventions, including the demobilisation and democratisation, can appear counterproductive: underdevelopment and war in poor countries was the trigger for the rash of peace agreements at the turn of the century, and yet in Congo the interventions have not resulted in development. The situation vindicates Mearsheimer's analysis of a first order threat: for as long as the pre-eminence of the USA is threatened, other threats do not register. A peace has been agreed in Congo that enables the first order threat – that posed by China – to be confronted. Other responses have been important in establishing the political economy, but weaknesses can be overlooked as their operational outcomes are not significant to global security.

Conclusions

This chapter has explored how changes in the global security environment impact on the Congolese economy by shaping its mechanisms and organisation. Since the end of the Cold War, global security has been defined by the interests of the USA and as such is intertwined with economic pre-eminence and neoliberalism. The transition in Congo included demobilisation and democratisation programmes, both of which adhered to the prevailing economic paradigm in their genesis but were patchily implemented. They did, though, license foreign parties to play roles that were influential in shaping the post-war political economy. The strategic importance of this is evident in the light of the need for a sturdy economic presence in Congo given the increasing strength of China.

In the past the impacts of global security on Congo's economy had implications for how security was experienced in Congo in framing abuse by Mobutu's security forces, the pillages of the early 1990s, subnational fighting and ultimately the wars. More recently, too, there are links between global security, the Congolese economy and the experience of security in Congo.

Three conflicts were identified at the outset of this chapter: the external violent competition for control of Congo's political and economic resources, the conflict between subnational groups, and the conflict between the leadership and the population. The peace agreed has reduced the violence involved in the external competition from its apex at the turn of the century, but has preserved the political economy that was established through violence. As the validity of the licences rests with the leadership which is in conflict with the population, foreign companies are implicated in forms of violence too and the agreed peace has delivered gains to the external economic competitors by resuscitating Congo's dependence on mineral exports.

With regard to the conflict between subnational groups, the transition has been neutral. The act of voting against the known power in the first rounds of the presidential elections suggests a heavy faultline between the east and the west of the country, but more significantly it indicates that few people feel represented by their leader and mediation of interests is unlikely. Meanwhile the wars continue in the east of the country and persistent insecurity presents opportunities for new conflicts. The Kivus and Ituri have absorbed the majority of emergency funding, but their politics have been sidelined by the political processes.

The third conflict – that between the leadership and the population – has been aggravated through the interventions made. Despite weaknesses in implementation, the demobilisation and democratisation had economic functions. In terms of the incentives for violent players, the poor were disarmed by the demobilisation: conditions for ex-combatants remain dire but they pose little threat outside Congo. Simultaneously the leadership has been bought out by the terms of the democratisation and has been strengthened vis-à-vis the population. This reinforces existing patterns of patrimonial power and causes difficulties for political and economic accountability.

The GDP growth is a positive sign within an economic analysis that conflates growth with development and peace. Examination of the processes involved reveals that the growth in Congo has been disconnected from domestic politics and development and has been achieved through violence. The implication is not simply that a more critical approach should be taken to the resurgent model of business for development, but that a more critical approach needs to be applied to notions of global security that impose further insecurities on already vulnerable populations.

Notes

1 The research for this chapter was funded by the British Academy.
2 The Democratic Republic of Congo was the Congo at Independence, and Zaïre between 1971 and 1997.
3 Dominant security needs also determined how the domestic economy was exploited. During the Second World War, Congo contributed the uranium for the nuclear bombs that were dropped on Hiroshima and Nagasaki.
4 Mobutu's exhortation 'débrouillez-vous' indicated that the state was not going to pay salaries and it was up to its employees to find their way. It is often translated into English as 'fend for yourself' but it includes an element of 'help yourself' too.
5 http://www.dfid.gov.uk/news/files/speeches/g8-business-action-africa.asp (accessed 08/01/09).
6 For example, Clare Short, the UK Secretary of State for international development at the time, claimed 'Africa is Europe's near abroad. If it is in trouble, that trouble and conflict will spread across the world. For example, bin Laden was in Sudan before he went to Afghanistan' (Hansard 06/02/02:300WH).
7 The International Committee in Support of the Transition (CIAT) comprised Angola, Belgium, Canada, China, France, Gabon, Mozambique, Nigeria, Russian Federation, South Africa, United Kingdom of Great Britain and Northern Ireland, United States, Zambia, the African Union/ African Commission and the European Union/ European Commission.
8 http://www.mdrp.org/drc.htm (accessed 29/09/08).
9 http://www.radiookapi.net/index.php?i = 53&a = 20462 (accessed 29/09/08).
10 http://www.mdrp.org/PDFs/DRC_Newsletter_0608.pdf (accessed 29/09/08).
11 Famously, the Mbudi Accord was signed on 20 February 2004, following pay negotiations between the Trade Unions and the transitional government, but it was not honoured.
12 Interviews June–September 2008 with state officials and traders in Kimbanseke, Kinshasa.
13 Budget from 01/07/05 to 30/06/06, http://www.monuc.org/News.aspx?newsID = 11533&menuOpened = About+MONUC (accessed 05/01/09).

14 Interviews June–September 2008 with traders and company staff in Kinshasa and Mbujimayi.
15 The subject of Joseph Kabila's background and interest became a major part of the election discourse with allegations commonly made – and particularly by Bemba – that he was of Rwandan and/or Tutsi origin (Mantuba-Ngoma *et al.*, 2006, 48).
16 The exceptions are Equateur, which was Bemba's stronghold and subsequently supported him in the election, and southern Katanga, which was never taken by the RCD but voted with the east of the country (Weiss, 2007, 151).
17 Some commodities, notably coltan, were of significance to security, but exploitation was not hindered – and in many ways was assisted – by the war.
18 http://www.moneyweb.co.za/mw/view/mw/en/page66?oid = 169240&sn = Detail (accessed 10/01/09).
19 http://www.china.org.cn/english/features/focac/183553.htm (accessed 10/01/09).
20 http://www.ft.com/cms/s/0/d66142e4–66d9–11dc-a218–0000779fd2ac.html (accessed 13/01/09).

References

Boshoff, H. (2004). 'Overview of Security Sector Reform processes in the DRC.' *African Security Review* 13(4).
Boyce, J. K. and L. Ndikumana (2001). 'Is Africa a net creditor? New estimates of capital flight from severely indebted Sub-Saharan African countries, 1970–96,' *Journal of Development Studies*, 38(2), 27–56.
Clark, J. F. (2002). *The African Stakes of the Congo War*. New York, Palgrave Macmillan.
Collier, P. (2000). Doing Well out of War: an Economic Perspective. *Greed and Grievance: Economic Agendas in Civil Wars*. D. M. Malone and M. R. Berdal. Boulder, Col., Lynne Rienner Publishers: 91–111.
Collier, P., and V. L. Elliott, *et al.*, (2003). *Breaking the Conflict Trap*. Washington, World Bank and Oxford University Press.
DFID (2008). Democratic Republic of Congo. Country Plan. London, Department for International Development: http://www.dfid.gov.uk/pubs/files/DRC-countryplan08–10.pdf.
Dibwe dia Mwembu, D. (2001). *Histoire des conditions de vie des travailleurs de l'Union Minière du Haut Katanga/ Gécamines (1910–1999)*. Lubumbashi, Presses Universaires de Lubumbashi.
Duffield, M. (2001). *Global Governance and the New Wars. The Merging of Development and Security*. London and New York, Zed Books.
Dunning, T. (2005). 'Resource Dependence, Economic Performance and Political Stability.' *Journal of Conflict Resolution* 49(4): 451–82.
Ekwa, M. (2004). *L'école trahie*. Kinshasa DRC, Editions Cadicec. Imprimerie Mediaspaul.
Fierke, K. M. (2007). *Critical Approaches to International Security*. Cambridge and Malden, Polity.
Hesselbein, G. (2007). The Rise and Decline of the Congolese State. An Analytical Narrative on State-Making. *Working Paper No. 21*. London, Crisis States Research Centre.
Hochschild, A. (1999). *King Leopold's Ghost: A Story of Greed, Terror, and Heroism in Colonial Africa*. New York, Mariner Books.

Hoover, J. P. (2005). The Lubumbashi Looting as a Microcosm of Zaïre's Looting, Senior Thesis Seminar, Professor Pohlandt-McCormick, 5 December.

HRW (2005). The Curse of Gold. http://www.hrw.org/en/reports/2005/06/01/curse-gold, Human Rights Watch.

ICG (2003). Rwandan Hutu rebels in the Congo: A New Approach to Disarmament and Reintegration. 23 May 2003. Africa Report No. 63. Nairobi/Brussels, International Crisis Group.

—— (2005a). The Congo's Transition is Failing: Crisis in the Kivus. Africa Report No. 91. 30 March 2005. Nairobi/ Brussels, International Crisis Group.

—— (2005b). A Congo Action Plan. Africa Briefing No. 34. Nairobi/Brussels 19 October 2005, International Crisis Group.

—— (2005c). Congo: Deal with the FDLR Threat Now. International Crisis Groups – New Media Release 14 September 2005. Brussels/Washington, CrisisWebNews.

IRC (2008). Mortality in the Democratic Republic of Congo. An Ongoing Crisis. New York, International Rescue Committee: http://www.theirc.org/resources/2007/2006–7_congomortalitysurvey.pdf.

IRIN (2008). DRC: Another Rebel Group Gives Up Arms: http://www.irinnews.org/Report.aspx?ReportId = 70449.

Jackson, S. (2002). 'Making a Killing: Criminality and Coping in Kivu War Economy.' *Review of African Political Economy* 29(93/94): 517–36.

La Revue (2006). 'Portrait: Le vrai Kabila.' www.jeuneafrique.com (Juillet/Août).

Le Carre, J. and J. Stearns (2006). Getting Congo's Wealth To Its People. *Boston Globe.* Boston: http://www.crisisgroup.org/home/index.cfm?id = 4587.

Lutundula Commission (2005). Assemblee Nationale Commission Spéciale Chargée de l'Examen de la Validité des Conventions a Caractere Economique et Financier. Conclues pendant les Guerres de 1996–97 et de 1998: http://www.freewebs.com/congo-kinshasa/.

Malengana, C. N-N. (2001). *Nationalité et citoyenneté au Congo-Kinshasa: le cas du Kivu.* Paris, L'Harmattan.

Mantuba-Ngoma, P. M., T. Hanf, and B. Schlee (Eds.) (2006). *La République Démocratique du Congo: Une Démocratisation au Bout du Fusil. Publications de la Fondation Konrad Adenauer.* Kinshasa.

Marriage, Z. (2007). 'Flip-flop Rebel Dollar Soldier. Demobilisation in the Democratic Republic of Congo.' *Conflict, Security and Development* 7(2).

Mearsheimer, J. J. (2002). *The Tragedy of Great Power Politics.* New York London, W. W. Norton.

MSF-Belgium (2005). Excess Mortality and Exclusion from Healthcare: Let's Not Turn Away from the Crisis in the Democratic Republic of the Congo. http://www.msf.org.hk/fs/view/downloadables/latest-news/2005/3012/DRC_05Report.doc. Brussells, Médecins Sans Frontières Belgium.

Nest, M., F. Grignon, and E.F. Kisangani (2006). *The Democratic Republic of Congo. Economic Dimensions of War and Peace.* Colorado, Lynne Rienner.

Nzongola-Ntalaja, G. (2002). *The Congo from Leopold to Kabila. A People's History.* London and New York, Zed Books.

ODI, C. Huggins, H. Mushara, P.M. Kamungi, J.S. Oketch, K. Vlassenroot (2005). 'Conflict in the Great Lakes Region – How is it linked with land and migration.' *Natural Resource Perspectives* (Number 96, March 2005).

Palermo, S. (1997). *Pour l'amour de mon peuple. Cent ans d'évangélisation au Haut-Zaïre 1897–1997.* (In two volumes) Rome, Edizioni Dehoniane Roma.

Putzel, J., S. Lindemann, *et al.*, (2008). Drivers of Change in the Democratic Republic of Congo: The Rise and Decline of the State and Challenges for Reconstruction. A Literature Review. *Working Paper No. 26. Development as State-Making*. London, Crisis States Research Centre.

UN (2001). Report of the UN expert Panel on the Illegal exploitation of natural resources and other forms of wealth of the Democratic Republic of the Congo. S/2001/357. United Nations: http://www.reliefweb.int/rw/rwb.nsf/AllDocsByUNID/ab11819fbac78bf985256a3000655c44.

—— (2006). Final Report of the Group of Experts on the DRC. S/2007/423, United Nations.

U.S. News and World Report (1992). In Zaïre, a Big Man Still Rules the Roost. *10 August 1992*.

Weiss, H. (2007). 'Voting for Change in the DRC.' *Journal of Democracy* 18(2): 138–51.   http://muse.jhu.edu/login?uri=/journals/journal_of_democracy/v018/18.2 weiss.html.

Wrong, M. (2001). *In the footsteps of Mr Kurtz: living on the brink of disaster in Mobutu's Congo*. New York, HarperCollins Publishers.

17 Mbimbos, Zvipamuzis and 'primitive accumulation' in Zimbabwe's violent mineral economy

Crisis, chaos and the state

David Moore and Showers Mawowa

As May 2009 drew to a close an 'interim transitional government', more commonly known after the supposed South African precedent as the 'government of national unity' (GNU) in Zimbabwe had been in existence for just over 100 days. This particular form of governance had been established in mid-February to allow the Movement for Democratic Change (MDC) the opportunity to share Zimbabwe's rule for two to five years until a new constitution would be formed laying the groundwork for new elections. The MDC had struggled for nearly a decade in the face of electoral fraud, brutal force and spiralling economic meltdown to gain state power from the Zimbabwe African National Union-Patriotic Front (ZANU-PF), which had been ruling Zimbabwe since it entered the realm of majority rule in 1980. Independent observers contend that the opposition party won the March 2008 election (as it had all elections since 2000), but Robert Mugabe remained in his presidential position in a government cobbled together after months of negotiations 'facilitated' by the once president of South Africa, Thabo Mbeki.

The GNU could be characterised only very generously as one of 'dual power'. The MDC's inability to enforce many of the agreements – ranging from the release of imprisoned political activists to guarantees of a free press – preceding the pact indicated something less than equal quotients of political control, let alone its 'sharing'. Signifying the GNU's fragility, on May 29 Prime Minister Morgan Tsvangirai and Deputy Prime Minister Arthur Mutambara sent a letter to the Southern African Development Community (SADC), which had been allocated the task of breaking deadlocks between Zimbabwe's GNU parties, asking it to among other things 'intercede . . . and solve as a matter of urgency' the problem presented by the fact that the governor of the Reserve Bank Gideon Gono, arguably the Zimbabwean second most responsible for the country's socio-economic crisis, had been re-appointed by President Robert Mugabe illegally and therefore should go (Zimonline.co.za May 29, 2009). Tsvangirai, who had moved since the 1980s through union ranks to attain the position of Prime Minister and the supposedly executive position of chair of 'the council of ministers' in the GNU, and Mutambara, once a university student activist, then a 'rocket scientist' and later leader of the break-away 'MDC-M', addressed their letter to two other opponents locked in the embrace of a political party rent asunder: SADC chair Jacob Zuma, the recently elected president of South Africa and Thabo Mbeki, ousted by Zuma in the months before, but still SADC's special facilitator for Zimbabwe. Zimbabwe's delicate transition was teetering, then, on a decision to be made by Africa's emergent hegemon. Much depended on whether or not two arch-enemies could agree on a way forward for their northern neighbour (Moore, 2009a).

This indication of Zimbabwe's lack of sovereignty – ironic because its president's public discourse was heavy on 'we will never be a colony again' rhetoric – was reinforced by the fact that it had no currency. A decade of printing more and more bank notes, until in 2008 the inflation rate reached into the billions, rendered that symbol of a country's financial power absolutely worthless. Thus it was eliminated. From early 2009 all of Zimbabwe's monetary transactions, including debts and savings from the past, were carried out in American dollars, South African rand, the odd British pound, and pulas from Botswana in adjacent areas (Thornycroft, 2009). Finance Minister Tendai Biti, an MDC MP, the party's secretary-general, a lawyer by training and like Mutambara a graduate of radical university politics, was struggling to pay government employees 'allowances' of US$100 per month in the face of advanced capitalist governments' refusal to advance anything but humanitarian aid to the crisis plagued state-society complex (Cox, 1987) that, it was estimated, would need $8.3billion to approach a semblance of its former economic self. In efforts to convince international financial and development institutions that its intents were honourable, the Zimbabwean GNU offered the International Monetary Fund $100,000 every quarter towards its $131million in arrears (Zimonline May 25, 2009).

Yet it was doubtful if such amounts of aid would be forthcoming without Gono's removal. Gono was widely reputed to have driven Zimbabwe to ruin with his profligate printing of dollars, which served (until they were worthless) to accelerate the creation of a crony class of bureaucrats and 'entrepreneurs' dependent on access to the Reserve Bank and thus the ability to become very rich with quick trips to the parallel market's money traders. Given Gono's proximity to the president's power (reputedly from the president's wife's village and close to her, he was rumoured to have started Mugabe's dependence on 'forex' when he headed one of the many banks mushrooming in the 1990s, the days of the 'economic structural adjustment programme' or ESAP), his disappearance would have indicated a return to the prudent values that ironically appeared in his puritanically-toned annual reports, as well as a significant diminution of presidential power. However, Gono's money-printing and forex skills had gained him many friends, including in the military, and even a (slight) chance of gaining the presidency when its 85-year old incumbent retired or died. Zimbabwe's economic and political future, then, lay not only in the hands of a president and his predecessor to its south. It depended on whether or not what was often called a 'casino economy' could be put on the straight and narrow through the removal of one man who epitomised its precarious gambling condition.

This chapter will illustrate in some detail one particular aspect of Zimbabwe's socio-economic crisis and how the politics of such economies become violent. It will examine two instances of Zimbabwe's 'informalised' mineral economy – the violent nature of which is symbolised by reports of hundreds of informal diamond miners being murdered by the army (Sithole, 2009). It will perform a genealogy of informal gold and diamond mining in two quite different parts of Zimbabwe during its political and economic crisis, and how networks of state and party power were entwined in this 'informality' as Zimbabwe's state and society approached chaos and indeed the brink of war. This 'micro' analysis is embedded in a larger context, of course, on which it is necessary to elaborate and to attempt to offer a theoretical explanation. First, then, there is the large question of how Zimbabwe reached its 2009 condition.

The narrative of Zimbabwe's economic decline is relatively well-known. Structural adjustment policies in the 1990s accelerated the development of a financial and service based capitalist class whilst unemployment, inequalities and poverty increased (Gibbon, 1995; Kanyenze, 2004). A group of liberation war veterans emerged in 1997 amidst scandal and anger to force Robert Mugabe – almost literally by gunpoint, given that they had kidnapped some of ZANU-PF's politburo members – to agree to huge pensions and guarantees of accelerated land reform. When the land reclamation scheme and the payment schedule for the pensions were gazetted in parliament the Zimbabwean dollar lost 75 per cent of its value, beginning its downward slide. A donor conference was held in 1998 but the promises made there were abandoned (save a US$50 million World Bank promise for some pilot projects) almost simultaneously with the Zimbabwean state's decision to help defend Laurent Kabila's DRC against Rwandan and Ugandan backed rebels, with 13,000 troops at a cost of US$1million per day. Sporadic land invasions began; a few *relatively* autonomous from the state (Sadomba, 2008). By 2000, in the face of a failed constitutional referendum and electoral challenges from the MDC, the ruling party took control of the 'war veterans' and the approximately 1,500 large scale commercial farms were invaded. World Bank and IMF loans were not repaid; inward flows were stopped.

After a decade of steady decline amidst political malfeasance and extensive human rights abuses to fend off the MDC challenge, aid agencies estimated in early 2009 that 5 million people were starving, migration organisations guessed that more than 3 million Zimbabweans were in exile (with their remittances supporting more than half of those remaining); employment statistics indicated less than 10 per cent in formal work, and a cholera epidemic raged due to poor water and sewerage infrastructure. The GNU of the MDC and ZANU-PF was formed due to intense pressure from SADC's facilitators in negotiations carried out in Pretoria. The MDC had won a parliamentary election in March 2008 but withdrew from a presidential runoff in June due to excessive ruling party violence. By September it agreed to enter the GNU, amidst widespread scepticism of its ability to control the generals in charge of the Joint Operations Command, who were benefiting excessively from the 'chaos' described in this chapter – but no longer by their access to official exchange rates (Raftopoulos and Phimister, 2004; Davies, 2004; Moore, 2007a; UNDP, 2008; Bond, 2009). The question hovering over Zimbabwe in mid-2009 was whether the fissures in the ruling party would explode into a full-blown civil war instead of the simmering accumulation-based conflict indicated in this chapter, or if the 'government of national unity' would allow a new dispensation and structure of accumulation to emerge.

To approach theoretical understanding of the Zimbabwean crisis, one could do worse than rely on the words of the well-known Zimbabwean political economist Ibbo Mandaza as he wrote in a May 2009 synopsis of the GNU's first 100 days. For him, the teetering nature of the compromise was rooted in

> the very nature of the post-colonial state itself . . . a hostage and dependent formation, insecure because of the lack of an anchor class . . . independent of the state, and for whom the state is virtually the be-all-and-end-all for the leadership and the bureaucratic bourgeoisie as a whole.
>
> For most state actors, there is hardly a life after life in the state; and for those in particular for whom the state has been the source of a parasitic and patronised existence, exit is almost a non-option. Transition becomes a terrain of intense contestation and conflict, between those trying to stay in and those determined to get in.
>
> This is why . . . since Independence in 1980, but particularly in the period from the mid-1990s onwards, the Zimbabwean state has survived on the twin-pillars of violence (or the threat of it) and patronage. Violence or the threat of it is an integral part of any state in the contemporary world.
>
> But, in the Zimbabwean context, state-sponsored violence became almost the state's *raison d'être* in the face of growing political opposition at home, flagging economic fortunes, international isolation, and the inevitable siege mentality that was now the order of the day
>
> (Mandaza, 2009).

Mandaza's analysis, rooted in his 1986 idea of a 'schizophrenic state' caught between the formalities of governance and the realities of settler-state capital's power (Mandaza, 1986; Moore, 2004b), does not try to explain what difference, conceptually, theoretically, or empirically, a formal opposition makes. Aside from the not considering questions of opposition, Mandaza's critique stands aside other academics' more moralistic stances hinging on the idea of 'justice' of land for the tillers and ZANU-PF's attempts to rectify history's wrongdoings. Mahmood Mamdani, for example, in spite of trying to call for a more 'complex' reading of the Zimbabwean crisis instead of human rights activists' whinging, relies on the justice and land trope to explain the 'popular support' for African leaders such as Mugabe and Idi Amin. In the process he places unprecedented power in the hands of individual leaders rather than actually examining the complexities of which he speaks (Mamdani, 2008, 2009; cf. Moore, 2009b). This perspective falls in line with the prolific output of 'agrarian patriot' scholars such as Sam Moyo and Paris Yeros, combining their enthusiasm for 'fast-track' land reform with a belief that in Zimbabwe the National Democratic Revolution has progressed to Phase II (Moyo and Yeros, 2005, 2007; Yeros, 2002; cf. Davies, 2004, Moore, 2007). According to these writers, the pursuit of this ideal combined with the defence of Laurent Kabila's Democratic Republic of Congo in 1998 inspired the 'west' to impose the sanctions on Zimbabwe that have driven it to such economic despair, and for the imperialists to impose their 'puppets' on the noble Zimbabwean masses.

Mamdani's structural intricacies turn out to rest ultimately on his enthusiasm for a normative and perhaps essentialist sense of 'African justice', in the Zimbabwean case centring on land. He writes of a ruling party 'championing' land reform in memory of the 'historic struggles' underpinning it; of 'authoritarian rulers' utilising forms of 'demagoguery' to project themselves as 'champions of mass justice . . . successfully rallying those to whom justice had been denied by the colonial system' and who 'not surprisingly' dispense justice mirroring the 'racialised injustice of the colonial system' (Mamdani, 2008). He is not as supportive of the ZANU-PF regime as he thinks his critics think, but tries to understand its ruinous policies with a singular vision of 'land to the tillers'. In the end his efforts to undermine the democratic naivety of his peers in North America serve to elevate beyond his reach the demagoguery he tries to similarly ridicule. The theory only recently on offer to explain cases such as Zimbabwe, however, was not a great deal better. It is the task of political economy to re-orient the vision of idealists everywhere, be they latter day *Narodnya Volya* or starry-eyed liberal democrats. This chapter is a small contribution to that mission.

A brief survey of 'radical' political economy literature on Africa and some conservative responses to it suggests both the richness and the lacunae of the field. The earlier phases of this literature were mostly silent on the question of violence, accumulation and class struggle in spite of being ostensibly rooted in the thoughts of the man who predicted capitalism's emergence with blood dripping from every pore. Perhaps because the *dependentista* roots of much of this thinking precluded even capitalism's early stages from visiting Africa's shores, it thus neglected that mode of production's birth pains. As for those hoping for a form of 'socialism' to fill the vacuum, perchance they were entranced by Julius Nyerere's invocation of its utopian variants. Bleaker visions such as Gavin Kitching's and Bill Freund's, rooted in the recognition that industrialisation and capitalism do not emerge without violence and that even then Africa's political and economic élites may not be up to the task, suggested this was nothing less than pie in the sky (Kitching, 1982, 2000; Freund, 1981; Moore, 2006).

However, the consequences of Nyerere's idealism may have been other than those of failed modernism, brutal even in its letdown (Scott, 1998): the academic flurry at the University of Dar es Salaam during his presidency has left an enduring political economy tradition. It may be ironic that the brief for a new political economy of accumulation is underpinned by a now classical tradition in African political economy that emanates from debates inspired by Mamdani's early work on class formation in Uganda and the Tanzanian context in which it originated (Arrighi and Saul, 1973; Mamdani, 1976; Shivji, 1977; Saul, 1974, 1976, 1979; Freund, 1981). These enduring works focused on the relation of emerging classes, the states they made (and that made them), and the ideological debates stemming from these processes. They were forged in contrast and conflict with a 'people vs. imperialism' perspective that too often merged the people with the states ostensibly ruling in their interests against the former colonial powers and their corporate appendages (Tandon, 1982).

John Saul's work on the 'overdeveloped state' summarises this discussion well. Saul simultaneously decried the African state's tendency to augment the fortunes of what Shivji called the silent class struggles of the bureaucratic bourgeoisie, and also somewhat romantically hoped that it would serve the desires of a political and ideological 'x' class if an alliance with the working class and peasantry would allow the conditions for something like socialism to emerge. However, the focus on the post-colonial state in Africa tended to concentrate overwhelmingly on the state and its *wabenzis* rather than the ways in which they related to class formation in society at large. Thus this work could be seen to have paved the way for a more conservative form of political economy that blamed Africa's malaise on a corruption-prone group of rent-seekers whilst ignoring the vicissitudes of the global political economy in the late 1970s and the 1980s that threw all statist projects into disarray, leading to a 'lost development decade' that only benefited a class better integrated into global financial circuits than before (Bates, 2005; Van der Walle, 2001; cf. Gibbon, Bangura and Ofsted, 1992).

Now the possibility of breathing life into this aging amalgam of academic activism, radical political sociological and cynical American political economy – including a plethora of banal analyses of 'failed states' – has manifested itself with a vibrant, albeit somewhat self-consciously melancholic, reinvention of even older modes of political economy: those of Karl Marx's ideas of 'primitive accumulation'. Christopher Cramer's seminal *Civil War is Not a Stupid Thing* enters the literature concerning the political economy of war in Africa on the shoulders of a series of works challenging liberal verities, rent-seeker parables, and humanitarian efforts on the gruesome subject (Cramer, 2006; De Waal, 1997; Duffield, 2001, 2002; Reno, 1999). It may not be coincidental that this work has appeared almost simultaneously with United Nations efforts to develop the idea of the international 'responsibility to protect' whilst African dictators assert their sovereign right to despoil, in the pattern of their European forefathers (Tilly, 1994; Moore, 2004a). The lasting value of this 'R2P' discourse will probably not be based in what Cramer calls the fantasies for the reconstruction of war-torn Africa (Cramer, 2006; Cramer and Goodhand, 2002).

It may be, instead, on the way it forces political economists' attention to the intricate ways in which patterns of accumulation emerge, based on Cramer's twist on Gramsci's idea of the 'war of position'. Cramer's notion of the war of position analyses how relatively new African classes – with access to a disintegrating state, or in the wake of advanced stages of decay, lots of weapons – take power and gather wealth in the vortexes of African post-Cold War and post-structural adjustment state-society complexes in ways that encourage both violence-based accumulation projects. Such an approach forces one to examine both the micro-modes of the production of war and wealth, and, through the networks deriving from them, the political economy of party-states and global power. In a world conjuncture wherein commodities rise and fall with the fortunes of financial reconfiguration, in the context of the ebbing and flowing of power and economy from an ailing United States of America to a muscular China, fledgling African social formations enter the construction of capitalism with new characteristics indeed.

This study of some of Zimbabwe's local manifestations of contemporary crisis and their links to a reconfiguration of the social relations of class, party and state, could be conceived as part of this project of rebuilding a 'political economy' for Africa. The continent is poised on the petards of a process of primitive accumulation that offers neither guarantees for 'progress' to a relatively self-sustaining process of capitalist development, nor for a future of permanent destruction and despair only offering hope to kleptocrats of Mobutuesque and Mugabeite hue (Gray, 2007; *Sunday Times*, 2009). This chapter, a combination of ethnography and economic anthropology within an attempt to theorise Zimbabwe's crisis of the ruling party and the state it is carrying with it to its uncertain fate, is an effort to ascertain the contours of chaotic accumulation. It does not, however, deign to guess the trajectory of those outlines. Zimbabwe's developmental path is uncertain. It is dependant to a great degree on how its own governance structures – ruined almost beyond recognition by nearly a decade of deliberate destruction – are reconfigured immediately. In the longer term Zimbabwe's fate rests on how regional and global forces realign in the wake of a world-wide financial crisis. In this instance, continued 'neo-liberal' global policies and South African economic dominance may lead to a teleology of basic resource extraction and the further crumbling of the remnants of a 'formal' economy that was relatively well established in Rhodesia and the early days of Zimbabwe, courtesy of white settler capital and propitious global structures (Arrighi, 1966; Wield in Stoneman, 1981). Yet in the context of a global 'new deal' (Bello, 2008) there may be space for a 'developmental state' that could rebuild the alliances between domestic industrial capital and the state classes that gave Rhodesia and Zimbabwe some of the characteristics of a 'semi-peripheral' state-society complex, with admittedly negative racial contours (Stoneman and Cliffe, 1989; Bond, 1998).

The chances for Bello's global social democracy are not great, but no matter what happens outside the admittedly porous borders of a small social formation just north of Africa's economic hegemon, a reconciliatory, sound, and 'progressive' governance structure would have to emanate from the GNU shared by the former ruling party and its MDC challenger. Starting by dismantling the Joint Operations Command, (*Observer* 2009), it would have to combine will and skill to redirect Zimbabwe's political economy of chaos. The trajectory of the rest of Africa's political economy may appear to vindicate the negative and almost racist analyses of writers such as Patrick Chabal, Jean-Pierre Daloz, and Jean-François Bayart, who have tried to convince scholars that the forms of accumulation one sees in Zimbabwe's crisis are indeed how 'Africa works' (Bayart, 1993; Chabal and Daloz, 1999; and for a slight change Chabal, 2009); for them the 'criminalisation of the state' is the *status-quo* that has arisen from the instrumentalisation of disorder constituting the African élites' mode of accumulation and consumption. In late 2004, when Zimbabwe was about halfway into a downward slide to the generation of the mode of accumulation indicated by the case studies below, a Cameroonian political scientist not averse to the above perspective remarked during his visit to Harare: 'This city is not very Africanised yet.' If 'Africanisation' means falling into academic clichés that are deeper than the potholes now marking all of Zimbabwe's cities and more pernicious than the hunger, cholera and HIV/AIDs that were killing approximately 3,500 Zimbabweans during the week in which the Zimbabwean president's wife bought a residence in Hong Kong worth £4million and went north to China to investigate the possibilities of establishing a diamond processing factory (*Sunday Times*, 2009), then academics must begin to take clichés more seriously than they have previously. To do this, scholars of African political economy in general and Zimbabwe can emphasise the *universal* attributes – in their diverse particularities – of capitalism's birth.

These epistemological and political prospects are matters for academic speculation as well as hurried efforts at reform from the organic intellectuals in states, international development agencies, and civil society (Moore, 2007b) who hustle to create a decent future through the modalities of Zimbabwe's 'transitional government' while hearing the echoes of lectures long past (Keynes in Cockett, 1995: 112). There is no conjecture, however, on the really existing patterns of accumulation by chaotic means that have emerged during Zimbabwe's interregnum. It is the real political economy of Zimbabwe's new mineral mining and marketing that will now be explored in this chapter.

The paradox

With the exception of diamonds and platinum, Zimbabwe's formal mining sector declined precipitously throughout the 2000s. Seven mining companies closed operations in the month of November 2008 alone. In 2000, Zimbabwe produced almost ten times more gold as it did eight years later. At the turn of the new millennium Zimbabwe – Africa's third biggest producer of gold – sold 2,259 kilograms of gold to the international market. Eight years later, 267 kilograms were sold (*Business Times*, 2008: 1). The late 2008 suspension of the South African owned Metallon Gold's five mines, accounting for 55 per cent of Zimbabwe's total gold production, reduced that output further. The sale of other minerals took on a similar pattern. This decline was disharmonious with global trends signified by booming commodity prices for most of the period in question, prompting Saunders to characterise it as one of Zimbabwe's painful paradoxes (Saunders, 10, 2008).

Note, however, that the decline was in formal/official production. This may not have reflected an overall decline in mining activity, but a shift to 'informal' means of production. As indicated above, several mines shut down due to the operational constraints within the legal and policy regime. Metallon Gold, for example, claimed the non payment of US$18.3 million by the country's reserve bank (the monopoly buyer of gold in the country) as the main reason for its closure: for the six months in mid-2008 it had failed to supply the monthly US$23million needed for two of Metallon's mines to run. The central bank's – a key state institution – inability to channel funds through 'normal' channels indicated a major constraint on both large and small miners. In the face of its failure, informal mining and trade was a competitive and efficient option. As in Zimbabwe's cities, where *siya so* or 'leave it alone and anything goes' was the rule of trade and production, so too in the parts of the country where gold and diamonds were the stock in trade.

The rate of mineral smuggling in Zimbabwe rivalled the proportions found in Africa's conflict societies. According to Zimbabwe's central bank, in 2007:

> Gold smuggled out of the country over the last 5 years averages 15 tonnes/year worth over US$400m/year ... Diamonds worth over US$800million [were smuggled, as were] ... other minerals ... to the tune of about US$200million per year. Fertilisers, chemicals, fuel and other items have been smuggled or traded in corrupt ways ... to the tune of not less than US$250million/year.
>
> (Gono, 2007: 5–6)

Gono observed that the above instances of corruption amounted to US$1.7 billion a year. This figure surpassed the country's total mineral exports; indeed it was more than all national exports (Reserve Bank of Zimbabwe, 2008: 11–15).

The diamond mining in Eastern Zimbabwe's Marange area and informal gold mining in the central Zimbabwe town of Kwekwe gave credence to Gono's concerns.[1] The two cases mirrored and epitomised the unregulated and disorderly accumulation patterns typifying post-2000 Zimbabwe. Since September 2006 the diamond fiasco in Eastern Zimbabwe was popularised in the media. At its consummation one journalist described the Marange diamond rush as the largest in Africa in the past hundred years (Thornycroft, 2006). Yet a similar scenario prevailed in Kwekwe and surrounding areas; in fact beginning much earlier, seemingly unbeknown or overlooked by most media. Since the early 2000s the informal mining and trade of gold virtually eclipsed formal mining and agriculture as the main economic activity in this part of Zimbabwe. The extensive and disordered nature of gold panning production in this region was etched with trenches on national roads, railway lines, public and private premises. By October 2001 the *Midlands Observer* estimated the number of people involved in gold panning activities in Kwekwe and surrounding areas to be nearly 600,000 (24 October, 2001).[2]

The behaviour of Zimbabwe's ruling elite in illegal gold mining in Kwekwe and the acrimony in Marange diamond mining illustrated Cramer's 'war of position' albeit in a state-society complex not fully in battle. The reliance on non-market modalities and force as instruments of accumulation can be explained at one level by the absence of an enforced property regime and the lack of regulation: the haphazard and often discretional enforcement and application of laws pertaining to illegal mining. In this unfolding imbroglio, deaths and injuries due to violence between panners themselves, the police and the army, or through mining accidents were common (*newzimbabwe.com*, 24 November 2008; *Midlands Observer*, 14 February 2003 and 14 May 2007). Concern was raised over ruling party politicians' exploitation of gold panners, indicating another level of explanation: the restructuring of the party-state classes as 'normal' means of accumulation disappeared in the wake of Zimbabwe's crisis. As the state's monopoly on property regulation dissipated and its internal mechanisms of control over the use of force weakened, informality in production and coercion became imbricated throughout material society.

Structures, networks and power

The form, structure and organisation of Zimbabwe's illegal mining were opaque. Since 2000 smuggling went far beyond rural survival. Accumulation networks starting from the mining site to the external markets were constructed and shaped by Zimbabwe's militarist authoritarian party-state and a political economy of crisis. An official at Zimbabwe's Harare International airport attested to the increased smuggling – euphemistically referred to as 'facilitation' – at the airport.

There is a network. It starts from some very big people, people we see on

TV, to ordinary handlers and customs people. Everybody gets a piece . . . 'It is nothing complicated. Couriers, sometimes security companies, arrive with stuff, and everybody knows the routine. They know which handlers to target and which points to avoid through the chain' [of clearing goods].

(*Financial Gazette*, 8 March 2008).

The authoritarianism of Zimbabwe's party state became more salient as it increased its involvement in the illegal amassing of wealth. Unlike other degenerated states where a full-blown political economy of conflict obtained, in spite of the crisis the Zimbabwean state maintained a relatively coherent and functionally cohesive state superstructure. As of 2009 its war of accumulation and state restructuring was not yet pervasive, and its intensification could have been forestalled. Yet the state's involvement in illegal mining and trade led it to becoming a site for contestation over these resources: control of the 'superstructure' was increasingly contested by those within the party-state in order to selectively enforce laws to their advantage.

The illegal mining was characterised by 'syndicates' consisting of groups of miners working together.[3] These often developed to become a form of organised resistance unit against law enforcers and rival groups. Others co-operated with various police and army officers. Syndicates were linked to members of the party-state elite working with a regional business partner, and a local villager. In some cases, syndicates followed ZANU-PF factional lines. In 2007 more than 80 groups operated in Kwekwe and surrounding areas alone, whilst Marange hosted a mélange of them with thousands of individual panners. In Marange military and police involvement went beyond demanding bribes and raiding the panners' booty to actually digging for diamonds. Top army generals sent 'undercover troops to plunder the precious stones' (*ZimDaily*, 6 October 2008).

As of 2008 many relatively autonomous diggers were replaced by soldiers paid in Zimbabwean dollars whilst their masters traded their diamonds for foreign currency. Towards the end of the year, however, many of these soldiers sold their products directly because they were paid only infrequently, and then in useless currency: it was clear that the generals' access to foreign currency was diminishing. Rumours that a failed December 2008 assassination attempt on General Perence Shiri, a member of the Joint Operational Command (JOC), was not due to 'politics' but diamond disputes, indicated the links between 'politics' and plunder economics, even if they may not 'true'. Some observers suggested that the fact that the soldiers were evading their commander's demands – whilst simultaneously their peers were rioting in major cities because they had to wait so long in queues to cash in their almost worthless pay-slips – contributed to the JOC's acquiescence to the South African brokered 'government of national unity' in early 2009.

In the Kwekwe area, with a salary in 2007 of less than US$20 a month it is not surprising that the police and army cashed in on miners. Rather than enforcing state licensing fees, tariffs and customs duties, they managed access to mining sites. On its part, the state seemed not to be interested in curtailing this corruption. Instead, its members saw this as a means to subsidise their poor salaries: their leaders realised such informal actions may have averted military insurrection. In Kwekwe, police charged illegal gold panners an equivalent of 200 South African Rand per hour of digging for gold in a tunnel. Panners, grateful to the police for managing access, creating order, and averting violent conflict, would pay the fees and enter in groups of eight to ten at a time. Junior officers competed to be deployed at extraction sites, often soliciting senior officers responsible for deployment, to later share the booty. At one site in rural Kwekwe the police operated in two day shifts in order to accommodate each other.

Similarly the army and police regarded deployment in Marange as an unparalleled opportunity. Off duty officers found their way to the site unceremoniously. In May 2008, the standard bribe rate for a panner caught in a police/army raid was US$100. Hence the online *Zimdaily* (8 December 2006) noted that the deployed soldiers 'will never be able to thank their lucky stars enough, for many would by the end of their tour of duty here have become super rich from stealing the same diamonds they are here to safeguard'. Security men were reported to hire villagers to help extract the diamonds. One soldier was quoted in the newspaper as saying '*Varume hatingafi nenyota makumbo ari mumvura*' ('guys we can't die of thirst while standing in water').

The way in which Zimbabwe's crisis and conflict mode of accumulation was linked to the party-state can be illustrated with one gold mining site in rural Kwekwe, observed in mid-2007. Rival syndicates aligned to two factions of Zimbabwe's ruling party contested one site. One was linked to Emmerson Mnangagwa, the ZANU-PF Secretary for Administration and by 2009 defence minister in Zimbabwe's transitional government. Mnangagwa – regarded by many as heir-apparent to the country's president – was also responsible for managing the ZANU-PF companies, a position that afforded him extensive links in the 'capital world', especially with ZANU-PF's white capitalist colleagues.[4] The Mnangagwa syndicate, as it was referred by local residents, co-opted a local villager who owned the homestead within which part of the gold mining site lies. Mr Mazenge thus legitimised their presence. Mnangagwa's brother-in-law, One Comfort, was responsible for the day to day management of the syndicate. The extracted gold was reportedly smuggled to South Africa through Zimbabwe's most famous gold dealer, Mac Milan (also connected to Mnangagwa), and other foreign connections.

Across the meadow was another syndicate led by the local headman. He worked with RBZ senior officials, a Gweru businessman (also a ZANU-PF member), and Midlands' former provincial mining commissioner. The headman held a prospecting licence and a claim registration certificate obtained from the mining commissioner.[5] He claimed that Mazenge would be relocated to make way for his 'legal claim'. The contingent plots were both located within part of the contested mining site. In June 2006 the headman's homestead was fenced by Fidelity Printers, RBZ's gold buying arm, ostensibly to establish a gold buying centre. This centre was not built. The bank appears to have been manipulated in order to disqualify rivals. Furthermore the area was guarded by the ZANU-PF linked Fawcet Security Company twenty four hours a day.

Between the panners and external markets one finds the buyers. Apparently independent local buyers are often 'front men' for big chiefs. These sometimes have to compete with external buyers though the latter seldom become involved without establishing sufficient connections locally and within the Zimbabwe party state. Not surprisingly foreigners arrested for smuggling are often surreptitiously deported without any litigation (*The Herald*, 11 December 2008: 1). In 2007, when the country was experiencing currency shortages, a joint fact finding mission in Marange, including police and Mutare court officials, impounded a vehicle loaded with sealed piles of brand new Zimbabwe dollar notes amounting to trillions. The notes had consistent serial numbers suggesting they were coming straight from the Reserve Bank of Zimbabwe. Clearly this could only be the work of someone with access to the central bank.

Combined with factional strife amongst Zimbabwe's ruling elites, the need to secure the flow of illegal minerals at every stage from the mining site to the external markets has made control of both state and relevant security highly contentious. The post-2000 period has seen increased interest by those in the ZANU-PF hierarchy in establishing private security firms. So heightened has been the contest that JOC, consisting of senior government officials, police chiefs, the prison service head and military figures now presides over the awarding of contracts to provide airport security. In early March 2008 at least three security companies with links to one ZANU-PF faction were stripped of lucrative airport security contracts by the JOC, on allegations of facilitating the smuggling of minerals through Harare International Airport (*Financial Gazette*, March 8 2008). The decision followed an embarrassing seizure of 121kgs of gold earmarked for the United Arab Emirates that had passed through the Zimbabwe airport (with a Zimbabwean man, Ernest Moore, suspected of links with top Zimbabwe politicians). Other senior ZANU-PF members accused the JOC, whose members are Mugabe loyalists, of using the incident to elbow out security companies owned by individuals aligned to Vice President Joyce Mujuru's faction, widely perceived to be critical of Mugabe.

The story of the late William Nhara, once the Principal Director in a non-Portfolio ministry and ZANU-PF Harare provincial spokesperson, is emblematic of the political and economic dimensions of Cramer's 'war of position', but at a level somewhat removed from the sites of production in rural Kwekwe and Marongwe. Nhara was arrested for allegedly trying to help a Lebanese business partner smuggle 10,700 carats of diamonds past airport customs checks. Nhara's trial took a dramatic twist, indicative of the 'godfather' nature of Zimbabwe's semi-feudal political economy, when he pleaded with Mugabe for mercy. Local observers were bemused at this plea, given the provincial party's reputation as critical of Mugabe's continued reign and the suspicion of working with the retired general-in-chief Solomon Mujuru's faction to push for Mugabe's exit at the annual ZANU-PF 2006 Congress. Nhara died before the conclusion of his trial, but not before an airport officer commented on his case: 'That guy was just unlucky. He's obviously a small timer and he didn't follow the right channels.' Apart from gold and gemstones, other contraband, including cigarettes, were routed routinely through airport security.

In a pattern that shows a worrying descent towards warlordism, panner groups fight over access to mining sites. These 'wars' involve as many as 400 in the case of Kwekwe gold mining (*The Midlands Observer*, 3 October 2003, 1) and thousands of smugglers in Marange diamonds. On the last week of November 2003 the Amaveni residential area in Kwekwe was turned into a 'war zone' as local panners fought with the 'Vampire group' of gold panners from another area over mining rights granted by council (*The Midlands Observer* 7 November 2003). The Vampire group, which was said to derive its name from its mode of operation, has allegedly 'caused havoc and instilled fear in the registered syndicates'. Notably, the Vampire group, like several gangster leaders in Kwekwe, was alleged to have links with 'powerful individuals within the *police* force' and thus 'does its activities without fear of reprisals from law enforcers' (*The Midlands Observer*, 2003). This explains why the locals resort to taking the law into their own hands.

Aside from the panners' violence, the Zimbabwean state was the biggest perpetrator of violence on illegal miners, let alone the violent clashes between army and police in Chiadzwa. A blitz code-named 'Operation *Hakudzokwi*' ('no smuggler will return alive') in Chiyadzwa in December 2008 may have marked the zenith of Zimbabwe's brutal clampdown of diamond mining. Mugabe's spokesperson in the state-run newspaper, writing under the pseudonym Natheniel Manheru celebrated 'mass murders' (*New Zimbabwe*, 24, 11, 2008) by army and police as a 'shock therapy . . . to reassert [government] authority in the wild, wild West'. RBZ chief Gono never missed a public forum to condemn illegal mining activity and warn those involved to stop. The Zimbabwe police, often jointly with the military and prison services carried out anti-smuggling operations such as *Chikorokoza Chapera* (literally meaning 'illegal mining has ended') or *mari yawanda* ('too much money') in which scores of illegal miners were killed and thousands arrested, their shacks ransacked and some suffocated as tear gas was administered into the mining tunnels (Zimonline, May 14, 2007; *The Midlands Observer*, 14 February 2003, 1).

This excessive brutality masked the Zimbabwean elites' involvement in mineral smuggling. In reality the state's policy and actions with regard to illegal trade were haphazard, contradictory and at best ambivalent. The state vacillated between banning the illicit minerals trade altogether and controlling and managing it. Some of the raids target the support bases for Zimbabwe's opposition MDC. Despite these efforts gold panning thrived, indeed it was curious to note that despite these clampdowns the Zimbabwe government still bought the minerals from illegal panners. In September 2006 Deputy Minister of Mines Tinos Rusere personally visited the diamond digging sites, urging on the informal miners to carry on digging and sell their gems to the Mineral Marketing Corporation of Zimbabwe (Saunders, 2007, 12). At a meeting involving the Ministry of Mines secretary, the city of Kwekwe Mayor, small scale gold miners and buyers, the Ministry of Mines promised to overhaul the mining legislation to 'empower the historically disadvantaged small scale miners' and to regulate illegal gold mining and trade, (*The Midlands Observer*, 3 June 2003). 'We are not saying that they should cease their activities forthwith, but that they should be wary of the dangers associated . . .', (*The Midlands Observer*, 24 October 2003, 2) the police spokesperson for Kwekwe commented after a miner had drowned in a disused mining tunnel at Turtle mine in Silobela.

The RBZ position on gold panning activities, *Chikorokoza* ('illegal gold miner'), was less satisfactory for a bank known for its avowed hard line stance against illicit economic activities. The bank's practice of giving special licences to designated agents to buy gold where the activities are concentrated in the name of 'decentralisation of Gold buying' was self-contradictory and self defeating (Gono, 2004, 28). In his July 2004 statement Gono notes that '176 custom millers and 38 Agents are working together with Fidelity Printers and Refiners (the gold buying arm of RBZ)' (Gono, 2004, 20). The ostensible rationale was that this would 'reduce grey market activities' (in other words, corruption) but by registering buyers – most of whom are surrogates for senior ZANU-PF officials' licences – the bank was tolerating illegal miners and thus encouraging panning, effectively contradicting its clampdown on 'illegal' gold trading activities. Moreover, most of the buyers remain unregistered. According to one buyer based in Totororo (who works closely with a ZANU-PF councillor and deputy mayor for Chegutu) there are very few if any registered buyers. Ironically, the RBZ has no problems accepting gold from these buyers during the rare times they sell to the bank.

These contests mirrored a broader national pattern. There were several cases where members of the ruling elite clashed on farm occupations, mining interests and other business spheres. Mujuru and Mnangagwa, the main contenders to Mugabe's 'throne', were known to have a long running rivalry over both formal and informal mining interests. Gideon Gono's presidential ambitions introduced another dimension (with none of the myths of 'liberation war hero' attached) to this multifaceted accumulation/power matrix. Gono often used his unchecked powers as the reserve bank governor to weed out perceived enemies from Zimbabwe's economic landscape. Clashes between ZANU-PF party leadership and the army chiefs pointed to the growing power of the armed forces in Zimbabwe's emergent forms of accumulation. Because of the illegal and contested nature of this accumulation, reliance on coercion and use of the state to selectively apply laws was central. The resort to violence was evident at all levels of the accumulation structure.

Conclusion

In the absence of a strictly and consistently policed accumulation order, a form of disorder and violence identical to capitalism's teething years prevailed. The apparent difference between accumulation Zimbabwe-style and the original form of capitalism is that in the latter a *modus vivendi* guaranteeing property rights emerged, thus arresting the violent contests that ensued from the disorder. According to Rousseau, 'the true founder of civil society was the first man who, having enclosed a piece of land, thought of saying "This is mine", and came across people simple enough to believe him' (1994, 55; Andreasson, 2004). What happens if a man encloses a piece of land and says 'this is mine' – but does not come across people simple enough to believe the claim, and who contest it? This might explain the violent conflict accompanying capitalism's teething years. It could also provide a clue as to the gist of the violence in Zimbabwe.

A pursuit of the liberal definition of property may be enlightening in this regard. Property begins with one enclosing (from others) something (a piece of land for example) and claiming ownership thereof. As Locke put it, 'he by his labour does, as it were, enclose it from the Common' (1967, 308). Rousseau's epigram above suggests that there must be acceptance – wilful or through subjugation – by those excluded. Without this, contest is inevitable. It could be, then, that with regards to gold mining claims in Zimbabwe and indeed the diamond fiasco in the eastern part of that country, those who attempted to enclose are yet to meet people simple enough to believe their claims. Or, the state capable of legislating closure on land and property acquisition is yet to emerge. A variant of Marx's notion of primitive accumulation or primary accumulation marked by violent dispossessions, which he equates to the original sin, may have started in Zimbabwe. Cramer's positional struggles mark these battles (Marx, 431, 1972; Cramer, 2006). Zimbabwe's low level violence was a modality through which the contest for property was being resolved. It may – or may not, if one believes that there is an inherent African 'ubuntu' that negates the notion of private property and thus 'western greed' (Metz, 2007) – have given birth to an enclosed form of market accumulation.

The violence characterising informal gold and diamond mining in Zimbabwe suggests a twisted tale of primitive accumulation. One twist in the tale (or tail) is the 'racial' dimension, given that the official Zimbabwean discourse concerned itself with the 'land' and the whites who once owned it. This process could be conceptualised as one in which an emergent 'black bourgeoisie', along with a few misled 'war veterans', a few thousand small commodity producers, and thousands more subsistence farmers, tried to take over a formerly white dominated and capitalist oriented social formation. Yet the process is also twisted when one leaves the racial paradigm and enters the mining fields. It is characterised by many reversals. A new government might have implemented the ZANU-PF ideologues' worst nightmares by bringing back private property and thus the white farmers and transnational mining corporations. Overt civil war may have ensued if the ZANU-PF factions repeated their 1970s infighting. A newly articulated blend of modes of production merging 'primitive communalism', feudalism and capitalism once again (Wolpe, 1972; Hart, 2007) could have emerged in the wake of either a successful 'transitional government' or a war increasing the 2008–9 levels of violence exponentially. Whether or not the chaos played its midwifery role is undetermined, but the appearance of market civilisation in Zimbabwe was far from imminent (Moore, 2007a).

Nevertheless, the above theoretical premise does assist the theorising of contemporary Zimbabwe's political economy. The reliance on militaristic modalities concurs with universal accounts of initial capitalist accumulation, relying on non-market modalities (Marx in Bond, 2007:1). After dismantling the semi-capitalist *status quo* in the 2000s, Zimbabwe appeared to be locked in this process as new forms of capital accumulation emerged out of the ashes of the old. More negatively, there is every indication that most conflict ridden and economically 'backward' societies in the developing world are locked in a state of permanent primitive accumulation. It is thus proposed here that violent conflicts in Africa are in fact twisted processes of primitive accumulation through which property rights are still contested and *may* be emerging.[6] State actors, with their access to global networks, foreign currency, and the means of coercion, play crucial roles in this process – far beyond that of simply 'rent-seeking'; and far beyond that of mobilising the masses and their dreams for land and liberty. These related premises, building on theories of the post-colonial state and modernised variants of primitive accumulation, aid a proper disentangling of the contradictory responses by the Zimbabwe state to the smuggling and the violence in the 'informal' but state-linked mineral sector.

Thus those (e.g. Mamdani, 2008) who utter the truism that African rulers combine consent and coercion as they go about their business should investigate the contours of the Centaur – the half man, half beast marking the state and the processes of accumulation over which it presides and participates – as closely as Gramsci and his predecessors desired (Gramsci, 1937, 1992). Otherwise, they risk slipping into the banalities of scholarship about Africa that have blemished the social science landscape around the world.

Notes

1 Eastern Zimbabwe and Central Zimbabwe can also be referred to as Manicaland and Midlands provinces respectively.
2 This 600,000 figure might be an exaggeration and should be treated with caution considering that according to the Central Statistics Office KweKwe Metro in 2005

had a population of 60,000. However it points to the level of increase in panning activities.
3 A cursory examination of the illegal mining language reveals much about the social relations evolving out of the work. For example terms like 'front' suggest someone is secretly behind the illegal mining deals, whereas terms like *Mbimbo* (a feared strong man leading a mafia) suggest conflicts of access and warlordism, while *Zvipamuzi* (slave) suggests exploitation. Much more suggestive jargon abounds in this realm.
4 These include John Bredenkamp, Muller Conrad 'Billy' Rautenbach, and Thai businesswoman Nalinee Joy Taveesin. In early 2009 they were included in the US government's sanctions list of Zimbabwean politicians and business people working with them.
5 In what could be a case of accumulation rivalry in ZANU-PF, the mining commissioner was once arrested for corruption on the awarding of a mining claims certificate. He was released and later transferred to Masvingo.
6 Even if they do emerge, there is no guarantee that they will generate growth and development, as Hernando de Soto (2004) believes.

References

Andreasson, S. (2006) 'Stand and Deliver: Private Property and the Politics of Global Dispossession', *Political Studies*, 54: 3–22.
Arrighi, G. (1966) 'The Political Economy of Rhodesia,' *New Left Review*, I, 39: 35–65.
—— and Saul, J. (1973) *Essays on the Political Economy of Africa*, New York: Monthly Review Press.
Bates, R. (1989; 2nd edn 2005) *Beyond the Miracle of the Market: The Political Economy of Agrarian Development in Kenya*, Cambridge: Cambridge University Press.
Bayart, J-F. (1993) *The State in Africa: The Politics of the Belly, London: Longman.*
Bayart, J-F., Ellis, S. and Hibou B. (1999), *The Criminalization of the State in Africa*, Oxford: James Currey.
Bello, W. (2008) 'The Coming Capitalist Consensus', *Foreign Policy in Focus*, Online. Available HTTP: <http://fpif.org/fpiftxt/5765>
Bond, P. (1998) *Uneven Zimbabwe: A Study of Finance, Development and Underdevelopment*, Trenton: Africa World Press.
—— (2007) 'Introduction: Two Economies – or One System of Superexploitation', *Africanus: Journal of Development Studies*, 37: 1–22.
Bond, P. (2009) 'Mamdani on Zimbabwe sets back Civil Society,' *Concerned African Scholars Bulletin*, 82, 36–41.
Chabal, P. (2009) *Africa: The Politics of Suffering and Smiling*, London and Scottsville: Zed Press and University of KwaZulu-Natal Press.
Chabal P. and Daloz, J-P. (1999) *Africa Works: Disorder as Political Instrument*. Oxford: James Currey.
Cockett, R. (1995) *Thinking the Unthinkable: Think-Tanks and the Counter-Revolution, 1931–1983*, London.
Cox, R. (1987) *Production, Power, and World Order: Social Forces in the Making of History*. New York: Columbia University Press.
Cramer, C. (2006) *Civil War is Not a Stupid Thing: Understanding Violence in Developing Countries*, London: Hurst and Co.

—— and Goodhand, J. (2002) 'Try Again, Fail Again, Fail Better? War, the State, and the "Post-conflict" Challenge in Afghanistan', *Development and Change*, 33: 885–909.

Davies, R. (2004) 'Memories of Underdevelopment: A Personal Interpretation of Zimbabwe's Economic Decline,' B. Raftopoulos and T. Savage (eds.) *Zimbabwe: Injustice and Political Reconciliation*, Cape Town: Institute of Justice and Reconciliation.

De Soto, H. (2000) *The Mystery of Capital: Why Capitalism Triumphs in the West and Fails Everywhere Else*, London: Bantam.

De Waal, A. (1997) *Famine Crimes: Politics and the Disaster Relief Industry in Africa*, London: James Currey.

Duffield, M. (2001) *Global Governance and the New Wars: The Merging of Development and Security*, London, Zed Books.

—— (2002) 'Social Reconstruction and the Radicalisation of Development: Aid as a Relation of Global Liberal Governance,' *Development and Change*, 33: 1049–71.

Duval-Smith, A. (2009) 'Power Sharing in Zimbabwe Threatened by Five-man Cabal', *Observer*, February 15.

Freund, W. (1981) 'Class Conflict, Political Economy and the Struggle for Socialism in Tanzania', *African Affairs*, 80: 483–99.

Gibbon, P. (ed.) (1995) *Structural Adjustment and the Working Poor in Zimbabwe*, Uppsala: Nordiska Afrikainstitutet.

Gibbon, P., Bangura, Y. and Ofstad, A. (1992) *Authoritarianism, Democracy and Adjustment: The Politics of Economic Change in Sub-Saharan Africa*, Uppsala: Nordiska Afrikainstitutet.

Gono, G. (2007) 'Promoting Indigenous Economic Empowerment', address to the Extraordinary Session of ZANU-PF Congress in Harare, 14 December 2007.

Gramsci, A. (1937; Columbia edn. 1992) *Prison Notebooks: Vol. 1*, J. Buttigieg (ed.) New York: Columbia University Press.

Gray, J. (2007) *Black Mass: Apocalyptic Religion and the Death of Utopia*, Toronto: Doubleday.

Hart, G. (2007) 'Changing Concepts of Articulation: Political Stakes in South Africa Today', *Review of African Political Economy*, 34: 85–101.

Harvey, D. (2003) *The New Imperialism*, Oxford: Oxford University Press.

Kanyenze, G. (2004) 'The Zimbabwean Economy 1980–2003: a ZCTU Perspective', D. Harold-Barry, (ed.), *Zimbabwe: The Past is the Future*, Harare: Weaver Press.

Kitching, G. (1982) *Development and Underdevelopment in Historical Perspective*, London: Methuen.

—— (2000) 'Why I Gave Up African Studies', *African Studies Review and Newsletter*, 22: 21–6.

—— (2003) 'Jagged Fragments: Imperialism, Racism, Hurt, and Honesty', *African Studies Quarterly* 7.

Locke, J. (1690; 1967) *Two Treatises of Government*, Cambridge: Cambridge University Press.

MacGaffey, J. (1989) 'Issues and Methods in the Study of African Economies', in J. MacGaffey (ed.) *The Real Economy of Zaire: The Contribution of Smuggling and Other Unofficial Activities to National Wealth*, London: James Currey.

Mamdani, M. (1976) *Politics and Class Formation in Uganda*, New York: Monthly Review Press.

—— (2008) 'Lessons of Zimbabwe', *London Review of Books*, 30, Online. Available HTTP: http://www.lrb.co.uk/v30/n23/mamd01_.html> (accessed December 4 2008).

—— (2009) 'Letters', *London Review of Books*, 31, Online. Available HTTP: http://www.lrb.co.uk/v31/n01/letters.html> (accessed January 5 2009).

Mandaza, I. (1986) 'Introduction', Mandaza (ed.) *Zimbabwe: The Political Economy of Transition, 1980–1986*, Dakar: Codresia.

—— (2009) 'Zimbabwe's Transitional Govt: The First 100 Days', *Zimbabwe Independent*, May 21.

Marx, K. (1867; 1972) 'The So-Called Primitive Accumulation', in R. C. Tucker (ed.) *The Marx-Engels Reader*, 2nd edn, New York: Norton.

Mawowa, S. (2007) 'Tapping into the Chaos: State, Crisis and Accumulation', unpublished M.A. Thesis, University of KwaZulu-Natal.

Metz, T. (2007) 'Toward an African Moral Theory', *The Journal of Political Philosophy*, 15: 321–41.

Moore, D. (2001) 'Is the Land the Economy and the Economy the Land? Primitive Accumulation in Zimbabwe,' *Journal of Contemporary African Studies*, 19: 253–66.

—— (2004a) 'The Second Age of the Third World: From Primitive Accumulation to Public Goods?' *Third World Quarterly*, 25: 87–109.

—— (2004b) 'Marxism and Marxist Intellectuals in Schizophrenic Zimbabwe: How Many Rights for Zimbabwe's Left? A Comment,' *Historical Materialism*, 12: 405–25.

—— (2007a) ' "Intellectuals" Interpreting Zimbabwe's Primitive Accumulation: Progress to Market Civilisation?', *Safundi*, 8: 199–222.

—— (2007b) (ed.) *The World Bank: Development, Poverty, Hegemony*, Scottsville: University of KwaZulu-Natal Press.

—— (2009a) 'Now Onus is on SA to Deliver: Power-sharing Arrangement Makes Regional Sovereign Responsible for Building a Decent Dispensation', *Cape Times*, February 3.

—— (2009b) 'Mamdani's Enthusiasms', *Association of Concerned African Scholars Bulletin*, 81: 59–64.

—— (2006) 'The Radicalised State: Zimbabwe's Interrupted Revolution', *Review of African Political Economy*, 111: 103–21.

—— (2007) 'The Zimbabwe Question and the Two Lefts', *Historical Materialism*, 15: 171–204.

Moyo, S. and Yeros, P. (eds.) (2005) *Reclaiming the Land: The Resurgence of Rural Movements in Africa, Asia and Latin America*, London: Zed Books.

—— (2007) 'The Zimbabwe Question and the Two Lefts', *Historical Materialism*, 15: 171–204.

Newzimbabwe.com, 24 November 2008, Online. Available HTTP: <www.new zimbabwe.com> Accessed December 12, 2008.

Observer, February 15, 2009.

Raftopoulos, B., and Phimister, I., (2004), 'Zimbabwe Now: The Political Economy of Crisis and Coercion', *Historical Materialism*, 12: 355–82.

Reno, W. (1999) *Warlord Politics and African States*, Boulder: Lynne Rienner.

Rousseau, J-J. (1754; 1994) *Discourse on the Origin of Inequality*, Oxford: Oxford University Press.

Sadomba, W. (2008) 'War Veterans in Zimbabwe's Land Occupations: Complexities of a liberation Movement in an African Post Colonial Settler Society', PhD. Dissertation, Wageningen University.

Saul, J. (1974) 'The State in Post-Colonial Societies: Tanzania,' in J. Saville and R. Miliband (eds.) *Socialist Register 1974*, London: Merlin; reprinted in Saul, *State and Revolution in Eastern Africa*. New York: Monthly Review Press, 1979.

—— (1976) 'The Unsteady State: Uganda, Obote and General Amin,' *Review of African Political Economy*, 5: 12–38, reprinted in Saul, *State and Revolution in Eastern Africa*. New York: Monthly Review Press, 1979.

Saunders, R. (2007) 'Mining and Crisis in Zimbabwe', *Fatal Transactions*, Online. Available HTTP: <http://www.fataltransactions.org/cgi-bin/dbp.cgi?db = cmsp&ID = 92> (accessed 4 December 2008).

—— (2008) 'Painful Paradoxes: Mining, Crisis and Regional Capital in Zimbabwe' *At Issue Ezine*, Online. Available HTTP: <http://www.africafiles.org/printableversion. asp?id = 18663> (accessed 10 November 2008).

Scott, J. C. (1998) *Seeing Like a State: How Certain Schemes to Improve the Human Condition Have Failed*. New Haven, CT: Yale University Press.

Shivji, I. (1973) *The Silent Class Struggle*, Dar es Salaam: Tanzania Publishing House.

Sithole, C. (2009) *Harare Accused of Brutal Crackdown on Diamond Prospectors*. Institute for War and Peace Reporting, ZCR No. 186, 25 March.

Stoneman, C. and Cliffe, L. (1989) *Zimbabwe: Politics, Economics, Society*, London: Pinter.

Swain, J. and Sheridan, M. (2009) 'Grasping Grace Puts Diamond Business on Her Shopping List', *Sunday Times* (SA) 15 February.

Tandon, Y. (ed.) (1982), *University of Dar es Salaam Debate on Class, State and Imperialism*, Dar es Salaam: Tanzania Publishing House.

The Business Times (Johannesburg) 9 November 2008.

The Financial Gazette (Harare), 8 March 2008.

The Herald (Harare) 11 December 2008.

The Midlands Observer (Gweru) 24 October 2001; 14 February 2003; 3 June 2003; 24 October 2003; 14 May 2007;14 May 2007.

The Reserve Bank of Zimbabwe (2008) 'Half Year Monetary Policy Statement', July.

—— (2004) *Monetary Policy Statement: The First Quarter to 31 March 2004* (March).

—— (2004a) *Monetary Policy Statement: The Second Quarter to 30 June 2004* (July).

The Sunday Times (Johannesburg) 15 February 2009.

The ZimDaily, 8 December 2006; 6 October 2008; 7 October 2008; 21 October 2008, Online. Available HTTP: <www.zimdaily.com>, accessed 23 October 2008.

Thornycroft, P. (2009) 'Get a Credit Card – They Work, says Confident Biti', *Sunday Independent* (Johannesburg), May 24, p. 11.

Tilly, C. (1994) 'States and Nationalism in Europe 1492–1992', *Theory and Society*, 23: 131–46.

United Nations Development Programme (2008), *Comprehensive Economic Recovery in Zimbabwe: A Discussion Document*, Harare: UNDP.

Van de Walle, N. (2001) *African Economies and the Politics of Permanent Crisis: 1979–1999*, Cambridge: Cambridge University Press.

Wield, D. (1981) 'Manufacturing Industry', in C. Stoneman (ed.) *Zimbabwe's Inheritance*, Basingstoke and Harare: Macmillan and College Press.

Wolpe, H. (1972), 'Capitalism and Cheap Labour-Power: From Segregation to Apartheid', *Economy and Society*, 1: 425–56; reprinted in H. Wolpe (ed.) *The Articulation of Modes of Production*, London: Routledge and Kegan Paul, 1980.

Yeros, P. (2002), 'Zimbabwe and the Dilemmas of the Left', *Historical Materialism*, 11: 3–15.
Zimonline, 14 May, 2007, Online. Available HTTP: <zimonline.com>, accessed 13 November 2008.

Guide to Further Reading

Arrighi, A. and Saul, J. (1973) *Essays on the Political Economy of Africa*, New York: Monthly Review Press.
Bond, P. (1998) *Uneven Zimbabwe: A Study of Finance, Development and Under-development*, Trenton: Africa World Press.
Cramer, C. (2006) *Civil War is Not a Stupid Thing: Understanding Violence in Developing Countries*, London: Hurst and Co.
Gramsci, A. (1937; Columbia edn. 1992) *Prison Notebooks: Vol. 1*, J. Buttigieg (ed.) New York: Columbia University Press.
Mawowa, S. (2007) 'Tapping into the Chaos: State, Crisis and Accumulation', unpublished M.A. Thesis, University of KwaZulu-Natal.
Moore, D. (2007) ' "Intellectuals" Interpreting Zimbabwe's Primitive Accumulation: Progress to Market Civilisation?', *Safundi*, 8:199–222.
Moyo, S. and Yeros, P. (eds.) (2004) *Reclaiming the Land: The Resurgence of Rural Movements in Africa, Asia and Latin America*, London: Zed Books.
Raftopoulos, B., and Phimister, I., (2004), 'Zimbabwe Now: The Political Economy of Crisis and Coercion', *Historical Materialism*, 12: 355–82.
Wolpe, H. (1972), 'Capitalism and Cheap Labour-Power: From Segregation to Apartheid', *Economy and Society*, 1: 425–56; reprinted in H. Wolpe (ed.) *The Articulation of Modes of Production*, London: Routledge and Kegan Paul, 1980

18 Good governance and growth in Africa

What can we learn from Tanzania?

Hazel Gray and Mushtaq Khan

Popular struggles for social justice in Africa and elsewhere are often couched in terms of demands for better governance. But the new consensus over 'good governance' supported by international financial institutions represents a much narrower programme of reform based on neoclassical economic theory. This agenda focuses on developing governance attributes in Africa that are theoretically supposed to enhance growth by making markets more efficient. Some of these governance capabilities (such as measures to improve government accountability or lower corruption) appear to coincide with goals supported by social justice movements for better governance. But the reasons for supporting these are very different in the official good governance agenda, and the way they are supported can make the achievement of social goals even more difficult. This chapter outlines the theoretical and methodological basis of the good governance agenda and sets out an alternative understanding of the links between growth and governance in Africa.

The good governance reforms are based on a particular way of understanding economic development that draws on new institutional economics and new political economy. It assumes that political stability and economic development in developing countries can be based on institutions of political representation, accountability and market competition. In making these assumptions it ignores not only much of the history of economic, political and social transformations through which industrial societies have emerged, it also reads economic and political theory very selectively. The danger is that in confusing desirable outcomes (such as low corruption, a good rule of law and accountability) with the preconditions that are required to achieve political stability and economic growth in poor countries, the good governance agenda can, in many contexts, result in lost opportunities for meaningful reform, or even worse. The first section examines some of these theoretical issues and the second section examines the implementation of the good governance agenda in Tanzania and some of its effects.

Good governance: some theoretical issues

The roots of the modern 'good governance' agenda lie in theoretical developments within the new institutional economics developed by North and Thomas (1973), North (1990), Olson (1982; 1997; 2000), Williamson (1985), Milgrom and Roberts (1992) and Bates (1984; 1989; 2001). These models established the importance of stable property rights for the functioning of a market economy. Good governance also drew on theories of rents and rent seeking that date back to the work of Krueger (1974), Posner (1975) and Bhagwati (1982). These theories claimed subsidies, market restrictions and other sources of 'rents' or politically created incomes were highly damaging for market economies. And finally, it drew on new political economy theories that supported democracies on the grounds that they helped to establish property rights and reduced rent seeking such as North (1990) and Olson (2000). The theoretical argument was that democratic accountability reduced the possibility of corruption and rent seeking, this in turn enabled a rule of law and stable property rights to be enforced, and these were essential for reducing transaction costs in markets, thereby allowing economic growth (Khan, 2004, 2006b, 2007).

These theoretical arguments were backed up by numerous econometric studies that purported to show a positive relationship between improvements in good governance and various measures of economic performance, in particular economic growth. While governance quality is difficult to measure directly, the new paradigm has been helped by the development of proxy measures for complex governance capabilities such as the rule of law and the stability of property rights. These proxies involve both 'objective' measures such as counting the number of corruption cases brought to court as well as 'subjective' measures that often use survey data from credit risk agencies who interview business people about their perceptions and experience of different aspects of governance.

The best known of these data sets are the World Wide Governance Indicators (WGI) produced by the World Bank but many data sets are now available. In terms of these measures, most countries in Africa perform badly on all of the key areas of concern of the good governance agenda. The WGI indicators place the vast majority of African countries in the bottom fiftieth percentile of their six dimensions of governance meaning that Africa performs worse than any other region, except the former Soviet Union (World Bank, 2008). In the Corruption Perceptions Index (CPI), produced by Transparency International, 30 out of the 47 countries where corruption was measured in Africa were found to have rampant corruption while only three, Botswana, Cape Verde and Mauritius, scored above the global average for corruption (Transparency International, 2008).

In many ways it has become difficult to confront the argument for the good governance agenda in Africa. This is partly because it has attained the status of 'conventional wisdom' in much of the discourse on development and has been espoused by African leaders, reflected in commitments in NEPAD and the AU, as well as being central to donor conditionality (Mkapa, 2008). More importantly, it taps into the popular aspirations of millions across the continent who face the burden of poor governance on a daily basis and who want their leaders to be held to account through genuinely democratic political systems. Nevertheless, despite the proliferation of quantitative studies and policy conditionality based on its conclusions, serious questions have been raised about the validity of the good governance agenda, both from within the mainstream and from heterodox economic approaches.

A major area of dispute concerns the empirical evidence, particularly the econometric models, used to support the good governance agenda. A basic problem is that the econometric approaches cannot definitively show that good governance is required for growth rather than the reverse, that growth and rising levels of per capita income are necessary for sustainable improvements in good governance (Khan, 2004). In particular, case studies of successful development in poor countries show that none of these countries achieved significant improvements in good governance *before* they began their economic transformations. Think of South Korea and Taiwan in the 1960s, Thailand and Malaysia in the 1980s, China in the 1990s amongst many other examples. The relationships found in many econometric studies between good governance and growth could therefore be spurious, caused by measurement error, reverse causation, poor model specification and data mining by dedicated researchers looking for combinations of countries and periods which support their theories. In addition, econometric studies that question these results are typically ignored.

For instance, Sachs *et al.*, (2004) provide an econometric analysis that standardizes the measurement of governance by level of income and finds that, in fact, many African countries are actually well governed according to their level of income. And while the Sachs *et al.* study finds a weak relationship between improvements in good governance and growth when all countries are looked at together, African countries have a more significant negative dummy. This can be interpreted in two ways. Either governance does not matter much for African countries, which is the interpretation that the authors support. Alternatively, the governance capabilities that the good governance approach focuses on may be less important for developing countries and the governance weaknesses that African countries suffer from may be very different from the ones identified in the good governance approach. The second possibility is supported by historical analyses of the governance capabilities that allowed a few developing countries to emerge from poverty to prosperity in the last 50 years.

Heterodox economics (and some developments within mainstream neo-classical economics) provide the theoretical framework for explaining the importance of these alternative governance capabilities for achieving prosperity and therefore eventually achieving good governance characteristics. In the context of significant market failures in developing countries, it is not surprising that growth has depended on state capabilities of addressing market failures (Amsden, 1989; Wade, 1990). Interventions to correct market failures inevitably create rents, because rents can be defined as incomes that are directly the result of state interventions (Khan, 2000b, 2000a). Thus, far from requiring the removal of all rents and rent seeking, success in development may require state capabilities to manage rents and rent seeking such that growth-enhancing rents could be managed and growth-reducing rents could be removed.

This heterodox approach has focused on the critical importance of rents and interventions that successful developing countries have used to overcome market failures limiting the acquisition of technology and the organization of learning-by-doing in productive activities. Growth in developing countries requires catching up through the acquisition of new technologies and learning to use these new technologies rapidly. Learning how to use modern technologies is an expensive process that entails extra costs until higher levels of productivity are achieved. In developing countries the weakness of markets and in particular capital markets means that these processes face significant market failures and success requires state action to facilitate technology acquisition and indeed to overcome other significant market failures (Khan, 2007, 2008). Addressing these problems requires significant governance capacities in managing rents but these capabilities are typically entirely ignored in the good governance approach.

The problem with intervention and rent-creation is that some rent seeking is inevitable. In developing countries much of this rent seeking may be illegal, and take the form of different types of corruption. Some types of corruption impose costs but do not significantly distort the intervention while other types of corruption can distort the implementation of the intervention to the extent that potentially beneficial effects are wiped out or even reversed. Growth-enhancing governance therefore requires institutional and political capabilities for limiting the damaging variants of corruption even if overall corruption cannot be significantly reduced in the short to medium term (Khan, 2006a). Most of the examples of successful rent creation of this sort come from Asia, however, this type of rent creation was also important in many African development plans prior to the liberalization drive of the 1980s (Mkandawire, 2001). However, in many cases across Africa, state created rents served no purpose other than to create incomes for state functionaries and politicians. Nevertheless, the drive to wipe out all state created rents has reduced the institutional and political capacity of many African countries to deal with significant market failures (Khan and Gray, 2006).

However, corruption in developing countries is not just related to potentially growth-enhancing rents. If that was the only problem, it would be possible to address this problem by gradually legalizing the rent seeking associated with these rents, in much the same way as the rent seeking associated with many socially desirable rents in advanced countries is legalized through the political process. The more fundamental problem is that many aspects of poor governance in developing countries are linked to interventions and rents that are potentially necessary for growth or political stability but which cannot be easily legalized. Two important types of such interventions are the 'interventions' that manage non-market asset allocations and that manage political stability in developing countries (Khan, 2004, 2006a, 2006b).

Non-market asset transfers are sometimes described as *primitive accumulation* and this process has implications that are very similar to conventional state-created rents. Primitive accumulation in low income countries is driven by the fact that many critical assets, in particular land, are in low productivity traditional sectors and as a result of their low productivity, their owners do not have the resources to pay for the definition and protection of clear property rights. In the course of economic transformation, the transactions that can re-allocate resources to emerging productive sectors are often not possible through conventional market processes precisely because property titles are missing or badly defined or heavily contested. Many of the significant asset re-allocations in developing countries happen through political processes rather than through market ones. These non-market processes can be legal (such as land reform), quasi legal (political influence guiding market transfers) or entirely illegal (asset grabbing). But clearly quite apart from the avarice of the politically powerful, there are structural reasons why market-based asset transfers cannot be relied upon in developing countries. Once again, critical governance capabilities are required to ensure that these non-market transfers are socially beneficial and not socially damaging. In contrast, the good governance approach urges developing countries to achieve the property right stability that is impossible to achieve at early stages of development.

Primitive accumulation in African countries manifests itself in various ways including land policies, the framework of regulation surrounding natural resource extraction, compulsory purchase orders and appropriations undertaken as part of privatization policies. In some cases even forms of taxation, subsidies and price fixing assist forms of primitive accumulation as they accelerate the transfer of assets to particular classes or groups. Historical evidence suggests that in high growth developers' property rights were *not* stable across the board but rather assets were systematically transferred to productive investors while in less dynamic developers, assets remained in the hands of unproductive expropriators (Qian, 2003, Brenner, 1985). The governance policy question for many African countries is why primitive accumulation often remains stuck in cycles of predation without the emergence of a more productive asset structure.

The process of political stabilization also involves significant transfers in all countries and these are rents by definition. In most rich countries political stabilization is primarily achieved through redistribution of fiscal resources through open transfers discussed in Khan (2005). Given the limited scope for fiscal transfers and the lack of political legitimacy of many of the groups that pose the greatest threat to political stability in low income countries, political stabilization typically cannot be achieved solely through the creation of legal rents. Instead, political stability in developing countries depends on off-budget transfers and non-legal rent creation for critical clients and constituencies through the patron-client networks operated by political parties and groups in power. The state's capacity to manage political stabilization in these ways is clearly critical for economic growth, and the types of rents that are created also have an effect on growth because some types of rents can be very damaging while others are much less so. It appears that political rent creation is very damaging in many African countries, descending in some cases to conditions of civil war and predation by competing groups of warlords.

The assumption of the good governance agenda is that problems of political stabilization can be solved through democratization and the attempt to manage political stability through fiscal transfers as in industrialized countries. This prescription is not very useful because the economic basis of such a fiscal strategy does not yet exist. Developing countries, including African countries, can only tax a much smaller share of their GDP because of the small share of modern activities, and their per capita incomes are also much lower. Thus, clientelism in Africa is not special at all but rather a feature of all developing countries. Unfortunately, a number of authors have pointed to specific African cultural factors or the absence of democracy in Africa to explain the prevalence of patron-client politics and 'neo-patrimonialism' (Hyden and Williams, 1994; Médard, 2002). Rather, while patron-client politics are common to *all* developing countries, the success of particular patron-client structures in achieving stability and growth differs significantly.

The problems of political stabilization in developing countries therefore have to be addressed through other types of governance capabilities that draw on the experience of successful countries in the developing world. Whether democratic or not, successful developing countries have had high levels of political corruption and political stabilization through patron-client networks. Adapting their governance capabilities to the conditions of specific African countries is a very different task from the exclusive focus on democratization and accountability that the good governance approach espouses.

Weaknesses in growth-enhancing governance in Africa may have more to do with state fragmentation. The institutional fragmentation of the state can result in predatory behaviour because different parts of the state can behave in uncoordinated ways, thereby resulting in short term predatory behaviour. The historical reasons for state fragmentation in Africa have been studied by Mamdani (1996) who argues that different patterns of direct and indirect rule by colonial governments established fragmented and bifurcated states in Africa. The problem of institutional fragmentation cannot however be solved by simply changing formal organizational structures of the state but is more likely to require fundamental changes in the political configurations underpinning the state.

The political fragmentation of the powerful classes and groups underpinning the state is often an important underlying cause of persistent institutional fragmentation of the state. Political fragmentation in developing countries frequently takes the form of multiple well-organized factions each seeking to gain power and rents for itself but failing to achieve enough stability to take a long-term view. As a result, political competition can result in the creation of many damaging rents in the process of primitive accumulation and political stabilization. Somewhat different political organizations can achieve greater political stability either through the inclusion of the most powerful groups within a single party or the emergence of a small number of equally powerful groups that have a credible prospect of cycling in and out of power. In these cases, political stabilization and primitive accumulation can lead to much more developmental rents. Changing the political organization of factions in these ways falls well outside the remit of most good governance type reforms. However differences in governance capabilities in these areas are probably much more important in explaining the differential performance of developing countries than good governance capabilities which are missing in virtually all developing countries. The next section explores some of these issues in the context of the good governance agenda in Tanzania.

Good governance and Tanzania

After 20 years of economic and political reforms, including market liberalization, the introduction of multiparty elections and extensive transparency and accountability reforms, Tanzania is often described as one of the more successful examples of good governance reforms in Africa (Utz, 2007). At the start of the reform process Tanzania was identified as having poor governance across the whole spectrum of state activities (World Bank, 2001) and the *Presidential Inquiry into Corruption* identified widespread corruption at all levels of government (United Republic of Tanzania, 1996). Major efforts were made to reduce rent seeking within the realm of public finance. Success in this area has been rewarded with high levels of foreign aid which have been increasingly channelled as direct budget support through the government's budgetary system (United Republic of Tanzania, 2005). A ring-fenced and very generous fiscal incentive structure was introduced to attract foreign investment into natural resource extraction which triggered a massive inflow of FDI into the sector, making Tanzania the fifth largest recipient of FDI on the continent.

In more recent years, some progress also seems to have been made in addressing cases of grand corruption involving senior politicians and business people. In 2007 the Prime Minister resigned over allegations of corruption over a contract for private power provision and the governor of the central bank resigned over allegations of the theft of billions of shillings of government funds from the Bank of Tanzania in 2006. Cases were also brought to court against two former finance ministers and the ex-permanent secretary of the ministry of finance over abuses of public office. Overall, improvements in governance are credited as part of the reason for Tanzania's improving rates of GDP growth, from an average 2 per cent during the period from 1985 to 1995 to over 5 per cent for the period from 1996 to 2005.

The story of Tanzania's success with good governance reforms is however more complicated than this picture would suggest. While certain areas of poor governance appear to have been effectively addressed through market promoting reforms and by enhancing the transparency and accountability of the state, there are critical areas of governance in Tanzania that have either not been affected or that fall outside the good governance agenda completely. These critical areas include land management and industrial policy and natural resource management. The reason for this differentiated performance can be traced both to the nature of policy advice but also to the institutional and political configuration of the state.

Good governance successes

Probably the most successful areas of good governance reform in Tanzania have been in public finances. Initially reforms of public finance focused on neo-liberal macroeconomic stabilization with cuts in public expenditure to reduce inflation, extensive privatization and the 'rationalization' of the tax system to promote private sector growth and foreign investment. Drastic cuts in government spending were initiated and government expenditures as a percentage of GDP fell from 27 per cent in 1992 to 11 per cent by 1998. The inflation rate was brought down from 32.4 per cent in 1986 to 14.4 per cent by 1998 (Bigsten and Danielson, 2001). From the mid-1990s these stabilization reforms were accompanied by good governance reforms that sought to address the pervasive corruption, lack of transparency and accountability, inefficient market distortions and endemic rent seeking affecting public finances (United Republic of Tanzania, 1996; World Bank, 2001; United Republic of Tanzania, 2003, 2004).

The budget process was seen to be highly politicized and numerous cases of corruption both on the revenue and expenditure side of the budget were documented by the *Presidential Inquiry into Corruption* (United Republic of Tanzania, 1996; World Bank, 2001). The cases identified involved bureaucratic and political corruption and even cases of outright predation and theft. On the expenditure side of the budget, there appeared to be significant 'off budget' expenditures not accounted for to the public or covered in the official budget document (World Bank, 2001). Off budget expenditures are notoriously difficult to identify given their covert nature but in Tanzania they may have included loans to the ruling party, hidden government projects and aid funded projects that were not included in the budget estimates.

These weaknesses were identified as a major constraint on Tanzania's development objectives (World Bank, 2001) and public expenditure reforms featured increasingly in donor conditionality. This was also driven by the shift amongst Tanzania's largest donors in aid modality away from project based finance to direct (or 'general') budget support (United Republic of Tanzania, 2005). The grant of aid money into the general budget allowed greater aid flows to be directed to African countries like Tanzania, but to make this politically acceptable to taxpayers in advanced countries providing the aid, a lot of effort was put into aligning developing country budget priorities to development commitments contained in the IMF/World Bank approved Poverty Reduction Strategy. An array of complementary reform programmes including the Civil Service Reform Programme, the Public Financial Management Reform Programme, the Public Expenditure Review, Legal Sector Reform Programme and the Accountability, Transparency and Integrity Programme were introduced. These led to extensive institutional and organizational changes in the ways that public finances operated.

In 1996 major institutional reforms of the revenue authority were introduced. The aims of the reform were to remove political influence, raise salaries and provide greater transparency and accountability of tax officials. Control of the revenue authority was removed from the Ministry of Finance. The Tanzania Revenue Authority (TRA) was established as an independent institution in order to insulate the TRA from political pressure and to move it outside the control of the civil service. Existing staff were dismissed and though most were subsequently re-employed, this was on different terms with more attractive wages and easier processes for dismissal. The aim was to raise the opportunity cost of corruption for bureaucrats. The tax exemption regime also underwent significant reforms to reduce the overall number of exemptions and to increase transparency in the exemption process. Subsequently, there was a significant fall in exemptions granted directly to private individuals and companies from around 35 per cent of total exemptions in 1998 to around 11 per cent in 2003. But there has been a sharp increase in the number of exemptions granted through the Tanzania Investment Centre from around 12 per cent in 1998 to 35 per cent in 2003 (Levin, 2005).

Major reforms of the public expenditure management system included the introduction of the cash budget, which limited payments to available cash on a monthly basis, and the introduction of a centralized computerized payments system through the Integrated Financial Management System (IFMS). Transparency and accountability were strengthened with the development of a medium-term expenditure framework (MTEF) and the establishment of the Public Expenditure Review (PER) with government and donor participation. An expenditure tracking system was put in place to reduce leakages at service delivery level. Further, efforts were made to put a greater proportion of the previously 'off budget' aid financed projects through the official system (United Republic of Tanzania, 2001). Annual reviews by the Controller and Auditor General pointed to significant improvement in the financial management of the budget, with fewer audit queries over time (United Republic of Tanzania, 2007). Successive Public Expenditure Reviews have also reported a fall in off budget expenditures.

The initial outcome of the revenue reforms was a decline in corruption and an increase in reported revenue from 11 per cent of GDP in 1995/96 to more than 12 per cent in 1996/97. However in three subsequent years tax revenue declined as a percentage of GDP and there were reports of corruption increasing again within the revenue authority (Fjeldstad, 2002). While tax revenues as a percentage of GDP started to rise again after 2000, the tax to GDP ratio remained low compared to other African countries with a similar economic structure. Cross-country analyses of tax-revenue performance suggest that Tanzania should be capable of generating tax-revenue of around 18 per cent of GDP (Bevan, 2001) rather than the 11–13 per cent that has been the norm since the reforms (Levin, 2005). Tax buoyancy has also remained low, suggesting that tax evasion and discretionary exemptions were still having a major impact on reducing tax revenue (Bigsten and Danielson, 2001). Political scandals concerning exemptions have also continued through the reform period. Some of the forms of rent seeking within the revenue system therefore appear to be much more difficult to root out with these types of governance reforms.

Similarly, while expenditure reforms have undoubtedly reduced some forms of political rent seeking in the budget, there are still some areas that remain beyond the influence of the good governance agenda. For example, some areas of government activity such as Defence, Police, the Prime Minister's office and the State House have their own budgeting systems and are not on-line within the IFMS system. Further, there have been a number of examples of large and, in some cases, dubious purchases outside the official budgetary process including the purchase of a national air traffic control system from the British company BAE, the construction of a national stadium and new parliamentary buildings that were not subject to the official government-donor scrutiny process of the PER. Thus, the claim that all off-budget expenditures have been eradicated requires further investigation.

Nevertheless, rent seeking in public finance appears to have been significantly modified by the governance reform agenda. There are however, other areas of rent seeking that have not been so amenable to these sorts of reforms. The focus on removing rents may have weakened the chances of building up capacity to manage other forms of rent processes in areas critical to Tanzania's growth prospects. Further, Tanzania's capacities to reduce certain forms of rent seeking are not simply about transparency and accountability but also relate to underlying political features of Tanzania. The underlying political drivers of rent seeking are important to understand in order to identify alternative strategies of growth-enhancing governance reform.

Perhaps the most important area where rent reduction strategies appear to have had adverse effects on developing the capacity to manage vital rent processes is in technology acquisition, in particular in manufacturing. As in most developing countries, trade policy has become the central focus of industrialization. Tanzanian manufacturing suffered severe disinvestment for most of the period of liberalization but started to pick up from the late 1990s.

However this subsequent growth was overwhelmingly in low value added manufacturing. Most of the previous tools of industrial policy to encourage diversification and productivity growth were jettisoned as cumulative reforms have restricted the role of the state to provide, at best, a much narrower range of trade related incentives to the manufacturing sector. The major initiative in this area was the introduction of Economic Processing Zones (EPZs) in 2002 and the launch of the Mini-Tiger Plan in December 2004.

The EPZs initiative suffered from a number of critical limitations. This was partly because while the legal framework for the provision of incentives was in place, the state was not able to ensure the quality and reliability of services available in the EPZs. In 2005, of the three EPZs established in Dar es Salaam, only one had sufficient infrastructure. Basic facilities such as electricity and roads were lacking in the other two (World Bank, 2005). Unreliable power and water supplies and undependable infrastructure, expensive administration costs and high raw material costs were listed as reasons for the lack of investment in these EPZs (World Bank, 2005). The central state was clearly aware of these deficiencies but lacked the political capability to induce the appropriate agencies of the state to provide the required services.

Another area where the state appears to lack essential capabilities for managing rent processes is in the vital area of natural resources. Natural resources potentially generate significant rents and African states need to develop capabilities for negotiating a fair share of these rents for the national economy and for managing the revenues coming from natural resources for long-term economic development. While the Tanzanian investment framework for natural resources offered relatively secure property rights and low taxes and did attract a large inflow of FDI into the sector, there are serious concerns that the state was too generous in its terms and agreed to a very low share of the rents for the domestic economy (Butler, 2004). While government revenues have increased from mining, they are still relatively low at around 3 per cent of GDP and significantly behind the target of 10 per cent of GDP. In 2006 the government launched a review of the terms offered to mining companies. Subsequently there were a number of 'goodwill' side payments by the mining companies to the government (Mines and Communities, 2007) and in March 2007 the review concluded that there was no basis for a change in the terms applicable to foreign investors in the mining sector.

There has also been little progress on the generation of backward and forward linkages from the mining sector, despite the intentions expressed in the Mining Policy. The aim was to expand the lapidary industry to encourage higher value added activities. The policy faced critical problems in terms of implementation. The intention to impose a tax on the export of uncut Tanzanite was not seen through. Previous initiatives to promote lapidary activities such as the 1996 government regulation which sought to require all foreign dealers to set up lapidary operations also failed. Further, the intention to grant EPZ status to lapidary industries has not received the required practical support from the government (Lange, 2006).

Another crucial area where governance capabilities need to be developed is for managing the rents associated with land policy. The government introduced a legal framework for land which attempted to address the dual challenges of securing social justice for small holders and traditional land-owners while creating an efficient market for land. These competing pressures meant that the implementation of the new land policy has been quite confused and in reality 'land reform' has often been occurring through the actions of private individuals engaging in illegal or quasi-legal non-market transfers with local political support, but without the direct oversight or planning of the central state. These types of transfers are clearly a variant of primitive accumulation. Over the period of liberalization local level struggles over land have become more important as accumulation strategies have shifted downwards as the economic activities of the central state have been reduced (Gibbon, 1995; Kelsall, 2000).

Thus, village level elites, working with individual central state politicians have often used the new laws which strengthen Village Council control over community based lands to transfer property rights to new investors. The lack of oversight means that these transfers have not necessarily been in line with Tanzania's development plans. As we described earlier, there are good theoretical reasons to expect these land transfers at early stages of development to have a large non-market element. The real question for countries like Tanzania is whether these transfers are likely to lead to the eventual emergence of productive sectors and the social cost of achieving such a transformation.

The political context

The apparent capacity of the Tanzanian state to control or limit some forms of rents while struggling to manage other rent processes relates both to the policy imperatives it has worked under, but also point to underlying institutional and political opportunities and challenges for the state. One of the most important features about Tanzania's political economy, which marks it out from many other African countries, is the relatively high degree of institutional and political coordination within the state. This is largely related to the history of the ruling political party, the CCM, which came to power as the Tanganyika National Union (TANU) after an anti-colonial struggle that swept it into office in 1961. In 1963 President Nyerere announced that Tanzania would become a one party state under TANU. The control of the party over the state was achieved through three main methods. First, the party was institutionalized from the central National Executive Committee (NEC) down to rural communities with the establishment of 10-cell party units at the village level. Second, the party penetrated the state bureaucracy so that the entire civil service was in effect at the direction of the party (Goulbourne, 1979). Since the introduction of multi-party politics in 1992 there has been a formal de-linking of the party from the state administration; however, in practice the two are still very much intertwined (Kelsall, 2003).

The third reason was the fact that other institutions which could have become oppositional centres of power, such as co-operatives and the army were integrated into the party.

The apparent party strength also relates to the fact that opposition from CCM factions within parliament was muted due to the punitive mechanisms available to the party whip (Mmuya, 1998) and the fact that most of the important decisions on rents occurred outside parliamentary debate. Methods of elite control within the party were very strong. The NEC and the Central Committee took on the role of controlling the elite within the party. The Central Committee controlled party patronage through monitoring the activities of members and recommending appointments and removals of party officers or even expulsion of members (Van Cranenburg, 1990; Skinlo, 2007). Tight elite control even at the very top is evident from the fact that there have been quite regular culls of senior members of cabinet and the party if they were found to have been engaged in corruption during the liberalization period.

The advent of multiparty elections has not threatened the hegemonic position of the CCM within the state. In fact, CCM has increased its control in each round of multi-party elections. Over time, the opposition parties have suffered from a lack of funding and internal divisions and have received a lower percentage of the vote in each subsequent national election. The CCM has increased its parliamentary representation from 78 per cent in the first multiparty elections in 1995 to 87 per cent in 2005. The well developed and inclusive institutional structures of the CCM party have been able to largely contain factional competition. This gives the state a degree of central political control that has allowed it to pursue rent reduction in certain areas, without threatening the political position of the CCM party. Reducing rent seeking in public finances also presented a large payoff to the central state in terms of increased aid flows directly through the budget which made it worth while for the state to pursue this agenda.

Beyond these institutional reasons there are also reasons related to Tanzania's wider social and economic structure. The low level of rural economic differentiation during the socialist Ujamaa period and the lack of industrialization led to more muted factional competition as the rural elite and intermediate classes that often play the role of political entrepreneurs were less strong in Tanzania. In a longer historical perspective, the comparatively short period of struggle for independence and its predominantly peaceful nature circumscribed the legacy of political organization in Tanzania. The more subdued level of political organization outside the structures of the CCM is also part of the reason why opposition parties have had very little impact on the strength of the CCM within the state. Within the CCM this also means that power within the party is more diffuse and no one faction can raise enough political support to completely dominate other factions within the party.

The diffuse power structure within the CCM is one of the reasons why power within the party seems to be centralized in Tanzania, as there appear to be few solid blocks of opposition within the party. However, while factions are weak, the centre seems to lack power when it comes to overruling internal factions that coalesce to protect other forms of rent and transfers. This is evident from some of the cases of grand corruption that have come to light where the top leadership was not able to override networks within the party who supported deals that were manifestly bad for the interests of the country and indeed for the leadership (Khan and Gray, 2006).

The capacity of the state to manage rents related to land and industrial policy are complicated by the historically difficult relationship between the CCM and the business sector. Prior to independence the party was led by quite a narrow section of intermediate class groups who entrenched their power through the party-state during the Ujamaa socialist period (Shivji, 1976). During this period, the party officially disavowed capitalist development in its pursuit of a more egalitarian socialist economy. The private business sector which was dominated by foreign capitalists and the Asian-Tanzanian commercial class was effectively cut out of the extensive rents created during Ujamaa while the nascent rural capitalist class was suppressed through the policy of villagization and the interdiction of independent co-operatives.

While the state's attitude to the private sector has changed dramatically during the liberalization period, the domestic African capitalist class is still very small and many of the new growth sectors, such as mining, are dominated by foreign capital. The links between the private sector and the Party are becoming increasingly evident (Kelsall, 2003) yet the state's management of rents and transfers to support Tanzania's domestic businesses remain politically complicated. Further, while the state appears to have been successful in terms of offering certain forms of subsidies and incentives to attract foreign capital, this has mainly remained in profitable areas such as natural resources and some low value added manufacturing. To bring about a shift into more productive activities would require the state to engage in a more complex system of encouragement and disciplining of domestic capitalists. These governance capabilities are arguably vital for long-term economic development, but the political space for it has to be created internally and is likely to be opposed by powerful donors.

Conclusions

Good governance reforms are based on theoretical propositions that are unrealistic for most if not all developing countries. However, some developing countries like Tanzania have done well with good governance reforms for a while because reforms of public finances allowed donors to pump significantly greater aid flows through national budgets. In addition, more transparent protection for foreign investors allowed greater FDI in natural resources. The question though is whether domestic productive capacities are being significantly enhanced. The implementation of good governance reforms was supposed to make the economy as a whole more efficient, benefiting all sectors through greater market efficiency. There is little evidence of such a broad based economic takeoff in countries like Tanzania. The development of a domestic African capitalism with local entrepreneurs who are able to compete in global markets is not much in evidence.

The historical evidence of sustained development and the analysis of heterodox economics suggests there are good reasons why markets by themselves are unlikely to result in the development of national capitalism. This is because markets in developing countries face significant market failures. Domestic capitalists with limited initial capabilities are unlikely to be able to access capital markets to finance relatively long periods of learning, or to acquire the assets and land they require in relatively inefficient asset markets. Addressing these market failures requires high levels of governance capabilities of a very different type. We have described these as growth-enhancing governance capabilities. There is no blueprint for these capabilities because the appropriate capabilities depend on the specific market failures that particular countries face, but also on the political constraints that determine the types of interventions that are likely to work in different contexts.

Interestingly, many features of Tanzania's political system are relatively favourable because of its relatively successful history of nation-building and party building. Despite this, the internal factions of the ruling party appear to be diffuse and difficult to discipline. The development of significant rent management capabilities would require improved capabilities to discipline internal political factions so that the allocation of some significant rents can be made on explicitly developmental criteria. This in turn requires a very different discourse about governance priorities so that the political consensus could slowly be constructed to allow some of these growth-enhancing governance capabilities to be strengthened. The real danger of the good governance agenda is that the space for these important governance discussions has been significantly reduced by defining good governance as *the* governance reform agenda for developing countries.

References

Amsden, Alice 1989. *Asia's Next Giant: South Korea and Late Industrialization.* Oxford: Oxford University Press.

Bates, Robert H. 1984. *Markets and States in Tropical Africa: The Political Basis of Agricultural Policies.* Berkeley: University of California Press.

—— 1989. *Beyond the Miracle of the Market: The Political Economy of Agrarian Development in Kenya.* Cambridge: Cambridge University Press.

—— 2001. *Prosperity and Violence: The Political Economy of Development.* New York: W.W. Norton.

Bevan, David 2001. *Tanzania Pubic Expenditure Review 2000/2001: The Fiscal Deficit and Sustainability of Fiscal Policy.* PER Working Group: Dar es Salaam.

Bhagwati, Jagdish N. 1982. Directly Unproductive, Profit-seeking (DUP) Activities, *Journal of Political Economy* 90 (5): 988–1002.

Bigsten, Arne and Anders Danielson 2001. *Is the Ugly Duckling Finally Growing Up?* A Report for the OECD project "Emerging Africa" No. 120. Nordiska Afrikainstitutet: Uppsala.

Brenner, Robert 1985 The Agrarian Roots of European Capitalism, in T.H. Aston and C. H. E. Philpin, (eds) *The Brenner Debate: Agrarian Class Structure and Economic Development in Pre-Industrial Europe*. Cambridge: Cambridge University Press.

Butler, Paula 2004. Tanzania: Liberalisation of Investment and the Mining Sector – Analysis of the Content and Certain Implications of the Tanzania 1998 Mining Act, in Bonnie Campell (ed.) *Regulating Mining in Africa: For Whose Benefit? Discussion Paper 26*, Uppsala: Nordiska Afrikainstitutet.

Fjeldstad, Odd-Helge 2002. *Fighting Fiscal Corruption: The Case of the Tanzania Revenue Authority*. Working Paper No. 2002: 3. Chr. Michelsen Institute (CMI): Bergen.

Gibbon, Peter (ed.) 1995. *Liberalised Development in Tanzania*. Uppsala: Nordiska Afrikainstitutet.

Goulbourne, Henry 1979. The Role of the Political Party in Tanzania since the Arusha Declaration, in Henry Goulbourne (ed.) *Politics and State in the Third World*, London: Macmillan.

Hyden, Goran and Donald C. Williams 1994. A Community Model of African Politics: Illustrations from Nigeria and Tanzania, *Comparative Studies in Society and History* 36 (1): 68–96.

Kelsall, Tim 2000. Governance, Local Politics and Districtization in Tanzania, *African Affairs* 99 (397): 533–51.

—— 2003. Governance, Democracy and Recent Political Struggles in Tanzania, *Commonwealth and Comparative Politics* 41 (2): 55–82.

Khan, Mushtaq H. 2000a. Rent-seeking as Process, in Mushtaq H. Khan and K.S. Jomo (eds) *Rents, Rent-Seeking and Economic Development: Theory and Evidence in Asia*, Cambridge: Cambridge University Press.

—— 2000b. Rents, Efficiency and Growth, in Mushtaq H. Khan, and K.S. Jomo (eds) *Rents, Rent-Seeking and Economic Development: Theory and Evidence in Asia*, Cambridge: Cambridge University Press.

—— 2004. State Failure in Developing Countries and Strategies of Institutional Reform, in Bertil Tungodden, Nicholas Stern and Ivar Kolstad (eds) *Annual World Bank Conference on Development Economics Europe (2003): Toward Pro-Poor Policies: Aid Institutions and Globalization*, Proceedings of Annual World Bank Conference on Development Economics, Oxford: Oxford University Press and World Bank. Available HTTP: <http://www-wds.worldbank.org/servlet/WDS_I Bank_Servlet?pcont = details&eid = 000160016_20040518162841>

—— 2005. Markets, States and Democracy: Patron-Client Networks and the Case for Democracy in Developing Countries, *Democratization* 12 (5): 705–25.

—— 2006a. Determinants of Corruption in Developing Countries: the Limits of Conventional Economic Analysis, in Susan Rose-Ackerman (ed.) *International Handbook on the Economics of Corruption*, Cheltenham: Edward Elgar.

—— 2006b. *Governance and Anti-Corruption Reforms in Developing Countries: Policies, Evidence and Ways Forward*. G-24 Discussion Paper Series: Research Papers for the Intergovernmental Group of Twenty-Four on International Monetary Affairs and Development No. 42. United Nations Conference on Trade and Development: New York and Geneva. Available HTTP: <http://www.unctad.org/en/docs/gdsmdpbg2420064_en.pdf>

—— 2007. Governance, Economic Growth and Development since the 1960s, in José Antonio Ocampo, K.S. Jomo and Rob Vos (eds) *Growth Divergences: Explaining Differences in Economic Performance*, Hyderabad, London and Penang: Orient Longman, Zed Books and Third World Network. Available HTTP: <http://www.un.org/esa/desa/papers/2007/wp54_2007.pdf>

—— 2008. Governance and Development: The Perspective of Growth-Enhancing Governance, in GRIPS Development Forum (ed.) *Diversity and Complementarity in Development Aid: East Asian Lessons for African Growth*, Tokyo: National Graduate Institute for Policy Studies. Available HTTP: <http://mercury.soas.ac.uk/users/mk17/Docs/GRIPS.pdf>

Khan, Mushtaq H. and Hazel Gray 2006. *State Weakness in Developing Countries and Strategies of Institutional Reform: Operational Implications for Anti-Corruption Policy and a Case Study of Tanzania.* Paper commissioned by the Department for International Development (DFID). School of Oriental and African Studies (SOAS) University of London: London. Available HTTP: <http://mercury.soas.ac.uk/users/mk17/Docs/Anti%20Corruption%20Policy%20and%20Tanzania%20Khan%20Gray%201.pdf>

Krueger, Anne O. 1974. The Political Economy of the Rent-Seeking Society, *American Economic Review* 64 (3): 291–303.

Lange, Siri 2006. *Benefit Streams from Mining in Tanzania: Case Studies from Geita and Mererani.* CMI Report No. R 2006:11. Chr. Michelsen Institute: Bergen.

Levin, Jorgen 2005. *Taxation in Tanzania – Revenue Performance and Incidence.* Country Economic Report No. 2005: 4. Swedish International Development Cooperation Agency (SIDA): Stockholm.

Mamdani, Mahmood 1996. *Citizen and Subject: Contemporary Africa and the Legacy of Late Colonialism.* London: James Currey.

Médard, Jean-François 2002. Corruption in the Neo-Patrimonial States of Sub-Saharan Africa, in Arnold J. Heidenheimer and Michael Johnston (eds) *Political Corruption: Concepts and Contexts*, Third Edition, New Brunswick: Transaction Publishers.

Milgrom, Paul and John Roberts 1992. *Economics, Organization and Management.* New Jersey: Prentice Hall.

Mines and Communities 2007. *Africa Update 30th March 2007*, 17th December 2007. Available HTTP: <http://www.minesandcommunities.org/Action/press1420.htm>

Mkandawire, Thandika 2001. Thinking About Developmental States in Africa, *Cambridge Journal of Economics* 25 (3): 289–314.

Mkapa, Benjamin William 2008. *Leadership for Growth, Development and Poverty Reduction: An African Viewpoint and Experience.* Commission on Growth and Development Working Paper No. 8. The World Bank: Washington DC.

Mmuya, Max 1998. *Tanzania Political Reform in Eclipse: Crisis and Cleavages in Political Parties.* Friedrich Ebert Stiftung: Dar es Salaam.

North, Douglass C. 1990. *Institutions, Institutional Change and Economic Performance.* Cambridge: Cambridge University Press.

North, Douglass C. and Robert P. Thomas 1973. *The Rise of the Western World: A New Economic History.* Cambridge: Cambridge University Press.

Olson, Mancur 1982. *The Rise and Decline of Nations.* London: Yale University Press.

—— 1997. The New Institutional Economics: The Collective Choice Approach to Economic Development in Christopher Clague (ed.) *Institutions and Economic Development*, Baltimore: Johns Hopkins University Press.

—— 2000. Dictatorship, Democracy and Development, in Mancur Olson and Satu Kähkönen (eds) *A Not-so-Dismal Science: A Broader View of Economies and Societies*, Oxford: Oxford University Press.

Posner, Richard A. 1975. The Social Costs of Monopoly and Regulation, *Journal of Political Economy* 83 (4): 807–27.

Qian, Yingi 1993. How Reform Worked in China, in Rodrik, Dani *In Search of Prosperity: Analytical Narratives on Economic Growth*, Princeton: Princeton University Press.

Sachs, Jeffrey D., John W. McArthur, Guido Schmidt-Traub, Margaret Kruk, Chandrika Bahadur, Michael Faye and Gordon McCord 2004. Ending Africa's Poverty Trap, *Brookings Papers on Economic Activity* 1: 117–240.

Shivji, Issa 1976. *Class Struggles in Tanzania*. London: Heinemann.

Skinlo, Tor-Einar Holvik 2007. *"Old" and "New" Authoritarianism in Tanzania – Theoretical, Methodological and Empirical Considerations*. Department of Comparative Politics. The University of Bergen: Bergen.

Transparency International 2008. Corruption Perceptions Index 2008. Available HTTP: <http://www.transparency.org/policy_research/surveys_indices/cpi/2008>

United Republic of Tanzania 1996. *The Report of the Presidential Inquiry into Corruption in Tanzania*. Volume I and II. Government Printers: Dar es Salaam.

—— 2001. *Tanzania Assistance Strategy*. Government of Tanzania: Dar es Salaam.

—— 2003. *National Trade Policy: Trade Policy for a Competitive Economy and Export Led Growth*. Government of Tanzania: Dar es Salaam.

—— 2004. *Tanzania's Third Phase Government Fight Against Corruption: Implementing The National Anti-Corruption Strategy and Action Plans 2001–2004*. Good Governance Co-ordination Unit, President's Office. Government Printers: Dar es Salaam.

—— 2005. *Tanzania Assistance Strategy Implementation Report 2002/03–2004/05*, November 2005. Government Printers: Dar es Salaam.

—— 2007. *Report of the Controller and Auditor General On the Financial Statements of Public Authorities and Other Bodies for the Financial year ended 30th June 2007*. National Auit Office: Dar es Salaam.

Utz, Robert J. (ed.) 2007. *Sustaining and Sharing Economic Growth in Tanzania*. Washington DC: The World Bank.

Van Cranenburg, Oda 1990. *The Widening Gyre: The Tanzanian One-Party State and Policy Towards Rural Co-operatives*. Leiden: Eubron Delft.

Wade, Robert 1990. *Governing the Market: Economic Theory and the Role of Government in East Asian Industrialization*. Princeton: Princeton University Press.

Williamson, Oliver E. 1985. *The Economic Institutions of Capitalism*. New York: Free Press.

World Bank 2001. *Tanzania at the Turn of the Century: From Reform to Sustained Growth and Poverty Reduction*. World Bank Country Study. Washington DC: The World Bank.

—— 2005. *Report on the Diagnostic Trade Integration Study, Prepared under the Integrated Framework for Trade-Related Technical Assistance to Least Developed Countries*. Dar es Salaam: The World Bank.

—— 2008. *Worldwide Governance Indicators (WGI)*. Washington DC: The World Bank Institute.

19 Management of the CFA franc in West Africa

From an imposed extroversion to chosen extroversion?

Kako Nubukpo[1]

Introduction[2]

The African Financial Community (CFA – communauté financière africaine) franc is a striking illustration of the continuing colonial and post-colonial linkage between France and the franc zone, an area essentially made up of its former West and Central African colonies. This currency is particular in that it was created without any prior economic convergence between the nations which share it and that its daily use defies current transparency regulations of international monetary and financial authorities. The lack of any social control from the populations which use the currency as well as the inflexibility of its peg to the euro raise the question of its role in the continued extroversion of African economies and their weak structural growth.

The case of the West African Economic and Monetary Union (UEMOA – Union Economique et Monétaire Ouest Africaine),[3] a grouping of eight States which, among others, all use the CFA franc and the Central Bank of West African States (BCEAO – Banque Centrale des États de l'Afrique de l'Ouest) is striking: indeed, never before has an economic and monetary union followed so strictly policies inspired by monetarism, referred to as 'competitive deflation'. In the UEMOA, the objective of the monetary policy led by the BCEAO is to ensure price stability with the aim of preserving the currency's internal and external value. Since 1989 the monetary policy has been more market-driven, entrenching the option of indirect control of bank liquidity. The interest rate, becoming the preferred instrument of monetary policy, is therefore given a primary role, especially since credit control was abandoned in January 1994.

The present article aims to provide a coherent framework with which to explain the main paradoxes of the monetary policy conducted by the BCEAO, the practical consequence of which is the weak economic growth experienced by the UEMOA zone.

Extrovert management of economic and monetary policy

The history of monetary relations between France and Africa[4] highlights the fact that political rationality always dominated economic rationality in the strictest sense: before the creation of the UMOA in 1962, it suggests the perfect congruency between the need to export low cost raw materials from the colonies to Metropolitan France and the gradual build-up of the CFA franc's monopoly over endogenous African currencies (Julienne, 1988, Diallo, 2005). However, after its creation, the UMOA was above all about maintaining the umbilical cord between France and its newly independent colonies. This is evidenced by the fact that the most nationalist among francophone African leaders at the time made a point of either not entering the Union (as was the case for Guinea under Sekou Touré and Togo under Sylvanus Olympio), or to leave it soon after its creation (as for Mali under Modibo Keita who left the UMOA in July 1962).

The failure to define economic convergence criteria and the lack of proper thought to what should constitute an optimal monetary zone – which, let us recall, precedes the economic and monetary union – confirms the UMOA/UEMOA's[5] eminently political character right from its inception. By the time that UEMOA countries had to undergo structural adjustment programmes in the 1980s, a tacit, if not formal, collusion was established between France, anxious to show its independence from the Bretton Woods institutions, and the authorities of the African countries in the franc zone, in order to reject the idea of a devaluation of the CFA franc and opt instead for a policy of 'real adjustment'. The UMOA/UEMOA countries, due to their disastrous economic fundamentals, were forced to implement painful reforms without being able to benefit from the level of freedom that monetary flexibility offers, while having to compete with English- and Portuguese-speaking West African countries with which they had long historical economic ties.

The 'monetary adjustment' or devaluation of the CFA franc in January 1994 was, at least on the surface, the first deed of renunciation from France, now forced to adhere to the diktat of the Bretton Woods institutions, in line with what is commonly called 'the Abidjan doctrine' (Hibou, 1995).[6] In fact, France was once again preserving its interests, which now coincided with a more or less openly accepted neo-liberalist approach, as evidenced by the independence of the Banque de France in 1992 and the signing of the Maastricht treaty, precursor to the Central European Bank and the euro, all of which took place in the context of a redirecting of government development aid towards Central and Eastern European countries (CECE).

Likewise, the West African monetary authorities and heads of States of the UEMOA zone also benefited from the double 'shield' of the IMF and French Treasury by choosing to position themselves as 'good pupils of the monetary orthodoxy' – the *ne plus ultra* of the African elite's extroversion – rather than bear the risk and responsibility of freedom of mind by opting for an endogenous thinking process towards an appropriate monetary policy in

West Africa. Seen as proof of this is the contrast between the publicity surrounding the planned creation of a single currency for all of West Africa (French, English and Portuguese-speaking countries) by 2005 under the auspices of the ECOWAS,[7] and the complete inertia on the part of West African governments on this matter for the past 10 years.

UEMOA's current monetary authorities tend to follow a policy of combating inflation caused by non-monetary external shocks (for example, inflation imported from France, caused by climatic disasters or rising oil prices), with tools adapted to heavily monetarised economies. Likewise, the liberalisation of the banking sector in the UEMOA, in a context of overliquidity and extroversion of retail banks, contribute to weakening the effectiveness of monetary policy. In addition, the [inflexibility] cost of the CFA's fixed peg to the euro as an impediment to growth cannot be overlooked.

UEMOA monetary management system

The main aim of monetary policy as carried out by the BCEAO is to preserve the currency's internal and external value. This policy has undergone several transformations, in 1975, October 1989 and October 1993, aligning UEMOA's new monetary management system closer to market mechanisms, thereby favouring indirect liquidity control methods.

The BCEAO's monetary policy (2002, a) is based on the use of the emitting bank's own key interest rates, on a renovated monetary market and on the liberalisation of bank conditions. In support of these tools, a system of minimum reserves makes it possible to modify the banking system's behaviour and act on the cost of credit. The UMOA/UEMOA's experience of monetary integration is atypical inasmuch as the establishment of a common currency in May 1962 preceded the realisation of the economic conditions for its sustainability, especially the effective existence of prescribed regulations for macroeconomic convergence and good management. The existing monetary cooperation with France is illustrated by a mechanism referred to as the 'transactions account'[8] which contributes to guaranteeing a fixed parity between the CFA franc and the euro. In this context, the search for price stability is presented as an objective likely to ensure the long term sustainability of the exchange rate and the competitiveness of the UEMOA economies. Furthermore, with its heavy exposure to external supply side shocks (climatic hazards, volatile commodity prices), the franc zone has had to face various asymmetric fluctuations to which the common monetary policy has had to react.

A study[9] was carried out to describe and evaluate the impact of the BCEAO's key interest rate movements on growth and inflation between 1989 and 1999 (Nubukpo, 2002). Given the low impact of the BCEAO's monetary policy on growth and inflation within the UEMOA, its main findings call for an improved understanding of how monetary policy translates into the real sector within the UEMOA environment. It also calls for an honest appraisal of the implications of the institutional framework when evaluating the performance of the UEMOA's monetary policy, while highlighting the paradoxes brought about by this context.

The absence of a growth objective in the BCEAO's missions

The BCEAO chose an inflation target of 2 per cent as the main objective for UEMOA's monetary policy.[10] This choice is a direct result of the pegging of the CFA franc to the euro, as this same target is set by the European Central Bank (ECB). However, in a fixed foreign exchange regime with free movement of capital, it is impossible for the BCEAO to substantially deviate for any length of time from the monetary policy followed by the anchor zone, namely the euro, as is evidenced by Mundell's 'triangle of impossibility' theory. This institutional link, inherited from the cooperation agreements between France and the UMOA/UEMIA, therefore restricts the BCEAO's capacity to set its monetary policy objective independently. Indeed, in a fixed foreign exchange regime inflation contributes, through the loss of competitiveness it generates, to the gradual deterioration of external accounts and the overvaluation of the exchange rate, thereby weakening the parity between the currencies.

Of course, the inflation target of 2 per cent chosen by the BCEAO, identical to that of the European Central Bank, seems intrinsically linked to the constraints that go with a fixed exchange rate between the two zones. It cannot be considered problematic if one assumes that 'what is good for the euro zone is good for the CFA zone'. Yet this assumption, precisely, could be wrong: while the inflation target could be pertinent for the euro zone, (even though it is heavily criticised by Keynesian economists),[11] it may prove most unsuitable for the UEMOA zone. Indeed, the challenges faced by these developing countries are much more complex and the currency's potential contribution to achieving economic growth should be given more thought. The setting of such an inflation target may indeed appear excessively restrictive for economies which require GDP growth rates in the order of 7 per cent to reach the millennium goals (MDG), in particular the pledge of reducing poverty by half by 2015.

It is surprising that the Central Bank of the UEMOA zone (BCEAO) limits itself to controlling inflation, with no concern for either economic growth or development. There is certainly no lack of empirical research on the subject. The debate surrounding the Phillips curve, for example, has been fuelled by the simultaneous pursuit of both objectives, i.e. the necessity to establish an arbitrage between inflation and economic growth. Moreover, various empirical studies, carried out particularly on economies in transition (Calvo and Coricelli, 1993, Coricelli, 1998, Ould-Ahmed, 1999) demonstrated that restrictive monetary policies had a recessive macroeconomic impact[12] while neo-structuralist models (Van Wijnbergen, 1983, a and b) insist on the negative side-effects of restrictive monetary policies in developing economies.

The BCEAO therefore seems to favour an exchange rate objective to the detriment of economic growth. Seen from such an angle, it is a currency board rather than an actual central bank as it does not have control of its monetary policy. Therefore, the question is to understand why the UEMOA authorities made this choice. The answer is two-fold. First, the absence of any independent management of the currency and exchange rate allows for certain levels of intellectual laziness and routine to prevail – bureaucratic behaviour *par excellence*, brought to light in the case of the UEMOA by Nguessan (1996). Second, UEMOA's monetary policies seem to have widely opted for philosophy of 'extroversion',[13] by developing an almost visceral attachment to the idea of a 'strong' CFA franc which would indicate the good health of the West African economies and their conformity to the international macroeconomic imperatives. Therefore, at the creation of the UMOA in 1962, shortly after independence, the choice of a fixed exchange rate between the French franc and the CFA franc, whether freely made or imposed, was never questioned. The conclusion one can draw from this is that the desire to be pegged to a strong currency, which can be interpreted as a residual attachment to the empire, was symbolised, even openly proclaimed, through a formal monetary link with the former colonial power, France. Here, the extroversion is directly evidenced by the fact that the external monetary link appears, ultimately, to take precedence over internal relations, as indicated by the priority given to the exchange rate objective over the growth objective. More precisely, the primacy given to a 'proper' kind of international integration, symbolised by this very specific monetary relation, has led to internal relations being managed in such a way that it does not endanger the stability and parity of the exchange rate. De facto, this choice perpetuates the primacy of consumption over production, the implicit premium in favour of consumption, which moreover, is imported consumption, yet another form of the preference for an extrovert management of economic relations.

Excessive foreign exchange reserves

The 2005 franc Zone report[14] quotes a record figure of 6,300 billion CFAF of reserves held by the central banks of the franc zone with the French Treasury. For BCEAO alone, these reserves represented more than 3,000 billion CFAF, amounting to a monetary emission cover rate of more than 110 per cent! It is important to note that the 'transactions account' agreements which tie the BCEAO to the French treasury only require a monetary emission cover rate of 20 per cent. As a consequence of this situation, the BCEAO is willingly giving up considerable financial means that could be useful for growth within the UEMOA, in favour of holding excessive foreign exchange reserves, the most obvious result being the improvement of its cash flow position through the income produced by its deposits. Some economists such as Nguessan, 1996, used the theory of bureaucracy in an attempt to explain the rationale of this behaviour. In the absence of any real control over the BCEAO's management, the UEMIA's monetary authorities were more interested in maintaining personal privileges than in maximising collective well-being.

It is, however, important to take this further and use the framework of political economic analysis to attempt to provide a plausible additional explanation to this paradox (Hibou, 1996, 1997). When looking at the apathetical responses to the mishandlings of the transactions accounts, what appears to be at stake is perhaps not France's support to a group of developing countries towards which it feels a particular responsibility as a result of its colonial history, nor a deliberate desire to maintain a 'French preserve', the weakness of which paradoxically requires the establishment of large exchange reserves as a precaution. It is rather, as we see it, the logical consequence of an extrovert management of the UEMOA's economies. Indeed, the monetary authorities of the zone seem to dread only one thing – the devaluation of CFA franc. The devaluation of 1994 was perceived as a blow to their image of 'modern' central bankers, obsessed as they are, in line with their European counterparts, with the need for a 'strong' currency, combating inflation, rejecting any counter-cyclic character of monetary policy and benefiting, in addition, from the favourable import conditions offered by an overvalued and stable currency. It is not possible to understand otherwise why the current exchange rate between the CFA franc and the euro persists, even though all serious analysts of the franc zone, in keeping with the 'letter of the Agence Française de Développement economists' of July 2006, have been in agreement for several years that this exchange rate seriously harms the competitiveness of the agricultural sector, especially the West African cotton sector badly affected by a long-term global decline (Nubukpo and Keita, 2006). As a result of the depreciation of the US dollar against the euro, the CFA franc is now a vastly overvalued currency for the UEMOA economies, particularly when considering their overall weakness and the challenges that they are facing.

The illusion of the 'final victory' against a non-monetary form of inflation, maintained by the monetary authorities of the UEMOA, and the holding of excessive foreign exchange reserves by the BCEAO with the French treasury, form part of the same logic – that of a double submission, initially enforced but increasingly voluntary, of the public authorities of the UEMOA to the International Monetary Fund on the one hand and to France on the other, with no regard for the interests of the populations of their countries. It is otherwise difficult to explain the 'conspiracy of silence' which currently prevails, when confronted with the internal and external inefficiency of the monetary policy used within the UEMOA and with the absurd character of the link between the CFA franc and the French treasury (budgetary agreements), long after the French franc ceased to exist, and when France's monetary policy is now managed in Frankfurt (headquarters of the ECB).

The cartel of French banks

Another motive for the inefficiency of the monetary policy carried out by the BCEAO is the heavily oligopolistic structure of the UEMOA's banking sector, causing a degree of viscosity of the banks' overdraft interest rates (Diop, 1998). UEMOA's banks do not actually need the BCEAO to roll-over loans – not only are they over-liquid (400 billion CFA francs), but they also overtly display cooperative behaviour. An overt system of mutual assistance (through the interbank market of the UEMOA) and tacit collusion (hence the expression 'French bank cartel' commonly used among UEMOA financiers) has established itself between the banking institutions which are essentially subsidiaries of large French banking groups and whose main objective is to maximise short-term profits. This leads them to favour the granting of credit to highly profitable newly privatised, or about to be privatised state companies, while reducing long term financing commitments, and/or reducing their exposure to small and medium enterprises. In this light, the extremely low number of subregional banks operating within the UEMOA, and the bankruptcy of 'development' banks overcome by chronic bad management, acts as a deterrent to the establishment of a true partnership for the development of the region.

Hardly any of the banks have to follow the lead of BCEAO when it lowers its key interest rates. Whenever needed, they can rely on their head offices in Paris for any foreign exchange transactions, and only drip-feed foreign exchange back home, applying a technique referred to as *novation*.[15] Once again, this demonstrates the extrovert character of the zone's monetary and financial system, here in the form the autonomous behaviour of its banking actors, constrained as they are by international standards defined outside their area of intervention. The way the UEMOA's banking system operates bears a striking resemblance to the historical trading economy, when Africa provided commodities for its European colonial masters, while banks were there to ensure that financial transactions, the counterparty of material transactions, were conducted properly.

The external inefficiency of UEMOA's monetary policy

The external inefficiency is linked to the inadequacy between the institutional architecture of the UEMOA zone (the CFA franc's peg to the euro) and the objectives of any economic policy in economic and monetary union (countercyclic function, reaction to asymmetrical shocks, economies' need for convergence). Indeed, in a context of free movement of capital and a fixed exchange rate, any 'small' economy's anchoring to a much larger zone means the monetary policy of the 'small' economy will lose its autonomy (Mundell, 1961). Therefore, the leaders of the BCEAO are made to follow the movements of the European Central Bank's (ECB) key interest rates even when the economic cycle of the UEMOA does not justify such a movement. At best, this policy is inefficient; at worst, it is harmful. In the first quarter of 2000, when the BCEAO was forced to increase its key interest rates to follow an increase made by the ECB for internal reasons within the euro zone, it had to issue a press release requesting the UEMOA's retail banks not to pass on the increase to their overdraft rates!

The apparent schizophrenia of the UEMOA's monetary authorities becomes particularly clear when the explanatory framework of the pre-eminence of a logic of extroversion is applied: the liberalisation of the financial system and the adoption of international monetary management standards are carried out as much to adhere to the injunctions of the Bretton Woods institutions (1989, then 1994) as to take pride in being a 'credible' monetary zone even though the environmental conditions are not met. To overcome the disastrous consequences of a poorly prepared financial liberalisation, every trick seems to be allowed. This might be illustrated, for example, by the persistence of the 'monetary programme': indeed, before the liberalisation of the financial system, the UEMOA's management of bank credit required the BCEAO to allocate each country with a provisional volume of credit to be granted by the banking system of the said country to its economy over a given year. This practice was put into place every November, during a meeting called the 'monetary programme'. This rightfully consecrated a policy of quantity management, (credit volume allocated to the different national banking systems) in a context where prices (interest rates) had little bearing. Whereas in noting the obvious failure of the financial liberalisation, the 'monetary programme' is still in place and continues to allocate the volume of liquidity to be granted by national banking systems to their economies. We find ourselves, therefore, in a system where price management (interest rates) is theoretically responsible for regulating the volume of bank liquidities, but where in reality the former credit control system persists.

The paradox is striking, as monetary authorities proclaim their liberalism while determining both prices and quantities. This monetary heritage dating back to the colonial period has been maintained by the African leaders of the franc zone. They favour the superiority of international legitimacy over internal legitimacy in terms of standards, ideas and regulations deemed to be 'good', 'fair' or 'legitimate'. This hierarchy carries severe consequences and has led certain economists to ask African authorities to end this 'monetary repression' (Tchundjang Pouemi, 1979) or 'monetary trap' (Monga and Tchatchouang, 1996).

The extraversion of monetary management in the UEMOA zone is only a reflection of the zone's real economies. Indeed, basic, single-produce specialisation of international trade (production and export of unprocessed commodities, cash crops sent to the former colonial power), inherited from colonial times, continues to characterise trade between West Africa and the rest of the world. African cotton-based economies, for example, due to the inertia caused by their extraversion (the UEMOA zone processes less than 5 per cent of its cotton fibre production) are struggling to use agriculture as a vehicle for development, particularly with regard to food sovereignty, despite certain cotton/cereal complementaries. As things stand, the UMEOA zone uses foreign exchange reserves provided by the export of agricultural and mining raw materials (cotton, cacao, gold, etc.) to import essential food products. Importing food is, of course, actually made easier as a result of the CFA franc's peg to the euro. And thus the UEMOA gets trapped into economic dependency, given that the current monetary regime does not serve as a vehicle for development, but rather perpetuates a cycle of dependency on the former colonial power. Moreover, due to the depreciation of the US dollar against the euro/CFA, African cotton sectors have lost between 35 and 40 per cent of their export competitiveness over the past three years. This observation is a measure of the silent conspiracy surrounding the management of the franc zone: indeed, the few economists who feel compelled to question why some of the weakest economies in the world (UEMOA) should be pegged to the strongest currency (euro), merely suggest that the CFA franc be devalued, as in 1994. Yet, economies competing with the UEMOA countries, particularly English-speaking African and Asian economies, which have a floating exchange rate system, needed only to depreciate their currencies in order to solve the price competitiveness issues that were looming on the horizon with UEMOA countries.

Finally, in terms of sovereignty, which includes the right to mint coins and print money, it is surprising that the CFA franc is still physically minted and printed in France in factories in the South-West (Pessac, near Bordeaux in the Aquitaine region) and the centre (Chamallières, near Clermont-Ferrand in the Auvergne). This subcontracting relationship between the BCEAO and the Banque de France can, at the very least, be considered unusual. It is yet another, symbolic manifestation of the UEMOA's economies dependency on the former colonial power. Almost fifty years after becoming independent, it seems surprising that the States of the UEMOA zone would still have not been able to develop the technical expertise, or demonstrate sufficient political will-power, for the minting and printing of CFA Francs to be physically based within the UEMOA zone. Moreover, in light of the difficulties outlined before, in terms of the African franc zone's actual capacity to manage its currency in an endogenous manner, it seems relevant to ask just how opportune a single currency for the UEMOA is, let alone the possibility of a single currency for the whole of the African continent. The challenges to address are numerous, not only in terms of the need for extraversion of the real economy and the currency itself, but also in terms of the type of governance required to manage a single currency for dozens of countries. At this stage, it seems as though these challenges will be very hard to overcome for the current African leadership.

Conclusion: what is the future of the CFA franc?

The resolutely monetarist management of the CFA franc, in an environment to which it is hardly suited, based on the holding of foreign exchange reserves as excessive as they are unnecessary, is becoming increasingly pro-cyclic and is accumulating harmful effects, damaging the prospects of growth within the UEMOA zone. However, a brutal devaluation, such as took place in 1994, would not provide a permanent resolution to the structural problems created by the CFA franc's peg to the euro. Furthermore, this would be difficult to justify in light of the BCEAO's high level of foreign reserves with the French Treasury. Rather, questions should be asked about the relevance of the foreign exchange regime and the costs of an extroverted monetary management to African populations. Indeed, in a strict economic sense, it seems more reasonable to envisage a floating exchange rate system within a certain fluctuation band to be determined between the authorities of the UEMOEA zone and those of the euro zone. This system would have the advantage of ensuring that the BCEAO authorities are given a gradual but proper training in effective monetary management, and to send, through a less rigid exchange rate, regular indications to the people of the countries concerned on the overall state of their economies. Such a system would also cease to favour a privileged, import-hungry urban class currently benefiting from a strong and convertible currency, while the UEMOA's main challenge is to make the millions of small producers who battle daily to survive competition and be self-sufficient.

In order to achieve this, a profound reflection is needed on the nature, contents and pertinence of the monetary cooperation agreements linking France and the countries of the franc zone. More than ever, the question of the coherence of public policies in a context of a multi-faceted extroversion is acutely relevant for the member states of the franc zone.

Notes

1 Associate professor in Economics at the University of Lomé (Togo). Former Head of Department at the Head Offices of the Central Bank of West African States (BCEAO) and Economist at the Centre for International Cooperation in Agronomical Research for Development (CIRAD), Montpellier (France). Contract: nubukpo@cirad.fr
2 The author would like to thank Béatrice Hibou, Olivier Vallée and anonymous reporters for their precious comments and advice on the early versions of this article. However, the author alone is responsible for the opinions expressed in the present documents and for any errors or omissions which it may contain.
3 The UEMOA is made up of eight countries: Benin, Burkina Faso, Ivory Coast, Guinea Bissau, Mali, Niger, Senegal and Togo.
4 Refer to 'Histoire de l'UMOA' issued in three volumes, published in 2000 by the BCEAO and the Memoirs of the first French Governor of the BCEAO Robert Julienne, published in 1988 by *L'Harmattan*.
5 The treaty incorporating the West African Monetary Union (UMOA) dates from May 1962, whereas the treaty which incorporates the UEMOA only dates from January 1994. Contrary to common belief, the UEMOA treaty did not replace that of the UMOA. Both treaties coexist and the UMOA's treaty still serves as a legal basis for strictly monetary issues. However, in the present article we have chosen, except for a few specific cases, to only mention the UEMOA for the reader's

convenience. By using the UEMOA treaty we are able to evoke both the real issues and the monetary and financial issues. Furthermore, it is intended that the two treaties will eventually be unified.

6 The 'Abidjan Doctrine', still referred to as the 'Balladur doctrine', was theorised and above all applied at the beginning of the 1990s when it was admitted that no African country in the franc zone is in a delicate position with the conditionalities of the International Monetary Fund and/or the World Bank would not be able to claim any financial support whatsoever from France.

7 Economic Community of West African States, created in 1975. Regroups all of the 16 West African countries except for Mauritania.

8 To determine the ins and outs of the operation of a 'transactions account' see Hugon (1999, p.19) and Claveranne (2005, p.50).

9 The results of the study were validated by the monetary authorities of the zone and published in the BCEAO's 'Annual Report', 2002b, pp.20–1.

10 The BCEAO claims to be more virtuous than the UEMOA which chose an inflation target of 3 per cent as part of the macroeconomic convergence criteria. We can question why the issuing agent, the BCEAO, has a different inflation target than that given by the UMOA/UEMOA's Council of Ministers, officially responsible for defining the monetary policy of the zone.

11 See Report No. 59 of the Economic Analysis Council (EAC, 2006).

12 In particular, Ould-Ahmed (1999) illustrates this observation through the analysis of two waves of restrictive monetary policies in Russia between 1993 and 1999.

13 Bayart (1999) gives a stimulating view on Africa's 'dependent' extroversion and its consequences on development.

14 For a commentary on this report, see the article entitled '*La zone Franc croule sous l'argent*', S. Gharbi, Jeune Afrique No. 2384, of 17 to 23 September 2006, p. 69.

15 In the UEMOA statutes any bank whose activities generate the acquisition of foreign currencies must repatriate these currencies to the BCEAO in order to increase, if only for a day, the UEMOA's net level of external assets. However, more often that not, the banks of the Union use the argument that they need these currencies at their disposal to carry out any potential transactions which require the exit of currencies from the UEMOA zone, to not perform this repatriation. In doing so, they apply the principle of 'novation', which means that they do not repatriate the balance of their transactions in foreign currencies. This is a flagrant breach of the monetary control regulations in place within the UEMOA.

References

Agence Française de Développement, 2006, 'Quel avenir pour le coton africain ?' *La Lettre des économistes de l'AFD* N§13, Juillet, 11pp.

Banque Centrale des Etats de l'Afrique de l'Ouest (BCEAO), 2000, *Histoire de l'UMOA*, tomes 1 à 3, Editions G. Israël, Paris.

Bayart, J.F., 1999, 'L'Afrique dans le monde : une histoire d'extraversion', *Critique Internationale* no. 5, automne, pp. 97–120.

BCEAO, 2002a, *Evaluation de la mise en oeuvre du dispositif de gestion monétaire de la Banque Centrale des Etats de l'Afrique de l'Ouest et réflexions pour un renforcement de son efficacité*, mimeo, BCEAO, Direction du Crédit, Dakar, Février.

—— , 2002, b, *Rapport Annuel*, Imprimerie de la BCEAO, Dakar, 137pp.

Conseil d'Analyse Economique, 2006, *Politique économique et croissance en Europe*, Rapport no. 59, P. Aghion, E. Cohen et J. Pisani-Ferry, La Documentation Française, Paris, 2006, 305pp.

Calvo, G.A. and Coricelli, F., 1993, 'Output Collapse in Eastern Europe: The Role of Credit', *IMF Staff Papers*, no.1, vol. 40, Mars, pp.32–52.

Claverannem, B., 2005, *La Zone Franc : au-delà de la monnaie,* Economica, Paris, 236pp.

Coricelli, F., 1998, *Macroeconomic Policies and the Development of Markets in Transition Economies,* Budapest, Central European University Press.

Diop, P.L., 1998, 'L'impact des taux directeurs de la BCEAO sur les taux débiteurs des banques', *Notes d'Information et Statistiques,* Banque Centrale des Etats de l'Afrique de l'Ouest, no. 483–84, juillet-août-septembre, 19pp.

Hibou, B., 1995, 'La politique économique de la France en zone franc', *Politique africaine,* no. 58, juin, Karthala, Paris, pp.25–40

Jeune Afrique, 2006, 'La Zone Franc croule sous l'argent', par Samir Gharbi, no. 2384, du 17 au 23 septembre, p.69.

Julienne, R., 1988, *Vingt ans d'Union monétaire ouest africaine*, L'Harmattan, Paris.

Monga, C. and Tchatchouang, J.C., 1996, *Sortir du piège monétaire*, Economica, Paris.

Mundell, R.A., 1961, 'A Theory of Optimum Currency Areas', *American Economic Review,* no. 4.

N'Guessan, T., 1996, *Gouvernance et politique monétaire : à qui profitent les banques centrales de la Zone Franc ?* L'Harmattan, collection 'bibliothèque du développement', Paris, 208pp.

Nubukpo, K., 2002, 'L'impact de la variation des taux d'intérêt directeurs de la BCEAO sur l'inflation et la croissance dans l'UMOA', *Notes d'Information et Statistiques,* Série 'Etudes et Recherches', no. 526, BCEAO, Dakar, juin, 32p. (Disponible à l'adresse électronique http://www.bceao.int/internet/bcweb.nsf/files/er30.pdf)

Ould-Ahmed, P., 1999, 'Politiques monétaires, comportements bancaires et crises de financement en Russie: les vicissitudes des années 90', *Revue d'Etudes Comparatives Est-Ouest,* no. 2–3, vol. 30, pp. 89–121.

Tchundjang Pouemi, J., 1979, *Monnaie, servitude et liberté : la répression monétaire de l'Afrique,* Editions MENAIBUC, Yaoundé; deuxième édition, 2ème trimestre, Paris, 285pp.

Van Wijnbergen, S., 1983, a, 'Credit Policy, Inflation and Growth in a Financially Repressed Economy', *Journal of Development Economics,* vol.13, no.1–2, August, pp. 45–65.

——, 1983, b, 'Interest Rate Management in LDCs', *Journal of Monetary Economics,* vol. 12, no. 3, September, pp. 433–52.

Part IV
New directions

20 Africa's urban revolution and the informal economy

Keith Hart

Africa in the twentieth century

Africa has become poorer in the last half-century, but, from being the most sparsely populated continent around 1900, Africa's seventh of the world's population now equals its share of the total land mass; and urbanization there is fast approaching the global average of around 50 per cent. We need to understand this 'urban revolution' of unprecedented speed and scale; and specifically to identify how Africa's urban economies might act as a spring-board for economic development in the coming century. The continent is divided into three disparate regions – North, South and Middle (West, Central and East Africa); but a measure of convergence between them is now taking place.

A preoccupation with Africa's post-colonial failure to 'develop' – or to 'take-off' – has obscured what really happened there in the twentieth century. The rise of cities has been accompanied by the formation of weak and venal states, locked into dependency on foreign powers and leaving the urban masses largely to their own devices. The latter have generated spontaneous markets to meet their own needs and these have come to be understood as an 'informal economy'. Whatever its value in bringing to light hitherto invisible economic activities, this concept is largely negative, focusing on whatever is not regulated by state bureaucracy and law. It tells us nothing about the social organization of these practices. In order to understand Africa's twentieth-century experience – the extraordinary compression of contradictory social developments within a short period – we must first take a long view of the region's divergence from the general historical trajectory of the Eurasian land mass.

Africa's traditional societies and agrarian civilization

I distinguish between three broad types of social formation: 'egalitarian societies' based on kinship; 'agrarian civilization' in which urban elites control the mass of rural labour by means of the state and class power; and 'national capitalism', where markets and capital accumulation are regulated by central bureaucracies in the national interest. Although Africa south of the Sahara has a more complex history than can be captured neatly by this typology, its dominant institutions before the modern period may best be understood in terms of the classless type based on kinship institutions. The second type, agrarian civilization, covered most of Europe, Asia, the Middle East and North Africa for the last few millennia. National capitalism within Africa has only taken root so far in South Africa, until recently for the benefit of whites only (Hart and Padayachee below). For a time after independence, Kenya was touted as a coming capitalist power. This was never realized, but the country has remained a centre for commercial innovation. Middle Africa, particularly after independence, made a belated transition to the Old Regime of agrarian civilization, while Europe and North America, followed by much of Asia, embraced national capitalism. This brought North and Middle Africa closer together as pre-industrial class societies, while South Africa has drawn closer to the rest of Africa since the coming of majority rule.

Jack Goody (1976, see Hart, 2006a) has tried to explain how and why African societies diverged before the modern period from their counterparts in Europe and Asia. He concluded that all the agrarian civilizations of Eurasia shared a common origin in the 'urban revolution' of Mesopotamia 5,000 years ago (Childe, 1954). This pattern also extended to Egypt and the Mediterranean littoral long ago. By the eleventh century, Cairo was the hub of a mercantile civilization stretching from Spain to India. The rise of cities was accompanied by the formation of states whose function was to supervise a new kind of class society, in which a narrow urban elite extracted agricultural surpluses from an increasingly servile rural labour force. Goody showed how forms of kinship and marriage reflected property relations that were themselves made possible by more intensive technologies, such as the plough and irrigation. Sub-Saharan Africa, he held, had largely missed out on this urban revolution along with its agricultural technology, higher population density and unequal property relations. This accounts for why traditional African forms of kinship and marriage are so distinctive and their societies were, relatively speaking, classless. Even where a measure of stratification existed, redistribution through kinship institutions prevented the emergence of classes based on different styles of consumption.

The contrast between egalitarian societies built on kinship and unequal societies based on state power and class division goes back to L. H. Morgan (1877) and before him to Jean-Jacques Rousseau (1754). It cannot be applied unambiguously to Africa and Eurasia before the modern age, even if we try to isolate Black Africa from its Northern and Southern extremities. The Atlantic and Indian Ocean slave trades generated coastal urban enclaves in both West and East Africa. The medieval civilization of the West African Sahel was a significant part of the Islamic world. Of the Yoruba agro-cities that emerged as a result of nineteenth-century warfare, Ibadan's population had reached 200,000 by the onset of colonial rule. These examples of pre-colonial urbanization (Freund, 2007) were rightly emphasized when the anti-colonial revolution delivered independence to most African countries from the 1950s.

Even so, large swathes of Middle Africa entered the modern era with a minimal urban population and the dominant institutions of their societies owed a lot more to kinship than to class differences. Indigenous states were commonplace in the early modern period, many of them emerging in response to the political, economic and demographic upheavals provoked by European imperial expansion. But, in a dozen volumes, Goody documents how most African societies south of the Sahara diverged from the pattern of agrarian civilization typical of pre-industrial Eurasia. This institutional pattern included territorial states, embattled cities, landed property, warfare, racism, bureaucratic administration, literacy, impersonal money, long-distance trade, work as a virtue, world religion and the nuclear family; and its grip on modern world society is still strong (Hart, 2002), since national capitalism everywhere incorporated elements of the Old Regime.

Of course, if traditional African societies appeared to be more equal than their European counterparts, it does not mean that inequality was wholly absent there. Friedrich Engels (1884) made much of the progressive subordination of women, first in tribal societies of farmers and herders, later in pre-industrial states and finally in capitalist societies. A body of more recent Marxist and feminist scholarship (e.g. Meillassoux, 1981) extended this analysis to the conflict between African males of different ages, with polygamous elders commanding young men's labour through control of access to marriageable women who were in their turn condemned to do most of the work without effective political representation. Gender and generation differences accordingly take on huge salience in African societies.

Africa's urban revolution

In 1900, Africa probably had less than 2 per cent of its inhabitants living in cities, under the global average before the industrial revolution. By 2000, a sustained population explosion has seen the urban share rise to almost half, compressing into one century what took twice as long elsewhere and from a much more rural base. Since Africa's population is still growing much faster than other regions at 2.5 per cent per annum, so too is its relative size in the world, if not yet its purchasing power (around 2 per cent of the world economy). In short, Africa experienced in the twentieth century its own version of an urban revolution that it had largely avoided before. This means not just the unprecedented proliferation of cities, but also that the whole package of pre-industrial class society was installed there more or less for the first time: states, new urban elites, intensification of agriculture and a political economy based on the extraction of rural surpluses. Any strategy for African development now must build on the social conditions that came into being when nominally independent nation-states were built on an economic foundation of pre-industrial agriculture (Hart, 1982).

The anti-colonial revolution unleashed extravagant hopes for the transformation of an unequal world. These have not yet been realized for most

Africans who are still waiting for political institutions that will guarantee their full participation as equals in world society. By most accounts African economies have not fared well since independence. But the model of development they were expected to adopt was 'national capitalism', the attempt to manage markets and accumulation through central bureaucracies with the general interest of citizens in mind. Development in this sense never had a chance to take root in Africa. For the first half century, African peoples were shackled by colonial empire and in the second, their new nations struggled to keep afloat in a world economy organized by and for the major powers, then engaged in the Cold War.

The assumption was that a change in ownership of the state would deliver economic development to African peoples, regardless of conditions in the world at large. Frantz Fanon took a different view. In *The Wretched of the Earth*, written from the depths of Algeria's own anti-colonial struggle, he spoke prophetically of the 'pitfalls of national consciousness' which would undermine Africa's post-colonial states and especially of the weakness of the new middle class who led them:

> From the beginning the national bourgeoisie directs its efforts towards (economic) activities of the intermediary type. The basis of its strength is found in its aptitude for trade and small business enterprises, and for securing commissions. It is not its money that works, but its business acumen. It does not go in for investments and it cannot achieve that accumulation of capital necessary to the birth and blossoming of an authentic bourgeoisie.
>
> (Fanon, 1970:144)

In other words, Africa's new leaders thought they were generating modern economies, with ambitions for public expenditure to match, but in reality they were erecting fragile states whose economic base was the same backward agriculture as before. As Fanon predicted, this weakness inexorably led them to exchange the democratic legitimacy of the independence struggle for dependence on foreign powers. These ruling elites first relied on revenues from agricultural exports, then on loans contracted under dubious circumstances, finally on the financial monopoly that came from being licensed to supervise their country's relations with global capitalism. But this bonanza was switched off in the 1980s, when foreign capital felt that it could dispense with the mediation of local state powers and concentrated on collecting debts from them. Many governments were made bankrupt and some simply collapsed into civil war.

It is hardly surprising that hopes for African democracy soon flew out of the window, to be replaced by a norm of dictatorship, whether civil or military. Concentration of political power at the centre led to primate urbanization, as economic demand became synonymous with the expenditures of a presidential kleptocracy. Political scientists have long written of the patrimonial norm for African states without pushing the analysis far or deep enough. The growth of cities should normally lead to an expanded level of rural-urban exchange, as farmers supply food to city-dwellers and in turn buy the latter's manufactures and services with the proceeds (Steuart, 1767, see Hart, 1982). But this progressive division of labour was stifled at birth in post-colonial Africa by the dumping of cheap subsidized food from North America and Europe and of cheap manufactures from Asia. For 'structural adjustment' meant that African national economies had no protection from the strong winds of world trade. The result was that a peasantry subjected to political extraction and violence was forced to choose between stagnation at home and migration to the main cities or abroad. Somehow the cities survived on the basis of markets that emerged spontaneously to recycle the money concentrated at the top and to meet the population's needs for food, shelter, clothing and transport. As Fanon pointed out, there is no shortage of business acumen, just of capital. These markets are the key to understanding the economic potential of Africa's urban revolution.

Urban commerce and the informal economy[1]

The idea of an informal economy came out of the lives of poor African city-dwellers. After the modernization boom of the 1960s, the notion that poor countries could become rich by emulating 'us' gave way to gloomier scenarios, fed by zero-sum theories of underdevelopment, dependency and 'the world system' (Wallerstein, 1974). In development policy-making circles, this trend manifested itself as fear of 'Third World urban unemployment'. It was noted that cities there were growing rapidly, but without comparable growth in jobs, conceived of as regular employment by government and the corporations. At this time, it was universally believed that only the state could lead an economy towards development and growth. There were a few liberal economists around, but their influence on policy was minimal. The question was therefore: how are 'we' (the bureaucracy and its academic advisors) going to provide the people with the jobs, health, housing etc that they need? And what will happen if we don't? The spectre of urban riots and even revolution raised its head. Anyone who visited these sprawling cities, however, would see a rather different picture. Their streets were teeming with life, a constantly shifting crowd of hawkers, porters, taxi-drivers, beggars, pimps, pickpockets, hustlers – all of them getting by without the benefit of a 'real job'.

There was no shortage of names for this kind of early-modern street economy. Terms like 'underground', 'unregulated', 'hidden', 'black' and 'second' economies abounded. Clifford Geertz's (1963) analysis of entrepreneurship in Indonesia was exemplary. The majority of a town's inhabitants were occupied in a street economy that he labelled 'bazaar-type'. In contrast, the 'firm-type' economy consisted largely of western corporations who benefited from the protection of state law. These had *form* in Weber's (1981) sense of 'rational enterprise', substituting calculation for speculation and above all minimizing risk. National bureaucracy lent these firms a measure of protection from competition, thereby allowing the systematic accumulation of capital. The bazaar on the other hand was individualistic and competitive, so that accumulation was well-nigh impossible. According to Geertz, some Reform Muslim entrepreneurs were rational and calculating enough; but they were denied the institutional protection of state bureaucracy granted to the existing corporations. He pointed out the irony of a neoclassical economics that studies the decisions of individuals in competitive markets like the bazaar, while treating as anomalous the dominant monopolies protected by state bureaucracy. The discipline found this model in the late nineteenth century, when a bureaucratic revolution was transforming mass production and distribution along corporate lines. At the same time the more powerful states awarded new privileges to big corporations and society took its modern form as national capitalism.

My paper, 'Informal income opportunities and urban employment in Ghana', was written for a 1971 conference (Hart, 1973). Before it was published, an International Labour Office report (ILO, 1972) launched the idea of an 'informal sector' in Kenya. I argued that Accra's poor were not 'unemployed'. They worked, often casually, for erratic and generally low returns; but they were definitely working. What distinguished these self-employed earnings from wage employment was the degree of *rationalization* of working conditions (Weber, 1978). An ability to stabilize economic returns within a bureaucratic form made them more calculable and regular for the workers as well as for their bosses. That stability was in turn guaranteed by the state's laws, which only extended so far into the depths of Ghana's economy. 'Formal' incomes came from regulated economic activities and 'informal' incomes, both legal and illegal, lay beyond regulation. I did not identify the informal economy with a place or a class or even whole persons. Everyone in Accra, but especially in the slums, tried to combine the two sources of income. Informal opportunities ranged from market gardening and brewing through every kind of trade to gambling, theft and political corruption. My focus was on what people generated out of the circumstances of their everyday lives. The laws and offices of state bureaucracy only made their search for self-preservation and improvement more difficult.

The ILO Kenya report suggested that self-employed or informal incomes might reduce the gap between those with and without jobs and so could contribute to a more equitable income distribution than was apparent from official statistics. Following a shift in World Bank policy, they advocated 'growth with redistribution', that is, helping the poor out of the proceeds of economic expansion. By now the multilateral institutions were worried about potential social explosions. A vogue for promoting the informal sector as a source of employment creation – in the most optimistic scenario capable of lifting a poor economy by the bootstraps – took off in the 1970s. The dominant paradigm of development was still Keynesian and it was still assumed to be the state's responsibility.

My aim was to insert a concrete description of irregular economic activity into the ongoing debates of professionals in the development industry. The ILO Kenya report, however, did set out to coin a concept, 'the informal sector', and it subsequently became a keyword organizing a new segment of the academic and policy-making bureaucracy. So the idea of an informal economy could be said to have had a double provenance that reflected its two sides: bureaucracy (the ILO report) and the people (an urban ethnography). Its association with the sprawling slums of Third World cities was strong at this time. Less attention was paid then to my observation that the commanding heights of the informal economy lay at the centres of political power, in the corrupt fortunes of public office-holders who often owned the taxis or the housing operated by the small fry.

The informal economy in development discourse

The 'informal economy' is the antithesis of 'national capitalism' or rather of its intellectual arm, 'macroeconomics'. Beginning as a way of conceptualizing the unregulated activities of the marginal poor in Third World cities, the informal sector became recognized as a universal feature of the modern economy. Independence from the state's rules unites practices as diverse as home improvement, street trade, squatter settlements, open source software, illegal drugs trafficking, political corruption, and offshore banking. Most economists have approached the informal economy in quantitative terms as a sector of small-scale, low-productivity, low-income activities without benefit of advanced machines, whereas I stress the reliability of income streams and the presence or absence of bureaucratic *form*.

The 1980s saw a major shift in world economy following the lead of Reagan and Thatcher. The state was no longer seen as the great provider. Rather 'the market', freed from as many encumbrances as possible, was the only engine of growth. The informal economy was reinvented as a zone of free commerce, competitive because it was unregulated. This coincided with the imposition of structural adjustment policies aiming to reduce public expenditures and throwing responsibility on to the invisible self-help schemes of the people themselves. By now, the rhetoric and reality of development had been effectively abandoned as the poor countries suffered the largest income drain in their history, through repayment of debts incurred during the wild banking boom of the 1970s.

What happened next could never have been anticipated around 1970: in the name of the free market, deregulation of national capitalism led to the radical informalization of world economy. Money went offshore and banking was increasingly unsupervised; corporations outsourced and downsized, in the process making work more casual and precarious; public functions were privatized; the drugs and illicit arms trades took off; the global war over intellectual property became the main site of capitalist struggle; and whole countries, such as Mobutu's Zaire, abandoned any pretence of formality in their economic affairs. Today, illegal drugs are the most valuable commodity traded internationally. Finance, until recently, slipped out of its political shackles. The armaments industry became the corrupt core of western governments. Grey markets for goods imitating well-known brands and unlicensed reproductions were labelled 'piracy'. The irrational borders of nation-states are riddled with smuggling.

The informal economy is now considered to be a feature of the industrial countries too, ranging from domestic do-it-yourself to the criminal economy of disaffected youth. Even before the Soviet Union's collapse, it was clear that the command economy had spawned a flourishing black market, antecedent of the criminal mafias and oligarchs who now dominate the Russian economy. In Europe, the dissident left has long had a slogan: 'Think red, work black, vote green'. Meanwhile, the collapse of the state in many Third World countries has led to the whole economy becoming informal. In many parts of Africa soldiers loot at will, while politicians fill foreign bank accounts. Or take Jamaica, which in the 1970s was a model 'middle-income' developing economy. At one point the value of illegal marijuana sales was higher than the country's three leading legitimate industries (tourism, bauxite and garments) taken together. No wonder politics was carried out by armed gangsters and youths left school early to learn hustling on the street.

Meanwhile, the attitude of international agencies towards informality changed. There is now substantial inward investment in some poor countries and foreign businesses feel the lack of an effective regulatory environment. This means boosting national bureaucracies which were deliberately undermined by structural adjustment. Now the call is for regulation and standardization. This is partly to secure a measure of economic order within particular countries; but transnational corporations and the international agencies also have a need for standardization between countries, so that they don't have to adapt procedures to local circumstances every time. Clearly national and local institutions are now becoming globalized. Informality is often seen as a *threat* to private sector development. Business corporations are undercut by informal operators who pay no taxes, evade costly regulations and take advantage of numerous devices, legal and illegal, to reduce their prices. Accordingly, whereas the informal economy was once seen as a positive factor in development, it is now more likely to be represented as an obstacle. Today the model of success for the world's ruling elites is still the highly bureaucratic type of economy achieved by Western countries only in the second half of the twentieth century (De Soto, 2000).

The dialectics of form

How might African governments encourage the evolution of the 'informal economy' towards more dynamic forms of urban commerce? 'Form' is *the rule*, an idea of what ought to be universal in social life; and for most of the twentieth century the dominant forms were those of bureaucracy, particularly national bureaucracy. The idea of an 'informal economy' is entailed in the institutional effort to organize society along formal lines. The twentieth century saw a general experiment in impersonal society that anchored bureaucracy in state-made laws carrying the threat of punishment. The dominant bureaucratic forms were conventionally divided according to ownership into public and private sectors. This uneasy alliance of governments and corporations is now sometimes classified as 'the formal sector'. Ostensibly, they share conformity to the rule of law.

The formal and informal economies appear to be separate entities because of the use of the term 'sector'. This gives the impression that the two are located in different places, like agriculture and manufacturing, whereas both the bureaucracy and its antithesis contain the formal/informal dialectic within as well as between them. There is a widespread perception of a class war between the bureaucracy and the people. It was not supposed to be like this. Modern bureaucracy was invented as part of a democratic political project to give citizens equal access to what was theirs as a right. It still has the ability to coordinate public services on a scale that is beyond the reach of individuals and most groups. And that is good enough reason to explore ways of linking the two more effectively. Many economic practices appear to be informal because their forms are largely invisible to the bureaucratic gaze. How then might non-conformist economic activities relate to the formal order? In four ways: as *division, content, negation* and *residue*.

The moral economy of capitalist societies is based on the attempt to keep impersonal and personal spheres of social life separate (Hart, 2005). The establishment of a formal public sphere entailed creating another one based on domestic privacy. The two constitute complementary halves of a single whole. Most people divide themselves every day between production and consumption, paid and unpaid work, submission to impersonal rules in the office and the free play of personality at home. Money links the two sides; their interaction is an endless process of separation and integration, *division*. The division of the sexes into male and female is the master metaphor for this dialectic of complementary unity.

For any rule to be translated into human action, something else must be brought into play, such as personal judgement. Informality is built into bureaucratic forms as unspecified *content*. Viable solutions to administrative problems always contain processes invisible to the formal order. For example, workers sometimes engage in a 'work-to-rule'. They follow their job descriptions to the letter without any of the informal practices that allow these abstractions to function. Everything grinds to a halt. Or take a chain of commodities from production by a transnational corporation to final consumption in Africa. At several points, from the factories to the docks to the supermarkets and on the street, invisible actors fill gaps the bureaucracy cannot handle directly. Informal processes are indispensable to the trade.

Of course, some activities break the law, through a breach of health and safety regulations, tax evasion, smuggling, the use of child labour, selling without a licence and so on. The third way that informal activities relate to formal organization is as its *negation*. Rule-breaking takes place both within bureaucracy and outside it; and so the informal is often illegal. This compromises attempts to promote the informal sector as a legitimate economic sphere, since it is hard to draw a line between colourful women selling oranges on the street and the gangsters (not to mention policemen!) who exact tribute from them. When the rule of law is weak, the forms that emerge in its place are often criminal in character.

The fourth category is not so obviously related to the formal order as the rest. Some informal activities exist in parallel, as *residue*. They are separate from bureaucracy. It would be stretching the logic of the formal/informal pair to include peasant economy, housework and so on within the rubric of 'informality'. Yet the social forms endemic to these often shape informal economic practices and vice versa. Is society just one thing – one state with its rule of law – or can it tolerate legal pluralism, leaving some institutions to their own devices? European empires, faced with scarce administrative resources, once turned to 'indirect rule' as a way of incorporating subject peoples into their systems of government on a semi-autonomous basis (Mamdani, 1996). Supervision of indigenous customary forms was delegated to appointed chiefs and headmen, reserving the key levers of power to the colonial regime. Anthropologists played their part in this (Asad, 1973). Any serious attempt to link formal and informal economies today would require a similar openness to plural forms.

On the usefulness of informality

Africa cannot afford a development model based only on the West's bureaucratic societies and the 'informal economy' is a bureaucratic concept. I have often wondered if it has advanced or retarded our understanding of development. The first criticism of the concept is that it is insufficiently dynamic. This might be because in the Cold War we lived under the threat of a nuclear holocaust (Hart, 1992). No-one wanted the two sides to move, since all life on the planet might then be placed in jeopardy. In any case, the sides did move – at several levels. So another criticism is that the label 'informal' says what these activities are not, but not what they are. For a development policy involving both sides, it will not do to lump everything together in a catch-all phrase whose chief virtue is that it allows bureaucrats to claim they understand what they never could. We need rather to expose the positive principles organizing the informal economy and to place them within a suitably broad historical framework. This is not to deny that there are political and analytical uses for the idea, particularly within international bureaucracies, such as lobbying for women's rights and conditions of work (WIEGO), as well as intellectual uses that continue to generate important empirical work in Africa, India and elsewhere (Skinner above).

It has never been resolved whether the informal economy refers to casual labour in formal enterprises or not. This has become more pressing in the context of widespread deregulation, as outlined above. Neoliberal economic policies since the 1980s fostered massive informalization of national and global economies, by reducing state controls and promoting the gigantic flows of credit and debt known as 'the markets'. Extension of the scope of informality to embrace rich and poor countries, government and business, casual labour and the self-employed, corruption and crime, when taken with the wholesale devolution of central bureaucracies compared with 40 years ago, leaves a question-mark over its continuing usefulness today.

The label 'informal' may be popular because it is both positive and negative. To act informally is to be free and flexible; but it also refers to what people are not doing – not wearing conventional dress, not being regulated by the state. The informal economy allows academics and bureaucrats to incorporate the teeming street life of exotic cities into their abstract models without having to know what people are really doing. The idea lends the appearance of conceptual unity to whatever goes on outside the bureaucracy. Fearing its own isolation in a 'planet of slums' (Davis, 2006), the bureaucracy oscillates between offering partnership to the informals and hounding them off the streets. We need to know how formal bureaucracy works in practice and, even more important, what social forms have emerged to organize the informal economy. It is now time to examine the institutional particulars sustaining whatever takes place beyond the law.

This brings me back to the categories of relations between formal and informal economies.

Division

The idea of interdependent, but separate halves of a social whole – in this case, the formal-informal dualism – is intrinsic to much development discourse. It is at best a way of launching discourse and soon limits critical enquiry.

Content

If informality is often the unspecified content of abstract forms, this favours accepting the legitimacy of many informal practices and leaving more to people's imagination.

Negation

When the state is weak, the informal is often also illegal. The obvious response is to crack down on rule-breakers; but in general such initiatives are unsystematic and merely cosmetic. The biggest offenders escape and the law is made an ass. The number of legal offences could profitably be reduced, if existing regulation is ineffective.

Residue

Governments might fruitfully adopt a hands-off approach towards semi-autonomous communities within their jurisdiction. But administrative decentralization poses a threat to weak states. These considerations, taken together, provide an abstract framework for thinking about how bureaucracy and the people might enter a new partnership for development. Nowhere is this issue more pressing than in Africa, where the question is largely one of organizing the urban informal economy as a launching pad for sustained economic growth in the coming decades.

The future of African urban commerce[2]

Africa's urban informal economy everywhere supplies food, housing and transport; education, health and other basic services; mining, manufactures and engineering; and trade at every level, including transnational commerce and foreign exchange. But its scope varies between the continent's regions. In West/Central Africa, where white settlement was minimal, the cities were substantially an indigenous creation and their markets were always unregulated. Foreign middlemen like the Lebanese minority flourished largely outside colonial administrative controls. The great ports of the Atlantic seaboard enjoy a degree of mercantile freedom that ensures they will play an important part in Africa's commercial growth. Today Angolan women jump on planes heading for London, Paris, Dubai and Rio, where they stock up on luxury goods for resale in the streets of Luanda. In Southern Africa, and to a lesser extent the East and North, cities were built by a white settler class who often imposed strict controls on the movement and activities of the indigenous population. The informal economy in South Africa today is distinctive in being hedged in by rules designed to promote modern industry. Elsewhere, in Zimbabwe, Mozambique and even in Kenya, the state has long played a more controlling role than would be considered normal today in Lagos, Cotonou or Dakar.

The state's relationship to economy has been transformed since independence. African nation-states have learnt the hard way that they are not free to choose their own forms of political economy. When the world was divided between the Rooseveltian consensus and the Soviet bloc in the first three decades after 1945 (what the French call *les trente glorieuses*), state ownership of production and control of distribution seemed to offer the best chance of defending the national interest against colonial and neo-colonial predators. After the 1970s, the mania for privatization led to ownership being ceded to individual corporations, often with a colonial past. Structural adjustment forced governments to abandon public service provision, to lay off many workers and to allow the free circulation of commodities and money. In the Congo, Angola, Somalia, Liberia and Sierra Leone, failed states and civil wars encouraged informal mining and trade, concentrating wealth and power in the hands of warlords and their followers. The restoration of peace in some areas usually came with the return of limited bureaucratic controls over distribution. The situation is highly dynamic and variable.

Tax collection in Africa never attained the regularity it has long achieved in Europe and Asia. Cathérine Coquéry-Vidrovitch once claimed that an 'African mode of production' was based on seizing revenues from long-distance trade rather than producing for local consumption. But this could be said of most pre-industrial states; and it is a measure of Africa's failure to adopt the model of 'national capitalism' that governments still rely on whatever resources they can extract from the import-export trade. The new urban classes that have arisen to control and live off these revenues, usually under a patrimonial regime propped up by foreign powers, constitute an old regime ripe for liberal revolution (Bayart, 2009).

The use of a term like 'patrimonialism' reminds us that the new states and class structures of Africa's urban revolution are entangled in kinship systems that remain indispensable to any understanding of how the informal economy works as social organization. The recruitment of dependents from 'home' allows the new urban middle classes to pass off exploitation of cheap labour as an egalitarian model of African kinship. Formal bureaucracy, on the other hand, is hostile to kinship, since the institution originated in the early modern drive to escape from a society based on personal relations. In that public context kinship is normally viewed as corruption. On the other hand, 'family business' has never lost favour and child labour is still acceptable there, if not when employed by transnational corporations. In the absence of a welfare state, Africans must rely on kinship to see them through the life cycle of birth, marriage, childrearing, old age and death; and this reinforces the traditional power of elders in the face of rural-urban migration on the part of youth and women (Goody, 1958).

To speak of economic growth in the future begs the question of what Africa's new urban populations could produce. So far, African countries have relied on exporting raw materials, when they could. Minerals clearly have a promising future owing to scarce supplies and rising demand; but the world market for food and other agricultural products is skewed by western farm subsidies and prices are further depressed by the large number of poor farmers seeking entry. Conventionally, African governments have aspired to manufacturing exports as an alternative, but here they face intense competition from Asia. But the world market for services is booming and perhaps greater opportunities for supplying national, regional and global markets exist there.

There was a time when most services were performed personally on the spot; but today, as a result of the digital revolution in communications, they increasingly link producers and consumers at distance. The fastest-growing sector of world trade is the production of culture: entertainment, education, media, software and a wide range of information services. The future of the human economy lies in the infinite scope for us to do things for each other – like singing songs or telling stories – that need not take a tangible form. The largest global television audiences are for sporting events like the World Cup or the Olympic Games. The United States's three leading exports are now films, music and software. Any move to enter this market will be confronted by transnational corporations and the governments who support them. Nevertheless, there is a lot more to play for here and the terrain is not as rigidly mapped out as in agriculture and manufactures. Africans are also exceptionally well-placed to compete here because of global audiences' proven preference for their music and plastic arts.

Why do you think Hollywood is where it is? A century ago, film-makers on the East Coast struggled under Thomas Edison's monopolies of electrical products; so some of them escaped to the Far West and kicked off the film industry there with as little regulation as possible. For his first Mickey Mouse cartoon, Walt Disney ripped off a Buster Keaton film, 'Steamboat Willie' (not to mention Aesop's fables). Now the Disney Corporation sues Chinese cartoonists for illegal appropriation of the Mickey Mouse logo. The world's third largest producer of films (some would say the second) is now Lagos in Nigeria ('Nollywood'). Most of their films cost no more than $5,000, a pattern reminiscent of Hollywood when W.G. Griffith was king. American popular culture is still that country's most successful export. There is no reason why it could not be for Africans too, if they can solve problems of transnational payment that have hitherto eluded them.

Africa must escape soon from varieties of Old Regime that owe a lot to the legacy of slavery, colonialism and apartheid; but conditions there can no longer be attributed solely to these ancient causes. The example of earlier commercial revolutions, reinforced by endogenous developments in economy, technology, religion and the arts, could offer fresh solutions for African underdevelopment. It has long been acknowledged that the rise of capitalism in Europe drew heavily on religion as one of its motors. Max Weber (1981) insisted that an economic revolution of this scope could only take root through a much broader cultural revolution. If Africa's informal economy has the potential to evolve into a more dynamic engine of urban commerce, what might be the cultural grounds for such a development? The basis for Africa's future economic growth must be the cultural production of its cities. This in turn rests on:

1   The energy of youth and women
2   The religious revival
3   The explosion of the modern arts
4   The communications revolution
5   The new African diaspora linked to sub-national identities

First, African societies, traditional and modern, have been dominated by older men. Women have benefited less from their opportunities and are less tied to their burdens. In many cases they have been quicker to exploit the commercial freedoms of the neoliberal international economy. Even when men and boys have plunged whole countries into civil war, thereby removing state guarantees from economic life, an informal economy resting on women's trade has often kept open basic supply lines. The social reality of Africa's cities is a young population without enough to do and a growing generation gap. The energies of youth must be harnessed more effectively and the chances of doing so are greater if the focus of economic development is on something that interests them, like popular culture.

Second, the religious revival in Africa – Christian, Muslim and traditional – has immense significance for economic development. This is often founded on young people's rejection of the social models and political options offered by their parents' generation. Fundamentalist and less extreme varieties of religion make a different kind of connection to world society than that offered by the nation-state, based on the assumption of American dominance or its opposite. They help to fill the moral void of contemporary politics and often offer well-tried recipes for creative economic organization. Christian churches are usually organized and supported by women, even if their leadership is often male.

Third, in all the talk of poverty, war and AIDS, the western media rarely report the extraordinary vitality of the modern arts in post-colonial Africa: novels, films, music, theatre, painting, sculpture, dance and their application in commercial design. There has been an artistic explosion in the last half-century, drawing on traditional sources, but also responding to the complexity of the contemporary world. One recent example is the 'Africa Remix' exhibition that toured Europe and Japan, a hundred installations from Johannesburg to Cairo, showing the modernity of contemporary African art. The African novel, along with comparable regions like India, leads the world. I have already mentioned the creativity of the film industry.

Fourth, Africa largely missed the first two phases of the machine revolution, based on the steam engine and electric grids; but the third phase, the digital revolution in communications whose most tangible product is the internet, offers Africans very different conditions of participation that they are already taking up avidly. In origin a means of communication for scientists and the military, the internet is now primarily a global marketplace with very unusual characteristics. Like the informal economy, it is largely unregulated; but this market freedom is harnessed to the most advanced technologies of our era. The internet has also generated new conditions for managing networks spanning home and abroad by radically shortening the time taken by communication and exchange at distance. The extraordinarily rapid adoption of mobile phones has made Africa a worldwide crucible for innovation, such as the first multinational network in East Africa and the use of phones there for purposes of banking, dealing and circulating price information. Nor should we neglect the role of television as a transnational means of widening perceptions of community.

Fifth, in the last half-century a new African diaspora has emerged, based on economic migration to America, Europe and nowadays Asia. These migrants are usually known away from home by their national identity, but many of them by-pass the national level when maintaining close relationships with their specific regions of origin. They are often highly educated, with experience of the corporate business world, while retaining links to relatives living in the informal economy at home. One consequence of neoliberal reforms has been that transnational exchange is now much easier, drawing at once on indigenous knowledge of local conditions and the expertise acquired by migrants and their families in the West. Remittances from abroad are of immense importance and are bound to play a major role in Africa's economic future.

How might these separate factors generate sustainable forms of enterprise capable of raising African economies to new levels? Economic success is always a contingent synthesis of existing and new conditions. There is no one model of successful enterprise, just many stories of economic innovation waiting to be discovered by those who will look. Thus the Mourides, a Sufist order founded almost a century ago, constitute an informal state with the state of Senegal (Cruise O'Brien, 1971). Their international trading operations are capable of influencing national economies, as when they recently shifted shoe supplies to the USA from Italy to China. A similar network of North African Muslims has been running cars and car parts illegally from Europe to Africa through Marseille on such a scale that the French car industry moved some of its production South to meet the demand. Pioneering communications enterprises in Kenya and Ghana are beginning to be noticed for their exciting ability to tailor modern technologies to local demand. The Nollywood phenomenon offers morality plays to global audiences at an affordable price. We might do well by trying to understand this development.

Conclusion: a key moment in economic history

It is a truism that the global economic crisis of 2008–9 has brought with it another swing in the balance between state and market comparable to that which took place in the watershed of the 1970s. An erstwhile spokesman for neo-liberal markets like South Africa's Trevor Manuel can now announce a revival of public planning within strong state institutions. The prospects of a new deal enabling some sort of transition from what has been called Africa's urban informal economy to sustained commercial growth is thus highly moot. Just as structural adjustment in the 1980s opened up space for small traders at the expense of the 'bureaucratic bourgeoisie', it would be surprising if the present moment did not entail a crackdown on 'informality', with a renewed emphasis on tax collection and the funding of public enterprises. There are precedents, however, for a more friendly approach on the part of governments. Thus President Chiluba of Zambia established a street vendors' desk in his office and removed some of the bureaucratic obstacles affecting at least this sector.[3] At the other extreme, South Africa's attempt to produce 'world-class' cities for the 2010 soccer World Cup has unleashed a bureaucratic war against informal traders and transport operators, exacerbated in some cases by the targeting of foreigners in so-called xenophobic riots. Informal operators have often been quicker to use mobile phones and other information technologies for purposes of transnational trade than bureaucratic firms. It would be a pity if this spin-off from neo-liberalism were stifled by a new dirigisme. This chapter does not offer predictions of likely scenarios in the coming decades. It has rather sought to illuminate the development possibilities thrown up by the historical pattern of rapid urbanization, informal market growth and states resembling Europe's Old Regime in Africa during the second half of the twentieth century.

Notes

1 The ground covered in this and the next two sections overlaps with Hart (2006b).
2 I have largely abandoned references in support of this speculative section. Clearly what follows is not a work of scholarship.
3 Owen Sichone: personal communication. I am grateful for this and many other constructive suggestions made by him on an earlier draft of this chapter.

References

Asad, Talal ([1973] 1995) *Anthropology and the Colonial Encounter*, Prometheus Books, Amherst NY.
Bayart, Jean-François (2009) *The State in Africa*, Polity, Cambridge.
Childe, Gordon (1954) *What Happened in History*, Penguin, Harmondsworth.
Coquéry-Vidrovitvh, Cathérine (1969) *Recherches sur un Mode de Production Africain*, La Pensée, Paris.
Cruise O'Brien, Donal (1971) *The Mourides of Senegal: The Political and Economic Organization of an Islamic Brotherhood*, Clarendon, Oxford.
De Soto, Hernando (2000) *The Mystery of Capital: Why Capitalism Triumphs in the West and Fails Everywhere Else*, Bantam, London.
Engels, Friedrich (1884) *The Origin of the Family, Private Property and the State*. London: Lawrence and Wishart.
Fanon, Frantz (1970) *The Wretched of the Earth*, Monthly Review Press, New York.
Freund, Bill (2007) *The African City: A History*, Cambridge University Press, Cambridge UK.
Geertz, Clifford (1963) *Peddlers and Princes*, Chicago University Press, Chicago.
Goody, Jack (ed.) (1958) *The Development Cycle in Domestic Groups*, Cambridge University Press, Cambridge UK.
—— (1976) *Production and Reproduction: A Comparative Study of the Domestic Domain*, Cambridge University Press, Cambridge UK.
Hart, Keith (1973) Informal income opportunities and urban employment in Ghana, *Journal of Modern African Studies*, 11.3, 61–89.
—— (1982) *The Political Economy of West African Agriculture*. Cambridge University Press, Cambridge UK.

—— (1992) Market and state after the Cold War: The Informal Economy Reconsidered, in R. Dilley (ed.) *Contesting Markets*, Edinburgh University Press, Edinburgh, 214–27.

—— (2002) World society as an old regime, in C. Shore and S. Nugent (eds) *Elite Cultures: Anthropological Approaches*, Routledge, London, 22–36.

—— (2005) *The Hit Man's Dilemma: or business, personal and impersonal*, Prickly Paradigm, Chicago.

—— (2006a) Agrarian civilization and world society, in D. Olson and M. Cole (eds) *Technology, Literacy and the Evolution of Society: Implications of the work of Jack Goody*, Lawrence Erlbaum, Mahwah, NJ, 29–48.

—— (2006b) Bureaucratic Form and the Informal Economy, in B. Guha-Khasnobis, R. Kanbur and E. Ostrom (eds) *Linking the Formal and Informal Economy: Concepts and Policies*, Oxford University Press, Oxford.

International Labour Office (1972) *Incomes, Employment and Equality in Kenya*, ILO, Geneva.

Mamdani, Mahmood (1996) *Citizen and Subject: Contemporary Africa and the Legacy of Late Colonialism*, Princeton University Press, Princeton NJ.

Meillassoux, Claude (1981) *Maidens, Meal and Money: Capitalism and the Domestic Community*, Cambridge University Press, Cambridge UK.

Morgan, Lewis H. (1964 [1877]) *Ancient Society*, Bellknapp, Cambridge MA.

Rousseau, Jean-Jacques (1984 [1754]) *Discourse on Inequality*, Penguin, Harmondsworth.

Wallerstein, Immanuel (1974) *The Modern World System*, Academic Press, New York.

Weber, Max (1978) *Economy and Society*, G. Roth and C. Wittich (eds), University of California Press, Berkeley CA.

—— (1981) *General Economic History*, Transaction Books, New Brunswick NJ.

21 Impacts and challenges of a growing relationship between China and sub-Saharan Africa

Raphael Kaplinsky, [1] *Dorothy McCormick,* [2] *and Mike Morris* [3]

Introduction

The existing literature is clear that China is impacting on sub-Saharan Africa (SSA). What is not clear is the precise nature of that impact. Does it come mainly from trade in cheap manufactured goods? Does it come from China's seemingly insatiable hunger for oil and minerals? What countries benefit and in what sectors? What role do Chinese companies operating in Africa play? How beneficial is Chinese aid and/or international cooperation? Who is losing out, and why?

Most of the literature focuses on trade but other interactions also generate positive or negative impacts. Of the many possibilities, we have identified foreign direct investment, production, and aid as potential channels of impact. In the following pages, we attempt first to take stock of our knowledge. We do by subjecting the most common forms of interaction between China and SSA to a comprehensive and detailed analysis using a systematic framework. We then use this analysis to identify the gaps in our knowledge and suggest ways of bridging them. The paper uses secondary data from a number of sources, including the International Monetary Fund, the World Bank, the US Department of Commerce, as well as published materials and relevant websites.

China's relations with Africa in the modern era have passed through three distinct phases. The first phase followed the Bandung Conference of Non-Aligned Nations in 1955, and resulted in almost four decades of what might be termed 'Third World Solidarity'. Partly driven by its ideological rivalry with the Soviet Union, China offered decolonising Africa moral and political support, in some cases coupled with limited military support and aid.[4] The period from the mid-1990s onwards – the subject of the analysis below – represents the second phase of Chinese involvement with SSA. Following a substantial growth in China's trade with Africa, and China's growing need for resources, large and predominantly state-owned enterprises (SOEs) entered SSA as investors and as contractors to Chinese-aid-funded projects in infrastructure and public buildings. The third and emergent phase of Chinese interaction with SSA is one involving small and medium sized, predominantly private-sector, enterprises. These comprise a mixture of firms. Some are incorporated in China and have extended their operations from China to SSA. Others have been started *ab initio* in SSA.

These largely coordinated sallies into SSA have led many observers to characterise China as 'having a strategy for Africa', not least in the context of the three-yearly Forum on China Africa Cooperation (FOCAC) conferences. (A mirroring characterisation is that whilst China may have a strategy for Africa, Africa lacks a strategy for China.) The fourth and currently emerging phase of Chinese interaction with Africa is one in which small and medium sized enterprises, often started by Chinese who had previously been employed in large scale investments by SOEs, have broken away from the coordinated pack of interventions and act as largely autonomous entrepreneurs (Mohan and Kale, 2007; Gu, 2009).

Framework for analysing impact

Although there are a number of *channels* through which China's impacts may be transmitted, we focus on three main channels that appear to be particularly pertinent at the present time: first, trade flows; second, FDI flows, technology transfer and integration in global value chains; and third, aid flows. There may also be impacts transmitted through the environment, financial flows, or participation in institutions of regional and global governance (IDS 2006).

In each channel, China-SSA relations may be either *complementary or competitive* (or indeed both). In trade, for example, China may provide SSA with appropriate capital goods and cheap consumer goods, and SSA may supply China with the commodities it requires to fuel its continued economic expansion. The relationship is complementary because both countries gain from it. However, imports of consumer goods to SSA may displace local producers, leading to sectorally competitive impacts on workers and entrepreneurs.

The distinction between the *direct and indirect* impacts is less obvious, and its significance is less widely recognised. Direct impacts through charting direct trade flows between China and SSA are relatively simple, clear, and easily measured. The indirect impacts occur as a result of China's relations with third countries, working their way indirectly through to SSA. For example, China's demand for commodities may raise their global prices, and even though a country like Ethiopia does not export animal feed to China (a direct relationship), it sells animal feeds into a global market in which prices have been raised by China's growing imports (indirect impact). The indirect impacts of China on SSA are sometimes much more substantial than the direct impacts. However, almost all of the analysis of the impact of China on SSA focuses on direct, bilateral relations, and hence tends to miss these important issues.

Table 21.1 integrates these three sets of factors into a synthetic framework to assess the overall impact of China on SSA. As will be shown below, our attempt to complete this synthetic matrix has resulted in several empty cells, and it is unclear to what extent this represents the pattern of China's impact on SSA or the underdeveloped state of our knowledge on these impacts.

Channels of impact

Trade

One of the main features of China's rapid growth has been its deepening trade orientation, with the trade-GDP ratio in excess of 70 per cent, well above the 'norm' for large countries. Within this, China has become a major exporter of manufactures and a significant importer of commodities. Trade between China and SSA is a small proportion of each region's total trade, but its rapid growth suggests that the trade channel is a significant source of impact. Trade values quintupled from close to $10billion in 2002 to more than $40billion in 2005, to more than $50billion by 2007 and rising by 46 per cent to $109billion in 2008.

Table 21.1 A synthetic framework for assessing the impact of China on SSA

Channel	Impact		
Trade		Direct	Indirect
	Complementary		
	Competitive		
Production and FDI		Direct	Indirect
	Complementary		
	Competitive		
Aid		Direct	Indirect
	Complementary		
	Competitive		

Table 21.2 Trade with China as a proportion of trade with industrialised countries (%)

	1990	1997	2001	2005	2006	2007
SSA Exports to China	0.56	4.08	6.46	15.01	17.82	19.48
SSA Imports From China	2.60	5.50	9.78	17.86	20.29	25.65

Source: Calculated from IMF Dots, accessed 17 February 2009

In 1990 SSA's exports to China were less than 1 per cent of its exports to industrialised countries, but by 2007 this percentage had risen to 19 per cent. Similarly SSA's imports from China, which were 2.6 per cent of its imports from industrialised countries in 1990, had risen to over 25 per cent by 2007. Since 2001, imports from China have been expanding more slowly than exports, allowing SSA's trade balance with China to turn from negative to positive (Kaplinsky and Farooki, 2008).

SSA's exports to China are mainly fuelled by China's growing demand for commodities (Kaplinsky and Farooki, 2008). The share in total SSA commodity exports to China of oil, iron ore, cotton, diamonds and logs grew from less than 50 per cent to more than 80 per cent between 1995 and 2005. The overwhelming bulk and most rapidly-growing export was oil. SSA manufactured exports to China were mostly from South Africa. But even in this case, nearly all products were derived from basic metals. Whilst Africa is in trade surplus with China in aggregate, its non-oil trade is in sharp deficit.

For some SSA economies, the importance of China as a direct destination of exports grew particularly rapidly. Exports to China account for between 86 and 100 per cent of all oil exports for Angola, Sudan, Nigeria, and Congo. A similar picture is true for the DRC, which sends 99.6 per cent of its basic metal exports to China. On the import side, only seven SSA countries source a significant share of their total imports from China. In 2007 the most import-dependent SSA economies on China were Angola (33 per cent of imports), South Africa (19 per cent), Sudan (13 per cent) and the DRC (8 per cent) (Kaplinsky and Farooki, 2008). Almost all were manufactured products.

What about potential bilateral trade between China and SSA? The evidence on the direct trade links suggests that, on the export side, SSA gains from China's demand for commodities, and on the import side, it gains cheap and appropriate consumer and capital goods. Outside of textiles, timber and cotton, there appears to be little trade between China and SSA in intermediate goods and little incorporation of China and SSA into coordinated global value chains. Jenkins and Edwards (2006) argue that most of these imports into SSA have substituted for imports from outside SSA, with the possible exception of Ethiopia and Nigeria, suggesting little displacement of domestic production and few negative impacts on employment and local production. These conclusions suggest a synergistic link between SSA and China, reflecting the optimism prevailing in some circles on the potential opportunities opened for SSA by China's rapid trade expansion (World Bank 2004b).

However, we suggest three major reasons for more cautious conclusions. The analyses of Jenkins and Edwards and the World Bank are conducted on 3-digit SITC trade data. Whilst this shows notable aggregate trends, it hides some important specific impacts which only show up with different, firm-level methodologies. For example, domestically produced clothing and furniture manufactures in both Ghana and South Africa are being displaced by imports from China (Kaplinsky and Morris, 2008). Similar anecdotal evidence can be found with regard to clothing and footwear manufacture in many SSA economies. In Ethiopia, a study of 96 micro, small and medium domestic producers reported that as a consequence of Chinese competition, 28 per cent were forced into bankruptcy, and 32 per cent downsized activity. The average size of micro enterprises fell from 7 to 4.8 employees, and of SMEs, from 41 to 17 (Tegegne, 2007).

Of greater concern are the potential effects on future production. Here, particularly in the case of light consumer goods, there are important and adverse long-term implications for SSA industrialisation (Kaplinsky and Morris, 2008). What 'spaces' will they be able to move into as their economies grow and they seek to diversify?

However, the most important indicator of caution stems from the *indirect* impact of China's trade with SSA. China's trade footprint is so large that it is in itself altering global prices, and this has significant impacts on SSA. The problem is that these indirect trade impacts are much more difficult to analyse, which is why almost all of the analysis so far has been on the growth and impact of direct trade links.

Most assessment of the impact of indirect trade links have focused on their effects on product prices (Kaplinsky and Santos-Paulino, 2006), the similarity (or lack of it) between SSA's and China's exports (Jenkins and Edwards, 2006), and the identification of winners and losers from trade with China (Stevens and Kennan, 2006). The fact that these have been done at fairly high levels of trade aggregation tends to mask the severity of China's indirect impact on SSA manufactured exports. The actual impacts are better seen by examining particular sectors and products.

By far the most significant recent manufactured export from SSA has been clothing and textiles, largely as a result of the United States Africa Growth and Opportunity Act (AGOA) preferences. Table 21.3 shows not just significant export growth, but growing reliance on the US market. For some SSA economies, these rapidly-growing exports have become especially significant. In 2002 clothing and textile exports accounted for 50 per cent of Lesotho's GDP. In Kenya, in 2004 employment in the clothing EPZ enterprises was equivalent to 20 per cent of formal sector manufacturing employment.

The primary driver for these growing clothing and textile exports has been trade preferences in general and the US AGOA preference scheme in particular. AGOA's derogation on the rules of origin allows SSA exporters to import inputs from outside the AGOA region or the US.[5] This derogation has been extended on a number of occasions to 2012. The derogation has allowed countries with weak or non-existent textile industries to boost employment and exports through clothing production.

The final integration of the textile sector into WTO rules involved the removal of all quotas, effective 1 January 2005. This opened the US market to imports from China, which had previously been subject to quotas. All of the countries that had been exporting textiles under AGOA experienced a decline in exports following the removal of quotas. Nevertheless, the outcome of quota-removal has not been quite as catastrophic as many had anticipated.

Table 21.3 Growth of SSA clothing and textile exports, 2000–7

		World	US% share
Kenya	2004	326,959	90.5
	2005	301,505	89.9
	2006	311,210	89.9
	2007	289,239	90.5
Lesotho	2004	496,953	97.0
	2005	415,671	94.0
	2006	433,286	94.0
	2007	431,624	93.2
Madagascar	2004	577,637	59.9
	2005	538,212	51.6
	2006	593,652	42.8
	2007	684,103	45.0
Mauritius	2004	1,023,068	23.5
	2005	850,242	19.7
	2006	897,603	14.0
	2007	977,916	12.4
Swaziland	2004	200,031	94.3
	2005	169,814	94.8
	2006	147,638	96.3
	2007	146,912	96.7
South Africa	2004	932,950	20.2
	2005	727,791	14.0
	2006	633,240	14.9
	2007	458,780	13.4

Source: COMTRADE database accessed via World Integrated Trade Solution (WITS) 19 September 2008

By value, overall AGOA textile exports fell by 26 per cent between 2004 and 2006 (www.agoa.info). Kenya fared best, with its 2006 exports at 95 per cent of their 2004 value. Lesotho, Swaziland, and Madagascar had 2006 exports of 85, 75, and 73 per cent of 2004 values respectively. By contrast, partly as a result of falling unit-prices, China's share in the same product markets increased, suggesting a direct exclusionary impact by China on SSA in third-country markets (Kaplinsky and Morris, 2008).

The main reason why SSA's overall export performance was not as bad as expected relates to the degree of effective subsidy offered to AGOA producers in the US. The nominal rates of tariff on the clothing products which AGOA countries export to the US range between 16 and 32 per cent. However, in nearly all cases AGOA clothing products can use (duty-free) fabrics and other inputs from outside SSA in manufacturing their clothing. These imported inputs account for up to 60 per cent of costs. Therefore, the implicit 'effective rate of subsidy' is substantially higher than the nominal rates of protection would suggest. These effective rates range between 27 and 84 per cent for representative exported products (Kaplinsky and Morris, 2008).

This rate of subsidy allows AGOA clothing producers to compete in the US market. This is because scales are low in SSA plants, and many SSA economies suffer from poor bureaucratic and physical infrastructure. But there is also pervasive evidence that many SSA clothing plants have low levels of productivity because of poor organisational procedures, low levels of skill and inadequate management within plants (Manchester Trade Team, 2005; Barnes *et al.*, 2006).

The impact of competition from China in third-country markets on poverty and livelihoods is very substantial. Some of this is positive, insofar as reduced prices of clothing imports enhances the consumption power of consumers. But the negative impacts are also very significant. With minimal backward linkages into textiles, the major conduit for income-dispersal in the clothing industry has been through direct employment. The scale of job-losses arising from the end of MFA quotas is alarming (Table 21.4).[6] It is not just the degree of job loss, but the nature of the jobs which have gone. Most workers are women, hence severe impacts on families, and in the absence of alternative employment, this decline has major poverty implications. We also know from global experience that rapid economic growth can be a significant factor in reducing poverty levels, and the loss to both GDP and exports arising from a sharp contraction of the clothing sector will have a further negative impact on poverty levels.

The employment decline largely omits employment losses in micro and small units for which exact numbers are not readily available. Chinese clothing imports have not only reduced domestic production, but have also displaced imports from neighbouring countries, many of which were previously produced by small-scale tailors, dressmakers, and knitters (for Kenya, see McCormick *et al.*, 2007).

FDI and production

Chinese investment in Africa has also increased dramatically, driven by both resource and market considerations. Although our data on FDI is more limited than on trade, we piece together a rough picture of Chinese

Table 21.4 Employment decline in clothing sector, 2004–5

	2004	*2005*	*% decline*
Kenya	34,614	31,745	9.3
Lesotho	54,000	40,000	25.9
Swaziland	28,000	16,000	42.9

Source: Kaplinsky and Morris, 2008

investments in Africa.[7] There was little Chinese foreign direct investment (FDI) in Africa until around 1990. Then from \$20million per year in the early 1990s, Chinese FDI in Africa jumped to close to \$100million in 2000 and reached more than \$1billion in 2006 (Zafar, 2007). This represents a growth rate higher than Chinese FDI to any other part of the world.

Chinese FDI is qualitatively different in kind from European and North American sourced FDI. Historically, Western and Japanese FDI in SSA has come from privately-owned corporations focused on profit maximisation, generally with relatively short time-horizons. By contrast, much of Chinese FDI in SSA comes from wholly or partially state-owned firms with access to very low-cost capital, and operating with much longer time-horizons. Many Chinese investments are linked to achieving strategic objectives, focused on long-term access to raw materials, and closely bundled with aid.

Furthermore, Chinese FDI is at least partly driven by an active government policy (UNCTAD, 2007). Currently Chinese companies enjoy four types of incentives: special and general tax incentives, credit and loans, foreign exchange allowances, and a favourable import and export regime. China's FDI to Africa has been further supported by common efforts by the Chinese and African governments, such as high level government and business visits, meetings, summits, joint committees, bilateral agreements, and various investment promotion activities.

Chinese FDI mainly takes the form of equity joint ventures with local entrepreneurs and/or national parastatals (Economist Intelligence Unit, 2005; UNCTAD, 2007). Some are multi-million-dollar joint ventures with local counterparts – in the energy and resource sectors, in Sudan, Nigeria, Gabon, Angola, Mali, and Zambia, and in manufacturing, including textile factories in Tanzania and Nigeria, and soya and prawn processing in Mozambique (UNCTAD, 2007; Bosten, 2006). In other cases, the investment and scale of operations are much smaller. In some SSA economies, small-scale entrepreneurial investment is presaged by the construction of specialised shopping malls retailing Chinese goods.

The Chinese have become highly visible in infrastructure construction and rehabilitation. Here it is not clear how much Chinese economic activity in SSA comprises FDI, how much is a result of winning commercial tenders, how much is linked to Chinese aid, and how much is part of integrated production networks between Chinese and SSA firms. Participation in infrastructure and construction projects ranges from stadiums in West Africa, to presidential palaces (in Kinshasa), dams (a \$650million tender for River Nile Merowe Dam project), pipelines (Sudan), roads, railways and government buildings.

By 2005, the Chinese had invested in 48 African countries (UNCTAD, 2007). Table 21.4 shows the number of projects and investment amounts for the top 14 recipients. Zambia, South Africa, Mali, and Tanzania top the list, with the remaining countries receiving relatively small amounts.

Most SSA investment in China comes from South Africa, with a number

Table 21.5 Top 14 SSA Countries receiving Chinese FDI
(1979–2001)

Country	Investments		Investment amount	
	No.	*%*	*Thousand US$*	*%*
Zambia	17	3.8	134,126	18.5
South Africa	83	18.5	110,849	15.3
Mali	5	1.1	58,122	8.0
Tanzania	14	3.1	39,483	5.4
Zimbabwe	11	2.5	33,257	4.6
Nigeria	33	7.4	31,144	4.3
D.R. Congo	7	1.6	24,242	3.3
Ghana	17	3.8	19,212	2.6
Kenya	21	4.7	18,475	2.5
Gabon	11	2.5	17,045	2.3
Benin	4	0.9	16,723	2.3
Mauritius	20	4.5	16,657	2.3
Côte d'Ivoire	13	2.9	16,033	2.2
Cameroon	15	3.3	15,851	2.2
Africa total	448		726,532	

Source: World Bank, 2004a

of large South African firms having a growing presence. This includes SABMiller (now the world's second largest brewing company), which has invested more than $400million in China since 1994, and has equity in 30 local breweries (Goldstein, 2004). Other large investors are SASOL, joining local Chinese investors in two very large coal-to-petroleum plants (each at more than $3billion) in the North West Province of China, Kumba Resources (part of Anglo American) in the production of zinc, SAPPI (also Anglo American, in paper), Polifin in chemicals and ABSA and NEDCOR in the financial sector.

Aid

Since the 1990s China's aid is increasingly directed towards broad strategic goals of developing links with resource-rich SSA economies (Muekalia, 2004; Kaplinsky *et al.*, 2007; Brookes and Shin, 2006; Pan, 2006; Tull, 2006). China's Africa Policy, adopted in 2006, bases China-Africa relations on five principles: Sincerity, equality, mutual benefit, solidarity, and common development. It also reiterates the one-China principle as the political foundation for the establishment and development of China's relations with African countries and regional organisations (China, 2006a; Guoqiang, 2007). This was further elaborated in the Beijing Summit (November 2006), which affirmed 'a new type of strategic partnership' between China and Africa (King, 2006).

Chinese aid to SSA can be grouped into six categories. The first is financial assistance for key investments. As of mid-2005, the Chinese government had provided aid to approximately 800 individual projects. Second, and linked to the first, China cancelled $1.2billion in debts owed by 31 African countries in 2004, and has continued to use debt relief as an aid tool. Third China's African Human Resources Development Fund had provided training in China to 9,400 Africans by the end of 2004, and a further 3,800 places were planned for each of 2005 and 2006. Fifteen thousand six hundred scholarships were offered to 52 SSA countries in 2005 (China, 2006b). Fourth, China has provided technical assistance to SSA – more than 600 teachers and more than 15,000 Chinese doctors have worked in 52 SSA countries, including 1,100 present at the end of 2004. Fifth, China has instituted a programme of tariff exemption for 29 SSA economies, covering 190 products, including food, textiles, minerals and machinery. The policy took effect at the beginning of 2005, and coverage has since been extended to 400 items. Finally, China has in very recent years begun to provide peace-keeping forces to SSA.

Infrastructure aid is useful because of Africa's general need for rehabilitation, expansion, and updating of infrastructure. Debt relief is valuable because freed up resources can be applied to other needs at the discretion of the government. Nevertheless, both have been controversial. Many infrastructure projects have been linked to resource extraction, and subject to criticism on environmental grounds. Some construction projects, like stadiums and government office buildings, have been seen as contributing little to long-term development or poverty reduction, not only because of the nature of the project, but also because they are tied to Chinese inputs and/or do not adhere to good labour practices. Debt relief, like general budget support, is most useful when the country has a clear development agenda into which the freed resources can be channelled. In its absence, debt relief runs the risk of wasting resources or propping up oppressive governments.

More generally Chinese aid has been criticised for failing to pay attention to a range of issues pertaining to good governance, human rights, environmental protection, and social justice (Bosshard, 2008; Zafar, 2007; Oya, 2006; Tull, 2006). There is evidence that this is beginning to change. China EXIM Bank, the country's official export credit agency and major lender to Africa, adopted an environmental policy in November 2004 (Bosshard, 2008). Although still general, it is clearly a step in the right direction. The Chinese government is also moving cautiously towards greater collaboration with Western donors, especially around issues of environmental sustainability (Lancaster, 2007). At the same time, it is clear that China does not want to lose its distinctive character as a donor with a special understanding and sympathy for Africa's development challenges. How this will be worked out, especially in the areas of human rights and social justice, remains to be seen (McCormick, 2008).

Channels in aggregate

These channels are interrelated. China's trade impact (direct and indirect) in clothing and textiles, for example, is closely linked to the integration of SSA and Chinese firms in coordinated global value chains, and China's growing aid programme appears to be closely related to its need for traded commodities.

We also noted a great danger of focusing on the present, the known and the measurable impacts. Moreover, partly because there is a great need to search for a solution to SSA's problems, and partly because the direct bilateral links are easier to see than the indirect, there is a danger of focusing unduly on the positive opportunities and neglecting the potentially negative disruptive impacts of China's growing impact on SSA.

What can be said in aggregate about China's impact on SSA? Table 21.6 presents some of the major conclusions emerging from our review of the three key channels:

- We are unable to fill all the 'cells' in this framework. For example, it is possible that there will be indirect complementary effects in the FDI/ production channel, and it is conceivable that Chinese-coordinated global value chains producing in the Middle East may source inputs from plants located in SSA. Does this inability to fill cells reflect the absence of impacts, unmeasured impacts, or poorly manifested impacts?
- Direct impacts are easily evidenced, both with regard to complementary and competitive effects. By contrast, indirect impacts are more difficult to evidence and much more difficult to measure.
- Data on the trade channel is much better than the production/FDI and aid channels. Is this a function of our lack of knowledge and/or the availability of global trade data, or does the trade impact assert itself first and most significantly?

Table 21.6 China and SSA: an elaborated synthetic view of three main channels, and complementary-competitive and direct-indirect impacts

Channel	Impacts		
		Direct	*Indirect*
Trade	Complementary	• Inputs for industries • Cheap consumption goods	• Higher global prices for SSA exports
	Competitive	• Displacement of existing and potential local producers by cheap Chinese products	• Competition in external markets – falling prices and falling market shares

(Continued Overleaf)

Table 21.6 Continued

Channel	Impacts		
		Direct	Indirect
Production and FDI	Complementary	• Chinese FDI in SSA, particularly in fragile states • Cheap and appropriate capital goods • Technology transfer • Integration in global value chains, particularly in clothing • Low-cost infrastructure	
	Competitive	• Displacement of existing and potential local producers • Less spin-off to local economy than other foreign contractors • Use of scarce resources	• Competition for global FDI and production platforms • Disinvestment and relocation by other foreign investors (for example, clothing and furniture)
		Direct	Indirect
Aid	Complementary	• Grants and concessional finance • Technical assistance • Training • Tariff exemptions • Debt relief	
	Competitive		Chinese aid to Latin America creates productive capacity which competes with SSA producers and lowers export prices

• With the exception of competitive effects in manufacturing through the trade channel, the balance of existing evidence tends to support the view that the positive impacts ('opportunities') are probably more important than the negative impacts ('threats'). But it is unclear whether this is a function of the availability of evidence, or the real world.

- It is difficult to generalise across countries and sectors. They might experience the impacts in each of these three channels in very different ways. For example, commodity exporters in SSA may gain from rising commodity prices (complementary indirect effects), whilst SSA commodity importers may suffer from the very same price rise (competitive indirect effects). Five economies account for more than 80 per cent of all SSA's oil and gas exports, 12 economies for more than 80 per cent of mineral exports, and 22 economies for more than 80 per cent of agricultural exports.
- We have no available methodology for providing a 'net outcome', even for individual countries and regions. This is partly because some impacts are not measurable, and partly because they involve trade-offs between winners (consumers buying cheap clothing imports) and losers (displaced domestic producers of clothing), often within the same country.

Drawing the issues together

We now address the implications for policy in five key areas. We do not offer detailed prescriptions for change but, instead aim to see these as promoting the basis for discussions with key stakeholders, within SSA and China, and with interested organisations and multi-lateral agencies elsewhere. The key issues are:

1   The challenges posed to industrial policy and sectoral choice
2   Reacting to changing patterns of poverty and income distribution
3   Global and regional links
4   Thinking about the future
5   Filling the knowledge gaps

Challenges posed to industrial policy and sectoral choice

SSA is most clearly challenged by China's impact on its industrial sector. China's impact on SSA industrialisation arises from its growing exports affecting SSA on two related and threatening fronts – competition in internal markets for domestically-oriented manufacturers, and competition in external markets from export-oriented industry.

Most is known about this in the clothing, textiles, furniture and footwear sectors. Chinese imports, are problematic for domestic manufacturers. Ghanaian furniture exporters find it increasingly difficult to compete with Chinese imports, as do South African clothing manufacturers (Kaplinsky and Morris, 2008). A similar pattern can be found in the Ethiopian footwear sector (Tegegne, 2007) and the Kenyan clothing sector (Kamau, 2007). Although data is scarce, discussions with manufacturers and retailers in a number of SSA economies with domestic manufacturing sectors suggest that import penetration is increasing in all markets, and in most of the traded-goods manufactured sectors.

However, the challenge to SSA industry is much more substantial than these current impacts might suggest. This is because its industry is currently poorly developed, and often largely confined to the food-processing industry (where products degrade over time and have a high transport-to-value ratio), building materials (a high transport-to-value ratio and producing customised products) and the informal manufacturing sector (producing to low levels of quality and largely using waste materials). The real policy challenge is not to existing industry, but to potential industry: what space is there for SSA manufacturing to expand in the future? What implications does this have for the growth of dynamic capabilities, learning externalities and structural transformation?

What can be done? First, there is scope for improving the productivity of existing industries, often by working with value chains rather than individual firms. Detailed firm-level analysis of productivity in the clothing sector in South Africa (Barnes, 2006) and in COMESA (Manchester Trade Team, 2005) reveal the nature of these productivity gaps. Kaplinsky and Morris (2006) also report evidence of significant productivity improvements following the introduction of training schemes in Lesotho. Competitiveness in all sectors is a moving target, and for various reasons, few SSA industries have hitherto been able to address this challenge of building dynamic capabilities. There is, however, no intrinsic reason why this should be the case, and there is thus considerable scope for effective industrial policies.

Trade is a second area of policy intervention. Here there may be a need for selective protection on the import side. But, as we saw in the earlier discussion of AGOA exports, SSA requires continued preferential treatment against China in external markets. AGOA has been extended to 2012, but this remains a temporary solution. SSA governments would do well to develop active industrial policies that provide incentives to deepening value added in the textiles sector.

A further important lesson is for SSA producers to be less concerned about the sector of production and more focused on identifying niches where they can build barriers to entry to Chinese producers through the development of innovative capabilities. In manufacturing this may be increasingly difficult as Chinese competences grow, whereas in horticulture and services, including knowledge-intensive services, relative capabilities may be high, as in the case of Kenya's horticulture sector, South Africa's medical sector, and East Africa's wildlife tourism sector.

Reacting to changing patterns of poverty and income distribution

Trade-related income poverty and distribution impacts can be significant (McCulloch *et al.*, 2002). Although little is known about the detailed impact on China's trade on SSA patterns of income distribution, there are reasons to believe that it could be substantial.

On the positive side, Chinese manufactured imports benefit consumers, particularly low-income consumers. This is a global phenomenon, since the decline in prices of basic manufactures is a primary factor holding inflation at bay in many OECD economies. Many SSA manufacturers complain that Chinese products are displacing locally-produced commodities. In many countries, the primary displacement effect is on imports of manufactures from other, non-SSA economies, with wholesalers and retailers switching their sourcing to cheap Chinese suppliers often with major positive impacts on consumer welfare. In South Africa, for example, whilst the overall price index increased by 30 per cent between 2000 and 2005, that of clothing fell by 5 per cent. Significantly, as in the case of the Ethiopian shoe industry, some of this price decline was due to lower cost imports from China but competition from Chinese manufactures also forced local manufacturers to upgrade their competitiveness (Morris, 2007).

There are also rapidly-emerging negative consequences of Chinese trade on income distribution. On the one hand, employment in many labour-intensive manufacturing sectors is being lost, not only in export-oriented enterprises, but also in micro and small units targeting the local market. On the other hand, the rise in commodity production is associated both with capital-intensive technologies, and because of the large-scale of commodity production, to highly-concentrated forms of ownership. This is not an intrinsic problem of all primary production, since many soft-commodities (tea, coffee, cotton and horticulture) are labour-intensive and locally-owned, but, hitherto, most commodity exports to China have been oil and hard commodities, particularly basic metals.

There is an additional global dimension to these emerging patterns of income distribution, since manufacturing incomes are either largely local within SSA (labour) or flow to firms based in low- and middle-income Asian economies. By contrast, with the exception of South Africa, commodity production almost exclusively occurs through the operations of foreign transnational firms. A mitigating factor with regard to the distributional consequences of commodity production is that it is relatively easy to tax, providing revenues to governments. But the use of these state revenues does not necessarily suggest that their poverty and distributional impacts are positive. Moreover, a legacy of the Washington Consensus Structural Adjustment Programmes has been the transfer of many mines to foreign ownership, often coupled with tax holidays. Consequently, many of the fruits of the recent China-induced commodity-boom were lost to African countries. In Zambia, for example, little of the rise in copper prices accrued to domestic parties, least of all to the state coffers (Weekes, 2008).

Global and regional integration

Historically, most of SSA's trade links have been with the former metropolitan powers, either directly with the UK and France, or more generally with Europe and North America. These links have been strengthened through the development of various forms of preferential trade arrangements (Lome-Cotonou, AGOA, EPAs and FTAs).

Two major developments are disturbing these historical patterns. First, there appears to be a naturally growing regional market in southern Africa, reflecting regional externalities in production (Evans *et al.*, 2006). But, secondly, the rapid growth in trade between SSA and China suggests a growing 'magnetic pull' from the East, posing a major policy challenge to SSA. In the context of stretched policy and administrative systems, and given the growing importance of regional ties in the global economy, who should they link with, and what forms of linkage might this involve? Should they aim to go North, go East or stay local?

Here it is possible to distinguish between what might be termed 'passive integration' and 'active integration'. The former refers to the removal of barriers to trade, as in the case of FTAs and WTO-orchestrated multilateral trade liberalisation. Positive integration involves targeted policies focusing on particular forms of market imperfections (for example, promoting learning about China and its language), strengthening poor infrastructure constraining particular geographical links, and actively seeking to develop various forms of 'deep integration' in China-SSA global value chains. It may also involve the development of particular patterns of trade preference, as in the recent Chinese initiative to lower tariffs on imports of manufactures from the least developed SSA economies.

SSA economies need to develop explicit policies in these areas involving a 'joined-up' mix of economic and political initiatives. As SSA loosens its links with Europe and North America, it will also be necessary for countries to determine how much weight they wish to place on intra-continental regional links, and how much on forging new regional links with China and other Asian countries.

Thinking about the future – developing 'dynamic capabilities'

For SSA economies the capacity to change, to grasp opportunities and to minimise threats is critical – referred to as the development of 'dynamic capabilities'. It involves a combination of search capabilities, strategic-formulation capabilities and implementation capabilities, as well as the capacity to change continually as new threats and opportunities arise.

Many of the dynamic capabilities required to meet these challenges are prefigured in the policy-related issues discussed above. An additional capability is the ability of SSA producers to anticipate future opportunities and threats opened up by sustained Chinese expansion. For example, one emerging opportunity is the promotion of Chinese tourism. By 2006 China had granted tourist destination status to 26 African countries (People's Daily Online, 6 November 2006). The number of Chinese tourists to Africa reached 110,000 in 2005, doubling the 2004 figure. With the growth in Chinese per capita incomes, tourism will accelerate. This has clear links to the manufacturing sector in the form of opportunities for producers of many items needed to establish and operate a tourist destination – furniture, textiles, uniforms, processed food and beverages, soaps and cleaning supplies.

Another possibility refers to China's food needs. At 3,040, China's per capita calorie consumption is on average 90 per cent of that in the high income economies (Chen *et al.*, 2006), so future import needs are likely to reflect a change in the composition of food consumption rather than a significant increase in its volume. So far, China has sourced very little food from SSA, partly because it has imported intermediates such as animal feed to support its own meat-producing sector. Most of the feed imported so far has been soya, and the primary origin of these imports has been from Latin America (Jenkins *et al.*, 2006), and SSA has gained little from this trade in animal-feeds.

This raises a series of strategic issues for SSA food producers, which require careful consideration, informed by data rather than wild speculation. Will China continue to produce its own meat? Will its growing per capita income lead it to import horticultural products, fish and chicken? If so, will these imports come directly from eastern and southern African economies which have a demonstrated comparative advantage, or will SSA gain indirectly from China's growing imports from a supply-constrained global economy?

These examples of tourism and soya are just that – examples. They represent future possibilities. At the same time, it is also necessary to anticipate future threats. A major potential problem for many SSA economies lies in the escalation of energy prices. Constrained global supplies and rapidly growing demand from China and India pushed prices far above previous estimates. So, too, the prices of other SSA imports, including food, might climb to new highs.

Filling the knowledge gaps

We know more about the questions to be addressed than on the nature of China's impact. There are significant knowledge gaps, and unless these are filled, policy and capability development will be undermined and may be misdirected.

We can conclude with some confidence that the three primary channels of transmission are indeed trade, FDI/production and aid, and that we know more about the direct impacts than the indirect impacts. In order to understand China's growing involvement in SSA, it is as important to focus on the geostrategic and political imperatives, as on the narrow pursuit of financial gain. But, other than this, we cannot at present draw any conclusions with confidence. We cannot assess whether on balance China's impact is likely to be positive or negative, and for which countries and regions, and for which particular stakeholders in particular countries and regions.

In order to establish a good foundation for policy development, key knowledge gaps suggest at least seven different types of research:

1 Base-line studies to assess the changing future impact of China on SSA.
2 Analyses of the determinants of SSA competitiveness and the steps required to enhance productivity (for example, in clothing, textiles, footwear and furniture, as well as in export-oriented food crops).
3 A more thorough assessment of indirect impacts of China's trade on SSA, facilitating the development of appropriate policies for providing special and differential treatment to low income SSA economies in global markets.
4 Studies aimed at determining the impact of China on consumer welfare, income distribution and absolute poverty levels in SSA, through an analysis of the consumer benefits derived from cheaper imports, and the distributional implications of a switch in specialisation away from labour-intensive manufactures to capital intensive commodities.
5 Studies that distinguish generic from sub-regional and country-specific impacts, aiding the classification of different types of SSA economies.
6 An analysis of the extent of Chinese migrants in SSA, their origins, their sectors of activity and their synergistic role with the entry of Chinese state-owned enterprises in Africa's resource and infrastructure sectors.
7 Research into likely future areas of threat and opportunity.

Conclusions

There is a growing realisation that China's present and potential impact on SSA is both far-reaching and complex. Our synthetic framework, whilst disentangling the impact of three major channels and their various effects, has produced only a partial picture of China's impact on SSA. This is at least partly because of gaps in our knowledge. Some of these gaps result from lack of data, but others arise because the organisation of Chinese society means that the channels are intertwined in ways not immediately obvious to outsiders. This appears to be especially true of the production and aid channels, but may also apply to trade. The result is that some potentially important areas of impact may be misunderstood or missed altogether.

China's public pronouncements convey a desire for a relationship of South–South cooperation, of one developing country helping another (King, 2006). Such a two-way relationship can only be fruitful if both parties respect one another and are ready to listen and learn from each other's experience. The relationship also needs to be underpinned by an understanding of how the actions of one are likely to affect the life of the other. Only then will genuine partnerships be possible.

Notes

1 The Open University, UK.
2 Institute for Development Studies, University of Nairobi, Kenya.
3 University of Cape Town and University of KwaZulu-Natal, South Africa.
4 The most visible project was the Tanzam railway linking Zambia with Tanzania in an attempt to free Central Africa from dependency on apartheid South Africa's transport infrastructure.
5 Only South Africa is excluded from the derogation on the rules of origin.
6 South African job losses have been excluded from Table 21.3 as they are due to a complex web of factors leading to a lack of international competiveness: exclusion from AGOA derogation, an appreciating exchange rate, high labour costs, inefficient production, surge in Chinese and other imported clothing and fabric.
7 There are two official sources of data on FDI from China: the Ministry of Commerce (MOFCOM) and the State Administration of Foreign Exchange (SAFE). The most recent detailed analysis of Chinese outward FDI has been provided by UNCTAD (2007) using both of these sources.

References

AGOA.info (2008) 'Country Information – Mali.' www.agoa.info (accessed 5 February 2008).

Barnes, J., M. Morris and M. Gastrow (2006) 'An Assessment of the South African Clothing Industry's Operational Competitiveness Relative to a Set of International Competitors', mimeo.

Bosshard, P. (2008) 'China's Environmental Footprint in Africa.' SAII China in Africa Policy Briefing No. 3. Cape Town: South African Institute of International Affairs.

Bosten, E. (2006) 'China's Engagement in the Construction Industry of Southern Africa: The Case of Mozambique'. Paper Prepared for the Asian and other Drivers of Global Change Workshop, St. Petersburg, January 19–20 (available at www.ids.ac.uk/asiandrivers).

Brookes, P. and Shin, Ji Hye. (2006) 'China's Influence in Africa: Implications for the United States.' *Backgrounder* No. 1916. Washington: The Heritage Foundation.

Chen, M-X., A. Goldstein, N. Pinaud and H. Reisen (2005), 'China and India: What's in it for Africa?' mimeo. Paris: OECD Development Centre.

China (2006a) 'China's African Policy' Beijing: Ministry of Foreign Affairs, People's Republic of China, www.fmprc.gov.cn/eng/zxxx/t230615htm (accessed 10 September 2006).

—— (2006b) 'Ministry: China to Increase Aid to Africa.' (http://english.sina.com/china/1/2006/0107/60908.html, accessed 3rd March 2006).

Economist Intelligence Unit (2005) 'Mali.' Country Profile. London: The Economist Intelligence Unit, Ltd.

Evans, D., R. Kaplinsky and S. Robinson (2006), 'Deep and Shallow Integration in Asia: Towards a Holistic Account'. R. Kaplinsky (ed.) 'Asian Drivers: Opportunities and Threats', *IDS Bulletin*, 37(1): 12–22.

Goldstein, A. (2004). *Regional Integration, FDI and Competitiveness in Southern Africa*, Paris: OECD Development Centre.

Gu, Jing (2009) 'China's Private Enterprises in Africa and the Implications for African Development', mimeo, Brighton: Institute of Development Studies.

Guoquiang, Qi. (2007) 'China's Foreign Aid: Structure, Policies, Practice, and Trend.' Thought Piece Submitted by Panellist at Conference on *New Directions in Development Assistance*, organised by the University of Oxford and Cornell University, 11–12 June, Oxford.

IDS Asian Drivers Team (2006) 'The Impact of the Asian Drivers on the Developing World'. R. Kaplinsky (ed.) 'Asian Drivers: Opportunities and Threats', *IDS Bulletin*, 37(1): 3–11.

Jenkins, R. and C. Edwards (2005) 'The Effect of China and India's Growth and Trade Liberalisation on Poverty in Africa.' Department for International Development, DCP 70, London: DFID.

Jenkins, R. and C. Edwards (2006) 'The Economic Impacts of China and India on sub-Saharan Africa: Trends and Prospects', Journal of Asian Economics, 17(2): 207–25.

Jenkins, E., Dussel Peters and M. Moreira (2006) 'The Impact of China on Latin America'. Agenda-setting paper prepared for DFID, Brighton: Institute of Development Studies.

Kamau, P. (2007) 'The Developmental Impact of Asian Drivers on Kenya, with Particular Emphasis on Clothing and Textile Manufacturing.' Draft paper prepared for OECD Development Centre.

Kaplinsky, R. and M. Morris (2006) 'Dangling by a Thread: How Sharp are the Chinese Scissors?', *Paper prepared for Africa Policy Division, DFID*, Brighton: Institute of Development Studies.

Kaplinsky, R. and A. Santos-Paulino (2006) 'A Disaggregated Analysis of EU Imports: The Implications for the Study of Patterns of Trade and Technology.' *Cambridge Journal of Economics* 30: 589–611.

Kaplinsky, R. and M. Z. Farooki (2008) 'Africa's Cooperation with New and Emerging Development Partners: Options for Africa's Development', *Report prepared for The Office of Special Advisor on Africa (OSAA)*, Department of Economic and Social Affairs (DESA), the United Nations, Milton Keynes, Development Policy and Practice, Open University.

Kaplinsky, R. and M. Morris (2008) 'Do the Asian Drivers Undermine Export-Oriented Industrialisation in SSA', *World Development* Special Issue on Asian Drivers and their Impact on Developing Countries, 36 (2), pp. 254–73.

Kaplinsky, R., D. McCormick and M. Morris (2007). 'The Impact of China on Sub Saharan Africa'. Working Paper No. 291. Brighton: Institute of Development Studies.

King, K. (2006) 'Aid Within the Wider China-Africa Partnership: A View from the Beijing Summit.' mimeo, available from www.cctr.ust.hk/china-africa/papers/Kenneth.King.pdf

Lancaster, C. (2007) 'The Chinese Aid System.' CGD Essay. Washington: Centre for Global Development.

McCormick, D. (2008) 'China and India as Africa's New Donors: Understanding the Impact of Aid on Development.' *Review of African Political Economy*, Issue 115, March, pp. 73–92.

McCormick, D., P. Kimuyu, and M.N. Kinyanjui (2007) 'Textiles and Clothing: Global Players and Local Struggles.' In D. McCormick, P.O. Alila, and M. Omosa,

Business in Kenya: Institutions and Interactions. Nairobi: University of Nairobi Press.

McCulloch, N., L. A. Winters and X. Cirera (2002) *Trade Liberalisation and Poverty: A Handbook*, London: Centre for Economic Policy Research.

Manchester Trade Team (2005), 'Impact of the End of MFA Quotas and COMESA's Textile and Apparel Exports under AGOA: Can the Sub-Saharan Africa Textile and Apparel Industry Survive and Grow in the Post-MFA World?' Report prepared for USAID East and Central Africa Global Competitiveness Trade Hub.

Mohan, G. and D. Kale (2007) The Invisible Hand of South-South globalisation: A Comparative Analysis of Chinese Migrants in Africa, Report to the Rockefeller Foundation, Milton Keynes: Development Policy and Practice, Open University. http://asiandrivers.open.ac.uk/documents/Rockefeller%20Report%20on%20 Chinese%20diasporas%2010th%20Oct%203.pdf Morris, M. (2007), 'The rapid increase of Chinese imports: how do we assess the industrial, labour and socio-economic implications?', *Paper delivered at the 20th Annual Labour Law Conference, Sandton Convention Centre*, 4th July.

Muekalia, Domingos Jardo (2004) 'Africa and China's Strategic Partnership.' *Africa Security Review* 13(1): 5–11.

Oya, Carlos (2006) *The Political Economy of Development Aid as Main Source of Foreign Finance for Poor African Countries: Loss of Policy Space and Possible Alternatives from East Asia*, London: SOAS.

Pan, E. (2006) 'China, Africa, and Oil.' www.cfr.org/publication/9557 (accessed 10 September 2006).

Stevens, Christopher, and Jane Kennan (2006) 'How to Identify the Trade Impact of China on Small Countries', *Institute of Development Studies Bulletin*, 37(1): 33–42.

Tegegne, G. (2006) 'Asian Imports and Coping Strategies of Medium, Small and Micro Firms: The Case of Footwear Sector in Ethiopia. Chinese Imports and the Ethiopian Shoe Industry.' *Journal of Modern African Studies* 45(4): 647–79.

Tegegne, Gebre-Egziabher (2007) 'Impacts of Chinese Imports and Coping Strategies of Local Producers: The Case of Small Scale Footwear Enterprises in Ethiopia', *Journal of Modern African Studies*, 45 (4).

Tull, D. M. (2006) 'China's Engagement in Africa: Scope, Significance, and Consequences.' *Journal of Modern African Studies* 44(3): 459–79.

UNCTAD (2007) 'Asian Foreign Direct Investments in Africa: Towards a New Era of Cooperation among Developing Countries.' UNCTAD/ITE/IIA/2007/1. New York and Geneva: United Nations.

Weekes, J. (2008) 'Economic affects of copper prices on the Zambian economy: Exchange rate regime and Kwacha Appreciation', *Paper presented at Workshop in Memory of Alf Maizels*, School of Oriental and Asian Studies, London, 18–19th September.

World Bank, (2004a) *Patterns of Africa-Asia Trade and Investment, Potential for Ownership and Partnership.* Volume 1 and Volume 2, Africa Region Private Sector Group. Washington: World Bank.

——, (2004b) *Country Analytical Briefs with Compendium of Country-Specific Analysis of Africa-Asia Trade Complementarity.* Africa Region Private Sector Group. Washington: World Bank.

Zafar, A. (2007) 'The Growing Relationship Between China and SSA: Macroeconomic, Trade, Investment and Aid Links.' *World Bank Research Observer* 22(1): 103–30.

22 South Africa in Africa

From national capitalism to regional integration

Keith Hart and Vishnu Padayachee

> Stability in the region and, as a result, development and democracy, will only be achieved when a regional hegemon is prepared to underwrite these objectives. So long as that does not happen, South Africa's economic goals will remain compromised. For, as President Thabo Mbeki has often stated, the fate of a democratic South Africa is inextricably bound up with what happens in the rest of the continent.
>
> (Habib and Selinyane, 2005:9)

> The democratization of South Africa has opened up the space to develop regional systems including the active involvement of civil society as a co-driver of the process.
>
> (Muchie *et al.*, 2006:18)

Why South Africa needs Africa

In *Architects of Poverty* (2009), Moeletsi Mbeki, brother of the former President of South Africa, asks why Africans remain so poor compared with the rest of the world. He blames African political elites which from the days of slavery have enriched themselves at the expense of their own people by serving the interests of foreign powers whose only concern is to exploit their countries' human and natural resources. National politicians today continue this process of accumulation without development throughout Africa. He includes South Africa's African National Congress (ANC) government in this critique, claiming that Black Economic Empowerment (BEE), the enrichment of a few black individuals with the right political connections, is similarly a pay-off by the white-controlled corporations of the 'Minerals-Energy Complex' (Fine and Rustomjee, 1996) for adopting economic policies favourable to their interests at the expense of those of the black masses.

Mbeki claims that the ANC was always marginal to the struggle against apartheid within South Africa itself and now relies on powerful paymasters for its ability to rule. The industrial economy launched by Afrikaner nationalists in mid-century has been run down over the last two decades and most South Africans remain poor, without meaningful jobs or the skills to better themselves. This economic strategy is going nowhere, he says, and it has already begun to provoke widespread unrest. Switching leaders from his brother to Jacob Zuma is merely cosmetic. The ANC remains what it always was, an African nationalist elite clinging to power without any programme for an economy capable of advancing the poor majority of citizens.

Drawing on the example of successful countries such as those of Scandinavia and Switzerland, Mbeki argues that the route to modern development lies in a commitment to manufacturing linked to investment in education and skills for citizens. Partnerships need to be formed at first with foreign capitalist firms who possess up-to-date technologies, but with a view to the eventual indigenization of ownership and control. This model was adopted by the Afrikaners, but for their own exclusive benefit, and it underlies China's recent success. The only comparable African case, apart from South Africa's flawed example, is Mauritius whose economy is now based on hi-tech textile manufactures and tourism. He appears sceptical of regional cooperation as a way of increasing the size of the home market. In other words, what we call 'national capitalism' (see the following section) remains the only viable path to a country's development, but the political class in charge has to be genuinely committed to the interests of all its citizens.

We accept some of Mbeki's political critique, but reject his main economic strategy. It is true that Africa's underdevelopment today may be substantially attributed to the self-serving actions of a fragmented political class that is for sale to the highest foreign bidder or indeed to any bidder. And the ANC government has followed a depressingly familiar route, when one considers the global legitimacy it inherited from the anti-apartheid struggle and the potential of the South African economy. But we do not agree that the Afrikaner model of import-substituting industrialization, which was the predominant paradigm of its time, remains a viable option in today's world or that it makes the most of South Africa's existing advantages. Whereas national capitalism remains a possibility for countries such as China that have already tested their industries in the world market, the past three decades of neoliberal globalization also saw the emergence of large trading blocs offering a measure of protection for nation-states against the harsh winds of globalization (the European Union being the most striking example). Accordingly, we offer here a strategy for South Africa, its immediate neighbours and the African continent based on the premise of a need for greater regional integration.

A shift from economic development conceived narrowly as a national project to a more inclusive process of regional cooperation, ultimately involving Africa as a whole, is unlikely to succeed if the only actors are the existing ruling powers, the political class identified by Moeletsi Mbeki as the main cause of Africa's fragmented vulnerability and persistent underdevelopment. African people – and South Africa is notable for this – have generated a plethora of social movements, which for shorthand we could call 'civil society', whose dynamism comes from having largely by-passed national bureaucracy in reaching out to the contemporary world. These movements are commercial, artistic, intellectual, religious, political, technical and much more besides. What they currently lack is an overarching vision of Africa's drive for emancipation of the sort that made Pan African resistance to colonial empire the world's most inclusive political movement in the first half of the twentieth century.

The development of modern civilization is founded on the twin pillars of democracy and science, on establishing government by the people for the people and on the drive to acquire systematic knowledge of the world adequate to that task. Until Africans have made a significant contribution to both projects, the world society we live in will continue to assign them bottom place on racial grounds. South Africa is indispensable to any such project; its people's own aspirations to modernity require them to abandon the principle of national capitalism in order to embrace this more inclusive cause.

In the *Introduction* to this volume we identified some persistent problems with thinking about African political economy. The first was a tendency to lump the continent's many regions together in a vague abstraction, 'Africa', which is then made the subject of oversimplified general theories, themselves often swinging between polarized extremes. The second problem concerns how 'development' has often been represented as a leap from one idea to its negation, whereas historical reality is always a more gradual shift in emphasis. The third concerns glib notions of political agency, as if development were a free choice from a smorgasbord of historical or comparative examples, regardless of the constraints imposed by world political economy at a given moment. The South African case encourages politicians and intellectuals to adopt such positions, and if anything to exaggerate them, especially when it comes to the country's relationship to the rest of Africa.

Cecil Rhodes and his contemporaries saw South Africa as a launching pad for British imperialism in the continent as a whole. Then, as the world retreated from imperialism to a national model of capitalism, South Africa withdrew too. This sense of a 'white man's country' isolated from the 'dark continent' peaked in the decades after the Second World War when extreme segregationist policies provoked worldwide rejection of the apartheid regime. The ANC's accession to power opened up a new phase of South Africa's potential leadership of a drive towards African unity, as once envisaged by independence movements, and it was captured by Thabo Mbeki's slogan of an 'African renaissance'. But the ANC's actual strategy combined openness to neoliberal globalization with policies that strengthened the opposition between the 'rainbow nation' and other Africans. South Africa's poor citizens, faced with the enrichment of a few blacks and their own continuing economic exclusion, were invited to identify with the beneficiaries of apartheid against their African neighbours who had supported them in the struggle. In all likelihood, Jacob Zuma's regime will feel obliged to address the needs of poor black citizens; and this would reflect a worldwide turn at present from economic liberalism to more intervention by the state.

We wish to explore, therefore, how South Africa might assume a role of political and economic leadership in Africa, starting with its own hinterland. This requires us to dispense with the myths surrounding that relationship, by identifying what South Africa's relations with Africa and the world really have been, both when it was thought to stand apart from the continent and now when it is included. Any sustainable future for Africa as a whole must be consistent with effective solutions to South Africa's long-running attempt to evolve from an export-oriented mining enclave to a modern industrial economy. To this end, we draw on a critique of the concept of 'national capitalism', the dominant model of 'development' in the twentieth century. South Africa is the only country in Africa to have come close to implementing this model, and then only with the benefits of whites in mind. If the rest of Africa remains in a pre-industrial stage of agrarian civilization, as Hart argues above, economic relations with South Africa must acknowledge this unequal development, while relying on regional integration as a source of mediation between extremes.

It is not enough, therefore, to seek answers to the conundrum of development within South Africa or any other individual country, as is the norm. For at least a century and a half, it has been an integral part of world society, first pioneering what became racial exclusion while supplying the gold that sustained the international economy, then offering an introverted example of white supremacy, before emerging as the 'rainbow nation', the only instance of national capitalism in Africa. South Africa's history is so different from its neighbours that most commentators are understandably content to focus on what happens exclusively within its boundaries. But the South African case cries out for a global and regional perspective to complement its national history, if only as a way of addressing how and why the ANC embraced nationalism and neoliberal globalization simultaneously, probably to the detriment of both.

In what follows, we first explain what we mean by national capitalism. Then we identify the persistent problem of South Africa's economic history: its contradictory attempt to make the transition from a mining enclave to a modern economy. The British imperialism that gave birth to modern South Africa was succeeded by two variants of national capitalism: the racially exclusive version devised by the Afrikaner National Party and that pursued by the ANC since the mid-1990s. At this time of global economic crisis, the underlying problem of South Africa's development remains unsolved.

Regional integration is one path towards a solution; but South Africa has a complicated history of relations within its own region. We propose a more active African strategy for South Africa as a precondition for its own transition to economic democracy. Such a strategy must start with rationalizing relations within the Southern African Development Community (SADC), which now includes countries as far afield as the Congo, Tanzania and Mauritius, with the aim of freeing up the movement of people, goods and money within the region. Such a regional perspective must also embrace African unity in a meaningful way. Rather than return to a mid-century model of industrial development, we base South Africa's (and Africa's) economic future on cultural services such as entertainment, education, media, software and information, along with finance, communications, transport, construction, energy and minerals.

National capitalism in the long twentieth century

'National capitalism' is our term for the modern synthesis of the nation-state and industrial capitalism: the institutional attempt to manage money, markets and accumulation through central bureaucracy within a cultural community of national citizens. It is linked to the rise of large corporations as the dominant form of capitalist organization and is in essence Hegel's recipe in *The Philosophy of Right* (1821, 1952 reprint), namely that only state power can contain the excesses of capitalism, while markets in turn limit the excesses of political power. Society should be managed by an educated bureaucratic elite in the national interest. Marx certainly did not envisage anything of this sort, but Weber recognized such a synthesis in Germany's historical experience of the alliance between Rhineland capitalism and Prussian bureaucracy. 'National capitalism' is still the dominant social form in our world, even if the transnational aspects of neoliberal globalization over the last three decades have obscured that fact.

The 1860s saw a transport and communications revolution (steamships, continental railways and the telegraph) that decisively opened up the world economy. At the same time a series of political revolutions gave the leading powers of the coming century the institutional means of organizing industrial capitalism. Capitalism has always rested on an unequal contract between owners of large amounts of money and those who make and buy their products. This contract depends on an effective threat of punishment if workers withhold their labour or buyers fail to pay up. The owners cannot make that threat alone: they need the support of governments, laws, prisons, police, even armies. By the mid-nineteenth century, it became clear that the machine revolution was pulling unprecedented numbers of people into the cities, where they added a wholly new dimension to traditional problems of crowd control. The political revolutions of the 1860s, from the American civil war to the Meiji Restoration and German unification, were based on a new and explicit alliance between capitalists and the military landlord class to form states capable of managing industrial workforces and of taming the criminal gangs that had taken over large swathes of the main cities.

Before long, governments provided new legal conditions for the operations of large corporations, ushering in mass production and consumption through a bureaucratic revolution. The national system became general after the First World War and was the dominant social form of twentieth-century civilization. Its apogee or 'golden age' (Hobsbawm, 1994) was the period 1948–73. This was a time of strong states and economic expansion when the idea of 'development' (poor nations growing richer with the help of the already rich) replaced colonial empire for most Third World countries. When, shortly before his downfall, Richard Nixon announced that "We are all Keynesians now", he was reflecting a universal belief then that governments had a responsibility to manage national capitalism in the interests of all citizens.

The 1970s were a watershed in world economic history. United States expenditure on its unwinnable war in Vietnam generated huge imbalances in the world's money flows, leading to a breakdown of the fixed parity exchange-rate system devised at Bretton Woods in 1944. America's departure from the gold standard in 1971 triggered a free-for-all in world currency markets, leading in 1975 to the invention of money market futures in Chicago to stabilize export prices for Midwestern farmers. At the same time, the world economy was plunged into depression in 1973 by the formation of OPEC and a hefty rise in the price of oil. 'Stagflation' (high unemployment and inflation) increased, opening the way for conservatives such as Reagan and Thatcher to revive the strategy of giving economic priority to the 'market' rather than the 'state'. The economic conditions of three decades ago and the policies devised then find their denouement in the global economic crisis today.

Apart from being based on a new ruling class alliance, national capitalism was committed to mobilizing citizens of all classes, and especially the new urban working class, in the drive for economic modernization. This meant principally taking the high wage, high productivity route to industrial capitalism, with some political support for unions and workplace democracy. It also meant the development of a national education system capable of raising work standards in an industrial economy that relied increasingly on sophisticated machines; a welfare state capable of meeting all citizens' needs for social security, health, housing and basic transport in some degree; and a commitment to containing wealth inequality engendered by markets through redistributive taxation, unemployment benefits and equal pricing of utilities across all regions.

South Africa embarked in the twentieth century on a bizarre variant of this programme, national capitalism for whites only. The failure of apartheid in the 1970s and 1980s, as national capitalism everywhere entered the turbulent waters of neoliberal globalization, is closely related to the inherent contradictions of trying to build a modern economy where the majority are deliberately excluded from the working class bargain on which national capitalism was normatively founded. It is not surprising then that South Africans of all classes tend to stress the unique character of their national society or that the comparative study of capitalism has often been built around paradigmatic national cases (Britain, the USA, France, Japan, S. Korea, etc.). What makes national capitals distinctive is the specific character of the class alliance that marked the emergence of capitalism in each country (see Padayachee, 2008). Whatever its general features, pre-existing social and cultural forms have always been incorporated into making it work.

Overcoming the limits of a mining enclave economy

South Africa was and still is for the most part a poor, dry country. Apart from a scattering of hunter-gatherers, it was only settled by African herders and farmers quite late, in the last millennium. Since then its history has been made by migrants. The Dutch East India Company made a refuelling station at the Cape in 1652 and explicitly sought to restrict colonial settlement there. During the Napoleonic Wars, the British seized control of the Cape Colony and the following decade, the 1820s, saw the birth of the peoples who dominated South African history in the nineteenth century and after: an influx of British migrants secured the area for the Empire and forced the Dutch to move inland to form the Afrikaner republics, while Shaka and his successors formed the Zulu nation. All three peoples subsequently fought wars against each other, with victory of sorts going to the British against the other two. South Africa did not develop a staple export comparable to Australian wool or Canadian timber. All this changed with the discovery of diamonds at Kimberley in 1867, shortly followed by gold in the Rand. Suddenly from the 1880s South Africa was a major exporter of minerals, notably supplying much of the gold that secured international trade before the First World War.

The British annexed the Transvaal and the Orange Free State and for three decades from the 1880s, South Africa participated fully in an age of financial globalization driven by imperial rivalry, with Britain at its centre. As Lewis (1978) argues, this was when the world economy took on a distinctively racial character with European and Asian migrants divided between high- and low-wage areas. South Africa was one of the main places where these streams converged (especially in Natal as a result of mass recruitment of Indian indentured labour) and the policies of racial discrimination employed there were intensified as a growing body of African migrants went to work on the mines and commercial farms. This was when Cecil Rhodes found a stage for his vision of an Africa united under British rule 'from Cape to Cairo'; and the British theorist of imperialism, J.A. Hobson celebrated the adventurous spirit and business acumen of the men who headed the companies around Johannesburg then:

> Never have I been so struck with the intellect and the audacious enterprise and foresight of great business men as here. Nor are these qualities confined to the Beits and Barnatos and other great capitalists; the town bristles and throbs with industrial and commercial energy. The utter dependence upon financial 'booms' and 'slumps' conjoined with the strain and kaleidoscopic changes of the political situation, has bred by selection and by education a type of man and of society which is as different from that of Manchester as the latter is from the life of Hankow or Buenos Ayres.
>
> (1900:13)

The Union was formed in 1910 as a compromise between the two main white groups and the end of three decades of financial imperialism in 1913–14 provided the next watershed moment, a break whose economic and political impact reinforced greater isolation in South Africa. Anglo-American, the country's dominant economic force in the twentieth century, was formed in 1917, marking a transition from imperial finance to a 'South African' economy aspiring to greater self-sufficiency. In other words, 1914 saw an end to that earlier phase of globalization and the beginning of the trend we call 'national capitalism' which flourished until the 1970s.

Afrikaner nationalism was a force before and after the Boer Wars. The Pact government of 1924, representing the white working class in general and the Afrikaner rural/urban poor in particular, launched national capitalism for the whites after the caesura of the First World War, focusing especially on large state enterprises. For them, maintaining the colour bar was everything, even though the explicit interest of capital was sometimes the opposite. Where the interests of the two converged was in a drive, led by Anglo-American, to diversify the South African economy, with a view especially to securing local supplies of mining inputs such as explosives, coal, steel and electricity. The result was the development of an industrial core to the South African economy, focusing on minerals and utilities, that was subsequently dubbed 'the mineral-energy complex' or MEC (Fine and Rustomjee, 1996; see also M. Mbeki, 2009). In the 1930s nascent Afrikaner business, political and cultural groups led a savings movement which later provided a launching pad for Afrikaner capital. After the war, Anglo-American played a leading role in the establishment of South Africa's modern capital market by, among other things, setting up the National Finance Corporation. In the 1960s, anticipating what became knows as 'Black Economic Empowerment', Anglo sold off some of its gold-mining interests to Afrikaner capital – the companies formed through these arrangements have gone on to be become global giants and include the resources conglomerate BHP Billiton, now listed in Melbourne and London.

The boom of 1948–73 matched exactly the growth of the world economy at the time and South Africa slipped into depression when the world did. The development of manufacturing and utilities in that period always depended on subsidies from gold exports since they ran a persistent balance of payments deficit. South Africa's gold supply ran out when demand for it did. This was disguised in the 1970s by the eight-fold rise on the gold price after the United States moved off the gold standard in 1971. The crisis became obvious in the 1980s when the gold price fell. 'The engine of South Africa's economic growth had stalled' (Feinstein, 2005). The oil-induced world depression after the energy crisis of 1973, hostility to the apartheid regime and the beginning of what later became significant capital outflows merely exacerbated this trend. South Africa's low industrial efficiency and high costs of production now faced rising demands from a more militant African labour force. The dual economy was bankrupt and its perpetrators knew it.

This was the immediate context for a negotiated settlement with the African majority.

The transition to African majority rule thus took place when the South African economy was running out of steam, without the volume and value of gold exports that supported growth for a century from the 1870s, with a failing attempt at industrial diversification and the legacy of a cheap labour policy that excluded most of the country's inhabitants from full participation in the modern economy. The ANC soon opted for policies consistent with neoliberal globalization which led to even greater economic inequality and the rapid decline of home-made manufactures in the face of cheap Asian imports. The services economy, especially finance, shopping malls, communications and security, boomed. But the country's underlying economic malaise, exacerbated by the global recession, persists and the evidence of social unrest is everywhere.

The ANC's Freedom Charter of 1955 included a proposal to nationalize the mines; and, after its legalization in 1991, the Macro-Economic Research Group (MERG, an economic think tank of the movement), came up with some fairly radical economic policies, consistent with the ANC's past. But white capital had other ideas: when Sanlam sold off part of its insurance business (Metropolitan Life) to black businessmen, this set a precedent for BEE as a major plank of ANC government policy (which it had never been before). Its 1994 election manifesto was based on the Reconstruction and Development Programme (RDP), an ambitious plan to mobilize the energies of South Africa's poor black majority through devolved and integrated development. But the Growth Employment and Redistribution policy (GEAR), introduced without negotiation in 1996, marked a sudden shift to conformity with the demands of neoliberal globalization. Presumably the government wished to pursue what it felt was a credible strategy for global markets when faced with a falling currency and in the absence of an approved macro-economic framework (Padayachee, 2005).

By the late 1990s, a number of major South African corporations listed their headquarters overseas. The early 2000s saw steady and sustained growth but without increased employment and with rising inequality, not only between the races, but also within the Black population. The ANC government recognized the need for development of education, training and skills. But its uneasy commitment to both globalization and national capitalism led to tension between nationals and non-nationals. Problems in the townships over utilities culminated in xenophobic conflict and violence in May 2008.

Charles Feinstein (2005) has provided a well-conceived account of South Africa's experiment in national capitalism for whites only. He argues that it was the country's failure to extend the principle of citizenship to Africans that underlay its inability to make a successful transition to industrial modernity. For him, as for us, this project hinges on developing the home market: by equalizing income across the classes; building a national system of education in support of industrialization; extending citizenship to the work-place (unions, bargaining, etc.); and caring for the health, welfare and housing of all the people. Marx (in *Capital* volume 1, 1979) held that capitalism in its progressive form takes the path of what he called 'relative surplus value', with the emphasis on increasing labour efficiency, mainly through machines. Reliance on cheap labour ('absolute surplus value', a variety of sweatshop capitalism with affinity to feudal methods of extracting surpluses from peas-ants) offers one way into the international economy, but improved productiv-ity is the only way of staying in. Development through a mining or plantation enclave separated from the rest of the local economy is the opposite of national capitalism and it does not offer a route to modernity. South Africa was an enclave export economy of a special kind (gold) with aspirations to modernity for the whites. But the gold ran out by the 1970s. And the limited success of Afrikaner national capitalism in establishing industrial manu-factures and utilities has since suffered a reverse under ANC stewardship.

So for Feinstein what makes South African capitalism special is this combination of a gold bonanza with instituted racial inequality: the economic recipe was unlimited demand for the principal export (including windfalls from time to time) and low wages for labour whose supply paradoxically was scarce. Comparing South Africa with Newly Industrializing Countries in Europe, Asia and Latin America as well as with the old Commonwealth, he shows how gold masked the contradictions of failure to follow an inclusive national path until the 1970s and especially the 1980s. This problem has not gone away with ANC rule and may have been exacerbated. In what follows we consider how South Africa's relations with the rest of Africa are central to any lasting solution.

South Africa's relations with Africa

History has conspired to isolate South Africa from the rest of the continent or at least it often seems like that. Cecil Rhodes' vision of an Africa united by British imperialism from 'the Cape to Cairo' briefly found its adherents and South Africa's metropolis was for many decades London. But the logic of nation-state formation always pulled the South African economy inwards and Anglo-American's concentration of economic power in the twentieth century was expressed in fairly systematic promotion of industrial and finan-cial diversification within the national economy. The most misleading aspect of the conventional description concerns the apartheid regime's presumptive isolation. In fact, the World Bank made substantial loans to South Africa in the 1950s and for a time it was second only to Mobutu's Zaire as an African recipient of IMF credits (Padayachee, 1990). As an American ally against the Communist threat during the Cold War, South Africa's security interests led it, for example under Vorster's and Botha's leadership, to establish fairly close ties with a constellation of African states in the 1970s and 1980s, mainly in southern Africa.

The Union of South Africa is 100 years old. It is important to recall that, like other British dominions, its structure was federal, bringing together provinces with highly disparate histories, geography and populations, as well as being linked to a patchwork of territories under British rule within and beyond its boundaries. As part of the aspiration to coordinate and rationalize this patchwork, a South African customs union (SACU) was formed in 1889 (Fourie and Rossouw, 2009: 5), the oldest of its kind in Africa involving what became Botswana, Lesotho, Swaziland, Namibia and South Africa itself. For most of its existence, this union was tightly controlled from Pretoria; but, as part of Thabo Mbeki's push to make relations with South Africa's neighbours more equal, democratic and consensual, SACU headquarters were moved to Namibia in 2004 (Daniel et al., 2005: 566) and members were granted more independence in their dealings with other countries. This arrangement is now in disarray since the smaller countries have signed separate agreements with the European Union which in effect allow them to act as ports of trade for European goods, subverting South Africa's attempts to control their entry and draw revenues from their importation. Now relations within SACU are at a low, proof, if any were needed, that any moves towards greater regional integration will have to acknowledge South Africa's unequal weight.

At the same time, the Southern African Development Community (SADC) has been expanded since the fall of apartheid to include Angola, Botswana, the Democratic Republic of Congo, Lesotho, Madagascar, Malawi, Mauritius, Mozambique, Namibia, Seychelles, South Africa, Swaziland, Tanzania, Zambia and Zimbabwe. This makes SADC potentially the largest regional economy in Africa, one moreover that is naturally dominated by South Africa. But the reality within the region at present is a maze of national restrictions on the movement of people, goods and money, crosscut by bilateral deals of bewildering variety (see Fourie and Rossouw, 2009 and Figure 22.1 below). Under the ANC, South Africa has increased, rather than reduced a sense of division between its own citizens and the many Africans who come there to live and work. Nevertheless, we argue that SADC remains the best chance for South Africa to coordinate economic policy with its neighbours. This would mean breaking with 'capitalism in one country' and its plethora of confusing and contradictory bilateral deals. In fact, under President Mbeki, nothing much happened at the level of SADC, since his attention was firmly focused on reforming regional cooperation at the continental level.

Thabo Mbeki's idea of an 'African renaissance' expressed the reasonable belief that a black majority government in South Africa might be a leading catalyst for an African economic revival based on greater political coordination between what have been, since independence, isolated nation-states that constituted easy pickings for the world's great powers. His diplomatic energy was unstinted and, as a result, the Organization of African Unity in Addis Ababa was reconstituted as the African Union (AU), with as its economic arm the New Partnership for Africa's Development (NEPAD) based in

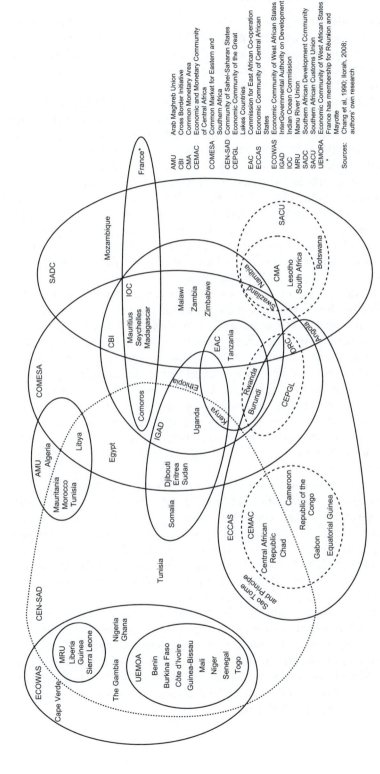

Figure 22.1 Overlapping regional arrangements in Africa.

Source: Fourie and Rossouw (2009)

Johannesburg and as its political arm the African Peer Review Mechanism (APRM). A Pan African Parliament (PAP), composed of representatives nominated by member states, also sits in Johannesburg. The principal measures anticipated are a single currency for Africa as a whole, a continental central bank and trade harmonization.

South Africa's economic relations with the rest of Africa under the ANC have not been standing still, but at the same time trade with Africa follows a similar pattern now to what it was under the apartheid regime. The main innovation has been an increased emphasis on a bilateral alliance with Africa's other great power, Nigeria, mainly it seems an exchange of oil supplies for manufactures and services. South African investment has diversified in the last two decades, especially in East Africa, where hotels, retail, communications, security and minerals have been the main sectors. In a recent development, Ghana and Nigeria have drawn on South African expertise in biometric identity and finance to attempt to build elaborate national systems linked to credit whose prospects of success seem implausible (Breckenridge n.d.). Although names like MTN and Shop Rite are now familiar in East, West and Central Africa, most outward investment is still within the expanded SADC. Half of South Africa's African investments are in Mozambique, with Mauritius next, mostly at the expense of Zimbabwe. Exchange controls on South African firms have been relaxed for African investments. The Johannesburg Stock Exchange (JSE) is now linked to Nairobi. South African banks are financing oil exploration in the Democratic Republic of Congo (DRC), Nigeria, Angola and Gabon. Some BEE firms have been active in the Congo, where the huge energy project of the Inga Dam led by the power utility, Eskom, is one sign of the DRC's growing importance for South Africa's expansion within the region. (See Daniel et al., 2003, Daniel et al., 2005 and Clapham et al., 2001 for these economic relations with Africa.)

Finally, India, Brazil and South Africa have formed a South-South alliance (IBSA) aimed at increasing trade and investment between them and perhaps influencing world economic councils together. But the existing level of common economic activity is embarrassingly small and the three countries were not even able to reach agreement for the Doha round of global trade negotiations. There is nothing to stop any of them from forming a bilateral alliance with China, for example, that would further undermine their precarious unity. In any case, such initiatives are inconsistent with those of regional integration and African unity and South Africa's economic policies in those respects were haphazard as a result. These generally reflected the interests of the minerals-energy complex more than the investment opportunities that South African capital found in Africa after the demise of apartheid. Above all, Thabo Mbeki's leadership was aimed exclusively at the very political class that has failed Africa so often since independence and he did not factor the forces of civil society into his plans.

An African strategy for South Africa

As Daniel Bell once said, 'The national state has become too small for the big problems in life and too big for the small problems' (1991: 225). One answer is to rely more on *subsidiarity*. This is one of the features of *federalism*, whereby sovereignty is constitutionally divided between a central governing authority and constituent political units (like states or provinces). The principle of devolving power to the lowest effective authority is one condition for wider political association among previously sovereign entities. Federalism has been around for as long as the nation-state, if not longer; but, as we have seen, the assumption of a national monopoly over political economy is deeply rooted in contemporary civilization. Most of the largest countries are federal in constitution, but this has not prevented them from behaving like nation-states of late.

Before gaining independence from colonial rule, Africa's political leaders often embraced the pan-African ideal, the unity of all people of African descent in a drive to recover control of their land from white imperialists. This movement, the most inclusive of its day, reflected the division of world society between European empires. The anti-colonial revolution, starting in Asia after 1945, took place when world society was being reformed as so many nominally sovereign nation-states. It did not take long for the Pan African idea to be replaced by what Fanon called 'national consciousness' (1970) and the continent was eventually divided into 53 states, most of whose boundaries were historically contingent. The new ruling elites probably never had strong ties to their subject populations and, once the legitimacy conferred by independence waned, they were forced to turn for material support to old foreign masters and some new ones. Moeletsi Mbeke's caricature, with which we began this essay, is too close for comfort and Jean-François Bayart's account of 'the politics of the belly' in *The State in Africa* (2009) is depressingly accurate. Despite occasional claims for the 'green shoots of democracy' in Africa, the political norm is weak, fragmented states, ruled from the top down by presidential kleptocrats in league with foreign extractive, commercial and military interests. These 'sovereigns' pack the decision-making bodies of the world's ruling institutions only to serve the interests of their paymasters, not those of their own people. At a time when North America, Europe, Asia and Latin America are forming regional trading blocs to cope with globalization, Africa suffers from a labyrinthine confusion of regional associations which do little to strengthen their members' bargaining power in world markets.

This is how Africa looks from the top. The situation on the ground is rather different, where African peoples have for centuries developed patterns of trans-border movement and exchange which persist despite their rulers' attempts to force economy and society into national cages. This is one major reason why so much of the African economy is held to be 'informal': state regulations are routinely ignored, with the result that half the population and most economic activity are made formally criminal and an absurd proportion of governmental effort is wasted on trying to apply unenforceable rules. The answer to this chaos is classical liberalism, the drive to establish the widest area possible of free trade and movement with minimal regulation by the authorities. Unfortunately, the last three decades of neo-liberal globalization have done much to discredit this recipe; and we too favour redistributive policies undertaken in the tradition of social democracy, especially at this time of global economic crisis. But we hold nevertheless that the boundaries of free commerce *and* of state intervention, for South Africa's sake as well as those of its smaller African neighbours, should be pushed outwards beyond the limits of the existing sovereignties.

South Africans like to think of their country as big and powerful, which it is when compared with its neighbours and even the rest of Africa. But it has nothing like the geographical size and economic clout of the United States, Japan, China, Germany, Britain, France, Russia, India or Brazil. Its population of under 50 millions is dwarfed by countries like Nigeria, Pakistan, Indonesia and Bangladesh; and the legacy of racial division which excluded and still excludes the majority of citizens from most benefits leaves South Africa some way behind countries like South Korea, Australia and Canada as an economic power. Africa is now the fastest-growing segment of the human population, a seventh of the total with only a fiftieth of its purchasing power. Even so, Asian manufacturers have not been as slow as their European and American counterparts to target the African market, while competing for a larger share of the continent's minerals. It seems obvious that South Africa needs to abandon the old imperial idea of being a white man's country linked to other lands of new settlement through the London metropolis. But how might it pursue a rational policy of integration with its African hinterland?

The first step should not be to seek economic coordination at the most inclusive level of the African continent as a whole. We do not agree that a single currency and central bank are appropriate to this stage of Africa's development, given the disparities between member states. The global economic crisis has shown up vividly the limitations of such institutions for the eurozone, with countries like Ireland, Spain and Greece sacrificed to a central policy set by Germany and France, whereas Britain, Switzerland, Sweden, Norway and even Iceland have been able to take monetary measures suited to their own circumstances. The existing pattern of regional associations needs to be rationalized with the aim of simplifying administration and abolishing conflict between rules at different levels of association.

In South Africa's case, this should probably mean abandoning SACU in order to concentrate on building up SADC as a customs union with one set of rules for all members. At present visas are still required for travel between many SADC countries and a maze of bilateral deals and tariff barriers make a mockery of the idea of an 'economic community'. A new model of integration within the Southern African region (eventually extending to East Africa) would have to break with the historical constraints imposed by existing bodies. Selective tariffs need urgently to be reduced within SADC, but this would not prevent protectionist measures being introduced at the regional level, where necessary. A consistent policy of trade liberalization would free up the movement of people, goods and capital within the region and allow existing informal practices to conform more closely to economic rules. Only then does it make sense to reach out to other African regions such as the Economic Community of West African States (ECOWAS). The political elites cannot be kept out of such a process, but the driving force for regional integration on this scale would have to be a broad-based social movement. In making this point, our emphasis differs from those of both the Mbeki brothers.

'Africa' is still a significant category in world affairs and these piece-meal steps towards regional integration would still benefit from a revival of the pan-African impulse that Thabo Mbeki tried to kindle. The AU and especially its economic arm, NEPAD, have a role to play in persuading the rest of the world that Africa's poverty is a drag on the growth of the global economy. If the continent's infant agricultural, manufacturing and service industries are to be given a chance to develop, there must be agreement at the level of multilateral institutions such as the WTO that Africa deserves special protection, at least for a period. Such arguments are unlikely to be persuasive coming from an Africa irrationally divided as at present. The continental and regional strategies need to be pursued side by side.

We have stressed here and elsewhere the potential of the arts, culture, education, science and sport in Africa's future development. African policy-makers need to think outside the box of their existing obsession with recapitulating the development stages of the old industrial economies. The continent's educational and scientific institutions could make a significant contribution to this process if they made a serious effort to overcome the institutional legacy of colonial and postcolonial society. Rather than revert to a mid-century industrial policy, we would argue that South Africa's hi-tech services sectors have a comparative advantage in Africa, complementary to Asian manufactures. Unlike Moeletse Mbeki, therefore, we do not fault the ANC for accepting this trend.

Traditional African societies could be said to have supported economies whose object was the production of life embodied in human beings. Hence the importance for many of them of cattle used to secure the reproduction of kin groups through marriage. Modern capitalist economies have as their object the accumulation of money through the production of inanimate things for sale. But in recent decades, the fastest growing sector of world trade has been in cultural commodities: services such as entertainment, education, media, software and information, along with explosive growth in the exchange of money itself and in the means of movement or transport. These trends make the economy more about what people do for each other (services) than the physical objects that go into making up their material livelihood. It could be said that, after the early phase of industrialization, the predominant focus of the world economy will revert to the production of human beings. There is no limit to the stories we can tell each other or to the pleasure we can derive from watching performers excel at what they do. Africa is well-placed to leapfrog the industrial phase of capitalist development from which it was largely excluded. South Africa, which for a time aspired to join in that industrial phase, should not pine for a return to shoe factories and chemical plants. The future of South African commerce with Africa and the world lies elsewhere.

South Africa must be a driver of regional integration and continental revival, if these objectives are to stand any chance of even partial success. But what constellation of political and economic interests might push the country in that direction? Nelson Mandela's vision of a 'rainbow nation' has come under severe strain in the last 15 years. South Africa is still a racially divided economy with an extremely advanced sector focused on mining, finance, security and retail ('walls and malls'); but a more racially mixed elite is surrounded by black poverty. Economic growth since 2000 has fed this divide, with the consequence that South Africa remains a world leader in inequality. The economy is too small to go it alone and its racist past still weighs heavily. The premise of national capitalism will not produce the expansion that is needed nor will nostalgia for the days of Afrikaner industrialization subsidized by gold.

Hosting the Football World Cup competition in 2010 has generated a lot of positive and negative hype; but the event is also a symbol of the contemporary world. Africa is at least a meaningful unity as regards this competition and the television audience generated by the cup final will be as large as the planet's total population half a century ago. Only an economic vision attuned to the reality of world society today can begin to address the long haul to a federal Africa, led by a South Africa that is more true to its own federal roots than the 'rainbow nation' ever was.

References

Bell, Daniel (1991): *The Winding Passage: Sociological Essays and Journeys.* New Brunswick, NJ: Transaction Books.

Breckenridge, Keith (n.d.) Banking on the poor: the adoption of the South African model of biometric identity registration in contemporary Africa (unpublished paper, University of KwaZulu-Natal, Durban).

Clapham, Christopher, G. Mills, Anna Morner and Elizabeth Sidiropoulos (2001): *Regional Integration in Southern Africa.* Johannesburg: South African Institute of International Affairs Publications.

Daniel, John, V. Naidoo and S. Naidu (2003): The South Africans have arrived: post-apartheid corporate expansion into Africa. In J. Daniel, A. Habib and R. Southall (eds.) *The State of the Nation 2003–2004.* Cape Town: HSRC Press.

Daniel, John, Jessica Lutchman and Sanusha Naidu (2005): South Africa and Nigeria, two unequal centres in a periphery. In J. Daniel, Roger Southall and Jessica Lutchman (eds.) *The State of the Nation 2004–2005.* Cape Town: HSRC Press.

Fanon, Frantz (1970): *The Wretched of the Earth*, London.

Feinstein, Charles (2005): *An Economic History of South Africa: Conquest, Discrimination and Development*. Cambridge: Cambridge University Press.

Fine, Ben and Zavareh Rustomjee (1996): *The Political Economy of South Africa, from Minerals-energy Complex to Industrialisation*. Johannesburg: Witswatersrand University Press.

Fourie, Johan and Jannie Rossouw (2009): Is regional integration pro-poor? Lessons from an intraregional comparison in the Southern African Development Community. Paper for presentation at the sixth African Finance Journal and African Finance Association Conference. Cape Town.

Habib, Adam and N. Selinyane (2005): Constraining the unconstrained: civil society and South Africa's hegemonic obligations in Africa. In W. Carlsnaes and P. Nel (eds.) *South Africa's Foreign Policy in the Post-apartheid Era*. Johannesburg.

Hart, Keith and Vishnu Padayachee (2000): Indian enterprise in Durban, South Africa: local and global history in the long twentieth century. *Comparative Studies in Society and History*. Vol. 42, No. 4.

Hegel, Georg W.F. (1821, reprint 1952): *The Philosophy of Right*. London: Oxford University Press.

Hobsbawm, Eric. (1994): *The Age of Extremes: The Short Twentieth Century, 1914–1991*. London: Michael Joseph.

Hobson, J.A. (1900): *The War in South Africa, Its causes and Effects*. London: John Nisbet.

Lewis, Arthur. (1978): *The Evolution of the International Economic Order*. Princeton: Princeton University Press.

Marx, Karl (1979 reprint): *Capital*, Vol. 1. Harmondsworth, UK: Penguin Books in association with New Left Review.

Mbeki, Moeletsi (2009): *Architects of Poverty: Why African Capitalism Needs Changing*. Johannesburg: Picador Africa.

Muchie, Mammo, Adam Habib and Vishnu Padayachee (2006): African integration and civil society, the case of the African union. *Transformation* #61.

Padayachee, Vishnu (1989): South Africa's international financial relations, 1970–87: history, crisis and transformation. Unpublished PhD thesis, University of Natal, Durban.

—— (2005): The South African economy. *Social Research*. Vol. 72, No. 3.

—— (2008): Capitalism of a special type? South African capitalism before and after 1994. *Journal Fur Entwicklungspolitik*. Vol. xxiv 4.

Index